The
Random House
Spanish
Dictionary

Ordinal/Ordinales

first	1st / 1º	primero
second	2nd / 2º	segundo
third	3rd / 3º	tercero
fourth	4th / 4º	cuarto
fifth	5th / 5º	quinto
sixth	6th / 6º	sexto
seventh	7th / 7º	séptimo
eighth	8th / 8º	octavo
ninth	9th / 9º	noveno
tenth	10th / 10º	décimo

DENISE
ist schön

Weights and Measures/Pesos y Medidas

1 centímetro	=	.3937 inches
1 metro	=	39.37 inches
1 kilómetro	=	.621 mile
1 centigramo	=	.1543 grain
1 gramo	=	15.432 grains
1 kilogramo	=	2.2046 pounds
1 tonelada	=	2.204 pounds
1 centilitro	=	.338 ounces
1 litro	=	1.0567 quart (liquid); .908 quart (dry)
1 kilolitro	=	264.18 gallons

1 inch	=	2.54 centímetros
1 foot	=	.305 metros
1 mile	=	1.61 kilómetros
1 grain	=	.065 gramos
1 pound	=	.455 kilogramos
1 ton	=	.907 toneladas
1 ounce	=	2.96 centilitros
1 quart	=	1.13 litros
1 gallon	=	4.52 litros

The
Random House
Spanish
Dictionary

SPANISH – ENGLISH
ENGLISH – SPANISH

ESPAÑOL – INGLÉS
INGLÉS – ESPAÑOL

Edited by
Donald F. Solá
Cornell University

Under the General Editorship of
Professor Frederick B. Agard,
Cornell Unversity

RANDOM HOUSE
NEW YORK

1987 Printing

Library of Congress Catalog Card Number: 67-20648

ISBN: 0-394-40064-X
Manufactured in the United States of America

Foreword

This bilingual dictionary has been designed as a practical tool for the general use of the English-speaking learner of Spanish and the Spanish-speaking learner of English. Travelers and students will find that this up-to-date and accurate reference work has been carefully prepared to meet their everyday needs.

The editors have taken great care to make this dictionary as useful and informative as possible for its size and scope — we hope you will enjoy making the most of it.

Prefacio

Este diccionario bilingüe se presenta como instrumento práctico destinado al uso del hispano-hablante que aprende inglés y del anglo-hablante que aprende español. Los viajeros así como los estudiantes encontrarán aquí una obra de consulta puesta al día para llenar correctamente sus requisitos cotidianos. Los editores se han esforzado en hacer este librito todo lo más útil e informativo posible, en vista de su tamaño y su alcance. Esperamos, pues, que le sea del máximo provecho.

Concise Pronunciation Guide

Spanish Letter	Pronunciation
a	Like English *a* in *father*.
b, v	At beginning of word group and after *m* or *n*, like English *b*. Elsewhere, like English *v*, but pronounced with both lips instead of upper teeth and lower lip.
c	Before *e* or *i*, like English *th* in *thin* (in Northern Spain); like Spanish *s* (in Southern Spain and the Americas); elsewhere, like English *k* in key.
ch	Like English *ch* in *child*.
d	At beginning of word group and after *n* or *l*, like English *d*. Elsewhere, like English *th* in *either*.
e	Like English *e* in *bet*.
f	As in English.
g	Before *e* or *i*, the same as Spanish *j*. Elsewhere, like English *g* in *get*.
gu	Before *e* or *i*, like English *g* in *get*. Elsewhere, like English *gw* in *Gwynn*.
gü	Like English *gw* in *Gwynn*.
h	Silent.
i	Like English *i* in *machine*, but more clipped. Before or after another vowel, like English *y* (except when accented).
j	Like English *h*, but more rasping.
k	Like English *k*.
l	Like English *l* in *like*, but with the tongue behind the upper front teeth.
ll	Like English *lli* in *million* (in Northern Spain); like Spanish *y* (in Southern Spain and the Americas).
m	As in English.

Spanish Letter	Pronunciation
n	As in English.
ñ	Like English *ny* in *canyon*.
o	Approximately like English *o* in *vote*, but more clipped.
p	As in English.
qu	Like English *k*.
r	Not at all like American English *r*; a quick flap of the tongue-tip on the roof of the mouth.
rr	A strongly "rolled" or trilled version of Spanish *r*.
s	Like English *s* in *lease*.
t	As in English.
u	Like English *oo* in *boot*, but more clipped. Before or after another vowel, like English *w* (except when accented).
v	See *b* above.
x	Like English *x*; although before consonants many speakers pronounce it like Spanish *s*; like Spanish *j* (in Mexican Indian words).
y	Approximately like English *y* in *yes*.
z	Like English *th* in *thin* (in Northern Spain); like English *s* in *lease* (in Southern Spain and the Americas).

Spanish Accentuation

In a number of words spoken stress is marked by an accent(´):*nación, país, médico, día*.

Words which are not so marked are, generally speaking, stressed on the next-to-the-last syllable if they end in a vowel, *n*, or *s*; and on the last syllable if they end in a consonant other than *n* or *s*.

Note: An accent is placed over some words to distinguish them from others having the same spelling and pronunciation but differing in meaning.

Spanish Irregular Verbs

Infinitive	Present	Future	Preterit	Past Part.
andar	ando	andaré	anduve	andado
caber	quepo	cabré	cupe	cabido
caer	caigo	caeré	caí	caído
conducir	conduzco	conduciré	conduje	conducido
dar	doy	daré	di	dado
decir	digo	diré	dije	dicho
estar	estoy	estaré	estuve	estado
haber	he	habré	hube	habido
hacer	hago	haré	hice	hecho
ir	voy	iré	fui	ido
jugar	juego	jugaré	jugué	jugado
morir	muero	moriré	morí	muerto
oír	oigo	oiré	oí	oído
poder	puedo	podré	pude	podido
poner	pongo	pondré	puse	puesto
querer	quiero	querré	quise	querido
saber	sé	sabré	supe	sabido
salir	salgo	saldré	salí	salido
ser	soy	seré	fui	sido
tener	tengo	tendré	tuve	tenido
traer	traigo	traeré	traje	traído
valer	valgo	valdré	valí	valido
venir	vengo	vendré	vine	venido
ver	veo	veré	vi	visto

Las Formas del Verbo Inglés

1. Se forma la 3ª persona singular del tiempo presente exactamente al igual que el plural de los sustantivos, añadiendo **-es** o **-s** a la forma sencilla según las mismas reglas, así:

(1)	teach	pass	wish	fix	buzz
	teaches	passes	wishes	fixes	buzzes
(2)	place	change	judge	please	freeze
	places	changes	judges	pleases	freezes

(3a)	find	sell	clean	hear	love	buy	know
	finds	sells	cleans	hears	loves	buys	knows
(3b)	think	like	laugh	stop	hope	meet	want
	thinks	likes	laughs	stops	hopes	meets	wants
(4)	cry	try	dry	carry	deny		
	cries	tries	dries	carries	denies		

Cinco verbos muy comunes tienen 3ª persona singular irregular:

(5)	go	do	say	have	be
	goes	does	says	has	is

2. Se forman el tiempo pasado y el participio de modo igual, añadiendo a la forma sencilla la terminación **-ed** o **-d** según las reglas que siguen.

(1) Si la forma sencilla termina en **-d** o **-t**, se le pone **-ed** como sílaba aparte:

end	fold	need	load
ended	folded	needed	loaded
want	feast	wait	light
wanted	feasted	waited	lighted

(2) Si la forma sencilla termina en cualquier otra consonante, se añade también **-ed** pero sin hacer sílaba aparte:

(2a)	bang	sail	seem	harm	earn	weigh
	banged	sailed	seemed	harmed	earned	weighed
(2b)	lunch	work	look	laugh	help	pass
	lunched	worked	looked	laughed	helped	passed

(3) Si la forma sencilla termina en **-e**, se le pone sólo **-d**:

(3a)	hate	taste	waste	guide	fade	trade
	hated	tasted	wasted	guided	faded	traded
(3b)	free	judge	rule	name	dine	scare
	freed	judged	ruled	named	dined	scared
(3c)	place	force	knife	like	hope	base
	placed	forced	knifed	liked	hoped	based

(4) Una **-y** final que sigue a cualquier consonante se cambia en **-ie** al añadir la **-d** del pasado/participio:

cry	try	dry	carry	deny
cried	tried	dried	carried	denied

3. Varios verbos muy comunes forman el tiempo pasado y el participio de manera irregular. Pertenecen a tres grupos.

(1) Los que tienen una sola forma irregular para tiempo pasado y participio, como los siguientes:

bend	bleed	bring	build	buy
bent	bled	brought	built	bough
catch	creep	deal	dig	feed
caught	crept	dealt	dug	fed

feel	fight	find	flee	get
felt	fought	found	fled	got
hang	have	hear	hold	keep
hung	had	heard	held	kept
lead	leave	lend	lose	make
led	left	lent	lost	made
mean	meet	say	seek	sell
meant	met	said	sought	sold
send	shine	shoot	sit	sleep
sent	shone	shot	sat	slept
spend	stand	strike	sweep	teach
spent	stood	struck	swept	taught

(2) Los que tienen una forma irregular para el tiempo pasado y otra forma irregular para el participio, como los siguientes:

be	beat	become	begin	bite
was	beat	became	began	bit
been	beaten	become	begun	bitten
blow	break	choose	come	do
blew	broke	chose	came	did
blown	broken	chosen	come	done
draw	drink	drive	eat	fall
drew	drank	drove	ate	fell
drawn	drunk	driven	eaten	fallen
fly	forget	freeze	give	go
flew	forgot	froze	gave	went
flown	forgotten	frozen	given	gone
grow	hide	know	ride	ring
grew	hid	knew	rode	rang
grown	hidden	known	ridden	rung
rise	run	see	shake	shrink
rose	ran	saw	shook	shrank
risen	run	seen	shaken	shrunk
sing	sink	speak	steal	swear
sang	sank	spoke	stole	swore
sung	sunk	spoken	stolen	sworn
swim	tear	throw	wear	write
swam	tore	threw	wore	wrote
swum	torn	thrown	worn	written

(3) Los que no varían del todo, la forma sencilla funcionando también como pasado/participio; entre éstos son de mayor frecuencia:

bet	burst	cast	cost	cut
hit	hurt	let	put	quit
read	set	shed	shut	slit
spit	split	spread	thrust	wet

El Plural del Sustantivo Inglés

A la forma singular se añade la terminación **-es** o **-s** de acuerdo con las reglas siguientes.

(1) Si el singular termina en **-ch**, **-s**, **-sh**, **-x** o **-z**, se le pone **-es** como sílaba aparte:

match	glass	dish	box	buzz
matches	glasses	dishes	boxes	buzzes

(2) Si el singular termina en **-ce**, **-ge**, **-se** o **-ze**, se le pone una **-s** que con la vocal precedente forma sílaba aparte:

face	page	house	size
faces	pages	houses	sizes

(3) Una **-y** final que sigue a cualquier consonante se cambia en **-ie** al ponérsele la **-s** del plural:

sky	city	lady	ferry	penny
skies	cities	ladies	ferries	pennies

(4) Los siguientes sustantivos comunes tienen plural irregular:

man	woman	child	foot	mouse	goos
men	women	children	feet	mice	gees
wife	knife	life	half	leaf	deer
wives	knives	lives	halves	leaves	deer

Money/Dinero

UNIT OF CURRENCY/MONEDA

Argentina	peso	**Guatemala**	quetzal
Belize	dollar	**Honduras**	lempira
Bolivia	peso	**Mexico**	peso
Brazil	cruzeiro	**Nicaragua**	córdoba
Canada	dollar	**Panama**	balboa
Chile	escudo	**Paraguay**	guaraní
Colombia	peso	**Peru**	sol
Costa Rica	colón	**Philippines**	peso
Cuba	peso	**Puerto Rico**	dollar
Dominican		**Spain**	peseta
** Republic**	peso	**United States**	dollar
Ecuador	sucre	**Uruguay**	peso
El Salvador	colón	**Venezuela**	bolívar

Days of the Week/Días de la Semana

Sunday	domingo
Monday	lunes
Tuesday	martes
Wednesday	miércoles
Thursday	jueves
Friday	viernes
Saturday	sábado

Months/Meses

January	enero	July	julio
February	febrero	August	agosto
March	marzo	September	septiembre
April	abril	October	octubre
May	mayo	November	noviembre
June	junio	December	diciembre

English Abbreviations/Abreviaturas Inglesas

a.	adjective
abbr.	abbreviation
adv.	adverb
aero.	aeronautical
agr.	agriculture
anat.	anatomy
art.	article
auto.	automotive
biol.	biology
bot.	botany
Carib.	Caribbean
chem.	chemistry
coll.	colloquial
com.	commercial
conj.	conjunction
dem.	demonstrative
econ.	economics
elec.	electrical
esp.	especially
f.	feminine
fig.	figurative
fin.	finance
geog.	geography
govt.	government
gram.	grammar
interj.	interjection
interrog.	interrogative
leg.	legal
m.	masculine
mech.	mechanics
med.	medicine
Mex.	Mexico
mil.	military
mus.	musical
n.	noun
naut.	nautical
phot.	photography
pl.	plural
pol.	politics
prep.	preposition
pron.	pronoun
punct.	punctuation
rel.	relative, religion
S.A.	Spanish America
theat.	theater
v.	verb

SPANISH-ENGLISH

A

a, *prep.* to; at.
abacero, *m.* grocer.
abad, *m.* abbot.
abadía, *f.* abbey.
abajo, *adv.* down; downstairs.
abandonar, *v.* abandon.
abanico, *m.* fan. **—abanicar,** *v.*
abaratar, *v.* cheapen.
abarcar, *v.* comprise; clasp.
abastecer, *v.* supply, provision.
abatido, *a.* dejected, despondent.
abatir, *v.* depress, dishearten.
abdicar, *v.* abdicate.
abdomen, *m.* abdomen.
abeja, *f.* bee.
abejarrón, *m.* bumblebee.
abertura, *f.* opening, aperture, slit.
abeto, *m.* fir.
abierto, *a.* open; overt.
abismo, *m.* abyss, chasm.
ablandar, *v.* soften.
abochornar, *v.* embarrass.
abogado, *m.* lawyer, attorney.
abolengo, *m.* ancestry.
abolición, *f.* abolition.
abolladura, *f.* dent. **—abollar,** *v.*
abominable, *a.* abominable.
abominar, *v.* abhor.
abonar, *v.* pay; fertilize.
abonarse, *v.* subscribe.
abono, *m.* fertilizer; subscription.
aborrecer, *v.* hate, loathe, abhor.
aborto, *m.* abortion.
abovedar, *v.* vault.
abrasar, *v.* burn.
abrazar, *v.* embrace; clasp.
abrazo, *m.* embrace.
abreviar, *v.* abbreviate, abridge, shorten.
abreviatura, *f.* abbreviation.
abrigar, *v.* harbor, shelter.
abrigarse, *v.* bundle up.
abrigo, *m.* overcoat; shelter; *(pl.)* wraps.
abril, *m.* April.
abrir, *v.* open; (med.) lance.
abrochar, *v.* clasp.

abrojo, *m.* thorn.
abrumar, *v.* overwhelm, crush, swamp.
absceso, *m.* abscess.
absolución, *f.* absolution; acquittal.
absoluto, *a.* absolute; downright.
absolver, *v.* absolve, pardon.
absorbente, *a.* absorbent.
absorber, *v.* absorb.
absorción, *f.* absorption.
abstenerse, *v.* abstain; refrain.
abstinencia, *f.* abstinence.
abstracción, *f.* abstraction.
abstraer, *v.* abstract.
absurdo, 1. *a.* absurd. **2.** *m.* absurdity.
abuela, *f.* grandmother.
abuelo, *m.* grandfather; *(pl.)* grandparents.
abultado, *a.* bulky.
abultamiento, *m.* bulge. **—abultar,** *v.*
abundancia, *f.* abundance, plenty.
abundante, *a.* abundant, plentiful.
abundar, *v.* abound.
aburrido, *a.* boring, tedious.
aburrimiento, *m.* boredom.
aburrir, *v.* bore.
abusar, *v.* abuse, misuse.
abusivo, *a.* abusive.
abuso, *m.* abuse.
abyecto, *a.* abject, low.
acá, *adv.* here.
acabar, *v.* finish. **a. de . . . ,** to have just . . . .
academia, *f.* academy.
académico, *a.* academic.
acaecer, *v.* happen.
acanalar, *v.* groove.
acaparar, *v.* hoard; monopolize.
acariciar, *v.* caress, stroke.
acaso, *m.* chance. **por si a.,** just in case.
acceder, *v.* accede.
accesible, *a.* accessible.
acceso, *m.* access, approach.
accesorio, *a.* accessory.
accidental, *a.* accidental.

accidente, *m.* accident, wreck.
acción, *f.* action, act; (com.) share of stock.
acechar, *v.* ambush, spy on.
aceite, *m.* oil.
aceitoso, *a.* oily.
aceituna, *f.* olive.
aceleración, *f.* acceleration.
acelerar, *v.* accelerate, speed up.
acento, *m.* accent.
acentuar, *v.* accent, accentuate, stress.
acepillar, *v.* brush; plane (wood).
aceptable, *a.* acceptable.
aceptación, *f.* acceptance.
aceptar, *v.* accept.
acequia, *f.* ditch.
acera, *f.* sidewalk.
acerca de, *prep.* about, concerning.
acercar, *v.* bring near.
acercarse, *v.* approach, come near, go near.
acero, *m.* steel.
acertar, *v.* guess right. **a. en**, hit (a mark).
acertijo, *m.* puzzle, riddle.
acidez, *f.* acidity.
ácido, **1.** *a.* sour. **2.** *m.* acid.
aclamación, *f.* acclamation.
aclamar, *v.* acclaim.
aclarar, *v.* brighten; clarify, clear up.
acoger, *v.* welcome, receive.
acogida, *f.* welcome, reception.
acometer, *v.* attack.
acomodador, *m.* usher.
acomodar, *v.* accommodate, fix up.
acompañamiento, *m.* accompaniment; following.
acompañar, *v.* accompany.
acondicionar, *v.* condition.
aconsejable, *a.* advisable.
aconsejar, *v.* advise.
acontecer, *v.* happen.
acontecimiento, *m.* event, happening.
acorazado, *m.* battleship.
acordarse, *v.* remember, recollect.
acortar, *v.* shorten.
acosar, *v.* beset, harry.
acostar, *v.* lay down; put to bed.
acostarse, *v.* lie down; go to bed.
acostumbrado, *a.* accustomed; customary.

acostumbrar, *v.* accustom.
acrecentar, *v.* increase.
acreditar, *v.* accredit.
acreedor -ra, *n.* creditor.
acróbata, *m.* acrobat.
actitud, *f.* attitude.
actividad, *f.* activity.
activista, *a. & n.* activist.
activo, *a.* active.
acto, *m.* act.
actor, *m.* actor.
actriz, *f.* actress.
actual, *a.* present.
actuar, *v.* act.
acuarela, *f.* watercolor.
acuario, *m.* aquarium.
acuático, *a.* aquatic.
acuchillar, *v.* slash, knife.
acudir, *v.* rally; hasten; be present.
acuerdo, *m.* accord, agreement settlement. **de a.**, in agreement agreed.
acumulación, *f.* accumulation.
acumular, *v.* accumulate.
acuñar, *v.* coin, mint.
acupuntura, *f.* acupuncture.
acusación, *f.* accusation, charge
acusado -da, *a. & n.* accused; defendant.
acusador -ra, *n.* accuser.
acusar, *v.* accuse; acknowledge.
acústica, *f.* acoustics.
achicar, *v.* diminish, dwarf; humble.
adaptación, *f.* adaptation.
adaptar, *v.* adapt.
adecuado, *a.* adequate.
adelantado, *a.* advanced; fas (clock).
adelantamiento, *m.* advancement, promotion.
adelantar, *v.* advance.
adelante, *adv.* ahead, forward onward, on.
adelanto, *m.* advancement, progress, improvement.
adelgazar, *v.* make thin.
ademán, *m.* attitude; gesture.
además, *adv.* in addition, besides also.
adentro, *adv.* in, inside.
adepto, *a.* adept.
aderezar, *v.* prepare; trim.
adherirse, *v.* adhere, stick.
adhesivo, *a.* adhesive.
adición, *f.* addition.

adicional, *a.* additional, extra.
adicto, *a. & m.* addicted; addict.
adiós, *m. & interj.* good-bye, fare-well.
adivinar, *v.* guess.
adjetivo, *m.* adjective.
adjunto, *a.* enclosed.
administración, *f.* administration.
administrador, *m.* administrator.
administrar, *v.* administer; manage.
administrativo, *a.* administrative.
admirable, *a.* admirable.
admiración. *f.* admiration; wonder.
admirar, *v.* admire.
admisión, *f.* admission.
admitir, *v.* admit, acknowledge.
adolescencia, *f.* adolescence, youth.
adolescente, *a.* adolescent.
adónde, *adv.* where.
adondequiera, *conj.* wherever.
adopción, *f.* adoption.
adoptar, *v.* adopt.
adoración, *f.* worship, love, adoration. **—adorar,** *v.*
adormecer, *v.* drowse.
adornar, *v.* adorn; decorate.
adorno, *m.* adornment, trimming.
adquirir, *v.* acquire, obtain.
adquisición, *f.* acquisition, attainment.
aduana, *f.* custom house, customs.
aducto. *m.* input.
adujada, *f.* (naut.) coil of rope.
adulación, *f.* flattery.
adular, *v.* flatter.
adulterar, *v.* adulterate.
adulterio, *m.* adultery.
adulto, *a. & m.* adult.
adusto, *a.* gloomy; austere.
adverbio, *m.* adverb.
adversario, *m.* adversary.
adversidad, *f.* adversity.
adverso, *a.* adverse.
advertencia, *f.* warning.
advertir, *v.* warn; notice.
adyacente, *a.* adjacent.
aéreo, *a.* aerial; air.
aeromoza, *f.* stewardess, flight attendant.
aeroplano, *m.* airplane.
aeropuerto, *m.* airport.
aerosol, *m.* aerosol, spray.

afable, *a.* affable, pleasant.
afanarse, *v.* toil.
afear, *v.* deface, mar, deform.
afectación, *f.* affectation.
afectar, *v.* affect.
afecto, *m.* affection, attachment.
afeitada, *f.* shave. **—afeitarse,** *v.*
afeminado, *a.* effeminate.
afición, *f.* fondness, liking; hobby.
aficionado -da, *n.* fan, devotee; amateur.
aficionarse a, *v.* become fond of.
afilado, *a.* sharp.
afilar, *v.* sharpen.
afiliación, *f.* affiliation.
afiliado, *m.* affiliate. **—afiliar,** *v.*
afinar, *v.* polish, tune up.
afinidad, *f.* relationship.
afirmación, *f.* affirmation, statement.
afirmar, *v.* affirm, assert.
afirmativa, *f.* affirmative. **—afirmativo,** *a.*
aflicción, *f.* affliction; sorrow, grief.
afligido, *a.* sorrowful, grieved.
afligir, *v.* grieve, distress.
aflojar, *v.* loosen.
afortunado, *a.* fortunate, successful, lucky.
afrenta, *f.* insult, outrage, affront. **—afrentar,** *v.*
afrentoso, *a.* shameful.
africano -na, *a. & n.* African.
afuera, *adv.* out, outside.
afueras, *f.,pl.* suburbs.
agacharse, *v.* squat, crouch; cower.
agarrar, *v.* seize, grasp, clutch.
agarro, *m.* clutch, grasp.
agencia, *f.* agency.
agente, *m.* agent, representative.
ágil, *a.* agile, spry.
agitación, *f.* agitation, ferment.
agitado, *a.* agitated; excited.
agitador, *m.* agitator.
agitar, *v.* shake, agitate, excite.
agobiar, *v.* oppress, burden.
agosto, *m.* August.
agotamiento, *m.* exhaustion.
agotar, *v.* exhaust, use up, sap.
agradable, *a.* agreeable, pleasant.
agradar, *v.* please.
agradecer, *v.* thank; appreciate, be grateful for.

agradecido, *a.* grateful, thankful.

agradecimiento, *m.* gratitude, thanks.

agravar, *v.* aggravate, make worse.

agravio, *m.* wrong. **—agraviar,** *v.*

agregado, *a. & m.* aggregate.

agregar, *v.* add; gather.

agresión, *f.* aggression; (leg.) battery.

agresivo, *a.* aggressive.

agresor, *m.* aggressor.

agrícola, *a.* agricultural.

agricultor, *m.* farmer.

agricultura, *f.* agriculture, farming.

agrio, *a.* sour.

agrupar, *v.* group.

agua, *f.* water. **—aguar,** *v.*

aguacate, *m.* avocado, alligator pear.

aguantar, *v.* endure, stand, put up with.

aguardar, *v.* await; expect.

aguardiente, *m.* brandy.

agudo, *a.* sharp, keen, shrill, acute.

agüero, *m.* omen.

águila, *f.* eagle.

aguja, *f.* needle.

agujero, *m.* hole.

aguzar, *v.* sharpen.

ahí, *adv.* there.

ahogar, *v.* drown; choke; suffocate.

ahondar, *v.* deepen.

ahora, *adv.* now.

ahorcar, *v.* hang (execute).

ahorrar, *v.* save, save up; spare.

ahorros, *m.pl.* savings.

ahumar, *v.* smoke.

airado, *a.* angry, indignant.

aire, *m.* air. **—airear,** *v.*

aislamiento, *m.* isolation.

aislar, *v.* isolate.

ajedrez, *m.* chess.

ajeno, *a.* alien; someone else's.

ají, *m.* chili.

ajo, *m.* garlic.

ajustado, *a.* adjusted; trim; exact.

ajustar, *v.* adjust.

ajuste, *m.* adjustment, settlement.

al, *contr.* of **a** + **el.**

ala, *f.* wing; brim (of hat).

alabanza, *f.* praise. **—alabar,** *v.*

alabear, *v.* warp.

alambique, *m.* still.

alambre, *m.* wire. **a. de púas,** barbed wire.

alarde, *m.* boasting, ostentation.

alargar, *v.* lengthen; stretch out.

alarma, *f.* alarm. **—alarmar,** *v.*

alba, *f.* daybreak, dawn.

albanega, *f.* hair net.

albañil, *m.* bricklayer; mason.

albaricoque, *m.* apricot.

albergue, *m.* shelter. **—albergar,** *v.*

alborotar, *v.* disturb, make noise, brawl, riot.

alboroto, *m.* brawl, disturbance, din, tumult.

álbum, *m.* album.

alcachofa, *f.* artichoke.

alcalde, *m.* mayor.

alcance, *m.* reach; range, scope.

alcanfor, *m.* camphor.

alcanzar, *v.* reach, overtake, catch.

alcayata, *f.* spike.

alce, *m.* elk.

alcoba, *f.* bedroom; alcove.

alcohol, *m.* alcohol.

alcohólico, *a.* alcoholic.

aldaba, *f.* latch.

aldea, *f.* village.

alegación, *f.* allegation.

alegar, *v.* allege.

alegrar, *v.* make happy, brighten. **alegrarse,** *v.* be glad.

alegre, *a.* gay, cheerful, merry.

alegría, *f.* gaiety, cheer.

alejarse, *v.* move away, off.

alemán -ana, *a. & n.* German.

Alemania, *f.* Germany.

alentar, *v.* cheer up, encourage.

alergia, *f.* allergy.

alerta, *adv.* on the alert.

aleve, alevoso, *a.* treacherous.

alfabeto, *m.* alphabet.

alfalfa, *f.* alfalfa.

alfarería, *f.* pottery.

alférez, *m.* (naval) ensign.

alfil, *m.* (chess) bishop.

alfiler, *m.* pin.

alfombra, *f.* carpet, rug.

alforja, *f.* knapsack; saddlebag.

algarabía, *f.* jargon; din.

álgebra, *f.* algebra.

algo, *pron. & adv.* something, somewhat; anything.

algodón, *m.* cotton.

alguien, *pron.* somebody, someone; anybody, anyone.

algún -no -na, *a. & pron.* some; any.

alhaja, *f.* jewel.

aliado, *a. & m.* allied; ally. **— aliar,** *v.*

alianza, *f.* alliance.

alicates, *m.pl.* pliers.

aliento, *m.* breath. **dar a.,** encourage.

aligerar, *v.* lighten.

alimentar, *v.* feed, nourish.

alimento, *m.* nourishment, food.

alinear, *v.* line up; (pol.) align.

alisar, *v.* smooth.

alistamiento, *m.* enlistment.

alistar, *v.* make ready, prime.

alistarse, *v.* get ready; (mil.) enlist.

aliviar, *v.* alleviate, relieve, ease.

alivio, *m.* relief.

alma, *f.* soul.

almacén, *m.* department store; storehouse.

almacenaje, *m.* storage.

almacenar, *v.* store.

almanaque, *m.* almanac.

almeja, *f.* clam.

almendra, *f.* almond.

almíbar, *m.* syrup.

almidón, *m.* starch. **—almidonar,** *v.*

almirante, *m.* admiral.

almohada, *f.* pillow.

almuerzo, *m.* lunch. **—almorzar,** *v.*

alojamiento, *m.* lodging, accommodations.

alojar, *v.* lodge, house.

alojarse, *v.* stay, room.

alquiler, *m.* rent. **—alquilar,** *v.*

alrededor, *adv.* around.

alrededores, *m.pl.* environs.

altanero, *a.* haughty.

altar, *m.* altar.

altavoz, *m.* loudspeaker.

alteración, *f.* alteration.

alterar, *v.* alter.

alternativa, *f.* alternative. **—alternativo,** *a.*

alterno, *a.* alternate. **—alternar,** *v.*

alteza, *f.* highness.

altivo, *a.* proud, haughty; lofty.

alto, 1. *a.* high, tall; loud. **2.** *m.* height, story (house).

altura, *f.* height, altitude.

alud, *m.* avalanche.

aludir, *v.* allude.

alumbrado, *m.* lighting.

alumbrar, *v.* light.

aluminio, *m.* aluminum.

alumno -na, *n.* student, pupil.

alusión, *f.* allusion.

alza, *f.* rise; boost.

alzar, *v.* raise, lift.

allá, *adv.* there. **más a.,** beyond, farther on.

allanar, *v.* flatten, smooth, plane.

allí, *adv.* there. **por a.,** that way.

ama, *f.* housewife, mistress (of house). **a. de llaves,** housekeeper.

amable, *a.* kind; pleasant, sweet.

amalgamar, *v.* amalgamate.

amamantar, *v.* suckle, nurse.

amanecer, 1. *m.* dawn, daybreak. **2.** *v.* dawn; awaken.

amante, *m.* lover.

amar, *v.* love.

amargo, *a.* bitter.

amargón, *m.* dandelion.

amargura, *f.* bitterness.

amarillo, *a.* yellow.

amarradero, *m.* mooring.

amarrar, *v.* hitch, moor, tie up.

amartillar, *v.* hammer; cock (a gun).

amasar, *v.* knead, mold.

ámbar, *m.* amber.

ambarino, *a.* amber.

ambición, *f.* ambition.

ambicionar, *v.* aspire to.

ambicioso, *a.* ambitious.

ambiente, *m.* environment, atmosphere.

ambigüedad, *f.* ambiguity.

ambiguo, *a.* ambiguous.

ambos, *a. & pron.* both.

ambulancia, *f.* ambulance.

amenaza, *f.* threat, menace.

amenazar, *v.* threaten, menace.

ameno, *a.* pleasant.

americana, *f.* suit coat.

americano -na, *a. & n.* American.

ametralladora, *f.* machine gun.

amigable, *a.* amicable, friendly.

amígdala, *f.* tonsil.

amigo -ga, *n.* friend.

amistad, *f.* friendship.

amistoso, *a.* friendly.

amniocéntesis, *m.* amniocentesis.

amo, *m.* master.

amonestaciones, *f.pl.* banns.
amonestar, *v.* admonish.
amoníaco, *m.* ammonia.
amontonar, *v.* amass, pile up.
amor, *m.* love. **a. propio,** self-esteem.
amorío, *m.* romance, love affair.
amoroso, *a.* amorous; loving.
amortecer, *v.* deaden.
amparar, *v.* aid, befriend; protect, shield.
amparo, *m.* protection.
ampliar, *v.* enlarge; elaborate.
amplificar, *v.* amplify.
amplio, *a.* ample, roomy.
ampolla, *f.* bubble; bulb; blister.
amputar, *v.* amputate.
amueblar, *v.* furnish.
analfabeto, *a. & m.* illiterate.
análisis, *m. or f.* analysis.
analizar, *v.* analyze.
analogía, *f.* analogy.
análogo, *a.* similar, analogous.
anarquía, *f.* anarchy.
anatomía, *f.* anatomy.
ancho, *a.* wide, broad.
anchoa, *f.* anchovy.
anchura, *f.* width, breadth.
anciano -na, *a. & m.* old, aged (person).
ancla, *f.* anchor. **—anclar,** *v.*
anclaje, *m.* anchorage.
andamio, *m.* scaffold.
andar, *v.* walk; move, go.
andén, *m.* (railroad) platform.
andrajoso, *a.* ragged, uneven.
anécdota, *f.* anecdote.
anegar, *v.* flood, drown.
anestesia, *f.* anesthetic.
anexar, *v.* annex.
anexión, *f.* annexation.
anfitrión, *m.* host.
ángel, *m.* angel.
angosto, *a.* narrow.
anguila, *f.* eel.
angular, *a.* angular.
ángulo, *m.* angle.
angustia, *f.* anguish, agony.
angustiar, *v.* distress.
anhelar, *v.* long for.
anidar, *v.* nest, nestle.
anillo, *m.* ring; circle.
animación, *f.* animation; bustle.
animado, *a.* animated, lively; animate.
animal, *a. & m.* animal.

ánimo, *m.* state of mind, spirits; courage.
aniquilar, *v.* annihilate, destroy.
aniversario, *m.* anniversary.
anoche, *adv.* last night.
anochecer, **1.** *m.* twilight, nightfall. **2.** *v.* get dark.
anónimo, *a.* anonymous.
anormal, *a.* abnormal.
anotación, *f.* annotation.
anotar, *v.* annotate.
ansia, ansiedad, *f.* anxiety.
ansioso, *a.* anxious.
antagonismo, *m.* antagonism.
antagonista, *m. & f.* antagonist; opponent.
anteayer, *adv.* day before yesterday.
antebrazo, *m.* forearm.
antecedente, *a. & m.* antecedent.
anteceder, *v.* precede.
antecesor, *m.* ancestor.
antemano. de a., in advance.
antena, *f.* antenna.
anteojos, *m.pl.* eyeglasses.
antepasado, *m.* ancestor.
anterior, *a.* previous, former.
antes, *adv.* before; formerly.
anticipación, *f.* anticipation.
anticipar, *v.* anticipate; advance.
anticonceptivo, *a. & n.* contraceptive.
anticuado, *a.* antiquated, obsolete.
antídoto, *m.* antidote.
antigüedad, *f.* antiquity; antique.
antiguo, *a.* former; old; antique.
antílope, *m.* antelope.
antinuclear, *a.* antinuclear.
antipatía, *f.* antipathy.
antipático, *a.* disagreeable, nasty.
antiséptico, *a. & m.* antiseptic.
antojarse. se me antoja . . . etc., I desire . . ., take a fancy to . . ., etc.
antojo, *m.* whim, fancy.
antorcha, *f.* torch.
antracita, *f.* anthracite.
anual, *a.* annual, yearly.
anudar, *v.* knot; tie.
anular, *v.* annul, void.
anunciar, *v.* announce; proclaim; advertise.
anuncio, *m.* announcement; advertisement.
añadir, *v.* add.
añil, *m.* bluing.

año, *m.* year.

apacible, *a.* peaceful, peaceable.

apaciguamiento, *m.* appeasement.

apaciguar, *v.* appease; placate.

apagado, *a.* dull.

apagar, *v.* extinguish, quench, put out.

aparador, *m.* buffet, cupboard.

aparato, *m.* apparatus; machine; appliance, set.

aparecer, *v.* appear, show up.

aparejo, *m.* rig. **—aparejar,** *v.*

aparentar, *v.* pretend; profess.

aparente, *a.* apparent.

apariencia, aparición, *f.* appearance.

apartado, 1. *a.* aloof; separate. **2.** *m.* post-office box.

apartamento, *m.* apartment. **a. en propiedad,** condominium.

apartar, *v.* separate; remove.

aparte, *adv.* apart; aside.

apartheid, *m.* apartheid.

apasionado, *a.* passionate.

apatía, *f.* apathy.

apearse, *v.* get off, alight.

apedrear, *v.* stone.

apelación, *f.* appeal. **—apelar,** *v.*

apellido, *m.* family name.

apenas, *adv.* scarcely, hardly.

apéndice, *m.* appendix.

apercibir, *v.* prepare, warn.

aperitivo, *m.* appetizer.

aperos, *m.pl.* implements.

apetecer, *v.* desire, have appetite for.

apetito, *m.* appetite.

ápice, *m.* apex.

apilar, *v.* stack.

apio, *m.* celery.

aplacar, *v.* appease; placate.

aplastar, *v.* crush, flatten.

aplaudir, *v.* applaud, cheer.

aplauso, *m.* applause.

aplazar, *v.* postpone, put off.

aplicable, *a.* applicable.

aplicado, *a.* industrious, diligent.

aplicar, *v.* apply.

aplomo, *m.* aplomb, poise.

apoderado, *m.* attorney.

apoderarse de, *v.* get hold of, seize.

apodo, *m.* nickname. **—apodar,** *v.*

apologético, *a.* apologetic.

apoplejía, *f.* apoplexy.

aposento, *m.* room, flat.

apostar, *v.* bet, wager.

apóstol, *m.* apostle.

apoyar, *v.* support, prop; lean.

apoyo, *m.* support; prop; aid; approval.

apreciable, *a.* appreciable.

apreciar, *v.* appreciate, prize.

aprecio, *m.* appreciation, regard.

apremio, *m.* pressure, compulsion.

aprender, *v.* learn.

aprendiz, *m.* apprentice.

aprensión, *f.* apprehension.

aprensivo, *a.* apprehensive.

apresurado, *a.* hasty, fast.

apresurar, *v.* hurry, speed up.

apretado, *a.* tight.

apretar, *v.* squeeze, press; tighten.

apretón, *m.* squeeze.

aprieto, *m.* plight, predicament.

aprobación, *f.* approbation, approval.

aprobar, *v.* approve.

apropiación, *f.* appropriation.

apropiado, *a.* appropriate. **— apropiar,** *v.*

aprovechar, *v.* profit by.

aprovecharse, *v.* take advantage.

aproximado, *a.* approximate.

aproximarse a, *v.* approach.

aptitud, *f.* aptitude.

apto, *a.* apt.

apuesta, *f.* bet, wager, stake.

apuntar, *v.* point, aim; prompt; write down.

apunte, *m.* annotation, note; promptings, cue.

apuñalar, *v.* stab.

apurar, *v.* hurry; worry.

apuro, *m.* predicament, scrape, trouble.

aquel, aquella, *dem. a.* that.

aquél, aquélla, *dem. pron.* that (one); the former.

aquello, *dem. pron.* that.

aquí, *adv.* here. **por a.,** this way.

aquietar, *v.* allay; lull, pacify.

ara, *f.* altar.

árabe, *a. & n.* Arab, Arabic.

arado, *m.* plow. **—arar,** *v.*

arándano, *m.* cranberry.

araña, *f.* spider. **a. de luces,** chandelier.

arbitración, *f.* arbitration.

arbitrador -ra, *n.* arbitrator.

arbitraje, *m.* arbitration.

arbitrar, v. arbitrate.
arbitrario, a. arbitrary.
árbitro, m. arbiter, umpire, referee.
árbol, m. tree; mast.
arbusto, m. bush, shrub.
arca, f. chest; ark.
arcada, f. arcade.
arcaico, a. archaic.
arce, m. maple.
arcilla, f. clay.
arco, m. arc; arch; (archer's) bow. **a. iris,** rainbow.
archipiélago, m. archipelago.
archivo, m. archive; file. **—archivar,** v.
arder, v. burn.
ardid, m. stratagem, cunning.
ardiente, a. ardent, burning, fiery.
ardilla, f. squirrel.
ardor, m. ardor, fervor.
arduo, a. arduous.
área, f. area.
arena, f. sand; arena.
arenoso, a. sandy.
arenque, m. herring.
arete, n. earring.
argentino -na, a. & n. Argentine.
argüir, v. dispute, argue.
árido, a. arid.
aristocracia, f. aristocracy.
aristócrata, f. aristocrat.
aristocrático, a. aristocratic.
aritmética, f. arithmetic.
arma, f. weapon, arm.
armadura, f. armor; reinforcement; framework.
armamento, m. armament.
armar, v. arm.
armario, m. cabinet, bureau, wardrobe.
armazón, m. framework, frame.
armería, f. armory.
armisticio, m. armistice.
armonía, f. harmony.
armonioso, a. harmonious.
armonizar, v. harmonize.
arnés, m. harness.
aroma, f. aroma, fragrance.
aromático, a. aromatic.
arpa, f. harp.
arquear, v. arch.
arquitecto, m. architect.
arquitectura, f. architecture.
arquitectural, a. architectural.
arrabal, m. suburb.

arraigar, v. take root, settle.
arrancar, v. pull out, tear out; start up.
arranque, m. dash, sudden start; fit of anger.
arrastrar, v. drag.
arrebatar, v. snatch, grab.
arrebato, m. sudden attack, fit of anger.
arrecife, m. reef.
arreglar, v. arrange; repair; fix; adjust, settle.
arreglárselas, v. manage, shift for oneself.
arreglo, m. arrangement, settlement.
arremeter, v. attack.
arrendar, v. rent.
arrepentimiento, m. repentance.
arrepentirse, v. repent.
arrestar, v. arrest.
arresto, m. arrest.
arriba, adv. up; upstairs.
arriendo, m. lease.
arriero, m. muleteer.
arriesgar, v. risk.
arrimarse, v. lean.
arrodillarse, v. kneel.
arrogancia, f. arrogance.
arrogante, a. arrogant.
arrojar, v. throw, hurl; shed.
arrollar, v. roll, coil.
arroyo, m. brook; gully; gutter.
arroz, m. rice.
arruga, f. ridge; wrinkle.
arrugar, v. wrinkle, crumple.
arruinar, v. ruin, destroy, wreck.
arsenal, m. arsenal; armory.
arsénico, m. arsenic.
arte, m. (f. in pl.) art, craft; wiliness.
arteria, f. artery.
artesa, f. trough.
artesano, m. artisan, craftsman.
ártico, a. arctic.
articulación, f. articulation; joint.
articular, v. articulate.
artículo, m. article.
artífice, m. & f. artisan.
artificial, a. artificial.
artificio, m. artifice, device.
artificioso, a. affected.
artillería, f. artillery.
artista, m. & f. artist.
artístico, a. artistic.
arzobispo, m. archbishop.
as, m. ace.
asado, m. roast.

asaltador, *m.* assailant.

asaltar, *v.* assail, attack.

asalto, *m.* assault. **—asaltar,** *v.*

asamblea, *f.* assembly.

asar, *v.* roast; broil, cook (meat).

asaz, *adv.* enough; quite.

ascender, *v.* ascend, go up; amount.

ascenso, *m.* ascent.

ascensor, *m.* elevator.

ascensorista, *m.* & *f.* (elevator) operator.

asco, *m.* nausea; disgusting thing. **qué a.,** how disgusting.

aseado, *a.* tidy. **—asear,** *v.*

asediar, *v.* besiege.

asedio, *m.* siege.

asegurar, *v.* assure; secure.

asegurarse, *v.* make sure.

asemejarse a, *v.* resemble.

asentar, *v.* settle; seat.

asentimiento, *m.* assent. **—asentir,** *v.*

aseo, *m.* neatness, tidiness.

aserción, *f.* assertion.

aserrar, *v.* saw.

asesinar, *v.* assassinate; murder, slay.

asesinato, *m.* assassination, murder.

asesino -na, *n.* murderer, assassin.

aseveración, *f.* assertion.

aseverar, *v.* assert.

asfalto, *m.* asphalt.

así, *adv.* so, thus, this way, that way. **a. como,** as well as. **a. que,** as soon as.

asiático -ca, *a.* & *n.* Asiatic.

asiduo, *a.* assiduous.

asiento, *m.* seat; chair; site.

asignar, *v.* assign; allot.

asilo, *m.* asylum, sanctuary.

asimilar, *v.* assimilate.

asir, *v.* grasp.

asistencia, *f.* attendance, presence.

asistir, *v.* be present, attend.

asno, *m.* donkey.

asociación, *f.* association.

asociado, *m.* associate, partner.

asociar, *v.* associate.

asolar, *v.* desolate; burn, parch.

asoleado, *a.* sunny.

asomar, *v.* appear, loom up, show up.

asombrar, *v.* astonish, amaze.

asombro, *m.* amazement, astonishment.

aspa, *f.* reel. **—aspar,** *v.*

aspecto, *m.* aspect.

aspereza, *f.* harshness.

áspero, *a.* rough, harsh.

aspiración, *f.* aspiration.

aspirador, *m.* vacuum cleaner.

aspirar, *v.* aspire.

aspirina, *f.* aspirin.

asqueroso, *a.* dirty, nasty, filthy.

asta, *f.* shaft.

asterisco, *m.* asterisk.

astilla, *f.* splinter, chip. **—astillar,** *v.*

astillero, *m.* dry dock.

astro, *m.* star.

astronauta, *m.* astronaut.

astronomía, *f.* astronomy.

astucia, *f.* cunning.

astuto, *a.* astute, sly, shrewd.

asumir, *v.* assume.

asunto, *m.* matter, affair, business; subject.

asustar, *v.* frighten, scare, startle.

atacar, *v.* attack, charge.

atajo, *m.* shortcut.

ataque, *m.* attack, charge; spell, stroke.

atar, *v.* tie, bind, fasten.

atareado, *a.* busy.

atascar, *v.* stall, stop, obstruct.

ataúd, *m.* casket, coffin.

atavío, *m.* dress; gear, equipment.

atemorizar, *v.* frighten.

atención, *f.* attention.

atender, *v.* heed; attend to, wait on.

atenerse a, *v.* count on, depend on.

atentado, *m.* crime, offense.

atento, *a.* attentive, courteous.

ateo, *m.* atheist.

aterrizar, *v.* land.

atesorar, *v.* hoard.

atestar, *v.* witness.

atestiguar, *v.* attest, testify.

atinar, *v.* hit upon.

atisbar, *v.* scrutinize, pry.

Atlántico, *m.* Atlantic.

atlántico, *a.* Atlantic.

atlas, *m.* atlas.

atleta, *m.* athlete.

atlético, *a.* athletic.

atletismo, *m.* athletics.

atmósfera, *f.* atmosphere.

atmosférico, a. atmospheric.

atómico, a. atomic.

átomo, m. atom.

atormentar, v. torment, plague.

atornillar, v. screw.

atracción, f. attraction.

atractivo, 1. a. attractive. **2.** m. attraction.

atraer, v. attract; lure.

atrapar, v. trap, catch.

atrás, adv. back; behind.

atrasado, a. belated; backward; slow (clock).

atrasar, v. delay, retard; be slow.

atraso, m. delay; backwardness; (pl.) arrears.

atravesar, v. cross.

atreverse, v. dare.

atrevido, a. daring, bold.

atrevimiento, m. boldness.

atribuir, v. attribute, ascribe.

atributo, m. attribute.

atrincherar, v. entrench.

atrocidad, f. atrocity, outrage.

atronar, v. deafen.

atropellar, v. trample; fell.

atroz, a. atrocious.

aturdir, v. daze, stun, bewilder.

audacia, f. audacity.

audaz, a. audacious, bold.

audible, a. audible.

audiovisual, a. audiovisual.

auditorio, m. audience.

aula, f. classroom, hall.

aullar, v. howl, bay.

aullido, m. howl.

aumentar, v. augment; increase, swell.

aun, aún, adv. still; even. **a. cuando,** even though, even if.

aunque, conj. although, though.

áureo, a. golden.

aureola, f. halo.

aurora, f. dawn.

ausencia, f. absence.

ausentarse, v. stay away.

ausente, a. absent.

auspicio, m. auspice.

austeridad, f. austerity.

austero, a. austere.

austríaco -ca, a. & n. Austrian.

auténtico, a. authentic.

auto, automóvil, m. auto, automobile.

autobús, m. bus.

automático, a. automatic.

autonomía, f. autonomy.

autor, m. author.

autoridad, f. authority.

autoritario, a. authoritative.

autorizar, v. authorize.

auxiliar, 1. a. auxiliary. **2.** v. assist, aid.

auxilio, m. aid, assistance.

avaluar, v. evaluate, appraise.

avance, m. advance. **—avanzar,** v.

avaricia, f. avarice.

avariento, a. miserly, greedy.

avaro -ra, a. & m. miser; miserly.

ave, f. bird.

avena, f. oat.

avenida, f. avenue; flood.

avenirse, v. compromise; agree.

aventajar, v. surpass, get ahead of.

aventar, v. fan; scatter.

aventura, f. adventure.

aventurar, v. venture, risk, gamble.

aventurero, a. & m. adventurous; adventurer.

avergonzado, a. ashamed, abashed.

avergonzar, v. shame, abash.

avería, f. damage. **—averiar,** v.

averiguar, v. ascertain, find out.

aversión, f. aversion.

avestruz, m. ostrich.

aviación, f. aviation.

aviador -ra, n. aviator.

ávido, a. avid; eager.

avión, m. airplane.

avisar, v. notify, let know; warn, advise.

aviso, m. notice, announcement; advertisement; warning.

avispa, f. wasp.

avivar, v. enliven, revive.

aya, f. governess.

ayatola, m. ayatollah.

ayer, adv. yesterday.

ayuda, f. help, aid. **—ayudar,** v.

ayudante, a. assistant, helper; adjutant.

ayuno, m. fast. **—ayunar,** v.

ayuntamiento, m. city hall.

azada, f., **azadón,** m. hoe.

azafata, f. stewardess, flight attendant.

azar, m. hazard, chance. **al a.,** at random.

azotar, v. whip, flog; belabor.

azote, m. scourge, lash.

azúcar, m. sugar.

azul, *a.* blue.
azulado, *a.* azure.
azulejo, *m.* tile; bluebird.

B

baba, *f.* drivel, **—babear,** *v.*
babador, *m.* bib.
babucha, *f.* slipper.
bacalao, *m.* codfish.
bacía, *f.* washbasin.
bacterias, *f.pl.* bacteria.
bacteriología, *f.* bacteriology.
bachiller -ra, *n.* bachelor (degree).
bahía, *f.* bay.
bailador -ra, *n.* dancer.
bailar, *v.* dance.
bailarín -ina, *n.* dancer.
baile, *m.* dancing, dance.
baja, *f.* fall (in price); (mil.) casualty.
bajar, *v.* lower; descend.
bajeza, *f.* baseness.
bajo, 1. *prep.* under, below. 2. *a.* low; short; base.
bala, *f.* bullet; ball; bale.
balada, *f.* ballad.
balancear, *v.* balance; roll, swing, sway.
balanza, *f.* balance; scales.
balbuceo, *m.* stammer; babble. **—balbucear,** *v.*
balcón, *m.* balcony.
balde, *m.* bucket, pail. **de b.,** gratis. **en b.,** in vain.
balística, *f.* ballistics.
balompié, *m.* football.
balón, *m.* football; (auto.) balloon tire.
baloncesto, *m.* basketball.
balota, *f.* ballot, vote, **—balotar,** *v.*
balsa, *f.* raft.
bálsamo, *m.* balm.
baluarte, *m.* bulwark.
ballena, *f.* whale.
bambolearse, *v.* sway.
bambú, *n.* bamboo.
banal, *a.* banal, trite.
banana, *f.* banana.
banano, *m.* banana tree.
bancarrota, *f.* bankruptcy.
banco, *m.* bank; bench; school of fish.
banda, *f.* band.

bandada, *f.* covey; flock.
bandeja, *f.* tray.
bandera, *f.* flag; banner; ensign.
bandido, *m.* bandit.
bando, *m.* faction.
bandolero, *m.* bandit, robber.
banquero, *m.* banker.
banqueta, *f.* stool; (Mex.) sidewalk.
banquete, *m.* feast, banquet.
banquillo, *m.* stool.
bañera, *f.* bathtub.
baño, *m.* bath; bathroom.
bañar, *v.* bathe.
baraja, *f.* pack of cards; game of cards.
baranda, *f.* railing, banister.
barato, *a.* cheap.
barba, *f.* beard; chin.
barbacoa, *f.* barbecue; stretcher.
barbaridad, *f.* barbarity; (Am.) excess (in anything).
bárbaro, *a.* barbarous; crude.
barbería, *f.* barbershop.
barbero, *m.* barber.
barca, *f.* (small) boat.
barcaza, *f.* barge.
barco, *m.* ship, boat.
barniz, *m.* varnish. **—barnizar,** *v.*
barómetro, *m.* barometer.
barón, *m.* baron.
barquilla, *f.* (naut.) log.
barra, *f.* bar.
barraca, *f.* hut, shed.
barrear, *v.* bar, barricade.
barreno, *m.* blast, blasting. **—barrenar,** *v.*
barrer, *v.* sweep.
barrera, *f.* barrier.
barricada, *f.* barricade.
barriga, *f.* belly.
barril, *m.* barrel; cask.
barrio, *m.* district, ward, quarter.
barro, *m.* clay, mud.
base, *f.* base; basis. **—basar,** *v.*
bastante, 1. *a.* enough, plenty of. 2. *adv.* enough; rather, quite.
bastar, *v.* suffice, be enough.
bastardo -a, *a. & n.* bastard.
bastear, *v.* baste.
bastidor, *m.* wing (in theater).
bastón, *m.* (walking) cane.
bastos, *m.pl.* clubs (cards).
basura, *f.* refuse, dirt; garbage; junk.
basurero, *m.* scavenger.
batalla, *f.* battle. **—batallar,** *v.*

batallón, *m.* battalion.
batata, *f.* sweet potato.
bate, *m.* bat. —**batear**, *v.*
batería, *f.* battery.
batido, *m.* (cooking) batter.
batir, *v.* beat; demolish; conquer.
baúl, *m.* trunk.
bautismo, *m.* baptism.
bautista, *m. & f.* Baptist.
bautizar, *v.* Christen, baptize.
bautizo, *m.* baptism.
baya, *f.* berry.
bayoneta, *f.* bayonet.
beato, *a.* blessed.
bebé, *m.* baby.
beber, *v.* drink.
bebible, *a.* drinkable.
bebida, *f.* drink, beverage.
beca, *f.* grant, scholarship.
becado -da, *n.* scholar.
becerro, *m.* calf; calfskin.
beldad, *f.* beauty.
belga, *a. & n.* Belgian.
Bélgica, *f.* Belgium.
belicoso, *a.* warlike.
beligerante, *a. & n.* belligerent.
bellaco, **1.** *a.* sly, roguish. **2.** *m.* rogue.
belleza, *f.* beauty.
bello, *a.* beautiful.
bellota, *f.* acorn.
bendecir, *v.* bless.
bendición, *f.* blessing, benediction.
bendito, *a.* blessed.
beneficio, *m.* benefit. —**beneficiar**, *v.*
beneficioso, *a.* beneficial.
benevolencia, *f.* benevolence.
benévolo, *a.* benevolent.
benigno, *a.* benign.
beodo, *a.* drunk.
berenjena, *f.* eggplant.
beso, *m.* kiss. —**besar**, *v.*
bestia, *f.* beast, brute.
betabel, *m.* beet.
Biblia, *f.* Bible.
bíblico, *a.* Biblical.
biblioteca, *f.* library.
bicarbonato, *m.* bicarbonate.
bicicleta, *f.* bicycle.
bien, **1.** *adv.* well. **2.** *n.* good; (*pl.*) possessions.
bienestar, *m.* well-being, welfare.
bienhechor -ra, *n.* benefactor.
bienvenida, *f.* welcome.
bienvenido, *a.* welcome.

biftec, *m.* steak.
bifurcación, *f.* fork. —**bifurcar**, *v.*
bigamia, *f.* bigamy.
bígamo -a, *n.* bigamist.
bigotes, *m.pl.* mustache.
bilis, *f.* bile.
billar, *m.* billiards.
billete, *m.* ticket; bank note, bill.
billón, *m.* billion.
biodegradable, *a.* biodegradable.
biografía, *f.* biography.
biología, *f.* biology.
biombo, *m.* screen.
bisel, *m.* bevel. —**biselar**, *v.*
bisonte, *m.* bison.
bisté, **bistec**, *m.* steak.
bizarro, *a.* brave; generous; smart.
bizcocho, *m.* biscuit, cake.
blanco, **1.** *a.* white; blank. **2.** *m.* white; target.
blandir, *v.* brandish, flourish.
blando, *a.* soft.
blanquear, *v.* whiten; bleach.
blasfemar, *v.* blaspheme, curse.
blasfemia, *f.* blasphemy.
blindado, *a.* armored.
blindaje, *m.* armor.
bloque, *m.* block. —**bloquear**, *v.*
bloqueo, *m.* blockade. —**bloquear**, *v.*
blusa, *f.* blouse.
bobo -ba, *a. & n.* fool; foolish.
boca, *f.* mouth.
bocado, *m.* bit; bite, mouthful.
bocanada, *f.* puff (of smoke); mouthful (of liquor).
bocina, *f.* horn.
bochorno, *m.* sultry weather; embarrassment.
boda, *f.* wedding.
bodega, *f.* wine cellar; (naut.) hold; grocery store.
bofetada, *f.* **bofetón**, *m.* slap.
boga, *f.* vogue; fad.
bogar, *v.* row (a boat).
bohemio -a, *a. & n.* Bohemian.
boicoteo, *m.* boycott. —**boicotear**, *v.*
boina, *f.* beret.
bola, *f.* ball.
bolera, *f.* bowling alley.
boletín, *m.* bulletin.
boleto, *m.* ticket. **b. de embarque**, boarding pass.
boliche, *m.* bowling alley.
boliviano -a, *a. & n.* Bolivian.

bolos, *m.pl.* bowling.
bolsa, *f.* purse; stock exchange.
bolsillo, *m.* pocket.
bollo, *m.* bun, loaf.
bomba, *f.* pump; bomb; gas station.
bombardear, *v.* bomb; bombard, shell.
bombear, *v.* pump.
bombero, *m.* fireman.
bombilla, *f.* (light) bulb.
bonanza, *f.* prosperity; fair weather.
bondad, *f.* kindness; goodness.
bondadoso, *a.* kind, kindly.
bonito, *a.* pretty.
bono, *m.* bonus; (fin.) bond.
boqueada, *f.* gasp; gape. **—boquear**, *v.*
boquilla, *f.* cigarette holder.
bordado, *m.*, **bordadura**, *f.* embroidery.
bordar, *v.* embroider.
borde, *m.* border, rim, edge, brink, ledge.
borla, *f.* tassel.
borracho, *a.* drunk.
borrachón, *m.* drunkard.
borrador, *m.* eraser.
borradura, *f.* erasure.
borrar, *v.* erase, rub out.
borrasca, *f.* squall, storm.
borrico, *m.* donkey.
bosque, *m.* forest, wood.
bostezo, *m.* yawn. **—bostezar**, *v.*
bota, *f.* boot.
botalón, *m.* (naut.) boom.
botánica, *f.* botany.
botar, *v.* throw out, throw away.
bote, *m.* boat; can, box.
botica, *f.* pharmacy, drugstore.
boticario, *m.* pharmacist, druggist.
botín, *m.* booty, plunder, spoils.
boto, *a.* dull, stupid.
botón, *m.* button.
botones, *m.* bellboy (in a hotel).
bóveda, *f.* vault.
boxeador, *m.* boxer.
boxeo, *m.* boxing. **—boxear**, *v.*
boya, *f.* buoy.
boyante, *a.* buoyant.
bozal, *m.* muzzle.
bramido, *m.* roar, bellow. **—bramar**, *v.*
brasileño -ña, *a. & n.* Brazilian.
bravata, *f.* bravado.

bravear, *v.* bully.
braza, *f.* fathom.
brazada, *f.* (swimming) stroke.
brazalete, *m.* bracelet.
brazo, *m.* arm.
brea, *f.* tar, pitch.
brecha, *f.* gap, breach.
bregar, *v.* scramble.
breña, *f.* rough country with brambly shrubs.
Bretaña, *f.* Britain.
breve, *a.* brief, short. **en b.**, shortly, soon.
brevedad, *f.* brevity.
bribón, *m.* rogue, rascal.
brida, *f.* bridle.
brigada, *f.* brigade.
brillante, **1.** *a.* brilliant, shiny. **2.** *m.* diamond.
brillo, *m.* shine, glitter. **—brillar**, *v.*
brinco, *m.* jump; bounce, skip. **—brincar**, *v.*
brindis, *m.* toast. **—brindar**, *v.*
brío, *m.* vigor.
brioso, *a.* vigorous, spirited.
brisa, *f.* breeze.
británico, *a.* British.
brocado, *m.* brocade.
brocha, *f.* brush.
broche, *m.* brooch, clasp, pin.
broma, *f.* joke. **—bromear**, *v.*
bronce, *m.* bronze; brass.
bronquitis, *f.* bronchitis.
brotar, *v.* gush; sprout; bud.
brote, *m.* bud, shoot.
bruja, *f.* witch.
brújula, *f.* compass.
bruma, *f.* mist.
brumoso, *a.* misty.
brusco, *a.* brusque; abrupt, curt.
brutal, *a.* savage, brutal.
brutalidad, *f.* brutality.
bruto, **1.** *a.* brutish; ignorant. **2.** *m.* blockhead.
bucear, *v.* dive.
bueno, *a.* good, fair; well (in health).
buey, *m.* ox, steer.
búfalo, *m.* buffalo.
bufanda, *f.* scarf.
bufón -ona, *n.* fool, buffoon, clown.
buho, *m.* owl.
buhonero, *m.* peddler, vender.
bujía, *f.* spark plug.
bulevar, *m.* boulevard.

bulto, *m.* bundle; lump.
bullicio, *m.* bustle, noise.
bullicioso, *a.* boisterous, noisy.
buñuelo, *m.* bun.
buque, *m.* ship.
burdo, *a.* coarse.
burgés -esa, *a. & n.* bourgeois.
burla, *f.* mockery; fun.
burlador, *m.* trickster, jokester.
burlar, *v.* mock, deride.
burlarse de, *v.* scoff at; make fun of.
burro, *m.* donkey.
busca, *f.* search, pursuit, quest.
buscar, *v.* seek, look for; look up.
busto, *m.* bust.
butaca, *f.* armchair; (theat.) orchestra seat.
buzo, *m.* diver.
buzón, *m.* mailbox.

C

cabal, *a.* exact; thorough.
cabalgar, *v.* ride horseback.
caballeresco, *a.* gentlemanly, chivalrous.
caballería, *f.* cavalry; chivalry.
caballeriza, *f.* stable.
caballero, *m.* gentleman; knight.
caballete, *m.* sawhorse; easel; ridge (of roof).
caballo, *m.* horse.
cabaña, *f.* cabin; booth.
cabecear, *v.* pitch (as a ship).
cabecera, *f.* head (of bed, table).
cabello, *m.* hair.
caber, *v.* fit into, be contained in. **no cabe duda,** there is no doubt.
cabeza, *f.* head; warhead.
cabildo, *m.* city hall.
cabizbajo, *a.* downcast.
cablegrama, *m.* cablegram.
cabo, *m.* end; (geog.) cape; (mil.) corporal. **llevar a c.,** carry out, accomplish.
cabra, *f.* goat.
cacahuete, *m.* peanut.
cacao, *m.* cocoa; chocolate.
cacerola, *f.* pan, casserole.
cachorro, *m.* cub; puppy.
cada, *a.* each, every.
cadáver, *m.* corpse.
cadena, *f.* chain.
cadera, *f.* hip.
cadete, *m.* cadet.

caer, *v.* fall.
café, *m.* coffee; café.
cafetal, *m.* coffee plantation.
cafetera, *f.* coffee pot.
caída, *f.* fall, drop; collapse.
caimán, *m.* alligator.
caja, *f.* box, case.
cajero -ra, *n.* cashier.
cajón, *m.* drawer.
cal, *f.* lime.
calabaza, *f.* calabash, pumpkin.
calabozo, *m.* jail, cell.
calambre, *m.* cramp.
calamidad, *f.* calamity, disaster.
calcetín, *m.* sock.
calcio, *m.* calcium.
calcular, *v.* calculate, figure.
cálculo, *m.* calculation, estimate.
caldera, *f.* kettle, caldron; boiler.
caldo, *m.* broth.
calefacción, *f.* heat, heating.
calendario, *m.* calendar.
calentar, *v.* heat, warm.
calidad, *f.* quality, grade.
caliente, *a.* hot, warm.
calificar, *v.* qualify.
calma, *f.* calm, quiet.
calmado, *a.* calm.
calmante, *a.* soothing, calming.
calmar, *v.* calm, quiet, lull, soothe.
calor, *m.* heat, warmth. **tener c.,** to be hot, warm; feel hot, warm. **hacer c.,** to be hot, warm (weather).
calorífero, *m.* radiator.
calumnia, *f.* slander. —**calumniar,** *v.*
caluroso, *a.* warm, hot.
calvario, *m.* Calvary.
calvo, *a.* bald.
calzado, *m.* footwear.
calzar, *v.* wear (as shoes).
calzoncillos, *m.pl.* shorts.
calzones, *m.pl.* trousers.
callado, *a.* silent, quiet.
callarse, *v.* quiet down; keep still; stop talking.
calle, *f.* street.
callejón, *m.* alley.
callo, *m.* callus, corn.
cama, *f.* bed.
cámara, *f.* chamber; camera.
camarada, *m. & f.* comrade.
camarera, *f.* chambermaid; waitress.
camarero, *m.* steward; waiter.

camarón, *m.* shrimp.

camarote, *m.* stateroom, berth.

cambiar, *v.* exchange, change, trade; cash.

cambio, *m.* change, exchange. **en c.,** on the other hand.

cambista, *m.* banker, broker.

cambur, *m.* banana.

camello, *m.* camel.

camilla, *f.* stretcher.

caminar, *v.* walk.

caminata, *f.* tramp, hike.

camino, *m.* road; way.

camión, *m.* truck.

camisa, *f.* shirt.

camisería, *f.* haberdashery.

camiseta, *f.* undershirt; T-shirt.

campamento, *m.* camp.

campana, *f.* bell.

campanario, *m.* bell tower, steeple.

campaneo, *m.* chime.

campaña, *f.* campaign.

campeón, *m.* champion.

campeonato, *m.* championship.

campesino -na, *n.* peasant.

campestre, *a.* country, rural.

campo, *m.* field; (the) country.

Canadá, *m.* Canada.

canadiense, *a.* & *n.* Canadian.

canal, *m.* canal; channel.

canalla, *f.* rabble.

canario, *m.* canary.

canasta, *f.* basket.

cáncer, *m.* cancer.

canciller, *m.* chancellor.

canción, *f.* song.

candado, *m.* padlock.

candela, *f.* fire; light; candle.

candelero, *m.* candlestick.

candidato -ta, *n.* candidate; applicant.

candidatura, *f.* candidacy.

canela, *f.* cinnamon.

cangrejo, *m.* crab.

caníbal, *m.* cannibal.

canje, *m.* exchange, trade. **—canjear,** *v.*

cano, *a.* gray.

canoa, *f.* canoe.

cansado, *a.* tired, weary.

cansancio, *m.* fatigue.

cansar, *v.* tire, fatigue, wear out.

cantante, *m.* & *f.* singer.

cantar, 1. *m.* song. **2.** *v.* sing.

cántaro, *m.* pitcher.

cantera, *f.* (stone) quarry.

cantidad, *f.* quantity, amount.

cantina, *f.* bar, tavern; restaurant.

canto, *m.* chant, song, singing; edge.

caña, *f.* cane, reed; sugar cane.

cañón, *m.* canyon; cannon; gun barrel.

caoba, *f.* mahogany.

caos, *m.* chaos.

caótico, *a.* chaotic.

capa, *f.* cape, cloak; coat (of paint).

capacidad, *f.* capacity; capability.

capacitar, *v.* enable.

capataz, *m.* foreman.

capaz, *a.* capable, able.

capellán, *m.* chaplain.

caperuza, *f.* hood.

capilla, *f.* chapel.

capital, *m.* capital. *f.* capital (city).

capitalista, *a.* & *n.* capitalist.

capitán, *m.* captain.

capitular, *v.* yield.

capítulo, *m.* chapter.

capota, *f.* hood.

capricho, *m.* caprice; fancy; whim.

caprichoso, *a.* capricious.

cápsula, *f.* capsule.

capturar, *v.* capture.

capucha, *f.* hood.

capullo, *m.* cocoon.

cara, *f.* face.

caracol, *m.* snail.

carácter, *m.* character.

característica, *f.* characteristic.

característico, *a.* characteristic.

caramba, mild exclamation.

caramelo, *m.* caramel; candy.

carátula, *f.* dial.

caravana, *f.* caravan.

carbón, *m.* carbon; coal.

carbonizar, *v.* char.

carburador, *m.* carburetor.

carcajada, *f.* burst of laughter.

cárcel, *f.* prison, jail.

carcelero, *m.* jailer.

carcinogénico, *a.* carcinogenic.

cardenal, *m.* cardinal.

carecer, *v.* lack.

carestía, *f.* scarcity; famine.

carga, *f.* cargo; load, burden; freight.

cargar, *v.* carry; load; charge.

cargo, *m.* load; charge, office.

caricia, *f.* caress.
caridad, *f.* charity.
cariño, *m.* affection, fondness.
cariñoso, *a.* affectionate, fond.
carisma, *m.* charisma.
caritativo, *a.* charitable.
carmesí, *a. & m.* crimson.
carnaval, *m.* carnival.
carne, *f.* meat, flesh; pulp.
carnero, *m.* ram; mutton.
carnicería, *f.* meat market; massacre.
carnicero, *m.* butcher.
carnívoro, *a.* carnivorous.
caro, *a.* dear, costly, expensive.
carpa, *f.* tent.
carpeta, *f.* folder; briefcase.
carpintero, *m.* carpenter.
carrera, *f.* race; career.
carreta, *f.* wagon, cart.
carrete, *m.* reel, spool.
carretera, *f.* road, highway.
carril, *m.* rail.
carrillo, *m.* cart (for baggage or shopping).
carro, *m.* car, automobile; cart.
carroza, *f.* chariot.
carruaje, *m.* carriage.
carta, *f.* letter; (*pl.*) cards.
cartel, *m.* placard, poster; cartel.
cartera, *f.* pocketbook, handbag, wallet; portfolio.
cartero, *m.* mailman, postman.
cartón, *m.* cardboard.
cartucho, *m.* cartridge; cassette.
casa, *f.* house, dwelling; home.
casaca, *f.* dress coat.
casado, *a.* married.
casamiento, *m.* marriage.
casar, *v.* marry, marry off.
casarse, *v.* get married. **c. con,** marry.
cascabel, *m.* jingle bell.
cascada, *f.* waterfall, cascade.
cascajo, *m.* gravel.
cascanueces, *m.* nutcracker.
cascar, *v.* crack, break, burst.
cáscara, *f.* shell, rind, husk.
casco, *m.* helmet; hull.
casera, *f.* landlady; housekeeper.
caserío, *m.* settlement.
casero, 1. *a.* homemade. **2.** *m.* landlord, superintendent.
caseta, *f.* cottage, hut.
casi, *adv.* almost, nearly.
casilla, *f.* booth; ticket office; pigeonhole.

casino, *m.* club; clubhouse.
caso, *m.* case. **hacer c. a,** pay attention to.
casorio, *m.* informal wedding.
caspa, *f.* dandruff.
casta, *f.* caste.
castaña, *f.* chestnut.
castaño, 1. *a.* brown. **2.** *m.* chestnut tree.
castañuela, *f.* castanet.
castellano, *a. & m.* Castillian.
castidad, *f.* chastity.
castigar, *v.* punish.
castigo, *m.* punishment.
castillo, *m.* castle.
castizo, *a.* pure, genuine; noble.
casto, *a.* chaste.
castor, *m.* beaver.
casual, *adj.* accidental, coincidental.
casualidad, *f.* coincidence. **por c.,** by chance.
casuca, *f.* hut, shanty, hovel.
catadura, *f.* act of tasting; appearance.
catalán, *a. & m.* Catalonian.
catálogo, *m.* catalogue. **—catalogar,** *v.*
catar, *v.* taste; examine, try; bear in mind.
catarata, *f.* cataract, waterfall.
catarro, *m.* head cold.
catástrofe, *f.* catastrophe.
catecismo, *m.* catechism.
cátedra, *f.* professorship.
catedral, *f.* cathedral.
catedrático, *m.* professor.
categoría, *f.* category.
categórico, *a.* categorical.
catequizar, *v.* catechize.
catolicismo, *m.* Catholicism.
católico -ca, *a. & n.* Catholic.
catorce, *a. & pron.* fourteen.
catre, *m.* cot.
cauce, *m.* riverbed; ditch.
caución, *f.* precaution; security, guarantee.
cauchal, *m.* rubber plantation.
caucho, *m.* rubber.
caudal, *m.* means, fortune; (*pl.*) holdings.
caudaloso, *a.* prosperous, rich.
caudillaje, *m.* leadership; tyranny.
caudillo, *m.* leader, chief.
causa, *f.* cause. **—causar,** *v.*
cautela, *f.* caution.

cauteloso, *m.* cautious.
cautivar, *v.* captivate.
cautiverio, *m.* captivity.
cautividad, *f.* captivity.
cautivo -va, *a. & n.* captive.
cauto, *a.* cautious.
cavar, *v.* dig.
caverna, *f.* cavern, cave.
cavernoso, *a.* cavernous.
cavidad, *f.* cavity, hollow.
cavilar, *v.* criticize, cavil.
cayado, *m.* shepherd's staff.
cayo, *m.* small rocky islet, key.
caza, *f.* hunting, pursuit, game.
cazador, *m.* hunter.
cazar, *v.* hunt.
cazatorpedero, *m.* destroyer.
cazo, *m.* ladle, dipper; pot.
cazuela, *f.* crock.
cebada, *f.* barley.
cebo, *m.* bait. **—cebar**, *v.*
cebolla, *f.* onion.
ceceo, *m.* lisp. **—cecear**, *v.*
cecina, *f.* dried beef.
cedazo, *m.* sieve, sifter.
ceder, *v.* cede; transfer; yield.
cedro, *m.* cedar.
cédula, *f.* decree. **c. personal**, identification card.
céfiro, *m.* zephyr.
cegar, *v.* blind.
ceguedad, ceguera, *f.* blindness.
ceja, *f.* eyebrow.
cejar, *v.* go backwards; yield, retreat.
celada, *f.* trap; ambush.
celaje, *m.* appearance of the sky.
celar, *v.* watch carefully, guard.
celda, *f.* cell.
celebración, *f.* celebration.
celebrante, *m.* officiating priest.
celebrar, *v.* celebrate, observe.
célebre, *a.* celebrated, noted, famous.
celebridad, *f.* fame; celebrity; pageant.
celeridad, *f.* speed, rapidity.
celeste, *a.* celestial.
celestial, *a.* heavenly.
célibe, **1.** *a.* unmarried. **2.** *m. & f.* unmarried person.
celo, *m.* zeal; (*pl.*) jealousy.
celosía, *f.* Venetian blind.
celoso, *a.* jealous; zealous.
céltico, *a.* Celtic.
célula, *f.* (biol.) cell.
celuloide, *m.* celluloid.

cellisca, *f.* sleet. **—cellisquear**, *v.*
cementar, *v.* cement.
cementerio, *m.* cemetery.
cemento, *m.* cement.
cena, *f.* supper.
cenagal, *m.* swamp, marsh.
cenagoso, *a.* swampy, marshy, muddy.
cenar, *v.* dine, eat.
cencerro, *m.* cowbell.
cendal, *m.* thin, light cloth; gauze.
cenicero, *m.* ashtray.
ceniciento, *a.* ashen.
cenit, *m.* zenith.
ceniza, *f.* ash, ashes.
censo, *m.* census.
censor, *m.* critic.
censura, *f.* reproof, censure; censorship.
censurable, *a.* objectionable.
censurar, *v.* censure, criticize.
centavo, *m.* cent.
centella, *f.* thunderbolt, lightning.
centellear, *v.* twinkle, sparkle.
centelleo, *m.* sparkle.
centenar, *m.* (a) hundred.
centenario, *a.* centennial, centenary.
centeno, *m.* rye.
centígrado, *a.* centigrade.
centímetro, *m.* centimeter.
céntimo, *m.* cent.
centinela, *m.* sentry, guard.
central, *a.* central.
centrar, *v.* center.
céntrico, *a.* central.
centro, *m.* center.
centroamericano -na, *a. & n.* Central American.
ceñidor, *m.* belt, sash; girdle.
ceñir, *v.* gird.
ceño, *m.* frown.
ceñudo, *a.* frowning, grim.
cepa, *f.* stump.
cepillo, *m.* brush; plane. **—cepillar**, *v.*
cera, *f.* wax.
cerámica, *f.* ceramics.
cerca, **1.** *adv.* near. **2.** *f.* fence, hedge.
cercado, *m.* enclosure; garden.
cercamiento, *m.* enclosure.
cercanía, *f.* proximity.
cercano, *a.* near, nearby.
cercar, *v.* surround.

cercenar, v. clip; lessen, reduce.

cerciorar, v. make sure; affirm.

cerco, m. hoop; siege.

cerda, f. bristle.

cerdo, m. hog.

cerdoso, a. bristly.

cereal, a. & m. cereal.

cerebro, m. brain.

ceremonia, f. ceremony.

ceremonial, a. & m. ceremonial, ritual.

ceremonioso, a. ceremonious.

cereza, f. cherry.

cerilla, f., **cerillo,** m. match.

cerner, v. sift.

cero, m. zero.

cerrado, a. cloudy; obscure; stupid.

cerradura, f. lock.

cerrajero, m. locksmith.

cerrar, v. close, shut.

cerro, m. hill.

cerrojo, m. latch, bolt.

certamen, m. contest; competition.

certero, a. accurate, exact; certain, sure.

certeza, f. certainty.

certidumbre, f. certainty.

certificado, m. certificate.

certificar, v. certify; register (a letter).

cerúleo, a. cerulean, sky-blue.

cervecería, f. brewery; beer saloon.

cervecero, m. brewer.

cerveza, f. beer.

cesante, a. unemployed.

cesar, v. cease.

césped, m. sod, lawn.

cesta, f., **cesto,** m. basket.

cetrino, a. yellow, lemon-colored.

cetro, m. scepter.

cicatero, a. stingy.

cicatriz, f. scar.

cicatrizar, v. heal.

ciclamino, m. cyclamate.

ciclo, m. cycle.

ciclón, m. cyclone.

ciego -ga, 1. a. blind. **2.** n. blind person.

cielo, m. heaven; sky, heavens; ceiling.

ciempiés, m. centipede.

cien, ciento, a. & pron. hundred.
por c., per cent.

ciénaga, f. swamp, marsh.

ciencia, f. science.

cieno, m. mud.

científico, 1. a. scientific. **2.** n. scientist.

cierre, m. fastener, snap, clasp.

cierto, a. certain, sure, true.

ciervo, m. deer.

cierzo, m. northerly wind.

cifra, f. cipher, number. **—cifrar,** v.

cigarra, f. locust.

cigarrera, cigarrillera, f. cigarette case.

cigarrillo, m. cigarette.

cigarro, m. cigar; cigarette.

cilíndrico, a. cylindrical.

cilindro, m. cylinder.

cima, f. summit, peak.

cimarrón, 1. a. wild, untamed. **2.** m. runaway slave.

címbalo, m. cymbal.

cimbrar, v. shake, brandish.

cimientos, m.pl. foundation.

cinc, m. zinc.

cincel, m. chisel. **—cincelar,** v.

cinco, a. & pron. five.

cincuenta, a. & pron. fifty.

cincha, f. (harness) cinch. **—cinchar,** v.

cine, m. movies; movie theater.

cíngulo, m. girdle.

cínico, a. & n. cynical; cynic.

cinta, f. ribbon, tape; (movie) film.

cintilar, v. glitter, sparkle.

cinto, m. belt; girdle.

cintura, f. waist.

cinturón, m. belt.

ciprés, m. cypress.

circo, m. circus.

circuito, m. circuit.

circulación, f. circulation.

circular, 1. a. & m. circular. **2.** v. circulate.

círculo m. circle, club.

circundante, a. surrounding.

circundar, v. encircle, surround.

circunferencia, f. circumference.

circunlocución, n. circumlocution.

circunscribir, v. circumscribe.

circunspección, n. decorum, propriety.

circunspecto, a. circumspect.

circunstancia, f. circumstance.

circunstante, m. bystander.

circunvecino, *a.* neighboring, adjacent.

cirio, *m.* candle.

ciruela, *f.* plum; prune.

cirugía, *f.* surgery.

cirujano, *m.* surgeon.

cisne, *m.* swan.

cisterna, *f.* cistern.

cita, *f.* citation; appointment, date.

citación, *f.* citation; (legal) summons.

citar, *v.* cite, quote; summon; make an appointment with.

ciudad, *f.* city.

ciudadanía, *f.* citizenship.

ciudadano -na, *n.* citizen.

ciudadela, *f.* fortress, citadel.

cívico, *a.* civic.

civil, *a. & n.* civil; civilian.

civilidad, *f.* politeness, civility.

civilización, *f.* civilization.

civilizador, *a.* civilizing.

civilizar, *v.* civilize.

cizallas, *f.pl.* shears. —**cizallar**, *v.*

cizaña, *f.* weed; vice.

clamar, *v.* clamor.

clamor, *m.* clamor.

clamoreo, *m.* persistent clamor.

clamoroso, *a.* clamorous.

clandestino, *a.* secret, clandestine.

clara, *f.* white (of egg).

claraboya, *m.* skylight; bull's-eye.

clarear, *v.* clarify; become light, dawn.

claridad, *f.* clarity.

clarificar, *v.* clarify.

clarín, *m.* bugle, trumpet.

clarinete, *m.* clarinet.

clarividencia, *f.* clairvoyance.

claro, *a.* clear; bright; light (in color); of course.

clase, *f.* class; classroom; kind, sort.

clásico, *a.* classic, classical.

clasificar, *v.* classify, rank.

claustro, *m.* cloister.

cláusula, *f.* clause.

clausura, *f.* cloister; inner sanctum.

clavado, *m.* dive.

clavar, *v.* nail, peg, pin.

clave, *f.* code; (mus.) key.

clavel, *m.* carnation.

clavetear, *v.* nail.

clavija, *f.* pin, peg.

clavijero, *m.* hatrack.

clavo, *m.* nail, spike.

clemencia, *f.* clemency.

clemente, *a.* merciful.

clerecía, *f.* clergy.

clerical, *a.* clerical.

clérigo, *m.* clergyman.

clero, *m.* clergy.

cliente, *m. & f.* customer, client.

clientela, *f.* clientele, practice.

clima, *m.* climate.

clímax, *m.* climax.

clínica, *f.* clinic.

clíper, *m.* clipper ship.

cloaca, *f.* sewer.

cloquear, *v.* cluck, cackle.

cloqueo, *m.* cluck.

cloro, *m.* chlorine.

club, *m.* club, association.

clueca, *f.* brooding hen.

coacción, *n.* compulsion.

coagular, *v.* coagulate, clot.

coágulo, *m.* clot.

coalición, *f.* coalition.

coartar, *v.* limit.

cobarde, *a. & n.* cowardly; coward.

cobardía, *f.* cowardice.

cobertizo, *m.* shed.

cobertor, *m.*, **cobija**, *f.* blanket.

cobertura, *f.* cover, wrapping.

cobijar, *v.* cover; protect.

cobrador, *m.* collector.

cobranza, *f.* collection or recovery of money.

cobrar, *v.* collect; charge; cash.

cobre, *m.* copper.

cobrizo, *a.* coppery.

cobro, *m.* collection or recovery of money.

coca, *f.* coca leaves.

cocaína, *f.* cocaine.

cocal, *m.* coconut plantation.

cocear, *v.* kick; resist.

cocer, *v.* cook, boil, bake.

cocido, *m.* stew.

cociente, *m.* quotient.

cocimiento, *m.* cooking.

cocina, *f.* kitchen.

cocinar, *v.* cook.

cocinero -ra, *n.* cook.

coco, *m.* coconut; coconut tree.

cocodrilo, *m.* crocodile.

coctel, *m.* cocktail.

coche, *m.* coach; car, automobile.

cochera, *f.* garage.

cochero, *m.* coachman; cab driver.

cochinada, *f.* filth; herd of swine.

cochino, *m.* pig, swine.

codazo, *m.* nudge with the elbow.

codicia, *f.* avarice, greed; lust.

codiciar, *v.* covet.

codicioso, *a.* covetous; greedy.

código, *m.* (law) code.

codo, *m.* elbow.

codorniz, *f.* quail.

coetáneo, *a.* contemporary.

cofrade, *m.* fellow member of a club, etc.

cofre, *m.* coffer; chest; trunk.

coger, *v.* catch; pick; take.

cogote, *m.* nape.

cohecho, *m.* bribe. **—cohechar,** *v.*

coheredero, *m.* co-heir.

coherente, *a.* coherent.

cohesión, *f.* cohesion.

cohete, *m.* fire cracker, rocket.

cohibición, *n.* restraint; repression.

cohibir, *v.* restrain; repress.

coincidencia, *f.* coincidence.

coincidir, *v.* coincide.

cojear, *v.* limp.

cojera, *m.* limp.

cojín, *m.* cushion.

cojinete, *m.* small cushion, pad.

cojo, *a.* lame.

col, *f.* cabbage.

cola, *f.* tail; glue; line, queue. **hacer c.,** stand in line.

colaboración, *f.* collaboration.

colaborar, *v.* collaborate.

coladera, *f.* strainer.

colador, *m.* colander, strainer.

colapso, *m.* collapse, prostration.

colar, *v.* strain; drain.

colateral, *a.* collateral.

colcha, *f.* bedspread, quilt.

colchón, *m.* mattress.

colear, *v.* wag the tail.

colección, *f.* collection, set.

coleccionar, *v.* collect.

colecta, *f.* collection (a prayer).

colectivo, *a.* collective.

colector, *m.* collector.

colega, *m. & f.* colleague.

colegial, *m.* college student.

colegiatura, *f.* college scholarship.

colegio, *m.* (private) school, college.

colegir, *v.* infer, deduce.

cólera, *f.* rage, wrath.

colérico, *adj.* angry, irritated.

coleto, *m.* leather jacket.

colgador, *m.* rack, hanger.

colgaduras, *f.,pl.* drapery.

colgante, *a.* hanging.

colgar, *v.* hang up, suspend.

colibrí, *m.* hummingbird.

coliflor, *f.* cauliflower.

coligarse, *v.* band together, unite.

colilla, *f.* butt of a cigar or cigarette.

colina, *f.* hill, hillock.

colinabo, *m.* turnip.

colindante, *a.* neighboring, adjacent.

colindar, *v.* neighbor, abut.

coliseo, *m.* theater; coliseum.

colisión, *f.* collision.

colmar, *v.* heap up, fill liberally.

colmena, *f.* hive.

colmillo, *m.* eyetooth; tusk; fang.

colmo, *m.* height, peak, extreme.

colocación, *f.* place, position; employment, job; arrangement.

colocar, *v.* place, locate, put, set.

colombiano -na, *a. & n.* Colombian.

colon, *m.* colon (of intestines).

colonia, *f.* colony.

colonial, *a.* colonial.

colonización, *f.* colonization.

colonizador, *m.* colonizer.

colonizar, *v.* colonize.

colono, *m.* colonist; tenant farmer.

coloquio, *m.* conversation, talk.

color, *m.* color. **—colorar,** *v.*

coloración, *f.* coloring.

colorado, *a.* red, ruddy.

colorar, *v.* color, paint; dye.

colorete, *m.* rouge.

colorido, *m.* color, coloring. **—colorir,** *v.*

colosal, *a.* colossal.

columbrar, *v.* discern.

columna, *f.* column, pillar, shaft.

columpiar, *v.* swing.

columpio, *m.* swing.

collado, *m.* hillock.

collar, *m.* necklace; collar.

coma, *f.* coma; comma.

comadre, *f.* midwife; gossip; close friend.

comadreja, *m.* weasel.

comandancia, *m.* command; command post.

comandante, *m.* commandant; commander; major.

comandar, *v.* command.

comandita, *f.* silent partnership.

comanditario, *m.* silent partner.

comando, *m.* command.

comarca, *f.* region; border, boundary.

comba, *f.* bulge.

combar, *v.* bend; bulge.

combate, *m.* combat. —**combatir,** *v.*

combatiente, *a. & m.* combatant.

combinación, *f.* combination; (lady's) slip.

combinar, *v.* combine.

combustible, 1. *a.* combustible. **2.** *m.* fuel.

combustión, *f.* combustion.

comedero, *m.* trough.

comedia, *f.* comedy; play.

comediante, *m.* actor; comedian.

comedido, *a.* polite, courteous; obliging.

comedirse, *v.* to be polite or obliging.

comedor, *m.* dining room. **coche c.,** dining car.

comendador, *m.* commander.

comensal, *m.* member of a household.

comentador, *m.* commentator.

comentario, *m.* commentary.

comento, *m.* comment. —**comentar,** *v.*

comenzar, *v.* begin, start, commence.

comer, *v.* eat, dine.

comercial, *a.* commercial.

comerciante, *m.* merchant, trader, businessman.

comerciar, *v.* trade, deal, do business.

comercio, *m.* commerce, trade, business.

comestible, 1. *a.* edible. **2.** *m. (pl.)* groceries, provisions.

cometa, *m.* comet. *f.* kite.

cometer, *v.* commit.

cometido, *m.* commission; duty; task.

comezón, *f.* itch.

comicios, *m.pl.* primary elections.

cómico -ca, *a. & m.* comic, comical; comedian.

comida, *f.* food; dinner; meal.

comidilla, *f.* light meal; gossip.

comienzo, *m.* beginning.

comilitona, *f.* banquet.

comilón, *m.* glutton; heavy eater.

comillas, *f.pl.* quotation marks.

comisario, *m.* commissary.

comisión, *f.* commission. —**comisionar,** *v.*

comisionado, *m.* agent, commissioner.

comisionar, *v.* commission.

comiso, *m.* (law) confiscation of illegal goods.

comistrajo, *m.* mess, hodgepodge.

comité, *m.* committee.

comitiva, *f.* retinue.

como, *conj. & adv.* like, as.

cómo, *adv.* how.

cómoda, *f.* bureau, chest (of drawers).

cómodamente, *adv.* conveniently.

comodatario, *m.* pawnbroker.

comodato, *m.* loan.

comodidad, *f.* convenience, comfort; commodity.

cómodo, *a.* comfortable; convenient.

comodoro, *m.* commodore.

compacto, *a.* compact.

compadecer, *v.* be sorry for, pity.

compadraje, *m.* clique.

compadre, *m.* close friend.

compaginar, *v.* put in order; arrange.

companage, *m.* cold lunch.

compañerismo, *m.* companionship.

compañero -ra, *n.* companion, partner.

compañía, *f.* company.

comparable, *a.* comparable.

comparación, *f.* comparison.

comparar, *v.* compare.

comparativamente, *adv.* comparatively.

comparativo, *a.* comparative.

comparecer, *v.* appear.

comparendo, *m.* summons.

comparsa, *f.* carnival masquerade; retinue.

compartimiento, *m.* compartment.

compartir, *v.* share.

compás, *m.* compass; beat, rhythm.

compasar, *v.* measure exactly.

compasible, *a.* compassionate.

compasión, *f.* compassion.

compasivo, *a.* compassionate.

compatibilidad, *f.* compatibility.

compatible, *a.* compatible.

compatriota, *m. & f.* compatriot.

compeler, *v.* compel.

compendiar, *v.* summarize; abridge.

compendiariamente, *adv.* briefly.

compendio, *m.* summary; abridgment.

compendiosamente, *adv.* briefly.

compensación, *f.* compensation.

compensar, *v.* compensate.

competencia, *f.* competence; competition.

competente, *a.* competent.

competentemente, *adv.* competently.

competición, *f.* competition.

competidor, *a. & n.* competitive; competitor.

competir, *v.* compete.

compilación, *f.* compilation.

compilar, *v.* compile.

compinche, *m.* pal.

complacencia, *f.* complacency.

complacer, *v.* please, oblige, humor.

complaciente, *a.* pleasing, obliging.

complejidad, *f.* complexity.

complejo, *a. & n.* complex.

complemento, *m.* complement; (gram.) object.

completamente, *adv.* completely.

completamiento, *m.* completion, finish.

completar, *v.* complete.

completo, *a.* complete, full, perfect.

complexidad, *f.* complexity.

complexión, *f.* nature, temperament.

complexo, *a.* complex, intricate.

complicación, *f.* complication.

complicado, *a.* complicated.

complicar, *v.* complicate.

cómplice, *m. & f.* accomplice, accessory.

complicidad, *f.* complicity.

complot, *m.* conspiracy.

componedor, *m.* typesetter.

componenda, *f.* compromise; settlement.

componente, *a. & m.* component.

componer, *v.* compose; fix, repair.

componible, *a.* reparable.

comportable, *a.* endurable.

comportamiento, *m.* behavior.

comportarse, *v.* behave.

comporte, *m.* behavior.

composición, *f.* composition.

compositivo, *a.* synthetic; composite.

compositor -ra, *n.* composer.

compostura, *f.* composure; repair; neatness.

compota, *f.* (fruit) sauce.

compra, *f.* purchase. **ir de compras,** to go shopping.

comprador -ra, *n.* buyer, purchaser.

comprar, *v.* buy, purchase.

comprehensivo, *a.* comprehensive.

comprender, *v.* comprehend, understand; include, comprise.

comprensibilidad, *f.* comprehensibility.

comprensible, *a.* understandable.

comprensión, *f.* comprehension, understanding.

comprensivo, *m.* comprehensive.

compresa, *f.* medical compress.

compresión, *f.* compression.

comprimir, *v.* compress.

comprobación, *f.* proof.

comprobante, 1. *a.* proving. **2.** *m.* proof.

comprobar, *v.* prove; verify, check.

comprometer, *v.* compromise.

comprometerse, *v.* become engaged.

compromiso, *m.* compromise; engagement.

compropietario, *m.* co-owner.

compuerta, *f.* floodgate.

compuesto, *m.* composition; compound.

compulsión, *f.* compulsion.

compulsivo, *a.* compulsive.

compunción, *f.* compunction.

compungirse, *v.* regret, feel remorse.

computación, *f.* computation.

computador, *m.* computer.

computar, *v.* compute.

cómputo, *m.* computation.

comulación, *f.* cumulation.

comulgar, *v.* take communion.

comulgatorio, *m.* communion altar.

común, *a.* common, usual.

comunal, *m.* common people.

comunero, *m.* commoner.

comunicable, *a.* communicable.

comunicación, *f.* communication.

comunicante, *m. & f.* communicant.

comunicar, *v.* communicate; convey.

comunicativo, *a.* communicative.

comunidad, *f.* community.

comunión, *f.* communion.

comunismo, *m.* communism.

comunista, *a. & n.* communistic; communist.

comúnmente, *adv.* commonly; usually; often.

con, *prep.* with.

concavidad, *f.* concavity.

cóncavo, 1. *a.* concave. **2.** *m.* concavity.

concebible, *a.* conceivable.

concebir, *v.* conceive.

conceder, *v.* concede.

concejal, *m.* councilman.

concejo, *m.* city council.

concento, *m.* harmony.

concentración, *f.* concentration.

concentrar, *v.* concentrate.

concepción, *f.* conception.

conceptible, *a.* conceivable.

concepto, *m.* concept; opinion.

concerniente, *a.* concerning.

concernir, *v.* concern.

concertar, *v.* arrange.

concertina, *f.* concertina.

concesión, *f.* concession.

conciencia, *f.* conscience; consciousness; consciousness.

concienzudo, *a.* conscientious.

concierto, *m.* concert.

conciliación, *f.* conciliation.

conciliador, *m.* conciliator.

conciliar, *v.* conciliate.

concilio, *m.* council.

concisión, *f.* conciseness.

conciso, *a.* concise.

concitar, *v.* instigate, stir up.

conciudadano, *m.* fellow citizen.

concluir, *v.* conclude.

conclusión, *f.* conclusion.

conclusivo, *a.* conclusive.

concluso, *a.* concluded; closed.

concluyentemente, *adv.* conclusively.

concomitante, *a.* concomitant, attendant.

concordador, *m.* moderator; conciliator.

concordancia, *f.* agreement, concord.

concordar, *v.* agree; put or be in accord.

concordia, *f.* concord, agreement.

concretamente, *adv.* concretely.

concretar, *v.* summarize.

concretarse, *v.* limit oneself to.

concreto, *a. & m.* concrete.

concubina, *f.* concubine, mistress.

concupiscente, *a.* lustful.

concurrencia, *f.* assembly; attendance; competition.

concurrente, *a.* concurrent.

concurrido, *a.* heavily attended or patronized.

concurrir, *v.* concur; attend.

concurso, *m.* contest, competition; meeting.

concha, *f.* (sea) shell.

conde, *m.* (title) count.

condecente, *a.* appropriate, proper.

condecoración, *f.* decoration; medal; badge.

condecorar, *v.* decorate with a medal.

condena, *f.* prison sentence.

condenación, *f.* condemnation.

condenar, *v.* condemn; damn; sentence.

condensación, *f.* condensation.

condensar, *v.* condense.

condesa, *f.* countess.

condescendencia, *f.* condescension.

condescender, *v.* condescend, deign.

condescendiente, *a.* condescending.

condición, *f.* condition.

condicional, *a.* conditional.

condicionalmente, *adv.* conditionally.

condimentar, *v.* season, flavor.

condimento, *m.* condiment, seasoning, dressing.

condiscípulo, *m.* schoolmate.

condolencia, *f.* condolence, sympathy.

condolerse de, *v.* sympathize with.

condómino, m. co-owner.
condonar, v. condone.
cóndor, m. condor (bird).
conducción, f. conveyance.
conducente, a. conducive.
conducir, v. conduct, escort, lead; drive.
conducta, f. conduct, behavior.
conducto, m. pipe, conduit; sewer.
conductor, m. driver; conductor.
conectar, v. connect.
conejera, f. rabbit warren; place of ill repute.
conejo, m. rabbit.
conexión, f. connection; coupling.
conexivo, a. connective.
conexo, a. connected, united.
confalón, m. ensign, standard.
confección, f. workmanship; ready-made article; concoction.
confeccionar, v. concoct.
confederación, f. confederation.
confederado, a. & m. confederate.
confederar, v. confederate, unite, ally.
conferencia, f. lecture; conference.
conferenciante, m. & f. lecturer, speaker.
conferenciar, v. confer.
conferencista, m. & f. lecturer, speaker.
conferir, v. confer.
confesar, v. confess.
confesión, f. confession.
confesionario, m. confessional.
confesor, m. confessor.
confetti, m.pl. confetti.
confiable, a. dependable.
confiado, a. confident; trusting.
confianza, f. confidence, trust, faith.
confiar, v. entrust; trust, rely.
confidencia, f. confidence, secret.
confidencial, a. confidential.
confidente, m. & f. confidant.
confidentemente, adv. confidently.
confín, m. confine.
confinamiento, m. confinement.
confinar, v. confine, imprison; border on.
confirmación, f. confirmation.
confirmar, v. confirm.

confiscación, f. confiscation.
confiscar, v. confiscate.
confitar, v. sweeten; make into candy or jam.
confite, m. candy.
confitería, f. confectionery; candy store.
confitura, f. confection.
conflagración, f. conflagration.
conflicto, m. conflict.
confluencia, f. confluence, junction.
confluir, v. flow into each other.
conformación, f. conformation.
conformar, v. conform.
conforme, 1. a. acceptable, right, as agreed; in accordance, in agreement. **2.** conj. according as.
conformidad, f. conformity; agreement.
conformismo, m. conformism.
conformista, m. conformist.
confortar, v. comfort.
confraternidad, m. brotherhood, fraternity.
confricar, v. rub.
confrontación, f. confrontation.
confrontar, v. confront.
confucianismo, m. Confucianism.
confundir, v. confuse; puzzle, mix up.
confusamente, adv. confusedly.
confusión, f. confusion, mix-up; clutter.
confuso, a. confused; confusing.
confutación, n. disproof.
confutar, v. refute, disprove.
congelable, a. congealable.
congelación, f. congealment; deep freeze.
congelado, a. frozen, congealed.
congelar, v. congeal, freeze.
congenial, a. congenial; analogous.
congeniar, v. be congenial.
congestión, f. congestion.
conglomeración, f. conglomeration.
congoja, f. grief, anguish.
congraciamiento, m. flattery; ingratiation.
congraciar, v. flatter; ingratiate oneself.
congratulación, f. congratulation.
congratular, v. congratulate.
congregación, f. congregation.
congregar, v. congregate.

congresista, *m. & f.* congressional representative.

congreso, *m.* congress; conference.

conjetura, *f.* conjecture. **—conjeturar,** *v.*

conjetural, *a.* conjectural.

conjugación, *f.* conjugation.

conjugar, *v.* conjugate.

conjunción, *f.* union; conjunction.

conjuntamente, *adv.* together, jointly.

conjunto. 1. *a.* joint, unified. **2.** *m.* whole.

conjuración, *f.* conspiracy, plot.

conjurado, *m.* conspirator, plotter.

conjurar, *v.* conjure.

conllevador, *m.* helper, aide.

conmemoración, *f.* commemoration; remembrance.

conmemorar, *v.* commemorate.

conmemorativo, *a.* commemorative, memorial.

conmensal, *m.* messmate.

conmigo, *adv.* with me.

conmilitón, *m.* fellow soldier.

conminación, *f.* threat, warning.

conminar, *v.* threaten.

conminatorio, *a.* threatening, warning.

conmiseración, *f.* sympathy.

conmoción, *f.* commotion, stir.

conmovedor, *a.* moving, touching.

conmover, *v.* move, affect, touch.

conmutación, *f.* commutation.

conmutador, *m.* electric switch.

conmutar, *v.* exchange.

connotación, *f.* connotation.

connotar, *v.* connote.

connubial, *a.* connubial.

connubio, *m.* matrimony.

cono, *m.* cone.

conocedor -ra, *n.* expert, connoisseur.

conocer, *v.* know, be acquainted with; meet, make the acquaintance of.

conocible, *a.* knowable.

conocido -da, 1. *a.* familiar, well known. **2.** *n.* acquaintance, person known.

conocimiento, *m.* knowledge, acquaintance; consciousness.

conque, *conj.* so then; and so.

conquista, *f.* conquest.

conquistador, *m.* conqueror.

conquistar, *v.* conquer.

consabido, *a.* aforesaid.

consagración, *f.* consecration.

consagrado, *a.* consecrated.

consagrar, *v.* consecrate, dedicate, devote.

consanguinidad, *f.* consanguinity.

consciente, *a.* conscious, aware.

conscientemente, *adv.* consciously.

conscripción, *f.* conscription for military service.

consecución, *f.* attainment.

consecuencia, *f.* consequence.

consecuente, *a.* consequent; consistent.

consecuentemente, *adv.* consequently.

consecutivamente, *adv.* consecutively.

consecutivo, *a.* consecutive.

conseguir, *v.* obtain, get, secure; succeed in, manage to.

conseja, *n.* fable.

consejero -ra, *n.* adviser, counselor.

consejo, *m.* council; counsel (piece of) advice.

consenso, *m.* consensus.

consentido, *a.* spoiled, bratty.

consentimiento, *m.* consent.

consentir, *v.* allow, permit.

conserje, *m.* superintendent, keeper.

conserva, *f.* conserve, preserve.

conservación, *f.* conservation.

conservador, *a. & m.* conservative.

conservar, *v.* conserve.

conservativo, *a.* conservative, preservative.

conservatorio, *m.* conservatory.

considerable, *a.* considerable, substantial.

considerablemente, *adv.* considerably.

consideración, *f.* consideration.

consideradamente, *adv.* considerably.

considerado, *a.* considerate.

considerando, *conj.* whereas.

considerar, *v.* consider.

consigna, *f.* watchword.

consignación, *f.* consignment.

consignar, *v.* consign.

consignatorio, m. consignee; trustee.

consigo, adv. with herself, with himself, with oneself, with themselves, with yourself, with yourselves.

consiguiente, 1. a. consequent. **2.** m. consequence.

consiguientemente, adv. consequently.

consistencia, f. consistency.

consistente, a. consistent.

consistir, v. consist.

consistorio, m. consistory.

consocio, m. associate; partner; comrade.

consola, f. console.

consolación, f. consolation.

consolar, v. console.

consolativo, a. consolatory.

consolidación, n. consolidation.

consolidado, a. consolidated.

consolidar, v. consolidate.

consonancia, f. agreement, accord, harmony.

consonante, a. & n. consonant.

consonar, v. rhyme.

consorte, m. & f. consort, mate.

conspicuo, a. conspicuous.

conspiración, f. conspiracy, plot.

conspirador -ra, n. conspirator.

conspirar, v. conspire, plot.

constancia, f. perseverance; record.

constante, a. constant.

constantemente, adv. constantly.

constar, v. consist; be clear, be on record.

constelación, f. constellation.

consternación, f. consternation.

consternar, v. dismay.

constipación, f. head cold.

constipado, a. having a head cold.

constitución, f. constitution.

constitucional, a. constitutional.

constitucionalidad, f. constitutionality.

constituir, v. constitute.

constitutivo, m. constituent.

constituyente, a. constituent.

constreñidamente, adv. compulsively; with constraint.

constreñimiento, m. compulsion; constraint.

constreñir, v. constrain.

constricción, f. constriction.

construcción, f. construction.

constructivo, a. constructive.

constructor, m. builder.

construir, v. construct, build.

consuelo, m. consolation.

cónsul, m. consul.

consulado, m. consulate.

consular, a. consular.

consulta, f. consultation.

consultación, f. consultation.

consultante, m. & f. consultant.

consultar, v. consult.

consultivo, a. consultative.

consultor, m. adviser.

consumación, f. consummation; end.

consumado, a. consummate, downright.

consumar, v. consummate.

consumidor, m. consumer.

consumir, v. consume.

consumo, m. consumption.

consunción, m. consumption, tuberculosis.

contabilidad, f. accounting, bookkeeping.

contabilista, contable, m. & f. accountant.

contacto, m. contact.

contado, m. **al c.,** (for) cash.

contador -ra, n. accountant, bookkeeper.

contagiar, v. infect.

contagio, m. contagion.

contagioso, a. contagious.

contaminación, f. contamination, pollution.

contaminar, v. contaminate, pollute.

contar, v. count; relate, recount, tell. **c. con,** count on.

contemperar, v. moderate.

contemplación, f. contemplation.

contemplador -ra, n. thinker.

contemplar, v. contemplate.

contemplativamente, adv. thoughtfully.

contemplativo, a. contemplative.

contemporáneo -nea, a. & n. contemporary.

contención, f. contention.

contencioso, a. quarrelsome; argumentative.

contender, v. cope, contend; conflict.

contendiente, m. & f. contender.

contenedor -ra, n. tenant.

contener, v. contain; curb, control.

contenido, m. contents.

contenta, f. endorsement.

contentamiento, m. contentment.

contentar, v. content, satisfy.

contentible, a. contemptible.

contento, 1. a. contented, happy. **2.** m. contentment, satisfaction, pleasure.

contérmino, a. adjacent, abutting.

contestable, a. disputable.

contestación, f. answer. —**contestar,** v.

contextura, f. texture.

contienda, f. combat; match; strife.

contigo, adv. with you.

contiguamente, adv. closely.

contiguo, a. adjoining, next.

continencia, f. continence, moderation.

continental, a. continental.

continente, m. continent; mainland.

continentemente, adv. in moderation.

contingencia, f. contingency.

contingente, a. contingent; incidental.

continuación, f. continuation. a c., thereupon, hereupon.

continuamente, adv. continuously.

continuar, v. continue, keep on.

continuidad, f. continuity.

continuo, a. continual; continuous.

contorcerse, v. writhe, twist.

contorción, f. contortion.

contorno, m. contour; profile; outline; neighborhood.

contra, prep. against.

contraalmirante, m. rear admiral.

contraataque, m. counterattack.

contrabalancear, v. counterbalance.

contrabandear, v. smuggle.

contrabandista, m. smuggler.

contrabando, m. contraband, smuggling.

contracción, f. contraction.

contracepción, f. contraception, birth control.

contractual, a. contractual.

contradecir, v. contradict.

contradicción, f. contradiction.

contradictorio, adj. contradictory.

contraer, v. contract; shrink.

contrahacedor -ra, n. imitator.

contrahacer, v. forge.

contralor, m. comptroller.

contramandar, v. countermand.

contraorden, f. countermand.

contraparte, f. counterpart.

contrapesar, v. counterbalance, offset.

contrapeso, m. counterweight.

contrapunto, m. counterpoint.

contrariamente, adv. contrarily.

contrariar, v. contradict; vex; antagonize; counteract.

contrariedad, f. contrariness; opposition; contradiction; disappointment; trouble.

contrario, a. & n. contrary, opposite.

contrarrestar, v. resist; counteract.

contrasol, m. sunshade.

contraste, m. contrast. —**contrastar,** v.

contratar, v. engage, contract.

contratiempo, m. accident; misfortune.

contratista, m. contractor.

contrato, m. contract.

contribución, f. contribution; tax.

contribuir, v. contribute.

contribuyente, m. contributor; taxpayer.

contrición, f. contrition.

contristar, v. afflict.

contrito, a. contrite, remorseful.

control, m. control. —**controlar,** v.

controversia, f. controversy.

controversista, m. disputant.

controvertir, v. dispute.

contumacia, f. stubbornness.

contumaz, adj. stubborn.

contumelia, f. contumely; abuse.

conturbar, v. trouble, disturb.

contusión, f. contusion; bruise.

convalecencia, f. convalescence.

convalecer, v. convalesce.

convaleciente, a. convalescent.

convecino, adj. near, close.

convencedor, adj. convincing.

convencer, v. convince.

convencimiento, *m.* conviction, firm belief.

convención, *f.* convention.

convencional, *a.* conventional.

conveniencia, *f.* suitability; advantage, interest.

conveniente, *a.* suitable; advantageous, opportune.

convenio, *m.* pact, treaty; agreement.

convenir, *v.* assent, agree, concur; be suitable, fitting, convenient.

convento, *m.* convent.

convergencia, *f.* convergence.

convergir, *v.* converge.

conversación, *f.* conversation.

conversar, *v.* converse.

conversión, *f.* conversion.

convertible, *a.* convertible.

convertir, *v.* convert.

convexidad, *f.* convexity.

convexo, *a.* convex.

convicción, *f.* conviction.

convicto, *adj.* guilty.

convidado -da, *n.* guest.

convidar, *v.* invite.

convincente, *a.* convincing.

convite, *m.* invitation, treat.

convocación, *f.* convocation.

convocar, *v.* convoke, assemble.

convoy, *m.* convoy, escort.

convoyar, *v.* convey; escort.

convulsión, *f.* convulsion.

convulsivo, *adj.* convulsive.

conyugal, *adj.* conjugal.

cónyuge, *n.* spouse, mate.

coñac, *m.* cognac, brandy.

cooperación, *f.* cooperation.

cooperador, *adj.* cooperative.

cooperar, *v.* cooperate.

cooperativo, *a.* cooperative.

coordinación, *f.* coordination.

coordinar, *v.* coordinate.

copa, *f.* goblet.

copartícipe, *m.* partner.

copete, *m.* tuft; toupee.

copia, *f.* copy. —**copiar,** *v.*

copiadora, *f.* copier.

copioso, *a.* copious.

copista, *m.* copyist.

copla, *f.* popular song.

coplero, *m.* poetaster.

cópula, *f.* connection.

coqueta, *f.* flirt. —**coquetear,** *v.*

coraje, *m.* courage, bravery; anger.

coral, 1. *a.* choral. **2.** *m.* coral.

coralino, *a.* coral.

corazón, *m.* heart.

corazonada, *f.* foreboding.

corbata, *f.* necktie.

corbeta, *f.* corvette.

corcova, *f.* hump, hunch.

corcovado, *m.* hunchback.

corcho, *m.* cork.

cordaje, *m.* rigging.

cordel, *m.* string, cord.

cordero, *m.* lamb.

cordial, *a.* cordial, hearty.

cordialidad, *f.* cordiality.

cordillera, *f.* mountain range.

cordón, *m.* cord; (shoe) lace.

cordura, *f.* sanity.

coreografía, *f.* choreography.

corista, *f.* chorus girl.

corneja, *f.* crow.

córneo, *a.* horny.

corneta, *f.* bugle, horn, cornet.

corniforme, *a.* horn-shaped.

cornisa, *f.* cornice.

cornucopia, *f.* cornucopia.

coro, *m.* chorus; choir.

corola, *f.* corolla.

corolario, *m.* corollary.

corona, *f.* crown, halo, wreath.

coronación, *f.* coronation.

coronamiento, *m.* completion of a task.

coronar, *v.* crown.

coronel, *m.* colonel.

coronilla, *f.* small crown.

corporación, *f.* corporation.

corporal, *adj.* corporeal, bodily.

corpóreo, *a.* corporeal.

corpulencia, *f.* corpulence.

corpulento, *a.* corpulent, stout.

corpuscular, *a.* corpuscular.

corpúsculo, *m.* corpuscle.

corral, *m.* corral, pen, yard.

correa, *f.* belt, strap.

corrección, *f.* correction.

correcto, *a.* correct, proper, right.

corrector, *m.* corrector, proofreader.

corredera, *f.* race course.

corredizo, *a.* easily untied.

corredor, *m.* corridor; runner.

corregible, *a.* corrigible.

corregidor, *m.* corrector; magistrate, mayor.

corregir, *v.* correct.

correlación, *f.* correlation.

correlacionar, *v.* correlate.

correlativo, a. correlative.
correo, m. mail.
correoso, a. leathery.
correr, v. run.
correría, f. raid; escapade.
correspondencia, f. correspondence.
corresponder, v. correspond.
correspondiente, a. & m. corresponding; correspondent.
corresponsal, m. correspondent.
corretaje, m. brokerage.
correvedile, m. tale bearer; gossip.
corrida, f. race. **c. (de toros),** bullfight.
corrido, a. abashed; expert.
corriente, 1. a. current, standard. **2.** f. current, stream. m. **al c.,** informed, up to date.
corrobación, f. corroboration.
corroborar, v. corroborate.
corroer, v. corrode.
corromper, v. corrupt.
corrompido, adj. corrupt.
corrupción, f. corruption.
corruptela, f. corruption, vice.
corruptibilidad, f. corruptibility.
corruptor, m. corrupter.
corsario, m. corsair.
corsé, m. corset.
corso, m. piracy.
cortadillo, m. small glass.
cortado, a. cut.
cortadura, f. cut.
cortante, a. cutting, sharp, keen.
cortapisa, f. obstacle.
cortaplumas, m. penknife.
cortar, v. cut, cut off, cut out.
corte, f. court, m. cut.
cortedad, f. smallness; shyness.
cortejar, v. pay court to, woo.
cortejo, m. court; courtship; sweetheart.
cortés, a. civil, courteous, polite.
cortesana, f. courtesan.
cortesano. 1. a. courtly, courteous. **2.** m. courtier.
cortesía, f. courtesy.
corteza, f. bark; rind; crust.
cortijo, m. farmhouse.
cortina, f. curtain.
corto, a. short.
corva, f. bend of the knee.
cosa, f. thing. **c. de,** a matter of, roughly.

cosecha, f. crop, harvest. —**cosechar,** v.
coser, v. sew, stitch.
cosmético, a. & m. cosmetic.
cosmopolita, a. & n. cosmopolitan.
coso, m. arena for bull fights.
cosquilla, f. tickle. —**cosquillar,** v.
cosquilloso, a. ticklish.
costa, f. coast; cost, expense.
costado, m. side.
costal, m. sack, bag.
costanero, a. coastal.
costar, v. cost.
costarricense, a. & n. Costa Rican.
coste, m. cost, price.
costear, v. defray, sponsor; sail along the coast of.
costilla, f. rib; chop.
costo, m. cost, price.
costoso, a. costly.
costra, f. crust.
costumbre, f. custom, practice, habit.
costura, f. sewing; seam.
costurera, f. seamstress, dressmaker.
cota de malla, coat of mail.
cotejar, v. compare.
coteleta, f. cutlet.
cotidiano, a. daily; everyday.
cotillón, m. cotillion.
cotización, f. quotation.
cotizar, v. quote (a price).
coto, m. enclosure; boundary.
cotón, m. printed cotton cloth.
cotufa, f. Jerusalem artichoke.
coturno, m. buskin.
covacha, f. small cave.
coxal, a. of the hip.
coy, m. hammock.
coyote, m. coyote.
coyuntura, f. joint; juncture.
coz, f. kick.
crac, m. failure.
cráneo, m. skull.
craniano, a. cranial.
crapuloso, a. drunken.
crasiento, a. greasy, oily.
craso, a. fat; gross.
cráter, m. crater.
craza, f. crucible.
creación, f. creation.
creador -ra, a. & n. creative; creator.
crear, v. create.

creativo, *a.* creative.
crébol, *m.* holly tree.
crecer, *v.* grow, grow up; increase.
creces, *f.pl.* increase, addition.
crecidamente, *adv.* abundantly.
crecido, *a.* increased, enlarged; swollen.
creciente, 1. *a.* growing. **2.** *f.* crescent.
crecimiento, *m.* growth.
credenciales, *f.pl.* credentials.
credibilidad, *f.* credibility.
crédito, *m.* credit.
credo, *m.* creed, belief.
crédulamente, *adv.* credulously, gullibly.
credulidad, *f.* credulity.
crédulo, *a.* credulous.
creedero, *a.* credible.
creedor, *a.* credulous, believing.
creencia, *f.* belief.
creer, *v.* believe; think.
creíble, *a.* credible, believable.
crema, *f.* cream.
cremación, *f.* cremation.
cremallera, *f.* zipper.
cremar, *v.* cremate.
crémor tártaro, cream of tartar.
creosota, *f.* creosote.
crepitar, *v.* crackle.
crepuscular, *a.* of or like the dawn or dusk.
crepúsculo, *m.* dusk, twilight.
crescendo, *m.* crescendo.
crespo, *a.* crisp; curly.
crespón, *m.* crepe.
cresta, *f.* crest.
crestado, *a.* crested.
creta, *f.* chalk.
cretáceo, *a.* chalky.
cretinismo, *m.* cretinism.
cretino, *m. & a.* cretin.
cretona, *f.* cretonne.
creyente, 1. *a.* believing. **2.** *n.* believer.
creyón, *m.* crayon.
cría, *f.* (stock) breeding; young (of an animal), litter.
criada, *f.* girl servant, maid.
criadero, *m.* (agr.) nursery.
criado -da, *m.* servant.
criador, *a.* fruitful, prolific.
crianza, *f.* breeding; upbringing.
criar, *v.* raise, rear; breed.
criatura, *f.* creature; infant.
criba, *f.* sieve; crib.

cribado, *a.* sifted.
cribar, *v.* sift.
crimen, *m.* crime.
criminal, *a. & m.* criminal.
criminalidad, *f.* criminality.
criminalmente, *adv.* criminally.
criminoso, *a.* criminal.
crin, *f.* mane of a horse.
crinolina, *f.* crinoline.
criocirugía, *f.* cryosurgery.
criollo -lla, *a. & n.* native; creole.
cripta, *f.* crypt.
criptografía, *f.* cryptography.
crisantemo, *m.* chrysanthemum.
crisis, *f.* crisis.
crisma, *f.* chrism.
crisol, *m.* crucible.
crispamiento, *m.* twitch, contraction.
crispar, *v.* contract (the muscles); twitch.
crista, *f.* heraldic crest.
cristal, *m.* crystal; lens.
cristalería, *f.* glassware.
cristalino, *a.* crystalline.
cristalización, *f.* crystallization.
cristalizar, *v.* crystallize.
cristianar, *v.* baptize.
cristiandad, *f.* Christendom.
cristianismo, *m.* Christianity.
cristiano -na, *a. & n.* Christian.
Cristo, *m.* Christ.
criterio, *m.* criterion; judgment.
crítica, *f.* criticism; critique.
criticable, *a.* blameworthy.
criticador, *a.* critical.
criticar, *v.* criticize.
crítico, *a. & m.* critical; critic.
croar, *v.* croak.
crocante, *m.* peanut brittle.
crocidar, *v.* crow.
crocodilo, *m.* crocodile.
cromático, *a.* chromatic.
cromo, *m.* chromium.
cromotipia, *f.* color printing.
crónica, *f.* chronicle.
crónico, *a.* chronic.
cronicón, *m.* concise chronicle.
cronista, *m.* chronicler.
cronología, *f.* chronology.
cronológicamente, *adv.* chronologically.
cronológico, *a.* chronologic.
cronómetro, *m.* chronometer.
croqueta, *f.* croquette.
croquis, *m.* sketch; rough outline.

crótalo, *m.* rattlesnake; castanet.
cruce, *m.* crossing, crossroads, junction.
crucero, *m.* cruiser.
crucífero, *a.* cross-shaped.
crucificado, *a.* crucified.
crucificar, *v.* crucify.
crucifijo, *m.* crucifix.
crucifixión, *f.* crucifixion.
crudamente, *adv.* crudely.
crudeza, *f.* crudeness.
crudo, *a.* crude, raw.
cruel, *a.* cruel.
crueldad, *f.* cruelty.
cruelmente, *adv.* cruelly.
cruentamente, *adv.* bloodily.
cruento, *a.* bloody.
crujía, *f.* corridor.
crujido, *m.* creak.
crujir, *v.* crackle, creak; rustle.
crúorico, *a.* bloody.
crup, *m.* croup.
crustáceo, *n. & a.* crustacean.
cruz, *f.* cross.
cruzada, *f.* crusade.
cruzado -da, *n.* crusader.
cruzamiento, *m.* crossing.
cruzar, *v.* cross.
cruzarse con, *v.* to (meet and) pass.
cuaderno, *m.* notebook.
cuadra, *f.* block; (hospital) ward.
cuadradamente, *adv.* exactly, precisely; completely, in full.
cuadradillo, *m.* lump of sugar.
cuadrado, *a. & m.* square.
cuadrafónico, *a.* quadraphonic.
cuadragésima, *f.* Lent.
cuadragésimo, *a.* Lenten.
cuadrángulo, *m.* quadrangle.
cuadrante, *m.* quadrant; dial.
cuadrar, *v.* square; suit.
cuadricular, *a.* in squares.
cuadrilátero, *a.* quadrilateral.
cuadrilla, *f.* band, troop, gang.
cuadrinieto, *n.* great-grandchild.
cuadro, *m.* picture; painting; frame. **a cuadros**, checked, plaid.
cuadro de servicio, timetable.
cuadrúpedal, *a.* quadruped.
cuádruplo, *a.* fourfold.
cuajada, *f.* curd.
cuajamiento, *m.* coagulation.
cuajar, *v.* coagulate; overdecorate.
cuajo, *m.* rennet; coagulation.
cuakerismo, *m.* Quakerism.

cuákero, *n. & a.* Quaker.
cual, *rel. pron.* which.
cuál, *a. & pron.* what, which.
cualidad, *f.* quality.
cualitativo, *a.* qualitative.
cualquiera, *a. & pron.* whatever, any; anyone.
cuando, *conj.* when.
cuando, *adv.* when. **de cuando en cuando**, from time to time.
cuantía, *f.* quantity; amount.
cuantiar, *v.* estimate.
cuantidad, *f.* quantity.
cuantiosamente, *adv.* abundantly.
cuantioso, *a.* abundant.
cuantitativo, *a.* quantitative.
cuanto, *a., adv. & pron.* as much as, as many as; all that which. **en c.**, as soon as. **en c. a**, as for. **c. antes**, as soon as possible. **c. más . . . tanto más**, the more . . . the more. **unos cuantos**, a few.
cuánto, *a. & adv.* how much, how many.
cuaquerismo, *m.* Quakerism.
cuáquero, *n. & a.* Quaker.
cuarenta, *a. & pron.* forty.
cuarentena, *f.* quarantine.
cuaresma, *f.* Lent.
cuaresmal, *a.* Lenten.
cuarta, *f.* quarter; quadrant; quart.
cuartana, *f.* ague.
cuartear, *v.* divide into quarters.
cuartel, *m.* (mil.) quarters; barracks; (naut.) hatch. **c. general**, headquarters. **sin c.**, giving no quarter.
cuartelada, *f.* military uprising.
cuarterón, *n. & a.* quadroon.
cuarteto, *m.* quartet.
cuartillo, *m.* pint.
cuarto, **1.** *a.* fourth. **2.** *m.* quarter; room.
cuarto de baño, bathroom.
cuarto de dormir, bedroom.
cuarzo, *m.* quartz.
cuasi, *adv.* almost, nearly.
cuate, *a. & n.* twin.
cuatrero, *n.* cattle rustler.
cuatrillón, *n.* quadrillion.
cuatro, *a. & pron.* four.
cuatrocientos, *a. & pron.* four hundred.
cuba, *f.* cask, tub, vat.
cubano -na, *a. & n.* Cuban.

cubero, m. cooper.

cubertura, f. cover.

cubeta, f. small barrel, keg.

cúbico, a. cubic.

cubierta, f. cover; envelope; wrapping; tread (of a tire); deck.

cubiertamente, adv. secretly, stealthily.

cubierto, m. place (at table).

cubil, m. lair.

cubo, m. cube; bucket.

cubrecama, f. bedspread.

cubrir, v. cover.

cubrirse, v. put on one's hat.

cucaracha, f. cockroach.

cuclillo, m. cuckoo.

cuco, a. sly.

cucula, f. hood, cowl.

cuchara, f. spoon, tablespoon.

cucharada, f. spoonful.

cucharita, cucharilla, f. teaspoon.

cucharón, m. dipper, ladle.

cuchicheo, m. whisper. —**cuchichear,** v.

cuchilla, f. cleaver.

cuchillada, f. slash.

cuchillería, f. cutlery.

cuchillo, m. knife.

cucho, m. fertilizer.

cuchufleta, f. jest.

cuelga, f. cluster, bunch.

cuelgacapas, m. coat rack.

cuello, m. neck; collar.

cuenca, f. socket; (river) basin; wooden bowl.

cuenco, m. earthen bowl.

cuenta, f. account; bill. **darse c.,** to realize. **tener en c.,** to keep in mind.

cuentagotas, m. dropper (for medicine).

cuentista, m. informer.

cuento, m. story, tale.

cuerda, f. cord; chord; rope; string; spring (of clock). **dar c. a,** to wind (clock).

cuerdamente, adv. sanely; prudently.

cuerdo, a. sane; prudent.

cuerno, m. horn.

cuero, m. leather; hide.

cuerpo, m. body; corps.

cuervo, m. crow, raven.

cuesco, m. pit, stone (of fruit).

cuesta, f. hill, slope. **llevar a cuestas,** to carry on one's back.

cuestación, f. solicitation for charity.

cuestión, f. question; affair; argument.

cuestionable, a. questionable.

cuestionar, v. question; discuss, argue.

cuestionario, m. questionnaire.

cuete, m. firecracker.

cuetzale, m. quetzal.

cueva, f. cave; cellar.

cugujada, f. lark.

cuidado, m. care, caution, worry. **tener c.,** to be careful.

cuidadosamente, adv. carefully.

cuidadoso, a. careful, painstaking.

cuidante, n. caretaker, custodian.

cuidar, v. take care of.

cuita, f. trouble, care, grief.

cuitado, a. unfortunate; shy, timid.

cuitamiento, m. timidity.

culata, f. haunch, buttock; butt of a gun.

culatada, f. recoil.

culatazo, m. blow with the butt of a gun; recoil.

culebra, f. snake.

culero, a. lazy, indolent.

culinario, a. culinary.

culminación, f. culmination.

culminar, v. culminate.

culpa, f. fault, guilt, blame. **tener la c.,** to be at fault. **echar la culpa a,** to blame.

culpabilidad, f. guilt, fault, blame.

culpable, a. at fault, guilty, to blame.

culpar, v. blame, accuse.

cultamente, adv. politely, elegantly.

cultivable, a. arable.

cultivación, f. cultivation.

cultivador, m. cultivator.

cultivar, v. cultivate.

cultivo, m. cultivation; (growing) crop.

culto, 1. a. cultured, cultivated. **2.** m. cult; worship.

cultura, f. culture; refinement.

cultural, a. cultural.

culturar, v. cultivate.

cumbre, m. summit, peak.

cumpleaños, m.pl. birthday.

mplidamente, *adv.* completely.

mplido, *a.* polite, polished.

mplimentar, *v.* compliment.

mplimiento, *m.* fulfillment; ompliment.

mplir, *v.* comply; carry out, ulfill; reach (years of age).

mular, *v.* accumulate.

mulativo, *a.* cumulative.

úmulo, *m.* heap, pile.

una, *f.* cradle.

undir, *v.* spread; expand; propagate.

uneiforme, *a.* cuneiform, wedge-shaped.

uneo, *m.* rocking.

uña, *f.* wedge.

uñada, *f.* sister-in-law.

uñado, *m.* brother-in-law.

uñete, *m.* keg.

uociente, *m.* quotient.

uota, *f.* quota; dues.

uotidiano, *a.* daily.

upé, *m.* coupé.

upido, *m.* lover.

upo, *m.* share; assigned quota.

upón, *m.* coupon.

úpula, *f.* dome.

cura, *m.* priest. *f.* treatment, (medical) care. **c. de urgencia,** first aid.

curable, *a.* curable.

curación, *f.* healing; cure; (surgical) dressing.

curado, *a.* cured, healed.

curador, *m.* custodian; curator.

curandero, *m.* healer, medicine man.

curar, *v.* cure, heal, treat.

curativo, *a.* a curative, healing.

curia, *f.* ecclesiastical court.

curiosear, *v.* snoop, pry, meddle.

curiosidad, *f.* curiosity.

curioso, *a.* curious.

curro, *a.* showy, loud, flashy.

cursante, *n.* student.

cursar, *v.* frequent; attend to.

cursi, *a.* vulgar, shoddy, in bad taste.

curso, *m.* course.

curtidor, *m.* tanner.

curtir, *v.* tan.

curva, *f.* curve; bend.

curvatura, *f.* curvature.

cúspide, *f.* top, peak.

custodia, *f.* custody.

custodiar, *v.* guard, watch.

custodio, *m.* custodian.

cutáneo, *a.* cutaneous.

cutícula, *f.* cuticle.

cutis, *m.* or *f.* skin, complexion.

cuyo, *a.* whose.

CH

chabancano, *a.* clumsy.

chacal, *m.* jackal.

chacó, *m.* shako.

chacona, *f.* chaconne.

chacota, *f.* fun, mirth.

chacotear, *v.* joke.

chacra, *f.* small farm.

chafallar, *v.* mend badly.

chagra, *m.* rustic; rural person.

chal, *m.* shawl.

chalán, *m.* horse trader.

chaleco, *m.* vest.

chalet, *m.* chalet.

challí, *m.* challis.

chamada, *f.* brushwood.

chamarillero, *m.* gambler.

chamarra, *f.* coarse linen jacket.

chambelán, *m.* chamberlain.

champaña, *m.* champagne.

champú, *m.* shampoo.

chamuscar, *v.* scorch.

chancaco, *a.* brown.

chancear, *v.* jest, joke.

chanciller, *m.* chancellor.

chancillería, *f.* chancery.

chancla, *f.* old shoe.

chancleta, *f.* slipper.

chanclos, *m.pl.* galoshes.

chancro, *m.* chancre.

changador, *m.* porter, handyman.

chantaje, *m.* blackmail.

chantajista, *n.* blackmailer.

chanto, *m.* flagstone.

chantre, *m.* precentor.

chanza, *f.* joke, jest. **—chancear,** *v.*

chanzoneta, *f.* chansonette.

chapa, *f.* (metal) sheet, plate; lock.

chaparrada, *f.* shower.

chaparral, *m.* chaparral.

chaparreras, *f.pl.* chaps.

chaparrón, *m.* downpour.

chapear, *v.* veneer.

chapeo, *m.* hat.

chapitel, *m.* spire, steeple; (architecture) capital.

chapodar, *v.* lop.

chapón, *m.* inkblot.
chapotear, *v.* paddle or splash in the water.
chapoteo, *m.* splash.
chapucear, *v.* fumble, bungle.
chapucero, *a.* sloppy, bungling.
chapurrear, *v.* speak (a language) brokenly.
chapuz, *m.* dive; ducking.
chapuzar, *v.* dive, duck.
chaqueta, *f.* jacket, coat.
charada, *f.* charade.
charamusca, *f.* twisted candy stick.
charanga, *f.* military band.
charanguero, *m.* peddler.
charca, *f.* pool, pond.
charco, *m.* pool, puddle.
charla, *f.* chat; chatter, prattle. —charlar, *v.*
charladuría, *f.* chatter.
charlatán, *m.* charlatan.
charlatanismo, *m.* charlatanism.
charol, *m.* varnish.
charolar, *v.* varnish; polish.
charquear, *v.* jerk (beef).
charquí, *m.* jerked beef.
charrán, *a.* roguish.
chascarillo, *m.* risqué story.
chasco, *m.* disappointment, blow; practical joke.
chasis, *m.* chassis.
chasquear, *v.* fool, trick; disappoint; crack (a whip).
chasquido, *m.* crack (sound).
chata, *f.* bedpan.
chato, *a.* flat-nosed, pug-nosed.
chauvinismo, *m.* chauvinism.
chauvinista, *n.* & *a.* chauvinist.
chelín, *m.* shilling.
cheque, *m.* (bank) check.
chica, *f.* girl.
chicana, *f.* chicanery.
chicle, *m.* chewing gum.
chico, 1. *a.* little. 2. *m.* boy.
chicote, *m.* cigar; cigar butt.
chicotear, *v.* whip, flog.
chicha, *f.* an alcoholic drink.
chícharo, *m.* pea.
chicharra, *f.* cicada; talkative person.
chicharrón, *m.* crisp fried scrap of meat.
chichear, *v.* hiss in disapproval.
chichón, *m.* bump, bruise, lump.
chifladura, *f.* mania; whim; jest.

chiflar, *v.* whistle; become insane.
chiflido, *m.* shrill whistle.
chile, *m.* chili.
chileno -na, *a.* & *n.* Chilean.
chillido, *m.* shriek, scream; screech. —chillar, *v.*
chillón, *a.* shrill.
chimenea, *f.* chimney, smoke stack; fireplace.
china, *f.* pebble; maid; Chinese woman.
chinarro, *m.* large pebble, stone.
chinche, *f.* bedbug; thumbtack.
chinchilla, *f.* chinchilla.
chinchorro, *m.* fishing net.
chinela, *f.* slipper.
chinero, *m.* china closet.
chino -na, *a.* & *n.* Chinese.
chiquero, *m.* pen for pigs, goats, etc.
chiquito, 1. *a.* small, tiny. 2. *m.* small child.
chiribitil, *m.* small room, den.
chirimía, *f.* flageolet.
chiripa, *f.* stroke of good luck.
chirla, *f.* mussel.
chirle, *a.* insipid.
chirona, *f.* prison, jail.
chirrido, *m.* squeak, chirp. —chirriar, *v.*
chis, *interj.* hush!
chisgarabís, *n.* meddler; unimportant person.
chisguete, *m.* squirt, splash.
chisme, *m.* gossip. —chismear, *v.*
chismero, *m.* gossiper.
chismoso, *adj.* gossiping.
chispa, *f.* spark.
chispeante, *a.* sparkling.
chispear, *v.* sparkle.
chisporrotear, *v.* emit sparks.
chistar, *v.* mumble.
chiste, *m.* joke, gag; witty saying.
chistera, *f.* fish basket; top hat.
chistoso, *a.* funny, comic, amusing.
chito, *interj.* hush!
chiva, *f.* female goat.
chivato, *m.* kid, young goat.
chivo, *m.* male goat.
chocante, *a.* striking; shocking; unpleasant.
chocar, *v.* collide, clash, crash; shock.
chocarrear, *v.* joke, jest.

choclo, *m.* clog; overshoe; ear of corn.
chocolate, *m.* chocolate.
chocolatería, *f.* chocolate shop.
chochear, *v.* be in one's dotage.
chochera, *f.* dotage, senility.
chofer, chófer, *m.* chauffeur, driver.
chofeta, *f.* chafing dish.
cholo, *m.* half-breed.
chopo, *m.* black poplar.
choque, *m.* collision, clash, crash; shock.
chorizo, *m.* sausage.
chorrear, *v.* spout; drip.
chorro, *m.* spout; spurt, jet. **llover a chorros,** to pour (rain).
choto, *m.* calf, kid.
choza, *f.* hut, cabin.
chozno, *m.* great-grandson.
chubasco, *m.* shower, squall.
chubascoso, *a.* squally.
chuchería, *f.* trinket, knickknack.
chulería, *f.* pleasant manner.
chuleta, *f.* chop, cutlet.
chulo, *m.* rascal, rogue; joker.
chupa, *f.* jacket.
chupada, *f.* suction.
chupado, *a.* very thin.
chupaflor, *m.* hummingbird.
chupar, *v.* suck.
churrasco, *m.* roasted meat.
chuscada, *f.* joke, jest.
chusco, *a.* funny, humorous.
chusma, *f.* mob, rabble.
chuzo, *m.* pike.

D

dable, *a.* possible.
dactilógrafo, *m.* typewriter.
dádiva, *f.* gift.
dadivosamente, *adv.* generously.
dadivoso, *a.* generous, bountiful.
dador, *m.* giver.
dados, *m.pl.* dice.
daga, *f.* dagger.
dalia, *f.* dahlia.
daltonismo, *m.* color blindness.
dallador, *m.* lawn mower.
dallar, *v.* mow.
dama, *f.* lady.
damasco, *m.* apricot.
damisela, *f.* young lady, girl.
danés -esa, *a.* & *n.* Danish, Dane.

danza, *f.* (the) dance. **—danzar,** *v.*
danzante, *m.* dancer.
dañable, *a.* condemnable.
dañar, *v.* hurt, harm; damage.
dañino, dañoso, *a.* harmful.
daño, *m.* damage; harm.
dañoso, *a.* harmful.
dar, *v.* give; strike (clock). **d. a,** face, open on. **d. con,** find, locate.
dardo, *m.* dart.
dársena, *f.* dock.
datar, *v.* date.
dátil, *m.* date (fruit).
dativo, *m.* & *a.* dative.
datos, *m.pl.* data.
de, *prep.* of; from; than.
debajo, *adv.* underneath. **d. de,** under.
debate, *m.* debate.
debatir, *v.* debate, argue.
debe, *m.* debit.
debelación, *f.* conquest.
debelar, *v.* conquer.
deber, 1. *v.* owe; must; be to, be supposed to. **2.** *m.* obligation.
debido, *a.* due.
débil, *a.* weak, faint.
debilidad, *f.* weakness.
debilitación, *f.* weakness.
debilitar, *v.* weaken.
débito, *m.* debit.
debutante, *f.* debutante.
debutar, *v.* make a debut.
década, *f.* decade.
decadencia, *f.* decadence, decline, decay.
decadente, *a.* decadent, declining, decaying.
decaer, *v.* decay, decline.
decalitro, *m.* decaliter.
decálogo, *f.* m. decalogue.
decámetro, *m.* decameter.
decano, *m.* dean.
decantado, *a.* much discussed; overexalted.
decapitación, *f.* beheading.
decapitar, *v.* behead.
decencia, *f.* decency.
decenio, *m.* decade.
decente, *a.* decent.
decentemente, *adv.* decently.
decepción, *f.* disappointment; delusion.
decepcionar, *v.* disappoint, disillusion.
decibelio, *m.* decibel.

decididamente, *adv.* decidedly.
decidir, *v.* decide.
decigramo, *m.* decigram.
decilitro, *m.* deciliter.
décima, *f.* ten-line stanza.
decimal, *a.* decimal.
décimo, *a.* tenth.
decir, *v.* tell, say. **es d.,** that is (to say).
decisión, *f.* decision.
decisivamente, *adv.* decisively.
decisivo, *a.* decisive.
declamación, *f.* declamation, speech.
declamar, *v.* declaim.
declaración, *f.* declaration; statement; plea.
declarar, *v.* declare, state.
declarativo, *a.* declarative.
declinación, *f.* descent; decay; decline; declension.
declinar, *v.* decline.
declive, *m.* declivity, slope.
decocción, *f.* decoction.
decomiso, *m.* seizure, confiscation.
decoración, *f.* decoration, trimming.
decorado, *m.* (theat.) scenery, set.
decorar, *v.* decorate, trim.
decorativo, *a.* decorative, ornamental.
decoro, *m.* decorum; decency.
decoroso, *a.* decorous.
decrecer, *v.* decrease.
decrépito, *a.* decrepit.
decreto, *m.* decree. **—decretar,** *v.*
dechado, *m.* model; sample; pattern; example.
dedal, *m.* thimble.
dédalo, *m.* labyrinth.
dedicación, *f.* dedication.
dedicar, *v.* devote; dedicate.
dedicatoria, *f.* dedication, inscription.
dedo, *m.* finger, toe.
deducción, *f.* deduction.
deducir, *v.* deduce; subtract.
defectivo, *a.* defective.
defecto, *m.* defect, flaw.
defectuoso, *a.* defective, faulty.
defender, *v.* defend.
defensa, *f.* defense.
defensivo, *a.* defensive.
defensor, *m.* defender.
deferencia, *f.* deference.
deferir, *v.* defer.

deficiente, *a.* deficient.
déficit, *m.* deficit.
definición, *f.* definition.
definido, *a.* definite.
definir, *v.* define; establish.
definitivamente, *adv.* definitely.
definitivo, *a.* definite; definitive.
deformación, *f.* deformation.
deformar, *v.* deform.
deforme, *a.* deformed; ugly.
deformidad, *f.* deformity.
defraudar, *v.* defraud.
defunción, *f.* death.
degeneración, *f.* degeneration.
degenerado, *a.* degenerate. **—degenerar,** *v.*
deglutir, *v.* swallow.
degollar, *v.* behead.
degradación, *f.* degradation.
degradar, *v.* degrade, debase.
deidad, *f.* deity.
deificación, *f.* deification.
deificar, *v.* deify.
deífico, *a.* divine, deific.
deísmo, *m.* deism.
dejadez, *f.* neglect, untidiness; laziness.
dejado, *a.* untidy; lazy.
dejar, *v.* let, allow; leave. **d. de,** stop, leave off. **no d. de,** not fail to.
dejo, *m.* abandonment; negligence; aftertaste; accent.
del, *contr.* of **de** + **el.**
delantal, *m.* apron.
delante, *adv.* ahead, forward; in front.
delantero, *a.* forward, front, first.
delator, *m.* informer; accuser.
delegación, *f.* delegation.
delegado -da, *n.* delegate. **—delegar,** *v.*
deleite, *m.* delight. **—deleitar,** *v.*
deleitoso, *a.* delightful.
deletrear, *v.* spell; decipher.
delfín, *m.* dolphin; dauphin.
delgadez, *f.* thinness, slenderness.
delgado, *a.* thin, slender, slim, slight.
deliberación, *f.* deliberation.
deliberadamente, *adv.* deliberately.
deliberar, *v.* deliberate.
deliberativo, *a.* deliberative.
delicadamente, *adv.* delicately.
delicadeza, *f.* delicacy.
delicado, *a.* delicate, dainty.

delicia, f. delight; deliciousness.
delicioso, a. delicious.
delincuencia, f. delinquency.
delincuente. a. & m. delinquent; culprit, offender.
delineación, f. delineation, sketch.
delinear, v. delineate, sketch.
delirante, a. delirious.
delirar, v. rave, be delirious.
delirio, m. delirium; rapture, bliss.
delito, m. crime, offense.
delta, m. delta (of river).
demagogia, f. demagogy.
demagogo, n. demagogue.
demanda, f. demand, claim.
demandador -ra, n. plaintiff.
demandar, v. sue; demand.
demarcación, f. demarcation.
demarcar, v. demarcate, limit.
demás, a. & n. other; (the) rest (of). **por d.,** too much.
demasía, f. excess; audacity; iniquity.
demasiado, a. & adv. too; too much; too many.
demencia, f. dementia; insanity.
demente, a. demented.
democracia, f. democracy.
demócrata. m. & f. democrat.
democrático, a. democratic.
demoler, v. demolish, tear down.
demolición, f. demolition.
demonio, m. demon, devil.
demontre, m. devil.
demora, f. delay, **—demorar,** v.
demostración, f. demonstration.
demostrador, m. demonstrator.
demostrar, v. demonstrate, show.
demostrativo, a. demonstrative.
demudar, v. change; disguise, conceal.
denegación, f. denial, refusal.
denegar, v. deny, refuse.
dengue, m. prudishness; dengue.
denigración, f. defamation, disgrace.
denigrar, v. defame, disgrace.
denodado, a. brave, dauntless.
denominación, f. denomination.
denominar, v. name, call.
denotación, f. denotation.
denotar, v. denote, betoken, express.
densidad, f. density.
denso, a. dense.

dentado, a. toothed; serrated; cogged.
dentadura, f. set of teeth.
dental, a. dental.
dentífrico, m. dentifrice.
dentista, m. dentist.
dentistería, f. dentistry.
dentro, adv. within, inside. **d. de poco,** in a short while.
denuedo, m. bravery, courage.
denuesto, m. insult, offense.
denuncia, f. denunciation; declaration.
denunciación, f. denunciation.
denunciar, v. denounce.
deparar, v. offer; grant.
departamento, m. department, section.
departir, v. talk, chat.
dependencia, f. dependence; branch office.
depender, v. depend.
dependiente. a. & m. dependent; clerk.
depilatorio, a. depilatory.
deplorable, a. deplorable, wretched.
deplorablemente, adv. deplorably.
deplorar, v. deplore.
deponer, v. depose.
deportación, f. deportation; exile.
deportar, v. deport.
deporte, m. sport. **—deportivo,** a.
deposición, f. assertion, deposition; removal; movement.
depositante, m. & f. depositor.
depósito, m. deposit. **—depositar,** v.
depravación, f. depravation; depravity.
depravado, a. depraved, wicked.
depravar, v. deprave, corrupt, pervert.
depreciación, f. depreciation.
depreciar, v. depreciate.
depredación, f. depredation.
depredar, v. pillage, depredate.
depresión, f. depression.
depresivo, a. depressive.
deprimir, v. depress.
depurar, v. purify.
derecha. f. right (hand, side).
derechera, f. shortcut.
derecho, 1. a. right; straight. **2.** m. right; (the) law. **derechos,** (com.) duty.

derechura, *f.* straightness.

derelicto, *a.* abandoned, derelict.

deriva, *f.* (naut.) drift.

derivación, *f.* derivation.

derivar, *v.* derive.

derogar, *v.* derogate; repeal, abrogate.

derramamiento, *m.* overflow.

derramar, *v.* spill, pour, scatter.

derrame, *m.* overflow; discharge.

derretir, *v.* melt, dissolve.

derribar, *v.* demolish, knock down; bowl over, floor, fell.

derrocamiento, *m.* overthrow.

derrocar, *v.* overthrow; oust; demolish.

derrochar, *v.* waste.

derroche, *m.* waste.

derrota, *f.* rout, defeat. **—derrotar,** *v.*

derrumbamiento, derrumbe, *m.* collapse; landslide.

derrumbarse, *v.* collapse, tumble.

derviche, *m.* dervish.

desabotonar, *v.* unbutton.

desabrido, *a.* insipid, tasteless.

desabrigar, *v.* uncover.

desabrochar, *v.* unbutton, unclasp.

desacierto, *m.* error.

desacobardar, *v.* remove fear; embolden.

desacomodadamente, *adv.* inconveniently.

desacomodado, *a.* unemployed.

desacomodar, *v.* molest; inconvenience; dismiss.

desacomodo, *m.* loss of employment.

desconsejado, *a.* imprudent, ill advised, rash.

desaconsejar, *v.* dissuade.

desacordadamente, *adv.* unadvisedly.

desacordar, *v.* differ, disagree; be forgetful.

desacorde, *a.* discordant.

desacostumbradamente, *adv.* unusually.

desacostumbrado, *a.* unusual, unaccustomed.

desacostumbrar, *v.* give up a habit or custom.

desacreditar, *v.* discredit.

desacuerdo, *m.* disagreement.

desadeudar, *v.* pay one's debts.

desadormecer, *v.* waken, rouse.

desadornar, *v.* divest of ornament.

desadvertidamente, *adv.* inadvertently.

desadvertido, *a.* imprudent.

desadvertimiento, *m.* imprudence, rashness.

desadvertir, *v.* act imprudently.

desafección, *f.* disaffection.

desafecto, *a.* disaffected.

desafiar, *v.* defy; challenge.

desafinar, *v.* be out of tune.

desafío, *m.* defiance; challenge.

desaforar, *v.* infringe one's rights; be outrageous.

desafortunado, *a.* unfortunate.

desafuero, *m.* violation of the law; outrage.

desagraciado, *a.* graceless.

desagradable, *a.* disagreeable, unpleasant.

desagradablemente, *adv.* disagreeably.

desagradecido, *a.* ungrateful.

desagradecimiento, *m.* ingratitude.

desagrado, *m.* displeasure.

desagraviar, *v.* make amends.

desagregar, *v.* separate, disintegrate.

desagriar, *v.* mollify, appease.

desaguadero, *m.* drain, outlet; cesspool; sink.

desaguador, *m.* water pipe.

desaguar, *v.* drain.

desaguisado, *m.* offense; injury.

desahogadamente, *adv.* impudently; brazenly.

desahogado, *a.* impudent, brazen; cheeky.

desahogar, *v.* relieve.

desahogo, *m.* relief; nerve, cheek.

desahuciar, *v.* give up hope for; despair of.

desairado, *a.* graceless.

desaire, *m.* slight; scorn. **—desairar,** *v.*

desajustar, *v.* mismatch, misfit; make unfit.

desalar, *v.* hurry, hasten.

desalentar, *v.* make out of breath; discourage.

desaliento, *m.* discouragement.

desaliñar, *v.* disarrange; make untidy.

desaliño, *m.* slovenliness, untidiness.

desalivar, v. salivate.
desalmadamente, adv. mercilessly.
desalmado, a. merciless.
desalojamiento, m. displacement; dislodging.
desalojar, v. dislodge.
desalquilado, a. vacant, unrented.
desamar, v. cease loving.
desamasado, a. dissolve, undo.
desamistarse, v. quarrel, disagree.
desamor, m. disaffection, dislike; hatred.
desamorado, a. cruel; harsh; rude.
desamparador, m. deserter.
desamparar, v. desert, abandon.
desamparo, m. desertion, abandonment.
desamueblar, v. dismantle.
desandrajado, a. shabby, ragged.
desanimadamente, adv. in a discouraged manner; spiritlessly.
desanimar, v. dishearten, discourage.
desánimo, m. discouragement.
desanudar, v. untie; loosen; disentangle.
desapacible, a. rough, harsh; unpleasant.
desaparecer, v. disappear.
desaparición, f. disappearance.
desapasionadamente, adv. dispassionately.
desapasionado, a. dispassionate.
desapego, m. impartiality.
desapercibido, adj. unprepared.
desapiadado, a. merciless, cruel.
desaplicación, f. indolence, laziness; negligence.
desaplicado, a. indolent, lazy; negligent.
desaposesionar, v. dispossess.
desapreciar, v. depreciate.
desapretador, m. screwdriver.
desapretar, v. loosen; relieve, ease.
desaprisionar, v. set free, release.
desaprobación, f. disapproval.
desaprobar, v. disapprove.
desaprovechado, a. useless, profitless; backward.
desaprovechar, v. waste; be backward.
desarbolar, v. unmast.

desarmado, a. disarmed, defenseless.
desarmar, v. disarm.
desarme, m. disarmament.
desarraigar, v. uproot; eradicate; expel.
desarreglar, v. disarrange, mess up.
desarrollar, v. develop.
desarrollo, m. development.
desarropar, v. undress; uncover.
desarrugar, v. remove wrinkles from.
desaseado, a. dirty; disorderly.
desasear, v. make dirty or disorderly.
desaseo, m. dirtiness; disorder.
desasir, v. loosen; disengage.
desasociable, a. unsociable.
desasosegar, v. disturb.
desasosiego, m. uneasiness.
desastrado, a. ragged, wretched.
desastre, m. disaster.
desastroso, a. disastrous.
desatar, v. untie, undo.
desatención, f. inattention; disrespect; rudeness.
desatender, v. ignore; disregard.
desatentado, a. inconsiderate; imprudent.
desatinado, a. foolish; insane; wild.
desatino, m. blunder. —**desatinar**, v.
desautorizado, a. unauthorized.
desautorizar, v. deprive of authority.
desavenencia, f. disagreement, discord.
desaventajado, a. disadvantageous.
desayuno, m. breakfast. —**desayunarse**, v.
desazón, f. insipidity; uneasiness.
desazonado, a. insipid; uneasy.
desbandada, f. disbanding.
desbandarse, v. disband.
desbarajuste, m. disorder, confusion.
desbaratar, v. destroy.
desbastar, v. plane, smoothen.
desbocado, a. foul-spoken, indecent.
desbocarse, v. use obscene language.
desbordamiento, m. overflow; flood.

desbordar, v. overflow.

desbrozar, v. clear away rubbish.

descabal, a. incomplete.

descabalar, v. render incomplete; impair.

descabellado, a. absurd, preposterous.

descabezar, v. behead.

descaecimiento, m. weakness; dejection.

descafeinado, a. decaffeinated.

descalabrar, v. injure, wound (esp. the head).

descalabro, m. accident, misfortune.

descalzarse, v. take off one's shoes.

descalzo, a. shoeless; barefoot.

descaminado, a. wrong, misguided.

descaminar, v. mislead; lead into error.

descamisado, a. shirtless; shabby.

descanso, m. rest. **—descansar,** v.

descarado, a. saucy, fresh.

descarga, f. discharge.

descargar, v. discharge, unload, dump.

descargo, m. acquittal.

descarnar, v. skin.

descaro, m. gall, effrontery.

descarriar, v. lead or go astray.

descarrilamiento, m. derailment.

descarrilar, v. derail.

descartar, v. discard.

descascarar, v. peel; boast, brag.

descendencia, f. descent, origin; progeny.

descender, v. descend.

descendiente, m.& f. descendant.

descendimiento, m. descent.

descenso, m. descent.

descentralización, f. decentralizing.

descifrar, v. decipher, puzzle out.

descoco, m. boldness, brazenness.

descolgar, v. take down.

descolorar, v. discolor.

descolorido, a. pale, faded.

descollar, v. stand out; excel.

descomedido, a. disproportionate; rude.

descomedirse, v. be rude.

descomponer, v. decompose; break down, get out of order.

descomposición, f. discomposure; disorder, confusion.

descompuesto, a. impudent, rude.

descomulgar, v. excommunicate.

descomunal, a. extraordinary, huge.

desconcertar, v. disconcert, baffle.

desconcierto, m. confusion, disarray.

desconectar, v. disconnect.

desconfiado, a. distrustful.

desconfianza, f. distrust.

desconfiar, v. distrust, mistrust; suspect.

descongestionante, m. decongestant.

desconocer, v. ignore, fail to recognize.

desconocido -da, n. stranger.

desconocimiento, m. ingratitude; ignorance.

desconsolado, a. disconsolate, wretched.

desconsuelo, m. grief.

descontar, v. discount, subtract.

descontentar, v. dissatisfy.

descontento, m. discontent.

descontinuar, v. discontinue.

desconvenir, v. disagree.

descorazonar, v. dishearten.

descorchar, v. uncork.

descortés, a. discourteous, impolite, rude.

descortesía, f. discourtesy, rudeness.

descortezar, v. peel.

descoyuntar, v. dislocate.

descrédito, m. discredit.

describir, v. describe.

descripción, f. description.

descriptivo, a. descriptive.

descuartizar, v. dismember, disjoint.

descubridor, m. discoverer.

descubrimiento, m. discovery.

descubrir, v. discover; uncover; disclose.

descubrirse, v. take off one's hat.

descuento, m. discount.

descuidado, a. reckless, careless; slack.

descuido, m. neglect. **—descuidar,** v.

desde, prep. since; from. **d. luego,** of course.

desdén, m. disdain. **—desdeñar,** v.

desdeñoso, a. contemptuous, disdainful, scornful.

desdicha, f. misfortune.

deseable, a. desirable.

desear, v. desire, wish.

desecar, v. dry, desiccate.

desechar, v. scrap, reject.

desecho, m. remainder, residue; (pl.) waste.

desembalar, v. unpack.

desembarazado, a. free; unrestrained.

desembarazar, v. free; extricate; unburden.

desembarcar, v. disembark, go ashore.

desembocar, v. flow into.

desembolsar, v. disburse; expend.

desembolso, m. disbursement.

desemejante, a. unlike, dissimilar.

desempacar, v. unpack.

desempeñar, v. carry out; redeem.

desempeño, m. fulfillment.

desencajar, v. disjoint; disturb.

desencantar, v. disillusion.

desencanto, m. disillusion.

desencarcelar, v. set free; release.

desenfadado, a. free; unembarrassed; spacious.

desenfado, m. freedom; ease; calmness.

desengaño, m. disillusion. **—desengañar,** v.

desenlace, m. outcome, conclusion.

desenredar, v. disentangle.

desensartar, v. unthread.

desentenderse, v. overlook; avoid noticing.

desenterrar, v. disinter, exhume.

desenvainar, v. unsheath.

desenvoltura, f. impudence, boldness.

desenvolver, v. evolve, unfold.

deseo, m. wish, desire, urge.

deseoso, a. desirous.

deserción, f. desertion.

desertar, v. desert.

desertor, m. deserter.

desesperación, f. despair, desperation.

desesperado, a. desperate; hopeless.

desesperar, v. despair.

desfalcar, v. embezzle.

desfavorable, a. unfavorable.

desfigurar, v. disfigure, mar.

desfiladero, m. defile.

desfile, m. parade. **—desfilar,** v.

desgaire, m. slovenly appearance.

desgana, f. lack of appetite; repugnance.

desgarrar, v. tear, lacerate.

desgastar, v. wear away, waste, erode.

desgaste, m. wear; erosion.

desgracia, f. misfortune.

desgraciado, a. unfortunate.

desgranar, v. shell.

desgreñar, v. dishevel.

deshacer, v. undo, take apart, destroy.

deshacerse de, v. get rid of, dispose of.

deshecho, a. undone; wasted.

deshelar, v. thaw; melt.

desheredamiento, m. disinheriting.

desheredar, v. disinherit.

deshielo, m. thaw, melting.

deshinchar, v. reduce a swelling.

deshojarse, v. shed (leaves).

deshonestidad, f. dishonesty.

deshonesto, a. dishonest.

deshonra, f. dishonor.

deshonrar, v. disgrace; dishonor.

deshonroso, a. dishonorable.

desierto, m. desert, wilderness.

designar, v. appoint, name.

designio, m. purpose, intent.

desigual, a. uneven, unequal.

desigualdad, f. inequality.

desilusión, f. disappointment.

desinfección, f. disinfection.

desinfectar, v. disinfect.

desintegrar, v. disintegrate, zap.

desinterés, m. indifference.

desinteresado, a. disinterested, unselfish.

desistir, v. desist, stop.

desleal, a. disloyal.

deslealtad, f. disloyalty.

desleír, v. dilute, dissolve.

desligar, v. untie, loosen; free, release.

deslindar, v. make the boundaries of.

deslinde, *m.* demarcation.

desliz, *m.* slip; false step; weakness.

deslizarse, *v.* slide; slip; glide; coast.

deslumbramiento, *m.* dazzling glare; confusion.

deslumbrar, *v.* dazzle; glare.

deslustre, *m.* tarnish. **—deslustrar,** *v.*

desmán, *m.* mishap; misbehavior; excess.

desmantelar, *v.* dismantle.

desmañado, *a.* awkward, clumsy.

desmayar, *v.* dismay, appall.

desmayo, *m.* faint. **—desmayarse,** *v.*

desmejorar, *v.* make worse; decline.

desmembrar, *v.* dismember.

desmemoria, *f.* forgetfulness.

desmemoriado, *a.* forgetful.

desmentir, *v.* contradict, disprove.

desmenuzable, *a.* crisp, crumbly.

desmenuzar, *v.* crumble, break into bits.

desmesurado, *a.* excessive.

desmonetización, *f.* demonetization.

desmonetizar, *v.* demonetize.

desmontado, *a.* dismounted.

desmoralización, *f.* demoralization.

desmoralizar, *v.* demoralize.

desmoronar, *v.* crumble, decay.

desmovilizar, *v.* demobilize.

desnatar, *v.* skim.

desnaturalización, *f.* denaturalization.

desnaturalizar, *v.* denaturalize.

desnegamiento, *m.* denial, contradiction.

desnervar, *v.* enervate.

desnivel, *m.* unevenness or difference in elevation.

desnudamente, *adv.* nakedly.

desnudar, *v.* undress.

desnudez, *f.* bareness, nudity.

desnudo, *a.* bare, naked.

desnutrición, *f.* malnutrition.

desobedecer, *v.* disobey.

desobediencia, *f.* disobedience.

desobediente, *a.* disobedient.

desobedientemente, *adv.* disobediently.

desobligar, *v.* release from obligation; offend.

desocupado, *a.* idle, not busy; vacant.

desocupar, *v.* vacate.

desolación, *f.* desolation; ruin.

desolado, *a.* desolate. **—desolar,** *v.*

desollar, *v.* skin.

desorden, *m.* disorder.

desordenar, *v.* disarrange.

desorganización, *f.* disorganization.

desorganizar, *v.* disorganize.

despabilado, *a.* vigilant, watchful; lively.

despacio, *adv.* slowly.

despachar, *v.* dispatch, ship, send.

despacho, *m.* shipment; dispatch, promptness; office.

desparpajo, *m.* glibness; fluency of speech.

desparramar, *v.* scatter.

despavorido, *a.* terrified.

despecho, *m.* spite.

despedazar, *v.* tear up.

despedida, *f.* farewell; leave-taking; discharge.

despedir, *v.* dismiss, discharge; see off.

despedirse de, *v.* say good-bye to, take leave of.

despegar, *v.* unglue; separate.

despego, *m.* indifference; disinterest.

despejar, *v.* clear, clear up.

despejo, *m.* sprightly; clear; unobstructed.

despensa, *f.* pantry.

despensero, *m.* butler.

despeñar, *v.* throw down.

desperdicio, *m.* waste. **—desperdiciar,** *v.*

despertador, *m.* alarm clock.

despertar, *v.* wake, wake up.

despesar, *m.* dislike.

despicar, *v.* satisfy.

despidida, *f.* gutter.

despierto, *a.* awake; alert, wide-awake.

despilfarrado, *a.* wasteful, extravagant.

despilfarrar, *v.* waste, squander.

despilfarro, *m.* waste, extravagance.

despique, *m.* revenge.

desplazamiento, *m.* displacement.

desplegar, *v.* display; unfold.

desplome, *m.* collapse. —**desplomarse,** *v.*

desplumar, *v.* defeather, pluck.

despoblar, *v.* depopulate.

despojar, *v.* strip; despoil, plunder.

despojo, *m.* plunder, spoils; (*pl.*) remains, debris.

desposado, *a.* newly married.

desposar, *v.* marry.

desposeer, *v.* dispossess.

déspota, *m. & f.* despot.

despótico, *a.* despotic.

despotismo, *m.* despotism, tyranny.

despreciable, *a.* contemptible.

despreciar, *v.* spurn, despise, scorn.

desprecio, *m.* scorn, contempt.

desprender, *v.* detach, unfasten.

desprenderse, *v.* loosen, come apart. **d. de,** part with.

desprendido, *a.* disinterested.

despreocupado, *a.* unprejudiced.

desprevenido, *a.* unprepared, unready.

desproporción, *f.* disproportion.

despropósito, *m.* nonsense.

desprovisto, *a.* devoid.

después, *adv.* afterwards, later; then, next. **d. de, d. que,** after.

despuntar, *v.* blunt; remove the point of.

desquiciar, *v.* unhinge; disturb, unsettle.

desquitar, *v.* get revenge, retaliate.

desquite, *m.* revenge, retaliation.

destacamento, *m.* (mil.) detachment.

destacarse, *v.* stand out, be prominent.

destapar, *v.* uncover.

destello, *m.* sparkle, gleam.

destemplar, *v.* change; soften.

desteñir, *v.* fade, discolor.

desterrado -da, *n.* exile.

desterrar, *v.* banish, exile.

destierro, *m.* banishment, exile.

destilación, *f.* distillation.

destilar, *v.* distill.

destilería, *f.* distillery.

destinación, *f.* destination.

destinar, *v.* destine, intend.

destinatorio -ria, *n.* addressee.

destino, *m.* destiny, fate; destination.

destitución, *f.* dismissal; abandonment.

destituido, *a.* destitute.

destorcer, *v.* undo, straighten out.

destornillado, *a.* reckless, careless.

destornillador, *m.* screwdriver.

destraillar, *v.* unleash; set loose.

destral, *a.* hatchet.

destreza, *f.* cleverness, dexterity, skill.

destripar, *v.* eviscerate, disembowel.

destrísimo, *a.* extremely dexterous.

destronamiento, *m.* dethronement.

destronar, *v.* dethrone.

destrozador, *m.* destroyer, wrecker.

destrozar, *v.* destroy, wreck.

destrozo, *m.* destruction, ruin.

destrucción, *f.* destruction.

destructibilidad, *f.* destructibility.

destructible, *a.* destructible.

destructivamente, *adv.* destructively.

destructivo, *a.* destructive.

destruir, *v.* destroy; wipe out.

desuello, *m.* impudence.

desunión, *f.* disunion; discord; separation.

desunir, *v.* disconnect, sever.

desusadamente, *adv.* unusually.

desusado, *a.* archaic; obsolete.

desuso, *m.* disuse.

desvalido, *a.* helpless, destitute.

desvalijador, *m.* highwayman.

desván, *m.* attic.

desvanecerse, *v.* vanish; faint.

desvariado, *a.* delirious; disorderly.

desvarío, *m.* raving. —**desvariar,** *v.*

desvedado, *a.* free; unrestrained.

desveladamente, *adv.* watchfully, alertly.

desvelado, *a.* watchful; alert.

desvelar, *v.* be watchful; keep awake.

desvelo, *m.* vigilance; uneasiness.

desventaja, *f.* disadvantage.

desventar, *v.* let air out of.

desventura, f. misfortune.

desventurado, a. unhappy; unlucky.

desvergonzado, a. shameless, brazen.

desvergüenza, f. shamelessness.

desvestir, v. undress.

desviación, f. deviation.

desviado, a. devious.

desviar, v. divert; deviate.

desvío, m. detour; side track; indifference.

desvirtuar, v. decrease the value of.

deszumar, v. remove the juice from.

detalle, m. detail. **—detallar,** v.

detective, m. detective.

detención, f. detention, arrest.

detenedor, m. stopper; catch.

detener, v. detain, stop; arrest.

detenidamente, adv. carefully, slowly.

detenido, adv. stingy; thorough.

détente, f. detente.

detergente, a. detergent.

deterioración, f. deterioration.

deteriorar, v. deteriorate.

determinable, a. determinable.

determinación, f. determination.

determinar, v. determine.

determinismo, m. determinism.

determinista, n. & a. determinist.

detestable, a. detestable, hateful.

detestablemente, adv. detestably, hatefully, abhorrently.

detestación, f. detestation, hatefulness.

detestar, v. detest.

detonación, f. detonation.

detonar, v. detonate, explode.

detracción, f. detraction, defamation.

detractar, v. detract, defame, vilify.

detraer, v. detract.

detrás, adv. behind; in back.

detrimento, m. detriment, damage.

deuda, f. debt.

deudo -da, n. relative, kin.

deudor -ra, n. debtor.

Deuteronomio, m. Deuteronomy.

devalar, v. drift.

devanar, v. to wind, as on a spool.

devanear, v. talk deliriously, rave.

devaneo, m. frivolity; idle pursuit; delirium.

devantal, m. apron.

devastación, f. devastation, ruin, havoc.

devastador, m. devastator.

devastar, v. devastate.

devenir, v. happen, occur; become.

devoción, f. devotion.

devocionario, m. prayer book.

devocionero, a. devotional.

devolver, v. return, give back.

devorar, v. devour.

devotamente, adv. devotedly, devoutly, piously.

devoto, a. devout; devoted.

deyección, f. depression, dejection.

día, m. day. **buenos días,** good morning.

diabetes, f. diabetes.

diabético, a. diabetic.

diablear, v. play pranks.

diablo, m. devil.

diablura, f. mischief.

diabólicamente, adv. diabolically.

diabólico, a. diabolic, devilish.

diaconado, m. deaconship.

diaconía, f. deaconry.

diácono, m. deacon.

diacrítico, a. diacritic.

diadema, f. diadem, crown.

diáfano, a. transparent.

diafragma, m. diaphragm.

diagnosticar, v. diagnose.

diagonal, a. diagonal.

diagonalmente, adv. diagonally.

diagrama, m. diagram.

dialectal, a. dialectal.

dialéctico, a. dialectic.

dialecto, m. dialect.

diálogo, m. dialogue.

diamante, m. diamond.

diamantista, m. diamond cutter; jeweler.

diametral, a. diametric.

diametralmente, adv. diametrically.

diámetro, m. diameter.

diana, f. reveille.

diapasón, m. pitch; tuning fork.

diaplejía, f. paralysis.

diariamente, adv. daily.

diario, *a. & m.* daily; daily paper; diary; journal.

diarrea, *f.* diarrhea.

diatriba, *f.* diatribe, harangue.

dibujo, *m.* drawing, sketch. **—dibujar**, *v.*

dicción, *f.* diction.

diccionario, *m.* dictionary.

diccionarista, *n.* lexicographer.

diciembre, *m.* December.

dicotomía, *f.* dichotomy.

dictado, *m.* dictation.

dictador, *m.* dictator.

dictadura, *f.* dictatorship.

dictamen, *m.* dictate.

dictar, *v.* dictate; direct.

dictatoría, *f.* dictatorial; tyrannic.

dicha, *f.* happiness.

dicho, *m.* saying.

dichoso, *a.* happy; fortunate.

didáctico, *a.* didactic.

diecinueve, *a. & pron.* nineteen.

dieciocho, *a. & pron.* eighteen.

dieciséis, *a. & pron.* sixteen.

diecisiete, *a. & pron.* seventeen.

diente, *m.* tooth.

diestramente, *adv.* skillfully, ably; ingeniously.

diestro, *a.* dexterous, skillful; clever.

dieta, *f.* diet; allowance.

dietética, *f.* dietetic.

diez, *a. & pron.* ten.

diezmal, *a.* decimal.

diezmar, *v.* decimate.

difamación, *f.* defamation, smear.

difamar, *v.* defame, smear, libel.

difamatorio, *a.* defamatory.

diferencia, *f.* difference.

diferencial, *a. & f.* differential.

diferenciar, *v.* differentiate, distinguish.

diferente, *a.* different.

diferentemente, *adv.* differently.

diferir, *v.* differ; defer, put off.

difícil, *a.* difficult, hard.

difícilmente, *adv.* with difficulty or hardship.

dificultad, *f.* difficulty.

dificultar, *v.* make difficult.

dificultoso, *a.* difficult, hard.

difidencia, *f.* diffidence.

difidente, *a.* diffident.

difteria, *f.* diphtheria.

difundir, *v.* diffuse, spread.

difunto, *a.* deceased, dead, late.

difusamente, *adv.* diffusely.

difusión, *f.* diffusion, spread.

digerible, *a.* digestible.

digerir, *v.* digest.

digestible, *a.* digestible.

digestión, *f.* digestion.

digestivo, *a.* digestive.

digesto, *m.* digest or code of laws.

digitado, *a.* digitate.

digital, **1.** *a.* digital. **2.** *f.* foxglove.

dignación, *f.* condescension; deigning.

dignamente, *adv.* with dignity.

dignarse, *v.* condescend, deign.

dignidad, *f.* dignity.

dignificar, *v.* dignify.

dignatario, *m.* dignitary.

digno, *a.* worthy; dignified.

digresión, *f.* digression.

digresivo, *a.* digressive.

dij, dije, *m.* trinket, piece of jewelry.

dilación, *f.* delay.

dilapidación, *f.* dilapidation.

dilatación, *f.* dilatation, enlargement.

dilatar, *v.* dilate; delay; expand.

dilatoria, *f.* delay.

dilecto, *a.* loved.

dilema, *m.* dilemma.

diligencia, *f.* diligence, industriousness.

diligente, *a.* diligent, industrious.

diligentemente, *adv.* diligently.

dilogía, *f.* ambiguous meaning.

dilución, *f.* dilution.

diluir, *v.* dilute.

diluvial, *a.* diluvial.

diluvio, *m.* flood, deluge.

dimensión, *f.* dimension; measurement.

diminución, *f.* diminution.

diminuto, diminutivo, *a.* diminutive, little.

dimisión, *f.* resignation.

dimitir, *v.* resign.

Dinamarca, *f.* Denmark.

dinamarqués -esa, *a. & n.* Danish, Dane.

dinámico, *a.* dynamic.

dinamita, *f.* dynamite.

dinamitero, *m.* dynamiter.

dínamo, *m.* dynamo.

dinasta, *m.* dynast, king, monarch.

dinastía, f. dynasty.
dinástico, a. dynastic.
dinero, m. money, currency.
dinosauro, m. dinosaur.
diócesi, f. diocese.
Dios, m. God.
dios -sa, n. god, goddess.
diploma, m. diploma.
diplomacia, f. diplomacy.
diplomado -da, n. graduate.
diplomarse, v. graduate (from a school).
diplomática, f. diplomacy.
diplomático, a. & m. diplomat; diplomatic.
dipsomania, f. dipsomania.
diptongo, m. diphthong.
diputación, f. deputation, delegation.
diputado, m. deputy.
diputar, v. depute, delegate; empower.
dique, m. dike; dam.
dirección, f. direction; address; guidance; (com.) management.
directamente, adv. directly.
directo, a. direct.
director, m. director; manager.
dirigente, a. directing, controlling, managing.
dirigible, a. dirigible.
dirigir, v. direct; lead; manage.
dirigirse a, v. address; approach, turn to; head for.
dirruir, v. destroy, devastate.
disanto, m. holy day.
discantar, v. sing (esp. in counterpoint); discuss.
disceptación, f. argument, quarrel.
disceptar, v. argue, quarrel.
discernimiento, m. discernment.
discernir, v. discern.
disciplina, f. discipline.
disciplinable, a. disciplinable.
disciplinar, v. discipline, train, teach.
discípulo -la, n. disciple, follower; pupil.
disco, m. disk; (phonograph) record.
discontinuación, f. discontinuation.
discontinuar, v. discontinue, break off, cease.
discordancia, f. discordance.
discordar, v. disagree, conflict.

discordia, f. discord.
discoteca, f. disco, discotheque.
discreción, f. discretion.
discrecional, a. optional.
discrecionalmente, adv. optionally.
discrepancia, f. discrepancy.
discretamente, adv. discreetly.
discreto, a. discreet.
discrimen, m. risk, hazard.
discriminación, f. discrimination.
discriminar, v. discriminate.
disculpa, f. excuse; apology.
disculpar, v. excuse; exonerate.
disculparse, v. apologize.
discurrir, v. roam; flow; think; plan.
discursante, n. lecturer, speaker.
discursivo, a. discursive.
discurso, m. speech, talk.
discusión, f. discussion.
discutible, a. debatable.
discutir, v. discuss; debate; contest.
disecación, f. dissection.
disecar, v. dissect.
disección, f. dissection.
diseminación, f. dissemination.
diseminar, v. disseminate, spread.
disensión, f. dissension; dissent.
disenso, m. dissent.
disentería, f. dysentery.
disentir, v. disagree, dissent.
diseñador -ra, m. designer.
diseño, m. design. **—diseñar,** v.
disertación, f. dissertation.
disfamación, f. defamation.
disforme, a. deformed, monstrous, ugly.
disformidad, f. deformity.
disfraz, m. disguise. **—disfrazar,** v.
disfrutar, v. enjoy.
disfrute, m. enjoyment.
disgustar, v. displease; disappoint.
disgusto, m. displeasure; disappointment.
disidencia, f. dissidence.
disidente, a. & n. dissident.
disímil, a. unlike.
disimilitud, f. dissimilarity.
disimulación, f. dissimulation.
disimulado, a. dissembling, feigning; sly.
disimular, v. hide, dissemble.

disímulo, *m.* pretense.
disipación, *f.* dissipation.
disipado, *a.* dissipated; wasted; scattered.
disipar, *v.* waste; scatter.
dislexia, *f.* dyslexia.
dislocación, *f.* dislocation.
dislocar, *v.* dislocate; displace.
disminuir, *v.* diminish, lessen, reduce.
disociación, *f.* dissociation.
disociar, *v.* dissociate.
disolubilidad, *f.* dissolubility.
disoluble, *a.* dissoluble.
disolución, *f.* dissolution.
disolutemente, *adv.* dissolutely.
disoluto, *a.* dissolute.
disolver, *v.* dissolve.
disonancia, *f.* dissonance; discord.
disonante, *a.* dissonant; discordant.
disonar, *v.* be discordant; clash in sound.
disono, *a.* dissonant.
dispar, *a.* unlike.
disparadamente, *adv.* hastily, hurriedly.
disparar, *v.* shoot, fire (a weapon).
disparatado, *a.* nonsensical.
disparatar, *v.* talk nonsense.
disparate, *m.* nonsense, tall tale.
disparejo, *a.* uneven, unequal.
disparidad, *f.* disparity.
disparo, *m.* shot.
dispendio, *m.* extravagance.
dispendioso, *a.* expensive; extravagant.
dispensa, dispensación, *f.* dispensation.
dispensable, *a.* dispensable; excusable.
dispensar, *v.* dispense, excuse; grant.
dispensario, *m.* dispensary.
dispepsia, *f.* dyspepsia.
dispéptico, *a.* dyspeptic.
dispersar, *v.* scatter; dispel; disband.
dispersión, *f.* dispersion, dispersal.
disperso, *a.* dispersed.
displicente, *a.* unpleasant.
disponer, *v.* dispose. **d. de,** have at one's disposal.
disponible, *a.* available.

disposición, *f.* disposition; disposal.
dispuesto, *a.* disposed, inclined; attractive.
disputa, *f.* dispute, argument.
disputable, *a.* disputable.
disputador, *m.* disputant.
disputar, *v.* argue; dispute.
disquisición, *f.* disquisition.
distancia, *f.* distance.
distante, *a.* distant.
distantemente, *adv.* distantly.
distar, *v.* be distant, be far.
distención, *f.* distension, swelling.
distender, *v.* distend, swell, enlarge.
dístico, *m.* couplet.
distinción, *f.* distinction, difference.
distingo, *m.* restriction.
distinguible, *a.* distinguishable.
distinguido, *a.* distinguished, prominent.
distinguir, *v.* distinguish; make out, spot.
distintamente, *adv.* distinctly, clearly; differently.
distintivo, *a.* distinctive.
distinto, *a.* distinct, different.
distracción, *f.* distraction, pastime; absent-mindedness.
distraer, *v.* distract.
distraídamente, *adv.* absent-mindedly, distractedly.
distraído, *a.* absent-minded; distracted.
distribución, *f.* distribution.
distribuidor -ra, *n.* distributor.
distribuir, *v.* distribute.
distributivo, *a.* distributive.
distribuidor, *m.* distributor.
distrito, *m.* district.
disturbar, *v.* disturb, trouble.
disturbio, *m.* disturbance, outbreak; turmoil.
disuadir, *v.* dissuade.
disuasión, *f.* dissuasion; deterrence.
disuasivo, *a.* dissuasive.
disyunción, *f.* disjunction.
dityrambo, *m.* dithyramb.
diurno, *a.* diurnal.
diva, *f.* singer.
divagación, *f.* digression.
divagar, *v.* digress, ramble.
diván, *m.* couch.

divergencia, *f.* divergence.
divergente, *a.* divergent, differing.
divergir, *v.* diverge.
diversamente, *adv.* diversely.
diversidad, *f.* diversity.
diversificar, *v.* diversify, vary.
diversión, *f.* diversion, pastime.
diverso, *a.* diverse, different; (*pl.*) various, several.
divertido, *a.* humorous, amusing.
divertimiento, *m.* diversion; amusement.
divertir, *v.* entertain, amuse.
divertirse, *v.* enjoy oneself, have a good time.
dividendo, *m.* dividend.
divididero, *a.* divisible.
dividir, *v.* divide, separate.
divieso, *m.* (med.) boil.
divinamente, *adv.* divinely.
divinidad, *f.* divinity.
divinizar, *v.* deify.
divino, *a.* divine; heavenly.
divisa, *f.* badge, emblem.
divisar, *v.* sight, make out.
divisibilidad, *f.* divisibility.
divisible, *a.* divisible.
división, *f.* division.
divisivo, *a.* divisive.
diviso, *a.* divided.
divo, *m.* god.
divorcio, *m.* divorce. **—divorciar,** *v.*
divulgable, *a.* divulgable.
divulgación, *f.* divulgation.
divulgar, *v.* divulge, reveal.
dobladamente, *adv.* doubly.
dobladillo, *m.* hem of a skirt or dress.
dobladura, *f.* fold, bend.
doblar, *v.* fold; bend.
doble, *a.* double.
doblegable, *a.* flexible, foldable.
doblegar, *v.* fold, bend; yield.
doblez, *m.* fold; duplicity.
doblón, *m.* doubloon.
doce, *a. & pron.* twelve.
docena, *f.* dozen.
docente, *a.* educational
dócil, *a.* docile.
docilidad, *f.* docility, tractableness.
dócilmente, *adv.* docilely, meekly.
doctamente, *adv.* learnedly, profoundly.

docto, *a.* learned, expert.
doctor, *m.* doctor.
doctorado, *m.* doctorate.
doctoral, *a.* doctoral.
doctrina, *f.* doctrine.
doctrinador, *m.* teacher.
doctrinal, *m.* catechism.
doctrinar, *v.* teach.
documentación, *f.* documentation.
documental, *a.* documentary.
documento, *m.* document.
dogal, *m.* noose.
dogma, *m.* dogma.
dogmáticamente, *adv.* dogmatically.
dogmático, *m.* dogmatic.
dogmatismo, *m.* dogmatism.
dogmatista, *m.* dogmatist.
dogo, *m.* bulldog.
dolar, *v.* cut, chop, hew.
dólar, *m.* dollar.
dolencia, *f.* pain; disease.
doler, *v.* ache, hurt, be sore.
doliente, *a.* ill; aching.
dolor, *m.* pain; grief, sorrow, woe.
dolorido, *a.* painful, sorrowful.
dolorosamente, *adv.* painfully, sorrowfully.
doloroso, *a.* painful, sorrowful.
dolosamente, *adv.* deceitfully.
doloso, *a.* deceitful.
domable, *a.* that can be tamed or managed.
domar, *v.* tame; subdue.
dombo, *m.* dome.
domesticable, *a.* that can be domesticated.
domesticación, *f.* domestication.
domésticamente, *adv.* domestically.
domesticar, *v.* tame.
domesticidad, *f.* domesticity.
doméstico, *a.* domestic.
domicilio, *m.* dwelling, home, residence.
dominación, *f.* domination.
dominador, *a.* dominating.
dominante, *a.* dominant.
dominar, *v.* rule, dominate; master.
dómine, *m.* teacher.
domingo, *m.* Sunday.
dominio, *m.* domain; rule; power.
dominó, *m.* domino.

domo, m. dome.
Don, title used before a man's first name.
don, m. gift.
dona, f. woman.
donación, f. donation.
donador -ra, n. giver, donor.
donaire, m. grace.
donairosamente, adv. gracefully.
donairoso, a. graceful.
donante, n. giver, donor.
donar, v. donate.
donativo, m. donation, contribution; gift.
doncella, f. lass; maid.
donde, dónde, conj. & adv. where.
dondequiera, adv. wherever, anywhere.
donosamente, adv. gracefully, wittily.
donoso, a. graceful; witty.
donosura, f. gracefulness; wittiness.
Doña, title used before a lady's first name.
dorado, a. gilded.
dorador, m. gilder.
dorar, v. gild.
dórico, a. Doric.
dormidero, a. sleep-inducing; soporific.
dormido, a. asleep.
dormir, v. sleep.
dormirse, v. fall asleep, go to sleep.
dormitar, v. doze.
dormitorio, m. dormitory; bedroom.
dorsal, a. dorsal.
dorso, m. spine.
dos, a. & pron. two. **los d.,** both.
dosañal, a. biennial.
doscientos, a. & pron. two hundred.
dosel, m. canopy; platform, dais.
dosificación, f. dosage.
dosis, f. dose.
dotación, f. endowment; (naut.) crew.
dotador, m. donor.
dotar, v. endow; give a dowry to.
dote, m. dowry; (pl.) talents.
dragaminas, f. mine sweeper.
dragar, v. dredge; sweep.
dragón, m. dragon; dragoon.
dragonear, v. pretend to be.
drama, m. drama; play.

dramática, f. dramatics.
dramáticamente, adv. dramatically.
dramático, a. dramatic.
dramatizar, v. dramatize.
dramaturgo, m. playwright, dramatist.
drástico, a. drastic.
drenaje, m. drainage.
dríada, f. dryad.
driza, f. halyard.
droga, f. drug.
droguería, f. drugstore.
droguero, m. druggist.
dromedario, m. dromedary.
druida, m. Druid.
dualidad, f. duality.
dubitable, a. doubtful.
dubitación, f. doubt.
ducado, m. duchy.
ducal, a. ducal.
dúctil, a. ductile.
ductilidad, f. ductility.
ducha, f. shower (bath).
duda, f. doubt.
dudable, a. doubtful.
dudar, v. doubt; hesitate; question.
dudosamente, adv. doubtfully.
dudoso, a. dubious; doubtful.
duela, f. stave.
duelista, m. duelist.
duelo, m. duel; grief; mourning.
duende, m. elf, hobgoblin.
dueño -ña, n. owner; landlord, -lady; master, mistress.
dulce, 1. a. sweet. **agua d.,** fresh water. **2.** m. piece of candy; (pl.) candy.
dulcedumbre, f. sweetness.
dulcemente, adv. sweetly.
dulcería, f. confectionery; candy shop.
dulcificar, v. sweeten.
dulzura, f. sweetness; mildness.
duna, f. dune.
dúo, m. duet.
duodenal, a. duodenal.
duplicación, f. duplication; doubling.
duplicadamente, adv. doubly.
duplicado, a. & m. duplicate.
duplicar, v. double, duplicate, repeat.
duplicidad, f. duplicity.
duplo, a. double.
duque, m. duke.

duquesa, *f.* duchess.
durabilidad, *f.* durability.
durable, *a.* durable.
duración, *f.* duration.
duradero, *a.* lasting, durable.
duramente, *adv.* harshly, roughly.
durante, *prep.* during.
durar, *v.* last.
durazno, *m.* peach.
dureza, *f.* hardness.
durmiente, *a.* dormant.
duro, *a.* hard; stiff; stern; stale.
dux, *m.* doge.

E

e, *conj.* and.
ebanista, *m.* cabinetmaker.
ebanizar, *v.* give an ebony finish to.
ébano, *m.* ebony.
ebonita, *f.* ebonite.
ebrio, *a.* drunken, inebriated.
ebullición, *f.* boiling.
eclecticismo, *m.* eclecticism.
ecléctico, *a.* eclectic.
eclesiástico, *a. & m.* ecclesiastic.
eclipse, *m.* eclipse. —**eclipsar,** *v.*
eclipsis, *f.* ellipsis.
égloga, *f.* eclogue.
eco, *m.* echo.
ecología, *f.* ecology.
ecológico, *a.* ecological.
ecologista, *m. & f.* ecologist.
economía, *f.* economy; thrift. **e. política,** economics.
económicamente, *adv.* economically.
económico, *a.* economic; economical, thrifty.
economista, *m.* economist.
economizar, *v.* save, economize.
ecuación, *f.* equation.
ecuador, *m.* equator.
ecuanimidad, *f.* equanimity.
ecuatorial, *a.* equatorial.
ecuatoriano -na, *a. & n.* Ecuadorian.
ecuestre, *a.* equestrian.
ecuménico. *a.* ecumenical.
echada, *f.* throw.
echadillo, *m.* foundling; orphan.
echar, *v.* throw, toss; pour. **e. a,** start to. **e. a perder,** spoil, ruin. **e. de menos,** miss.
echarse, *v.* lie down.

edad, *f.* age.
edecán, *m.* aide-de-camp.
Edén, *m.* Eden.
edición, *f.* edition; issue.
edicto, *m.* edict, decree.
edificación, *f.* construction.
edificador, *n.* constructor; builder.
edificar, *v.* build.
edificio, *m.* edifice, building.
editar, *v.* publish, issue.
editor, *m.* publisher.
editorial, *a.* editorial.
edredón, *m.* quilt.
educación, *f.* upbringing, breeding; education.
educador, *m.* educator.
educar, *v.* educate, bring up; train.
educativo, *a.* educational.
educción, *f.* deduction.
educir, *v.* educe.
educto, *m.* output.
efectivamente, *adv.* actually, really.
efectivo, *a.* effective; actual, real. **en e.,** (com.) in cash.
efecto, *m.* effect.
efectuar, *v.* effect; cash.
eferente, *a.* efferent.
efervescencia, *f.* effervescence; zeal.
eficacia, *f.* efficacy.
eficaz, *a.* efficient, effective.
eficazmente, *adv.* efficaciously.
eficiencia, *f.* efficiency.
eficiente, *a.* efficient.
efigie, *f.* effigy.
efímera, *f.* May fly.
efímero, *a.* ephemeral, passing.
efulvio, *m.* effluvium.
efundir, *v.* effuse; pour out.
efusión, *f.* effusion.
egipcio -cia, *a. & n.* Egyptian.
Egipto, *f.* Egypt.
égira, *f.* hegira.
egoísmo, *m.* egoism, egotism, selfishness.
egoísta, *a. & n.* selfish, egoistic; egoist.
egotismo, *m.* egotism.
egotista, *m.* egotist.
egreso, *m.* expense, outlay.
eje, *m.* axis; axle.
ejecución, *f.* execution; performance; enforcement.

ejecutar, *v.* execute; enforce; carry out.

ejecutivo, *a.* & *m.* executive.

ejecutor, *m.* executor.

ejemplar, 1. *a.* exemplary. 2. *m.* copy.

ejemplificación, *f.* exemplification.

ejemplificar, *v.* illustrate.

ejemplo, *m.* example.

ejercer, *v.* exert; practice.

ejercicio, *m.* exercise, drill. — **ejercitar,** *v.*

ejercitación, *f.* exercise, training, drill.

ejercitar, *v.* exercise, train, drill.

ejército, *m.* army.

ejotes, *m.pl.* string beans.

el, *art.* & *pron.* the; the one.

él, *pron.* he, him; it.

elaboración, *f.* elaboration; working up.

elaborado, *a.* elaborate.

elaborador, *m.* manufacturer, maker.

elaborar, *v.* elaborate; manufacture; brew.

elación, *f.* elation; magnanimity; turgid style.

elasticidad, *f.* elasticity.

elástico, *m.* elastic.

elección, *f.* election; option, choice.

electivo, *a.* elective.

electo, *a.* elected, chosen, appointed.

electorado, *m.* electorate.

electoral, *a.* electoral.

electricidad, *f.* electricity.

electricista, *m.* electrician.

eléctrico, *a.* electric.

electrización, *f.* electrification.

electrocardiograma, *m.* electrocardiogram.

electrocución, *f.* electrocution.

electrocutar, *v.* electrocute.

electrodo, *m.* electrode.

electroimán, *m.* electromagnet.

electrólisis, *f.* electrolysis.

electrólito, *m.* electrolyte.

electrón, *m.* electron.

elefante, *m.* elephant.

elegancia, *f.* elegance.

elegante, *a.* elegant, smart, stylish, fine.

elegantemente, *adv.* elegantly.

elegía, *f.* elegy.

elegibilidad, *f.* eligibility.

elegible, *a.* eligible.

elegir, *v.* select, choose; elect.

elemental, *a.* elementary.

elementalmente, *adv.* elementally; fundamentally.

elementar, *a.* elementary.

elemento, *m.* element.

elevación, *f.* elevation; height.

elevador, *m.* elevator.

elevamiento, *m.* elevation.

elevar, *v.* elevate; erect, raise.

elidir, *v.* elide.

eliminación, *f.* elimination.

eliminar, *v.* eliminate.

elipse, *f.* ellipse.

elipsis, *f.* ellipsis.

elíptico, *a.* elliptic.

elocuencia, *f.* eloquence.

elocuente, *a.* eloquent.

elocuentemente, *adv.* eloquently.

elogio, *m.* praise, compliment. — **elogiar,** *v.*

elucidación, *f.* elucidation.

elucidar, *v.* elucidate.

eludir, *v.* elude.

ella, *pron.* she, her; it.

ello, *pron.* it.

ellos -as, *pron. pl.* they, them.

emaciación, *f.* emaciation.

emanar, *v.* emanate, stem.

emancipación, *f.* emancipation, freeing.

emancipador, *n.* emancipator.

emancipar, *v.* emancipate, free.

embajada, *f.* embassy; legation; (coll.) errand.

embajador, *m.* ambassador.

embalar, *v.* pack, bale.

embaldosado, *m.* tile floor.

embalsamador, *m.* embalmer.

embalsamar, *v.* embalm.

embarazada, *a.* pregnant.

embarazadamente, *adv.* embarrassedly.

embarazar, *v.* embarrass.

embarazo, *m.* embarrassment; pregnancy.

embarbascado, *a.* difficult; complicated.

embarcación, *f.* boat, ship; embarkation.

embarcadero, *m.* wharf, pier, dock.

embarcador, *m.* shipper, loader, stevedore.

embarcar, *v.* ship.

embarcarse, v. embark; sail.

embargador, m. one who impedes; one who orders an embargo.

embargante, a. impeding, hindering.

embargar, v. impede, restrain; (leg.) seize, embargo.

embargo, m. seizure, embargo. **sin e.,** however, nevertheless.

embarnizar, v. varnish.

embarque, m. shipment.

embarrador, m. plasterer.

embarrancar, v. get stuck in mud.

embarrar, v. plaster; besmear with mud.

embasamiento, m. foundation of a building.

embastecer, v. get fat.

embaucador, m. imposter.

embaucar, v. deceive, trick, hoax.

embaular, v. pack in a trunk.

embausamiento, m. amazement.

embebecer, v. amaze, astonish; entertain.

embeber, v. absorb; incorporate; saturate.

embelecador, m. imposter.

embeleco, m. fraud, perpetration.

embeleñar, v. fascinate, charm.

embelesamiento, m. rapture.

embelesar, v. fascinate, charm.

embeleso, m. rapture, bliss.

embellecer, v. beautify, embellish.

embestida, f. violent assault; attack.

emblandecer, v. soften; moisten; move to pity.

emblema, m. emblem.

emblemático, a. emblematic.

embocadura, f. narrow entrance; mouth of a river.

embocar, v. eat hastily; gorge.

embolia, f. embolism.

embolsar, v. pocket.

embonar, v. improve, fix, repair.

emborrachador, a. intoxicating.

emborrachar, v. get drunk.

emboscada, f. ambush.

emboscar, v. put or lie in ambush.

embotado, a. blunt, dull (edged). **—embotar,** v.

embotadura, f. bluntness; dullness.

embotellar, v. put in bottles.

embozado, v. muzzled; muffled.

embozar, v. muzzle; muffle.

embozo, m. muffler.

embrague, m. (auto.) clutch.

embravecer, v. be or make angry.

embriagado, a. drunken, intoxicated.

embriagar, v. intoxicate.

embriaguez, f. drunkenness.

embrión, m. embryo.

embrionario, a. embryonic.

embrochado, a. embroidered.

embrollo, m. muddle. **—embrollar,** v.

embromar, v. tease; joke.

embuchado, m. pork sausage.

embudo, m. funnel.

embuste, m. lie, fib.

embustear, v. lie, fib.

embustero -ra, m. liar.

embutir, v. stuff, cram.

emendación, f. emendation, change, correction.

emergencia, f. emergency.

emérito, a. emeritus.

emético, m. & a. emetic.

emigración, f. emigration.

emigrante, a. & n. emigrant.

emigrar, v. emigrate.

eminencia, f. eminence, height.

eminente, a. eminent.

emisario, m. emissary, spy; outlet.

emisión, f. issue; emission.

emisor, m. radio transmitter.

emitir, v. emit.

emoción, f. feeling, emotion, thrill.

emocional, a. emotional.

emocionante, a. exciting.

emocionar, v. touch, move, excite.

emolumento, m. emolument; perquisite.

empacar, v. pack.

empacho, m. shyness, timidity; embarrassment.

empadronamiento, m. census; list of taxpayers.

empalizada, f. palisade, stockade.

empanada, f. meat pie.

empañar, v. blur; soil, sully.

empapar, v. soak.

empapelado, m. wallpaper.

empaque, m. packing; appearance, mien.

empaquetar, v. pack, package.
emparejarse, v. match, pair off; level, even off.
emparentado, a. related by marriage.
emparrado, m. arbor.
empastadura, f. (dental) filling.
empastar, v. fill (a tooth).
empate, m. tie, draw. —empatarse, v.
empecer, v. hurt, harm, injure; prevent.
empedernir, v. harden.
empeine, m. groin; instep; hoof.
empellar, v. shove, jostle.
empellón, m. hard push, shove.
empeñar, v. pledge; pawn.
empeñarse en, v. persist in, be bent on.
empeño, m. persistence; pledge; pawning.
empeoramiento, m. deterioration.
empeorar, v. get worse.
emperador, m. emperor.
emperatriz, f. empress.
empernar, v. nail.
empero, conj. however.
emperramiento, m. stubbornness.
empezar, v. begin, start.
empinado, a. steep.
empinar, v. raise; exalt.
empíreo, a. celestial, heavenly; divine.
empíricamente, adv. empirically.
empírico, a. empirical.
empirismo, m. empiricism.
emplastarse, v. get smeared.
emplasto, m. salve.
emplazamiento, m. court summons.
emplazar, v. summon to court.
empleado -da, n. employee.
emplear, v. employ; use.
empleo, m. employment, job; use.
empobrecer, v. make or become impoverished.
empobrecimiento, m. impoverishment.
empolvado, a. dusty.
empolvar, v. powder.
empollador, m. incubator.
empollar, v. hatch.
emporcar, v. soil, make dirty.
emporio, m. emporium.
emprendedor, a. enterprising.

emprender, v. undertake.
empreñar, v. make pregnant; beget.
empresa, f. enterprise, undertaking.
empresario, m. impresario.
empréstito, m. loan.
empujón, m. push; shove. —empujar, v.
empuñar, v. grasp, seize; wield.
emulación, f. emulation; envy; rivalry.
emulador, m. emulator; rival.
émulo, a. rival. —emular, v.
emulsión, f. emulsion.
emulsionar, v. emulsify.
en, prep. in, on, at.
enaguas, f.pl. petticoat; skirt.
enajenable, a. alienable.
enajenación, f. alienation; derangement, insanity.
enajenar, v. alienate.
enamoradamente, adv. lovingly.
enamorado, a. in love.
enamorador, m. wooer; suitor; lover.
enamorarse, v. fall in love.
enano -na, n. midget; dwarf.
enardecer, v. inflame.
enastado, a. horned.
encabestrar, v. halter.
encabezado, m. headline.
encabezador, m. reaping machine.
encabezamiento, m. title; census; tax roll.
encabezar, v. head.
encachar, v. hide.
encadenamiento, m. connection, linkage.
encadenar, v. chain; link, connect.
encajar, v. fit in, insert.
encaje, m. lace.
encalar, v. whitewash.
encalvecer, v. lose one's hair.
encallarse, v. be stranded.
encallecido, a. hardened; calloused.
encaminar, v. guide; direct; be on the way to.
encandilar, v. dazzle; daze.
encantación, f. incantation.
encantado, a. charmed, fascinated, enchanted.
encantador, a. charming, delightful.

encante, m. public auction.

encanto, m. charm, delight. —**encantar,** v.

encapillado, m. clothes one is wearing.

encapotar, v. cover, cloak; muffle.

encaramarse, v. perch; climb.

encararse con, v. face.

encarcelación, f. imprisonment.

encarcelar, v. jail, imprison.

encarecer, v. recommend; extol.

encarecidamente, adv. extremely; ardently.

encargado, m. agent; attorney; representative.

encargar, v. entrust.

encargarse, v. take charge, be in charge.

encargo, m. errand; assignment; (com.) order.

encarnación, f. incarnation.

encarnado, a. red.

encarnar, v. embody.

encarnecer, v. grow fat or heavy.

encarnizado, a. bloody, fierce.

encarrilar, v. set right; put on the track.

encartar, v. ban, outlaw; summon.

encastar, v. improve by cross-breeding.

encastillar, v. be obstinate or unyielding.

encatarrado, a. suffering from a cold.

encausar, v. prosecute; take legal action against.

encauzar, v. channel; direct.

encefalitis, f. encephalitis.

encelamiento, m. envy, jealousy.

encenagar, v. wallow in mud.

encendedor, m. lighter.

encender, v. light; set fire to, kindle; turn on.

encendido, m. ignition.

encerado, a. oilcloth; tarpaulin.

encerar, v. wax.

encerrar, v. enclose; confine, shut in.

encía, f. gum.

encíclico, 1. a. encyclic. 2. f. encyclical.

enciclopedia, f. encyclopedia.

enciclopédico, a. encyclopedic.

encierro, m. confinement; enclosure.

encima, adv. on top. **e. de,** on. **por e. de,** above.

encina, f. oak.

encinta, a. pregnant.

enclavar, v. nail.

enclenque, a. frail, weak, sickly.

encogerse, v. shrink. **e. de hombros,** shrug the shoulders.

encogido, a. shy, bashful, timid.

encojar, v. make or become lame; cripple.

encolar, v. glue, paste, stick.

encolerizar, v. make or become angry.

encomendar, v. commend; recommend.

encomiar, v. praise, laud, extol.

encomienda, f. commission, charge; (postal) package.

encomio, m. encomium, eulogy.

enconar, v. irritate, annoy, anger.

encono, m. rancor, resentment.

enconoso, a. rancorous, resentful.

encontrado, a. opposite.

encontrar, v. find; meet.

encorajar, v. encourage; incite.

encorralar, v. corral.

encorvadura, f. bend, curvature.

encorvar, v. arch, bend.

encorvarse, v. stoop.

encrucijada, f. crossroads.

encuadrar, v. frame.

encubierta, f. secret, fraudulent.

encubrir, v. hide, conceal.

encuentro, m. encounter; match, bout.

encurtido, m. pickle.

enchapado, m. veneer.

enchufe, m. (elec.) plug, socket.

endeble, a. rail, weak, sickly.

enderezar, v. straighten; redress.

endiablado, a. devilish.

endibia, f. endive.

endiosar, v. deify.

endorso, endoso, m. endorsement.

endosador, m. endorser.

endosar, v. endorse.

endosatario, m. endorsee.

endulzar, v. sweeten; soothe.

endurar, v. harden; endure.

endurecer, v. harden.

enemigo -ga, f. foe, enemy.

enemistad, f. enmity.

éneo, a. brass.

energía, f. energy.

enérgicamente, *adv.* energetically.

enérgico, *a.* forceful; energetic.

enero, *m.* January.

enervación, *f.* enervation.

enfadado, *a.* angry.

enfadar, *v.* anger, vex.

enfado, *m.* anger, vexation.

énfasis, *m. or f.* emphasis, stress.

enfáticamente, *adv.* emphatically.

enfático, *a.* emphatic.

enfermar, *v.* make ill; fall ill.

enfermedad, *f.* illness, sickness, disease.

enfermera, *f.* nurse.

enfermería, *f.* sanitorium.

enfermo -ma, *a. & n.* ill, sick; sickly; patient.

enfilar, *v.* line up; put in a row.

enflaquecer, *v.* make thin; grow thin.

enfoque, *m.* focus. —**enfocar,** *v.*

enfrascamiento, *m.* entanglement.

enfrascar, *v.* entangle oneself.

enfrenar, *v.* bridle, curb; restrain.

enfrente, *adv.* across, opposite; in front.

enfriadera, *f.* icebox; cooler.

enfriar, *v.* chill, cool.

enfurecer, *v.* infuriate, enrage.

engalanar, *v.* adorn, trim.

enganchar, *v.* hook, hitch, attach.

engañar, *v.* deceive, cheat.

engaño, *m.* deceit; delusion.

engañoso, *a.* deceitful.

engarce, *m.* connection, link.

engastar, *v.* to put (gems) in a setting.

engaste, *m.* setting.

engatusar, *v.* deceive, trick.

engendrar, *v.* engender, beget, produce.

engendro, *m.* fetus, embryo.

englofar, *v.* be deeply absorbed.

engolosinar, *v.* allure, charm, entice.

engomar, *v.* gum.

engordador, *a.* fattening.

engordar, *v.* fatten; grow fat.

engranaje, *m.* (mech.) gear.

engranar, *v.* gear; mesh together.

engrandecer, *v.* increase, enlarge; exalt; exaggerate.

engrasación, *f.* lubrication.

engrasar, *v.* grease, lubricate.

engreído, *a.* conceited.

engreimiento, *m.* conceit.

engullidor, *m.* devourer.

engullir, *v.* devour.

enhebrar, *v.* thread.

enhestadura, *f.* raising.

enhestar, *v.* raise, erect, set up.

enhiesto, *a.* erect, upright.

enhorabuena, *f.* congratulations.

enigma, *m.* enigma, puzzle.

enigmáticamente, *adv.* enigmatically.

enigmático, *a.* enigmatic.

enjabonar, *v.* soap, lather.

enjalbegar, *v.* whitewash.

enjambradera, *f.* queen bee.

enjambre, *m.* swarm. —**enjambrar,** *v.*

enjaular, *v.* cage, coop up.

enjebe, *m.* lye.

enjuagar, *v.* rinse.

enjugar, *v.* wipe, dry off.

enjutez, *f.* dryness.

enjuto, *a.* dried; lean, thin.

enlace, *m.* attachment; involvement; connection.

enladrillador, *m.* bricklayer.

enlardar, *v.* baste.

enlazar, *v.* lace; join, connect; wed.

enlodar, *v.* cover with mud.

enloquecer, *v.* go insane; drive crazy.

enloquecimiento, *m.* insanity.

enlustrecer, *v.* polish, brighten.

enmarañar, *v.* entangle.

enmendación, *f.* emendation.

enmendador, *m.* emender, reviser.

enmendar, *v.* amend, correct.

enmienda, *f.* amendment; correction.

enmohecer, *v.* rust; mold.

enmohecido, *a.* rusty; moldy.

enmudecer, *v.* silence; become silent.

ennegrecer, *v.* blacken.

ennoblecer, *v.* ennoble.

enodio, *m.* young deer.

enojado, *a.* angry, cross.

enojarse, *v.* get angry.

enojo, *m.* anger. —**enojar,** *v.*

enojosamente, *adv.* angrily.

enorme, *a.* enormous, huge.

enormemente, *adv.* enormously; hugely.

enormidad, *f.* enormity; hugeness.

enraizar, v. take root, sprout.

enramada, f. bower.

enredado, a. entangled, snarled.

enredar, v. entangle, snarl; mess up.

enredo, m. tangle, entanglement.

enriquecer, v. enrich.

enrojecerse, v. color; blush.

enrollar, v. wind, coil, roll up.

enromar, v. make dull, blunt.

enronquecimiento, m. hoarseness.

enroscar, v. twist, curl, wind.

ensacar, v. put in a bag.

ensalada, f. salad.

ensaladera, f. salad bowl.

ensalmo, m. charm, enchantment.

ensalzamiento, m. praise.

ensalzar, v. praise, laud, extol.

ensamblar, v. join; unite; connect.

ensanchamiento, m. widening, expansion, extension.

ensanchar, v. widen, expand, extend.

ensangrentado, a. bloody; bloodshot.

ensañar, v. enrage, infuriate; rage.

ensayar, v. try out; rehearse.

ensayista, n. essayist.

ensayo, m. attempt; trial; rehearsal.

ensenada, f. cove.

enseña, f. ensign, standard.

enseñador, m. teacher.

enseñanza, f. education; teaching.

enseñar, v. teach, train; show.

enseres, m.pl. household goods.

ensilaje, m. ensilage.

ensillar, v. saddle.

ensordecer, v. deafen.

ensordecimiento, m. deafness.

ensuciar, v. dirty, muddy, soil.

ensueño, m. illusion, dream.

entablar, v. board up; initiate, begin.

entallador, m. sculptor, carver.

entapizar, v. upholster.

ente, m. being.

entenada, f. stepdaughter.

entenado, m. stepson.

entender, v. understand.

entendimiento, m. understanding.

entenebrecer, v. darken.

enterado, a. aware, informed.

enteramente, adv. entirely, completely.

enterar, v. inform.

enterarse, v. find out.

entereza, f. entirety; integrity; firmness.

entero, a. entire, whole, total.

enterramiento, m. burial, interment.

enterrar, v. bury.

entestado, a. stubborn, willful.

entibiar, v. to cool; moderate.

entidad, f. entity.

entierro, m. interment, burial.

entonación, f. intonation.

entonamiento, m. intonation.

entonar, v. chant; harmonize.

entonces, adv. then.

entono, m. arrogance; affectation.

entortadura, f. crookedness.

entortar, v. make crooked; bend.

entrada, f. entrance; admission, admittance.

entrambos, a. & pron. both.

entrante, a. coming, next.

entrañable, a. affectionate.

entrañas, f.pl. entrails, bowels; womb.

entrar, v. enter, go in, come in.

entre, prep. among; between.

entreabierto, a. ajar, half-open.

entreabrir, v. set ajar.

entreacto, m. intermission.

entrecejo, a. frowning.

entrecuesto, m. spine, backbone.

entredicho, m. prohibition.

entrega, f. delivery.

entregar, v. deliver, hand; hand over.

entrelazar, v. intertwine, entwine.

entremedias, adv. meanwhile; halfway.

entremés, m. side dish.

entremeterse, v. meddle, intrude.

entremetido, m. meddler; intermediary.

entrenador, m. coach. —**entrenar,** v.

entrenarse, v. train.

entrepalado, a. variegated; spotted.

entrerenglonar, v. interline.

entresacar, v. select, choose; sift.

entretanto, adv. meanwhile.

entretenedor, *m.* entertainer.

entretener, *v.* entertain, amuse; delay.

entretenimiento, *m.* entertainment, amusement.

entrevista, *f.* interview. —entrevistar, *v.*

entristecedor, *a.* sad.

entristecer, *v.* sadden.

entronar, *v.* enthrone.

entroncar, *v.* be related or connected.

entronización, *f.* enthronement.

entronque, *m.* relationship; connection.

entumecer, *v.* become or be numb; swell.

entusiasmado, *a.* enthusiastic.

entusiasmo, *m.* enthusiasm.

entusiasta, *m.* & *f.* enthusiast.

entusiástico, *a.* enthusiastic.

enumeración, *f.* enumeration.

enumerar, *v.* enumerate.

enunciación, *f.* enunciation; statement.

enunciar, *v.* enunciate.

envainar, *v.* sheathe.

envalentonar, *v.* encourage, embolden.

envanecimiento, *m.* conceit, vanity.

envasar, *v.* put in a container; bottle.

envase, *m.* container.

envejecer, *v.* age, grow old.

envejecimiento, *m.* oldness, age.

envenenar, *v.* poison.

envés, *m.* wrong side; back.

envestir, *v.* put in office; invest.

enviada, *f.* shipment.

enviado, *m.* envoy.

enviar, *v.* send; ship.

envidia, *f.* envy. —envidiar, *v.*

envidiable, *a.* enviable.

envidioso, *a.* envious.

envilecer, *v.* vilify, debase, disgrace.

envío, *m.* shipment.

envión, *m.* shove.

envoltura, *f.* wrapping.

envolver, *v.* wrap, wrap up.

enyesar, *v.* plaster.

enyugar, *v.* yoke.

eperlano, *m.* smelt (fish).

épica, *f.* epic writing.

épico, *a.* epic.

epicureísmo, *m.* Epicureanism.

epicúreo, *n.* & *a.* epicurean.

epidemia, *f.* epidemic.

epidémico, *a.* epidemic.

epidermis, *f.* epidermis.

epigrama, *m.* epigram.

epigramático, *a.* epigrammatic.

epilepsia, *f.* epilepsy.

epiléptico, *n.* & *a.* epileptic.

epílogo, *m.* epilogue.

episcopado, *m.* bishopric; episcopate.

episcopal, *a.* episcopal.

episódico, *a.* episodic.

episodio, *m.* episode.

epístola, *f.* epistle, letter.

epitafio, *m.* epitaph.

epitomadamente, *adv.* concisely.

epitomar, *v.* epitomize, summarize.

época, *f.* epoch, age.

epopeya, *f.* epic.

epsomita, *f.* Epsom salts.

equidad, *f.* equity.

equilibrado, *a.* stable.

equilibrio, *m.* equilibrium, balance.

equinoccio, *m.* equinox.

equipaje, *m.* luggage, baggage.

equipar, *v.* equip.

equiparar, *v.* compare.

equipo, *m.* equipment; team.

equitación, *f.* horsemanship.

equitativo, *a.* fair, equitable.

equivalencia, *f.* equivalence.

equivalente, *a.* equivalent.

equivaler, *v.* equal, be equivalent.

equivocación, *f.* mistake.

equivocado, *a.* wrong, mistaken.

equivocarse, *v.* make a mistake, be wrong.

equívoco, *a.* equivocal, ambiguous.

era, *f.* era, age.

erario, *m.* exchequer.

erección, *f.* erection; elevation.

eremita, *m.* hermit.

erguir, *v.* erect; straighten up.

erigir, *v.* erect, build.

erisipela, *f.* erysipelas.

erizado, *a.* bristly.

erizarse, *v.* bristle.

erizo, *m.* hedgehog; sea urchin.

ermita, *f.* hermitage.

ermitaño, *m.* hermit.

erogación, *f.* expenditure. —erogar, *v.*

erosión, *f.* erosion.

erótico, *a.* erotic.
erradicación, *f.* eradication.
erradicar, *v.* eradicate.
errado, *a.* mistaken, erroneous.
errante, *a.* wandering, roving.
errar, *v.* be mistaken.
errata, *f.* erratum.
errático, *a.* erratic.
erróneamente, *adv.* erroneously.
erróneo, *a.* erroneous.
error, *m.* error, mistake.
eructo, *m.* belch. —**eructar,** *v.*
erudición, *f.* scholarship, learning.
eruditamente, *adv.* learnedly.
erudito, *m.* scholar.
erupción, *f.* eruption; rash.
eruptivo, *a.* eruptive.
esbozo, *m.* outline, sketch. —**esbozar,** *v.*
escabechar, *v.* pickle; preserve.
escabel, *m.* small stool or bench.
escabroso, *a.* rough, irregular; craggy; rude.
escabullirse, *v.* steal away, sneak away.
escala, *f.* scale; ladder. **hacer e.,** to make a stop.
escalada, *f.* escalation.
escalador, *m.* climber.
escalar, *v.* climb; scale.
escaldar, *v.* scald.
escalera, *f.* stairs, staircase; ladder.
escalfado, *a.* poached.
escalofriado, *a.* chilled.
escalofrío, *m.* chill.
escalón, *m.* step.
escaloña, *f.* scallion.
escalpar, *v.* scalp.
escalpelo, *m.* scalpel.
escama, *f.* (fish) scale. —**escamar,** *v.*
escamondar, *v.* trim, cut; prune.
escampada, *f.* stampede.
escandalizar, *v.* shock, scandalize.
escandalizativo, *a.* scandalous.
escándalo, *m.* scandal.
escandaloso, *a.* scandalous; disgraceful.
escandinavo, *n.* & *a.* Scandinavian.
escandir, *v.* scan.
escanilla, *f.* cradle.
escañuelo, *m.* small footstool.
escapada, *f.* escapade.

escapar, *v.* escape.
escape, *m.* escape; (auto.) exhaust.
escápula, *f.* scapula.
escarabajo, *m.* black beetle; scarab.
escaramucear, *v.* skirmish; dispute.
escarbadientes, *m.* toothpick.
escarbar, *v.* scratch; poke.
escarcha, *f.* frost.
escardar, *v.* weed.
escarlata, *f.* scarlet.
escarmentar, *v.* correct severely.
escarnecedor, *m.* scoffer; mocker.
escarnecer, *v.* mock, make fun of.
escarola, *f.* endive.
escarpado, 1. *a.* steep. 2. *m.* bluff.
escarpe, *m.* escarpment.
escasamente, *adv.* scarcely; sparingly; barely.
escasear, *v.* be scarce.
escasez, *f.* shortage, scarcity.
escaso, *a.* scant; scarce.
escatimoso, *a.* malicious; sly, cunning.
escena, *f.* scene; stage.
escenario, *m.* stage (of theater); scenario.
escénico, *a.* scenic.
escépticamente, *adv.* skeptically.
escepticismo, *m.* skepticism.
escéptico -ca, *a.* & *n.* skeptic; skeptical.
esclarecer, *v.* clear up.
esclavitud, *f.* slavery; bondage.
esclavizar, *v.* enslave.
esclavo -va, *m.* slave.
escoba, *f.* broom.
escocés, *a.* & *n.* Scotch, Scottish; Scot.
Escocia, *f.* Scotland.
escofinar, *v.* rasp.
escoger, *v.* choose, select.
escogido, *a.* choice, select.
escogimiento, *m.* choice.
escolar, 1. *a.* scholastic, (of) school. 2. *m.* student.
escolasticismo, *m.* scholasticism.
escolta, *f.* escort. —**escoltar,** *v.*
escollo, *m.* reef.
escombro, *m.* mackerel.
escombros, *m.pl.* debris, rubbish.
esconce, *m.* corner.
escondedero, *m.* hiding place.

esconder, v. hide, conceal.

escondidamente, adv. secretly.

escondimiento, m. concealment.

escopeta, f. shotgun.

escopetazo, m. gunshot.

escoplo, m. chisel.

escorbuto, m. scurvy.

escorpena, f. grouper.

escorpión, m. scorpion.

escorzón, m. toad.

escribiente, m. & f. clerk.

escribir, v. write.

escritor -ra, n. writer, author.

escritorio, m. desk.

escritura, f. writing, handwriting.

escrófula, f. scrofula.

escroto, m. scrotum.

escrúpulo, m. scruple.

escrupuloso, a. scrupulous.

escrutinio, m. scrutiny; examination.

escuadra, f. squad; fleet.

escuadrón, m. squadron.

escualidez, f. squalor; poverty.

escuálido, a. squalid.

escualo, m. shark.

escuchar, v. listen; listen to.

escudero, m. squire.

escudo, m. shield; protection; coin of certain countries.

escuela, f. school.

escuerzo, m. toad.

esculpir, v. carve, sculpture.

escultor, m. sculptor.

escultura, f. sculpture.

escupidera, f. cuspidor.

escupir, v. spit.

escurridor, m. colander, strainer.

escurrir, v. drain off; wring out.

escurrirse, v. slip; sneak away.

ese, esa, dem. a. that.

ése, ésa, dem. pron. that (one).

esencia, f. essence; perfume.

esencial, a. essential.

esencialmente, adv. essentially.

esfera, f. sphere.

esfinge, f. sphinx.

esforzar, v. strengthen.

esforzarse, v. strive, exert oneself.

esfuerzo, m. effort; attempt; vigor.

esgrima, f. fencing.

eslabón, m. link (of a chain).

eslabonar, v. link, join, connect.

eslavo, a. & n. Slavic; Slav.

esmalte, m. enamel, polish. —esmaltar, v.

esmerado, a. careful, thorough.

esmeralda, f. emerald.

esmerarse, v. take pains, do one's best.

esmeril, m. emery.

eso, dem. pron. that.

esófago, m. esophagus.

esotérico, a. esoteric.

espacial, a. spatial.

espacio, m. space. —espaciar, v.

espaciosidad, f. spaciousness.

espacioso, a. spacious.

espada, f. sword; spade (in cards).

espadarte, m. swordfish.

espalda, f. back.

espaldera, f. espalier.

espantar, v. frighten, scare; scare away.

espanto, m. fright.

espantoso, a. frightening, frightful.

España, f. Spain.

español -ola, a. & n. Spanish; Spaniard.

esparcir, v. scatter, disperse.

espárrago, m. asparagus.

espartano, n. & a. Spartan.

espasmo, m. spasm.

espasmódico, a. spasmodic.

espata, f. spathe.

espato, m. spar (mineral).

espátula, f. spatula.

especia, f. spice. —especiar, v.

especial, a. special, especial.

especialidad, f. specialty.

especialista, m. & f. specialist.

especialización, f. specialization.

especialmente, adv. especially.

especie, f. species; sort.

especiería, f. grocery store.

especiero, m. grocer.

especificar, v. specify.

específico, a. specific.

espécimen, m. specimen.

especioso, a. neat; polished; specious.

espectáculo, m. spectacle, show.

espectador -ra, n. spectator.

espectro, m. specter, ghost.

especulación, f. speculation.

especulador, m. speculator.

especular, v. speculate.

especulativo, a. speculative.

espejo, m. mirror.

espelunca, *f.* dark cave, cavern.

espera, *f.* wait.

esperanza, *f.* hope, expectation.

esperar, *v.* hope; expect; wait, wait for, watch for.

espesar, *v.* thicken.

espeso, *a.* thick, dense, bushy.

espesor, *m.* thickness, density.

espía, *m. & f.* spy. **—espiar,** *v.*

espigón, *m.* bee sting.

espina, *f.* thorn.

espinaca, *f.* spinach.

espinal, *a.* spinal.

espinazo, *m.* spine.

espineta, *f.* spinet.

espino, *m.* briar.

espinoso, *a.* spiny, thorny.

espión, *m.* spy.

espionaje, *m.* espionage.

espiración, *f.* expiration.

espiral, *a. & m.* spiral.

espirar, *v.* expire; breathe, exhale.

espíritu, *m.* spirit.

espiritual, *a.* spiritual.

espiritualidad, *f.* spirituality.

espiritualmente, *adv.* spiritually.

espita, *f.* faucet, spigot.

espléndido, *a.* splendid.

esplendor, *m.* splendor.

espolear, *v.* incite, urge on.

espoleta, *f.* wishbone.

esponja, *f.* sponge.

esponjoso, *a.* spongy.

esponsales, *m.pl.* engagement, betrothal.

esponsalicio, *a.* nuptial.

espontáneamente, *adv.* spontaneously.

espontaneidad, *f.* spontaneity.

espontáneo, *a.* spontaneous.

espora, *f.* spore.

esporádico, *a.* sporadic.

esposa, *f.* wife.

esposar, *v.* shackle.

esposo, *m.* husband.

espuela, *f.* spur. **—espolear,** *v.*

espuma, *f.* foam. **—espumar,** *v.*

espumadera, *f.* colander.

espumajear, *v.* foam at the mouth.

espumajo, *m.* foam.

espumar, *v.* foam, froth; skim.

espumoso, *a.* foamy; sparkling (wine).

espurio, *a.* spurious.

esputar, *v.* spit, expectorate.

esputo, *m.* spit, saliva.

esquela, *f.* note.

esqueleto, *m.* skeleton.

esquema, *m.* scheme; diagram.

esquero, *m.* leather sack or pouch.

esquiciar, *v.* outline, sketch.

esquicio, *m.* rough sketch or outline.

esquife, *m.* skiff.

esquilar, *v.* fleece, shear.

esquilmo, *m.* harvest.

esquimal, *n. & a.* Eskimo.

esquina, *f.* corner.

esquivar, *v.* evade, shun.

estabilidad, *f.* stability.

estable, *a.* stable.

establecedor, *m.* founder, originator.

establecer, *v.* establish, set up.

establecimiento, *m.* establishment.

establero, *m.* groom.

establo, *m.* stable.

estaca, *f.* stake.

estación, *f.* station; season.

estacionamiento, *m.* parking.

estacionar, *v.* station; park (a vehicle).

estacionario, *a.* stationary.

estadista, *m.* statesman.

estadística, *f.* statistics.

estadístico, *a.* statistical.

estado, *m.* state; condition; status.

estafa, *f.* swindle, fake. **—estafar,** *v.*

estafeta, *f.* post office.

estagnación, *f.* stagnation.

estallar, *v.* explode; burst; break out.

estallido, *m.* crash; crack; explosion.

estampa, *f.* stamp. **—estampar,** *v.*

estampado, *m.* printed cotton cloth.

estampida, *f.* stampede.

estampilla, *f.* (postage) stamp.

estancado, *a.* stagnant.

estancar, *v.* stanch, stop, check.

estancia, *f.* stay; (S.A.) small farm.

estanciero -ra, *n.* small farmer.

estandarte, *m.* banner.

estanque, *m.* pool; pond.

estante, *m.* shelf.

estaño, *m.* tin. **—estañar,** *v.*

estar, v. be; stand; look.

estática, f. static.

estático, a. static.

estatua, f. statue.

estatura, f. stature.

estatuto, m. statute, law.

este, m. east.

este, esta, dem. a. this.

éste, ésta, dem. pron. this (one); the latter.

estelar, a. stellar.

estenografía, f. stenography.

estenógrafo -fa, n. stenographer.

estera, f. mat, matting.

estereofónico, a. stereophonic.

estéril, a. barren; sterile.

esterilidad, f. sterility, fruitless-ness.

esterilizar, v. sterilize.

estética, f. esthetics.

estético, a. esthetic.

estetoscopio, m. stethoscope.

estibador, m. stevedore.

estiércol, m. dung, manure.

estigma, m. stigma; disgrace.

estilo, m. style; sort.

estilográfica, f. (fountain) pen.

estima, f. esteem.

estimable, a. estimable, worthy.

estimación, f. estimation.

estimar, v. esteem; value; esti-mate; gauge.

estimular, v. stimulate.

estímulo, m. stimulus.

estío, m. summer.

estipulación, f. stipulation.

estipular, v. stipulate.

estirar, v. stretch.

estirpe, m. stock, lineage.

esto, dem. pron. this.

estocada, f. stab, thrust.

estofado, m. stew. —**estofar,** v.

estoicismo, m. stoicism.

estoico, n. & a. stoic.

estómago, m. stomach.

estorbar, v. bother, hinder, inter-fere with.

estorbo, m. hindrance.

estornudo, m. sneeze. —**estornu-dar,** v.

estrabismo, m. strabismus.

estrago, m. devastation, havoc.

estrangulación, f. strangulation.

estrangular, v. strangle.

estratagema, f. stratagem.

estrategia, f. strategy.

estratégico, a. strategic.

estrato, m. stratum.

estrechar, v. tighten; narrow.

estrechez, f. narrowness; tight-ness.

estrecho, 1. a. narrow, tight. **2.** m. strait.

estregar, v. scour, scrub.

estrella, f. star.

estrellamar, m. starfish.

estrellar, v. shatter, smash.

estremecimiento, m. shudder. — **estremecerse,** v.

estrenar, v. wear for the first time; open (a play).

estreno, m. debut, first perform-ance.

estrenuo, a. strenuous.

estreptococo, m. streptococcus.

estría, f. groove.

estribillo, m refrain.

estribo, m. stirrup.

estribor, m. starboard.

estrictamente, adv. strictly.

estrictez, f. strictness.

estricto, a. strict.

estrofa, f. stanza.

estropajo, m. mop.

estropear, v. cripple, damage, spoil.

estructura, f. structure.

estructural, a. structural.

estruendo, m. din, clatter.

estuario, m. estuary.

estuco, m. stucco.

estudiante -ta, n. student.

estudiar, v. study.

estudio, m. study; studio.

estudioso, a. studious.

estufa, f. stove.

estulto, a. foolish.

estupendo, a. wonderful, grand, fine.

estupidez, f. stupidity.

estúpido, a. stupid.

estupor, m. stupor.

estuque, m. stucco.

esturión, m. sturgeon.

etapa, f. stage.

éter, m. ether.

etéreo, a. ethereal.

eternal, a. eternal.

eternidad, f. eternity.

eterno, a. eternal.

ética, f. ethics.

ético, a. ethical.

etimología, f. etymology.

etiqueta, f. etiquette; tag, label.

étnico, a. ethnic.

etrusco, n. & a. Etruscan.

eucaristía, f. Eucharist.

eufemismo, m. euphemism.

eufonía, f. euphony.

Europa, f. Europe.

europeo -pea, a. & n. European.

eutanasia, f. euthanasia.

evacuación, f. evacuation.

evacuar, v. evacuate.

evadir, v. evade.

evangélico, a. evangelical.

evangelio, m. gospel.

evangelista, m. evangelist.

evaporación, f. evaporation.

evaporarse, v. evaporate.

evasión, f. evasion.

evasivamente, adv. evasively.

evasivo, a. evasive.

evento, m. event, occurrence.

eventual, a. eventual.

eventualidad, f. eventuality.

evicción, f. eviction.

evidencia, f. evidence.

evidenciar, v. prove, show.

evidente, a. evident.

evitación, f. avoidance.

evitar, v. avoid, shun.

evocación, f. evocation.

evocar, v. evoke.

evolución, f. evolution.

exacerbar, v. irritate deeply.

exactamente, adv. exactly.

exactitud, f. precision, accuracy.

exacto, a. exact, accurate.

exageración, f. exaggeration.

exagerar, v. exaggerate.

exagonal, a. hexagonal.

exaltación, f. exaltation.

exaltamiento, m. exaltation.

exaltar, v. exalt.

examen, m. test, examination.

examinar, v. test, examine.

exánime, a. spiritless, weak.

exasperación, f. exasperation.

exasperar, v. exasperate.

excavación, f. excavation.

excavar, v. excavate.

exceder, v. exceed, surpass; outrun.

excelencia, f. excellence.

excelente, a. excellent.

excéntrico, a. eccentric.

excepción, f. exception.

excepcional, a. exceptional.

excepto, prep. except, except for.

exceptuar, v. except.

excesivamente, adv. excessively.

excesivo, a. excessive.

exceso, m. excess.

excitabilidad, f. excitability.

excitación, f. excitement.

excitar, v. excite.

exclamación, f. exclamation.

exclamar, v. exclaim.

excluir, v. exclude, bar, shut out.

exclusión, f. exclusion.

exclusivamente, adv. exclusively.

exclusivo, a. exclusive.

excomulgar, v. excommunicate.

excomunión, f. excommunication.

excreción, f. excretion.

excremento, m. excrement.

excretar, v. excrete.

exculpar, v. exonerate.

excursión, f. excursion.

excursionista, n. excursionist.

excusa, f. excuse. **—excusar,** v.

excusado, m. toilet.

excusarse, v. apologize.

exención, f. exemption.

exento, a. exempt. **—exentar,** v.

exhalación, f. exhalation.

exhalar, v. exhale, breathe out.

exhausto, a. exhausted.

exhibición, f. exhibit, exhibition.

exhibir, v. exhibit, display.

exhortación, f. exhortation.

exhortar, v. exhort, admonish.

exhumación, f. exhumation.

exhumar, v. exhume.

exigencia, f. requirement, demand.

exigente, a. exacting, demanding.

exigir, v. require, exact, demand.

eximir, v. exempt.

existencia, f. existence; (econ.) supply.

existente, a. existent.

existir, v. exist.

éxito, m. success.

éxodo, m. exodus.

exoneración, f. exoneration.

exonerar, v. exonerate, acquit.

exorar, v. beg, implore.

exorbitancia, f. exorbitance.

exorbitante, a. exorbitant.

exorcismo, m. exorcism.

exornar, v. adorn, decorate.

exótico, a. exotic.

expansibilidad, *f.* expansibility.
expansión, *f.* expansion.
expansivo, *a.* expansive; effusive.
expatriación, *f.* expatriation.
expatriar, *v.* expatriate.
expectación, *f.* expectation.
expectorar, *v.* expectorate.
expedición, *f.* expedition.
expediente, *m.* expedient, means.
expedir, *v.* send off, ship; expedite.
expeditivo, *a.* speedy, prompt.
expedito, *a.* speedy, prompt.
expeler, *v.* expel, eject.
expendedor, *m.* dealer.
expender, *v.* expend.
expensas, *f.pl.* expenses, costs.
experiencia, *f.* experience.
experimentado, *a.* experienced.
experimental, *a.* experimental.
experimentar, *v.* experience.
experimento, *m.* experiment.
expertamente, *adv.* expertly.
experto, *a. & m.* expert.
expiación, *f.* atonement.
expiar, *v.* atone for.
expiración, *f.* expiration.
expirar, *v.* expire.
explanación, *f.* explanation.
explanar, *v.* make level.
expletivo, *n. & a.* expletive.
explicable, *a.* explicable.
explicación, *f.* explanation.
explicar, *v.* explain.
explicativo, *a.* explanatory.
explícitamente, *adv.* explicitly.
explícito, *adj.* explicit.
exploración, *f.* exploration.
explorador, *m.* explorer; scout.
explorar, *v.* explore; scout.
exploratorio, *a.* exploratory.
explosión, *f.* explosion; outburst.
explosivo, *a.* explosive.
explotación, *f.* exploitation.
explotar, *v.* exploit.
exponer, *v.* expose; set forth.
exportación, *f.* exportation; export.
exportador, *m.* exporter.
exportar, *v.* export.
exposición, *f.* exhibit; exposition; exposure.
expósito, *n.* foundling; orphan.
expresado, *a.* aforesaid.
expresamente, *adv.* clearly, explicitly.
expresar, *v.* express.

expresión, *f.* expression.
expresivo, *a.* expressive; affectionate.
expreso, *a. & m.* express.
exprimir, *v.* squeeze.
expropiación, *f.* expropriation.
expropiar, *v.* expropriate.
expulsar, *v.* expel, eject; evict.
expulsión, *f.* expulsion.
expurgación, *f.* expurgation.
expurgar, *v.* expurgate.
exquisitamente, *adv.* exquisitely.
exquisito, *a.* exquisite.
éxtasi, *m.* ecstasy.
extemporáneo, *a.* extemporaneous, impromptu.
extender, *v.* extend; spread; widen; stretch.
extensamente, *adv.* extensively.
extensión, *f.* extension, spread, expanse.
extenso, *a.* extensive, widespread.
extenuación, *f.* weakening; emaciation.
extenuar, *v.* extenuate.
exterior, *a. & m.* exterior; foreign.
exterminar, *v.* exterminate.
exterminio, *m.* extermination, ruin.
extinción, *f.* extinction.
extinguir, *v.* extinguish.
extinto, *a.* extinct.
extintor, *m.* fire extinguisher.
extirpar, *v.* eradicate.
extorsión, *f.* extortion.
extra, *n.* extra.
extracción, *f.* extraction.
extractar, *v.* summarize.
extracto, *m.* extract; summary.
extradición, *f.* extradition.
extraer, *v.* extract.
extranjero -ra, 1. *a.* foreign. **2.** *n.* foreigner; stranger.
extrañar, *v.* surprise; miss.
extraño, *a.* strange, queer.
extraordinariamente, *adv.* extraordinarily.
extraordinario, *a.* extraordinary.
extravagancia, *f.* extravagance.
extravagante, *a.* extravagant.
extraviado, *a.* lost, misplaced.
extraviarse, *v.* stray, get lost.
extravío, *m.* aberration, deviation.

extremadamente, *adv.* extremely.
extremado, *a.* extreme.
extremaunción, *f.* extreme unction.
extremidad, *f.* extremity.
extremista, *n. & a.* extremist.
extremo, *a. & m.* extreme, end.
extrínseco, *a.* extrinsic.
exuberancia, *f.* exuberance.
exuberante, *a.* exuberant.
exudación, *f.* exudation.
exudar, *v.* exude, ooze.
exultación, *f.* exultation.

F

fábrica, *f.* factory.
fabricación, *f.* manufacture, manufacturing.
fabricante, *m.* manufacturer, maker.
fabricar, *v.* manufacture, make.
fabril, *a.* making, building.
fábula, *f.* fable, myth.
fabuloso, *a.* fabulous.
facción, *f.* faction, party; *(pl.)* features.
faccioso, *a.* factious.
fácil, *a.* easy.
facilidad, *f.* facility, ease.
facilitar, *v.* facilitate, make easy.
fácilmente, *adv.* easily.
facsímil, *m.* facsimile.
factible, *a.* feasible.
factor, *m.* factor.
factótum, *m.* factotum; jack of all trades.
factura, *f.* invoice, bill.
facturar, *v.* check (baggage).
facultad, *f.* faculty; ability.
facultativo, *a.* optional.
fachada, *f.* façade, front.
faena, *f.* task; work.
faja, *f.* band; sash; zone.
falacia, *f.* fallacy; deceitfulness.
falda, *f.* skirt; lap.
falibilidad, *f.* fallibility.
falsear, *v.* falsify, counterfeit; forge.
falsedad, *f.* falsehood; lie; falseness.
falsificación, *f.* falsification; forgery.
falsificar, *v.* falsify, counterfeit, forge.
falso, *a.* false; wrong.

falta, *f.* error, mistake; fault; lack. **hacer f.**, to be lacking, to be necessary. **sin f.**, without fail.
faltar, *v.* be lacking, be missing; be absent.
faltriquera, *f.* pocket.
falla, *f.* failure, fault.
fallar, *v.* fail.
fallecer, *v.* pass away, die.
fallo, *m.* verdict.
fama, *f.* fame; reputation; glory.
familia, *f.* family; household.
familiar, *a.* familiar; domestic; (of) family.
familiaridad, *f.* familiarity, intimacy.
familiarizar, *v.* familiarize, acquaint.
famoso, *a.* famous.
fanal, *m.* lighthouse; lantern; lamp.
fanático -ca, *a. & n.* fanatic.
fanatismo, *m.* fanaticism.
fanfarria, *f.* bluster. —**fanfarrear**, *v.*
fango, *m.* mud.
fantasía, *f.* fantasy; fancy, whim.
fantasma, *m.* phantom; ghost.
fantástico, *a.* fantastic.
faquín, *m.* porter.
faquir, *m.* fakir.
farallón, *m.* cliff.
Faraón, *m.* Pharaoh.
fardel, *m.* bag; package.
fardo, *m.* bundle.
farináceo, *a.* farinaceous.
faringe, *f.* pharynx.
fariseo, *m.* pharisee, hypocrite.
farmacéutico, *a.* pharmacist.
farmacia, *f.* pharmacy.
faro, *m.* beacon; lighthouse; headlight.
farol, *m.* lantern; (street) light.
farra, *f.* spree.
fárrago, *m.* medley; hodgepodge.
farsa, *f.* farce.
fascinación, *f.* fascination.
fascinar, *v.* fascinate, bewitch.
fase, *f.* phase.
fastidiar, *v.* disgust; irk, annoy.
fastidio, *m.* disgust; annoyance.
fastidioso, *a.* annoying; tedious.
fatal, *a.* fatal.
fatalidad, *f.* fate; calamity, bad luck.
fatalismo, *m.* fatalism.
fatalista, *n. & a.* fatalist.

fatiga, f. fatigue. **—fatigar,** v.
fauno, m. faun.
favor, m. favor; behalf. **por f.,** please.
favorable, a. favorable.
favorablemente, adv. favorably.
favorecer, v. favor; flatter.
favoritismo, m. favoritism.
favorito -ta, a. & n. favorite.
faz, f. face.
fe, f. faith.
fealdad, f. ugliness, homeliness.
febrero, m. February.
febril, a. feverish.
fécula, f. starch.
fecundar, v. fertilize.
fecundidad, f. fecundity, fertility.
fecundo, a. fecund, fertile.
fecha, f. date. **—fechar,** v.
federación, f. confederacy.
federal, a. federal.
felicidad, f. happiness; bliss.
felicitación, f. congratulation.
felicitar, v. congratulate; compliment.
feligrés -esa, n. parishioner.
felón, m. felon.
felonía, f. felony.
felpa, f. plush.
felpudo, m. doormat.
femenino, a. feminine.
feminismo, m. feminism.
feminista, n. feminist.
fenecer, v. conclude; die.
fénix, m. phoenix; model.
fenomenal, a. phenomenal.
fenómeno, m. phenomenon.
feo, a. ugly, homely.
feracidad, f. feracity, fertility.
feraz, a. fertile, fruitful; copious.
feria, f. fair; market.
feriado, a. **día f.,** holiday.
fermentación, f. fermentation.
fermento, m. ferment. **—fermentar,** v.
ferocidad, f. ferocity, fierceness.
feroz, a. ferocious, fierce.
férreo, a. of iron.
ferrería, f. ironworks.
ferretería, f. hardware; hardware store.
ferrocarril, m. railroad.
fértil, a. fertile.
fertilidad, f. fertility.
fertilizar, v. fertilize.
férvido, a. fervid, ardent.

ferviente, a. fervent.
fervor, m. fervor, zeal.
fervoroso, a. zealous, eager.
festejar, v. entertain, fete.
festejo, m. feast.
festín, m. feast.
festividad, f. festivity.
festivo, a. festive.
fétido, adj. fetid.
feudal, a. feudal.
feudo, m. feud.
fiado, adj. on trust, on credit.
fianza, f. bail.
fiar, v. trust, sell on credit; give credit.
fiarse de, v. trust (in), rely on.
fiasco, m. fiasco.
fibra, f. fiber; vigor.
fibroso, a. fibrous.
ficción, f. fiction.
ficticio, a. fictitious.
ficha, f. slip, card; chip.
fidedigno, a. trustworthy.
fideicomisario, m. trustee.
fideicomiso, m. trust.
fidelidad, f. fidelity.
fideo, m. noodle.
fiebre, f. fever.
fiel, a. faithful.
fieltro, m. felt.
fiera, f. wild animal.
fiereza, f. fierceness, wildness.
fiero, a. fierce; wild.
fiesta, f. festival, feast; party.
figura, f. figure. **—figurar,** v.
figurarse, v. imagine.
figurón, m. dummy.
fijar, v. fix; set, establish; post.
fijarse en, v. notice.
fijeza, f. firmness.
fijo, a. fixed, stationary, permanent, set.
fila, f. row, rank, file, line.
filantropía, f. philanthropy.
filete, m. fillet.
film, m. film. **—filmar,** v.
filo, m. (cutting) edge.
filón, m. vein (of ore).
filosofía, f. philosophy.
filosófico, a. philosophical.
filósofo, m. philosopher.
filtro, m. filter. **—filtrar,** v.
fin, m. end, purpose, goal. **a f. de que,** in order that. **en f.,** in short. **por f.,** finally, at last.
final, **1.** a. final. **2.** m. end.
finalidad, f. finality.

finalmente, *adv.* at last.
financiero, 1. *a.* financial. **2.** *m.* financier.
finca, *f.* real estate; estate; farm.
finés, *a.* Finnish.
fineza, *f.* courtesy, politeness; fineness.
fingimiento, *m.* pretense.
fingir, *v.* feign, pretend.
fino, *a.* fine; polite, courteous.
firma, *f.* signature; (com.) firm.
firmamento, *m.* firmament, heavens.
firmar, *v.* sign.
firme, *a.* firm, fast, steady, sound.
firmemente, *adv.* firmly.
firmeza, *f.* firmness.
fisco, *m.* exchequer, treasury.
física, *f.* physics.
físico, *a. & n.* physical; physicist.
fisiología, *f.* physiology.
fláccido, *a.* flaccid, soft.
flaco, *a.* thin, gaunt.
flagelación, *f.* flagellation.
flagelar, *v.* flagellate, whip.
flagrancia, *f.* flagrancy.
flagrante, *a.* flagrant.
flama, *f.* flame; ardor, zeal.
flamante, *a.* flaming.
flamenco, *a.* flamingo.
flan, *m.* custard.
flanco, *m.* side; (mil.) flank.
flanquear, *v.* flank.
flaqueza, *f.* thinness; weakness.
flauta, *f.* flute.
flautín, *m.* piccolo.
flautista, *m. & f.* flutist, piper.
fleco, *m.* fringe; flounce.
flecha, *f.* arrow.
flechero, *m.* archer.
flema, *f.* phlegm.
flete, *m.* freight. —**fletar,** *v.*
flexibilidad, *f.* flexibility.
flexible, *a.* flexible, pliable.
flirtear, *v.* flirt.
flojo, *a.* limp; loose, flabby, slack.
flor, *f.* flower; compliment.
flora, *f.* flora.
floral, *a.* floral.
florecer, *v.* flower, bloom; flourish.
floreo, *m.* flourish.
florero, *m.* flower pot; vase.
floresta, *f.* forest.
florido, *a.* flowery; flowering.

florista, *m. & f.* florist.
flota, *f.* fleet.
flotante, *a.* floating.
flotar, *v.* float.
flotilla, *f.* flotilla, fleet.
fluctuación, *f.* fluctuation.
fluctuar, *v.* fluctuate.
fluente, *a.* fluent.
fluidez, *f.* fluency.
fluído, *a. & m.* fluid, liquid.
fluir, *v.* flow.
flujo, *m.* flow, flux.
flúor, *m.* fluorine.
fluorescencia, *f.* fluorescence.
fluorescente, *a.* fluorescent.
fobia, *f.* phobia.
foca, *f.* seal.
foco, *m.* focus, center.
fogata, *f.* bonfire.
fogón, *m.* hearth, fireplace.
fogosidad, *f.* vehemence, ardor.
fogoso, *a.* vehement, ardent.
folklore, *m.* folklore.
follaje, *m.* foliage.
folleto, *m.* pamphlet, booklet.
fomentar, *v.* develop, promote, further, foster.
fomento, *m.* fomentation.
fonda, *f.* eating house, inn.
fondo, *m.* bottom; back (part); background; (*pl.*) funds; finances. **a f.,** thoroughly.
fonética, *f.* phonetics.
fonético, *a.* phonetic.
fonógrafo, *m.* phonograph.
forastero -ra, 1. *a.* foreign, exotic. **2.** *n.* stranger.
forjar, *v.* forge.
forma, *f.* form, shape. —**formar,** *v.*
formación, *f.* formation.
formal, *a.* formal.
formaldehído, *m.* formaldehyde.
formalidad, *f.* formality.
formalizar, *v.* finalize; formulate.
formidable, *a.* formidable.
formidablemente, *adv.* formidably.
formón, *m.* chisel.
fórmula, *f.* formula.
formular, *v.* formulate, draw up.
formulario, *m.* form.
foro, *m.* forum.
forraje, *m.* forage, fodder.
forrar, *v.* line.
forro, *m.* lining.
fortalecer, *v.* fortify.

fortaleza, f. fort, fortress; fortitude.

fortificación, f. fortification.

fortitud, f. fortitude.

fortuitamente, adv. fortuitously.

fortuito, a. fortuitous.

fortuna, f. fortune; luck.

forúnculo, m. boil.

forzar, v. force, compel, coerce.

forzosamente, adv. compulsorily; forcibly.

forzoso, a. compulsory; necessary. **paro f.,** unemployment.

forzudo, a. powerful, vigorous.

fosa, f. grave.

fósforo, m. match; phosphorus.

fósil, m. fossil.

foso, m. ditch, trench; moat.

fotocopiadora, f. photocopier.

fotografía, f. photograph. —**fotografiar,** v.

frac, m. dress coat.

fracasar, v. fail.

fracaso, m. failure.

fracción, f. fraction.

fractura, f. fracture, break.

fragancia, f. fragrance; perfume; aroma.

fragante, a. fragrant.

frágil, a. fragile, breakable.

fragilidad, f. fragility.

fragmentario, a. fragmentary.

fragmento, m. fragment, bit.

fragor, m. noise, clamor.

fragoso, a. noisy.

fragua, f. forge. —**fraguar,** v.

fraile, m. monk.

frambuesa, f. raspberry.

francamente, adv. frankly, candidly.

francés, -esa, a. & n. French; Frenchman.

Francia, f. France.

franco, a. frank.

franela, f. flannel.

frangible, a. breakable.

franqueo, m. postage.

franqueza, f. frankness.

franquicia, f. franchise.

frasco, m. flask, bottle.

frase, f. phrase; sentence.

fraseología, f. phraseology; style.

fraternal, a. fraternal, brotherly.

fraternidad, f. fraternity, brotherhood.

fraude, m. fraud.

fraudulento, a. fraudulent.

frazada, f. blanket.

frecuencia, f. frequency.

frecuente, a. frequent.

frecuentemente, adv. frequently, often.

fregadero, m. sink.

fregadura, f. scouring, scrubbing.

fregar, v. scour, scrub, mop.

freír, v. fry.

fréjol, m. kidney bean.

frenesí, m. frenzy.

frenéticamente, adv. frantically.

frenético, a. frantic, frenzied.

freno, m. brake. —**frenar,** v.

frente, 1. f. forehead. **2.** m. front. **en f., al f.,** opposite, across. **f. a,** in front of.

fresa, f. strawberry.

fresca, f. fresh, cool air.

fresco, a. fresh; cool; crisp.

frescura, f. coolness, freshness.

fresno, m. ash tree.

fresquería, f. soda fountain.

friabilidad, f. brittleness.

friable, a. brittle.

frialdad, f. coldness.

fríamente, adv. coldly; coolly.

fricandó, m. fricandeau.

fricar, v. rub together.

fricción, f. friction.

friccionar, v. rub.

friega, f. friction.

frigidez, f. frigidity.

frígido, a. frigid.

frijol, m. bean.

frío, a. & n. cold. **tener f.,** to be cold, feel cold. **hacer f.,** to be cold (weather).

friolento, friolero, a. chilly; sensitive to cold.

friolera, f. trifle, trinket.

friso, m. frieze.

fritillas, f.pl. fritters.

frito, a. fried.

fritura, f. fritter.

frívolamente, adv. frivolously.

frivolidad, f. frivolity.

frívolo, a. frivolous.

frondoso, a. leafy.

frontera, f. frontier; border.

frotar, v. rub.

fructífero, a. fruitful.

fructificar, v. bear fruit.

fructuosamente, adv. fruitfully.

fructuoso, a. fruitful.

frugal, a. frugal, thrifty.

frugalidad, f. frugality; thrift.

frugalmente, adv. frugally, thriftily.

fruncir, v. gather, contract. **f. el entrecejo,** frown.

fruslería, f. trinket.

frustrar, v. frustrate, thwart.

fruta, f. fruit.

fruto, m. fruit; product; profit.

fucsia, f. fuchsia.

fuego, m. fire.

fuelle, m. bellows.

fuente, f. fountain; source; platter.

fuera, adv. without, outside.

fuero, m. statute.

fuerte, 1. a. strong; loud. **2.** m. fort.

fuertemente, adv. strongly; loudly.

fuerza, f. force, strength.

fuga, f. flight, escape.

fugarse, v. flee, escape.

fugaz, a. fugitive, passing.

fugitivo -va, a. & n. fugitive.

fulcro, m. fulcrum.

fulgor, m. gleam, glow. **—fulgurar,** v.

fulminante, a. explosive.

fumador, m. smoker.

fumar, v. smoke.

fumigación, f. fumigation.

fumigador, m. fumigator.

fumigar, v. fumigate.

fumoso, a. smoky.

función, f. function; performance, show.

funcionar, v. function, work, run.

funcionario, m. official, functionary.

funda, f. case, sheath, slipcover.

fundación, f. foundation.

fundador -ra, n. founder.

fundamental, a. fundamental, basic.

fundamentalmente, adv. fundamentally.

fundamento, m. base, basis, foundation.

fundar, v. found, establish.

fundición, f. foundry; melting, meltdown.

fundir, v. fuse; smelt.

fúnebre, a. dismal.

funeral, m. funeral.

funestamente, adv. sadly.

fungo, m. fungus.

furente, a. furious, enraged.

furia, f. fury.

furiosamente, adv. furiously.

furioso, a. furious.

furor, m. furor; fury.

furtivamente, adv. furtively.

furtivo, a. furtive, sly.

furúnculo, m. boil.

fusibilidad, f. fusibility.

fusible, m. fuse.

fusil, m. rifle, gun.

fusilar, v. shoot.

fusión, f. fusion; merger.

fusionar, v. unite, fuse, merge.

fútbol, m. football, soccer.

fútil, a. trivial.

futilidad, f. triviality.

futuro, a. & m. future.

futurología, f. futurology.

G

gabán, m. overcoat.

gabinete, m. closet; cabinet; study.

gacela, f. gazelle.

gaceta, f. gazette, newspaper.

gacetilla, f. personal news section of a newspaper.

gaélico, a. Gaelic.

gafas, f.pl. eyeglasses.

gaguear, v. stutter, stammer.

gaita, f. bagpipe.

gaje, m. salary; fee.

gala, f. gala, ceremony; (pl.) regalia. **tener a g.,** be proud of.

galán, m. gallant.

galano, a. stylishly dressed; elegant.

galante, a. gallant.

galantería, f. gallantry, compliment.

galápago, m. fresh-water turtle.

galardón, m. prize; reward.

gáleo, m. swordfish.

galera, f. wagon; shed.

galería, f. gallery, (theat.) balcony.

galés, n. & a. Welsh.

galgo, m. greyhound.

galillo, m. uvula.

galocha, f. galosh.

galón, m. gallon; (mil.) stripe.

galope, m. gallop. **—galopar,** v.

gallardete, m. pennant.

galleta, f. cracker.

gallina, f. hen.

gallinero, *m.* chicken coop.

gallo, *m.* rooster.

gambito, *m.* gambit.

gamuza, *f.* chamois.

gana, *f.* desire, wish, mind (to). **de buena g.,** willingly. **tener ganas de,** to feel like.

ganado, *m.* cattle.

ganador -ra, *n.* winner.

ganancia, *f.* gain, profit; (*pl.*) earnings.

ganapán, *m.* drudge.

ganar, *v.* earn; win; beat.

gancho, *m.* hook, hanger, clip, hairpin.

gandul -la, *n.* idler, tramp, hobo.

ganga, *f.* bargain.

gangrena, *f.* gangrene.

gansarón, *m.* gosling.

ganso, *m.* goose.

garabato, *m.* hook; scrawl, scribble.

garaje, *m.* garage.

garantía, *f.* guarantee; collateral, security.

garantizar, *v.* guarantee, secure, pledge.

garbanzo, *m.* chickpea.

garbo, *m.* grace.

garboso, *a.* graceful, sprightly.

gardenia, *f.* gardenia.

garfia, *f.* claw, talon.

garganta, *f.* throat.

gárgara, *f.* gargle. **—gargarizar,** *v.*

garita, *f.* sentry box.

garito, *m.* gambling house.

garlopa, *f.* carpenter's plane.

garra, *f.* claw.

garrafa, *f.* decanter, carafe.

garrideza, *f.* elegance, handsomeness.

garrido, *a.* elegant, handsome.

garrote, *m.* club, cudgel.

garrotillo, *m.* croup.

garrudo, *a.* powerful, brawny.

garza, *f.* heron.

gas, *m.* gas.

gasa, *f.* gauze.

gaseosa, *f.* carbonated water.

gaseoso, *a.* gaseous.

gasolina, *f.* gasoline.

gastar, *v.* spend; use up, wear out; waste.

gastritis, *f.* gastritis.

gastrónomo, *m.* glutton.

gastrónomo -ma, *n.* gourmet, epicure.

gatear, *v.* creep.

gatillo, *m.* trigger.

gato -ta, *n.* cat.

gaucho, *m.* Argentine cowboy.

gaveta, *f.* drawer.

gavilla, *f.* sheaf.

gaviota, *f.* sea gull.

gayo, *a.* merry, gay.

gazapera, *f.* rabbit warren.

gazapo, *m.* rabbit.

gazmoñada, *f.* prudishness.

gazmoño, *m.* prude.

gaznate, *m.* windpipe.

gelatina, *f.* gelatine.

gemelo -la, *n.* twin.

gemelos, *m.pl.* cuff links; opera glasses.

gemido, *m.* moan, groan, wail. — **gemir,** *v.*

genciana, *f.* gentian.

genealogía, *f.* genealogy, pedigree.

generación, *f.* generation.

generador, *m.* generator.

general, *a. & m.* general.

generalidad, *f.* generality.

generalización, *f.* generalization.

generalizar, *v.* generalize.

generalmente, *adv.* generally.

género, *m.* gender; kind; (*pl.*) goods, material.

generosidad, *f.* generosity.

generoso, *a.* generous.

génesis, *f.* genesis.

genial, *a.* genial; brilliant.

genio, *m.* genius; temper; disposition.

genitivo, *m.* genitive.

gente, *f.* people, folk.

gentil, *a.* gracious; graceful.

gentileza, *f.* grace, graciousness.

gentío, *m.* mob, crowd.

genuino, *a.* genuine.

geografía, *f.* geography.

geográfico, *a.* geographical.

geométrico, *a.* geometric.

geranio, *m.* geranium.

gerencia, *f.* management.

gerente, *m.* manager, director.

germen, *m.* germ.

germinar, *v.* germinate.

gerundio, *m.* gerund.

gesticulación, *f.* gesticulation.

gesticular, *v.* gesticulate, gesture.

gestión, *f.* conduct; effort.

gesto, *m.* gesture, facial expression.

gigante, *a.* & *m.* gigantic, giant.
gigantesco, *a.* gigantic, huge.
gimnasio, *m.* gymnasium.
gimnástica, *f.* gymnastics.
gimotear, *v.* whine.
ginebra, *f.* gin.
girado, *m.* (com.) drawee.
girador, *m.* (com.) drawer.
girar, *v.* revolve, turn, spin, whirl.
giratorio, *a.* rotary, revolving.
giro, *m.* whirl, turn, spin; (com.) draft. **g. postal,** money order.
gitano -na, *a.* & *n.* Gypsy.
glacial, *a.* glacial, icy.
gladiador, *m.* gladiator.
glándula, *f.* gland.
glasé, *m.* glacé.
glicerina, *f.* glycerine.
globo, *m.* globe; balloon.
gloria, *f.* glory.
glorieta, *f.* bower.
glorificación, *f.* glorification.
glorificar, *v.* glorify.
glorioso, *a.* glorious.
glosa, *f.* gloss. —**glosar,** *v.*
glosario, *m.* glossary.
glotón -ona, *a.* & *n.* gluttonous; glutton.
glutín, *m.* gluten; glue.
gobernación, *f.* government.
gobernador, *m.* governor.
gobernalle, *m.* rudder, tiller, helm.
gobernante, *m.* ruler.
gobernar, *v.* govern.
gobierno, *m.* government.
goce, *m.* enjoyment.
gola, *f.* throat.
golfo, *m.* gulf.
golondrina, *f.* swallow.
golosina, *f.* delicacy.
golpe, *m.* blow, stroke. **de g.,** suddenly.
golpear, *v.* strike, beat, pound.
gollete, *m.* upper portion of one's throat.
goma, *f.* rubber; gum; glue; eraser.
gonce, *m.* hinge.
góndola, *f.* gondola.
gordo, *a.* fat.
gordura, *f.* fatness.
gorila, *m.* gorilla.
gorja, *f.* gorge.
gorjeo, *m.* warble, chirp. —**gorjear,** *v.*
gorrión, *m.* sparrow.

gorro, *m.* cap.
gota, *f.* drop (of liquid).
gotear, *v.* drip, leak.
goteo, *m.* leak.
gotera, *f.* leak; gutter.
gótico, *a.* Gothic.
gozar, *v.* enjoy.
gozne, *m.* hinge.
gozo, *m.* enjoyment, delight, joy.
gozoso, *a.* joyful, joyous.
grabado, *m.* engraving, cut, print.
grabador, *m.* engraver.
grabar, *v.* engrave; record.
gracia, *f.* grace; wit, charm. **hacer g.,** to amuse, strike as funny. **tener g.,** to be funny, to be witty.
gracias, *f.pl.* thanks, thank you.
gracioso, *a.* witty, funny.
grada, *f.* step.
gradación, *f.* gradation.
grado, *m.* grade; rank; degree.
graduado -da, *n.* graduate.
gradual, *a.* gradual.
graduar, *v.* grade, graduate.
gráfico, *a.* graphic, vivid.
grafito, *m.* graphite.
grajo, *m.* jackdaw.
gramática, *f.* grammar.
gramo, *m.* gram.
gran, grande, *a.* big, large; great.
granada, *f.* grenade; pomegranate.
granar, *v.* seed.
grandeza, *f.* greatness.
grandiosidad, *f.* grandeur.
grandioso, *a.* grand, magnificent.
grandor, *m.* size.
granero, *m.* barn; granary.
granito, *m.* granite.
granizada, *f.* hailstorm.
granizo, *m.* hail. —**granizar,** *v.*
granja, *f.* grange; farm; farmhouse.
granjear, *v.* earn, gain; get.
granjero, *m.* farmer.
grano, *m.* grain; kernel.
granuja, *m.* waif, urchin.
grapa, *f.* clamp, clip.
grasa, *f.* grease, fat.
grasiento, *a.* greasy.
gratificación, *f.* gratification; reward; tip.
gratificar, *v.* gratify; reward; tip.
gratis, *adv.* gratis, free.
gratitud, *f.* gratitude.
grato, *a.* grateful; pleasant.
gratuito, *a.* gratuitous.

gravamen, *m.* tax; burden; obligation.
grave, *a.* grave, serious, severe.
gravedad, *f.* gravity, seriousness.
gravitación, *f.* gravitation.
gravitar, *v.* gravitate.
gravoso, *a.* burdensome.
Grecia, *f.* Greece.
greco, *a. & n.* Greek.
greda, *f.* clay.
gresca, *f.* revelry; quarrel.
griego -ga, *a. & n.* Greek.
grieta, *f.* opening; crevice, crack.
grifo, *m.* faucet.
grillo, *m.* cricket.
grima, *f.* fright.
gringo -ga, *n.* foreigner (usually North American).
gripa, gripe, *f.* grippe.
gris, *a.* gray.
grito, *m.* shout, scream, cry. —**gritar,** *v.*
grosella, *f.* currant.
grosería, *f.* grossness; coarseness.
grosero, *a.* coarse, vulgar, discourteous.
grotesco, *a.* grotesque.
grúa, *f.* crane.
gruesa, *f.* gross.
grueso, 1. *a.* bulky; stout; coarse, thick. **2.** *m.* bulk.
grulla, *f.* crane.
gruñido, *m.* growl, snarl, mutter. —**gruñir,** *v.*
grupo, *m.* group, party.
gruta, *f.* cavern.
guadaña, *f.* scythe. —**guadañar,** *v.*
guagua, *f.* (S.A.) baby; (Carib.) bus.
gualdo, *m.* yellow, golden.
guano, *m.* guano (fertilizer).
guante, *m.* glove.
guapo, *a.* handsome.
guarda, *m. or f.* guard.
guardabarros, *m.* fender.
guardacostas, *m.* revenue ship.
guardar, *v.* keep, store, put away; guard.
guardarropa, *f.* coat room.
guardarse de, *v.* beware of, avoid.
guardia, 1. *f.* guard; watch. **2.** *m.* policeman.
guardián, *m.* guardian, keeper, watchman.
guardilla, *f.* attic.
guarida, *f.* den.

guarismo, *m.* number, figure.
guarnecer, *v.* adorn.
guarnición, *f.* garrison; trimming.
guasa, *f.* joke, jest.
guayaba, *f.* guava.
gubernativo, *a.* governmental.
guerra, *f.* war.
guerrero, *m.* warrior.
guía, 1. *m. & f.* guide. **2.** *f.* guidebook, directory.
guiar, *v.* guide; steer, drive.
guija, *f.* pebble.
guillotina, *f.* guillotine.
guindar, *v.* hang.
guinga, *f.* gingham.
guiñada, *f.,* **guiño,** *m.* wink. —**guiñar,** *v.*
guión, *m.* dash, hyphen.
guirnalda, *f.* garland, wreath.
guisa, *f.* guise, manner.
guisado, *m.* stew.
guisante, *m.* pea.
guisar, *v.* cook.
guita, *f.* twine.
guitarra, *f.* guitar.
guitarrista, *n.* guitarist.
gula, *f.* gluttony.
gurú, *m.* guru.
gusano, *m.* worm, caterpillar.
gustar, *v.* please; taste.
gusto, *m.* pleasure; taste; liking.
gustoso, *a.* pleasant, tasteful.
gutural, *a.* guttural.

H

haba, *f.* bean.
habanera, *f.* Cuban dance melody.
haber, *v.* have. **h. de,** be to, be supposed to.
haberes, *m.pl.* property; worldly goods.
habichuela, *f.* bean.
hábil, *a.* skillful; capable; clever.
habilidad, *f.* ability; skill; talent.
habilidoso, *a.* able, skillful, talented.
habilitado, *m.* paymaster.
habilitar, *v.* qualify; supply, equip.
hábilmente, *adv.* ably.
habitación, *f.* dwelling; room.
habitante, *m. & f.* inhabitant.
habitar, *v.* inhabit; dwell.
hábito, *m.* habit; custom.

habitual, *a.* habitual.
habituar, *v.* accustom, habituate.
habla, *f.* speech.
hablador, *a.* talkative.
hablar, *v.* talk, speak.
haca, *f.* pony.
hacedor, *m.* maker.
hacendado, *m.* hacienda owner; farmer.
hacendoso, *a.* industrious.
hacer, *v.* do; make. **hace dos años,** etc., two years ago, etc.
hacerse, *v.* become, get to be.
hacia, *prep.* toward.
hacienda, *f.* property; estate; ranch; farm; (govt.) treasury.
hacha, *f.* ax, hatchet.
hada, *f.* fairy.
hado, *m.* fate.
halagar, *v.* flatter.
halar, *v.* haul, pull.
halcón, *m.* hawk, falcon.
haleche, *m.* anchovy.
hallado, *a.* found. **bien h.,** welcome. **mal h.,** uneasy.
hallar, *v.* find, locate.
hallarse, *v.* be located; happen to be.
hallazgo, *m.* find, thing found.
hamaca, *f.* hammock.
hambre, *f.* hunger. **tener h., estar con h.,** to be hungry.
hambrear, *v.* hunger; starve.
hambriento, *a.* starving, hungry.
haragán, *m.* idler, lazy person.
haraganear, *v.* loiter.
harapo, *m.* rag, tatter.
haraposo, *a.* ragged, shabby.
harem, *m.* harem.
harina, *f.* flour, meal.
harnero, *m.* sieve.
hartar, *v.* satiate.
harto, *a.* stuffed; fed up.
hartura, *f.* superabundance, glut.
hasta, 1. *prep.* until, till; as far as, up to. **h. luego,** good-bye, so long. **2.** *adv.* even.
hastío, *m.* distaste, loathing.
hato, *m.* herd.
hay, *v.* there is, there are. **h. que,** it is necessary to. **no h. de qué,** you're welcome, don't mention it.
haya, *f.* beech tree.
haz, *f.* bundle, sheaf; face.
hazaña, *f.* deed; exploit, feat.
hebdomadario, *a.* weekly.

hebilla, *f.* buckle.
hebra, *f.* thread, string.
hebreo -rea, *a.* & *n.* Hebrew.
hechicero -ra, *n.* wizard, witch.
hechizar, *v.* bewitch.
hechizo, *m.* spell.
hecho, *m.* fact; act; deed.
hechura, *f.* workmanship, make.
hediondez, *f.* stench.
helada, *f.* frost.
helado, *m.* ice cream.
helar, *v.* freeze.
helecho, *m.* fern.
hélice, *f.* propeller.
helio, *m.* helium.
hembra, *f.* female.
hemisferio, *m.* hemisphere.
hemoglobina, *f.* hemoglobin.
henchir, *v.* stuff.
hendedura, *f.* crevice, crack.
heno, *m.* hay.
hepática, *f.* liverwort.
heraldo, *m.* herald.
herbáceo, *a.* herbaceous.
herbívoro, *a.* herbivorous.
heredar, *v.* inherit.
heredero -ra, *n.* heir; successor.
hereditario, *a.* hereditary.
hereje, *m.* & *f.* heretic.
herejía, *f.* heresy.
herencia, *f.* inheritance; heritage.
herético, *a.* heretical.
herida, *f.* wound, injury.
herir, *v.* wound, injure.
hermafrodita, *a.* & *m.* hermaphrodite.
hermana, *f.* sister.
hermano, *m.* brother.
hermético, *a.* airtight.
hermoso, *a.* beautiful, handsome.
hermosura, *f.* beauty.
hernia, *f.* hernia, rupture.
héroe, *m.* hero.
heroico, *a.* heroic.
heroína, *f.* heroine.
heroísmo, *m.* heroism.
herradura, *f.* horseshoe.
herramienta, *f.* tool; implement.
herrería, *f.* blacksmith's shop.
herrero, *m.* blacksmith.
herrumbre, *f.* rust.
hertzio, *m.* hertz.
hervir, *v.* boil.
hesitación, *f.* hesitation.
heterogéneo, *a.* heterogeneous.
heterosexual, *a.* heterosexual.

hexágono, *m.* hexagon.
hez, *f.* dregs, sediment.
híbrido, *n. & a.* hybrid.
hidalgo -ga, *m.* noble.
hidalguía, *f.* nobility; generosity.
hidráulico, *a.* hydraulic.
hidrofobia, *f.* rabies.
hidrógeno, *m.* hydrogen.
hidropesía, *f.* dropsy.
hiedra, *f.* ivy.
hiel, *f.* gall.
hielo, *m.* ice.
hiena, *f.* hyena.
hierba, *f.* grass; herb; marijuana.
hierbabuena, *f.* mint.
hierro, *m.* iron.
hígado, *m.* liver.
higiene, *f.* hygiene.
higiénico, *a.* sanitary, hygienic.
higo, *m.* fig.
higuera, *f.* fig tree.
hija, *f.* daughter.
hijastro, *m.* stepchild.
hijo, *m.* son.
hila, *f.* line.
hilandero, *m.* spinner.
hilar, *v.* spin.
hilera, *f.* row, line, tier.
hilo, *m.* thread; string; wire; linen.
himno, *m.* hymn.
hincar, *v.* drive, thrust, sink.
hincarse, *v.* kneel down.
hinchar, *v.* swell.
hindú, *n. & a.* Hindu.
hinojo, *m.* knee.
hipnótico, *a.* hypnotic.
hipnotismo, *m.* hypnotism.
hipnotizar, *v.* hypnotize.
hipo, *m.* hiccough.
hipocresía, *f.* hypocrisy.
hipócrita, *a. & n.* hypocritical; hypocrite.
hipódromo, *m.* race track.
hipoteca, *f.* mortgage. **—hipotecar,** *v.*
hipótesis, *f.* hypothesis.
hirsuto, *a.* hairy, hirsute.
hispano, *a.* Hispanic, Spanish American.
Hispanoamérica, *f.* Spanish America.
hispanoamericano -na, *a. & n.* Spanish American.
histerectomía, *f.* hysterectomy.
histeria, *f.* hysteria.
histérico, *a.* hysterical.

historia, *f.* history; story.
historiador, *m.* historian.
histórico, *a.* historic, historical.
histrión, *m.* actor.
hocico, *m.* snout, muzzle.
hogar, *m.* hearth; home.
hoguera, *f.* bonfire, blaze.
hoja, *f.* leaf; sheet (of paper); pane; blade.
hajalata, *f.* tin.
hojalatero, *m.* tinsmith.
hojear, *v.* scan, skim through.
hola, *interj.* hello.
Holanda, *f.* Holland, Netherlands.
holandés -esa, *a. & n.* Dutch; Hollander.
holganza, *f.* leisure; diversion.
holgazán, 1. *a.* idle, lazy. **2.** *m.* idler, loiterer, tramp.
holgazanear, *v.* idle, loiter.
holografía, *f.* holography.
holograma, *m.* hologram.
hollín, *m.* soot.
hombre, *m.* man.
hombría, *f.* manliness.
hombro, *m.* shoulder.
homenaje, *m.* homage.
homeópata, *m.* homeopath.
homicidio, *m.* homicide.
homilía, *f.* homily.
homosexual, *a.* homosexual, gay.
honda, *f.* sling.
hondo, *a.* deep.
hondonada, *f.* ravine.
hondura, *f.* depth.
honestidad, *f.* modesty, unpretentiousness.
honesto, *a.* honest; pure; just.
hongo, *m.* fungus; mushroom.
honor, *m.* honor.
honorable, *a.* honorable.
honorario, 1. *a.* honorary. **2.** *m.* honorarium, fee.
honorífico, *a.* honorary.
honra, *f.* honor. **—honrar,** *v.*
honradez, *f.* honesty.
honrado, *a.* honest, honorable.
hora, *f.* hour, time (of day).
horadar, *v.* perforate.
horario, *m.* timetable, schedule.
horca, *f.* gallows; pitchfork.
horda, *f.* horde.
horizontal, *a.* horizontal.
horizonte, *m.* horizon.
hormiga, *f.* ant.
hormiguear, *v.* itch.

hormiguero, *m.* ant hill.
hornero -ra, *n.* baker.
hornillo, *m.* stove.
horno, *m.* oven; kiln.
horóscopo, *m.* horoscope.
horrendo, *a.* dreadful, horrendous.
horrible, *a.* horrible, hideous, awful.
horrido, *a.* horrid.
horror, *m.* horror.
horrorizar, *v.* horrify.
horroroso, *a.* horrible, frightful.
hortelano, *m.* horticulturist.
hospedaje, *m.* lodging.
hospedar, *v.* give or take lodgings.
hospital, *m.* hospital.
hospitalario, *a.* hospitable.
hospitalidad, *f.* hospitality.
hospitalmente, *adv.* hospitably.
hostia, *f.* host.
hostil, *a.* hostile.
hostilidad, *f.* hostility.
hotel, *m.* hotel.
hoy, *adv.* today. **h. día, h. en día,** nowadays.
hoya, *f.* dale, valley.
hoyo, *m.* pit, hole.
hoyuelo, *m.* dimple.
hoz, *f.* sickle.
hucha, *f.* chest, money box; savings.
hueco, 1. *a.* hollow, empty. **2.** *m.* hole, hollow.
huelga, *f.* strike.
huella, *f.* track, trace; footprint.
huérfano -na, *a. & n.* orphan.
huero, *a.* empty.
huerta, *f.* (vegetable) garden.
huerto, *m.* orchard.
hueso, *m.* bone; fruit pit.
huésped, *m. & f.* guest.
huesudo, *a.* bony.
huevo, *m.* egg.
huída, *f.* flight, escape.
huir, *v.* flee.
hule, *m.* oilcloth.
humanidad, *f.* humanity, mankind; humaneness.
humanista, *m.* humanist.
humanitario, *a.* humane.
humano, *a.* human; humane.
humareda, *f.* dense cloud of smoke.
humedad, *f.* humidity, moisture, dampness.

humedecer, *v.* moisten, dampen.
húmedo, *a.* humid, moist, damp.
humildad, *f.* humility, meekness.
humilde, *a.* humble, meek.
humillación, *f.* humiliation.
humillar, *v.* humiliate.
humo, *m.* smoke; (*pl.*) airs, affectation.
humor, *m.* humor, mood.
humorista, *m.* humorist.
hundimiento, *m.* collapse.
hundir, *v.* sink; collapse.
húngaro -ra, *a. & n.* Hungarian.
Hungría, *f.* Hungary.
huracán, *m.* hurricane.
huraño, *a.* shy, bashful.
hurgar, *v.* stir.
hurón, *m.* ferret.
hurraca, *f.* magpie.
hurtadillas, *f.pl.* **a h.,** on the sly.
hurtador, *m.* thief.
hurtar, *v.* steal, rob of; hide.
hurtarse, *v.* hide; withdraw.
husmear, *v.* scent, smell.
huso, *m.* spindle; bobbin.

I

ibérico, *a.* Iberian.
iberoamericano -na, *a. & n.* Latin American.
ida, *f.* departure; trip out. **i. y vuelta,** round trip.
idea, *f.* idea.
ideal, *a. & m.* ideal.
idealismo, *m.* idealism.
idealista, *m. & f.* idealist.
idear, *v.* plan, conceive.
idéntico, *a.* identical.
identidad, *f.* identity; identification.
identificar, *v.* identify.
idilio, *m.* idyll.
idioma, *m.* language.
idiota, *a. & n.* idiotic; idiot.
idotismo, *m.* idiom; idiocy.
idolatrar, *v.* idolize, adore.
idolo, *m.* idol.
idóneo, *a.* suitable, fit, apt.
iglesia, *f.* church.
ignición, *f.* ignition.
ignominia, *f.* ignominy, shame.
ignominioso, *a.* ignominious, shameful.
ignorancia, *f.* ignorance.
ignorante, *a.* ignorant.

ignorar, v. be ignorant of, not know.

ignoto, a. unknown.

igual, 1. a. equal; the same; (pl.) alike. **2.** m. equal.

igualar, v. equal; equalize; match.

igualdad, f. equality.

ijada, f. flank (of an animal).

ilegal, a. illegal.

ilegítimo, a. illegitimate.

ileso, a. unharmed.

ilícito, a. illicit, unlawful.

iluminación, f. illumination.

iluminar, v. illuminate.

ilusión, f. illusion.

ilusorio, a. illusive.

ilustración, f. illustration; learning.

ilustrador, m. illustrator.

ilustrar, v. illustrate.

ilustre, a. illustrious, honorable, distinguished.

imagen, f. image.

imaginación, f. imagination.

imaginar, v. imagine.

imaginario, a. imaginary.

imaginativo, a. imaginative.

imán, m. magnet; imam.

imbécil, a. & n. imbecile; stupid, foolish; fool.

imbuir, v. imbue, instil.

imitación, f. imitation.

imitador, m. imitator.

imitar, v. imitate.

impaciencia, f. impatience.

impaciente, a. impatient.

impar, a. unequal, uneven, odd.

imparcial, a. impartial.

impasible, a. impassive, unmoved.

impávido, adj. fearless, intrepid.

impedimento, m. impediment, obstacle.

impedir, v. impede, hinder, stop, obstruct.

impeler, v. impel; incite.

impensado, a. unexpected.

imperar, v. reign; prevail.

imperativo, a. imperative.

imperceptible, a. imperceptible.

imperdible, n. safety pin.

imperecedero, a. imperishable.

imperfecto, a. imperfect, faulty.

imperial, a. imperial.

imperialismo, m. imperialism.

impericia, f. inexperience.

imperio, m. empire.

imperioso, a. imperious, domineering.

impermeable, 1. a. waterproof. **2.** m. raincoat.

impersonal, a. impersonal.

impertinencia, f. impertinence.

ímpetu, m. impulse; impetus.

impetuoso, a. impetuous.

impiedad, f. impiety.

impío, a. impious.

implacable, a. implacable, unrelenting.

implicar, v. implicate, involve.

implorar, v. implore.

imponente, a. impressive.

imponer, v. impose.

importación, f. import, importing.

importancia, f. importance.

importador, m. importer.

importante, a. important.

importar, v. be important, matter; import.

importe, m. value, amount.

importunar, v. beg, importune.

imposibilidad, f. impossibility.

imposibilitado, a. helpless.

imposible, a. impossible.

imposición, f. imposition.

impostor, m. imposter, faker.

impotencia, f. impotence.

impotente, a. impotent.

imprecar, v. curse.

impreciso, adj. inexact.

impregnar, v. impregnate.

imprenta, f. press; printing house.

imprescindible, a. essential.

impresión, f. impression.

impresionable, a. emotional.

impresionar, v. impress.

impresor, m. printer.

imprevisión, f. oversight, thoughtlessness.

imprevisto, a. unexpected, unforeseen.

imprimir, v. print; imprint.

improbable, a. improbable.

improbo, a. dishonest.

improductivo, a. unproductive.

improperio, m. insult.

impropio, a. improper.

improvisación, f. improvisation.

improvisar, v. improvise.

improviso, a. unforeseen.

imprudencia, f. imprudence.

imprudente, *a.* imprudent, reckless.

impuesto, *m.* tax.

impulsar, *v.* prompt, impel.

impulsivo, *a.* impulsive.

impulso, *m.* impulse.

impureza, *f.* impurity.

impuro, *a.* impure.

imputación, *f.* imputation.

imputar, *v.* impute, attribute.

inaccesible, *a.* inaccessible.

inacción, *f.* inaction; inactivity.

inaceptable, *a.* unacceptable.

inactivo, *a.* inactive; sluggish.

inadecuado, *a.* inadequate.

inadvertencia, *f.* oversight.

inadvertido, *a.* inadvertent, careless; unnoticed.

inagotable, *a.* inexhaustible.

inalterado, *a.* unchanged.

inanición, *f.* starvation.

inanimado, *adj.* inanimate.

inapetencia, *f.* lack of appetite.

inaplicable, *a.* inapplicable; unfit.

inaudito, *a.* unheard of.

inauguración, *f.* inauguration.

inaugurar, *v.* inaugurate, open.

incandescente, *a.* incandescent.

incansable, *a.* tireless.

incapacidad, *f.* incapacity.

incapacitar, *v.* incapacitate.

incapaz, *a.* incapable.

incauto, *a.* unwary.

incendiar, *v.* set on fire.

incendio, *m.* fire, conflagration.

incertidumbre, *f.* uncertainty, suspense.

incesante, *a.* continual, incessant.

incidente, *m.* incident, event.

incienso, *m.* incense.

incierto, *a.* uncertain, doubtful.

incisión, *f.* incision, cut.

incitamiento, *m.* incitement, motivation.

incitar, *v.* incite, instigate.

incivil, *a.* impolite, rude.

inclemencia, *f.* inclemency.

inclemente, *a.* inclement, merciless.

inclinación, *f.* inclination, bent; slope.

inclinar, *v.* incline; influence.

inclinarse, *v.* slope; lean, bend over; bow.

incluir, *v.* include; enclose.

inclusivo, *a.* inclusive.

incluso, *prep.* including.

incógnito, *a.* unknown.

incoherente, *a.* incoherent.

incombustible, *a.* fireproof.

incomodar, *v.* disturb, bother, inconvenience.

incomodidad, *f.* inconvenience.

incómodo, *m.* uncomfortable; cumbersome; inconvenient.

incomparable, *a.* incomparable.

incompatible, *a.* incompatible.

incompetencia, *f.* incompetence.

incompetente, *a.* incompetent.

incompleto, *a.* incomplete.

incondicional, *a.* unconditional.

inconexo, *a.* incoherent; unconnected.

incongruente, *a.* not suitable.

inconsciencia, *f.* unconsciousness.

inconsciente, *a.* unconscious.

inconsecuencia, *f.* inconsistency.

inconsecuente, *a.* inconsistent.

inconsiderado, *a.* inconsiderate.

inconstancia, *f.* changeableness.

inconstante, *a.* changeable.

inconveniencia, *f.* unsuitability.

inconveniente, **1.** *a.* unsuitable. **2.** *m.* disadvantage; objection.

incorporar, *v.* incorporate, embody.

incorporarse, *v.* sit up.

incorrecto, *a.* incorrect, wrong.

incredulidad, *f.* incredulity.

incrédulo, *a.* incredulous.

increíble, *a.* incredible.

incremento, *m.* increase.

incubar, *v.* hatch.

inculto, *a.* uncultivated.

incurable, *a.* incurable.

incurrir, *v.* incur.

indagación, *f.* investigation, inquiry.

indagador, *m.* investigator.

indagar, *v.* investigate, inquire into.

indebido, *a.* undue.

indecencia, *f.* indecency.

indecente, *a.* indecent.

indeciso, *a.* undecided.

indefenso, *a.* defenseless.

indefinido, *a.* indefinite.

indeleble, *a.* indelible.

indemnizar, *v.* indemnify.

independencia, *f.* independence.

independiente, *a.* independent.

India, *f.* India.
indicación, *f.* indication.
indicar, *v.* indicate, point out.
indicativo, *a. & m.* indicative.
índice, *m.* index; forefinger.
indicio, *m.* hint, clue.
indiferencia, *f.* indifference.
indiferente, *a.* indifferent.
indígena, *a. & n.* native.
indigente, *a.* indigent, poor.
indignación, *f.* indignation.
indignado, *a.* indignant, incensed.
indignar, *v.* incense.
indigno, *a.* unworthy.
indio -dia, *a. & n.* Indian.
indirecto, *a.* indirect.
indiscreción, *f.* indiscretion.
indiscreto, *a.* indiscreet.
indiscutible, *a.* unquestionable.
indispensable, *a.* indispensable.
indisposición, *f.* indisposition, ailment; reluctance.
indistinto, *a.* indistinct, unclear.
individual, *a.* individual.
individualidad, *f.* individuality.
individuo, *a. & m.* individual.
indócil, *a.* headstrong, unruly.
índole, *f.* nature, character, disposition.
indolencia, *f.* indolence.
indolente, *a.* indolent.
indómito, *a.* untamed, wild; unruly.
inducir, *v.* induce, persuades.
indudable, *a.* certain, indubitable.
indulgencia, *f.* indulgence.
indulgente, *a.* indulgent.
indultar, *v.* free; pardon.
industria, *f.* industry.
industrial, *a.* industrial.
industrioso, *a.* industrious.
inédito, *a.* unpublished.
ineficaz, *a.* inefficient.
inepto, *a.* incompetent.
inequívoco, *a.* unmistakable.
inercia, *f.* inertia.
inerte, *a.* inert.
inesperado, *a.* unexpected.
inestable, *a.* unstable.
inevitable, *a.* inevitable.
inexacto, *a.* inexact.
inexperto, *a.* unskilled.
inexplicable, *a.* inexplicable, unexplainable.
infalible, *a.* infallible.

infame, *a.* infamous, bad.
infamia, *f.* infamy.
infancia, *f.* infancy; childhood.
infante, *m.* infant.
infantería, *f.* infantry.
infantil, *a.* infantile, childish.
infatigable, *a.* untiring.
infausto, *a.* unlucky.
infección, *f.* infection.
infeccioso, *a.* infectious.
infectar, *v.* infect.
infeliz, *a.* unhappy, miserable.
inferior, *a.* inferior; lower.
inferir, *v.* infer; inflict.
infernal, *a.* infernal.
infestar, *v.* infest.
infiel, *a.* unfaithful.
infierno, *m.* hell.
infiltrar, *v.* infiltrate.
infinidad, *f.* infinity.
infinito, *a.* infinite.
inflación, *f.* inflation.
inflamación, *f.* inflammation.
inflamar, *v.* inflame, set on fire.
inflar, *v.* inflate, pump up, puff up.
inflexible, *a.* inflexible, rigid.
inflexión, *f.* inflection.
infligir, *v.* inflict.
influencia, *f.* influence.
influenza, *f.* influenza, flu.
influir, *v.* influence, sway.
influyente, *a.* influential.
información, *f.* information.
informal, *a.* informal.
informar, *v.* inform; report.
informe, *m.* report; *(pl.)* information, data.
infortunio, *m.* misfortune.
infracción, *f.* violation.
infrascrito, *m.* signer, undersigned.
infringir, *v.* infringe, violate.
infructuoso, *a.* fruitless.
infundir, *v.* instil, inspire with.
ingeniería, *f.* engineering.
ingeniero, *m.* engineer.
ingenio, *m.* wit; talent.
ingeniosidad, *f.* ingenuity.
ingenioso, *a.* witty, ingenious.
ingenuidad, *f.* candor; naïveté.
ingenuo, *a.* ingenuous, naïve, candid.
Inglaterra, *f.* England.
ingle, *f.* groin.
inglés -esa, *a. & n.* English; Englishman.

ingratitud, f. ingratitude.
ingrato, a. ungrateful.
ingrediente, m. ingredient.
ingresar en, v. enter; join.
ingreso, m. entrance; (pl.) earnings, income.
inhábil, a. unskilled, incapable.
inhabilitar, v. disqualify.
inherente, a. inherent.
inhibir, v. inhibit.
inhumano, a. cruel, inhuman.
iniciador, m. initiator.
inicial, a. initial.
iniciar, v. initiate, begin.
iniciativa, f. initiative.
inicuo, a. wicked.
iniquidad, f. iniquity; sin.
injuria, f. insult. —**injuriar,** v.
injusticia, f. injustice.
injusto, a. unjust, unfair.
inmaculado, a. immaculate; pure.
inmediato, a. immediate.
inmensidad, f. immensity.
inmenso, a. immense.
inmersión, f. immersion.
inmigración, f. immigration.
inmigrante, a. & n. immigrant.
inmigrar, v. immigrate.
inminente, a. imminent.
inmoderado, a. immoderate.
inmodesto, a. immodest.
inmoral, a. immoral.
inmoralidad, f. immorality.
inmortal, a. immortal.
inmortalidad, f. immortality.
inmóvil, a. immobile, motionless.
inmundicia, f. dirt, filth.
inmune, a. immune.
inmunidad, f. immunity.
innato, a. innate, inborn.
innecesario, a. unnecessary, needless.
innoble, a. ignoble.
innocuo, a. innocuous.
innovación, f. innovation.
innumerable, a. innumerable, countless.
inocencia, f. innocence.
inocente, a. innocent.
inocular, v. inoculate.
inodoro, m. toilet.
inofensivo, a. inoffensive, harmless.
inolvidable, a. unforgettable.
inoportuno, a. inopportune.
inquietar, v. disturb, worry, trouble.

inquieto, a. anxious, uneasy, worried; restless.
inquietud, f. concern, anxiety, worry; restlessness.
inquilino -na, n. occupant, tenant.
inquirir, v. inquire into, investigate.
inquisición, f. inquisition, investigation.
insaciable, a. insatiable.
insalubre, a. unhealthy.
insano, a. insane.
inscribir, v. inscribe; record.
inscribirse, v. register, enroll.
inscripción, f. inscription; registration.
insecto, m. insect.
inseguro, a. unsure, uncertain; insecure, unsafe.
insensato, a. stupid, senseless.
insensible, a. unfeeling, heartless.
inseparable, a. inseparable.
inserción, f. insertion.
insertar, v. insert.
insidioso, a. insidious, crafty.
insigne, a. famous, noted.
insignia, f. insignia, badge.
insignificante, a. insignificant, negligible.
insincero, a. insincere.
insinuación, f. insinuation; hint.
insinuar, v. insinuate, suggest, hint.
insipidez, f. insipidity.
insípido, a. insipid.
insistencia, f. insistence.
insistente, a. insistent.
insistir, v. insist.
insolación, f. sunstroke.
insolencia, f. insolence.
insolente, a. insolent.
insólito, a. unusual.
insolvente, a. insolvent.
insomnio, m. insomnia.
insoportable, a. unbearable.
inspección, f. inspection.
inspeccionar, v. inspect, examine.
inspector, m. inspector.
inspiración, f. inspiration.
inspirar, v. inspire.
instalación, f. installation, fixture.
instalar, v. install, set up.
instantánea, f. snapshot.
instantáneo, a. instantaneous.

instante, a. & m. instant. **al i.,** at once.

instar, v. coax, urge.

instigar, v. instigate, urge.

instintivo, a. instinctive.

instinto, m. instinct.

institución, f. institution.

instituto, m. institute. —**instituir,** v.

institutriz, f. governess.

instrucción, f. instruction; education.

instructivo, a. instructive.

instructor, m. instructor.

instruir, v. instruct, teach.

instrumento, m. instrument.

insuficiente, a. insufficient.

insufrible, a. intolerable.

insular, a. island, insular.

insulto, m. insult. —**insultar,** v.

insuperable, a. insuperable.

insurgente, n. & a. insurgent, rebel.

insurrección, f. insurrection, revolt.

insurrecto, a. & m. insurgent.

intacto, a. intact.

integral, a. integral.

integridad, f. integrity; entirety.

íntegro, a. entire; upright.

intelecto, m. intellect.

intelectual, a. & n. intellectual.

inteligencia, f. intelligence.

inteligente, a. intelligent.

inteligible, a. intelligible.

intemperie, f. bad weather.

intención, f. intention.

intendente, m. manager.

intensidad, f. intensity.

intensificar, v. intensify.

intensivo, a. intensive.

intenso, a. intense.

intentar, v. attempt, try.

intento, m. intent.

interceptar, v. intercept.

intercesión, f. intercession.

interés, m. interest; concern; appeal.

interesante, a. interesting.

interesar, v. interest, appeal to.

interferencia, f. interference.

interino, a. temporary.

interior, 1. a. interior, inner; **2.** m. interior.

interjección, f. interjection.

intermedio, 1. a. intermediate. **2.** m. intermediary; intermission.

interminable, a. interminable, endless.

intermisión, f. intermission.

intermitente, a. intermittent.

internacional, a. international.

internarse en, v. enter into, go into.

interno, a. internal.

interpelar, v. ask questions; quiz.

interponer, v. interpose.

interpretación, f. interpretation.

interpretar, v. interpret; construe.

intérprete, m. & f. interpreter.

interrogación, f. interrogation.

interrogar, v. question, interrogate.

interrogativo, a. interrogative.

interrumpir, v. interrupt.

interrupción, f. interruption.

intersección, f. intersection.

intervalo, m. interval.

intervención, f. intervention.

intervenir, v. intervene, interfere.

intestino, m. intestine.

intimación, f. intimation, hint.

intimar, v. suggest, hint.

intimidad, f. intimacy.

intimidar, v. intimidate.

íntimo -ma, a. & n. intimate.

intolerable, a. intolerable.

intolerancia, f. intolerance, bigotry.

intolerante, a. intolerant.

intranquilo, a. uneasy.

intravenoso, a. intravenous.

intrepidez, f. daring.

intrépido, a. intrepid.

intriga, f. intrigue, plot, scheme. —**intrigar,** v.

intrincado, a. intricate, involved.

introducción, f. introduction.

introducir, v. introduce.

intruso -sa, n. intruder.

intuición, f. intuition.

inundación, f. flood. —**inundar,** v.

inútil, a. useless.

invadir, v. invade.

inválido -da, a. & n. invalid.

invariable, a. constant.

invasión, f. invasion.

invasor, m. invader.

invencible, a. invincible.

invención, f. invention.

inventar, v. invent; devise.

inventario, m. inventory.

inventivo, a. inventive.

invento, *m.* invention.
inventor, *m.* inventor.
invernáculo, *m.* greenhouse.
invernal, *a.* wintry.
inverosímil, *a.* improbable, unlikely.
inversión, *f.* inversion; (com.) investment.
inverso, *a.* inverse, reverse.
invertir, *v.* invert; reverse; (com.) invest.
investigación, *f.* investigation.
investigador, *m.* investigator.
investigar, *v.* investigate.
invierno, *m.* winter.
invisible, *a.* invisible.
invitación, *f.* invitation.
invitar, *v.* invite.
invocar, *v.* invoke.
involuntario, *a.* involuntary.
inyección, *f.* injection.
inyectar, *v.* inject.
ir, *v.* go. **irse,** go away, leave.
ira, *f.* anger, ire.
iracundo, *a.* wrathful, irate.
iris, *m.* iris. **arco i.,** rainbow.
Irlanda, *f.* Ireland.
irlandés -esa, *a. & n.* Irish; Irishman.
ironía, *f.* irony.
irónico, *a.* ironical.
irracional, *a.* irrational; insane.
irradiación, *f.* radiation.
irradiar, *v.* radiate.
irrazonable, *a.* unreasonable.
irregular, *a.* irregular.
irreligioso, *a.* irreligious.
irremediable, *a.* irremediable, hopeless.
irresistible, *a.* irresistible.
irresoluto, *a.* irresolute, wavering.
irrespectuoso, *a.* disrespectful.
irreverencia, *f.* irreverence.
irreverente, *adj.* irreverent.
irrigación, *f.* irrigation.
irrigar, *v.* irrigate.
irritación, *f.* irritation.
irritar, *v.* irritate.
irrupción, *f.* raid, attack.
isla, *f.* island.
isleño -ña, *n.* islander.
israelita, *n. & a.* Israelite.
Italia, *f.* Italy.
italiano -na, *a. & n.* Italian.
itinerario, *m.* itinerary; timetable.

izar, *v.* hoist.
izquierda, *f.* left (hand, side).
izquierdista, *n. & a.* leftist.
izquierdo, *a.* left.

J

jabalí, *m.* wild boar.
jabón, *m.* soap.
jabonar, *v.* soap.
jaca, *f.* nag.
jacinto, *m.* hyacinth.
jactancia, *f.* boast. **—jactarse,** *v.*
jactancioso, *a.* boastful.
jadear, *v.* pant, puff.
jaez, *m.* harness; kind.
jalar, *v.* haul, pull.
jalea, *f.* jelly.
jaletina, *f.* gelatin.
jamás, *adv.* never, ever.
jamón, *m.* ham.
Japón, *m.* Japan.
japonés -esa, *a. & n.* Japanese.
jaqueca, *f.* headache.
jarabe, *m.* syrup.
jaranear, *v.* jest; carouse.
jardín, *m.* garden.
jardinero -ra, *n.* gardener.
jarra, *f.* jar; pitcher.
jarro, *m.* jug, pitcher.
jaspe, *m.* jasper.
jaula, *f.* cage; coop.
jauría, *f.* pack of hounds.
jazmín, *m.* jasmine.
jefatura, *f.* headquarters.
jefe, *m.* chief, boss.
Jehová, *m.* Jehovah.
jengibre, *m.* ginger.
jerez, *m.* sherry.
jerga, *f.* slang.
jergón, *m.* straw bed.
jerigonza, *f.* jargon.
jeringa, *f.* syringe.
jeringar, *v.* inject; annoy.
jeroglífico, *m.* hieroglyph.
jesuita, *m.* Jesuit.
Jesús, *m.* Jesus.
jeta, *f.* snout.
jícara, *f.* cup.
jinete, *m.* horseman.
jingoísmo, *m.* jingoism.
jingoísta, *n. & a.* jingoist.
jira, *f.* tour, picnic, outing.
jirafa, *f.* giraffe.
jocundo, *a.* jovial.

jornada, f. journey; day's work.
jornal, m. day's wage.
jornalero, m. day laborer, workman.
joroba, f. hump.
jorobado, a. humpbacked.
joven, 1. a. young. **2.** m. & f. young person.
jovial, a. jovial, jolly.
jovilidad, f. joviality.
joya, f. jewel, gem.
joyelero, m. jewel box.
joyería, f. jewelry; jewelry store.
joyero, m. jeweler.
juanete, m. bunion.
jubilación, f. retirement; pension.
jubilar, v. retire, pension.
jubileo, m. jubilee, public festivity.
júbilo, m. glee, rejoicing.
jubiloso, a. joyful, gay.
judaico, a. Jewish.
judaísmo, m. Judaism.
judía, f. bean, string bean.
judicial, a. judicial.
judio -día, m. & n. Jewish; Jew.
juego, m. game; play; gambling; set. **j. de damas,** checkers.
juerga, f. spree.
jueves, m. Thursday.
juez, m. judge.
jugador -ra, n. player.
jugar, v. play; gamble.
juglar, m. minstrel.
jugo, m. juice.
jugoso, a. juicy.
juguete, m. toy, plaything.
juguetear, v. trifle.
juguetón, a. playful.
juicio, m. sense, wisdom, judgment.
juicioso, a. wise, judicious.
julio, m. July.
jumento, m. donkey.
junco, m. reed, rush.
junio, m. June.
junípero, m. juniper.
junquillo, m. jonquil.
junta, f. board, council; joint, coupling.
juntamente, adv. jointly.
juntar, v. join; connect; assemble.
junto, a. together. **j. a,** next to.
juntura, f. joint, juncture.
jurado, m. jury.
juramento, m. oath.

jurar, v. swear.
jurisconsulto, m. jurist.
jurisdicción, f. jurisdiction; territory.
jurisprudencia, f. jurisprudence.
justa, f. joust. **—justar,** v.
justicia, f. justice, equity.
justiciero, a. just.
justificación, f. justification.
justificadamente, adv. justifiably.
justificar, v. justify, warrant.
justo, a. right; exact; just; righteous.
juvenil, a. youthful.
juventud, f. youth.
juzgado, m. court.
juzgar, v. judge, estimate.

K, L, LL

káiser, m. kaiser.
karate, m. karate.
kepis, m. military cap.
kerosena, f. kerosene.
kilo, kilogramo, m. kilogram.
kilohertzio, m. kilohertz.
kilolitro, m. kiloliter.
kilómetro, m. kilometer.
kiosco, m. newsstand; pavilion.
la, 1. art. & pron. the; the one. **2.** pron. her, it, you; (pl.) them, you.
laberinto, m. labyrinth, maze.
labia, f. eloquence, fluency.
labio, m. lip.
labor, f. labor, work.
laborar, v. work; till.
laboratorio, m. laboratory.
laborioso, a. industrious.
labrador, m. farmer.
labranza, f. farming; farmland.
labrar, v. work, till.
labriego -ga, n. peasant.
laca, f. shellac.
lacio, a. withered; limp; straight.
lactar, v. nurse, suckle.
lácteo, a. milky.
ladear, v. tilt, tip; sway.
ladera, f. slope.
ladino, a. cunning, crafty.
lado, m. side. **al l. de,** beside. **de l.,** sideways.
ladra, f. barking. **—ladrar,** v.
ladrillo, m. brisk.
ladrón -ona, n. thief, robber.

lagarto, *m.* lizard; (Mex.) alligator.

lago, *m.* lake.

lágrima, *f.* tear.

lagrimear, *v.* weep, cry.

laguna, *f.* lagoon; gap.

laico, *a.* lay.

laja, *f.* stone slab.

lamentable, *a.* lamentable.

lamentación, *f.* lamentation.

lamentar, *v.* lament; wail; regret, be sorry.

lamento, *m.* lament, wail.

lamer, *v.* lick; lap.

lámina, *f.* print, illustration.

lámpara, *f.* lamp.

lampiño, *a.* beardless.

lana, *f.* wool.

lanar, *a.* woolen.

lance, *m.* throw; episode; quarrel.

lancha, *f.* launch; small boat.

lanchón, *m.* barge.

langosta, *f.* lobster; locust.

languidecer, *v.* languish, pine.

languidez, *f.* languidness.

lánguido, *a.* languid.

lanza, *f.* lance, spear.

lanzada, *f.* thrust, throw.

lanzar, *v.* throw, hurl; launch.

lañar, *v.* cramp; clamp.

lapicero, *m.* mechanical pencil.

lápida, *f.* stone; tombstone.

lápiz, *m.* pencil; crayon.

lapso, *m.* lapse.

lardo, *m.* lard.

largar, *v.* loosen; free.

largo, 1. *a.* long. **a lo l. de,** along. **2.** *m.* length.

largor, *m.* length.

largueza, *f.* generosity; length.

largura, *f.* length.

laringe, *f.* larynx.

larva, *f.* larva.

lascivia, *f.* lasciviousness.

lascivo, *a.* lascivious.

láser, *m.* laser.

laso, *a.* weary.

lástima, *f.* pity. **ser l.,** to be a pity, to be too bad.

lastimar, *v.* hurt, injure.

lastimoso, *a.* pitiful.

lastre, *m.* ballast. **—lastrar,** *v.*

lata, *f.* tin can; tin (plate); (coll.) annoyance, bore.

latente, *a.* latent.

lateral, *a.* lateral, side.

latigazo, *m.* lash, whipping.

látigo, *m.* whip.

latín, *m.* Latin (language).

latino, *a.* Latin.

latir, *v.* bet, pulsate.

latitud, *f.* latitude.

latón, *m.* brass.

laúd, *m.* lute.

laudable, *a.* laudable.

láudano, *m.* laudanum.

laurel, *m.* laurel.

lava, *f.* lava.

lavabo, lavamanos, *m.* washroom, lavatory.

lavandera, *f.* washerwoman, laundress.

lavandería, *f.* laundry.

lavar, *v.* wash.

lavatorio, *m.* lavatory.

laya, *f.* spade. **—layar,** *v.*

lazar, *v.* lasso.

lazareto, *m.* hospital; quarantine.

lazo, *m.* tie, knot; bow; loop.

le, *pron.* him, her, you; (*pl.*) them, you.

leal, *a.* loyal.

lealtad, *f.* loyalty, allegiance.

lebrel, *m.* greyhound.

lección, *f.* lesson.

lecito, *m.* yolk.

lector -ra, *n.* reader.

lectura, *f.* reading.

leche, *f.* milk.

lechería, *f.* dairy.

lechero, *m.* milkman.

lecho, *m.* bed, couch.

lechón, *m.* pig.

lechoso, *a.* milky.

lechuga, *f.* lettuce.

lechuza, *f.* owl.

leer, *v.* read.

legación, *f.* legation.

legado, *m.* bequest.

legal, *a.* legal, lawful.

legalizar, *v.* legalize.

legar, *v.* bequeath, leave, will.

legible, *a.* legible.

legión, *f.* legion.

legislación, *f.* legislation.

legislador, *m.* legislator.

legislar, *v.* legislate.

legislativo, *a.* legislative.

legislatura, *f.* legislature.

legítimo, *a.* legitimate.

lego, *m.* layman.

legua, *f.* league (measure).

legumbres, *f.pl.* vegetables.

lejano, *a.* distant, far-off.
lejía, *f.* lye.
lejos, *adv.* far. **a lo l.,** in the distance.
lelo, *a.* stupid, foolish.
lema, *m.* theme; slogan.
lengua, *f.* tongue; language.
lenguado, *m.* sole, flounder.
lenguaje, *m.* speech, language.
lenguaraz, *a.* talkative.
lente, *m. or f.* lens. *m.pl.* eyeglasses.
lenteja, *f.* lentil.
lentitud, *f.* slowness.
lento, *a.* slow.
leña, *f.* wood, firewood.
león, *m.* lion.
leopardo, *m.* leopard.
lerdo, *a.* dull-witted.
lesbiana, *f.* lesbian.
lesión, *f.* wound; damage.
letanía, *f.* litany.
letárgico, *a.* lethargic.
letargo, *m.* lethargy.
letra, *f.* letter (of alphabet); print; words (of a song).
letrado, 1. *a.* learned. **2.** *m.* lawyer.
letrero, *m.* sign, poster.
leva, *f.* (mil.) draft.
levadura, *f.* yeast, leavening, baking powder.
levantador, *m.* lifter; rebel, mutineer.
levantar, *v.* raise, lift.
levantarse, *v.* rise, get up; stand up.
levar, *v.* weigh (anchor).
leve, *a.* slight, light.
levita, *f.* frock coat.
léxico, *m.* lexicon, dictionary.
ley, *f.* law, statute.
leyenda, *f.* legend.
lezna, *f.* awl.
libación, *f.* libation.
libelo, *m.* libel.
libélula, *f.* dragonfly.
liberación, *f.* liberation, release.
liberal, *a.* liberal.
libertad, *f.* liberty, freedom.
libertador, *m.* liberator.
libertar, *v.* free, liberate.
libertinaje, *m.* licentiousness.
libertino, *m.* libertine.
libidine, *f.* licentiousness; lust.
libidinoso, *a.* libidinous; lustful.
libra, *f.* pound.

libranza, *f.* draft, bill of exchange.
librar, *v.* free, rid.
libre, *a.* free, unoccupied.
librería, *f.* bookstore.
librero, *m.* bookseller.
libreta, *f.* notebook; booklet.
libreto, *m.* libretto.
libro, *m.* book.
licencia, *f.* permission, license, leave; furlough.
licenciado -da, *n.* graduate.
licencioso, *a.* licentious.
lícito, *a.* lawful.
licor, *m.* liquor.
lid, *f.* fight. **—lidiar,** *v.*
líder, *m.* leader.
liebre, *f.* hare.
lienzo, *m.* linen.
liga, *f.* league, confederacy; garter.
ligadura, *f.* ligature.
ligar, *v.* tie, bind, join.
ligero, *a.* light; fast, nimble.
ligustro, *m.* privet.
lija, *f.* sandpaper.
lijar, *v.* sandpaper.
lima, *f.* file; lime.
limbo, *m.* limbo.
limitación, *f.* limitation.
límite, *m.* limit. **—limitar,** *v.*
limo, *m.* slime.
limón, *m.* lemon.
limonada, *f.* lemonade.
limonero, *m.* lemon tree.
limosna, *f.* alms.
limosnero -ra, *n.* beggar.
limpiabotas, *m.* bootblack.
limpiadientes, *m.* toothpick.
limpiar, *v.* clean, wash, wipe.
límpido, *a.* limpid, clear.
limpieza, *f.* cleanliness.
limpio, *m.* clean.
linaje, *m.* lineage, ancestry.
linaza, *f.* linseed.
lince, *a.* sharp-sighted, observing.
linchamiento, *m.* lynching.
linchar, *v.* lynch.
lindar, *v.* border, bound.
linde, *m.* boundary; landmark.
lindero, *m.* boundary.
lindo, *a.* pretty, lovely, nice.
línea, *f.* line.
lineal, *a.* lineal.
linfa, *f.* lymph.
lingüista, *m. & f.* linguist.

lingüístico, *a.* linguistic.
linimento, *m.* liniment.
lino, *m.* linen; flax.
linóleo, *m.* linoleum.
linterna, *f.* lantern; flashlight.
lío, *m.* pack, bundle; mess, scrape; hassle.
liquidación, *f.* liquidation.
liquidar, *v.* liquidate; settle up.
líquido, *a.* & *m.* liquid.
lira, *f.* lyre.
lírico, *a.* lyric.
lirio, *m.* lily.
lirismo, *m.* lyricism.
lis, *f.* lily.
lisiar, *v.* cripple, lame.
liso, *a.* smooth, even.
lisonja, *f.* flattery.
lisonjear, *v.* flatter.
lisonjero -ra, *f.* flatterer.
lista, *f.* list; stripe; menu.
listar, *v.* list; put on a list.
listo, *a.* ready; smart, clever.
listón, *m.* ribbon.
litera, *f.* litter, bunk, berth.
literal, *a.* literal.
literario, *a.* literary.
literato, *m.* literary person, writer.
literatura, *f.* literature.
litigación, *f.* litigation.
litigio, *m.* litigation; lawsuit.
litoral, *a.* coast.
litro, *m.* liter.
liturgia, *f.* liturgy.
liviano, *a.* light (in weight).
lívido, *a.* livid.
lo, *pron.* the; him, it, you; (*pl.*) them, you.
loar, *v.* praise, laud.
lobina, *f.* striped bass.
lobo, *m.* wolf.
lóbrego, *a.* murky; dismal.
local, 1. *a.* local. **2.** *m.* site.
localidad, *f.* locality; location; seat (in theater).
localizar, *v.* localize.
loción, *f.* lotion.
loco -ca, 1. *a.* crazy, insane, mad. **2.** *n.* lunatic.
locomotora, *f.* locomotive.
locuaz, *a.* loquacious.
locución, *f.* locution, expression.
locura, *f.* folly; madness, insanity.
lodo, *m.* mud.
lodoso, *a.* muddy.

lógica, *f.* logic.
lógico, *a.* logical.
lograr, *v.* achieve; succeed in.
logro, *m.* accomplishment.
lombriz, *f.* earthworm.
lomo, *m.* loin; back (of an animal).
lona, *f.* canvas.
longevidad, *f.* longevity.
longitud, *f.* longitude; length.
lonja, *f.* shop; market.
lontananza, *f.* distance.
loro, *m.* parrot.
losa, *f.* slab.
lote, *m.* lot, share.
lotería, *f.* lottery.
loza, *f.* china, crockery.
lozanía, *f.* freshness, vigor.
lozano, *a.* fresh, spirited.
lubricación, *f.* lubrication.
lubricar, *v.* lubricate.
lucero, *m.* (bright) star.
lúcido, *a.* lucid, clear.
luciente, *a.* shining, bright.
luciérnaga, *f.* firefly.
lucimiento, *m.* success; splendor.
lucir, *v.* shine, sparkle; show off.
lucrativo, *a.* lucrative, profitable.
lucha, *f.* fight, struggle; wrestling. **—luchar,** *v.*
luchador, *m.* fighter, wrestler.
luego, *adv.* right away; afterwards, next. **l. que,** as soon as. **desde l.,** of course. **hasta l.,** good-bye, so long.
lugar, *m.* place, spot; space, room.
lúgubre, *a.* gloomy; dismal.
lujo, *m.* luxury. **de l.,** de luxe.
lujoso, *a.* luxurious.
lumbre, *f.* fire; light.
luminoso, *a.* luminous.
luna, *f.* moon.
lunar, *m.* beauty mark; mole; polka dot.
lunático, *a.* & *n.* lunatic.
lunes, *m.* Monday.
luneta, *f.* (theat.) orchestra seat.
lustre, *m.* polish, shine. **—lustrar,** *v.*
lustroso, *a.* shiny.
luto, *m.* mourning.
luz, *f.* light. **dar a l.,** give birth to.
llaga, *f.* sore.
llama, *f.* flame; llama.
llamada, *f.* call; knock. **—llamar,** *v.*

llamarse, v. be called, be named.
se llama . . . etc., his name is . . . etc.

llamativo, a. gaudy, showy.

llamear, v. blaze.

llaneza, f. simplicity.

llano, 1. a. flat, level; plain. **2.** m. plain.

llanta, f. tire.

llanto, m. crying, weeping.

llanura, f. prairie, plain.

llave, f. key; wrench; faucet; (elec.) switch. **ll. inglesa,** monkey wrench.

llegada, f. arrival.

llegar, v. arrive; reach. **ll. a ser,** become, come to be.

llenar, v. fill.

lleno, a. full.

llenura, f. abundance.

llevadero, a. tolerable.

llevar, v. take, carry, bear; wear (clothes); **ll. a cabo,** carry out.

llevarse, v. take away, run away with. **ll. bien,** get along well.

llorar, v. cry, weep.

lloroso, a. sorrowful, tearful.

llover, v. rain.

llovido, m. stowaway.

llovizna, f. drizzle, sprinkle. — **llovíznar,** v.

lluvia, f. rain.

lluvioso, a. rainy.

M

maca, f. blemish, flaw.

macaco, a. ugly, horrid.

macareno, a. boasting.

macarrones, m.pl. macaroni.

macear, v. molest, push around.

maceta, f. vase; mallet.

macizo, 1. a. solid. **2.** m. bulk; flower bed.

macular, v. stain.

machacar, v. pound; crush.

machina, f. derrick.

machista, a. macho.

macho, m. male.

machucho, a. mature, wise.

madera, f. lumber; wood.

madero, m. beam, timber.

madrastra, f. stepmother.

madre, f. mother. **m. política,** mother-in-law.

madreperla, f. mother-of-pearl.

madriguera, f. burrow; lair, den.

madrina, f. godmother.

madroncillo, m. strawberry.

madrugada, f. daybreak.

madrugar, v. get up early.

madurar, v. ripen.

madurez, f. maturity.

maduro, a. ripe; mature.

maestría, f. mastery.

maestro, m. master; teacher.

mafia, f. mafia.

maganto, a. lethargic, dull.

magia, f. magic.

mágico, a. & m. magic; magician.

magistrado, m. magistrate.

magnánimo, a. magnanimous.

magnético, a. magnetic.

magnetismo, m. magnetism.

magnetófono, m. tape recorder.

magnificar, v. magnify.

magnificencia, f. magnificence.

magnífico, a. magnificent.

magnitud, f. magnitude.

magno, a. great, grand.

magnolia, f. magnolia.

mago, m. magician; wizard.

magosto, m. picnic, outing.

magro, a. meager; thin.

magullar, v. bruise.

— **mahometano, n. & a.** Mohammedan.

mahometismo, m. Mohammedanism.

maíz, m. corn.

majadero, a. & m. foolish; fool.

majar, v. mash.

majestad, f. majesty.

majestuoso, a. majestic.

mal, 1. adv. badly; wrong. **2.** m. evil, ill; illness.

mala, f. mail.

malacate, m. hoist.

malandanza, f. misfortune.

malaventura, f. misfortune.

malcomido, a. underfed; malnourished.

malcontento, a. disssatisfied.

maldad, f. badness; wickedness.

maldecir, v. curse, damn.

maldición, f. curse.

maldito, a. accursed, damned.

malecón, m. embankment.

maledicencia, f. slander.

maleficio, m. spell, charm.

malestar, m. indisposition.

maleta, f. suitcase, valise.

malévolo, a. malevolent.

maleza, f. weeds; underbrush.

malgastar, v. squander.

malhechor, m. malefactor, evildoer.

malhumorado, a. morose, ill-humored.

malicia, f. malice.

maliciar, v. suspect.

malicioso, a. malicious.

maligno, a. malignant, evil.

malo, a. bad; evil; wicked; naughty; ill.

malograr, v. miss, lose.

malparto, m. abortion, miscarriage.

malquerencia, f. hatred.

malquerer, v. dislike; bear ill will.

malsano, a. unhealthy; unwholesome.

malsín, m. malicious gossip.

malta, f. malt.

maltratar, v. mistreat.

malvado, **1.** a. wicked. **2.** m. villain.

malviz, m. redwing.

malla, f. mesh, net.

mallete, m. mallet.

mamá, f. mama, mother.

mamar, v. suckle; suck.

mamífero, m. mammal.

mampara, f. screen.

mampostería, f. masonry.

mamut, m. mammoth.

manada, f. flock, herd, drove.

manantial, m. spring (of water).

manar, v. gush, flow out.

mancebo, m. young man.

mancilla, f. stain; blemish.

manco, a. armless; one-armed.

mancha, f. stain, smear, blemish, spot. —**manchar**, v.

mandadero, m. messenger.

mandado, m. order, command.

mandamiento, m. commandment; command.

mandar, v. send; order, command.

mandatario, m. attorney; representative.

mandato, m. mandate, command.

mandíbula, f. jaw; jawbone.

mando, m. command, order; leadership.

mandón, a. domineering.

mandril, m. baboon.

manejar, v. handle, manage; drive (a car).

manejo, m. management; horsemanship.

manera, f. way, manner, means. **de m. que**, so, as a result.

manga, f. sleeve.

mangana, f. lariat, lasso.

manganeso, m. manganese.

mango, m. handle; mango (fruit).

mangosta, f. mongoose.

manguera, f. hose.

manguito, m. muff.

maní, m. peanut.

manía, f. mania, madness; hobby.

maníaco, maniático, a. & m. maniac.

manicomio, m. insane asylum.

manicura, f. manicure.

manifactura, f. manufacture.

manifestación, f. manifestation.

manifestar, v. manifest, show.

manifiesto, a. & m. manifest.

manija, f. handle; crank.

maniobra, f. maneuver. —**maniobrar**, v.

manipulación, f. manipulation.

manipular, v. manipulate.

maniquí, m. mannequin.

manivela, f. (mech.) crank.

manjar, m. food, dish.

manlieve, m. swindle.

mano, f. hand.

manojo, m. handful; bunch.

manómetro, m. gauge.

manopla, f. gauntlet.

manosear, v. handle, feel, touch.

manotada, f. slap, smack. —**manotear**, v.

mansedumbre, f. meekness, tameness.

mansión, f. mansion; abode.

manso, a. tame, gentle.

manta, f. blanket.

manteca, f. fat, lard; butter.

mantecado, m. ice cream.

mantecoso, a. buttery.

mantel, m. tablecloth.

mantener, v. maintain, keep; sustain; support.

mantenimiento, m. maintenance.

mantequera, f. butter dish; churn.

mantequilla, f. butter.

mantilla, f. mantilla; baby clothes.

mantillo, m. humus; manure.

manto, m. mantle, cloak.

manual, *a.* & *m.* manual.

manubrio, *m.* handle; crank.

manufacturar, *v.* manufacture; make.

manuscrito, *m.* manuscript.

manzana, *f.* apple; block (of street).

manzano, *m.* apple tree.

maña, *f.* skill; cunning; trick.

mañana, 1. *adv.* tomorrow. 2. *f.* morning.

mañanear, *v.* rise early in the morning.

mañero, *a.* clever; skillful; lazy.

mapa, *m.* map, chart.

mapache, *m.* raccoon.

mapurito, *m.* skunk.

máquina, *f.* machine.

maquinación, *f.* machination; plot.

maquinador, *m.* plotter, schemer.

maquinal, *a.* mechanical.

maquinar, *v.* scheme, plot.

maquinaria, *f.* machinery.

maquinista, *m.* machinist; engineer.

mar, *m. or f.* sea.

marabú, *m.* marabou.

maraña, *f.* tangle; maze; snarl; plot.

maravilla, *f.* marvel, wonder. —maravillarse, *v.*

maravilloso, *a.* marvelous, wonderful.

marbete, *m.* tag, label; check.

marca, *f.* mark, sign; brand, make.

marcar, *v.* mark; observe, note.

marcial, *a.* martial.

marco, *m.* frame.

marcha, *f.* march, progress. —marchar, *v.*

marchante, *m.* merchant; customer.

marcharse, *v.* go away, depart.

marchitable, *a.* perishable.

marchitar, *v.* fade, wilt, wither.

marchito, *a.* faded, withered.

marea, *f.* tide.

mareado, *a.* seasick.

marearse, *v.* get dizzy; be seasick.

mareo, *m.* dizziness, seasickness.

marfil, *m.* ivory.

margarita, *f.* pearl; daisy.

margen, *m. or f.* margin, edge, rim.

marido, *m.* husband.

marijuana, *f.* marijuana, pot, grass.

marimba, *f.* marimba.

marina, *f.* navy; seascape.

marinero, *m.* sailor, seaman.

marino, *a.* & *m.* marine, (of) sea; mariner, seaman.

marión, *m.* sturgeon.

mariposa, *f.* butterfly.

mariquita, *f.* ladybird.

mariscal, *m.* marshal.

marisco, *m.* shellfish; mollusk.

marítimo, *a.* maritime.

mármol, *m.* marble.

marmóreo, *a.* marble.

maroma, *f.* rope.

marqués, *m.* marquis.

marquesa, *f.* marquise.

Marte, *m.* Mars.

martes, *m.* Tuesday.

martillo, *m.* hammer. —martillar, *v.*

mártir, *m.* & *f.* martyr.

martirio, *m.* martyrdom.

martirizar, *v.* martyrize.

marzo, *m.* March.

mas, *conj.* but.

más, *v.* & *adv.* more, most; plus. no m., only.

masa, *f.* mass; dough.

masaje, *m.* massage.

mascar, *v.* chew.

máscara, *f.* mask.

mascarada, *f.* masquerade.

mascota, *f.* mascot; good-luck charm.

masculino, *a.* masculine.

mascullar, *v.* mumble.

masón, *m.* Freemason.

masticar, *v.* chew.

mástil, *m.* mast; post.

mastín, *m.* mastiff.

mastuerzo, *m.* fool, ninny.

mata, *f.* plant; bush.

matadero, *m.* slaughterhouse.

matador, *m.* matador.

matanza, *f.* killing, bloodshed, slaughter.

matar, *v.* kill, slay; slaughter.

matasanos, *m.* quack.

mate, *m.* checkmate; Paraguayan tea.

matemáticas, *f.pl.* mathematics.

matemático, *a.* mathematical.

materia, _f._ material; subject (matter).

material, _a. & m._ material.

materialismo, _m._ materialism.

materializar, _v._ materialize.

maternal, materno, _a._ maternal.

maternidad, _f._ maternity.

matiné, _f._ matinee.

matiz, _m._ hue, shade.

matizar, _v._ blend; tint.

matón, _m._ bully.

matorral, _m._ thicket.

matoso, _a._ weedy.

matraca, _f._ rattle. —**matraquear**, _v._

matrícula, _f._ registration; tuition.

matricularse, _v._ enroll, register.

matrimonio, _m._ matrimony, marriage, married couple.

matriz, _f._ womb; (mech.) die, mold.

matrona, _f._ matron.

maullar, _v._ mew.

máxima, _f._ maxim.

máxime, _a._ principally.

máximo, _a. & m._ maximum.

maya, _f._ daisy.

mayo, _m._ May.

mayonesa, _f._ mayonnaise.

mayor, **1.** _a._ larger, largest; greater, greatest; elder, eldest, senior. **m. de edad**, of age. **al por m.**, at wholesale. **2.** _m._ major.

mayoral, _m._ head shepherd; boss; foreman.

mayordomo, _m._ manager; butler, steward.

mayoría, _f._ majority, bulk.

mazmorra, _f._ dungeon.

mazorca, _f._ ear of corn.

me, _pron._ me; myself.

mecánico, _a. & m._ mechanical; mechanic.

mecanismo, _m._ mechanism.

mecanizar, _v._ mechanize.

mecanografía, _f._ typewriting.

mecanógrafo -fa, _f._ typist.

mecedor, _m._ swing.

mecedora, _f._ rocking chair.

mecer, _v._ rock; swing, sway.

mecha, _f._ wick; fuse.

mechón, _m._ lock (of hair).

medalla, _f._ medal.

médano, _m._ sand dune.

media, _f._ stocking.

mediación, _f._ mediation.

mediador, _m._ mediator.

mediados, _m.pl._ **a m. de**, about the middle of (a period of time).

medianero, _m._ mediator.

medianía, _f._ mediocrity.

mediano, _a._ medium; moderate; mediocre.

medianoche, _f._ midnight.

mediante, _prep._ by means of.

mediar, _v._ mediate.

medicamento, _m._ medicine, drug.

medicastro, _m._ quack.

medicina, _f._ medicine.

medicinar, _v._ treat (as a doctor).

médico, **1.** _a._ medical. **2.** _m._ doctor, physician.

medida, _f._ measure, step.

medidor, _m._ meter.

medio, **1.** _a._ half; mid, middle of. **2.** _m._ middle; means.

mediocre, _a._ mediocre.

mediocridad, _f._ mediocrity.

mediodía, _m._ midday, noon.

medioeval, _a._ medieval.

medir, _v._ measure, gauge.

meditación, _f._ meditation.

meditar, _v._ meditate.

mediterráneo, _a._ Mediterranean.

medrar, _v._ thrive.

medroso, _a._ fearful, cowardly.

megáfono, _m._ megaphone.

megahertzio, _m._ megahertz.

mejicano, _a. & m._ Mexican.

mejilla, _f._ cheek.

mejor, _a. & adv._ better; best. **a lo m.**, perhaps.

mejora, _f._, **mejoramiento**, _m._ improvement.

mejorar, _v._ improve, better.

mejoría, _f._ improvement; superiority.

melancolía, _f._ melancholy.

melancólico, _a._ melancholy.

melaza, _f._ molasses.

melena, _f._ mane; long or loose hair.

melindroso, _a._ fussy.

melocotón, _m._ peach.

melodía, _f._ melody.

melodioso, _a._ melodious.

melón, _m._ melon.

meloso, _a._ like honey.

mella, _f._ notch; dent. —**mellar**, _v._

mellizo -za, _n. & a._ twin.

membrana, _f._ membrane.

membrete, _m._ memorandum; letterhead.

membrillo, *m.* quince.
membrudo, *a.* strong, muscular.
memorable, *a.* memorable.
memorándum, *m.* memorandum; notebook.
memoria, *f.* memory; memoir; memorandum.
mención, *f.* mention. **—mencionar,** *v.*
mendigar, *v.* beg (for alms).
mendigo -a, *n.* beggar.
mendrugo, *m.* crumb, bit.
menear, *v.* shake, wag; stir.
menester, *m.* need, want; duty, task. **ser m.,** to be necessary.
menesteroso, *a.* needy.
mengua, *f.* decrease; lack; poverty.
menguar, *v.* abate, decrease.
menor, *a.* smaller, smallest; lesser, least; younger, youngest, junior. **m. de edad,** minor, under age. **al por m.,** at retail.
menos, *a. & adv.* less, least; minus. **a m. que,** unless. **echar de m.,** to miss.
menospreciar, *v.* cheapen; despise; slight.
mensaje, *m.* message.
mensajero -ra, *n.* messenger.
menstruar, *v.* menstruate.
mensual, *a.* monthly.
mensualidad, *f.* monthly income or allowance; monthly payment.
menta, *f.* mint, peppermint.
mentado, *a.* famous.
mental, *a.* mental.
mentalidad, *f.* mentality.
mente, *f.* mind.
mentecato, *a.* foolish, stupid.
mentir, *v.* lie, tell a lie.
mentira, *f.* lie, falsehood. **parece m.,** it seems impossible.
mentiroso, *a.* lying, untruthful.
mentol, *m.* menthol.
menú, *m.* menu.
menudeo, *a.* retail.
menudo, *a.* small, minute. **a m.,** often.
meñique, *a.* tiny.
meple, *m.* maple.
merca, *f.* purchase.
mercader, *m.* merchant.
mercaderías, *f.pl.* merchandise, commodities.
mercado, *m.* market.

mercancía, *f.* merchandise; (*pl.*) wares.
mercante, *a.* merchant.
mercantil, *a.* mercantile.
merced, *f.* mercy, grace.
mercenario -ria, *a. & m.* mercenary.
mercurio, *m.* mercury.
merecedor, *a.* worthy.
merecer, *v.* merit, deserve.
merecimiento, *m.* merit.
merendar, *v.* eat lunch.
merendero, *m.* lunchroom.
meridional, *a.* southern.
merienda, *f.* midday meal, lunch.
mérito, *m.* merit, worth.
meritorio, *a.* meritorious.
merla, *f.* blackbird.
merluza, *f.* haddock.
mermelada, *f.* marmalade.
mero, *a.* mere.
mes, *m.* month.
mesa, *f.* table.
meseta, *f.* plateau.
mesón, *m.* inn.
mesonero, *m.* innkeeper.
mestizo -za, *a. & n.* half-caste.
meta, *f.* goal, objective.
metabolismo, *m.* metabolism.
metafísica, *f.* metaphysics.
metáfora, *f.* metaphor.
metal, *m.* metal.
metálico, *a.* metallic.
metalurgia, *f.* metallurgy.
meteoro, *m.* meteor.
meteorología, *f.* meteorology.
meter, *v.* put (in).
meterse, *v.* interfere, meddle.
metódico, *a.* methodic.
método, *m.* method, approach.
metralla, *f.* shrapnel.
métrico, *a.* metric.
metro, *m.* meter (measure); subway.
metrópoli, *f.* metropolis.
mexicano -na, *a. & n.* Mexican.
mezcla, *f.* mixture; blend.
mezclar, *v.* mix; blend.
mezcolanza, *f.* mixture; hodgepodge.
mezquino, *a.* stingy; petty.
mi, *a.* my.
mí, *pron.* me; myself.
microbio, *m.* microbe, germ.
microficha, *f.* microfiche.
micrófono, *m.* microphone.
microforma, *f.* microform.

microscópico, a. microscopic.

microscopio, m. microscope.

miedo, m. fear. **tener m.,** fear, be afraid.

miedoso, a. fearful.

miel, f. honey.

miembro, m. member; limb.

mientras, conj. while. **m. tanto,** meanwhile. **m. más . . . más,** the more . . . the more.

miércoles, m. Wednesday.

miga, migaja, f. scrap, crumb.

migración, f. migration.

migratorio, a. migratory.

mil, a. & pron. thousand.

milagro, m. miracle.

milagroso, a. miraculous.

milicia, f. militia.

militante, a. militant.

militar, 1. a. military. **2.** m. military man.

militarismo, m. militarism.

milla, f. mile.

millar, m. (a) thousand.

millón, m. million.

millonario -ria, n. millionaire.

mimar, v. pamper, spoil (a child).

mimbre, f. willow; wicker.

mímico, a. mimic.

mimo, m. mime, mimic.

mina, f. mine. **—minar,** v.

mineral, a. & m. mineral.

minero, m. miner.

miniatura, f. miniature.

miniaturizar, v. miniaturize.

mínimo, a. & m. minimum.

ministerio, m. ministry; cabinet.

ministro, m. (govt.) minister, secretary.

minoría, f. minority.

minoridad, f. minority; nonage.

minucioso, a. minute; thorough.

minué, m. minuet.

minuta, f. minute; draft.

mío, a. mine.

miopía, f. myopia.

mira, f. gunsight.

mirada, f. look; gaze, glance.

miramiento, m. consideration; respect.

mirar, v. look, look at; watch. **m. a,** face.

miríada, f. myriad.

mirlo, m. blackbird.

mirón, m. bystander, observer.

mirra, f. myrrh.

mirto, m. myrtle.

misa, f. mass, church service.

misceláneo, a. miscellaneous.

miserable, a. miserable, wretched.

miseria, f. misery.

misericordia, f. mercy.

misericordioso, a. merciful.

misión, f. assignment; mission.

misionario -ria, misionero -ra, n. missionary.

mismo, 1. a. & pron. same; -self, -selves. **2.** adv. right, exactly.

misterio, m. mystery.

misterioso, a. mysterious, weird.

místico, a. & m. mystical, mystic.

mitad, f. half.

mítico, a. mythical.

mitigar, v. mitigate.

mitin, m. meeting.

mito, m. myth.

mitón, m. mitten.

mitra, f. miter (bishop's).

mixto, a. mixed.

mixtura, f. mixture.

mobiliario, m. household goods.

mocasín, m. moccasin.

mocedad, f. youthfulness.

moción, f. motion.

mocoso -sa, n. brat.

mochila, f. knapsack, backpack.

mocho, a. cropped, trimmed, shorn.

moda, f. mode, fashion, style.

modales, m.pl. manners.

modelo, m. model, pattern.

moderación, f. moderation.

moderado, a. moderate. **—moderar,** v.

modernizar, v. modernize.

moderno, a. modern.

modestia, f. modesty.

modesto, a. modest.

módico, a. reasonable, moderate.

modificación, f. modification.

modificar, v. modify.

modismo, m. (gram.) idiom.

modista, f. dressmaker; milliner.

modo, m. way, means.

modular, v. modulate.

mofarse, v. scoff, sneer.

mofletudo, a. fat-cheeked.

mohín, m. grimace.

moho, m. mold, mildew.

mohoso, a. moldy.

mojar, v. wet.

mojón, m. landmark; heap.

molde, m. mold, form.

molécula, f. molecule.

moler, v. grind, mill.

molestar, v. molest, bother, disturb, annoy, trouble.

molestia, f. bother, annoyance, trouble; hassle.

molesto, a. bothersome; annoyed; uncomfortable.

molicie, f. softness.

molinero, m. miller.

molino, m. mill.

molusco, m. mollusk.

mollera, f. top of the head.

momentáneo, a. momentary.

momento, m. moment.

mona, f. female monkey.

monarca, m. monarch.

monarquía, f. monarchy.

monarquista, n. & a. monarchist.

monasterio, m. monastery.

mondadientes, m. toothpick.

moneda, f. coin; money.

monetario, a. monetary.

monición, a. warning.

monigote, m. puppet.

monja, f. nun.

monje, m. monk.

mono -na, 1. a. (coll.) cute. **2.** m. & f. monkey.

monólogo, m. monologue.

monopatín, m. skateboard.

monopolio, m. monopoly.

monopolizar, v. monopolize.

monosílabo, m. monosyllable.

monotonía, f. monotony.

monótono, a. monotonous, dreary.

monstruo, m. monster.

monstruosidad, f. monstrosity.

monstruoso, a. monstrous.

monta, f. amount; price.

montaña, f. mountain.

montañoso, a. mountainous.

montar, v. mount, climb; amount; (mech.) assemble. **m. a caballo,** ride horseback.

montaraz, a. wild, barbaric.

monte, m. mountain, forest.

montón, m. heap, pile.

montuoso, a. mountainous.

montura, f. riding horse, mount.

monumental, a. monumental.

monumento, m. monument.

mora, f. blackberry.

morada, f. residence, dwelling.

morado, a. purple.

moral, 1. a. moral. **2.** f. morale.

moraleja, f. moral.

moralidad, f. morality, morals.

moralista, m. & f. moralist.

morar, v. dwell, live, reside.

mórbido, a. morbid.

mordaz, a. caustic; sarcastic.

mordedura, f. bite.

morder, v. bite.

moreno -na, a. & n. brown; dark-skinned; dark-haired, brunette.

morfina, f. morphine.

moribundo, a. dying.

morir, v. die.

morisco -ca, moro -ra, a. & n. Moorish; Moor.

morriña, f. sadness.

morro, m. bluff.

mortaja, f. shroud.

mortal, a. & m. mortal.

mortalidad, f. mortality.

mortero, m. mortar.

mortífero, a. fatal, mortal.

mortificar, v. mortify.

mortuario, a. funereal.

mosaico, a. & m. mosaic.

mosca, f. fly.

mosquito, m. mosquito.

mostacho, m. mustache.

mostaza, f. mustard.

mostrador, m. counter; showcase.

mostrar, v. show, display.

mote, m. nickname; alias.

motín, m. mutiny; riot.

motivo, m. motive, reason.

motocicleta, f. motorcycle.

motor, m. motor.

motorista, n. motorist.

movedizo, a. movable; shaky.

mover, v. move; stir.

movible, a. movable.

móvil, a. mobile.

movilización, f. mobilization.

movilizar, v. mobilize.

movimiento, m. movement, motion.

mozo, m. boy; servant, waiter, porter.

muaré, m. moiré.

mucoso, a. mucous.

muchacha, f. girl; maid (servant).

muchachez, m. boyhood, girlhood.

muchacho, m. boy.

muchedumbre, f. crowd, mob.

mucho, 1. *a.* much, many. **2.** *adv.* much.
muda, *f.* change.
mudanza, *f.* change; change of residence.
mudar, *v.* change, shift.
mudarse, *v.* change residence, move.
mudo -da, *a. & n.* mute.
mueble, *m.* piece of furniture; (*pl.*) furniture.
mueca, *f.* grimace.
muela, *f.* (back) tooth.
muelle, *m.* pier, wharf; (mech.) spring.
muerte, *f.* death.
muerto -ta, 1. *a.* dead. **2.** *n.* dead person.
muesca, *f.* notch; groove.
muestra, *f.* sample, specimen, sign.
mugido, *m.* lowing; mooing.
mugir, *v.* low, moo.
mugre, *f.* filth, dirt.
mugriento, *a.* dirty.
mujer, *f.* woman; wife.
mujeril, *a.* womanly, feminine.
mula, *f.* mule.
mulato, *a. & m.* mulatto.
muleta, *f.* crutch; prop.
mulo, *m.* mule.
multa, *f.* fine, penalty.
multicolor, *a.* many-colored.
multinacional, *a.* multinational.
múltiple, *a.* multiple.
multiplicación, *f.* multiplication.
multiplicar, *v.* multiply.
multiplicidad, *f.* multiplicity.
multitud, *f.* multitude, crowd.
mundanal, *a.* worldly.
mundano, *a.* worldly, mundane.
mundial, *a.* worldwide; (of the) world.
mundo, *m.* world.
munición, *f.* ammunition.
municipal, *a.* municipal.
muñeca, *f.* doll; wrist.
muñeco, *m.* doll; puppet.
mural, *a. & m.* mural.
muralla, *f.* wall.
murciélago, *m.* bat.
murga, *f.* musical band.
murmullo, *m.* murmur; rustle.
murmurar, *v.* murmur; rustle; grumble.
murta, *f.* myrtle.
musa, *f.* muse.

muscular, *a.* muscular.
músculo, *m.* muscle.
muselina, *f.* muslin.
museo, *m.* museum.
música, *f.* music.
musical, *a.* musical.
músico, *a. & m.* musical; musician.
muslo, *m.* thigh.
mustio, *a.* sad.
muta, *f.* pack of hounds.
mutabilidad, *f.* mutability.
mutación, *f.* mutation.
mutilación, *f.* mutilation.
mutilar, *v.* mutilate; mangle.
mutuo, *a.* mutual.
muy, *adv.* very.

N, Ñ

---

nabo, *m.* turnip.
nacar, *m.* mother-of-pearl.
nacarado, *a.* pearly.
nacer, *v.* be born.
naciente, *a.* rising.
nacimiento, *m.* birth.
nación, *f.* nation.
nacional, *a.* national.
nacionalidad, *f.* nationality.
nacionalismo, *m.* nationalism.
nacionalista, *n. & a.* nationalist.
nacionalización, *f.* nationalization.
nacionalizar, *v.* nationalize.
nada, 1. *pron.* nothing; anything. **de n.,** you're welcome. **2.** *adv.* at all.
nadador, *m.* swimmer.
nadar, *v.* swim.
nadie, *pron.* no one, nobody; anyone, anybody.
nafta, *f.* naphtha.
naipe, *m.* (playing) card.
naranja, *f.* orange.
naranjada, *f.* orangeade.
naranjo, *m.* orange tree.
narciso, *m.* daffodil; narcissus.
narcótico, *a. & m.* narcotic.
nardo, *m.* spikenard.
nariz, *f.* nose; (*pl.*) nostrils.
narración, *f.* account.
narrador, *m.* narrator.
narrar, *v.* narrate.
narrativo, *f.* narrative.
nata, *f.* cream.
natal, *a.* native, natal.

natalicio, *m.* birthplace.
natalidad, *f.* birth rate.
natilla, *f.* custard.
nativo, *a.* native; innate.
natural, 1. *a.* natural. **2.** *m. & f.* native. *m.* nature, disposition.
naturaleza, *f.* nature.
naturalidad, *f.* naturalness; nationality.
naturalista, *a. & m.* naturalistic; naturalist.
naturalización, *f.* naturalization.
naturalizar, *v.* naturalize, accustom.
naufragar, *v.* be shipwrecked; fail.
naufragio, *m.* shipwreck; disaster.
náufrago -ga, *a. & n.* shipwrecked (person).
náusea, *f.* nausea.
nausear, *v.* feel nauseous.
náutico, *a.* nautical.
navaja, *f.* razor; pen knife.
naval, *a.* naval.
nave, *f.* ship.
navegable, *a.* navigable.
navegación, *f.* navigation.
navegador, *m.* navigator.
navegante, *m.* navigator.
navegar, *v.* sail; navigate.
Navidad, *f.* Christmas.
navío, *m.* ship.
neblina, *f.* mist, fog.
nebuloso, *a.* misty; nebulous.
necedad, *f.* stupidity; nonsense.
necesario, *a.* necessary.
necesidad, *f.* necessity, need, want.
necesitado, *a.* needy, poor.
necesitar, *v.* need.
necio -cia, 1. *a.* stupid, silly. **2.** *n.* fool.
néctar, *m.* nectar.
nefando, *a.* nefarious.
negable, *a.* deniable.
negación, *f.* denial, negation.
negar, *v.* deny.
negarse, *v.* refuse, decline.
negativa, *f.* negative, refusal.
negativamente, *adv.* negatively.
negativo, *a.* negative.
negligencia, *f.* negligence, neglect.
negligente, *a.* negligent.
negociación, *f.* negotiation, deal.
negociador, *m.* negotiator.

negociante, *m.* businessman.
negociar, *v.* negotiate, trade.
negocio, *m.* trade; business.
negro -gra, 1. *a.* black. **2.** *m.* Black.
nene -na, *m.* baby.
neo, neón, *m.* neon.
nervio, *m.* nerve.
nervioso, *a.* nervous.
nervosamente, *adv.* nervously.
nesciencia, *f.* ignorance.
nesciente, *a.* ignorant.
neto, *a.* net.
neumático, 1. *a.* pneumatic. **2.** *m.* (pneumatic) tire.
neumonía, *f.* pneumonia.
neurótico, *a.* neurotic.
neutral, *a.* neutral.
neutralidad, *f.* neutrality.
neutro, *a.* neuter; neutral.
neutrón, *m.* neutron.
nevada, *a.* snowfall.
nevado, *a.* snow-white; snow-capped.
nevar, *v.* snow.
nevera, *f.* icebox.
nevoso, *a.* snowy.
ni, 1. *conj.* nor. **ni . . . ni,** neither . . . nor. **2.** *adv.* not even.
nicho, *m.* recess.
nido, *m.* nest.
niebla, *f.* fog; mist.
nieto -ta, *n.* grandchild.
nieve, *f.* snow.
nilón, *m.* nylon.
nimio, *adj.* stingy.
ninfa, *f.* nymph.
ningún -no -na, *a. & pron.* no, none, neither (one); any, either (one).
niñera, *f.* nursemaid.
niñez, *f.* childhood.
niño -ña 1. *a.* young; childish; childlike. **2.** *n.* child.
níquel, *m.* nickel.
niquelado, *a.* nickel-plated.
nítido, *a.* neat, clean, bright.
nitrato, *m.* nitrate.
nitro, *m.* niter.
nitrógeno, *m.* nitrogen.
nivel, *m.* level; grade. **—nivelar,** *v.*
no, 1. *adv.* not. **no más,** only. **2.** *interj.* no.
noble, *a. & n.* noble; nobleman.
nobleza, *f.* nobility; nobleness.
noción, *f.* notion, idea.

nocivo, *a.* harmful.

noctiluca, *f.* glowworm.

nocturno, *a.* nocturnal.

noche, *f.* night; evening.

Nochebuena, *f.* Christmas Eve.

nodriza, *f.* wet nurse.

nogal, *m.* walnut.

nombradía, *f.* fame.

nombramiento, *m.* appointment, nomination.

nombrar, *v.* name, appoint, nominate; mention.

nombre, *m.* name; noun.

nómina, *f.* list; payroll.

nominación, *f.* nomination.

nominal, *a.* nominal.

nominar, *v.* name.

non, *a.* uneven, odd.

nonada, *f.* trifle.

nordeste, *m.* northeast.

nórdico, *a.* Nordic.

norma, *f.* norm, standard.

normal, *a.* normal, standard.

normalidad, *f.* normality.

normalizar, *v.* normalize; standardize.

noroeste, *m.* northwest.

norte, *m.* north.

norteamericano -na, *a.* & *n.* North American.

Noruega, *f.* Norway.

noruego -ga, *a.* & *n.* Norwegian.

nos, *pron.* us; ourselves.

nosotros -as, *pron.* we, us; ourselves.

nostalgia, *f.* nostalgia, homesickness.

nostálgico, *a.* nostalgic.

nota, *f.* note; grade, mark.

notable, *a.* notable, remarkable.

notación, *f.* notation; note.

notar, *v.* note, notice.

notario, *m.* notary.

noticia, *f.* notice; piece of news; *(pl.)* news.

notificación, *f.* notification.

notificar, *v.* notify.

notorio, *a.* well-known.

novato -ta, *n.* novice.

novecientos, *a.* & *pron.* nine hundred.

novedad, *f.* novelty; piece of news.

novel, *a.* new, inexperienced.

novela, *f.* novel.

novelista, *m.* & *f.* novelist.

novena, *f.* novena.

noveno, *a.* ninth.

noventa, *a.* & *pron.* ninety.

novia, *f.* bride; sweetheart, fiancée.

noviazgo, *m.* engagement, match.

novicio -cia, *n.* novice, beginner.

noviembre, *m.* November.

novilla, *f.* heifer.

novio, *m.* bridegroom; sweetheart, fiancé.

nube, *f.* cloud.

nubile, *a.* marriageable.

nublado, *a.* cloudy.

nuclear, *a.* nuclear.

núcleo, *m.* nucleus.

nudo, *m.* knot.

nuera, *f.* daughter-in-law.

nuestro, *a.* our, ours.

nueva, *f.* news.

nueve, *a.* & *pron.* nine.

nuevo, *a.* new. **de n.,** again, anew.

nuez, *f.* nut; walnut.

nulidad, *f.* nonentity.

nulo, *a.* null, void.

numeración, *f.* numeration.

numerar, *v.* number.

numérico, *a.* numerical.

número, *m.* number; size (of shoe, etc.)

numeroso, *a.* numerous.

numismática, *f.* numismatics.

nunca, *adv.* never; ever.

nupcial, *a.* nuptial.

nupcias, *f.pl.* nuptials, wedding.

nutrición, *f.* nutrition.

nutrimiento, *m.* nourishment.

nutrir, *v.* nourish.

nutritivo, *a.* nutritious.

ñame, *m.* yam.

ñapa, *f.* something extra.

ñoñería, *f.* dotage.

ñoño, *a.* feeble-minded, senile.

O

o, *conj.* or. **o . . . o,** either . . . or.

oasis, *m.* oasis.

obedecer, *v.* obey, mind.

obediencia, *f.* obedience.

obediente, *a.* obedient.

obelisco, *m.* obelisk.

obertura, *f.* overture.

obeso, *a.* obese.

obispo, *m.* bishop.

obituario, *m.* obituary.

objeción, *f.* objection.

objetivo, *a.* & *m.* objective.
objeto, *m.* object. —**objetar,** *v.*
oblicuo, *a.* oblique.
obligación, *f.* obligation, duty.
obligar, *v.* oblige, require, compel; obligate.
obligatorio, *a.* obligatory, compulsory.
oblongo, *a.* oblong.
oboe, *m.* oboe.
obra, *f.* work. —**obrar,** *v.*
obrero -ra, *n.* worker, laborer.
obscenidad, *f.* obscenity.
obsceno, *a.* obscene.
obscurecer, *v.* obscure; darken.
obscuridad, *f.* obscurity; darkness.
obscuro, *a.* obscure; dark.
obsequiar, *v.* court; make presents to, fete.
obsequio, *m.* obsequiousness; gift; attention.
observación, *f.* observation.
observador, *m.* observer.
observancia, *f.* observance.
observar, *v.* observe, watch.
observatorio, *m.* observatory.
obsesión, *f.* obsession.
obstáculo, *m.* obstacle.
obstante, *adv.* **no o.,** however, yet, nevertheless.
obstar, *v.* hinder, obstruct.
obstetricia, *f.* obstetrics.
obstinación, *f.* obstinacy.
obstinado, *a.* obstinate, stubborn.
obstinarse, *v.* persist, insist.
obstrucción, *f.* obstruction.
obstruir, *v.* obstruct, clog, block.
obtener, *v.* obtain, get, secure.
obtuso, *a.* obtuse.
obvio, *a.* obvious.
ocasión, *f.* occasion; opportunity, chance. **de o.,** secondhand.
ocasional, *a.* occasional.
ocasionalmente, *adv.* occasionally.
ocasionar, *v.* cause, occasion.
occidental, *a.* western.
occidente, *m.* west.
océano, *m.* ocean.
ocelote, *m.* ocelot.
ocio, *m.* idleness, leisure.
ociosidad, *f.* idleness, laziness.
ocioso, *a.* idle, lazy.
ocre, *m.* ochre.
octava, *f.* octave.

octavo, *a.* eighth.
octogonal, *a.* octagonal.
octubre, *m.* October.
oculista, *m.* oculist.
ocultación, *f.* concealment.
ocultar, *v.* hide, conceal.
oculto, *a.* hidden.
ocupación, *f.* occupation.
ocupado, *a.* occupied; busy.
ocupante, *m.* occupant.
ocupar, *v.* occupy.
ocuparse de, *v.* take care of, take charge of.
ocurrencia, *f.* occurrence; witticism.
ocurrir, *v.* occur, happen.
ochenta, *a.* & *pron.* eighty.
ocho, *a.* & *pron.* eight.
ochocientos, *a.* & *pron.* eight hundred.
oda, *f.* ode.
odio, *m.* hate. —**odiar,** *v.*
odiosidad, *f.* odiousness; hatred.
odioso, *a.* obnoxious, odious.
odisea, *f.* odyssey.
oeste, *m.* west.
ofender, *v.* offend, wrong.
ofenderse, *v.* be offended, take offense.
ofensa, *f.* offense.
ofensiva, *f.* offensive.
ofensivo, *a.* offensive.
ofensor -ra, *n.* offender.
oferta, *f.* offer, proposal.
ofertorio, *m.* offertory.
oficial, *a.* & *m.* official; officer.
oficialmente, *adv.* officially.
oficiar, *v.* officiate.
oficina, *f.* office.
oficio, *m.* office; trade; church service.
oficioso, *a.* officious.
ofrecer, *v.* offer.
ofrecimiento, *m.* offer, offering.
ofrenda, *f.* offering.
oftalmía, *f.* ophthalmia.
ofuscamiento, *m.* obfuscation; bewilderment.
ofuscar, *v.* obfuscate; bewilder.
ogro, *m.* ogre.
oído, *m.* ear; hearing.
oír, *v.* hear; listen.
ojal, *m.* buttonhole.
ojalá, *interj.* expressing wish or hope. **o. que . . .** would that . . .
ojeada, *f.* glance; peep; look.

ojear, v. eye, look at, glance at, stare at.

ojeriza, f. spite; grudge.

ojiva, f. pointed arch; ogive.

ojo, m. eye. ¡Ojo! Look out!

ola, f. wave.

olaje, m. surge of waves.

oleada, f. swell.

oleo, m. oil; holy oil; extreme unction.

oleomargarina, f. oleomargarine.

oleoso, a. oily.

oler, v. smell.

olfatear, v. smell.

olfato, m. scent, smell.

oliva, f. olive.

olivar, m. olive grove.

olivo, m. olive tree.

olmo, m. elm.

olor, m. odor, smell, scent.

oloroso, a. fragrant, scented.

olvidadizo, a. forgetful.

olvidar, v. forget.

olvido, m. omission; forgetfulness.

olla, f. pot, kettle. **o. podrida,** stew.

ombligo, m. navel.

ominar, v. foretell.

ominoso, a. ominous.

omisión, f. omission.

omitir, v. omit, leave out.

ómnibus, m. bus.

omnipotencia, f. omnipotence.

omnipotente, a. almighty.

omnipresencia, f. omnipresence.

omnisciencia, f. omniscience.

omnívoro, a. omnivorous.

once, a. & pron. eleven.

onda, f. wave, ripple.

ondear, v. ripple.

ondulación, f. wave, undulation.

ondular, v. undulate, ripple.

onza, f. ounce.

opaco, a. opaque.

ópalo, m. opal.

opción, f. option.

ópera, f. opera.

operación, f. operation.

operar, v. operate; operate on.

operario -ria, n. operator; (skilled) worker.

operarse, v. have an operation.

operativo, a. operative.

opereta, f. operetta.

opiato, m. opiate.

opinar, v. opine.

opinión, f. opinion, view.

opio, m. opium.

oponer, v. oppose.

oporto, m. port (wine).

oportunidad, f. opportunity.

oportunismo, m. opportunism.

oportunista, n. & a. opportunist.

oportuno, a. opportune, expedient.

oposición, f. opposition.

opresión, f. oppression.

opresivo, a. oppressive.

oprimir, v. oppress.

oprobio, m. infamy.

optar, v. select, choose.

óptica, f. optics.

óptico, a. optic.

optimismo, m. optimism.

optimista, a. & n. optimistic; optimist.

óptimo, a. best.

opuesto, a. opposite; opposed.

opugnar, v. attack.

opulencia, f. opulence, wealth.

opulento, a. opulent, wealthy.

oración, f. sentence; prayer; oration.

oráculo, m. oracle.

orador, m. orator, speaker.

oral, a. oral.

orangután, m. orangutan.

orar, v. pray.

oratoria, f. oratory.

oratorio, a. oratorical.

orbe, m. orb; globe.

órbita, f. orbit.

orden, m. or f. order.

ordenador, m. computer; regulator.

ordenanza, f. ordinance.

ordenar, v. order; put in order; ordain.

ordeñar, v. milk.

ordinal, n. & a. ordinal.

ordinario, a. ordinary; common, usual.

oreja, f. ear.

orejera, f. earmuff.

orfanato, m. orphanage.

organdí, m. organdy.

orgánico, a. organic.

organismo, m. organism.

organista, m. & f. organist.

organización, f. organization.

organizar, v. organize.

órgano, m. organ.

orgía, f. orgy, revel.

orgullo, *m.* pride.
orgulloso, *a.* proud.
orientación, *f.* orientation.
oriental, *a.* Oriental; eastern.
orientar, *v.* orient.
oriente, *m.* orient, east.
orificación, *f.* gold filling (for tooth).
origen, *m.* origin; parentage, descent.
original, *a.* original.
originalidad, *f.* originality.
originalmente, *adv.* originally.
originar, *v.* originate.
orilla, *f.* shore; bank; edge.
orín, *m.* rust.
orina, *f.* urine.
orinar, *v.* urinate.
orines, *n.pl.* urine.
oriol, *m.* oriole.
orla, *f.* border; edging.
ornado, *a.* ornate.
ornamentación, *f.* ornamentation.
ornamento, *m.* ornament. —**ornamentar**, *v.*
ornar, *v.* ornament, adorn.
oro, *m.* gold.
orquesta, *f.* orchestra.
ortiga, *f.* nettle.
ortodoxo, *a.* orthodox.
ortografía, *f.* orthography, spelling.
ortóptero, *a.* orthopterous.
oruga, *f.* caterpillar.
orzuelo, *m.* sty.
os, *pron.* you (*pl.*); yourselves.
osadía, *f.* daring.
osar, *v.* dare.
oscilación, *f.* oscillation.
oscilar, *v.* oscillate, rock.
ósculo, *m.* kiss.
oscurecer, oscuridad, oscuro = **obscur-**.
oso, osa, *n.* bear.
ostentación, *f.* ostentation, showiness.
ostentar, *v.* show off.
ostentoso, *a.* ostentatious, flashy.
ostra, *f.* oyster.
ostracismo, *m.* ostracism.
otalgia, *f.* earache.
otero, *m.* hill, knoll.
otoño, *m.* autumn, fall.
otorgar, *v.* grant, award.
otro, *a. & pron.* other, another. **o.**

vez, again. **el uno al o.**, one another, each other.
ovación, *f.* ovation.
oval, ovalado, *a.* oval.
óvalo, *m.* oval.
ovario, *m.* ovary.
oveja, *f.* sheep.
ovejero, *m.* shepherd.
ovillo, *m.* ball of yarn.
oxidación, *f.* oxidation.
oxidar, *v.* oxidize; rust.
óxido, *m.* oxide.
oxígeno, *m.* oxygen.
oyente, *m.* hearer; (*pl.*) audience.
ozono, *m.* ozone.

P

pabellón, *m.* pavilion.
pabilo, *m.* wick.
paciencia, *f.* patience.
paciente, *a. & n.* patient.
pacificar, *v.* pacify.
pacífico, *a.* pacific.
pacifismo, *m.* pacifism.
pacifista, *n. & a.* pacifist.
pacto, *m.* pact, treaty.
padecer, *v.* suffer.
padrastro, *m.* stepfather.
padre, *m.* father; priest; (*pl.*) parents.
padrenuestro, *m.* paternoster.
padrino, *m.* godfather; sponsor.
paella, *f.* dish of rice with meat or chicken.
paga, *f.* pay, wages.
pagadero, *a.* payable.
pagador, *m.* payer.
paganismo, *m.* paganism.
pagano -na, *a. & n.* heathen, pagan.
pagar, *v.* pay, pay for.
página, *f.* page.
pago, *m.* pay, payment.
país, *m.* country, nation.
paisaje, *m.* landscape, scenery, countryside.
paisano -na, *n.* countryman; compatriot; civilian.
paja, *f.* straw.
pajar, *m.* barn.
pájaro, *m.* bird.
paje, *m.* page (person).
pala, *f.* shovel, spade.
palabra, *f.* word.
palabrero, *a.* talkative.

palabrista, *m.* talkative person.
palacio, *m.* palace.
paladar, *m.* palate.
paladear, *v.* taste; relish.
palanca, *f.* lever.
palangana, *f.* washbasin.
palco, *m.* theater box.
palenque, *m.* palisade.
palidecer, *v.* turn pale.
palidez, *f.* paleness.
pálido, *a.* pale.
paliza, *f.* beating.
palizada, *f.* palisade.
palma, palmera, *f.* palm (tree).
palmada, *f.* slap, clap.
palmear, *v.* applaud.
palo, *m.* pole, stick; suit (in cards); (naut.) mast.
paloma, *f.* dove, pigeon.
palpar, *v.* touch, feel.
palpitación, *f.* palpitation.
palpitar, *v.* palpitate.
paludismo, *m.* malaria.
palleta, *f.* mat, pallet.
pampa, *f.* (South America) prairie, plain.
pan, *m.* bread; loaf.
pana, *f.* corduroy.
pánacea, *f.* panacea.
panadería, *f.* bakery.
panadero -ra, *n.* baker.
panameño -ña, *a.* & *n.* Panamanian, of Panama.
panamericano, *a.* Pan-American.
páncreas, *m.* pancreas.
pandeo, *m.* bulge.
pandilla, *f.* band, gang.
panecillo, *m.* roll, muffin.
panegírico, *m.* panegyric.
pánico, *m.* panic.
panocha, *f.* ear of corn.
panorámico, *a.* panoramic.
pantalones, *m.pl.* trousers, pants.
pantalla, *f.* (movie) screen; lamp shade.
pantano, *m.* bog, marsh, swamp.
pantanoso, *a.* swampy, marshy.
pantera, *f.* panther.
pantomima, *f.* pantomime.
panza, *f.* belly, paunch.
pañal, *m.* diaper.
paño, *m.* piece of cloth.
pañuelo, *m.* handkerchief.
Papa, *m.* Pope.
papa, *f.* potato.
papá, *m.* papa, father.
papado, *m.* papacy.

papagayo, *m.* parrot.
papal, *a.* papal.
papel, *m.* paper; role, part.
papelera, *f.* file or folder for papers.
papelería, *f.* stationery store.
papera, *f.* mumps.
paquete, *m.* package.
par, 1. *a.* even, equal. **2.** *m.* pair; equal, peer. **abierto de p. en p.,** wide open.
para, *prep.* for; in order to. **p. que,** in order that. **estar p.,** to be about to.
parabién, *m.* greeting; congratulation.
parabrisa, *m.* windshield.
paracaídas, *m.* parachute.
parachoques, *m.* (auto.) bumper.
parada, *f.* stop, halt; parade.
paradero, *m.* whereabouts; stopping place.
paradigma, *m.* paradigm.
paradoja, *f.* paradox.
parafina, *f.* paraffin.
parafrasear, *v.* paraphrase.
paraguas, *m.* umbrella.
paraguayano -na, *n.* & *a.* Paraguayan.
paraíso, *m.* paradise.
paralelo, *a.* & *m.* parallel.
parálisis, *f.* paralysis.
paralizar, *v.* paralyze.
paramédico, *m.* paramedic.
parámetro, *m.* parameter.
parapeto, *m.* parapet.
parar, *v.* stop, stem, ward off; stay.
pararse, *v.* stop; stand up.
parasismo, *m.* paroxysm.
parasítico, *a.* parasitic.
parásito, *m.* parasite.
parcela, *f.* plot of ground.
parcial, *a.* partial.
parcialidad, *f.* partiality; bias.
parcialmente, *adv.* partially.
pardo, *a.* brown.
parear, *v.* pair, match, mate.
parecer, 1. *m.* opinion. **2.** *v.* seem, appear, look.
parecerse, *v.* look alike. **p. a,** look like.
parecido, *a.* similar.
pared, *f.* wall.
pareja, *f.* pair, couple; (dancing) partner.
parentela, *f.* kinfolk.

parentesco, *m.* parentage, lineage; kin.

paréntesis, *m.* parenthesis.

paria, *m.* outcast.

paridad, *f.* parity.

pariente, *n. & f.* relative.

parir, *v.* give birth to young.

parisiense, *n. & a.* Parisian.

parlamentario, *a.* parliamentary.

parlamento, *m.* parliament.

paro, *m.* stoppage; strike. **p. forzoso,** unemployment.

parodia, *f.* parody.

parodista, *m.* parodist.

paroxismo, *m.* paroxysm.

párpado, *m.* eyelid.

parque, *m.* park.

parra, *f.* grapevine.

párrafo, *m.* paragraph.

parranda, *f.* spree.

parrandear, *v.* carouse.

parrilla, *f.* grill.

párroco, *m.* parish priest.

parroquia, *f.* parish.

parroquial, *a.* parochial.

parsimonia, *f.* economy, thrift.

parsimonioso, *a.* economical, thrifty.

parte, *f.* part. **de p. de,** on behalf of. **alguna p.,** somewhere. **por otra p.,** on the other hand. **dar p. a,** to notify.

partera, *f.* midwife.

partición, *f.* distribution.

participación, *f.* participation.

participante, *m. & f.* participant.

participar, *v.* participate; announce.

participio, *m.* participle.

partícula, *f.* particle.

particular, 1. *a.* particular; private. **2.** *m.* particular; detail; individual.

particularmente, *adv.* particularly.

partida, *f.* departure; (mil.) party; (sport) game.

partidario -ria, *n.* partisan.

partido, *m.* side, party, faction; game, match.

partir, *v.* leave, depart; part, cleave, split.

parto, *m.* delivery, childbirth.

pasa, *f.* raisin.

pasado, 1. *a.* past; last. **2.** *m.* past.

pasaje, *m.* passage, fare.

pasajero -ra, 1. *a.* passing, transient. **2.** *n.* passenger.

pasamano, *m.* banister.

pasaporte, *m.* passport.

pasar, *v.* pass; happen; spend (time). **p. por alto,** overlook. **p. lista,** call the roll. **p. sin,** do without.

pasatiempo, *m.* pastime, hobby.

pascua, *f.* religious holiday; (*pl.*) Christmas (season). **P. Florida,** Easter.

paseo, *m.* walk, stroll; drive. —**pasear,** *v.*

pasillo, *m.* aisle; hallway.

pasión, *f.* passion.

pasivo, *a.* passive.

pasmar, *v.* astonish, astound, stun.

pasmo, *m.* spasm; wonder.

paso, 1. *a.* dried (fruit). **2.** *m.* pace, step; (mountain) pass.

pasta, *f.* paste; batter; plastic.

pastar, *v.* graze.

pastel, *m.* pastry; pie.

pastelería, *f.* pastry; pastry shop.

pasteurización, *f.* pasteurization.

pasteurizar, *v.* pasteurize.

pastilla, *f.* tablet, lozenge, drop.

pasto, *m.* pasture; grass.

pastor, *m.* pastor, shepherd.

pastorear, *v.* pasture, tend (a flock).

pastura, *f.* pasture.

pata, *f.* foot of (animal).

patada, *f.* kick.

patán, *m.* boor.

patanada, *f.* rudeness.

patata, *f.* potato.

patear, *v.* stamp, tramp, kick.

patente, *a. & m.* patent. —**patentar,** *v.*

paternal, paterno, *a.* paternal.

paternidad, *f.* paternity, fatherhood.

patético, *a.* pathetic.

patíbulo, *m.* scaffold, gallows.

patín, *m.* skate. —**patinar,** *v.*

patio, *m.* yard, court, patio.

pato, *m.* duck.

patria, *f.* native land.

patriarca, *m.* patriarch.

patrimonio, *m.* inheritance.

patriota, *m. & f.* patriot.

patriótico, *a.* patriotic.

patriotismo, *m.* patriotism.

patrocinar, *v.* patronize, sponsor.

patrón, *m.* patron; boss; (dress) pattern.

patrulla, *f.* patrol. **—patrullar,** *v.*

pausa, *f.* pause. **—pausar,** *v.*

pavesa, *f.* embers.

pavimentar, *v.* pave.

pavimento, *m.* pavement.

pavo, *m.* turkey. **p. real,** peacock.

payaso, *m.* clown.

paz, *f.* peace.

peatón -na, *m.* pedestrian.

peca, *f.* freckle.

pecado, *m.* sin. **—pecar,** *v.*

pecador -ra, *a. & n.* sinful; sinner.

pecera, *f.* aquarium, fishbowl.

peculiar, *a.* peculiar.

peculiaridad, *f.* peculiarity.

pechera, *f.* shirt front.

pecho, *m.* chest; breast; bosom.

pedagogía, *f.* pedagogy.

pedagogo, *m.* pedagogue, teacher.

pedal, *m.* pedal.

pedantesco, *a.* pedantic.

pedazo, *m.* piece.

pedernal, *m.* flint.

pedestal, *m.* pedestal.

pediatría, *f.* pediatrics.

pedicuro, *m.* chiropodist.

pedir, *v.* ask, ask for; request; apply for; order.

pedregoso, *a.* rocky.

pegajoso, *a.* sticky.

pegar, *v.* beat, strike; adhere, fasten, stick.

peinado, *m.* coiffure, hairdo.

peine, *m.* comb. **—peinar,** *v.*

peineta, *f.* (ornamental) comb.

pelagra, *f.* pellagra.

pelar, *v.* skin, pare, peel.

pelea, *f.* fight, row. **—pelearse,** *v.*

pelícano, *m.* pelican.

película, *f.* movie, motion picture, film.

peligrar, *v.* be in danger.

peligro, *m.* peril, danger.

peligroso, *a.* perilous, dangerous.

pelo, *m.* hair.

pelota, *f.* ball.

peltre, *m.* pewter.

peluca, *f.* wig.

peludo, *a.* hairy.

peluquería, *f.* hairdresser's shop, beauty parlor.

peluquero, *m.* hairdresser.

pellejo, *m.* skin, peel (of fruit).

pellizco, *m.* pinch. **—pellizcar,** *v.*

pena, *f.* pain, grief, trouble, woe; penalty. **valer la p.,** to be worthwhile.

penacho, *m.* plume.

penalidad, *f.* trouble; penalty.

pender, *v.* hang, dangle; be pending.

pendiente, 1. *a.* hanging; pending. **2.** *m.* incline, slope; earring, pendant.

pendón, *m.* pennant, flag.

penetración, *f.* penetration.

penetrar, *v.* penetrate, pierce.

penicilina, *f.* penicillin.

península, *f.* peninsula.

penitencia, *f.* penitence, penance.

penitenciaría, *f.* penitentiary.

penoso, *a.* painful, troublesome, grievous.

pensador -ra, *n.* thinker.

pensamiento, *m.* thought.

pensar, *v.* think; intend, plan.

pensativo, *a.* pensive, thoughtful.

pensión, *f.* pension; boardinghouse.

pensionista, *m. & f.* boarder.

pentagonal, *a.* pentagonal.

penuria, *f.* penury, poverty.

peña, *f.* rock.

peñascoso, *a.* rocky.

peón, *m.* unskilled laborer; infantryman.

peonada, *f.* group of laborers.

peonía, *f.* peony.

peor, *a.* worse, worst.

pepino, *m.* cucumber.

pepita, *f.* seed (in fruit).

pequeñez, *f.* smallness; trifle.

pequeño -ña, 1. *a.* small, little, short, slight. **2.** *n.* child.

pera, *f.* pear.

peral, *m.* pear tree.

perca, *f.* perch (fish).

percal, *m.* calico, percale.

percentaje, *m.* percentage.

percepción, *f.* perception.

perceptivo, *a.* perceptive.

percibir, *v.* perceive, sense; collect.

percha, *f.* perch; clothes hanger, rack.

perder, *v.* lose; miss; waste. **echar a p.,** spoil.

perdición, *f.* perdition, downfall.

pérdida, *f.* loss.

perdiz, *f.* partridge.

perdón, *m.* pardon, forgiveness.

perdonar, v. forgive, pardon; spare.

perdurable, a. enduring, everlasting.

perdurar, v. endure, last.

perecedero, a. perishable.

perecer, v. perish.

peregrinación, f. peregrination; pilgrimage.

peregrino -na, n. pilgrim.

perejil, m. parsley.

perenne, a. perennial.

pereza, f. laziness.

perezoso, a. lazy, sluggish.

perfección, f. perfection.

perfeccionar, v. perfect.

perfectamente, adv. perfectly.

perfecto, a. perfect.

perfidia, f. falseness, perfidy.

pérfido, a. perfidious.

perfil, m. profile.

perforación, f. perforation.

perforar, v. pierce, perforate.

perfume, m. perfume, scent. — **perfumar,** v.

pergamino, m. parchment.

pericia, f. skill, expertness.

perico, m. parakeet.

perímetro, m. perimeter.

periódico, 1. a. periodic. 2. m. newspaper.

periodista, m. journalist.

período, m. period.

periscopio, m. periscope.

perito -ta, a. & n. experienced; expert, connoisseur.

perjudicar, v. damage, hurt; impair.

perjudicial, a. harmful, injurious.

perjuicio, m. injury, damage.

perjurar, v. commit perjury.

perjurio, m. perjury.

perla, f. pearl.

permanecer, v. remain, stay.

permanencia, f. permanence; stay.

permanente, a. permanent.

permiso, m. permission; permit; furlough.

permitir, v. permit, enable, let, allow.

permuta, f. exchange; barter.

pernicioso, a. pernicious.

perno, m. bolt.

pero, conj. but.

peróxido, m. peroxide.

perpendicular, m. & a. perpendicular.

perpetración, f. perpetration.

perpetrar, v. perpetrate.

perpetuar, v. perpetuate.

perpetuidad, f. perpetuity.

perpetuo, a. perpetual.

perplejo, a. perplexed, puzzled.

perro -rra, n. dog.

persecución, f. persecution.

perseguir, v. pursue; persecute.

perseverancia, f. perseverance.

perseverar, v. persevere.

persiana, f. shutter, Venetian blind.

persistente, a. persistent.

persistir, v. persist.

persona, f. person.

personaje, m. personage; (theat.) character.

personal, 1. a. personal. 2. m. personnel, staff.

personalidad, f. personality.

personalmente, adv. personally.

perspectiva, f. perspective; prospect.

perspicaz, a. perspicacious, acute.

persuadir, v. persuade.

persuasión, f. persuasion.

persuasivo, a. persuasive.

pertenecer, v. pertain, belong.

pertinencia, f. pertinence.

pertinente, a. pertinent; relevant.

perturbar, v. perturb, disturb.

peruano -na, a. & n. Peruvian.

perversidad, f. perversity.

perverso, a. perverse.

pesadez, f. dullness, importunity.

pesadilla, f. nightmare.

pesado, a. heavy; dull, dreary, boring.

pésame, m. condolence.

pesar, 1. m. sorrow; regret. **a p. de,** in spite of. 2. v. weigh.

pesca, f. fishing; catch (of fish).

pescado, m. fish. — **pescar,** v.

pescador, m. fisherman.

pesebre, m. stall, manger, crib.

peseta, f. monetary unit of Spain.

pesimismo, m. pessimism.

pesimista, a. & n. pessimistic; pessimist.

peso, m. weight; load; peso (monetary unit).

pesquera, f. fishery.

pesquisa, f. investigation.

pestaña, *f.* eyelash.
pestañeo, *m.* wink, blink. **—pestañear,** *v.*
peste, *f.* plague.
pestilencia, *f.* pestilence.
pétalo, *m.* petal.
petición, *f.* petition.
petirrojo, *m.* robin.
petrel, *m.* petrel.
pétreo, *a.* rocky.
petrificar, *v.* petrify.
petróleo, *m.* petroleum.
petunia, *f.* petunia.
pez, *m.* fish (in the water). *f.* pitch, tar.
pezuña, *f.* hoof.
piadoso, *a.* pious.
pianista, *m. & f.* pianist.
piano, *m.* piano.
picadura, *f.* sting, bite, prick.
picamaderos, *m.* woodpecker.
picante, *a.* hot, spicy.
picaporte, *m.* latch.
picar, *v.* sting, bite, prick; itch; chop up, grind up.
pícaro -ra, 1. *a.* knavish, mischievous. **2.** *n.* rogue, rascal.
picarse, *v.* be offended, piqued.
picazón, *f.* itch.
pícea, *f.* spruce.
pico, *m.* peak; pick; beak; spout; small amount.
picotazo, *m.* peck. **—picotear,** *v.*
pictórico, *a.* pictorial.
pichón, *m.* pigeon, squab.
pie, *m.* foot. **al p. de la letra,** literally; thoroughly.
piedad, *f.* piety; pity, mercy.
piedra, *f.* stone.
piel, *f.* skin, hide; fur.
pierna, *f.* leg.
pieza, *f.* piece; room; (theat.) play.
pijamas, *m. or f.pl.* pajamas.
pila, *f.* pile, stack; battery; sink.
pilar, *m.* pillar, column.
píldora, *f.* pill.
piloto, *m.* pilot.
pillo, *m.* thief; rascal.
pimienta, *f.* pepper (spice).
pimiento, *m.* pepper (vegetable).
pináculo, *m.* pinnacle.
pincel, *m.* (artist's) brush.
pinchazo, *m.* puncture. **—pinchar,** *v.*
pingajo, *m.* rag, tatter.
pino, *m.* pine.

pinta, *f.* pint.
pintar, *v.* paint; portray, depict.
pintor -ra, *n.* painter.
pintoresco, *a.* picturesque.
pintura, *f.* paint; painting.
pinzas, *f.pl.* pincers, tweezers; claws.
piña, *f.* pineapple.
pío, *a.* pious; merciful.
piojo, *m.* louse.
pionero -ra, *n.* pioneer.
pipa, *f.* tobacco pipe.
pique, *m.* resentment, pique. **echar a p.,** sink (ship).
pira, *f.* pyre.
pirámide, *f.* pyramid.
pirata, *m.* pirate. **p. de aviones,** hijacker.
pisada, *f.* tread, step. **—pisar,** *v.*
piscina, *f.* fishpond; swimming pool.
piso, *m.* floor.
pista, *f.* trace, clue, track; racetrack.
pistola, *f.* pistol.
pistón, *m.* piston.
pitillo, *m.* cigarette.
pito, *m.* whistle. **—pitar,** *v.*
pizarra, *f.* slate; blackboard.
pizca, *f.* bit, speck; pinch.
pizza, *f.* pizza.
placentero, *a.* pleasant.
placer, 1. *m.* pleasure. **2.** *v.* please.
plácido, *a.* placid.
plaga, *f.* plague, scourge.
plagio, *m.* plagiarism; (S.A.) kidnapping.
plan, *m.* plan. **—planear,** *v.*
plancha, *f.* plate, slab, flatiron.
planchar, *v.* iron, press.
planeta, *m.* planet.
plano, 1. *a.* level, flat. **2.** *m.* plan; plane.
planta, *f.* plant; sole (of foot).
plantación, *f.* plantation.
plantar, *v.* plant.
plantear, *v.* pose, present.
plantel, *m.* educational institution; (agr.) nursery.
plasma, *f.* plasma.
plástico, *a. & m.* plastic.
plata, *f.* silver; (coll.) money.
plataforma, *f.* platform.
plátano, *m.* plantain, cooking banana.
platel, *m.* platter.

plática, f. chat, talk. **—platicar,** v.
platillo, m. saucer.
plato, m. plate, dish.
playa, f. beach, shore.
plaza, f. square. **p. de toros,** bull-ring.
plazo, m. term, deadline; installment.
plebe, f. common people; masses.
plebiscito, m. plebiscite.
plegadura, f. fold, pleat. **—plegar,** v.
pleito, m. lawsuit; dispute.
plenitud, f. fullness; abundance.
pleno, a. full. **en pleno . . .** in the middle of . . .
pliego, m. sheet of paper.
pliegue, m. fold, pleat, crease.
plomería, f. plumbing.
plomero, m. plumber.
plomizo, a. leaden.
plomo, m. lead; fuse.
pluma, f. feather; (writing) pen.
plumafuente, f. fountain pen.
plumaje, m. plumage.
plumero, m. feather duster; plume.
plumoso, a. feathery.
plural, a. & m. plural.
población, f. population; town.
poblador -ra, n. settler.
poblar, v. populate; settle.
pobre, a. & n. poor; poor person.
pobreza, f. poverty, need.
pocilga, f. pigpen.
poción, f. drink; potion.
poco, 1. a. & adv. little, not much, (pl.) few. **por p.,** almost, nearly. **2.** m. **un p. (de),** a little, a bit (of).
poder, 1. m. power. **2.** v. be able to, can; be possible, may, might. **no p. menos de,** not be able to help.
poderío, m. power, might.
poderoso, a. powerful, mighty, potent.
podrido, a. rotten.
poema, m. poem.
poesía, f. poetry; poem.
poeta, m. poet.
poético, a. poetic.
polaco -ca, a. & n. Polish; Pole.
polar, a. polar.
polaridad, f. polarity.
polea, f. pulley.

polen, m. pollen.
policía, f. police. m. policeman.
poligamia, f. polygamy.
polígloto -ta, a. n. polyglot.
polilla, f. moth.
política, f. politics; policy.
político, a. & m. politic; political; politician.
póliza, f. (insurance) policy; permit, ticket.
polizonte, m. policeman.
polo, m. pole; polo.
polonés, a. Polish.
Polonia, f. Poland.
polvera, f. powder box; powder puff.
polvo, m. powder; dust.
pólvora, f. powder, gunpowder.
pollada, f. brood.
pollería, f. poultry shop.
pollino, m. donkey.
pollo, m. chicken.
pompa, f. pomp.
pomposo, a. pompous.
ponche, m. punch (beverage).
ponchera, f. punch bowl.
ponderar, v. ponder.
ponderoso, a. ponderous.
poner, v. put, set, lay, place.
ponerse, v. put on; become, get; set (sun). **p. a,** start to.
poniente, m. west.
pontífice, m. pontiff.
popa, f. stern.
popular, a. popular.
popularidad, f. popularity.
populazo, m. populace; masses.
por, prep. by, through, because of; via; for. **p. qué,** why?
porcelana, f. porcelain, china-ware.
porcentaje, m. percentage.
porción, f. portion, lot.
porche, m. porch; portico.
porfiar, v. persist; argue.
pormenor, m. detail.
pornografía, f. pornography.
poro, m. pore.
poroso, a. porous.
porque, conj. because.
porqué, m. reason, motive.
porra, f. stick, club.
porrazo, m. blow.
portaaviones, m. aircraft carrier.
portador -ra, n. bearer.
portal, m. portal.
portar, v. carry.

portarse, v. behave, act.
portátil, a. portable.
portavoz, m. megaphone.
porte, m. bearing; behavior; postage.
portero, m. porter; janitor.
pórtico, m. porch.
portorriqueño -ña, n. & a. Puerto Rican.
portugués -esa, a. & n. Portuguese.
posada, f. lodge, inn.
posar, v. pose.
posdata, f. postscript.
poseer, v. possess, own.
posesión, f. possession.
posibilidad, f. possibility.
posible, a. possible.
posiblemente, adv. possibly.
posición, f. position, stand.
positivo, a. positive.
posponer, v. postpone.
postal, a. postal.
poste, m. post, pillar.
posteridad, f. posterity.
posterior, a. posterior, rear.
postizo, a. false, artificial.
postrado, a. prostrate. —**postrar,** v.
postre, m. dessert.
póstumo, a. posthumous.
postura, f. posture, pose; bet.
potable, a. drinkable.
potaje, m. porridge; pot stew.
potasa, f. potash.
potasio, m. potassium.
pote, m. pot, jar.
potencia, f. potency, power.
potencial, a. & f. potential.
potentado, m. potentate.
potente, a. potent, powerful.
potestad, f. power.
potro, m. colt.
pozo, m. well.
práctica, f. practice. —**practicar,** v.
práctico, a. practical.
pradera, f. prairie, meadow.
prado, m. meadow; lawn.
pragmátismo, m. pragmatism.
preámbulo, m. preamble.
precario, a. precarious.
precaución, f. precaution.
precaverse, v. beware.
precavido, a. cautious, guarded, wary.

precedencia, f. precedence, priority.
precedente, a. & m. preceding; precedent.
preceder, v. precede.
precepto, m. precept.
preciar, v. value, prize.
preciarse de, v. take pride in.
precio, m. price.
precioso, a. precious; beautiful, gorgeous.
precipicio, m. precipice, cliff.
precipitación, f. precipitation.
precipitar, v. precipitate, rush; throw headlong.
precipitoso, a. precipitous; rash.
precisar, v. fix, specify; be necessary.
precisión, f. precision; necessity.
preciso, a. precise; necessary.
precocidad, f. precocity.
precoz, a. precocious.
precursor -ra 1. a. preceding. **2.** n. precursor, forerunner.
predecesor, -ra, a. & n. predecessor.
predecir, v. predict, foretell.
predicación, f. sermon.
predicador, m. preacher.
predicar, v. preach; publish.
predicción, f. prediction.
predilecto, a. favorite, preferred.
predisponer, v. predispose.
predisposición, f. predisposition; bias.
predominante, a. prevailing, prevalent, predominant.
predominar, v. prevail, predominate.
predominio, m. predominance, sway.
prefacio, m. preface.
preferencia, f. preference.
preferentemente, adv. preferably.
preferible, a. preferable.
preferir, v. prefer.
prefijo, m. prefix; area code. —**prefijar,** v.
pregón, m. proclamation, cry.
pregonar, v. proclaim, cry out.
pregunta, f. question, inquiry. **hacer una p.,** to ask a question.
preguntar, v. ask, inquire.
preguntarse, v. wonder.
prehistórico, a. prehistoric.
prejuicio, m. prejudice.
prelacía, f. prelacy.

preliminar, *a.* & *m.* preliminary.
preludio, *m.* prelude.
prematuro, *a.* premature.
premeditación, *f.* premeditation.
premeditar, *v.* premeditate.
premiar, *v.* reward; award a prize to.
premio, *m.* prize, award; reward.
premisa, *f.* premise.
premura, *f.* pressure; urgency.
prenda, *f.* jewel; (personal) quality. **p. de vestir**, garment.
prender, *v.* seize, arrest, catch; attack, pin, clip. **p. fuego a**, set fire to.
prensa, *f.* printing press; (the) press.
prensar, *v.* press, compress.
preñado, *a.* pregnant.
preocupación, *f.* worry, preoccupation.
preocupar, *v.* worry, preoccupy.
preparación, *f.* preparation.
preparar, *v.* prepare.
preparativo, *m.* preparation.
preparatorio, *m.* preparatory.
preponderante, *a.* preponderant.
preposición, *f.* preposition.
prerrogativa, *f.* prerogative, privilege.
presa, *f.* capture; prey; (water) dam.
presagiar, *v.* presage, forebode.
presbiteriano -na, *n.* & *a.* Presbyterian.
presbítero, *m.* priest.
prescindir de, *v.* dispense with; omit.
prescribir, *v.* prescribe.
prescripción, *f.* prescription.
presencia, *f.* presence.
presenciar, *v.* witness, be present at.
presentable, *a.* presentable.
presentación, *f.* presentation; introduction.
presentar, *v.* present; introduce.
presente, *a.* & *m.* present.
preservación, *f.* preservation.
preservar, *v.* preserve, keep.
preservativo, *a.* & *m.* preservative.
presidencia, *f.* presidency.
presidencial, *a.* presidential.
presidente -ta, *n.* president.
presidio, *m.* prison; garrison.
presidir, *v.* preside.

presión, *f.* pressure.
preso, *m.* prisoner.
presta, *f.* mint (plant).
prestador, *m.* lender.
prestamista, *m.* & *f.* money lender.
préstamo, *m.* loan.
prestar, *v.* lend.
presteza, *f.* haste, promptness.
prestidigitación, *f.* sleight of hand.
prestigio, *m.* prestige.
presto, **1.** *a.* quick, prompt; ready. **2.** *adv.* quickly; at once.
presumido, *a.* conceited, presumptuous.
presumir, *v.* presume; boast; claim; be conceited.
presunción, *f.* presumption; conceit.
presunto, *a.* presumed; prospective.
presuntuoso, *a.* presumptuous.
presupuesto, *m.* motive, pretext; budget.
pretender, *v.* pretend; intend; aspire.
pretendiente, *m.* suitor; pretender (to throne).
pretensión, *f.* pretension; claim.
pretérito, *a.* & *m.* preterit, past (tense).
pretexto, *m.* pretext.
prevalecer, *v.* prevail.
prevención, *f.* prevention.
prevenir, *v.* prevent; forewarn; prearrange.
preventivo, *a.* preventive.
prever, *v.* foresee.
previamente, *adv.* previously.
previo, *a.* previous.
previsión, *f.* foresight. **p. social**, social security.
prieto, *a.* blackish, very dark.
primacía, *f.* primacy.
primario, *a.* primary.
primavera, *f.* spring (season).
primero, *a.* & *adv.* first.
primitivo, *a.* primitive.
primo -ma, *n.* cousin.
primor, *m.* beauty; excellence; lovely thing.
primoroso, *a.* exquisite, elegant; graceful.
princesa, *f.* princess.
principal, **1.** *a.* principal, main. **2.** *m.* chief, head, principal.

principalmente, *adv.* principally.

príncipe, *m.* prince.

principiar, *v.* begin, initiate.

principio, *m.* beginning, start; principle.

prioridad, *f.* priority.

prisa, *f.* hurry, haste. **darse p.,** hurry, hasten. **tener p.,** be in a hurry.

prisión, *f.* prison; imprisonment.

prisionero -ra, *n.* captive, prisoner.

prisma, *m.* prism.

prismático, *a.* prismatic.

privación, *f.* privation, want.

privado, *a.* private, secret; deprived.

privar, *v.* deprive.

privilegio, *m.* privilege.

pro, *m. or f.* benefit, advantage. **en p. de,** in behalf of. **en p. y en contra,** pro and con.

proa, *f.* prow, bow.

probabilidad, *f.* probability.

probable, *a.* probable, likely.

probablemente, *adv.* probably.

probar, *v.* try, sample; taste; test; prove.

probarse, *v.* try on.

probidad, *f.* honesty, integrity.

problema, *m.* problem.

probo, *a.* honest.

procaz, *a.* impudent, saucy.

proceder, *v.* proceed.

procedimiento, *m.* procedure.

procesar, *v.* prosecute; sue; process.

procesión, *f.* procession.

proceso, *m.* process; (court) trial.

proclama, proclamación, *f.* proclamation.

proclamar, *v.* proclaim.

procreación, *f.* procreation.

procrear, *v.* procreate.

procurar, *v.* try; see to it; get, procure.

prodigalidad, *f.* prodigality.

prodigar, *v.* lavish, squander, waste.

prodigio, *m.* prodigy.

pródigo, *a.* prodigal, profuse, lavish.

producción, *f.* production.

producir, *v.* produce.

productivo, *a.* productive.

producto, *m.* product.

proeza, *f.* prowess.

profanación, *f.* profanation.

profanar, *v.* defile, desecrate.

profanidad, *f.* profanity.

profano, *a.* profane.

profecía, *f.* prophecy.

proferir, *v.* utter, express.

profesar, *v.* profess.

profesión, *f.* profession.

profesional, *a.* professional.

profesor -ra, *n.* professor, teacher.

profeta, *m.* prophet.

profético, *a.* prophetic.

profetizar, *v.* prophesy.

proficiente, *a.* proficient.

profundamente, *adv.* profoundly, deeply.

profundidad, *f.* profundity, depth.

profundizar, *v.* deepen.

profundo, *a.* profound, deep.

profuso, *a.* profuse.

progenie, *f.* progeny, offspring.

programa, *m.* program; schedule.

progresar, *v.* progress, advance.

progresión, *f.* progression.

progresista, progresivo, *a.* progressive.

progreso, *m.* progress.

prohibición, *f.* prohibition.

prohibir, *v.* prohibit, forbid.

prohibitivo, *a.* prohibitive.

prole, *f.* progeny.

proletariado, *m.* proletariat.

proliferación, *f.* proliferation.

prolijo, *a.* prolix, tedious; long-winded.

prólogo, *m.* prologue; preface.

prolongar, *v.* prolong.

promedio, *m.* average.

promesa, *f.* promise.

prometer, *v.* promise.

prometido, *a.* promised; engaged (to marry).

prominencia, *f.* prominence.

promiscuamente, *adv.* promiscuously.

promiscuo, *a.* promiscuous.

promisorio, *a.* promissory.

promoción, *f.* promotion.

promover, *v.* promote, further.

promulgación, *f.* promulgation.

promulgar, *v.* promulgate.

pronombre, *m.* pronoun.

pronosticación, *f.* prediction, forecast.

pronosticar, *v.* predict, forecast.

pronóstico, *m.* prediction.
prontamente, *adv.* promptly.
prontitud, *f.* promptness.
pronto, 1. *a.* prompt; ready. **2.** *adv.* soon; quickly. **de p.,** abruptly.
pronunciación, *f.* pronunciation.
pronunciar, *v.* pronounce.
propagación, *f.* propagation.
propaganda, *f.* propaganda.
propagandista, *n.* propagandist.
propagar, *v.* propagate.
propicio, *a.* propitious, auspicious, favorable.
propiedad, *f.* property.
propietario -ria, *n.* proprietor; owner; landlord, landlady.
propina, *f.* gratuity, tip.
propio, *a.* proper, suitable; typical; (one's) own; -self.
proponer, *v.* propose.
proporción, *f.* proportion.
proporcionado, *a.* proportionate.
proporcionar, *v.* provide with, supply, afford.
proposición, *f.* proposition, offer; proposal.
propósito, *m.* purpose; plan; **a p.,** by the way, apropos; on purpose.
propuesta, *f.* proposal, motion.
prorrata, *f.* quota.
prórroga, *f.* renewal, extension.
prorrogar, *v.* renew, extend.
prosa, *f.* prose.
prosaico, *a.* prosaic.
proscribir, *v.* prohibit, proscribe, ban.
prosecución, *f.* prosecution.
proseguir, *v.* pursue; proceed, go on.
prosélito, *m.* proselyte.
prospecto, *m.* prospectus.
prosperar, *v.* prosper, thrive, flourish.
prosperidad, *f.* prosperity.
próspero, *a.* prosperous, successful.
prosternado, *a.* prostrate.
prostitución, *f.* prostitution.
prostituir, *v.* prostitute; debase.
prostituta, *f.* prostitute.
protagonista, *m. & f.* protagonist, hero, heroine.
protección, *f.* protection.
protector -ra, *a. & n.* protective; protector.

proteger, *v.* protect, safeguard.
protegido -da, *n.* protégé.
proteína, *f.* protein.
protesta, *f.* protest. **—protestar,** *v.*
protestante, *a. & n.* Protestant.
protocolo, *m.* protocol.
protuberancia, *f.* protuberance, lump.
provecho, *m.* profit, gain, benefit. **¡Buen provecho!** May you enjoy your meal!
provechoso, *a.* beneficial, advantageous, profitable.
proveer, *v.* provide, furnish.
provenir de, *v.* originate in, be due to, come from.
proverbial, *a.* proverbial.
proverbio, *m.* proverb.
providencia, *f.* providence.
providente, *a.* provident.
provincia, *f.* province.
provincial, *a.* provincial.
provinciano -na, *a. & n.* provincial.
provisión, *f.* provision, supply, stock.
provisional, *a.* provisional.
provocación, *f.* provocation.
provocador, *m.* provoker.
provocar, *v.* provoke, excite.
provocativo, *a.* provocative.
proximidad, *f.* proximity, vicinity.
próximo, *a.* next; near.
proyección, *f.* projection.
proyectar, *v.* plan, project.
proyectil, *m.* projectile, missile, shell.
proyecto, *m.* plan, project, scheme.
proyector, *m.* projector.
prudencia, *f.* prudence.
prudente, *a.* prudent.
prueba, *f.* proof; trial; test.
psicoanálisis, *m. or f.* psychoanalysis.
psicología, *f.* psychology.
psicológico, *a.* psychological.
psicólogo, *m.* psychologist.
psiquedélico, *a.* psychedelic.
psiquiatra, *m.* psychiatrist.
psiquiatría, *f.* psychiatry.
publicación, *f.* publication.
publicar, *v.* publish.
publicidad, *f.* publicity.
público, *a. & m.* public.

puchero, *m.* pot.
pudiente, *a.* powerful; wealthy.
pudín, *m.* pudding.
pudor, *m.* modesty.
pudoroso, *a.* modest.
pudrirse, *v.* rot.
pueblo, *m.* town, village; (the) people.
puente, *m.* bridge.
puerco -ca, *n.* pig.
pueril, *a.* childish.
puerilidad, *f.* puerility.
puerta, *f.* door; gate.
puerto, *m.* port, harbor.
puertorriqueño -ña, *a.* & *n.* Puerto Rican.
pues, 1. *adv.* well . . . **2.** *conj.* as, since, for.
puesto, *m.* appointment, post, job; place; stand. **p. que,** since.
pugilato, *m.* boxing.
pugna, *f.* conflict.
pugnacidad, *f.* pugnacity.
pugnar, *v.* fight; oppose.
pulcritud, *f.* beauty.
pulga, *f.* flea.
pulgada, *f.* inch.
pulgar, *m.* thumb.
pulir, *v.* polish; beautify.
pulmón, *m.* lung.
pulmonía, *f.* pneumonia.
pulpa, *f.* pulp.
púlpito, *m.* pulpit.
pulque, *m.* pulque (fermented maguey juice).
pulsación, *f.* pulsation, beat.
pulsar, *v.* pulsate, beat.
pulsera, *f.* wristband; bracelet; wristwatch.
pulso, *m.* pulse.
pulverizar, *v.* pulverize.
puma, *f.* puma.
pundonor, *m.* point of honor.
punta, *f.* point, tip, end.
puntada, *f.* stitch.
puntapié, *m.* kick.
puntería, *f.* (marksman's) aim.
puntiagudo, *a.* sharp-pointed.
puntillas, f.pl. de p., en p., on tip-toe.
punto, *m.* point; period; spot, dot. **dos puntos,** (punct.) colon. **a p. de,** about to. **al p.,** instantly.
puntuación, *f.* punctuation.
puntual, *a.* punctual, prompt.
puntuar, *v.* punctuate.
puñada, *f.* fist, blow.

puñado, *m.* handful.
puñal, *m.* dagger.
puñalada, *f.* stab.
puñetazo, *m.* punch, fist blow.
puño, *m.* fist; cuff; handle.
pupila, *f.* pupil (of eye).
pupitre, *m.* writing desk, school desk.
pureza, *f.* purity; chastity.
purgante, *m.* laxative.
purgar, *v.* purge, cleanse.
purgatorio, *m.* purgatory.
puridad, *f.* purity.
purificación, *f.* purification.
purificar, *v.* purify.
purismo, *m.* purism.
purista, *n.* purist.
puritanismo, *m.* puritanism.
puro, 1. *a.* pure. **2.** *m.* cigar.
púrpura, *f.* purple.
purpúreo, *a.* purple.
purulencia, *f.* purulence.
purulento, *a.* purulent.
pus, *m.* pus.
pusilánime, *a.* pusillanimous.
puta, *f.* prostitute.
putrefacción, *f.* putrefaction, rot.
putrefacto, *a.* putrid, rotten.
pútrido, *a.* putrid.
puya, *f.* goad.

Q

que, 1. *rel. pron.* who, whom; that, which. **2.** *conj.* than.
qué, 1. *a.* & *pron.* what. **por q., para q.,** why? **2.** *adv.* how.
quebrada, *f.* ravine, gully, gulch; stream.
quebradizo, *a.* fragile, brittle.
quebrar, *v.* break.
queda, *f.* curfew.
quedar, *v.* remain, be located; be left. **q. bien a,** be becoming to.
quedarse, *v.* stay, remain. **q. con,** keep, hold on to.
quedo, *a.* quiet; gentle.
quehacer, *m.* task; chore.
queja, *f.* complaint.
quejarse, *v.* complain, grumble.
quejido, *m.* moan.
quejoso, *a.* complaining.
quema, *f.* burning.
quemadura, *f.* burn.
quemar, *v.* burn.
querella, *f.* quarrel; complaint.

querencia, f. affection, liking.
querer, v. want, wish; will; love (a person). **q. decir,** mean. **sin q.,** without meaning to; unwillingly.
querido, a. dear, loved, beloved.
quesería, f. dairy.
queso, m. cheese.
quiebra, f. break, fracture; damage; bankruptcy.
quien, rel. pron. who, whom.
quién, interrog. pron. who, whom.
quienquiera, pron. whoever, whomever.
quietamente, adv. quietly.
quieto, a. quiet, still.
quietud, f. quiet, quietude.
quijada, f. jaw.
quijotesco, a. quixotic.
quilate, m. carat.
quilla, f. keel.
quimera, f. chimera, vision; quarrel.
química, f. chemistry.
químico, a. & m. chemical; chemist.
quimoterapía, f. chemotherapy.
quincalleri, f. hardware store.
quince, a. & pron. fifteen.
quinientos, a. & pron. five hundred.
quinina, f. quinine.
quinta, f. country home.
quinto, a. fifth.
quirúrgico, m. surgeon.
quiste, m. cyst.
quitamanchas, m. stain remover.
quitanieve, m. snowplow.
quitar, v. take away, remove.
quitarse, v. take off; get rid of.
quitasol, m. parasol, umbrella.
quizá, **quizás,** adv. perhaps, maybe.
quórum, m. quorum.

R

rábano, m. radish.
rabí, rabino, m. rabbi.
rabia, f. rage; grudge; rabies.
rabiar, v. rage, be furious.
rabieta, f. tantrum.
rabioso, a. furious; rabid.
rabo, m. tail.
racimo, m. bunch, cluster.

ración, f. ration. —**racionar,** v.
racionabilidad, f. rationality.
racional, a. rational.
racionalismo, m. rationalism.
racionalmente, adv. rationally.
racha, f. streak.
radar, m. radar.
radiación, f. radiation.
radiador, m. radiator.
radiante, a. radiant.
radical, a. & m. radical.
radicalismo, m. radicalism.
radicoso, a. radical.
radio, m. or f. radio.
radioactividad, f. radioactivity.
radioactivo, a. radioactive.
radiodifundir, v. broadcast.
radiodifusión, f. (radio) broadcasting.
ráfaga, f. gust (of wind).
raíz, f. root.
raja, f. rip; split, crack. —**rajar,** v.
ralea, f. stock, breed.
ralo, a. thin, scattered.
rama, f. branch, bough.
ramillete, m. bouquet.
ramo, m. branch, bough.
ramonear, v. browse.
rampa, f. ramp.
rana, f. frog.
rancidez, f. rancidity.
rancio, a. rancid, rank, stale, sour.
ranchero -ra, n. small farmer.
rancho, m. ranch.
rango, m. rank.
ranúnculo, m. ranunculus; buttercup.
ranura, f. slot.
rapacidad, f. rapacity.
rapaz, 1. a. rapacious. **2.** m. young boy.
rapé, m. snuff.
rápidamente, adv. rapidly.
rapidez, f. rapidity, speed.
rápido, 1. a. rapid, fast, speedy. **2.** m. express (train).
rapiña, f. robbery, plundering.
rapsodia, f. rhapsody.
raqueta, f. (tennis) racket.
rareza, f. rarity, freak.
raridad, f. rarity.
raro, a. rare, strange, unusual, odd, queer.
rasar, v. skim.
rascar, v. scrape; scratch.

rasgadura, *f.* tear, rip. **—rasgar,** *v.*

rasgo, *m.* trait.

rasgón, *m.* tear.

rasguño, *m.* scratch. **—rasguñar,** *v.*

raso, 1. *a.* plain. **soldado r.,** (mil.) private. **2.** *m.* satin.

raspar, *v.* scrape; erase.

rastra, *f.* trail, track. **—rastrear,** *v.*

rastrillar, *v.* rake.

rastro, *m.* track, trail, trace; rake.

rata, *f.* rat.

ratificación, *f.* ratification.

ratificar, *v.* ratify.

rato, *m.* while, spell, short time.

ratón, *m.* mouse.

ratonera, *f.* mousetrap.

raya, *f.* dash, line, streak, stripe.

rayar, *v.* rule, stripe; scratch; cross out.

rayo, *m.* lightning bolt; ray; flash.

rayón, *m.* rayon.

raza, *f.* race; breed, stock.

razón, *f.* reason; ratio. **a r. de,** at the rate of. **tener r.,** to be right.

razonable, *a.* reasonable, sensible.

razonamiento, *m.* argument.

razonar, *v.* reason.

reacción, *f.* reaction.

reaccionar, *v.* react.

reaccionario, *m.* reactionary.

reacondicionar, *v.* recondition.

reactivo, *a.* & *m.* reactive; (chem.) reagent.

reactor, *m.* reactor.

real, *a.* royal, regal; real, actual.

realdad, *f.* royal authority.

realeza, *f.* royalty.

realidad, *f.* reality.

realista, *a.* & *n.* realistic; realist.

realización, *f.* achievement, accomplishment.

realizar, *v.* accomplish; fulfill; effect; (com.) realize.

realmente, *adv.* in reality.

realzar, *v.* enhance.

reata, *f.* rope; lasso, lariat.

rebaja, *f.* reduction.

rebajar, *v.* cheapen; reduce (in price); lower.

rebanada, *f.* slice. **—rebanar,** *v.*

rebaño, *m.* flock, herd.

rebato, *m.* alarm; sudden attack.

rebelarse, *v.* rebel, revolt.

rebelde, *a.* & *n.* rebellious; rebel.

rebelión, *f.* rebellion, revolt.

reborde, *m.* border.

rebotar, *v.* rebound.

rebozo, *m.* shawl.

rebuscar, *v.* search thoroughly.

rebuznar, *v.* bray.

recado, *m.* message; errand.

recaída, *f.* relapse. **—recaer,** *v.*

recalcar, *v.* stress, emphasize.

recámara, *f.* (Mex.) bedroom.

recapitulación, *f.* recapitulation.

recapitular, *v.* recapitulate.

recatado, *m.* coy; prudent.

recelar, *v.* fear, distrust.

receloso, *a.* distrustful.

recepción, *f.* reception.

receptáculo, *m.* receptacle.

receptividad, *f.* receptivity.

receptivo, *a.* receptive.

receptor, *m.* receiver.

receta, *f.* recipe; prescription.

recetar, *v.* prescribe.

recibimiento, *m.* reception; cordiality.

recibir, *v.* receive.

recibo, *m.* receipt.

reciclar, *v.* recycle.

recidiva, *f.* relapse.

recién, *adv.* recently, newly, just.

reciente, *a.* recent.

recinto, *m.* enclosure.

recipiente, *m.* recipient.

reciprocación, *f.* reciprocation.

recíprocamente, *adv.* reciprocally.

reciprocar, *v.* reciprocate.

reciprocidad, *f.* reciprocity.

recitación, *f.* recitation.

recitar, *v.* recite.

reclamación, *f.* claim; complaint.

reclamar, *v.* claim; complain.

reclamo, *m.* claim; advertisement, advertising; decoy.

reclinar, *v.* recline, repose, lean.

recluta, *m.* recruit.

reclutar, *v.* recruit, draft.

recobrar, *v.* recover, salvage, regain.

recobro, *m.* recovery.

recoger, *v.* gather; collect; pick up.

recogerse, *v.* retire (for night).

recolectar, *v.* gather, assemble harvest.

recomendación, *f.* recommendation; commendation.

recomendar, *v.* recommend; commend.

recompensa, *f.* recompense; compensation.

recompensar, *v.* reward; compensate.

reconciliación, *f.* reconciliation.

reconciliar, *v.* reconcile.

reconocer, *v.* recognize; acknowledge; inspect, examine; (mil.) reconnoiter.

reconocimiento, *m.* recognition; appreciation, gratitude.

reconstituir, *v.* reconstitute.

reconstruir, *v.* reconstruct, rebuild.

record, *m.* (sports) record.

recordar, *v.* recall, recollect; remind.

recorrer, *v.* go over; read over; cover (distance).

recorte, *m.* clipping, cutting.

recostarse, *v.* recline, lean back, rest.

recreación, *f.* recreation.

recreo, *m.* recreation.

recriminación, *f.* recrimination.

rectangular, *a.* rectangular.

rectángulo, *m.* rectangle.

rectificación, *f.* rectification.

rectificar, *v.* rectify.

recto, *a.* straight; just, fair. **ángulo r.,** right angle.

recuento, *m.* recount.

recuerdo, *m.* memory, souvenir, remembrance; (pl.) regards.

reculada, *f.* recoil. —**recular,** *v.*

recuperación, *f.* recuperation.

recuperar, *v.* recuperate.

recurrir, *v.* revert; resort, have recourse.

recurso, *m.* resource; recourse.

rechazar, *v.* reject, spurn, discard.

rechinar, *v.* chatter.

red, *f.* net; trap.

redacción, *f.* (editorial) staff; composition (of written material).

redactar, *v.* draft, draw up; edit.

redactor, *m.* editor.

redada, *f.* netful, catch, haul.

redargución, *f.* retort. —**redargüir,** *v.*

redención, *f.* redemption, salvation.

redentor, *m.* redeemer.

redimir, *v.* redeem.

redoblante, *m.* drummer.

redonda, *f.* neighborhood, vicinity.

redondo, *a.* round, circular.

reducción, *f.* reduction.

reducir, *v.* reduce.

reembolso, *m.* refund. —**reembolsar,** *v.*

reemplazar, *v.* replace, supersede.

reencarnación, *f.* reincarnation.

reexaminar, *v.* reexamine.

reexpedir, *v.* forward (mail).

referencia, *f.* reference.

referéndum, *m.* referendum.

referir, *v.* relate, report on.

referirse, *v.* refer.

refinamiento, *m.* refinement.

refinar, *v.* refine.

refinería, *f.* refinery.

reflejar, *v.* reflect; think, ponder.

reflejo, *m.* reflection; glare.

reflexión, *f.* reflection, thought.

reflexionar, *v.* reflect, think.

reflujo, *m.* ebb; ebb tide.

reforma, *f.* reform. —**reformar,** *v.*

reformación, *f.* reformation.

reformador, *m.* reformer.

reforzar, *v.* reinforce, strengthen; encourage.

refractario, *a.* refractory.

refrán, *m.* proverb, saying.

refrenar, *v.* curb, rein; restrain.

refrescar, *v.* refresh, freshen, cool.

refresco, *m.* refreshment; cold drink.

refrigeración, *f.* refrigeration.

refrigerador, *m.* refrigerator.

refrigerar, *v.* refrigerate.

refuerzo, *m.* reinforcement.

refugiado -da, refugee.

refugiarse, *v.* take refuge.

refugio, *m.* refuge, asylum, shelter.

refulgencia, *f.* refulgence.

refulgente, *a.* refulgent.

refulgir, *v.* shine.

refunfuñar, *v.* mutter, grumble, growl.

refutación, *f.* refutation; rebuttal.

refutar, *v.* refute.

regadizo, *a.* irrigable.

regadura, *f.* irrigation.

regalar, *v.* give (a gift), give away.

regalo, *m.* gift, present, **con r.,** in luxury.

regañar, v. reprove; scold.

regaño, m. reprimand, scolding.

regar, v. water, irrigate.

regatear, v. haggle.

regateo, m. bargaining, haggling.

regazo, m. lap.

regencia, f. regency.

regeneración, f. regeneration.

regenerar, v. regenerate.

regente, m. regent.

régimen, m. regime; diet.

regimentar, v. regiment.

regimiento, m. regiment.

región, f. region.

regional, a. regional, sectional.

regir, v. rule; be in effect.

registrar, v. register; record; search.

registro, m. register; record; search.

regla, f. rule, regulation. **en r.,** in order.

reglamento, m. code of regulations.

regocijarse, v. rejoice, exult.

regocijo, f. rejoicing; merriment, joy.

regordete, a. chubby, plump.

regresar, v. go back, return.

regresión, f. regression.

regresivo, a. regressive.

regreso, m. return.

regulación, f. regulation.

regular, 1. a. regular; fair, middling. **2.** v. regulate.

regularidad, f. regularity.

regularmente, adv. regularly.

rehabilitación, f. rehabilitation.

rehabilitar, v. rehabilitate.

rehén, m. hostage.

rehusar, v. refuse; decline.

reina, f. queen.

reinado, m. reign. **—reinar,** v.

reino, m. kingdom; realm; reign.

reír, v. laugh.

reiteración, f. reiteration.

reiterar, v. reiterate.

reja, f. grating, grillwork.

relación, f. relation; account, report.

relacionar, v. relate, connect.

relajamiento, m. laxity, laxness.

relajar, v. relax, slacken.

relámpago, m. lightning; flash (of lightning).

relatador, m. teller.

relatar, v. relate, recount.

relativamente, adv. relatively.

relatividad, f. relativity.

relativo, a. relative.

relato, m. account, story.

relegación, f. relegation.

relegar, v. relegate.

relevar, v. relieve.

relicario, m. reliquary; locket.

relieve, m. (sculpture) relief.

religión, f. religion.

religiosidad, f. religiosity.

religioso -sa, 1. a. religious. **2.** m. member of a religious order.

reliquia, f. relic.

reloj, m. clock; watch.

relojería, f. watchmaker's shop.

relojero, m. watchmaker.

relucir, v. glow, shine; excel.

relumbrar, v. glitter, sparkle.

rellenar, v. refill; fill up, stuff.

relleno, m. stuffing.

remache, m. rivet. **—remachar,** v.

remar, v. row (a boat).

rematado, a. finished; sold.

remate, m. end, finish; auction. **de r.,** utterly.

remedador, m. imitator.

remedar, v. imitate.

remedio, m. remedy. **—remediar,** v.

remendar, v. mend, patch.

remesa, f. shipment; remittance.

remiendo, m. patch.

remilgado, a. prudish; affected.

reminiscencia, f. reminiscence.

remitir, v. remit.

remo, m. oar.

remolacha, f. beet.

remolcador, m. tug (boat).

remolino, m. whirl; whirlpool; whirlwind.

remolque, m. tow. **—remolcar,** v.

remontar, v. ascend, go up.

remontarse, v. get excited; soar. **r. a,** date from; go back to (in time).

remordimiento, m. remorse.

remotamente, adv. remotely.

remoto, a. remote.

remover, v. remove; stir; shake; loosen.

rempujar, v. jostle.

remuneración, f. remuneration.

remunerar, v. remunerate.

renacido, a. reborn, born-again.

renacimiento, m. rebirth; renaissance.

rencor, *m.* rancor, bitterness, animosity; grudge.

rencoroso, *a.* rancorous, bitter.

rendición, *f.* surrender.

rendido, *a.* weary, worn out.

rendir, *v.* yield; surrender, give up; win over.

renegado, *m.* renegade.

renglón, *m.* line; (com.) item.

reno, *m.* reindeer.

renombre, *m.* renown.

renovación, *f.* renovation, renewal.

renovar, *v.* renew; renovate.

renta, *f.* income; rent.

rentar, *v.* yield; rent for.

renuencia, *f.* reluctance.

renuente, *a.* reluctant.

renuncia, *f.* resignation; renunciation.

renunciar, *v.* resign; renounce, give up.

reñir, *v.* scold, berate; quarrel, wrangle.

reo, *a. & n.* criminal; convict.

reorganizar, *v.* reorganize.

reparación, *f.* reparation, atonement; repair.

reparar, *v.* repair; mend; stop, stay over. **r. en,** notice; consider.

reparo, *m.* repair; remark; difficulty; objection.

repartición, *f.,* **repartimiento, reparto,** *m.* division, distribution.

repartir, *v.* divide, apportion, distribute; (theat.) cast.

repaso, *m.* review. **—repasar,** *v.*

repatriación, *f.* repatriation.

repatriar, *v.* repatriate.

repeler, *v.* repel.

repente, *m.* **de r.,** suddenly; unexpectedly.

repentinamente, *adv.* suddenly.

repentino, *a.* sudden.

repercusión, *f.* repercussion.

repertorio, *m.* repertoire.

repetición, *f.* repetition.

repetidamente, *adv.* repeatedly.

repetir, *v.* repeat.

repisa, *f.* shelf.

réplica, *f.* reply; objection.

replicar, *v.* reply; answer back.

repollo, *m.* cabbage.

reponer, *v.* replace; repair.

reponerse, *v.* recover, get well.

reporte, *m.* report; news.

repórter, reportero, *m.* reporter.

reposado, *a.* tranquil, peaceful, quiet.

reposo, *m.* repose, rest. **—reposar,** *v.*

reposte, *f.* pantry.

represalia, *f.* reprisal.

representación, *f.* representation; (theat.) performance.

representante, *m.* representative, agent.

representar, *v.* represent; depict; (theat.) perform.

representativo, *a.* representative.

represión, *f.* repression.

represivo, *a.* repressive.

reprimenda, *f.* reprimand.

reprimir, *v.* repress, quell.

reproche, *m.* reproach. **—reprochar,** *v.*

reproducción, *f.* reproduction.

reproducir, *v.* reproduce.

reptil, *m.* reptile.

república, *f.* republic.

republicano -na, *a. & n.* republican.

repudiación, *f.* repudiation.

repudiar, *v.* repudiate; disown.

repuesto, *m.* spare part. **de r.,** spare.

repugnancia, *f.* repugnance.

repugnante, *a.* repugnant, repulsive.

repugnar, *v.* disgust.

repulsa, *f.* refusal; repulse.

repulsivo, *a.* repulsive.

reputación, *f.* reputation.

reputar, *v.* repute; appreciate.

requerir, *v.* require.

requesón, *m.* cottage cheese.

requisición, *f.* requisition.

requisito, *m.* requisite, requirement.

res, *f.* head of cattle.

resbalar, *v.* slide; slip.

resbaloso, *a.* slippery.

rescate, *m.* rescue, ransom. **—rescatar,** *v.*

rescindir, *v.* rescind.

resentimiento, *m.* resentment.

resentirse, *v.* resent.

reserva, *f.* reserve. **—reservar,** *v.*

reservación, *f.* reservation.

resfriado, *m.* (med.) cold.

resfriarse, *v.* catch cold.

resguardar, *v.* guard, protect.

residencia, *f.* residence, seat.

residente, *a. & n.* resident.

residir, v. reside.
residuo, m. remainder.
resignación, f. resignation.
resignar, v. resign.
resina, f. resin; rosin.
resistencia, f. resistance.
resistir, v. resist; endure.
resolución, f. resolution.
resolutivamente, adv. resolutely.
resolver, v. resolve; solve.
resonante, a. resonant.
resonar, v. resound.
resorte, m. (mech.) spring.
respaldar, v. endorse; back.
respaldo, m. back (of a seat).
respectivo, a. respective.
respecto, m. relation, proportion; **r. a**, concerning, regarding.
respetabilidad, f. respectability.
respetable, a. respectable.
respeto, m. respect. **—respetar**, v.
respetuosamente, adv. respectfully.
respetuoso, a. respectful.
respiración, f. respiration, breath.
respirar, v. breathe.
resplandecente, a. resplendent.
resplandor, m. brightness, glitter.
responder, v. respond, answer.
responsabilidad, f. responsibility.
responsable, a. responsible.
respuesta, f. answer, response, reply.
resquicio, m. crack, slit.
resta, f. subtraction, remainder.
restablecer, v. restore, reestablish.
restablecerse, v. recover, get well.
restar, v. remain; subtract.
restauración, f. restoration.
restaurante, m. restaurant.
restaurar, v. restore.
restitución, f. restitution.
restituir, v. restore, give back.
resto, m. remainder, rest; (pl.) remains.
restorán, m. restaurant.
restregar, v. scrape.
restricción, f. restriction.
restrictivo, a. restrictive.
restringir, v. restrict, curtail.
resucitar, v. resuscitate; resurrect.
resuelto, a. resolute.
resultado, m. result.

resultar, v. result; turn out; ensue.
resumen, m. résumé, summary, **en r.**, in brief.
resumir, v. sum up.
resurgir, v. resurge, reappear.
resurrección, f. resurrection.
retaguardia, f. rear guard.
retal, m. remnant.
retardar, v. retard, show.
retardo, m. delay.
retención, f. retention.
retener, v. retain, keep, withhold.
reticencia, f. reticence.
reticente, a. reticent.
retirada, f. retreat, retirement.
retirar, v. retire, retreat, withdraw.
retiro, m. retirement.
retorcer, v. wring.
retórica, f. rhetoric.
retórico, a. rhetorical.
retorno, m. return.
retozo, m. frolic, romp. **—retozar**, v.
retozón, a. frisky.
retracción, f. retraction.
retractor, v. retract.
retrasar, v. delay, set back; be slow.
retraso, m. delay, lag, slowness.
retratar, v. portray; photograph.
retrato, m. portrait, picture; photograph.
retreta, f. (mil.) retreat.
retrete, m. alcove; toilet.
retribución, f. retribution.
retroactivo, a. retroactive.
retroalimentación, f. feedback.
retroceder, v. recede, go back, draw back, back up.
retumbar, v. resound, rumble.
reumático, a. rheumatic.
reumatismo, m. rheumatism.
reunión, f. gathering, meeting, party; reunion.
reunir, v. gather, collect, bring together.
reunirse, v. meet, assemble, get together.
revelación, f. revelation.
revelar, v. reveal, betray; (phot.) develop.
reventa, f. resale.
reventar, v. burst; split apart.
reventón, m. blowout (of tire).
reverencia, f. reverence.

reverendo, *a.* reverend.

reverente, *a.* reverent.

revertir, *v.* revert.

revés, *m.* reverse; back, wrong side. **al r.,** just the opposite; inside out.

revisar, *v.* revise; review.

revisión, *f.* revision.

revista, *f.* magazine, periodical; review.

revivir, *v.* revive.

revocación, *f.* revocation.

revocar, *v.* revoke, reverse.

revolotear, *v.* hover.

revolución, *f.* revolution.

revolucionario -ria, *a. & m.* revolutionary.

revolver, *v.* revolve; stir, agitate.

revólver, *m.* revolver, pistol.

revuelta, *f.* revolt; turn.

rey, *m.* king.

reyerta, *f.* quarrel, wrangle.

rezar, *v.* pray.

rezongar, *v.* grumble; mutter.

ría, *f.* estuary.

riachuelo, *m.* creek.

riba, *f.* embankment.

rico, *a.* rich, wealthy; delicious.

ridiculamente, *adv.* ridiculously.

ridiculizar, *v.* ridicule.

ridículo, *a. & m.* ridiculous; ridicule.

riego, *m.* irrigation.

rienda, *f.* rein.

riesgo, *m.* risk, gamble.

rifa, *f.* raffle; lottery; scuffle.

rifle, *m.* rifle.

rígidamente, *adv.* rigidly.

rigidez, *f.* rigidity.

rígido, *a.* rigid, stiff.

rigor, *m.* rigor.

riguroso, *a.* rigorous, strict.

rima, *f.* rhyme. **—rimar,** *v.*

rincón, *m.* corner, nook.

rinoceronte, *m.* rhinoceros.

riña, *f.* quarrel, feud.

riñón, *m.* kidney.

río, *m.* river.

ripio, *m.* debris.

riqueza, *f.* wealth.

risa, *f.* laugh; laughter.

risco, *m.* cliff.

risibilidad, *f.* risibility.

risotada, *f.* peal of laughter.

risueño, *a.* cheerful, smiling.

rítmico, *a.* rhythmical.

ritmo, *m.* rhythm.

rito, *m.* rite.

ritual, *a. & m.* ritual.

rivalidad, *f.* rivalry.

rivera, *f.* brook.

rizado, *a.* curly.

rizo, *m.* curl. **—rizar,** *v.*

robar, *v.* rob, steal.

roble, *m.* oak.

roblón, *m.* rivet. **—roblar,** *v.*

robo, *m.* robbery, theft.

robustamente, *adv.* robustly.

robusto, *a.* robust.

roca, *f.* rock; cliff.

rociada, *f.* spray, sprinkle. **—rociar,** *v.*

rocío, *m.* dew.

rodar, *v.* roll; roam.

rodear, *v.* surround, encircle.

rodeo, *m.* turn, winding; roundup.

rodilla, *f.* knee.

rodillo, *m.* roller.

rodio, *m.* rhodium.

rododendro, *m.* rhododendron.

roedor, *m.* rodent.

roer, *v.* gnaw.

rogación, *f.* request, entreaty.

rogar, *v.* beg, plead with, supplicate.

rojizo, *a.* reddish.

rojo, *a.* red.

rollo, *m.* roll; coil.

romadizo, *m.* head cold.

romance, *m.* romance, ballad.

románico, *a.* Romance.

romano -na, *a. & n.* Roman.

romántico, *a.* romantic.

romería, *f.* pilgrimage; picnic.

romero -ra, *n.* pilgrim.

rompecabezas, *m.* puzzle (pastime).

romper, *v.* break, smash, shatter; sever; tear.

rompible, *a.* breakable.

ron, *m.* rum.

roncar, *v.* snore.

ronco, *a.* hoarse.

ronda, *f.* round.

rondar, *v.* prowl.

ronquido, *m.* snore.

ronzal, *m.* halter.

roña, *f.* scab; filth.

ropa, *f.* clothes, clothing. **r. blanca,** linen. **r. interior,** underwear.

ropero, *m.* closet.

rosa, f. rose. **r. náutica**, compass.

rosado, a. pink, rosy.

rosal, m. rose bush.

rosario, m. rosary.

rosbif, m. roast beef.

rosca, f. thread (of screw).

róseo, a. rosy.

rostro, m. face, countenance.

rota, f. defeat; (naut.) course.

rotación, f. rotation.

rotatorio, a. rotary.

rótulo, m. label. —**rotular**, v.

rotundo, a. round; sonorous.

rotura, f. break, fracture, rupture.

rozar, v. rub against; chafe; graze.

rubí, m. ruby.

rubio -bia, a. & n. blond.

rubor, m. blush; bashfulness.

rúbrica, f. caption; scroll.

rucho, m. donkey.

rudeza, f. rudeness; roughness.

rudimento, m. rudiment.

rudo, a. rude, rough.

rueda, f. wheel.

ruego, m. plea; entreaty.

rufián, m. ruffian.

rufo, a. sandy (colored).

rugir, v. bellow, roar.

rugoso, a. wrinkled.

ruibarbo, m. rhubarb.

ruido, m. noise.

ruidoso, a. noisy.

ruina, f. ruin, wreck.

ruinar, v. ruin, destroy.

ruinoso, a. ruinous.

ruiseñor, m. nightingale.

ruleta, f. roulette.

rumba, f. rumba (dance or music).

rumbo, m. course, direction.

rumor, m. rumor; murmur.

runrún, m. rumor.

ruptura, f. rupture, break.

rural, a. rural.

Rusia, f. Russia.

ruso -sa, a. & n. Russian.

rústico -ca, a. & n. rustic. **en r.**, paperback f.

ruta, f. route.

rutina, f. routine.

rutinario, a. routine.

S

sábado, m. Saturday.

sábalo, m. shad.

sábana, f. sheet.

sabañón, m. chilblain.

saber, **1.** n. knowledge. **2.** v. know; learn, find out; know how to; taste. **a s.**, namely, to wit.

sabiduría, f. wisdom; learning.

sabio, **1.** a. wise; scholarly. **2.** m. sage; scholar.

sable, m. saber.

sabor, m. flavor, taste, savor.

saborear, v. savor, relish.

sabotaje, m. sabotage.

sabroso, a. savory, tasty.

sabuesco, m. hound.

sacacorchos, m. corkscrew.

sacar, v. draw out; take out; take.

sacerdocio, m. priesthood.

sacerdote, m. priest.

saciar, v. satiate.

saco, m. sack, bag, pouch; suit coat, jacket.

sacramento, m. sacrament.

sacrificio, m. sacrifice. —**sacrificar**, v.

sacrilegio, m. sacrilege.

sacristán, m. sexton.

sacro, a. sacred, holy.

sacrosanto, a. sacrosanct.

sacudir, v. shake, jerk, jolt.

sádico, a. sadistic.

sadismo, m. sadism.

sagacidad, f. sagacity.

sagaz, a. sagacious, sage.

sagrado, a. sacred, holy.

sal, f. salt; (coll.) wit.

sala, f. room; living room, parlor; hall, auditorium.

salado, a. salted, salty; (coll.) witty.

salar, v. salt; steep in brine.

salario, m. salary, wages.

salchicha, f. sausage.

saldo, m. remainder, balance; (bargain) sale.

salero, m. salt shaker.

salida, f. exit, outlet; departure.

salir, v. go out, come out; set out, leave, start; turn out; result.

salirse de, v. get out of. **s. con la suya**, have one's own way.

salitre, *m.* saltpeter.

saliva, *f.* saliva.

salmo, *m.* psalm.

salmón, *m.* salmon.

salmuera, *f.* pickle; brine.

salobre, *a.* salty.

salón, *m.* parlor, living room; hall.

salpicar, *v.* spatter, splash.

salpullido, *m.* rash.

salsa, *f.* sauce; gravy.

saltamontes, *m.* grasshopper.

salteador, *m.* highwayman.

salto, *m.* jump, leap, spring. — **saltar,** *v.*

saltón, *m.* grasshopper.

salubre, *a.* salubrious, healthful.

salubridad, *f.* health.

salud, *f.* health.

saludable, *a.* healthful, wholesome.

saludar, *v.* greet; salute.

saludo, *m.* greeting; salutation; salute.

salutación, *f.* salutation.

salva, *f.* salvo.

salvación, *f.* salvation; deliverance.

salvador -ra, *n.* savior; rescuer.

salvaguardia, *m.* safeguard.

salvaje, *a. & m.* savage, wild (man).

salvamento, *m.* salvation; rescue.

salvar, *v.* save; salvage; rescue; jump over.

salvavidas, *m.* life preserver.

salvia, *f.* sage (plant).

salvo, 1. *a.* safe. **2.** *prep.* except, save (for). **s. que,** unless.

San, *title.* Saint.

sanar, *v.* heal, cure.

sanatorio, *m.* sanatorium.

sanción, *f.* sanction. **—sancionar,** *v.*

sandalia, *f.* sandal.

sandez, *f.* stupidity.

sandía, *f.* watermelon.

saneamiento, *m.* sanitation.

sangrar, *v.* bleed.

sangre, *f.* blood.

sangriento, *a.* bloody.

sanguinario, *a.* bloodthirsty.

sanidad, *f.* health.

sanitario, *a.* sanitary.

sano, *a.* healthy, sound, sane; healthful, wholesome.

santidad, *f.* sanctity, holiness.

santificar, *v.* sanctify.

santo -ta, 1. *a.* holy, saintly. **2.** *m.* saint.

Santo -ta, *title.* Saint.

santuario, *m.* sanctuary, shrine.

saña, *f.* rage, anger.

sapiente, *a.* wise.

sapo, *m.* toad.

saquear, *v.* sack, ransack, plunder.

sarampión, *m.* measles.

sarape, *m.* (Mex.) woven blanket; shawl.

sarcasmo, *m.* sarcasm.

sarcástico, *a.* sarcastic.

sardina, *f.* sardine.

sargento, *m.* sergeant.

sarna, *f.* itch.

sartén, *m.* frying pan.

satánico, *a.* satanic.

satélite, *m.* satellite.

satírico, *a. & m.* satirical; satirist.

satirizar, *v.* satirize.

sátiro, *m.* satyr.

satisfacción, *f.* satisfaction.

satisfacer, *v.* satisfy.

satisfactorio, *a.* satisfactory.

saturación, *f.* saturation.

saturar, *v.* saturate.

sauce, *m.* willow.

savia, *f.* sap.

saxófono, *m.* saxophone.

saya, *f.* skirt.

sazón, *f.* season; seasoning. **a la s.,** at that time.

sazonar, *v.* flavor, season.

se, *pron.* -self, -selves.

seca, *f.* drought.

secante, *a.* **papel s.,** blotting paper.

secar, *v.* dry.

sección, *f.* section.

seco, *a.* dry; curt.

secreción, *f.* secretion.

secretar, *v.* secrete.

secretaría, *f.* secretary's office; secretariat.

secretario -ra, *n.* secretary.

secreto, *a. & m.* secret.

secta, *f.* denomination, sect.

secuela, *f.* result; sequel.

secuestrar, *v.* abduct, kidnap; hijack.

secuestro, *m.* abduction, kidnapping.

secular, *a.* secular.

secundario, *a.* secondary.

sed, *f.* thirst. **tener s.**, **estar con s.**, to be thirsty.

seda, *f.* silk.

sedar, *v.* quiet, allay.

sedativo, *a.* & *m.* sedative.

sede, *f.* seat, headquarters.

sedentario, *a.* sedentary.

sedición, *f.* sedition.

sedicioso, *a.* seditious.

sediento, *a.* thirsty.

sedimento, *m.* sediment.

sedoso, *a.* silky.

seducir, *v.* seduce.

seductivo, *a.* seductive, alluring.

segar, *v.* reap, harvest; mow.

seglar, *m.* layman.

segmento, *m.* segment.

segregar, *v.* segregate.

seguida, *f.* succession. **en s.**, right away, at once.

seguido, *a.* consecutive.

seguir, *v.* follow; continue, keep on, go on.

según, **1.** *prep.* according to, **2.** *conj.* as.

segundo, *a.* & *m.* second. —**segundar**, *v.*

seguridad, *f.* safety, security; assurance.

seguro, **1.** *a.* safe, secure; sure, certain. **2.** *m.* insurance.

seis, *a.* & *pron.* six.

seiscientos, *a.* & *pron.* six hundred.

selección, *f.* selection, choice.

seleccionar, *v.* select, choose.

selecto, *a.* select, choice, elite.

selva, *f.* forest; jungle.

selvoso, *a.* sylvan.

sello, *m.* seal; stamp. —**sellar**, *v.*

semáforo, *m.* semaphore.

semana, *f.* week.

semanal, *a.* weekly.

semántica, *f.* semantics.

semblante, *m.* look, expression.

sembrado, *m.* sown field.

sembrar, *v.* sow, seed.

semejante, **1.** *a.* like, similar; such (a). **2.** *m.* fellowman.

semejanza, *f.* similarity, likeness.

semejar, *v.* resemble.

semilla, *f.* seed.

seminario, *m.* seminary.

senado, *m.* senate.

senador -ra, *n.* senator.

sencillez, *f.* simplicity; naturalness.

sencillo, *a.* simple, natural; single.

senda, *f.* **sendero**, *m.* path.

senectud, *f.* old age.

senil, *a.* senile.

seno, *m.* breast, bosom.

sensación, *f.* sensation.

sensacional, *a.* sensational.

sensato, *a.* sensible, wise.

sensibilidad, *f.* sensibility; sensitiveness.

sensible, *a.* sensitive; emotional.

sensitivo, *a.* sensitive.

sensual, *a.* sensual.

sensualidad, *f.* sensuality.

sentar, *v.* seat. **s. bien**, fit well, be becoming.

sentarse, *v.* sit, sit down.

sentencia, *f.* (court) sentence.

sentidamente, *adv.* feelingly.

sentido, *m.* meaning, sense; consciousness.

sentimental, *a.* sentimental.

sentimiento, *m.* sentiment, feeling.

sentir, *v.* feel, sense; hear; regret, be sorry.

seña, *f.* sign, indication; (*pl.*) address.

señal, *f.* sign, signal; mark.

señalar, *v.* designate, point out; mark.

señor, *m.* gentleman; lord; (title) Mr., Sir.

señora, *f.* lady; wife; (title) Mrs., Madam.

señorita, *f.* young lady; (title) Miss.

sépalo, *m.* sepal.

separación, *f.* separation, parting.

separadamente, *adv.* separately.

separado, *a.* separate. —**separar**, *v.*

septentrional, *a.* northern.

septiembre, *m.* September.

séptimo, *a.* seventh.

sepulcro, *m.* sepulcher.

sepultar, *v.* bury, entomb.

sepultura, *f.* grave.

sequedad, *f.* dryness.

sequía, *f.* drought.

ser, *v.* be.

serenata, *f.* serenade.

serenidad, *f.* serenity.

sereno, 1. *a.* serene, calm. **2.** *m.* dew; watchman.

serie, *f.* series, sequence.

seriedad, *f.* seriousness.

serio, *a.* serious. **en s.,** seriously.

sermón, *m.* sermon.

seroso, *a.* watery.

serpiente, *f.* serpent, snake.

serrano, *m.* mountaineer.

serrar, *v.* saw.

serrín, *m.* sawdust.

servicial, *a.* helpful, of service.

servicio, *m.* service; toilet.

servidor -ra, *n.* servant.

servidumbre, *f.* bondage; staff of servants.

servil, *a.* servile, menial.

servilleta, *f.* napkin.

servir, *v.* serve. **s. para,** be good for.

servirse, *v.* help oneself.

sesenta, *a. & pron.* sixty.

sesgo, *m.* slant. **—sesgar,** *v.*

sesión, *f.* session; sitting.

seso, *m.* brain.

seta, *f.* mushroom.

setecientos, *a. & pron.* seven hundred.

setenta, *a. & pron.* seventy.

seto, *m.* hedge.

severamente, *adv.* severely.

severidad, *f.* severity.

severo, *a.* severe, strict, stern.

sexismo, *m.* sexism.

sexista, *m. & a.* sexist.

sexo, *m.* sex.

sexto, *a.* sixth.

sexual, *a.* sexual.

si, *conj.* if; whether.

sí, 1. *pron.* -self, -selves. **2.** *interj.* yes.

sicómoro, *m.* sycamore.

sidra, *f.* cider.

siempre, *adv.* always. **para s.,** forever. **s. que,** whenever; provided that.

sierra, *f.* saw; mountain range.

siervo, *m.* slave; serf.

siesta, *f.* (afternoon) nap.

siete, *a. & pron.* seven.

sifón, *m.* siphon; siphon bottle.

siglo, *m.* century.

signatura, *f.* signature.

significación, *f.* significance.

significado, *m.* meaning.

significante, *a.* significant.

significar, *v.* signify, mean.

significativo, *a.* significant.

signo, *m.* sign, symbol; mark.

siguiente, *a.* following, next.

sílaba, *f.* syllable.

silbar, *v.* whistle; hiss, boo.

silbato, silbido, *m.* whistle.

silencio, *m.* silence, stillness.

silenciosamente, *a.* silently.

silencioso, *a.* silent, still.

silicato, *m.* silicate.

silicio, *m.* silicon.

silueta, *f.* silhouette.

silvestre, *a.* wild, uncultivated. **fauna s.,** wildlife.

silla, *f.* chair; saddle.

sillón, *m.* armchair.

sima, *f.* chasm; cavern.

simbólico, *a.* symbolic.

símbolo, *m.* symbol.

simetría, *f.* symmetry.

simétrico, *a.* symmetrical.

símil, similar, *a.* similar, alike.

similitud, *f.* similarity.

simpatía, *f.* congeniality; friendly feeling.

simpático, *a.* likeable, nice, congenial.

simple, *a.* simple.

simpleza, *f.* silliness; trifle.

simplicidad, *f.* simplicity.

simplificación, *f.* simplification.

simplificar, *v.* simplify.

simular, *v.* simulate.

simultáneo, *a.* simultaneous.

sin, *prep.* without.

sinagoga, *f.* synagogue.

sinceridad, *f.* sincerity.

sincero, *a.* sincere.

sincronizar, *v.* synchronize.

sindicato, *m.* syndicate; labor union.

síndroma, *m.* syndrome.

sinfonía, *f.* symphony.

sinfónico, *a.* symphonic.

singular, *a. & m.* singular.

siniestro, *a.* sinister, ominous.

sino, *conj.* but.

sinónimo, *m.* synonym.

sinrazón, *f.* wrong, injustice.

sinsabor, *m.* displeasure, distaste.

sintaxis, *f.* syntax.

síntesis, *f.* synthesis.

sintético, *a.* synthetic.

síntoma, *m.* symptom.

siquiera, *adv.* **ni s.,** not even.

sirena, *f.* siren.

sirviente -ta, *n.* servant.

sistema, *m.* system.
sistemático, *a.* systematic.
sistematizar, *v.* systematize.
sitiar, *v.* besiege.
sitio, *m.* site, location, place, spot.
situación, *f.* situation; location.
situar, *v.* situate; locate.
smoking, *m.* tuxedo, dinner jacket.
so, *prep.* under.
soba, *f.* massage. —**sobar,** *v.*
sobaco, *m.* armpit.
sobaquero, *f.* armhole.
soberano -na, *a. & m.* sovereign.
soberbia, *f.* arrogance.
soberbio, *a.* superb; arrogant.
soborno, *m.* bribe. —**sobornar,** *v.*
sobra, *f.* excess, surplus. **de sobra,** to spare.
sobrado, *m.* attic.
sobrante, *a. & m.* surplus.
sobre, 1. *prep.* about; above, over. **2.** *m.* envelope.
sobrecama, *f.* bedspread.
sobrecargo, *m.* supercargo.
sobredicho, *a.* aforesaid.
sobrehumano, *a.* superhuman.
sobrenatural, *a.* supernatural, weird.
sobrepasar, *v.* surpass.
sobresalir, *v.* excel.
sobretodo, *m.* overcoat.
sobrevivir, *v.* survive, outlive.
sobriedad, *f.* sobriety; moderation.
sobrina, *f.* niece.
sobrino, *m.* nephew.
sobrio, *a.* sober, temperate.
socarrén, *m.* eaves.
sociable, *a.* sociable.
social, *a.* social.
socialismo, *m.* socialism.
socialista, *a. & m.* socialistic; socialist.
sociedad, *f.* society; association.
socio -cia, *n.* associate, partner; member.
sociología, *f.* sociology.
socorro, *m.* help, aid. —**socorrer,** *v.*
soda, *f.* soda.
sodio, *m.* sodium.
sofá, *m.* sofa, couch.
sofisma, *m.* sophism.
sofista, *m.* sophist.
sofocación, *f.* suffocation.

sofocar, *v.* smother, suffocate, stifle, choke.
soga, *f.* rope.
soja, *f.* soybean.
sol, *m.* sun.
solada, *f.* dregs.
solanera, *f.* sunbath.
solapa, *f.* lapel.
solar, 1. *a.* solar. **2.** *m.* building lot.
solaz, *m.* solace, comfort. —**solazar,** *v.*
soldado, *m.* soldier.
soldar, *v.* solder, weld.
soledad, *f.* solitude, privacy.
solemne, *a.* solemn.
solemnemente, *adv.* solemnly.
solemnidad, *f.* solemnity.
soler, *v.* be in the habit of.
solicitador, *m.* solicitor.
solicitar, *v.* solicit; apply for.
solícito, *a.* solicitous.
solicitud, *f.* solicitude; application.
sólidamente, *adv.* solidly.
solidaridad, *f.* solidarity.
solidez, *f.* solidity.
solidificar, *v.* solidify.
sólido, *a. & m.* solid.
soliloquio, *m.* soliloquy.
solitario, *a.* solitary, lone.
solo, 1. *a.* only; single; alone; lonely. **a solas,** alone. **2.** *m.* solo.
sólo, *adv.* only, just.
soltar, *v.* release; loosen.
soltero -ra, *a. & n.* single, unmarried (person).
soltura, *f.* poise, ease, facility.
solubilidad, *f.* solubility.
solución, *f.* solution.
solucionar, *v.* solve, settle.
solvente, *a.* solvent.
sollozo, *m.* sob. —**sollozar,** *v.*
sombra, *f.* shade; shadow. —**sombrear,** *v.*
sombrero, *m.* hat.
sombrilla, *f.* parasol.
sombrío, *a.* somber, bleak, gloomy.
sombroso, *a.* shady.
someter, *v.* subject; submit.
somnolencia, *f.* drowsiness.
son, *m.* sound. —**sonar,** *v.*
sonata, *f.* sonata.
sondar, *v.* sound, fathom.
sonido, *m.* sound.
sonoridad, *f.* sonority.

sonoro, *a.* sonorous.

sonrisa, *f.* smile. —**sonreír**, *v.*

sonrojo, *m.* flush, blush. —**sonrojarse**, *v.*

soñador -ra, *a. & n.* dreamy; dreamer.

soñar, *v.* dream.

soñoliento, *a.* sleepy.

sopa, *f.* soup.

soplar, *v.* blow.

soplete, *m.* blowtorch.

soplo, *m.* breath; puff, gust.

soportar, *v.* abide, bear, stand.

soprano, *m. & f.* soprano.

sorbete, *m.* sherbet.

sorbo, *m.* sip. —**sorber**, *v.*

sordera, *f.* deafness.

sórdidamente, *adv.* sordidly.

sordidez, *f.* sordidness.

sórdido, *a.* sordid.

sordo, *a.* deaf; muffled, dull.

sordomudo -da, *a. & n.* deafmute.

sorpresa, *f.* surprise. —**sorprender**, *v.*

sorteo, *m.* drawing lots; raffle.

sortija, *f.* ring.

sosa, *f.* (chem.) soda.

soso, *a.* dull, insipid, tasteless.

sospecha, *f.* suspicion.

sospechar, *v.* suspect.

sospechoso, *a.* suspicious.

sostén, *m.* support; brassiere.

sostener, *v.* hold, support; maintain.

sostenimiento, *m.* sustenance.

sota, *f.* jack (in cards).

sótano, *m.* basement, cellar.

soto, *m.* grove.

soviet, *m.* soviet.

soya, *f.* soybean.

su, *a.* his, her, its, their, your.

suave, *a.* smooth; gentle, soft, mild.

suavidad, *f.* smoothness; gentleness, softness, mildness.

suavizar, *v.* soften.

subalterno, *a. & m.* subordinate.

subasta, *f.* auction.

subconsciencia, *f.* subconscious.

súbdito -ta, *m.* subject.

subida, *f.* ascent, rise.

subilla, *f.* awl.

subir, *v.* rise, climb, ascend, mount. **s. a,** amount to.

súbito, *a.* sudden.

subjetivo, *a.* subjective.

subjuntivo, *a. & m.* subjunctive.

sublimación, *f.* sublimation.

sublimar, *v.* elevate; sublimate.

sublime, *a.* sublime.

submarino, *a. & m.* submarine.

subordinación, *f.* subordination.

subordinado, *a. & m.* subordinate. —**subordinar**, *v.*

subrayar, *v.* underline.

subscribirse, *v.* subscribe; sign one's name.

subscripción, *f.* subscription.

subsecuente, *a.* subsequent.

subsidiario, *a.* subsidiary.

subsiguiente, *a.* subsequent.

substancia, *f.* substance.

substancial, *a.* substantial.

substantivo, *m.* substantive, noun.

substitución, *f.* substitution.

substituir, *v.* replace; substitute.

substitutivo, *a.* substitute.

substituto -ta, *n.* substitute.

substraer, *v.* subtract.

subterfugio, *m.* subterfuge.

subterráneo, 1. *a.* subterranean, underground. **2.** *m.* place underground; subway.

suburbio, *m.* suburb.

subvención, *f.* subsidy, grant.

subversión, *f.* subversion.

subversivo, *a.* subversive.

subvertir, *v.* subvert.

subyugación, *f.* subjugation.

subyugar, *v.* subjugate, quell.

succión, *f.* suction.

suceder, *v.* happen, occur, befall. **s. a,** succeed, follow.

sucesión, *f.* succession.

sucesivo, *a.* successive. **en lo s.,** in the future.

suceso, *m.* event.

sucesor -ra, *n.* successor.

suciedad, *f.* filth, dirt.

sucio, *a.* filthy, dirty.

suculento, *a.* succulent.

sucumbir, *v.* succumb.

sud, *m.* south.

sudamericano -na, *a. & n.* South American.

sudar, *v.* perspire, sweat.

sudeste, *m.* southeast.

sudoeste, *m.* southwest.

sudor, *m.* perspiration, sweat.

Suecia, *f.* Sweden.

sueco -ca, *a. & n.* Swedish; Swede.

suegra, *f.* mother-in-law.
suegro, *m.* father-in-law.
suela, *f.* sole.
sueldo, *m.* salary, wages.
suelo, *m.* soil; floor; ground.
suelto, *a.* loose; free; odd, separate.
sueño, *m.* sleep; sleepiness; dream. **tener s.,** to be sleepy.
suero, *m.* serum.
suerte, *f.* luck; chance; lot.
suéter, *m.* sweater.
suficiente, *a.* sufficient.
sufragio, *m.* suffrage.
sufrimiento, *m.* suffering, agony.
sufrir, *v.* suffer; undergo; endure.
sugerencia, *f.* suggestion.
sugerir, *v.* suggest.
sugestión, *f.* suggestion.
sugestionar, *v.* influence; hypnotize.
suicida, *m. & f.* suicide (person).
suicidarse, *v.* commit suicide.
suicidio, *m.* (act of) suicide.
Suiza, *f.* Switzerland.
suizo -za, *a. & n.* Swiss.
sujeción, *f.* subjection.
sujetar, *v.* hold, fasten, clip.
sujeto, 1. *a.* subject, liable. **2.** *m.* (gram.) subject.
sulfato, *m.* sulfate.
sulfuro, *m.* sulfide.
sultán, *m.* sultan.
suma, *f.* sum, amount. **en s.,** in short.
sumar, *v.* add up.
sumaria, *f.* indictment.
sumario, *m. & a.* summary.
sumergir, *v.* submerge.
sumersión, *f.* submersion.
sumisión, *f.* submission.
sumiso, *a.* submissive.
sumo, *a.* great, high, utmost.
suntuoso, *a.* sumptuous.
superar, *v.* overcome, surpass.
superficial, *a.* superficial, shallow.
superficie, *f.* surface.
superfluo, *a.* superfluous.
superhombre, *m.* superman.
superintendente, *m.* superintendent.
superior, 1. *a.* superior; upper, higher. **2.** *m.* superior.
superioridad, *f.* superiority.
superlativo, *m. & a.* superlative.
superstición, *f.* superstition.

supersticioso, *a.* superstitious.
supervisar, *v.* supervise.
supervivencia, *f.* survival.
suplantar, *v.* supplant.
suplementario, *a.* supplementary.
suplemento, *m.* supplement. — **suplementar,** *v.*
suplente, *a. & m.* substitute.
súplica, *f.* request, entreaty, plea.
suplicación, *f.* supplication; request, entreaty.
suplicar, *v.* request, entreat; implore.
suplicio, *m.* torture, ordeal.
suplir, *v.* supply.
suponer, *v.* suppose, pressume, assume.
suposición, *f.* supposition, assumption.
supremacía, *f.* supremacy.
supremo, *a.* supreme.
supresión, *f.* suppression.
suprimir, *v.* suppress; abolish.
supuesto, *a.* supposed. **por s.,** of course.
sur, *m.* south.
surco, *m.* furrow. — **surcar,** *v.*
surgir, *v.* arise; appear suddenly.
surtido, *m.* assortment; supply, stock.
surtir, *v.* furnish, supply.
susceptibilidad, *f.* susceptibility.
susceptible, *a.* susceptible.
suscitar, *v.* stir up.
suscri- = **subscri-**
suspender, *v.* withhold; suspend; fail (in a course).
suspensión, *f.* suspension.
suspenso, *m.* failing grade. **en s.,** in suspense.
suspicacia, *f.* suspicion, distrust.
suspicaz, *a.* suspicious.
suspicazmente, *adv.* suspiciously.
suspiro, *m.* sigh. — **suspirar,** *v.*
sustan- = **substan-**
sustentar, *v.* sustain, support.
sustento, *m.* sustenance, support, living.
susti- = **substi-**
susto, *m.* fright, scare.
sustraer- = **substraer.**
susurro, *m.* rustle; whisper. — **susurrar,** *v.*
sutil, *a.* subtle.
sutileza, sutilidad, *f.* subtlety.
sutura, *f.* suture.
suyo, *a.* his, hers, theirs, yours.

T

tabaco, *m.* tobacco.
tábano, *m.* horsefly.
tabaquería, *f.* tobacco shop.
taberna, *f.* tavern, bar.
tabernáculo, *m.* tabernacle.
tabique, *m.* dividing wall, partition.
tabla, *f.* board, plank; table, list.
tablado, *m.* stage, platform.
tablero, *m.* panel.
tableta, *f.* tablet.
tablilla, *f.* bulletin board.
tabú, *m.* taboo.
tabular, *a.* tabular.
tacaño, *a.* stingy.
tácitamente, *adv.* tacitly.
tácito, *a.* tacit.
taciturno, *a.* taciturn.
taco, *m.* heel (of shoe); billiard cue.
tacón, *m.* heel (of shoe).
táctico, *a.* tactical.
tacto, *m.* (sense of) touch; tact.
tacha, *f.* fault, defect.
tachar, *v.* find fault with; cross out.
tachuela, *f.* tack.
tafetán, *m.* taffeta.
taimado, *a.* sly.
tajada, *n.* cut, slice. **—tajar,** *v.*
tajea, *f.* channel.
tal, *a.* such. **con t. que.,** provided that. **t. vez,** perhaps.
taladrar, *v.* drill.
taladro, *m.* (mech.) drill.
talante, *m.* humor, disposition.
talco, *m.* talc.
talega, *f.* bag, sack.
talento, *m.* talent.
talón, *m.* heel (of foot); (baggage) check, stub.
talla, *f.* engraving; stature; size (of suit).
tallador -ra, *n.* engraver; dealer (at cards).
talle, *m.* figure; waist; fit.
taller, *m.* workshop, factory.
tallo, *m.* stem, stalk.
tamal, *m.* tamale.
tamaño, *m.* size.
tambalear, *v.* stagger, totter.
también, *adv.* also, too.
tambor, *m.* drum.
tamiz, *m.* sieve, sifter.

tampoco, *adv.* neither, either.
tan, *adv.* so.
tanda, *f.* turn, relay.
tándem, *m.* tandem bicycle.
tangencia, *f.* tangency.
tangible, *a.* tangible.
tango, *m.* tango (dance or music).
tanque, *m.* tank.
tanteo, *m.* estimate. **—tantear,** *v.*
tanto, 1. *a. & pron.* so much, so many; as much, as many. **entre t., mientras t.,** meanwhile. **por lo t.,** therefore. **un t.,** somewhat, a bit. **2.** *m.* point (in games); (*pl.*) score. **estar al t.,** to be up to date.
tañer, *v.* play (an instrument); ring (bells).
tapa, *f.* cap, cover. **—tapar,** *v.*
tapadero, *m.* stopper, lid.
tápara, *f.* caper.
tapete, *m.* small rug, mat, cover.
tapia, *f.* wall.
tapicería, *f.* tapestry.
tapioca, *f.* tapioca.
tapiz, *m.* tapestry; carpet.
tapizado (de pared), *m.* (wall) covering.
tapón, *m.* plug; cork.
taquigrafía, *f.* shorthand.
taquilla, *f.* ticket office; ticket window.
tara, *f.* hang-up.
tarántula, *f.* tarantula.
tararear, *v.* hum.
tardanza, *f.* delay; lateness.
tardar, *v.* delay; be late; (take of time). **a más t.,** at the latest.
tarde, 1. *adv.* late. **2.** *f.* afternoon.
tardío, *a.* late, belated.
tarea, *f.* task, assignment.
tarifa, *f.* rate; tariff; price list.
tarjeta, *f.* card.
tarta, *f.* tart.
tartamudear, *v.* stammer, falter.
tasa, *f.* rate.
tasación, *f.* valuation.
tasar, *v.* assess, appraise.
tasugo, *m.* badger.
tautología, *f.* tautology.
taxi, taxímetro, *m.* taxi.
taxista, *m.f.* taxi driver.
taxonomía, *f.* taxonomy.
taza, *f.* cup.
te, *pron.* you; yourself.
té, *m.* tea.

teátrico, *a.* theatrical.
teatro, *m.* theater.
tecla, *f.* key (of a piano, etc.).
técnica, *f.* technique.
técnicamente, *adv.* technically.
técnico, *a.* technical.
tecnología, *f.* technology.
techo, *m.* roof. —**techar,** *v.*
tedio, *m.* tedium, boredom.
tedioso, *a.* tedious.
teísmo, *m.* theism.
teja, *f.* tile.
tejado, *m.* roof.
tejer, *v.* weave; knit.
tejido, *m.* fabric; weaving.
tejón, *m.* badger.
tela, *f.* cloth, fabric, web. **t. metálica,** screen; screening.
telar, *m.* loom.
telaraña, *f.* cobweb.
telefonista, *m.* & *f.* (telephone) operator.
teléfono, *m.* telephone. —**telefonear,** *v.*
telégrafo, *m.* telegraph. —**telegrafiar,** *v.*
telegrama, *m.* telegram.
telescopio, *m.* telescope.
televisión, *f.* television.
telón, *m.* (theat.) curtain.
telurio, *m.* tellurium.
tema, *m.* theme, subject.
temblar, *v.* tremble, quake; shake, shiver.
temblor, *m.* tremor; shiver.
temer, *v.* fear, be afraid of, dread.
temerario, *a.* rash.
temeridad, *f.* temerity.
temerosamente, *adv.* timorously.
temeroso, *a.* fearful.
temor, *m.* fear.
témpano, *m.* kettledrum; iceberg.
temperamento, *m.* temperament.
temperancia, *f.* temperance.
temperatura, *f.* temperature.
tempestad, *f.* tempest, storm.
tempestuoso, *a.* tempestuous, stormy.
templado, *a.* temperate, mild, moderate.
templanza, *f.* temperance; mildness.
templar, *v.* temper; tune (an instrument).
templo, *m.* temple.
temporada, *f.* season, time, spell.

temporal, temporáneo, *a.* temporary.
temprano, *a.* & *adv.* early.
tenacidad, *f.* tenacity.
tenaz, *a.* tenacious, stubborn.
tenazmente, *adv.* tenaciously.
tendencia, *f.* tendency, trend.
tender, *v.* stretch, stretch out.
tendero -ra, *n.* shopkeeper, storekeeper.
tendón, *m.* tendon, sinew.
tenebrosidad, *f.* gloom.
tenebroso, *a.* dark, gloomy.
tenedor, *m.* keeper; holder; fork.
tener, *v.* have; own; hold. **t. que,** have to, must.
teniente, *m.* lieutenant.
tenis, *m.* tennis; (*pl.*) sneakers.
tenor, *m.* tenor.
tensión, *f.* tension, stress, strain.
tenso, *a.* tense.
tentación, *f.* temptation.
tentáculo, *m.* tentacle.
tentador, *a.* alluring, tempting.
tentar, *v.* tempt; lure; grope, probe.
tentativa, *f.* attempt.
tentativo, *a.* tentative.
teñir, *v.* tint, dye.
teología, *f.* theology.
teológico, *a.* theological.
teoría, *f.* theory.
teórico, *a.* theoretical.
terapéutico, *a.* therapeutic.
tercero, *a.* third.
tercio, *m.* third.
terciopelo, *m.* velvet.
terco, *a.* obstinate, stubborn.
termal, *a.* thermal.
terminación, *f.* termination; completion.
terminar, *v.* terminate, finish.
término, *m.* term; end.
terminología, *f.* terminology.
termómetro, *m.* thermometer.
termos, *m.* thermos.
ternero -ra, *n.* calf.
ternura, *f.* tenderness.
terquedad, *f.* stubbornness.
terraza, *f.* terrace.
terremoto, *m.* earthquake.
terreno, 1. *a.* earthly, terrestrial. **2.** *m.* ground, terrain; lot, plot.
terrible, *a.* terrible, awful.
terrífico, *a.* terrific.
territorio, *m.* territory.
terrón, *m.* clod, lump; mound.

terror, *m.* terror.

terso, *a.* smooth, glossy; terse.

tertulia, *f.* social gathering, party.

tesis, *f.* thesis.

tesorería, *f.* treasury.

tesorero -ra, *n.* treasurer.

tesoro, *m.* treasure.

testamento, *m.* will, testament.

testarudo, *a.* stubborn.

testificar, *v.* testify.

testigo, *m.* witness; testimony.

testimonial, *a.* testimonial.

testimonio, *m.* testimony.

teta, *f.* teat.

tetera, *f.* teapot.

tétrico, *a.* sad; gloomy.

texto, *m.* text.

textura, *f.* texture.

tez, *f.* complexion.

ti, *pron.* you; yourself.

tía, *f.* aunt.

tibio, *a.* lukewarm.

tiburón, *m.* shark.

tiemblo, *m.* aspen.

tiempo, *m.* time; weather; (gram.) tense.

tienda, *f.* shop, store; tent.

tientas, *f.pl.* **andar a t.,** to grope (in the dark).

tierno, *a.* tender.

tierra, *f.* land; ground; earth, dirt, soil.

tieso, *a.* taut, stiff, hard, strong.

tiesto, *m.* flower pot.

tiesura, *f.* stiffness; harshness.

tifo, *m.* typhus.

tifoideo, *f.* typhoid fever.

tigre, *m.* tiger.

tijeras, *f.pl.* scissors.

tila, *f.* linden.

timbre, *m.* seal, stamp; tone; (electric) bell.

timidamente, *adv.* timidly.

timidez, *f.* timidity.

tímido, *a.* timid, shy.

timón, *m.* rudder, helm.

tímpano, *m.* kettledrum; eardrum.

tina, *f.* tub, vat.

tinaja, *f.* jar.

tinta, *f.* ink.

tinte, *m.* tint, shade.

tintero, *m.* inkwell.

tinto, *a.* wine-colored; red (of wine).

tintorería, *f.* dry cleaning shop.

tintorero -ra, *n.* dyer; dry cleaner.

tintura, *f.* tincture; dye.

tiñoso, *a.* scabby; stingy.

tío, *m.* uncle.

tiovivo, *m.* merry-go-round.

típico, *a.* typical.

tipo, *m.* type, sort; (interest) rate; (coll.) guy, fellow.

tira, *f.* strip.

tirabuzón, *m.* corkscrew.

tirada, *f.* edition.

tiranía, *f.* tyranny.

tiránico, *m.* tyrannical.

tirano, *m.* tyrant.

tirante, 1. *a.* tight, taut; tense. **2.** *m.* (*pl.*) suspenders.

tirar, *v.* throw; draw; pull; fire (a weapon).

tiritar, *v.* shiver.

tiro, *m.* throw; shot.

tirón, *m.* pull. **de un t.,** at a stretch, at one stroke.

tísico, *n. & a.* consumptive.

tisis, *f.* consumption, tuberculosis.

titania, *m.* titanium.

títere, *m.* puppet.

titilación, *f.* twinkle.

titubear, *v.* stagger; totter; waver.

titulado, *a.* entitled; so-called.

titular, 1. *a.* titular. **2.** *v.* entitle.

título, *m.* title, headline.

tiza, *f.* chalk.

tiznar, *v.* smudge; stain.

toalla, *f.* towel. **t. sanitaria,** sanitary napkin.

toalleta, *f.* small towel.

tobillo, *m.* ankle.

tocadiscos, *m.* record player.

tocado, *m.* hairdo.

tocador, *m.* boudoir; dressing table.

tocante, *a.* touching. **t. a,** concerning, relative to.

tocar, *v.* touch; play (an instrument). **t. a uno,** be one's turn; be up to one.

tocayo, *m.* namesake.

tocino, *m.* bacon.

todavía, *adv.* yet, still.

todo, 1. *a.* all, whole. **todos los,** every. **2.** *pron.* all, everything. **con t.,** still, however. **del t.,** wholly; at all.

todopoderoso, *a.* almighty.

toldo, *m.* awning.

tolerancia, *f.* tolerance.
tolerante, *a.* tolerant.
tolerar, *v.* tolerate.
toma, *f.* taking, capture, seizure.
tomaína, *f.* ptomaine.
tomar, *v.* take; drink.
tomate, *m.* tomato.
tomillo, *m.* thyme.
tomo, *m.* volume.
tonada, *f.* tune.
tonel, *m.* barrel, cask.
tonelada, *f.* ton.
tonelaje, *m.* tonnage.
tónico, *a. & m.* tonic.
tono, *m.* tone, pitch, shade. **darse t.,** to put on airs.
tonsila, *f.* tonsil.
tonsilitis, *f.* tonsilitis.
tontería, *f.* nonsense, foolishness.
tonto -ta, *a. & n.* foolish, silly; fool.
topacio, *m.* topaz.
topar, *v.* run into. **t. con,** come upon.
tópico, 1. *a.* topical. **2.** *m.* topic.
topo, *m.* mole (animal).
toque, *m.* touch.
tórax, *m.* thorax.
torbellino, *m.* whirlwind.
torcer, *v.* twist; wind; distort.
toreador, *m.* toreador.
torero, *m.* bullfighter.
torio, *m.* thorium.
tormenta, *f.* storm.
tormento, *m.* torment.
tornado, *m.* tornado.
tornar, *v.* return; turn.
tornarse en, *v.* turn into, become.
torneo, *m.* tournament.
tornillo, *m.* screw.
toro, *m.* bull.
toronja, *f.* grapefruit.
torpe, *a.* awkward, clumsy; sluggish.
torpedero, *m.* torpedo boat.
torpedo, *m.* torpedo.
torre, *f.* tower.
torrente, *m.* torrent.
tórrido, *a.* torrid.
torta, *f.* cake; loaf.
tortilla, *f.* omelet; (Mex.) tortilla, pancake.
tórtola, *f.* dove.
tortuga, *f.* turtle.
tortuoso, *a.* tortuous.
tortura, *f.* torture. **—torturar,** *v.*
tos, *m.* cough. **—toser,** *v.*

tosco, *a.* coarse, rough, uncouth.
tosquedad, *f.* coarseness, roughness.
tostar, *v.* toast; tan.
total, *a. & m.* total.
totalidad, *f.* totality, entirety, whole.
totalitario, *a.* totalitarian.
totalmente, *adv.* totally; entirely.
tótem, *m.* totem.
tóxico, *a.* toxic.
trabajador -ra, 1. *a.* hardworking. **2.** *n.* worker.
trabajo, *m.* work; labor. **—trabajar,** *v.*
trabar, *v.* fasten, shackle; grasp; strike up.
tracción, *f.* traction.
tracto, *m.* tract.
tractor, *m.* tractor.
tradición, *f.* tradition.
tradicional, *a.* traditional.
traducción, *f.* translation.
traducir, *v.* translate.
traductor, *m.* translator.
traer, *v.* bring; carry; wear.
tráfico, *m.* traffic. **—traficar,** *v.*
tragar, *v.* swallow.
tragedia, *f.* tragedy.
trágicamente, *adv.* tragically.
trágico -ca, 1. *a.* tragic. **2.** *n.* tragedian.
trago, *m.* swallow; drink.
traición, *f.* treason, betrayal.
traicionar, *v.* betray.
traidor -ra, *a. & n.* traitorous; traitor.
traje, *m.* suit; dress; garb, apparel.
trama, *v.* plot (of a story).
tramador, *m.* weaver; plotter.
tramar, *v.* weave; plot, scheme.
trámite, *m.* (business) deal, transaction.
tramo, *m.* span, stretch, section.
trampa, *f.* trap, snare.
trampista, *m.* cheater; swindler.
trance, *m.* critical moment or stage. **a todo t.,** at any cost.
tranco, *m.* stride.
tranquilidad, *f.* tranquility, calm, quiet.
tranquilizante, *m.* tranquilizer.
tranquilizar, *v.* quiet, calm down.
tranquilo, *a.* tranquil, calm.
transacción, *f.* transaction.
transbordador, *m.* ferry.

transcribir, v. transcribe.

transcripción, f. transcription.

transcurrir, v. elapse.

transeúnte, a. & n. transient; passerby.

transexual, a. transsexual.

transferencia, f. transference.

transferir, v. transfer.

transformación, f. transformation.

transformar, v. transform.

transfusión, f. transfusion.

transgresión, f. transgression.

transgresor, m. transgressor.

transición, f. transition.

transigir, v. compromise, settle; agree.

transitivo, a. transitive.

tránsito, m. transit, passage.

transitorio, a. transitory.

transmisión, f. transmission; broadcast.

transmisora, f. broadcasting station.

transmitir, v. transmit; broadcast.

transparencia, f. transparency.

transparente, 1. a. transparent. 2. m. (window) shade.

transportación, f. transportation.

transportar, v. transport, convey.

transporte, m. transportation; transport.

tranvía, m. streetcar, trolley.

trapacero, n. cheat; swindler.

trapo, m. rag.

tráquea, f. trachea.

tras, prep. after; behind.

trasegar, v. upset, overturn.

trasero, a. rear, back.

traslado, m. transfer. —trasladar, v.

traslapo, m. overlap. —traslapar, v.

trasnochar, v. sit up all night.

traspalar, v. shovel.

traspasar, v. go beyond; cross; violate; pierce.

trasquilar, v. shear; clip.

trastornar, v. overturn, overthrow, upset.

trastorno, m. overthrow; upheaval.

tratado, m. treaty; treatise.

tratamiento, m. treatment.

tratar, v. treat, handle. t. de, deal with; try to; call (a name).

tratarse de, v. be a question of.

trato, m. treatment; manners; (com.) deal.

través, adv. a t. de, through, across. de t., sideways.

travesía, f. crossing; voyage.

travesti, m. transvestite.

travestido, a. disguised.

travesura, f. prank; mischief.

travieso, a. naughty, mischievous.

trayectoria, f. trajectory.

trazar, v. plan, devise; trace; draw.

trazo, n. plan, outline; line, stroke.

trébol, m. clover.

trece, a. & pron. thirteen.

trecho, m. space, distance, stretch.

tregua, f. truce, respite, lull.

treinta, a. & pron. thirty.

tremendo, a. tremendous.

tremer, v. tremble.

tren, m. train.

trenza, f. braid. —trenzar, v.

trepar, v. climb, mount.

trepidación, f. trepidation.

tres, a. & pron. three.

trescientos, a. & pron. three hundred.

triángulo, m. triangle.

tribu, f. tribe.

tribulación, f. tribulation.

tribuna, f. rostrum, stand; (pl.) grandstand.

tribunal, m. court, tribunal.

tributario, a. & m. tributary.

tributo, m. tribute.

triciclo, m. tricycle.

trigo, m. wheat.

trigonometría, f. trigonometry.

trigueño, a. swarthy, dark.

trilogía, f. trilogy.

trimestral, a. quarterly.

trinchar, v. carve (meat).

trinchera, f. trench, ditch.

trineo, m. sled; sleigh.

trinidad, f. trinity.

tripa, f. tripe, entrails.

triple, a. triple. —triplicar, v.

tripulación, f. (ship's) crew.

triste, a. sad, sorrowful; dreary.

tristemente, adv. sadly.

tristeza, f. sadness; gloom.

triunfal, a. triumphal.

triunfante, a. triumphant.

triunfo, *m.* triumph, trump. — **triunfar,** *v.*

trivial, *a.* trivial, commonplace.

trivialidad, *f.* triviality.

trocar, *v.* exchange; switch; barter.

trofeo, *m.* trophy.

trombón, *m.* trombone.

trompa, trompeta, *f.* trumpet, horn.

tronada, *f.* thunderstorm.

tronar, *v.* thunder.

tronco, *m.* trunk, stump.

trono, *m.* throne.

tropa, *f.* troop.

tropel, *m.* crowd, throng.

tropezar, *v.* trip, stumble, **t. con,** come upon, run into.

trópico, *a. & m.* tropical; tropics.

tropiezo, *m.* stumble; obstacle; slip, error.

trote, *m.* trot. —**trotar,** *v.*

trovador, *m.* troubadour.

trozo, *m.* piece, portion, fragment, selection, passage.

trucha, *f.* trout.

trueco, trueque, *m.* exchange, barter.

trueno, *m.* thunder.

tu, *a.* your.

tú, *pron.* you.

tuberculosis, *f.* tuberculosis.

tubo, *m.* tube, pipe.

tuerca, *f.* (mech.) nut.

tulipán, *m.* tulip.

tumba, *f.* tomb, grave.

tumbar, *v.* knock down.

tumbarse, *v.* tumble.

tumbo, *m.* tumble; somersault.

tumor, *m.* tumor; growth.

tumulto, *m.* tumult, commotion.

tumultuoso, *a.* tumultuous, boisterous.

tunante, *m.* rascal, rogue.

tunda, *f.* spanking, whipping.

túnel, *m.* tunnel.

tungsteno, *m.* tungsten.

túnica, *f.* tunic, robe.

tupir, *v.* pack tight, stuff; stop up.

turbación, *f.* confusion, turmoil.

turbamulta, *f.* mob; crowd.

turbar, *v.* disturb, upset; embarrass.

turbina, *f.* turbine.

turbio, *a.* turbid; muddy.

turco -ca, *a. & n.* Turkish; Turk.

turismo, *m.* touring, (foreign) travel.

turista, *m. & f.* tourist.

turno, *m.* turn; (work) shift.

turquesa, *f.* turquoise.

Turquía, *f.* Turkey.

turrón, *m.* nougat.

tusa, *f.* corncob; corn.

tutear, *v.* use the pronoun **tú,** etc., in addressing a person.

tutela, *f.* guardianship; aegis.

tutor, *m.* tutor; guardian.

tuyo, *a.* your, yours.

U

u, *conj.* or.

ubre, *f.* udder.

ufano, *a.* proud, haughty.

úlcera, *f.* ulcer.

ulterior, *a.* ulterior.

último, *a.* last, final; ultimate; latest. **por ú.,** finally.

ultraje, *m.* outrage. —**ultrajar,** *v.*

umbral, *m.* threshold.

umbroso, *a.* shady.

un, una, *art. & a.* a, an; one; (*pl.*) some.

unánime, *a.* unanimous.

unanimidad, *f.* unanimity.

unción, *f.* unction.

ungüento, *m.* ointment, salve.

único, *a.* only, sole; unique.

unicornio, *m.* unicorn.

unidad, *f.* unit; unity.

unificar, *v.* unify.

uniforme, *a. & m.* uniform.

uniformidad, *f.* uniformity.

unión, *f.* union; joining.

unir, *v.* unite, join.

universal, *a.* universal.

universalidad, *f.* universality.

universidad, *f.* university; college.

universo, *m.* universe.

uno, una, *pron.* one; (*pl.*) some.

untar, *v.* spread; grease; anoint.

uña, *f.* fingernail.

urbanidad, *f.* urbanity; good breeding.

urbano, *a.* urban; urbane; well-bred.

urbe, *f.* large city.

urgencia, *f.* urgency.

urgente, *a.* urgent, pressing. **entrega u.,** special delivery.

urgir, v. be urgent.
urna, f. urn; ballot box; (pl.) polls.
usanza, f. usage, custom.
usar, v. use; wear.
uso, m. use; usage; wear.
usted, pron. you.
usual, a. usual.
usualmente, adv. usually.
usura, f. usury.
usurero, m. usurer.
usurpación, f. usurpation.
usurpar, v. usurp.
utensilio, m. utensil.
útero, m. uterus.
útil, a. useful, handy.
utilidad, f. utility, usefulness.
utilizar, v. use, utilize.
útilmente, adv. usefully.
utópico, a. utopian.
uva, f. grape.

V

vaca, f. cow; beef.
vacaciones, f.pl. vacation, holidays.
vacancia, f. vacancy.
vacante, 1. a. vacant. 2. f. vacancy.
vaciar, v. empty; pour out.
vacilación, f. vacillation, hesitation.
vacilante, a. vacillating.
vacilar, v. falter, hesitate; waver; stagger.
vacío, 1. a. empty. 2. m. void, empty space.
vacuna, f. vaccine.
vacunación, f. vaccination.
vacunar, v. vaccinate.
vacuo, 1. a. empty, vacant. 2. m. vacuum.
vadear, v. wade through, ford.
vado, m. ford.
vagabundo, a. & m. vagabond.
vagar, v. wander, rove, roam; loiter.
vago -ga, 1. a. vague, hazy; wandering, vagrant. 2. n. vagrant, tramp.
vagón, m. railroad car.
vahído, m. dizziness.
vaina, f. sheath; pod.
vainilla, f. vanilla.
vaivén, m. vibration, sway.

vajilla, f. (dinner) dishes.
valentía, f. valor, courage.
valer, 1. m. worth. 2. v. be worth.
valerse de, v. make use of, avail oneself of.
valía, f. value.
validez, f. validity.
válido, a. valid.
valiente, a. valiant, brave, courageous.
valija, f. valise.
valioso, a. valuable.
valor, m. value, worth; bravery, valor; (pl., com.) securities.
valoración, f. appraisal.
valorar, v. value, appraise.
vals, m. waltz.
valsar, v. waltz.
valuación, f. valuation.
valuar, v. value; rate.
válvula, f. valve.
valla, f. fence, barrier.
valle, m. valley.
vándalo, m. vandal.
vanidad, f. vanity.
vanidoso, a. vain, conceited.
vano, a. vain; inane.
vapor, m. vapor; steam; steamer, steamship.
vaquero, m. cowboy.
vara, f. wand, stick, switch.
varadero, m. shipyard.
varar, v. launch; be stranded; run aground.
variable, a. variable.
variación, f. variation.
variar, v. vary.
variedad, f. variety.
varios, a. & pron. pl. various; several.
varón, m. man; male.
varonil, a. manly, virile.
vasallo, m. vassal.
vasectomía, f. vasectomy.
vasija, f. bowl, container (for liquids).
vaso, m. water glass; vase.
vástago, m. bud, shoot; twig; offspring.
vasto, a. vast.
vecindad, f. vecindario, m. neighborhood, vicinity.
vecino -na, a. & n. neighboring; neighbor.
vedar, v. forbid; impede.
vega, f. meadow.
vegetación, f. vegetation.

vegetal, *m.* vegetable.

vehemente, *a.* vehement.

vehículo, *m.* vehicle; conveyance.

veinte, *a. & pron.* twenty.

vejez, *f.* old age.

vejiga, *f.* bladder.

vela, *f.* vigil, watch; candle; sail.

velar, *v.* stay up, sit up; watch over.

velo, *m.* veil.

velocidad, *f.* velocity, speed; rate.

velomotor, *m.* motorbike, moped.

veloz, *a.* speedy, fast, swift.

vellón, *m.* fleece.

velloso, *a.* hairy; fuzzy.

velludo, *a.* downy.

vena, *f.* vein.

venado, *m.* deer.

vencedor -ra, *n.* victor.

vencer, *v.* defeat, overcome, conquer; (com.) become due, expire.

vencimiento, *m.* defeat.

venda, *f.* **vendaje**, *m.* bandage. — **vendar**, *v.*

vendedor -ra, *n.* seller, trader; sales clerk.

vender, *v.* sell.

vendimia, *f.* vintage.

veneno, *m.* poison.

venenoso, *a.* poisonous.

veneración, *f.* veneration.

venerar, *v.* venerate, revere.

venero, *m.* spring, origin.

véneto, *a.* Venetian.

venezolano, *a. & n.* Venezuelan.

vengador -ra, *n.* avenger.

venganza, *f.* vengeance, revenge.

vengar, *v.* avenge.

venida, *f.* arrival, advent, coming.

venidero, *a.* future; coming.

venir, *v.* come.

venta, *f.* sale; sales.

ventaja, *f.* advantage; profit.

ventajoso, *a.* advantageous; profitable.

ventana, *f.* window.

ventero, *m.* innkeeper.

ventilación, *f.* ventilation.

ventilador, *m.* ventilator, fan.

ventilar, *v.* ventilate, air.

ventoso, *a.* windy.

ventura, *f.* venture; happiness; luck.

ver, *v.* see. **tener que v. con**, have to do with.

vera, *f.* edge.

veracidad, *f.* truthfulness, veracity.

verano, *m.* summer. —**veranear** *v.*

veras, *f.pl.* **de v.**, really, truly.

veraz, *a.* truthful.

verbigracia, *adv.* for example.

verbo, *m.* verb.

verboso, *a.* verbose.

verdad, *f.* truth. **ser v.**, to be true

verdadero, *a.* true, real.

verde, *a.* green; risqué, off-color

verdor, *m.* greenness, verdure.

verdugo, *m.* hangman.

verdura, *f.* verdure, vegetation (*pl.*) vegetables.

vereda, *f.* path.

veredicto, *m.* verdict.

vergonzoso, *a.* shameful, embarrassing; shy, bashful.

vergüenza, *f.* shame; disgrace; embarrassment.

verificar, *v.* verify, check.

verja, *f.* grating, railing.

verosímil, *a.* likely, plausible.

verraco, *m.* boar.

verruga, *f.* wart.

versátil, *a.* versatile.

verse, *v.* look, appear.

versión, *f.* version.

verso, *m.* verse, stanza; line (of poetry).

verter, *v.* pour, spill; shed; empty.

vertical, *a.* vertical.

vertiente, *f.* slope; watershed.

vertiginoso, *a.* dizzy.

vértigo, *m.* vertigo, dizziness.

vestíbulo, *m.* vestibule, lobby.

vestido, *m.* dress; clothing.

vestigio, *m.* vestige, trace.

vestir, *v.* dress, clothe.

veterano -na, *a. & n.* veteran.

veterinario, *m.* veterinary.

veto, *m.* veto.

vetusto, *a.* ancient, very old.

vez, *f.* time; turn. **tal v.**, perhaps **a la v.**, at the same time. **en v. de** instead of. **una v.**, once. **otra v.** again.

vía, *f.* track; route, way.

viaducto, *m.* viaduct.

viajante, *a. & n.* traveling; traveler.

viajar, *v.* travel; journey, tour.

viaje, *m.* trip, journey, voyage; (*pl.*) travels.

viajero -ra, *n.* traveler; passenger.

viandas, *f.pl.* victuals, food.

víbora, *f.* viper.

vibración, *f.* vibration.

vibrar, *v.* vibrate.

vicepresidente, *m.* vice president.

vicio, *m.* vice.

vicioso, *a.* vicious; licentious.

víctima, *f.* victim.

victoria, *f.* victory.

victorioso, *a.* victorious.

vid, *f.* grapevine.

vida, *f.* life; living.

vídeo, *m.* videotape.

videodisco, *m.* videodisc.

vidrio, *m.* glass.

viejo -ja, *a.* & *n.* old; old person.

viento, *m.* wind. **hacer v.,** to be windy.

vientre, *m.* belly.

viernes, *m.* Friday.

viga, *f.* beam, rafter.

vigente, *a.* in effect (prices, etc.).

vigilante, *a.* & *m.* vigilant, watchful; watchman.

vigilar, *v.* guard, watch over.

vigilia, *f.* vigil, watchfulness; (rel.) fast.

vigor, *m.* vigor. **en v.,** in effect, in force.

vil, *a.* vile, low, contemptible.

vileza, *f.* baseness; vileness.

villa, *f.* town; country house.

villancico, *m.* Christmas carol.

villanía, *f.* villainy.

villano, *m.* boor.

vinagre, *m.* vinegar.

vínculo, *m.* link. **—vincular,** *v.*

vindicar, *v.* vindicate.

vino, *m.* wine.

viña, *f.* vineyard.

violación, *f.* violation.

violar, *v.* violate.

violencia, *f.* violence.

violento, *a.* violent; impulsive.

violeta, *f.* violet.

violín, *m.* violin.

violón, *m.* bass viol.

virar, *v.* veer, change course.

virgen, *f.* virgin.

viril, *a.* virile, manly.

virilidad, *f.* virility; manhood.

virtual, *a.* virtual.

virtud, *f.* virtue; efficacy, power.

virtuoso, *a.* virtuous.

viruela, *f.* smallpox.

visa, *f.* visa.

visaje, *m.* grimace.

visera, *f.* visor.

visible, *a.* visible.

visión, *f.* vision.

visionario -ria, *a.* & *n.* visionary.

visita, *f.* visit; visitor, caller.

visitación, *f.* visitation.

visitante, *a.* & *m.* visiting; visitor.

visitar, *v.* visit; inspect, examine.

vislumbre, *f.* glimpse.

viso, *m.* looks; outlook.

víspera, *f.* eve, day before.

vista, *f.* view; scene; sight.

vistazo, *m.* glance, glimpse.

vistoso, *a.* beautiful; showy.

visual, *a.* visual.

vital, *a.* vital.

vitalidad, *f.* vitality.

vitamina, *f.* vitamin.

vitando, *a.* hateful.

vituperar, *v.* vituperate; revile.

viuda, *f.* widow.

viudo, *m.* widower.

vivaz, *a.* vivacious, buoyant; clever.

víveres, *m.pl.* provisions.

viveza, *f.* animation, liveliness.

vívido, *a.* vivid, bright.

vivienda, *f.* (living) quarters, dwelling.

vivificar, *v.* vivify, enliven.

vivir, *v.* live.

vivo, *a.* live, alive, living; vivid; animated, brisk.

vocablo, *m.* word.

vocabulario, *m.* vocabulary.

vocación, *f.* vocation, calling.

vocal, 1. *a.* vocal. **2.** *f.* vowel.

vocear, *v.* vociferate.

vodevil, *m.* vaudeville.

volante, 1. *a.* flying. **2.** *m.* memorandum; (steering) wheel.

volar, *v.* fly; explode.

volcán, *m.* volcano.

volcar, *v.* upset, capsize.

voltear, *v.* turn, whirl; overturn.

voltio, *m.* volt.

volumen, *m.* volume.

voluminoso, *a.* voluminous.

voluntad, *f.* will.

voluntario -ria, *a.* & *n.* voluntary; volunteer.

voluntarioso, *a.* willful.

volver, *v.* turn; return, go back,

come back. **v. a hacer** (etc.), do (etc.) again.

volverse, *v.* turn around; turn, become.

vómito, *m.* vomit. **—vomitar,** *v.*

voracidad, *f.* voracity; greed.

voraz, *a.* greedy, ravenous.

vórtice, *m.* whirlpool.

vosotros -as, *pron.pl.* you; yourselves.

votación, *f.* voting, vote.

voto, *m.* vote; vow. **—votar,** *v.*

voz, *f.* voice; word. **a voces,** by shouting. **en v. alta,** aloud.

vuelco, *m.* upset.

vuelo, *m.* flight. **v. libre,** hang gliding.

vuelta, *f.* turn, bend; return. **a la v. de,** around. **dar una v.,** to take a walk.

vuestro, *a.* your, yours.

vulgar, *a.* vulgar, common.

vulgaridad, *f.* vulgarity.

vulgo, *m.* (the) masses, (the) common people.

vulnerable, *a.* vulnerable.

Y, Z

y, *conj.* and.

ya, *adv.* already; now; at once. **y. no,** no longer, any more. **y. que,** since.

yacer, *v.* lie.

yanqui, *a. & n.* North American.

yate, *m.* yacht.

yegua, *f.* mare.

yelmo, *m.* helmet.

yema, *f.* yolk (of an egg).

yerba, *f.* grass; herb.

yerno, *m.* son-in-law.

yerro, *m.* error, mistake.

yeso, *m.* plaster.

yo, *pron.* I.

yodo, *m.* iodine.

yoduro, *m.* iodide.

yugo, *m.* yoke.

yunque, *m.* anvil.

yunta, *f.* team (of animals).

zafarse, *v.* run away, escape. **z. de,** get rid of.

zafio, *a.* coarse, uncivil.

zafiro, *m.* sapphire.

zaguán, *m.* vestibule, hall.

zalamero -ra, *n.* flatterer, wheedler.

zambullir, *v.* plunge, dive.

zanahoria, *f.* carrot.

zanja, *f.* ditch, trench.

zapatería, *f.* shoe store; shoemaker's shop.

zapatero, *m.* shoemaker.

zapato, *m.* shoe.

zar, *m.* czar.

zaraza, *f.* calico; chintz.

zarza, *f.* bramble.

zarzuela, *f.* musical comedy.

zodíaco, *m.* zodiac.

zona, *f.* zone.

zoología, *f.* zoology.

zoológico, *a.* zoological.

zorro -rra, *n.* fox.

zozobra, *f.* worry, anxiety; capsizing.

zozobrar, *v.* capsize.

zumba, *f.* spanking.

zumbido, *m.* buzz, hum. **—zumbar,** *v.*

zumo, *m.* juice, sap.

zurcir, *v.* darn, mend.

zurdo, *a.* left-handed.

zurrar, *v.* flog, drub.

A

a, *art.* un, una.

abacus, *n.* ábaco *m.*

abandon, 1. *n.* desenfreno, abandono *m.* **2.** *v.* abandonar, desamparar.

abandoned, *a.* abandonado.

abandonment, *n.* abandonado, desamparo *m.*

abase, *v.* degradar, humillar.

abasement, *n.* degradación, humillación *f.*

abash, *v.* avergonzar.

abate, *v.* menguar, moderarse.

abatement, *n.* disminución *f.*

abbess, *n.* abadesa *f.*

abbey, *n.* abadía *f.*

abbot, *n.* abad *m.*

abbreviate, *v.* abreviar.

abbreviation, *n.* abreviatura *f.*

abdicate, *v.* abdicar.

abdication, *n.* abdicación *f.*

abdomen, *n.* abdomen *m.*

abdominal, *a.* abdominal.

abduct, *v.* secuestrar.

abduction, *n.* secuestración *f.*

abductor, *n.* secuestrador *m.*

aberrant, *a.* extraviado.

aberration, *n.* error, extravío *m.*

abet, *v.* apoyar, favorecer.

abetment, *n.* apoyo *m.*

abettor, *n.* cómplice *m. & f.*

abeyance, *n.* suspensión *f.*

abhor, *v.* abominar, odiar.

abhorrence, *n.* detestación *f.*; aborrecimiento *m.*

abhorrent, *a.* detestable, aborrecible.

abide, *v.* soportar. **to a. by,** cumplir con.

abiding, *a.* perdurable.

ability, *n.* habilidad *f.*

abject, *a.* abyecto; desanimado.

abjuration, *n.* renuncia *f.*

abjure, *v.* renunciar.

ablative, *a. & n.* (gram.) ablativo *m.*

ablaze, *a.* en llamas.

able, *a.* capaz; competente. **to be a.,** poder.

able-bodied, *a.* robusto.

ablution, *n.* ablución *f.*

ably, *adv.* hábilmente.

abnegate, *v.* repudiar; negar.

abnegation, *n.* abnegación; repudiación *f.*

abnormal, *a.* anormal.

abnormality, *n.* anormalidad, deformidad *f.*

abnormally, *adv.* anormalmente.

aboard, *adv.* a bordo.

abode, *n.* residencia *f.*

abolish, *v.* suprimir.

abolishment, *n.* abolición *f.*

abolition, *n.* abolición *f.*

abominable, *a.* abominable.

abominate, *v.* abominar, detestar.

abomination, *n.* abominación; enormidad *f.*

aboriginal, *a.* primitivo.

abortion, *n.* aborto *m.*

abortive, *a.* abortivo.

abound, *v.* abundar.

about, 1. *adv.* como. **about to,** para; a punto de. **2.** *prep.* de, sobre, acerca de.

about-face, *n.* (mil.) media vuelta.

above, 1. *adv.* arriba. **2.** *prep.* sobre; por encima de.

aboveboard, *a. & adv.* sincero, franco.

abrasion, *n.* raspadura *f.*; (med.) abrasión *f.*

abrasive, 1. *a.* raspante. **2.** *n.* abrasivo *m.*

abreast, *adv.* de frente.

abridge, *v.* abreviar.

abridgment, *n.* abreviación *f.*; compendio *m.*

abroad, *adv.* en el extranjero, al extranjero.

abrogate, *v.* abrogar, revocar.

abrogation, *n.* abrogación, revocación *f.*

abrupt, *a.* repentino; brusco.

abruptly, *adv.* bruscamente, precipitadamente.

abruptness, n. precipitación; brusquedad f.

abscess, n. absceso m.

abscond, v. fugarse.

absence, n. ausencia, falta f.

absent, a. ausente.

absentee, a. & n. ausente m.

absent-minded, a. distraído.

absinthe, n. absenta f.

absolute, a. absoluto.

absolutely, adv. absolutamente.

absoluteness, n. absolutismo m.

absolution, n. absolución f.

absolutism, n. absolutismo, despotismo m.

absolve, v. absolver.

absorb, v. absorber; preocupar.

absorbed, a. absorbido; absorto.

absorbent, a. absorbente.

absorbing, a. interesante.

absorption, n. absorción; preocupación f.

abstain, v. abstenerse.

abstemious, a. abstemio, sobrio.

abstinence, n. abstinencia f.

abstract, 1. n. resumen m. **2.** v. abstraer.

abstracted, a. distraído.

abstraction, n. abstracción f.

abstruse, a. abstruso.

absurd, a. absurdo, ridículo.

absurdity, n. absurdo m.

absurdly, adv. absurdamente.

abundance, n. abundancia f.

abundant, a. abundante.

abundantly, adv. abundantemente.

abuse, 1. n. abuso m. **2.** v. abusar de; maltratar.

abusive, a. abusivo.

abusively, adv. abusivamente, ofensivamente.

abut (on), v. terminar (en); lindar (con).

abutment, n. (building) estribo, contrafuerte m.

abyss, n. abismo m.

Abyssinian, a. & n. abisinio -ia.

academic, a. académico.

academy, n. academia f.

acanthus, n. (bot.) acanto m.

accede, v. acceder; consentir.

accelerate, v. acelerar.

acceleration, n. aceleración f.

accelerator, n. (auto.) acelerador m.

accent, 1. n. acento m. **2.** v. acentuar.

accentuate, v. acentuar.

accept, v. aceptar.

acceptability, n. aceptabilidad

acceptable, a. aceptable.

acceptably, adv. aceptablemente

acceptance, n. aceptación f.

access, n. acceso m., entrada f.

accessible, a. accesible.

accessory, 1. a. accesorio. **2.** n. cómplice m. & f.

accident, n. accidente m. **by a** por casualidad.

accidental, a. accidental.

accidentally, adv. accidentalmente, casualmente.

acclaim, v. aclamar.

acclamation, n. aclamación f.

acclimate, v. aclimatar.

acclivity, n. subida f.

accolade, n. acolada f.

accommodate, v. acomodar.

accommodating, a. bondadoso complaciente.

accommodation, n. servicio m. (pl.) alojamiento m.

accompaniment, n. acompañamiento m.

accompanist, n. acompañador m

accompany, v. acompañar.

accomplice, n. cómplice m. & f

accomplish, v. llevar a cabo; realizar.

accomplished, a. acabado, cumplido; culto.

accomplishment, n. realización f. logro m.

accord, 1. n. acuerdo m. **2.** v otorgar.

accordance, n.: **in a. with,** de acuerdo con.

accordingly, adv. en conformidad.

according to, prep. según.

accordion, n. (mus.) acordeón m

accost, v. dirigirse a.

account, n. relato m.; (com.) cuenta f. **on a. of,** a causa de. **on no a.,** de ninguna manera. **2.** v **a. for,** explicar.

accountable, a. responsable.

accountant, n. contador -ra.

accounting, n. contabilidad f.

accouter, v. equipar, ataviar.

accouterments, n. equipo, atavío m.

accredit, *v.* acreditar.

accretion, *n.* aumento *m.*

accrual, *n.* aumento, incremento *m.*

accrue, *v.* provenir; acumularse *m.*

accumulate, *v.* acumular.

accumulation, *n.* acumulación *f.*

accumulative, *a.* acumulativo.

accumulator *n.* acumulador *m.*

accuracy, *n.* exactitud, precisión *f.*

accurate, *a.* exacto.

accursed, *a.* maldito.

accusation, *n.* acusación *f.,* cargo *m.*

accusative, *a. & n.* acusativo *m.*

accuse, *v.* acusar.

accused, *a. & n.* acusado, procesado *m.*

accuser, *n.* acusador -ra.

accustom, *v.* acostumbrar.

accustomed, *a.* acostumbrado.

ace, 1. *a.* sobresaliente. 2. *n.* as *m.*

acerbity, *n.* acerbidad, amargura *f.*

acetate, *n.* (chem.) acetato *m.*

acetic, *a.* acético.

acetylene, 1. *a.* acetilénico. 2. *n.* (chem.) acetileno *m.*

ache, 1. *n.* dolor *m.* 2. *v.* doler.

achieve, *v.* lograr, llevar a cabo.

achievement, *n.* realización *f.;* hecho notable.

acid, *a. & n.* ácido *m.*

acidify, *v.* acidificar.

acidity, *n.* acidez *f.*

acidosis, *n.* (med.) acidismo *m.*

acid test, prueba decisiva.

acidulous, *a.* agrio, acídulo.

acknowledge, *v.* admitir (receipt) acusar.

acme, *n.* apogeo, colmo *m.*

acne, *n.* (med.) acne *m. & f.;* barros *m.pl.*

acolyte, *n.* acólito *m.*

acorn, *n.* bellota *f.*

acoustics, *n.* acústica *f.*

acquaint, *v.* familiarizar. **to be acquainted with,** conocer.

acquaintance *n.* conocimiento *m.* (person known) conocido -da. **to make the a. of,** conocer.

acquainted, be acquainted with, *v.* conocer.

acquiesce, *v.* consentir.

acquiescence, *n.* consentimiento *m.*

acquire, *v.* adquirir.

acquirement, *n.* adquisición *f.;* (pl.) conocimientos *m.pl.*

acquisition, *n.* adquisición *f.*

acquisitive, *a.* adquisitivo.

acquit, *v.* exonerar, absolver.

acquittal, *n.* absolución *f.*

acre, *n.* acre *m.*

acreage, número de acres.

acrid, *a.* acre, picante.

acrimonious, *a.* acrimonioso, mordaz.

acrimony, *n.* acrimonia, aspereza *f.*

acrobat, *n.* acróbata *m.*

across, 1. *adv.* a través, al otro lado. 2. *prep.* al otro lado de, a través de.

acrostic, *n.* acróstico *m.*

act, 1. *n.* acción *f.;* acto *m.* 2. *v.* actuar, portarse. **act as,** hacer de. **act on,** decidir sobre.

acting, 1. *a.* interino. 2. *n.* acción *f.;* (theat.) representación *f.*

actinism, *n.* actinismo *m.*

actinium, *n.* (chem.) actinio *m.*

action, *n.* acción *f.* **take a.,** tomar medidas.

activate, *v.* activar.

activation, *n.* activación *f.*

activator. *n.* (chem.) activador *m.*

active, *a.* activo.

activity, *n.* actividad *f.*

actor, *n.* actor *m.*

actress, *n.* actriz *f.*

actual, *a.* real, efectivo.

actuality, *n.* realidad, actualidad *f.*

actually, *adv.* en realidad.

actuary, *n.* actuario *m.*

actuate, *v.* impulsar, mover.

acumen, *n.* cacumen *m.,* perspicacia *f.*

acupuncture, *n.* acupuntura *f.*

acute, *a.* agudo; perspicaz.

acutely, *adv.* agudamente.

acuteness, *n.* agudeza *f.*

adage, *n.* refrán, proverbio *m.*

adamant, *a.* firme.

Adam's apple, nuez de la garganta.

adapt, *v.* adaptar.

adaptable, *a.* adaptable.

adaptability, *n.* adaptabilidad *f.*

adaptation, *n.* adaptación *f.*

adapter, n. (tech.) adaptador m.; (mech.) ajustador m.

adaptive, a. adaptable, acomodable.

add, v. agregar, añadir. **a. up,** sumar.

adder, n. víbora f.; serpiente m.

addict, n. adicto; ('fan') aficionado m.

addition, n. adición f. **in a. to,** además de.

additional, a. adicional.

addle, v. confundir.

address, 1. n. dirección f.; señas f.pl. (speech) discurso. **2.** v. dirigirse a.

addressee, n. destinatorio -ia.

adduce, v. aducir.

adenoid, a. adenoideo.

adept, a. adepto.

adeptly, adv. diestramente.

adeptness, n. destreza f.

adequacy, n. suficiencia f.

adequate, a. adecuado.

adequately, adv. adecuadamente.

adhere, v. adherirse, pegarse.

adherence, n. adhesión f.; apego m.

adherent, n. adherente, partidario m.

adhesion, n. adhesión f.

adhesive, a. adhesivo. **a. tape,** esparadrapo m.

adhesiveness, n. adhesividad f.

adieu, 1. interj. adiós. **2.** n. despedida f.

adjacent, a. adyacente.

adjective, n. adjectivo m.

adjoin, v. lindar (con).

adjoining, a. contiguo.

adjourn, v. suspender, levantar.

adjournment, n. suspensión f.; (leg.) espera f.

adjunct, n. adjunto m.; (gram.) atributo m.

adjust, v. ajustar, acomodar; arreglar.

adjuster, n. ajustador m.

adjustment, n. ajuste; arreglo m.

adjutant, n. (mil.) ayudante m.

administer, v. administrar.

administration, n. administración f.; gobierno m.

administrative, a. administrativo.

administrator, n. administrador m.

admirable, a. admirable.

admirably, adv. admirablemente.

admiral, n. almirante m.

admiralty, n. ministerio de marina.

admiration, n. admiración f.

admire, v. admirar.

admirer, n. admirador -ra; enamorado -da.

admiringly, adv. admirativamente.

admissible, a. admisible, aceptable.

admission, n. admisión; entrada f.

admit, v. admitir.

admittance, n. entrada f.

admittedly, adv. reconocidamente.

admixture, n. mezcla f.

admonish, v. amonestar.

admonition, n. admonición f.

adolescence, n. adolescencia f.

adolescent, n. & a. adolescente.

adopt, v. adoptar.

adoption, n. adopción f.

adorable, a. adorable.

adoration, n. adoración f.

adore, v. adorar.

adorn, v. adornar.

adornment, n. adorno m.

adrenalin, n. adrenalina f.

adrift, adv. a la ventura.

adroit, a. diestro.

adulate, v. adular.

adulation, n. adulación f.

adult, a. & n. adulto m.

adulterant, a. & n. adulterante m.

adulterate, v. adulterar.

adulterer, n. adúltero m.

adulteress, n. adúltera f.

adultery, n. adulterio m.

advance, 1. n. avance; adelanto m. **in a.,** de antemano, antes. **2.** v. avanzar, adelantar.

advanced, a. avanzado, adelantado.

advancement, n. adelantamiento m.; promoción f.

advantage, n. ventaja f. **take a. of,** aprovecharse de.

advantageous, a. provechoso, ventajoso.

advantageously, adv. ventajosamente.

advent, n. venida, llegada f.

adventitious, a. adventicio, espontáneo.

adventure, *n.* aventura *f.*

adventurer, *n.* aventurero *m.*

adventurous, *a.* aventurero, intrépido.

adventurously, *adv.* arriesgadamente.

adverb, *n.* adverbio *m.*

adverbial, *a.* adverbial.

adversary, *n.* adversario *m.*

adverse, *a.* adverso.

adversely, *adv.* adversamente.

adversity, *n.* adversidad *f.*

advert, *v.* hacer referencia a.

advertise, *v.* avisar, anunciar.

advertisement, *n.* aviso, anuncio *m.*

advertiser, *n.* anunciante, avisador *m.*

advertising, *n.* publicidad *f.*

advice, *n.* consejos *m.pl.*

advisability, *n.* prudencia, propiedad *f.*

advisable, *a.* aconsejable, prudente.

advisably, *adv.* prudentemente.

advise, *v.* aconsejar.

advisedly, *adv.* avisadamente, prudentemente.

advisement, *n.* consideración *f.;* **take under a.,** someter a estudio.

adviser, *n.* consejero *m.*

advocacy, *n.* abogacía; defensa *f.*

advocate, 1. *n.* abogado *m.* **2.** *v.* apoyar.

aegis, *n.* amparo *m.*

aerate, *v.* airear, ventilar.

aeration, *n.* aeración, ventilación *f.*

aerial, *a.* aéreo.

aerie, *n.* nido de águila.

aeronautics, *n.* aeronáutica *f.*

aerosol bomb, *n.* bomba insecticida.

afar, *adv.* lejos. **from a.,** de lejos, desde lejos.

affability, *n.* afabilidad, amabilidad *f.*

affable, *a.* afable.

affably, *adv.* afablemente.

affair, *n.* asunto *m.* **love a.,** aventura amorosa.

affect, *v.* afectar; (emotionally) conmover.

affectation, *n.* afectación *f.*

affected, *a.* artificioso.

affecting, *a.* conmovedor.

affection, *n.* cariño *m.*

affectionate, *a.* afectuoso, cariñoso.

affectionately, *adv.* afectuosamente, con cariño.

affiance, *v.* dar palabra de casamiento; **become affianced,** comprometerse.

affidavit, *n.* (leg.) declaración, deposición *f.*

affiliate, 1. *n.* afiliado *m.* **2.** *v.* afiliar.

affiliation, *n.* afiliación *f.*

affinity, *n.* afinidad *f.*

affirm, *v.* afirmar.

affirmation, *n.* afirmación, aserción *f.*

affirmative, 1. *n.* afirmativa *f.* **2.** *a.* afirmativo.

affirmatively, *adv.* afirmativamente, aseveradamente.

affix, 1. *n.* (gram.) afijo *m.* **2.** *v.* fijar, pegar, poner.

afflict, *v.* afligir.

affliction, *n.* aflicción *f.;* mal *m.*

affluence, *n.* abundancia, opulencia *f.*

affluent, *a.* opulento, afluente.

afford, *v.* proporcionar. **be able to a.,** tener con que comprar.

affront, 1. *n.* afrenta *f.* **2.** *v.* afrentar, insultar.

afield, *adv.* lejos de casa; lejos del camino; lejos del asunto.

afire, *adv.* ardiendo.

afloat, *adv.* (naut.) a flote.

aforementioned, aforesaid, *a.* dicho, susodicho.

afraid, *a.* **to be a.,** tener miedo, temer.

African, *n. & a.* africano -na.

aft, *adv.* (naut.) a popa, en popa.

after, 1. *prep.* después de. **2.** *conj.* después que.

aftermath, *n.* resultados *m.pl.,* consecuencias *f.pl.*

afternoon, *n.* tarde *f.* **good a.,** buenas tardes.

afterthought, *n.* idea tardía.

afterward(s), *adv.* después.

again, *adv.* otra vez, de nuevo. **to do a.,** volver a hacer.

against, *prep.* contra; en contra de.

agape, *adv.* con la boca abierta.

agate, *n.* ágata *f.*

age, 1. *n.* edad *f.* **of a.,** mayor de

edad. **old a.,** vejez *f.* **2.** *v.* envejecer.

aged, *a.* viejo, anciano, añejo.

ageism, *n.* discriminación contra las personas de edad.

ageless, *a.* sempiterno.

agency, *n.* agencia *f.*

agenda, *n.* agenda *f.,* orden *m.*

agent, *n.* agente; representante *m.*

agglutinate, *v.* aglutinar.

agglutination, *n.* aglutinación *f.*

aggrandize, *v.* agrandar; elevar.

aggrandizement, *n.* engrandecimiento *m.*

aggravate, *v.* agravar; irritar.

aggravation, *n.* agravamiento; empeoramiento *m.*

aggregate, *a.* & *n.* agregado *m.*

aggregation, *n.* agregación *f.*

aggression, *n.* agresión *f.*

aggressive, *a.* agresivo.

aggressively, *adv.* agresivamente.

aggressiveness, *n.* agresividad *f.*

aggressor, *n.* agresor *m.*

aghast, *a.* horrorizado.

agile, *a.* ágil.

agility, *n.* agilidad, ligereza, prontitud *f.*

agitate, *v.* agitar.

agitation, *n.* agitación *f.*

agitator, *n.* agitador *m.*

agnostic, *a.* & *n.* agnóstico *m.*

ago, *adv.* hace. **two days a.,** hace dos días.

agonized, *a.* angustioso.

agony, *n.* sufrimiento *m.;* angustia *f.*

agrarian, *a.* agrario.

agree, *v.* estar de acuerdo; convenir. **a. with one,** sentar bien.

agreeable, *a.* agradable.

agreeably, *adv.* agradablemente.

agreement, *n.* acuerdo *m.*

agriculture, *n.* agricultura *f.*

ahead, *adv.* adelante.

aid, **1.** *n.* ayuda *f.* **2.** *v.* ayudar.

aide, *n.* ayudante *m.*

ailing, *adj.* enfermo.

ailment, *n.* enfermedad *f.*

aim, **1.** *n.* puntería *f.;* (purpose) propósito *m.* **2.** *v.* apuntar.

aimless, *a.* sin objeto.

air, *n.* aire *m.* **by a.** por avión. **2.** *v.* ventilar, airear.

airbag, *n.* (in automobiles) saco de aire *m.*

air-conditioned, *a.* enfriado por aire.

air-conditioning, *n.* acondicionamiento del aire.

aircraft, *n.* máquina de volar.

aircraft carrier, *n.* portaaviones *m.*

airing, *n.* ventilación *f.*

airline, *n.* línea aérea.

airliner, *n.* avión de transporte.

airmail, *n.* correo aéreo.

airplane, *n.* avión, aeroplano *m.*

air pollution, *n.* contaminación atmosférica.

airport, *n.* aeropuerto *m.*

air pressure, presión atmosférica.

air raid, ataque aéreo.

airsick, *a.* mareado.

airtight, *a.* hermético.

aisle, *n.* pasillo *m.*

ajar, *a.* entreabierto.

akin, *a.* emparentado, semejante.

alacrity, *n.* alacridad, presteza *f.*

alarm, **1.** *n.* alarma *f.* **2.** *v.* alarmar.

alarmist, *n.* alarmista *m.* & *f.*

albino, *n.* albino -na.

album, *n.* álbum *m.*

alcohol, *n.* alcohol *m.*

alcoholic, *a.* alcohólico.

alcove, *n.* alcoba *f.*

ale, *n.* cerveza inglesa.

alert, **1.** *n.* alarma *f.* **on the a.,** alerta, sobre aviso. **2.** *a.* listo, vivo. **3.** *v.* poner sobre aviso.

alfalfa, *n.* alfalfa *f.*

algebra, *n.* álgebra *f.*

alias, *n.* alias *m.*

alibi, *n.* excusa *f.;* (leg.) coartada *f.*

alien, **1.** *a.* ajeno, extranjero. **2.** *n.* extranjero -ra.

alienate, *v.* enajenar.

alight, *v.* bajar, apearse.

align, *v.* alinear.

alike, **1.** *a.* semejante, igual. **2.** *adv.* del mismo modo, igualmente.

alimentary canal, *n.* tubo digestivo.

alive, *a.* vivo; animado.

alkali, *n.* (chem.) álcali, cali *m.*

alkaline, *a.* alcalino.

all, *a.* & *pron.* todo. **not at a.,** de ninguna manera, nada.

allay, *v.* aquietar.

allegation, *n.* alegación *f.*

allege, *v.* alegar; pretender.

allegiance, *n.* lealtad *f.;* (to country) homenaje *m.*
allegory, *n.* alegoría *f.*
allergy, *n.* alergia *f.*
alleviate, *v.* aliviar.
alley, *n.* callejón *m.* **bowling a.,** bolera *f.,* boliche *m.*
alliance, *n.* alianza *f.*
allied, *a.* aliado.
alligator, *n.* caimán *m.;* (Mex.) lagarto *m.* **a. pear,** aguacate *m.*
allocate, *v.* colocar, asignar.
allot, *v.* asignar.
allotment, *n.* lote, porción *f.*
allow, *v.* permitir, dejar.
allowance, *n.* abono *m.;* dieta *f.* **make a. for,** tener en cuenta.
alloy, *n.* mezcla *f.* (metal) aleación *f.*
all right, está bien.
allude, *v.* aludir.
allure, 1. *n.* atracción *f.* **2.** *v.* atraer, tentar.
alluring, *a.* tentador, seductivo.
allusion, *n.* alusión *f.*
ally, 1. *n.* aliado *m.* **2.** *v.* aliar.
almanac, *n.* almanaque *m.*
almighty, *a.* todopoderoso.
almond, *n.* almendra *f.*
almost, *adv.* casi.
alms, *n.* limosna *f.*
aloft, *adv.* arriba, en alto.
alone, *adv.* solo, a solas. **to leave a.,** dejar en paz.
along, *prep.* por; a lo largo de. **a. with,** junto con.
alongside, 1. *adv.* al lado. **2.** *prep.* junto a.
aloof, *a.* apartado.
aloud, *adv.* en voz alta.
alpaca, *n.* alpaca *f.*
alphabet, *n.* alfabeto *m.*
alphabetical, *a.* alfabético.
alphabetize, *v.* alfabetizar.
already, *adv.* ya.
also, *adv.* también.
altar, *n.* altar *m.*
alter, *v.* alterar.
alteration, *n.* alteración *f.*
alternate, 1. *a.* alterno. **2.** *n.* substituto -ta. **3.** *v.* alternar.
alternative, 1. *a.* alternativo. **2.** *n.* alternativa *f.*
although, *conj.* aunque.
altitude, *n.* altura *f.*
alto, *n.* contralto *m.*

altogether, *adv.* en junto; enteramente.
altruism, *n.* altruismo *m.*
alum, *n.* alumbre *m.*
aluminum, *n.* aluminio *m.*
always, *adv.* siempre.
amalgam, *n.* amalgama *f.*
amalgamate, *v.* amalgamar.
amass, *v.* amontonar.
amateur, *n.* aficionado -da.
amaze, *v.* asombrar; sorprender.
amazement, *n.* asombro *m.*
amazing, *a.* asombroso, pasmoso.
ambassador, *n.* embajador *m.*
amber, 1. *a.* ambarino **2.** *n.* ámbar *m.*
ambidextrous, *a.* ambidextro.
ambiguity, *n.* ambigüedad *f.*
ambiguous, *a.* ambiguo.
ambition, *n.* ambición *f.*
ambitious, *a.* ambicioso.
ambulance, *n.* ambulancia *f.*
ambush, 1. *n.* emboscada *f.* **2.** *v.* acechar.
ameliorate, *v.* mejorar.
amenable, *a.* tratable, dócil.
amend, *v.* enmendar.
amendment, *n.* enmienda *f.*
amenity, *n.* amenidad *f.*
American, *a. & n.* americano -na, norteamericano -na.
amethyst, *n.* amatista *f.*
amiable, *a.* amable.
amicable, *a.* amigable.
amid, *prep.* entre, en medio de.
amidships, *adv.* (naut.) en medio del navío.
amiss, *adv.* mal. **to take a.,** llevar a mal.
amity, *n.* amistad, armonía *f.*
ammonia, *n.* amoníaco *m.*
ammunition, *n.* munición *f.*
amnesia, *n.* (med.) amnesia *f.*
amnesty, *n.* amnistía *f.,* indulto *m.*
amniocentesis, *n.* amniocéntesis *m.*
amoeba, *n.* amiba *f.*
among, *prep.* entre.
amoral, *a.* amoral.
amorous, *a.* amoroso.
amorphous, *a.* amorfo.
amortize, *v.* (com.) amortizar.
amount, 1. *n.* cantidad, suma *f.* **2.** *v.* **a. to,** subir a.
ampere, *n.* (elec.) amperio *m.*
amphibian, *a. & n.* anfibio *m.*

amphitheater, *n.* anfiteatro, circo *m.*

ample, *a.* amplio; suficiente.

amplify, *v.* amplificar.

amputate, *v.* amputar.

amuse, *v.* entretener, divertir.

amusement, *n.* diversión *f.*

an, *art.* un, una.

anachronism, *n.* anacronismo, *m.*

analogous, *a.* análogo, parecido.

analogy, *n.* analogía *f.*

analysis, *n.* análisis *m. & f.*

analyst, *n.* analizador *m.*

analytic, *a.* analítico.

analyze, *v.* analizar.

anarchy, *n.* anarquía *f.*

anatomy, *n.* anatomía *f.*

ancestor, *n.* antepasado *m.*

ancestral, *a.* de los antepasados, hereditario.

ancestry, *n.* linaje, abolengo *m.*

anchor, 1. *n.* ancla *f.* **to weigh a.,** levar el ancla. **2.** *v.* anclar.

anchorage, *n.* (naut.) ancladero, anclaje *m.*

anchovy, *n.* anchoa *f.*

ancient, *a. & n.* antiguo.

and, *conj.* y, (before *i-, hi-*) e.

anecdote, *n.* anécdota *f.*

anemia, *n.* (med.) anemia *f.*

anesthetic, *n.* anestesia *f.*

anew, *adv.* de nuevo.

angel, *n.* ángel *m.*

anger, 1. *n.* ira *f.*, enojo *m.* **2.** *v.* enfadar, enojar.

angle, *n.* ángulo *m.*

angry, *a.* enojado, enfadado.

anguish, *n.* angustia *f.*

angular, *a.* angular.

aniline, *n.* (chem.) anilina *f.*

animal, *a.& n.* animal *m.*

animate, 1. *adj.* animado. **2.** *v.* animar.

animated, *a.* vivo, animado.

animation, *n.* animación, viveza *f.*

animosity, *n.* rencor *m.*

anise, *n.* anís *m.*

ankle, *n.* tobillo *m.*

annals, *n.pl.* anales *m.pl.*

annex, 1. *n.* anexo *m.*, adición *f.* **2.** *v.* anexar.

annexation, *n.* anexión, adición *f.*

annihilate, *v.* aniquilar, destruir.

anniversary, *n.* aniversario *m.*

annotate, *v.* anotar.

annotation, *n.* anotación *f.*, apunte *m.*

announce, *v.* anunciar.

announcement, *n.* anuncio, aviso *m.*

announcer, *n.* anunciador *m.;* (radio) anunciador, noticiador *m.*

annoy, *v.* molestar.

annoyance, *n.* molestia, incomodidad *f.*

annual, *a.* anual.

annuity, *n.* anualidad, pensión *f.*

annul, *v.* anular, invalidar.

anode, *n.* (elec.) ánodo *m.*

anoint, *v.* untar; (rel.) ungir.

anomalous, *a.* anómalo, irregular.

anonymous, *a.* anónimo.

another, *a. & pron.* otro.

answer, 1. *n.* contestación, respuesta *f.* **2.** *v.* contestar, responder. **a. for,** ser responsable de.

answerable, *a.* discutible, refutable.

ant, *n.* hormiga *f.*

antacid, *a. & n.* antiácido *m.*

antagonism, *n.* antagonismo *m.*

antagonist, *n.* antagonista *m.*

antagonistic, *a.* antagónico, hostil.

antagonize, *v.* contrariar.

antarctic, *a. & n.* antártico *m.*

antecedent, *a. & n.* antecedente *m.*

antedate, *v.* antedatar.

antelope, *n.* antílope *m.*, gacela *f.*

antenna, *n.* antena *f.*

anterior, *a.* anterior.

anteroom, *n.* antecámara *f.*

anthem, *n.* himno *m.;* (religious) antífona *f.*

anthology, *n.* antología *f.*

anthracite, *n.* antracita *f.*

anthrax, *n.* (med.) ántrax *m.*

anthropology, *n.* antropología *f.*

antiaircraft, *a.* antiaéreo.

antibody, *n.* anticuerpo *m.*

anticipate, *v.* esperar, anticipar.

anticipation, *n.* anticipación *f.*

anticlerical, *a.* anticlerical.

anticlimax, *n.* anticlímax *m.*

antidote, *n.* antídoto *m.*

antimony, *n.* antimonio *m.*

antinuclear, *a.* antinuclear.

antipathy, *n.* antipatía *f.*

antiquated, *a.* anticuado.

antique, 1. *a.* antiguo. **2.** *n.* antigüedad *f.*
antiquity, *n.* antigüedad *f.*
antiseptic, *a.* & *n.* antiséptico *m.*
antisocial, *a.* antisocial.
antitoxin, *n.* (med.) antitoxina *f.*
antler, *n.* asta *f.*
anvil, *n.* yunque *m.*
anxiety, *n.* ansia, ansiedad *f.*
anxious, *a.* inquieto, ansioso.
any, *a.* alguno; (at all) cualquiera; (after *not*) ninguno.
anybody, *pron.* alguien; (at all) cualquiera; (after *not*) nadie.
anyhow, *adv.* de todos modos; en todo caso.
anyone, *pron.* = anybody.
anything, *pron.* algo; (at all) cualquier cosa; (after *not*) nada.
anyway, *adv.* = anyhow.
anywhere, *adv.* en alguna parte; (at all) dondequiera; (after *not*) en ninguna parte.
apart, *adv.* aparte. **to take a.,** deshacer.
apartheid, *n.* apartheid *m.*
apartment, *n.* apartamento, piso *m.*
apathetic, *a.* apático.
apathy, *n.* apatía *f.*
ape, 1. *n.* mono *m.* **2.** *v.* imitar.
aperture, *n.* abertura *f.*
apex, *n.* ápice *m.*
aphorism, *n.* aforismo *m.*
apiary, *n.* apiario, abejar *m.*
apiece, *adv.* por persona; cada uno.
apologetic, *a.* apologético.
apologist, *n.* apologista *m.* & *f.*
apologize, *v.* excusarse, disculparse.
apology, *n.* excusa; apología *f.*
apoplectic, *a.* apoplético.
apoplexy, *n.* apoplejía *f.*
apostate, *n.* apóstata *m.* & *f.*
apostle, *n.* apóstol *m.*
apostolic, *a.* apostólico.
appall, *v.* espantar; desmayar.
apparatus, *n.* aparato *m.*
apparel, *n.* ropa *f.*
apparent, *a.* aparente; claro.
apparition, *n.* fantasma *f.*
appeal, 1. *n.* súplica *f.*; interés *m.*; (leg.) apelación *f.* **2.** *v.* apelar; suplicar; interesar.
appear, *v.* aparecer, asomar;

(seem) parecer; (leg.) comparecer.
appearance, *n.* apariencia *f.*, aspecto *m.*
appease, *v.* aplacar, apaciguar.
appeasement, *n.* apaciguamiento *m.*
appeaser, *n.* apaciguador, pacificador *m.*
appellant, *n.* apelante, demandante *m.*
appellate, *a.* (leg.) de apelación.
appendage, *n.* pertenencia *f.*
appendectomy, *n.* (med.) apendectomía *f.*
appendicitis, *n.* (med.) apendicitis *m.*
appendix, *n.* apéndice *m.*
appetite, *n.* apetito *m.*
appetizer, *n.* apertivo *m.*
appetizing, *a.* apetitivo.
applaud, *v.* aplaudir.
applause, *n.* aplauso *m.*
apple, *n.* manzana *f.* **a. tree,** manzano *m.*
applesauce, *n.* compota de manzana.
appliance, *n.* utensilio, aparato *m.*
applicable, *a.* aplicable.
applicant, *n.* suplicante *m.* & *f.*; candidato -ta.
application, *n.* solicitud *f.*
applied, *a.* aplicado. **a. for,** pedido.
appliqué, *n.* (sewing) aplicación *f.*
apply, *v.* aplicar. **a. for,** solicitar, pedir.
appoint, *v.* nombrar.
appointment, *n.* nombramiento, puesto *m.*
apportion, *v.* repartir.
apposition, *n.* (gram.) aposición *f.*
appraisal, *n.* valoración *f.*; apremio *m.*
appraise, *v.* avaluar, tasar; estimar.
appreciable, *a.* apreciable; notable.
appreciate, *v.* apreciar, estimar.
appreciation, *n.* aprecio; reconocimiento *m.*
apprehend, *v.* prender, capturar.
apprehension, *n.* aprensión *f.*
apprehensive, *a.* aprensivo.
apprentice, *n.* aprendiz *m.*

apprise, v. informar.
approach, 1. n. acceso; método m. **2.** v. acercarse.
approachable, a. accesible.
approbation, n. aprobación f.
appropriate, 1. a. apropiado. **2.** v. apropiar.
appropriation, n. apropiación f.
approval, n. aprobación f.
approve, v. aprobar.
approximate, 1. a. aproximado. **2.** v. aproximar.
approximately, adv. aproximadamente.
approximation, n. aproximación f.
appurtenance, n. pertenencia f.
apricot, n. albaricoque, damasco m.
April, n. abril m.
apron, n. delantal m.
apropos, adv. a propósito.
apt, a. apto; capaz.
aptitude, n. aptitud; facilidad f.
aquarium, n. acuario m., pecera f.
aquatic, a. acuático.
aqueduct, n. acueducto m.
aqueous, a. ácueo, acuoso, aguoso.
aquiline, a. aquilino, aguileño.
Arab, a. & n. árabe m. & f.
arable, a. cultivable.
arbitrary, a. arbitrario.
arbitrate, v. arbitrar.
arbitration, n. arbitraje m., arbitración f.
arbitrator, n. arbitrador -ra.
arbor, n. emparrado m.
arboreal, a. arbóreo.
arc, n. arco m.
arch, 1. n. arco m. **2.** v. arquear, encorvar.
archaeology, n. arqueología f.
archaic, a. arcaico.
archbishop, n. arzobispo m.
archdiocese, n. archidiócesis m.
archduke, n. archiduque m.
archer, n. arquero m.
archery, n. ballestería f.
archipelago, n. archipiélago m.
architect, n. arquitecto m.
architectural, a. arquitectural.
architecture, n. arquitectura f.
archive, n. archivo m.
archway, n. arcada f.
arctic, a. ártico.
ardent, a. ardiente.

ardor, n. ardor m., pasión f.
arduous, a. arduo, difícil.
area, n. área; extensión f.
area code, prefijo m.
arena, n. arena f.
Argentine, a. & n. argentino -na.
argue, v. disputar; sostener.
argument, n. disputa f.; razonamiento m.
argumentative, a. argumentoso.
aria, n. (mus.) aria f.
arid, a. árido, seco.
arise, v. surgir.
aristocracy, n. aristocracia f.
aristocrat, n. aristócrata m.
aristocratic, a. aristocrático.
arithmetic, n. aritmética f.
ark, n. arca f.
arm, 1. n. brazo m.; (weapon) arma f. **2.** v. armar.
armament, n. armamento m.
armchair, n. sillón m., butaca f.
armed forces, fuerzas militares.
armful, n. brazada f.
armhole, n. (sew.) sobaquera f.
armistice, n. armisticio m.
armor, n. armadura f., blindaje m.
armored, a. blindado.
armory, n. armería f., arsenal m.
armpit, n. sobaco m.
army, n. ejército m.
arnica, n. árnica f.
aroma, n. fragancia f.
aromatic, a. aromático.
around, prep. alrededor de, a la vuelta de; cerca de a **here,** por aquí.
arouse, v. despertar; excitar.
arraign, v. (leg.) procesar criminalmente.
arrange, v. arreglar; concertar; (mus.) adaptar.
arrangement, n. arreglo; orden m.
array, 1. n. orden; adorno m. **2.** v. adornar.
arrears, n. atrasos m.pl.
arrest, 1. n. detención f. **2.** v. detener, arrestar.
arrival, n. llegada f.
arrive, v. llegar.
arrogance, n. arrogancia f.
arrogant, a. arrogante.
arrogate, v. arrogarse, usurpar.
arrow, n. flecha f.
arrowhead, n. punta de flecha.

arsenal, *n.* arsenal *m.*

arsenic, *n.* arsénico *m.*

arson, *n.* incendio premeditado.

art, arte *m.* (*f.* in *pl.*); (skill) maña *f.*

arterial, *a.* arterial.

arteriosclerosis, *n.* arteriosclerosis *m.*

artery, *n.* arteria *f.*

artesian well, pozo artesiano *m.*

artful, *a.* astuto.

arthritis, *n.* artritis *f.*

artichoke, *n.* alcachofa *f.*

article, *n.* artículo *m.*

articulate, *a.* articular.

articulation, *n.* articulación *f.*

artifice, *n.* artificio *m.*

artificial, *a.* artificial.

artificially, *adv.* artificialmente.

artillery, *n.* artillería *f.*

artisan, *n.* artesano *m.*

artist, *n.* artista *m.* & *f.*

artistic, *a.* artístico.

artistry, *n.* arte *m.* & *f.*

artless, *a.* natural, cándido.

as, *adv.* & *conj.* como; **as . . . as . . .** tan . . . como.

asbestos, *n.* asbesto *m.*

ascend, *v.* ascender.

ascendancy, *n.* ascendiente *m.*

ascendant, *a.* ascendente.

ascent, *n.* subida *f.*, ascenso *m.*

ascertain, *v.* averiguar.

ascetic, 1. *a.* ascético. **2.** *n.* asceta *m.* & *f.*

ascribe, *v.* atribuir.

ash, *n.* ceniza *f.*

ashamed, *a.* avergonzado.

ashen, *a.* pálido.

ashore, *adv.* a tierra. **go a.,** desembarcar.

ashtray, *n.* cenicero *m.*

Asiatic, *a.* & *n.* asiático -ca.

aside, *adv.* al lado. **a. from,** aparte de.

ask, *v.* preguntar; invitar; (request) pedir. **a. for,** pedir. **a. a question,** hacer una pregunta.

askance, *adv.* de soslayo; con recelo.

asleep, *a.* dormido. **to fall a.,** dormirse.

asparagus, *n.* espárrago *m.*

aspect, *n.* aspecto *m.*, apariencia *f.*

asperity, *n.* aspereza *f.*

aspersion, *n.* calumnia *f.*

asphalt, *n.* asfalto *m.*

asphyxia, *n.* asfixia *f.*

asphyxiate, *v.* asfixiar, sofocar.

aspirant, *a.* & *n.* aspirante.

aspirate, *v.* aspirar.

aspiration, *n.* aspiración *f.*

aspirator, *n.* aspirador *m.*

aspire, *v.* aspirar. **a. to,** ambicionar.

aspirin, *n.* aspirina *f.*

ass, *n.* asno, burro *m.*

assail, *v.* asaltar, acometer.

assailant, *n.* asaltador *m.*

assassin, *n.* asesino *m.*

assassinate, *v.* asesinar.

assassination, *n.* asesinato *m.*

assault, 1. *n.* asalto *m.* **2.** *v.* asaltar, atacar.

assay, *v.* examinar; ensayar.

assemblage, *n.* asamblea *f.*

assemble, *v.* juntar, convocar; (mechanism) montar.

assembly, *n.* asamblea, concurrencia *f.*

assent, 1. *n.* asentimiento *m.* **2.** *v.* asentir, convenir.

assert, *v.* afirmar, aseverar. **a. oneself,** hacerse sentir.

assertion, *n.* aserción, aseveración *f.*

assertive, *a.* asertivo.

assess, *v.* tasar, avaluar.

assessor, *n.* asesor *m.*

asset, *n.* ventaja *f.* **assets,** (com.) capital *m.*

asseverate, *v.* aseverar, afirmar.

asseveration, *n.* aseveración *f.*

assiduous, *a.* asiduo.

assiduously, *adv.* asiduamente.

assign, *v.* asignar; destinar.

assignable, *a.* asignable, transferible.

assignation, *n.* asignación *f.*

assignment, *n.* misión; tarea *f.*

assimilate, *v.* asimilar.

assimilation, *n.* asimilación *f.*

assimilative, *a.* asimilativo.

assist, *v.* ayudar, auxiliar.

assistance, *n.* ayuda *f.*, auxilio *m.*

assistant, *n.* ayudante, asistente *m.*

associate, 1. *n.* socio *m.* **2.** *v.* asociar.

association, *n.* asociación; sociedad *f.*

assonance, *n.* asonancia *f.*

assort, *v.* surtir con variedad.

assorted, a. variado, surtido.

assortment, n. surtido m.

assuage, v. mitigar, aliviar.

assume, v. suponer; asumir.

assuming, a. presuntuoso. **a. that,** dado que.

assumption, n. suposición; (rel.) asunción f.

assurance, n. seguridad; confianza f.

assure, v. asegurar; dar confianza.

assured, 1. a. seguro. **2.** a. & n. (com.) asegurado m.

assuredly, adv. ciertamente.

aster, n. (bot.) aster m.

asterisk, n. asterisco m.

astern, adv. (naut.) a popa.

asteroid, n. asteroide m.

asthma, n. (med.) asma f.

astigmatism, n. astigmatismo m.

astir, adv. en movimiento.

astonish, v. asombrar, pasmar.

astonishment, n. asombro m., sorpresa f.

astound, v. pasmar, sorprender.

astral, a. astral, estelar.

astray, a. desviado.

astride, adv. a horcajadas.

astringent, a. & n. astringente m.

astrology, n. astrología f.

astronaut, n. astronauta m.

astronomy, n. astronomía f.

astute, a. astuto; agudo.

asunder, adv. en dos.

asylum, n. asilo, refugio m.

asymmetry, n. asimetría f.

at, prep. a, en; cerca de.

ataxia, n. (med.) ataxia f.

atheist, n. ateo m.

athlete, n. atleta m.

athletic, a. atlético.

athletics, n. atletismo m., deportes m.pl.

athwart, prep. á través de.

Atlantic, 1. a. atlántico. **2.** n. Atlántico m.

Atlantic Ocean, el mar atlántico.

atlas, n. atlas m.

atmosphere, n. atmósfera f.; (fig.) ambiente m.

atmospheric, a. atmosférico.

atoll, n. atolón m.

atom, n. átomo m.

atomic, a. atómico.

atomic bomb, bomba atómica.

atomic energy, energía atómica.

atomic theory, teoría atómica.

atomic weight, peso atómico.

atonal, a. (mus.) atonal.

atone, v. expiar, compensar.

atonement, n. expiación; reparación f.

atrocious, a. atroz.

atrocity, n. atrocidad f.

atrophy, 1. n. (med.) atrofia f. **2.** v. atrofiar.

atropine, n. (chem.) atropina f.

attach, v. juntar; prender; (hook) enganchar; (fig.) atribuir.

attaché, n. agregado m.

attachment, 1. enlace m.; accesorio m.; (emotional) afecto, cariño m.

attack, 1. n. ataque m. **2.** v. atacar.

attacker, n. asaltador m.

attain, v. lograr, alcanzar.

attainable, a. accesible, realizable.

attainment, n. logro m.; (pl.) dotes f.pl.

attempt, 1. n. ensayo; esfuerzo m.; tentativa f. **2.** v. ensayar intentar.

attend, v. atender; (a meeting) asistir a.

attendance, n. asistencia; presencia f.

attendant, 1. a. concomitante. **2.** n. servidor -ra.

attention, n. atención f.; obsequio m. **to pay a. to,** hacer caso a.

attentive, a. atento.

attentively, adv. atentamente.

attenuate, v. atenuar, adelgazar

attest, v. confirmar, atestiguar.

attic, n. desván m., guardilla f.

attire, 1. n. traje m. **2.** v. vestir

attitude, n. actitud f., ademán m

attorney, n. abogado, apoderado m.

attract, v. atraer. **a. attention,** llamar la atención.

attraction, n. atracción f., atractivo m.

attractive, a. atractivo; simpático.

attributable, a. atribuible, imputable.

attribute, 1. n. atributo m. **2.** v atribuir.

attrition, n. roce, desgaste m.; atrición f.

attune, v. armonizar.

auction, n. subasta f., (S.A.) venduta f.

auctioneer, n. subastador m., (S.A.) martillero m.

audacious, a. audaz.

audacity, n. audacia f.

audible, a. audible.

audience, n. auditorio, público m.; entrevista f.

audiovisual, a. audiovisual.

audit, v. revisar cuentas.

audition, n. audición f.

auditor, n. interventor, revisor m.

auditorium, n. sala f.; teatro m.

auditory, a. & n. auditorio m.

augment, v. aumentar.

augur, v. augurar, pronosticar.

August, n. agosto m.

aunt, n. tía f.

auspice, n. auspicio f.

auspicious, a. favorable; propicio.

austere, a. austero.

austerity, n. austeridad, severidad f.

Austrian, a. & n. austríaco -ca.

authentic, a. auténtico.

authenticate, v. autenticar.

authenticity, n. autenticidad f.

author, n. autor, escritor m.

authoritarian, a. & n. autoritario m.

authoritative, a. autoritario; autorizado.

authoritatively, adv. autorizadamente.

authority, n. autoridad f.

authorization, n. autorización f.

authorize, v. autorizar.

auto, n. auto, automóvil m.

autobiography, n. autobiografía f.

autocracy, n. autocracia f.

autocrat, n. autócrata m. & f.

autograph, n. autógrafo m.

automatic, a. automático.

automatically, adv. automáticamente.

automobile, n. automóvil, coche m.

automotive, a. automotriz.

autonomy, n. autonomía f.

autopsy, n. autopsia f.

autumn, n. otoño m.

auxiliary, a. auxiliar.

avail, 1. n. of no a., en vano. 2. v. a. oneself of, aprovechar.

available, a. disponible.

avalanche, n. alud m.

avarice, n. avaricia, codicia f.

avariciously, adv. avaramente.

avenge, v. vengar.

avenger, n. vengador -ra.

avenue, n. avenida f.

average, 1. a. medio; común. 2. n. promedio, término medio m. 3. v. calcular el promedio.

averse, a. adverso.

aversion, n. aversión f.

avert, v. desviar; impedir.

aviary, n. pajarera, avería f.

aviation, n. aviación f.

aviator, n. aviador -ra.

aviatrix, n. aviatriz f.

avid, a. ávido.

avocation, n. pasatiempo f.

avoid, v. evitar.

avoidable, a. evitable.

avoidance, n. evitación f.; (leg.) anulación f.

avow, v. declarar; admitir.

avowal, n. admisión f.

avowed, a. reconocido; admitido.

avowedly, adv. reconocidamente; confesadamente.

await, v. esperar, aguardar.

awake, a. despierto.

awaken, v. despertar.

award, 1. n. premio m. 2. v. otorgar.

aware, a. enterado, consciente.

awash, a. & adv. (naut.) a flor de agua.

away, adv. (see under verb: **go away, put away, take away,** etc.)

awe, n. pavor m.

awesome, a. pavoroso; aterrador.

awful, a. horrible, terrible, muy malo.

awhile, adv. por un rato.

awkward, a. torpe, desmañado; (fig.) delicado, embarazoso.

awning, n. toldo m.

awry, a. oblicuo, torcido.

ax, axe, n. hacha f.

axiom, n. axioma m.

axis, n. eje m.

axle, n. eje m.

ayatollah, n. ayatola m.

azure, a. azulado.

B

babble, 1. *n.* balbuceo, murmullo *m.* **2** *v.* balbucear.

babbler, *n.* hablador -ra, charlador -ra.

baboon, *n.* mandril *m.*

baby, *n.* nene, bebé *m.*

babyish, *a.* infantil.

bachelor, *n.* soltero *m.*

bacillus, *n.* bacilo, microbio *m.*

back, 1. *adv.* atrás. **to be b.,** estar de vuelta. **b. of,** detrás de. **2.** *n.* espalda *f.;* (of animal) lomo *m.*

backbone, *n.* espinazo *m.;* (fig.) firmeza *f.*

backer, *n.* sostenedor -ra.

background, *n.* fondo *m.* antecedentes *m.pl.*

backing, *n.* apoyo *m.,* garantía *f.*

backlash, *n.* repercusión negativa.

backlog, *n.* rezago *m.*

backpack, *n.* mochila *f.*

backstage, *n.* entre bastidores *m.*

backward, 1. *a.* atrasado. **2.** *adv.* hacia atrás.

backwardness, *n.* atraso *m.*

backwater, *n.* remolino *m.;* contracorriente *f.*

backwoods, *n.* monte *m.;* región apartada.

bacon, *n.* tocino *m.*

bacteria, *n.* bacterias *f.pl.*

bacteriologist, *n.* bacteriólogo *m.*

bacteriology, *n.* bacteriología *f.*

bad, *a.* malo.

badge, *n.* insignia, divisa *f.*

badger, 1. *n.* tejón *m.* **2.** *v.* atormentar.

badly, *adv.* mal.

badness, *n.* maldad *f.*

bad-tempered, *a.* de mal humor.

baffle, *v.* desconcertar.

bafflement, *n.* contrariedad; confusión *f.*

bag, 1. *n.* saco *m.;* bolsa *f.* **2.** *v.* ensacar, cazar.

baggage, *n.* equipaje *m.* **b. check,** talón *m.*

baggage cart (airport), carrillo para llevar equipaje.

baggy, *a.* abotagado; bolsudo; hinchado.

bagpipe, *n.* gaita *f.*

bail, 1. *n.* fianza *f.* **2.** *v.* desaguar.

bailiff, *n.* alguacil *m.*

bait, 1. *n.* cebo *m.* **2.** *v.* cebar.

bake, *v.* cocer en horno.

baker, *n.* panadero, hornero *m.*

bakery, *n.* panadería *f.*

baking, *n.* hornada *f.* **b. powder,** levadura *f.*

balance, *n.* balanza *f.;* equilibrio *m.;* (com.) saldo *m.*

balcony, *n.* balcón *m.;* (theat.) galería *f.*

bald, *a.* calvo.

baldness, *n.* calvicie *f.*

bale, 1. *n.* bala *f.* **2.** *v.* embalar.

balk, *v.* frustrar; rebelarse.

balky, *a.* rebelón.

ball, *n.* bola, pelota *f.;* (dance) baile *m.*

ballad, *n.* romance, *m.;* balada *f.*

ballast, 1. *n.* lastre *m.* **2.** *v.* lastrar.

ball bearing, *n.* cojinete de bolas *m.*

ballerina, *n.* bailarina *f.*

ballet, *n.* danza *f.;* ballet *m.*

ballistics, *n.* balística *f.*

balloon, *n.* globo *m.* **b. tire,** neumático de balón.

ballot, 1. *n.* balota *f.,* voto *m.* **2.** *v.* balotar, votar.

ballpoint pen, *n.* bolígrafo *m.*

ballroom, *n.* salón de baile *m.*

balm, *n.* bálsamo; ungüento *m.*

balmy, *a.* fragante; reparador; calmante.

balsa, *n.* bálsamo *m.*

balsam, *n.* bálsamo *m.*

balustrade, *n.* barandilla *f.*

bamboo, *n.* bambú *m.,* caña *f.*

ban, 1. *n.* prohibición *f.* **2.** *v.* prohibir; proscribir.

banal, *a.* trivial; vulgar.

banana, *n.* banana *f.,* cambur *m.* **b. tree,** banano, plátano *m.*

band, 1. *n.* venda *f.;* (of men) banda, cuadrilla, partida *f.* **2.** *v.* asociarse.

bandage, 1. *n.* vendaje *m.* **2.** *v.* vendar.

bandanna, *n.* pañuelo (grande) *m.;* bandana *f.*

bandbox, *n.* caja de cartón.

bandit, *n.* bandido -da.

bandmaster, *n.* músico mayor *m.*

bandstand, *n.* kiosco de música.

bang, 1. *interj.* ¡pum! **2.** *n.* ruido de un golpe. **3.** *v.* golpear ruidosamente.

banish, *v.* desterrar.

banishment, n. destierro m.

banister, n. pasamano m.

bank, 1. n. banco m.; (of a river) margen m. or f. **2.** v. depositar.

bankbook, n. libreta de depositos f.

banker, n. banquero m.

banking, 1. a. bancaria. **2.** n. banca f.

bank note, n. billete de banco m.

bankrupt, n. insolvente.

bankruptcy, n. bancarrota f.

banner, n. bandera f.; estandarte m.

banquet, n. banquete m.

banter, 1. n. choteo m.; zumba; burla f. **2.** v. chotear; zumbar; burlarse.

baptism, n. bautismo, bautizo m.

baptismal, a. bautismal.

Baptist, n. bautista m.

baptize, v. bautizar.

bar, 1. n. barra f.; obstáculo m.; (tavern) taberna f.; bar m. **2.** v. barrear; prohibir, excluir.

barbarian, 1. a. bárbaro. **2.** n. bárbaro -ra.

barbarism, n. barbarismo m., barbarie f.

barbarous, n. bárbaro, cruel.

barbecue, n. animal asado entero; (Mex.) barbacoa f.

barber, n. barbero m. **b. shop,** barberéa f.

barbiturate, n. barbiturado m.

bare, 1. a. desnudo; descubierto. **2.** v. desnudar; descubrir.

bareback, adv. sin silla.

barefoot(ed), a. descalzo.

barely, adv. escasamente, apenas.

bareness, n. desnudez f.; pobreza f.

bargain, 1. n. ganga f., compra ventajosa f.; contrato m. **2.** v. regatear; negociar.

barge, n. lanchón m., barcaza f.

baritone, n. barítono m.

barium, n. bario m.

bark, 1. n. corteza f.; (of dog) ladra f. **2.** v. ladrar.

barley, n. cebada f.

barn, n. granero m.

barnacle, n. lapa f.

barnyard, n. corral m.

barometer, n. barómetro m.

barometric, a. barométrico.

baron, n. barón m.

baroness, n. baronesa f.

baronial, a. baronial.

baroque, a. barroco.

barracks, n. cuartel m.

barrage, n. cortina de fuego f.

barred, a. excluido; prohibido.

barrel, n. barril m.; (of gun) cañón m.

barren, a. estéril.

barrenness, n. esterilidad f.

barricade, n. barricada, barrera f.

barrier, n. barrera f.; obstáculo m.

barroom, n. cantina f.

bartender, n. tabernero; cantinero m.

barter, 1. n. cambio, trueque m. **2.** v. cambiar, trocar.

base, 1. a. bajo, vil. **2.** n. base f. **3.** v. basar.

baseball, n. beisbol m.

baseboard, n. tabla de resguardo.

basement, n. sótano m.

baseness, n. bajeza, vileza f.

bashful, a. vergonzoso, tímido.

bashfully, adv. timidamente; vergonzosamente.

bashfulness, n. vergüenza; timidez f.

basic, a. fundamental, básico.

basin, n. bacía f.; (of river) cuenca f.

basis, n. base f.

bask, v. tomar el sol.

basket, n. cesta, canasta f.

bass, n. (fish) lobina f.; (mus.) bajo profundo m. **b. viol.** violón m.

bassinet, n. bacinete m.

bassoon, n. bajón m.

bastard, a. & n. bastardo; hijo natural m.

baste, v. (sew) bastear; (cooking) pringar.

bat, n. (animal) murciélago m.; (baseball) bate m. **2.** v. batear.

batch, n. cantidad de cosas.

bath, n. baño m.

bathe, v. bañar.

bather, n. bañista m.

bathing resort, n. balneario m.

bathing suit, n. traje de baño.

bathrobe, n. bata de baña f.

bathroom, n. cuarto de baño.

bathtub, n. bañera f.

baton, n. bastón m.; (mus.) batuta f.

battalion, *n.* batallón *m.*

batter, 1. *n.* (cooking) batido *m.;* (baseball) voleador *m.* **2.** *v.* batir; derribar.

battery, *n.* batería; (elec.) pila *f.*

batting, *n.* agramaje, moldeaje *m.*

battle, 1. *n.* batalla *f.;* combate *m.* **2.** *v.* batallar.

battlefield, *n.* campo de batalla.

battleship, *n.* acorazado *m.*

bauxite, *n.* bauxita *f.*

bawl, *v.* gritar; vocear.

bay, 1. *n.* bahía *f.* **2.** *v.* aullar.

bayonet, *n.* bayoneta *f.*

bazaar, *n.* bazar *m.,* feria *f.*

be, *v.* ser; estar. (See **hacer; hay; tener** in Sp.-Eng. section).

beach, *n.* playa *f.*

beacon, *n.* faro *m.*

bead, *n.* cuenta *f.; pl.* (rel.) rosario *m.*

beading, *n.* abalorio *m.*

beady, *a.* globuloso; burbujoso.

beak, *n.* pico *m.*

beaker, *n.* vaso con pico *m.*

beam, *n.* viga *f.;* (of wood) madero *m.;* (of light) rayo *m.*

beaming, *a.* radiante.

bean, *n.* haba, habichuela *f.,* frijol *m.*

bear, 1. *n.* oso -sa. **2.** *v.* llevar; (endure) aguantar.

bearable, *a.* sufrible; suportable.

beard, *n.* barba *f.*

bearded, *a.* barbado; barbudo.

beardless, *a.* lampiño; imberbe.

bearer, *n.* portador -ra.

bearing, *n.* porte, aguante *m.*

bearskin, *n.* piel de oso *f.*

beast, *n.* bestia *f.;* bruto *m.*

beat, 1. *n.* golpear; batir; pulsar; (in games) ganar, vencer.

beaten, *a.* vencido; batido.

beating, *n.* paliza *f.*

beau, *n.* novio *m.*

beautiful, *a.* hermoso, bello.

beautifully, *adv.* bellamente.

beautify, *v.* embellecer.

beauty, *n.* hermosura, belleza *f.* **b. parlor,** salón de belleza.

beaver, *n.* castor *m.*

becalm, *v.* calmar; sosegar; encalmarse.

because, *conj.* porque. **b. of,** a causa de.

beckon, *v.* hacer señas.

become, *v.* hacerse; ponerse.

becoming, *a.* propio, correcto; **be b.,** quedar bien, sentar bien.

bed, *n.* cama *f.;* lecho *m.;* (of river) cauce *m.*

bedbug, *n.* chinche *m.*

bedclothes, *n.* ropa de cama.

bedding, *n.* colchones *m.pl.*

bedfellow, *n.* compañero de cama *m.*

bedizen, *v.* adornar; aderezar.

bedridden, *a.* postrado (en cama).

bedrock, *n.* (mining) lecho de roca *m.;* (fig.) fundamento *m.*

bedroom, *n.* alcoba *f.;* (Mex.) recámara *f.*

bedside, *n.* lado de cama *f.*

bedspread, *n.* cubrecama, sobrecama *f.*

bedstead, *n.* armadura de cama *f.*

bedtime, *n.* hora de acostarse.

bee, *n.* abeja *f.*

beef, *n.* carne de vaca.

beefsteak, *n.* bistec, bisté *m.*

beehive, *n.* colmena *f.*

beer, *n.* cerveza *f.*

beeswax, *n.* cera de abejas.

beet, *n.* remolacha *f.;* (Mex.) betabel *m.*

beetle, *n.* escarabajo *m.*

befall, *v.* suceder, sobrevenir.

befitting, *a.* conveniente; propio; digno.

before, 1. *adv.* antes. **2.** *prep.* antes de; (in front of) delante de. **3.** *conj.* antes que.

beforehand, *adv.* de antemano.

befriend, *v.* amparar.

befuddle, *v.* confundir; aturdir.

beg, *v.* rogar, suplicar; (for alms) mendigar.

beget, *v.* engendrar; producir.

beggar, *n.* mendigo -ga; (Sp. Am.) limosnero -ra.

beggarly, *a.* pobre, miserable.

begin, *v.* empezar, comenzar, principiar.

beginner, *n.* principiante *m.*

beginning, *n.* principio, comienzo *m.*

begrudge, *v.* envidiar.

behalf: in, on b. of, a favor de, en pro de.

behave, *v.* portarse comportarse.

behavior, *n.* conducta *f.;* comportamiento *m.*

behead, v. decapitar.

behind, 1. adv. atrás, detrás. **2.** prep. detrás de.

behold, v. contemplar.

beige, a. crema.

being, n. existencia f.; (person) ser m.

bejewel, v. adornar con joyas.

belated, a. atrasado, tardío.

belch, 1. n. eructo m. **2.** v. vomitar; eructar.

belfry, n. campanario m.

Belgian, 1. a. belga. **2.** n. belga m. & f.

Belgium, n. Bélgica f.

belie, v. desmentir.

belief, n. creencia f.; parecer m.

believable, a. creíble.

believe, v. creer.

believer, n. creyente m.

belittle, v. dar poca importancia a.

bell, n. campana f.; (of house) campanilla f.; (electric) timbre m.

bellboy, n. mozo, botones m.

bellicose, a. guerrero.

belligerence, n. beligerancia f.

belligerent, a. & n. beligerante.

belligerently, adv. belicosamente.

bellow, v. bramar, rugir.

bellows, n. fuelle m.

belly, n. vientre m.; panza, barriga f.

belong, v. pertenecer.

belongings, n. propiedad f.

beloved, a. querido, amado.

below, 1. adv. debajo, abajo. **2.** prep. debajo de.

belt, n. cinturón m.

bench, n. banco m.

bend, 1. n. vuelta; curva f. **2.** v. encorvar, doblar.

beneath, 1. adv. debajo, abajo. **2.** prep. debajo de.

benediction, n. bendición f.

benefactor, n. bienhechor -ra.

benefactress, n. bienhechora f.

beneficial, a. provechoso, beneficioso.

beneficiary, n. beneficiario, beneficiado m.

benefit, 1. n. provecho, beneficio m. **2.** v. beneficiar.

benevolence, n. benevolencia f.

benevolent, a. benévolo.

benevolently, adv. benignamente.

benign, a. benigno.

benignity, n. benignidad; bondad f.

bent, 1. a. encorvado. **b. on,** resuelto a. **2.** n. inclinación f.

benzene, n. bencina f.

bequeath, v. legar.

bequest, n. legado m.

berate, v. reñir, regañar.

bereave, v. despojar; desolar.

bereavement, n. privación f.; despojo m.

berry, n. baya f.

berth, n. camarote m.; (naut.) litera f.; (for vessel) amarradero m.

beseech, v. suplicar; implorar.

beseechingly, adv. suplicantemente.

beset, v. acosar; rodear.

beside, prep. al lado de.

besides, adv. además, por otra parte.

besiege, v. sitiar; asediar.

besieged, a. sitiado.

besieger, n. sitiador m.

besmirch, v. manchar; deshonrar.

best, a. & adv. mejor. **at b.,** a lo más.

bestial, a. bestial; brutal.

bestir, v. incitar; intrigar.

best man, n. padrino de boda.

bestow, v. conferir.

bestowal, n. dádiva; presentación f.

bet, 1. n. apuesta f. **2.** v. apostar.

betoken, v. denotar, significar.

betray, v. traicionar; revelar.

betrayal, n. traición f.

betroth, v. contraer esponsales; prometer.

betrothal, n. esponsales m.pl.

better, 1. a. & adv. mejor. **2.** v. mejorar.

between, prep. entre, en medio de.

bevel, 1. n. cartabón m. **2.** v. cortar al sesgo.

beverage, n. bebida f.; (cold) refresco m.

bewail, v. llorar; lamentar.

beware, v. guardarse, precaverse.

bewilder, v. aturdir.

bewildered, a. descarriado.

bewildering, a. aturdente.

bewilderment, n. aturdimiento m.; perplejidad f.

bewitch, v. hechizar; embrujar.

beyond, prep. más allá de.

biannual, a. semianual; semestral.

bias, 1. n. parcialidad f.; prejuicio m. **on the b.,** al sesgo 2. v. predisponer, influir.

bib, n. babador m.

Bible, n. Biblia f.

Biblical, a. bíblico.

bibliography, n. bibliografía f.

bicarbonate, n. bicarbonato m.

bicentennial, a. & n. bicentenario m.

biceps, n. biceps m.

bicker, v. altercar.

bicycle, n. bicicleta f.

bicyclist, n. biciclista f.

bid, 1. n. proposición, oferta f. 2. v. mandar; ofrecer.

bidder, n. postor m.

bide, v. aguardar; esperar.

bier, n. ataúd m.

bifocal, a. bifocal.

big, a. grande.

bigamist, n. bígamo -ma.

bigamy, n. bigamia f.

bigot, n. persona intolerante.

bigotry, n. intolerancia f.

bilateral, a. bilateral.

bile, n. bilis f.

bilingual, a. bilingüe.

bilious, a. bilioso.

bill, 1. n. cuenta, factura f.; (money) billete m.; (of bird) pico m. 2. v. facturar.

billet, 1. n. billete m.; (mil.) boleta f. 2. v. aposentar.

billfold, n. cartera f.

billiard balls, n. bolas de billar.

billiards, n. billar m.

billion, n. billón m.

bill of health, n. certificado de sanidad.

bill of lading, n. conocimiento de embarque.

bill of sale, n. escritura de venta.

billow, n. ola; oleada f.

bimetallic, a. bimetálico.

bimonthly, a. & adv. bimestral.

bin, n. hucha f.; depósito m.

bind, v. atar; obligar; (book) encuadernar.

bindery, n. taller de encuadernación m.

binding, n. encuadernación f.

binocular, 1. a. binocular. 2. n.pl. gemelos m.pl.

biochemistry, n. bioquímica f.

biodegradable, a. biodegradable.

biofeedback, n. retroalimentación biológica.

biographer, n. biógrafo f.

biographical, a. biográfico.

biography, n. biografía f.

biological, a. biológico.

biologically, adv. biológicamente.

biology, n. biología f.

bipartisan, a. bipartito.

biped, n. bípedo m.

bird, n. pájaro m.; ave f.

bird of prey, n. ave de rapiña.

birth, n. nacimiento m. **give b. to,** dar a luz.

birth control, n. contracepción f.

birthday, n. cumpleaños m.

birthmark, n. estigma f., marca de nacimiento.

birthplace, n. natalicio m.

birth rate, n. natalidad f.

birthright, n. primogenitura f.

biscuit, n. bizcocho m.

bisect, v. bisecar.

bishop, n. obispo m.; (chess) alfil m.

bishopric, n. obispado m.

bismuth, n. bismuto m.

bison, n. bisonte m.

bit, n. pedacito m.; (mech.) taladro m.; (for horse) bocado m.; (computer) bit m.

bitch, n. perra f.

bite, 1. n. bocado m.; picada f. 2. v. morder; picar.

biting, a. penetrante; mordaz.

bitter, a. amargo.

bitterly, adv. amargamente; agriamente.

bitterness, n. amargura f.; rencor m.

bivouac, 1. n. vivaque m. 2. v. vivaquear.

biweekly, a. quincenal.

black, a. negro.

Black, n. (person) negro -gra; persona de color.

blackberry, n. mora f.

blackbird, n. mirlo m.

blackboard, n. pizarra f.

blacken, v. ennegrecer.

black eye, n. ojo amoratado.

blackguard, n. tunante; pillo m.

blackmail, 1. *n.* chantaje *m.* **2.** *v.* amenazar con chantaje.

black market, *n.* mercado negro.

blackout, *n.* oscurecimiento, apagamiento *m.*

blacksmith, *n.* herrero *m.*

bladder, *n.* vejiga *f.*

blade, *n.* (sword) hoja *f.;* (oar) pala *f.;* (grass) brizna *f.*

blame, *v.* culpar, echar la culpa a.

blameless, *a.* inculpable.

blanch, *v.* blanquear; escaldar.

bland, *a.* blando.

blank, *a.* & *n.* blanco.

blanket, *n.* manta *f.;* cobertor *m.*

blare, 1. *n.* sonido de trompeta. **2.** *v.* sonar como trompeta.

blaspheme, *v.* blasfemar.

blasphemer, *n.* blasfemo, blasfemador *m.*

blasphemous, *a.* blasfemo, impío.

blasphemy, *n.* blasfemia *f.*

blast, 1. *n.* barreno *m.;* (wind) ráfaga *f.* **2.** *v.* barrenar.

blatant, *a.* bramante.

blaze, 1. *n.* llama, hoguera *f.* **2.** *v.* encenderse en llama.

blazing, *a.* flameante.

bleach, *v.* blanquear.

bleachers, *n.* asientos al aire libre.

bleak, *a.* frío y sombrío.

bleakness, *n.* intemperie *f.*

bleed, *v.* sangrar.

blemish, 1. *n.* mancha *f.;* lunar *m.* **2.** *v.* manchar.

blend, 1. *n.* mezcla *f.* **2.** *v.* mezclar, combinar.

blended, *a.* mezclado.

bless, *v.* bendecir.

blessed, *a.* bendito.

blessing, *n.* bendición *f.*

blight, 1. *n.* plaga *f.;* tizón *m.* **2.** *v.* atizonar.

blind, *a.* ciego.

blindfold, *v.* vendar los ojos.

blinding, *a.* deslumbrante; ofuscante.

blindly, *adv.* ciegamente.

blindness, *n.* ceguedad, ceguera *f.*

blink, 1. *n.* guiñada *f.* **2.** *v.* guiñar.

bliss, *n.* felicidad *f.*

blissful, *a.* dichoso; bienaventurado.

blissfully, *adv.* felizmente.

blister, *n.* ampolla *f.*

blithe, *a.* alegre; jovial; gozoso.

blizzard, *n.* chubasco de nieve.

bloat, *v.* hinchar.

bloc, *n.* grupo (político); bloc.

block, 1. *n.* bloque *m.;* (street) manzana, cuadra *f.* **2.** *v.* bloquear.

blockade, 1. *n.* bloqueo *m.* **2.** *v.* bloquear.

blond, *a.* & *n.* rubio -ia.

blood, *n.* sangre *f.;* parentesco, linaje *m.*

bloodhound, *n.* sabueso *m.*

bloodless, *a.* exangüe; desangrado.

blood poisoning, *n.* envenenamiento de sangre.

blood pressure, *n.* presión arterial.

bloodshed, *n.* matanza *f.*

bloodthirsty, *a.* cruel, sanguinario.

bloody, *a.* ensangrentado, sangriento.

bloom, 1. *n.* flor *f.* **2.** *v.* florecer.

blooming, *a.* lozano; fresco.

blossom, 1. *n.* flor *f.* **2.** *v.* florecer.

blot, 1. *n.* mancha *f.* **2.** *v.* manchar.

blotch, 1. *n.* mancha, roncha *f.* **2.** *v.* manchar.

blotter, *n.* papel secante.

blouse, *n.* blusa *f.*

blow, 1. *n.* golpe *m.;* (fig.) chasco *m.* **2.** *v.* soplar.

blowout, *n.* reventón de neumático.

blubber, *n.* grasa de ballena.

bludgeon, *n.* porra *f.*

blue, *a.* azul; triste, melancólico.

bluebird, *n.* azulejo *m.*

blue jeans, *n.* jeans *m.pl.*

blueprint, *n.* heliografía *f.*

bluff, 1. *n.* risco *m.* **2.** *v.* alardear; baladronar.

bluing, *n.* añil *m.*

blunder, 1. *n.* desatino *m.* **2.** *v.* desatinar.

blunderer, *n.* desatinado *m.*

blunt, 1. *a.* embotado; descortés. **2.** *v.* embotar.

bluntly, *adv.* bruscamente.

bluntness, *n.* grosería *f.*

blur, 1. *n.* trazo confuso *m.* **2.** *v.* hacer indistinto.

blush, 1. *n.* rubor, sonrojo *m.* **2.** *v.* sonrojarse.

bluster, 1. n. fanfarria f. **2.** v. fanfarrear.

boar, n. verraco m. **wild b.,** jabalí.

board, 1. n. tabla; (govt.) consejo m.; junta f. **b. and room,** cuarto y comida, casa y comida. **2.** v. (ship) abordar.

boarder, n. pensionista m. & f.

boardinghouse, pensión f., casa de huéspedes.

boarding pass, n. boleto de embarque.

boast, 1. n. jactancia f. **2.** v. jactarse.

boaster, n. fanfarrón m.

boastful, a. jactancioso.

boastfulness, n. jactancia f.

boat, n. barco, buque, bote m.

boathouse, n. casilla de botes f.

boatswain, n. contramaestre m.

bob, v. menear.

bobbin, n. bobina f.

bobby pin, n. gancho m.

bodice, n. corpiño m.

bodily, a. corporal.

body, n. cuerpo m.

bodyguard, n. guardia de corps.

bog, n. pantano m.

Bohemian, a. & n. bohemio -mia.

boil, 1. n. (med.) divieso m. **2.** v. hervir.

boiler, n. marmita; caldera f.

boisterous, a. tumultuoso.

boisterously, adv. tumultuosamente.

bold, a. atrevido, osado.

boldface, n. (type) letra negra.

boldly, adv. audazmente; descaradamente.

boldness, n. atrevimiento m.; osadía f.

Bolivian, a. & n. boliviano -na.

bologna, n. salchicha f.

bolster, 1. n. travesero, cojín m. **2.** v. apoyar, sostener.

bolt, 1. n. perno m.; (of door) cerrojo m.; (lightning) rayo m. **2.** v. acerrojar.

bomb, 1. n. bomba f. **2.** v. bombardear.

bombard, v. bombardear.

bombardier, n. bombardero m.

bombardment, n. bombardeo m.

bomber, n. avión de bombardeo.

bombproof, a. a prueba de granadas.

bombshell, n. bomba f.

bonbon, n. dulce, bombón m.

bond, n. lazo m.; (com.) bono m.

bondage, n. esclavitud, servidumbre f.

bonded, a. garantizado.

bone, n. hueso m.

boneless, a. sin huesos.

bonfire, n. hoguera, fogata f.

bonnet, n. gorra f.

bonus, n. bono m.

bony, a. huesudo.

book, n. libro m.

bookbinder, n. encuadernador m.

bookcase, n. armario para libros.

bookkeeper, n. tenedor de libros.

bookkeeping, n. contabilidad f.

booklet, n. folleto m., libreta f.

bookseller, n. librero m.

bookstore, n. librería f.

boom, n. (naut.) botalón m.; prosperidad repentina.

boon, n. dádiva f.

boor, n. patán, rústico m.

boorish, a. villano.

boost, 1. n. alza; ayuda f. **2.** v. levantar, alzar; fomentar.

booster, n. fomentador m.

boot, n. bota f.

bootblack, n. limpiabotas m.

booth, n. cabaña; casilla f.

booty, n. botín m.

border, 1. n. borde m.; frontera f. **2.** v. b. on, lindar con.

borderline, 1. a. marginal. **2.** n. margen m.

bore, 1. n. lata f.; persona pesada. **2.** v. aburrir, fastidiar; (mech.) taladrar.

boredom, n. aburrimiento m.

boric acid, n. ácido bórico m.

boring, a. aburrido, pesado.

born, a. nacido. **be born,** nacer.

born-again, a. renacido.

borrow, v. pedir prestado.

bosom, n. seno, pecho m.

boss, n. jefe, patrón m.

botany, n. botánica f.

both, pron. & a. ambos, los dos.

bother, 1. n. molestia f. **2.** v. molestar, incomodar.

bothersome, a. molesto.

bottle, 1. n. botella f. **2.** v. embotellar.

bottom, n. fondo m.

boudoir, n. tocador m.

bough, n. rama f.

boulder, n. canto rodado.

boulevard, *n.* bulevar *m.*

bounce, 1. *n.* brinco *m.* 2. *v.* brincar; hacer saltar.

bound, 1. *n.* salto *m.* 2. *v.* limitar.

boundary, *n.* límite, lindero *m.*

bouquet, *n.* ramillete de flores.

bourgeois, *a. & n.* burgués.

bout, *n.* encuentro; combate *m.*

bow, 1. *n.* saludo *m.;* (of ship) proa *f.;* (archery) arco *m.;* (ribbon) lazo *m.* 2. *v.* saludar, inclinar.

bowels, *n.* intestinos *m.pl.;* entrañas *f.pl.*

bowl, 1. *n.* vasija *f.;* platón *m.* 2. *v.* jugar a los bolos. **b. over**, derribar.

bowlegged, *a.* perniabierto.

bowling, *n.* bolos *m.pl.*

box, 1. *n.* caja *f.;* (theat.) palco *m.* 2. *v.* (sports) boxear.

boxcar, *n.* vagón *m.*

boxer, *n.* boxeador, pugilista *m.*

boxing, *n.* boxeo *m.*

box office, *n.* taquilla *f.*

boy, *n.* muchacho, chico *m.*

boycott, 1. *n.* boicoteo *m.* 2. *v.* boicotear.

boyhood, *n.* muchachez *f.*

boyish, *a.* pueril.

boyishly, *adv.* puerilmente.

brace, 1. *n.* grapón *m.; pl.* tirantes *m.pl.* 2. *v.* reforzar.

bracelet, *n.* brazalete *m.*, pulsera *f.*

bracket, *n.* ménsula *f.*

brag, *v.* jactarse.

braggart, 1. *a.* jactancioso. 2. *n.* jaque *m.*

braid, 1. *n.* trenza *f.* 2. *v.* trenzar.

brain, *n.* cerebro, seso *m.*

brainy, *a.* sesudo, inteligente.

brake, 1. *n.* freno *m.* 2. *v.* frenar.

bran, *n.* salvado *m.*

branch, *n.* ramo *m.;* (of tree) rama *f.*

brand, *n.* marca *f.*

brandish, *v.* blandir.

brand-new, *a.* enteramente nuevo.

brandy, *n.* aguardiente, coñac *m.*

brash, *a.* impetuoso.

brass, *n.* bronce, latón *m.*

brassiere, *n.* corpiño, sostén *m.*

brat, *n.* mocoso *m.*

bravado, *n.* bravata *f.*

brave, *a.* valiente.

bravery, *n.* valor *m.*

brawl, 1. *n.* alboroto *m.* 2. *v.* alborotar.

brawn, *n.* músculo *m.*

bray, *v.* rebuznar.

brazen, *a.* desvergonzado.

Brazil, *n.* Brasil *m.*

Brazilian, *a. & n.* brasileño -ña.

breach, *n.* rotura, infracción *f.*

bread, *n.* pan *m.*

breadth, *n.* anchura *f.*

break, 1. *n.* rotura; pausa *f.* 2. *v.* quebrar, romper.

breakable, *a.* rompible, frágil.

breakage, *n.* rotura *f.*, destrozo *m.*

breakfast, 1. *n.* desayuno, almuerzo *m.* 2. *v.* desayunarse, almorzar.

breakneck, *a.* rápido, precipitado, atropellado.

breast, *n.* pecho, seno *m.*

breath, *n.* aliento; soplo *m.*

breathe, *v.* respirar.

breathless, *a.* desalentado.

breathlessly, *adv.* jadeantemente, intensamente.

bred, *a.* criado; educado.

breeches, *n.pl.* calzones; pantalones, *m.pl.*

breed, 1. *n.* raza *f.* 2. *v.* engendrar; criar.

breeder, *n.* criador *m.*

breeding, *n.* cría *f.*

breeze, *n.* brisa *f.*

breezy, *a.:* **it is b.**, hace brisa.

brevity, *n.* brevedad *f.*

brew, *v.* fraguar, elaborar.

brewer, *n.* cervecero *m.*

brewery, *n.* cervecería *f.*

bribe, 1. *n.* soborno, cohecho *m.* 2. *v.* sobornar, cohechar.

briber, *n.* sobornador *m.*

bribery, *n.* soborno, cohecho *m.*

brick, *n.* ladrillo *m.*

bricklayer, *n.* albañil *m.*

bridal, *a.* nupcial.

bride, *n.* novia *f.*

bridegroom, *n.* novio *m.*

bridesmaid, *n.* madrina de boda.

bridge, *n.* puente *m.*

bridged, *a.* conectado.

bridgehead, *n.* (mil.) cabeza de puente.

bridle, *n.* brida *f.*

brief, *a.* breve.

briefcase, *n.* maletín *m.*

briefly, *adv.* brevemente.
briefness, *n.* brevedad *f.*
brier, *n.* zarza *f.*
brig, *n.* bergantín *m.*
brigade, *n.* brigada *f.*
bright, *a.* claro, brillante.
brighten, *v.* abrillantar; alegrar.
brightness, *n.* resplandor *m.*
brilliance, *n.* brillantez *f.*
brilliant, *a.* brillante.
brim, *n.* borde *m.; (of hat)* ala *f.*
brine, *n.* salmuera *f.*
bring, *v.* traer. **b. about,** efectuar, llevar a cabo.
brink, *n.* borde *m.*
briny, *a.* salado.
brisk, *a.* vivo; enérgico.
briskly, *adv.* vivamente.
briskness, *n.* viveza *f.*
bristle, *n.* cerda *f.*
bristly, *a.* hirsuto.
Britain, *n.* **Great B.,** Gran Bretaña *f.*
British, *a.* británico.
British Empire, imperio británico.
British Isles, islas británicas.
Briton, *n.* inglés *m.*
brittle, *a.* quebradizo, frágil.
broad, *a.* ancho.
broadcast, 1. *n.* radiodifusión *n.* **2.** *v.* radiodifundir.
broadcaster, *n.* locutor *m.*
broadcloth, *n.* paño fino.
broaden, *v.* ensanchar.
broadly, *adv.* ampliamente.
broadminded, *a.* tolerante, liberal.
brocade, *n.* brocado *m.*
brocaded, *a.* espolinado.
broil, *v.* asar.
broiler, *n.* parilla *f.*
broken, *a.* roto, quebrado.
broken-hearted, *a.* angustiado.
broker, *n.* corredor, cambista *m.*
brokerage, *n.* corretaje *f.*
bronchial, *a.* bronquial.
bronchitis, *n.* bronquitis *f.*
bronze, *n.* bronce *m.*
brooch, *n.* broche *m.*
brood, 1. *n.* cría, progenie *f.* **2.** *v.* empollar; cobijar.
brook, *n.* arroyo *m.,* quebrada *f.*
broom, *n.* escoba *f.*
broomstick, *n.* palo de escoba.
broth, *n.* caldo *m.*
brothel, *n.* burdel *m.*

brother, *n.* hermano *m.*
brotherhood, *n.* fraternidad *f.*
brother-in-law, *n.* cuñado *m.*
brotherly, *a.* fraternal.
brow, *n.* ceja; frente *f.*
brown, *a.* pardo, moreno.
browse, *v.* ramonear.
bruise, 1. *n.* contusión *f.* **2.** *v.* magullar.
brunette, *a.* & *n.* moreno -na, trigueño -ña.
brush, *n.* cepillo *m.;* brocha *f.* **2.** *v.* cepillar.
brushwood, *n.* matorral *m.*
brusque, *a.* brusco.
brusquely, *adv.* bruscamente.
brutal, *a.* brutal.
brutality, *n.* brutalidad *f.*
brutalize, *v.* embrutecer.
brute, *n.* bruto *m.,* bestia *f.*
bubble, *n.* ampolla *f.*
bucket, *n.* cubo *m.*
buckle, *n.* hebilla *f.*
buckram, *n.* bucarán *m.*
bucksaw, *n.* sierra de bastidor.
buckshot, *n.* posta *f.*
buckwheat, *n.* trigo sarraceno.
bud, 1. *n.* brote *m.* **2.** *v.* brotar.
budding, *a.* en capullo.
budge, *v.* moverse.
budget, *n.* presupuesto *m.*
buffalo, *n.* búfalo *m.*
buffer, *n.* parachoques *m.*
buffet, *n.* bufet *m.; (furniture)* aparador *m.*
buffoon, *n.* bufón *m.*
bug, *n.* insecto *m.*
bugle, *n.* clarín *m.;* corneta *f.*
build, *v.* construir.
builder, *n.* constructor *m.*
building, *n.* edificio *m.*
bulb, *n.* bulbo *m.; (of lamp)* bombilla, ampolla *f.*
bulge, 1. *n.* abultamiento *m.* **2.** *v.* abultar.
bulk, *n.* masa *f.;* grueso *m.;* mayoría *f.*
bulkhead, *n.* frontón *m.*
bulky, *a.* grueso, abultado.
bull, *n.* toro *m.*
bulldog, *n.* perro de presa.
bullet, *n.* bala *f.*
bulletin, *n.* boletín *f.*
bulletproof, *a.* a prueba de bala.
bullfight, *n.* corrida de toros.
bullfighter, *n.* torero *m.*
bullfinch, *n.* pinzón real *m.*

bully, 1. *n.* rufián *m.* **2.** *v.* bravear.

bulwark, *n.* baluarte *m.*

bum, *n.* holgazán *m.*

bump, 1. *n.* golpe, choque *m.* **2.** *v.* **b. into,** chocar contra.

bumper, *n.* parachoques *m.*

bun, *n.* bollo *m.*

bunch, *n.* racimo; montón *m.*

bundle, 1. *n.* bulto *m.* **2.** *v.* **b. up,** abrigar.

bungalow, *n.* casa de un solo piso.

bungle, *v.* estropear.

bunion, *n.* juanete *m.*

bunk, *n.* litera *f.*

bunny, *n.* conejito *m.*

bunting, *n.* lanilla, banderas *f.*

buoy, *n.* boya *f.*

buoyant, *a.* boyante; vivaz.

burden, 1. *n.* carga *f.* **2.** *v.* cargar.

burdensome, *a.* gravoso.

bureau, *n.* (furniture) cómoda *f.*; departamento *m.*

burglar, *n.* ladrón *m.*

burglarize, *v.* robar.

burglary, *n.* robo *m.*

burial, *n.* entierro *m.*

burlap, *n.* arpillera *f.*

burly, *a.* corpulento.

burn, *v.* quemar; arder.

burner, *n.* mechero *m.*

burning, *a.* ardiente.

burnish, *v.* pulir; acicalar.

burrow, *v.* minar; horadar.

burst, *v.* reventar.

bury, *v.* enterrar.

bus, *n.* autobús *m.*

bush, *n.* arbusto *m.*

bushy, *a.* matoso; peludo.

business, *n.* negocios *m.pl.*; comercio *m.*

businesslike, *a.* directo.

businessman, *n.* comerciante *m.*

businesswoman, *n.* mujer de negocios.

bust, *n.* busto; pecho *m.*

bustle, *n.* bullicio *m.*; animación *f.*

busy, *a.* ocupado, atareado.

busybody, *n.* entremetido *m.*

but, *conj.* pero; sino.

butcher, *n.* carnicero *m.*

butchery, *n.* carnicería; matanza *f.*

butler, *n.* mayordomo *m.*

butt, *n.* punta *f.*; cabo extremo *m.*

butter, *n.* manteca, mantequilla *f.*

buttercup, *n.* ranúnculo *m.*

butterfat, *n.* mantequilla *f.*

butterfly, *n.* mariposa *f.*

buttermilk, *n.* suero (de leche) *m.*

button, *n.* botón *m.*

buttonhole, *n.* ojal *m.*

buttress, *n.* sostén; refuerzo *m.*

buxom, *a.* regordete.

buy, *v.* comprar.

buyer, *n.* comprador -ra.

buzz, 1. *n.* zumbido *m.* **2.** *v.* zumbar.

buzzard, *n.* gallinazo *m.*

buzzer, *n.* zumbador *m.*

buzz saw, *n.* sierra circular *f.*

by, *prep.* por; (near) cerca de, al lado de; (time) para.

by-and-by, *adv.* pronto; luego.

bygone, *a.* pasado.

bylaw, *n.* estatuto, reglamento *m.*

bypass, *n.* desvío *m.*

byproduct, *n.* producto accesorio *m.*

bystander, *n.* espectador; mirón *m.*

byte, *n.* en teoría de la información: ocho bits.

byway, *n.* camino desviado *m.*

C

cab, *n.* coche de alquiler.

cabaret, *n.* cabaret *m.*

cabbage, *n.* repollo *m.*

cabin, *n.* cabaña *f.*

cabinet, *n.* gabinete; ministerio *m.*

cabinetmaker, *n.* ebanista *m.*

cable, *n.* cable *m.*

cablegram, *n.* cablegrama *m.*

cache, *n.* escondite *m.*

cackle, 1. *n.* charla *f.*, cacareo *m.* **2.** *v.* cacarear.

cacophony, *n.* cacofonía *f.*

cactus, *n.* cacto *m.*

cad, *n.* persona vil.

cadaver, *n.* cadáver *m.*

cadaverous, *a.* cadavérico.

cadence, *n.* cadencia *f.*

cadet, *n.* cadete *m.*

cadmium, *n.* cadmio *m.*

cadre, *n.* núcleo; (mil.) cuadro *m.*

café, *n.* café, cantina *f.*

cafeteria, n. cafetería f.
caffeine, n. cafeína f.
cage, 1. n. jaula f. **2.** v. enjaular.
caged, a. enjaulado.
caisson, n. arcón m.; (mil.) furgón m.
cajole, v. lisonjear; adular.
cake, n. torta f.; bizcocho m.
calamitous, a. calamitoso.
calamity, n. calamidad f.
calcify, v. calcificar.
calcium, n. calcio m.
calculable, a. calculable.
calculate, v. calcular.
calculating, a. interesado.
calculation, n. calculación f.; cálculo m.
calculus, n. cálculo m.
caldron, n. caldera f.
calendar, n. calendario m.
calf, n. ternero m.
calfskin, n. piel de becerro.
caliber, n. calibre m.
calico, n. percal m.
caliper, n. calibrador m.
calisthenics, n. calistenia, gimnasia f.
calk, v. calafatear; rellenar.
calker, n. calafate m.
call, 1. n. llamada f. **2.** v. llamar.
calligraphy, n. caligrafía f.
calling, n. vocación f.
calling card, n. tarjeta (de visita) f.
callously, adv. insensiblemente.
callow, a. sin experiencia.
callus, n. callo m.
calm, 1. a. tranquilo, calmado. **2.** n. calma f. **3.** v. calmar.
calmly, adv. serenamente.
calmness, n. calma f.
caloric, a. calórico.
calorie, n. caloría f.
calorimeter, n. calorímetro m.
calumniate, v. calumniar.
calumny, n. calumnia f.
Calvary, n. Calvario m.
calve, v. parir (la vaca).
calyx, n. cáliz m.
camaraderie, n. compañerismo m., compadrería f.
cambric, n. batista f.
camel, n. camello m.
camellia, n. camelia f.
camel's hair, n. piel de camello.
cameo, n. camafeo m.
camera, n. cámara f.

camouflage, n. camuflaje m.
camouflaging, n. simulacro, disfraz m.
camp, 1. n. campamento m. **2.** v. acampar.
campaign, n. campaña f.
camper, n. acampado m.
campfire, n. fogata de campamento.
camphor, n. alcanfor m.
camphor ball, n. bola de alcanfor.
campus, n. campo de colegio (o universidad) m.
can, v. (be able) poder.
can, 1. n. lata f. **2.** v. conservar en latas.
Canada, n. Canadá m.
Canadian, a. & n. canadiense.
canal, n. canal m.
canalize, v. canalizar.
canard, n. embuste m.
canary, n. canario m.
cancel, v. cancelar.
cancellation, n. cancelación f.
cancer, n. cáncer m.
candelabrum, n. candelabro m.
candid, a. cándido, sincero.
candidacy, n. candidatura f.
candidate, n. candidato -ta.
candidly, adv. candidamente.
candidness, n. candidez; sinceridad f.
candied, a. garapiñado.
candle, n. vela f.
candlestick, n. candelero m.
candor, n. candor m.; sinceridad f.
candy, n. dulces m.pl.
cane, n. caña f.; (for walking) bastón m.
canine, a. canino.
canister, n. frasco m.; lata f.
canker, n. llaga; úlcera f.
cankerworm, n. oruga f.
canned, a. envasado.
canner, n. envasador m.
cannery, n. fábrica de conservas alimenticias f.
cannibal, n. caníbal m.
cannon, n. cañón m.
cannonade, n. cañoneo m.
cannoneer, n. cañonero m.
canny, a. sagaz; prudente.
canoe, n. canoa f.
canon, n. canon m.; (rel.) canónigo m.
canonical, a. canónico.

canonize, v. canonizar.

canopy, n. dosel m.

cant, n. hipocresía f.

cantaloupe, n. melón m.

canteen, n. cantina f.

canter, 1. n. medio galope m. **2.** v. galopar.

cantonment, n. (mil.) acuartelamiento m.

canvas, n. lona f.

canyon, n. cañon, desfiladero m.

cap, 1. n. tapa f.; (headwear) gorro m. **2.** v. tapar.

capability, n. capacidad f.

capable, a. capaz.

capably, adv. hábilmente.

capacious, a. espacioso.

capacity, n. capacidad f.

cape, n. capa f., (geog.) cabo m.

caper, n. zapateta f.; (bot.) alcaparra f.

capillary, a. capilar.

capital, n. capital m.; (govt.) capital f.

capitalism, n. capitalismo m.

capitalist, n. capitalista m.

capitalistic, a. capitalista.

capitalization, n. capitalización f.

capitalize, v. capitalizar.

capitulate, v. capitular.

capon, n. capón m.

caprice, n. capricho m.

capricious, a. caprichoso.

capriciously, adv. caprichosamente.

capriciousness, n. capricho m.

capsize, v. zozobrar, volcar.

capsule, n. cápsula f.

captain, n. capitán m.

caption, n. título m.; (motion pictures) subtítulo m.

captious, a. capcioso.

captivate, v. cautivar.

captivating, a. encantador.

captive, n. cautivo -va, prisionero -ra.

captivity, n. cautividad f.

captor, n. apresador m.

capture, 1. n. captura f. **2.** v. capturar.

car, n. coche, carro m.; (of train) vagón, coche m. **baggage c.,** vagón de equipajes. **parlor c.,** coche salón.

carafe, n. garrafa f.

caramel, n. caramelo m.

carat, n. quilate m.

caravan, n. caravana f.

caraway, n. alcaravea f.

carbide, n. carburo m.

carbine, n. carabina f.

carbohydrate, n. hidrato de carbono.

carbon, n. carbón m.

carbon dioxide, anhídrido carbónico.

carbon monoxide, monóxido de carbono.

carbon paper, n. papel carbón m.

carbuncle, n. carbunclo m.

carburetor, n. carburador m.

carcinogenic, a. carcinogénico.

card, n. tarjeta f. **playing c.,** naipe m.

cardboard, n. cartón m.

cardiac, a. cardíaco.

cardigan, n. chaqueta de punto.

cardinal, 1. a. cardinal. **2.** n. cardenal m.

care, 1. n. cuidado. **2.** v. **c. for,** cuidar.

careen, v. carenar; encharse de costado.

career, n. carrera f.

carefree, a. descuidado.

careful, a. cuidadoso. **be. c.,** tener cuidado.

carefully, adv. cuidadosamente.

carefulness, n. esmero; cuidado m.; cautela f.

careless, a. descuidado.

carelessly, adv. descuidadamente; negligentemente.

carelessness, n. descuido m.

caress, 1. n. caricia f. **2.** v. acariciar.

caretaker, n. guardián m.

cargo, n. carga f.

caricature, n. caricatura f.

caries, n. caries f.

carload, n. furgonada, vagonada.

carnal, a. carnal.

carnation, n. clavel m.

carnival, n. carnaval m.

carnivorous, a. carnívoro.

carol, n. villancico m.

carouse, v. parrandear.·

carpenter, n. carpintero m.

carpet, n. alfombra f.

carpeting, n. alfombrado m.

car pool, n. uso habitual, por varias personas, de un automóvil perteneciente a una de ellas.

carriage, n. carruaje; (bearing) porte m.

carrier, n. portador -ra.

carrier pigeon, n. paloma mensajera.

carrot, n. zanahoria f.

carrousel, n. volantín m.

carry, v. llevar, cargar. **c. out,** cumplir, llevar a cabo.

cart, n. carreta f.

cartage, n. acarreo, carretaje m.

cartel, n. cartel m.

cartilage, n. cartílago m.

carton, n. caja de cartón.

cartoon, n. caricatura f.

cartoonist, n. caricaturista m.

cartridge, n. cartucho m.

carve, v. esculpir; (meat) trinchar.

carver, n. tallador; grabador m.

carving, n. entalladura f.; arte de trinchar. **c. knife,** trinchante m.

cascade, n. cascada f.

case, n. caso m.; (box) caja f. **in any c.,** sea como sea.

cash, 1. n. dinero contante. **2.** v. efectuar, cambiar.

cashier, n. cajero -ra.

cashmere, n. casimir f.

casino, n. casino m.

cask, n. barril m.

casket, n. ataúd m.

casserole, n. cacerola f.

cassette, n. cassette m., cartucho m.

cast, 1. n. (theat.) reparto de papeles. **2.** v. echar; (theat.) repartir.

castanet, n. castañuela f.

castaway, n. náufrago m.

caste, n. casta f.

caster, n. tirador m.

castigate, v. castigar.

Castilian, a. castellano.

cast iron, n. hierro colado m.

castle, n. castillo m.

castoff, a. descartado.

casual, a. casual.

casually, adv. casualmente.

casualness, n. casualidad f.

casualty, n. víctima f.; (mil.) baja f.

cat, n. gato -ta.

cataclysm, n. cataclismo m.

catacomb, n. catacumba f.

catalogue, n. catálogo m.

catapult, n. catapulta f.

cataract, n. catarata f.

catarrh, n. catarro m.

catastrophe, n. catástrofe m.

catch, v. alcanzar, atrapar, coger.

catchy, a. contagioso.

catechism, n. catequismo m.

catechize, v. catequizar.

categorical, a. categórico.

category, n. categoría f.

cater, v. abastecer; proveer. **c. to,** complacer.

caterpillar, n. gusano m.

catgut, n. cuerda (de tripa).

catharsis, n. purga f.

cathartic, 1. a. catártico; purgante. **2.** n. purgante m.

cathedral, n. catedral f.

cathode, n. cátodo m.

Catholic, 1. a. católico. **2.** n. católico -ca.

Catholicism, n. catolicismo m.

catnap, n. siesta corta.

catsup, n. salsa de tomate.

cattle, n. ganado m.

cattleman, n. ganadero m.

cauliflower, n. coliflor m.

causation, n. causalidad f.

cause, n. causa f.

causeway, n. calzada f.; terraplén m.

caustic, a. cáustico.

cauterize, v. cauterizar.

cautery, n. cauterio m.

caution, n. cautela f.

cautious, a. cauteloso.

cavalcade, n. cabalgata f.

cavalier, n. caballero m.

cavalry, n. caballería f.

cave, cavern, n. caverna f.

cave-in, n. hundimiento m.

caviar, n. caviar m.

cavity, n. hueco m.

cayman, n. caimán m.

cease, v. cesar.

ceaseless, a. incesante.

cedar, n. cedro m.

cede, v. ceder.

ceiling, n. cielo m.

celebrant, n. celebrante m.

celebrate, v. celebrar.

celebration, n. celebración f.

celebrity, n. persona célebre.

celerity, n. celeridad; prontitud f.

celery, n. apio m.

celestial, a. celeste.

celibacy, n. celibato m.

celibate, a. & n. célibe m.

cell, *n.* celda *f.*; (biol.) célula *f.*

cellar, *n.* sótano *m.*

cellist, *n.* celista *m.*

cello, *n.* violoncelo *m.*

cellophane, *n.* celofán *m.*

cellular, *a.* celular.

celluloid, *n.* celuloide *m.*

cellulose, 1. *a.* celuloso. **2.** *n.* celulosa *f.*

Celtic, *a.* céltico.

cement, *n.* cemento *m.*

cemetery, *n.* cementerio *m.*; campo santo *m.*

censor, *n.* censor *m.*

censorious, *a.* severo; crítico.

censorship, *n.* censura *f.*

censure, 1. *n.* censura *f.* **2.** *v.* censurar.

census, *n.* censo *m.*

cent, *n.* centavo *m.*, céntimo *m.*

centenary, *a.* & *n.* centenario *m.*

centennial, *a.* & *n.* centenario *m.*

center, *n.* centro *m.*

centerfold, *n.* página central desplegable en una revista.

centerpiece, *n.* centro de mesa.

centigrade, *a.* centígrado.

centigrade thermometer, termómetro centígrado.

central, *a.* central.

Central American, *a.* & *n.* centroamericano -na.

centralize, *v.* centralizar.

century, *n.* siglo *m.*

century plant, *n.* maguey *f.*

ceramic, *a.* cerámico.

ceramics, *n.* cerámica *f.*

cereal, *n.* cereal *m.*

cerebral, *a.* cerebral.

ceremonial, *n.* ceremonial.

ceremonious, *a.* ceremonioso.

ceremony, *n.* ceremonia *f.*

certain, *a.* cierto, seguro.

certainly, *adv.* sin duda, seguramente.

certainty, *n.* certeza *f.*

certificate, *n.* certificado *m.*

certification, *n.* certificación *f.*

certified, *a.* certificado.

certify, *v.* certificar.

certitude, *n.* certeza *f.*

cessation, *n.* cesación *f.*, discontinuación *f.*

cession, *n.* cesión *f.*

chafe, *v.* irritar.

chafing dish, *n.* escalfador *m.*

chagrin, *n.* disgusto *m.*

chain, 1. *n.* cadena *f.* **2.** *v.* encadenar.

chair, *n.* silla *f.*

chairman, *n.* presidente *m.*

chairperson, *n.* presidente -ta; persona que preside.

chalk, *n.* tiza *f.*

challenge, 1. *n.* desafío *m.* **2.** *v.* desafiar.

challenger, *n.* desafiador *m.*

chamber, *n.* cámara *f.*

chamberlain, *n.* camarero *m.*

chambermaid, *n.* camarera *f.*

chameleon, *n.* camaleón *m.*

chamois, *n.* gamuza *f.*

champagne, *n.* champán *m.*, champaña *f.*

champion, 1. *n.* campeón *m.* **2.** defender.

championship, *n.* campeonato *m.*

chance, *n.* oportunidad, ocasión *f.* **by c.,** por casualidad, por acaso. **take a c.,** aventurarse.

chancel, *n.* antealtar *m.*

chancellery, *n.* cancillería *f.*

chancellor, *n.* canciller *m.*

chandelier, *n.* araña de luces.

change, 1. *n.* cambio; (from a bill) moneda *f.* **2.** *v.* cambiar.

changeability, *n.* mutabilidad *f.*

changeable, *a.* variable, inconstante.

changer, *n.* cambiador *m.*

channel, 1. *n.* canal *m.* **2.** *v.* encauzar.

chant, 1. *n.* canto llano *m.* **2.** *v.* cantar.

chaos, *n.* caos *m.*

chaotic, *a.* caótico.

chap, 1. *n.* (coll.) tipo *m.* **2.** *v.* rajar.

chapel, *n.* capilla *f.*

chaperon, *n.* dueña *f.*

chaplain, *n.* capellán *m.*

chapter, *n.* capítulo *m.*

char, *v.* carbonizar.

character, *n.* carácter *m.*

characteristic, 1. *a.* característico. **2.** *n.* característica *f.*

characterization, *n.* caracterización *f.*

characterize, *v.* caracterizar.

charcoal, *n.* carbón leña.

charge, 1. *n.* acusación *f.*; ataque *m.* **2.** *v.* cargar; acusar; atacar.

chariot, *n.* carroza *f.*

charisma, *n.* carisma *m.*

charitable, *a.* caritativo.

charitableness, *n.* caridad *f.*

charitably, *adv.* caritativamente.

charity, *n.* caridad *f.;* (alms) limosna *f.*

charlatan, *n.* charlatán -na.

charlatanism, *n.* charlatanería *f.*

charm, **1.** *n.* encanto *m.;* (witchcraft) hechizo *m.* **2.** *v.* encantar; hechizar.

charming, *a.* encantador.

charred, *a.* carbonizado.

chart, *n.* mapa *m.*

charter, **1.** *n.* carta *f.* **2.** *v.* alquilar.

charter flight, vuelo charter *m.*

chase, **1.** *n.* caza *f.* **2.** *v.* cazar; perseguir.

chaser, *n.* perseguidor *m.*

chasm, *n.* abismo *m.*

chassis, *n.* chasis *m.*

chaste, *a.* casto.

chasten, *v.* corregir, castigar.

chastise, *v.* castigar.

chastisement, *n.* castigo *m.*

chastity, *n.* castidad, pureza *f.*

chat, **1.** *n.* plática, charla *f.* **2.** *v.* platicar, charlar.

chateau, *n.* castillo *m.*

chattels, *n.pl.* bienes *m.*

chatter, **1.** *v.* cotorrear; (teeth) rechinar. **2.** *n.* cotorreo *m.*

chatterbox, *n.* charlador *m.*

chauffeur, *n.* chofer *m.*

cheap, *a.* barato.

cheapen, *v.* rebajar, menospreciar.

cheaply, *adv.* barato.

cheapness, *n.* baratura *f.*

cheat, *v.* engañar.

cheater, *n.* engañador *m.*

check, **1.** *n.* verificación *f.;* (bank) cheque *m.;* (restaurant) cuenta *f.;* (chess) jaque *m.* **2.** *v.* verificar.

checkers, *n.* juego de damas.

checkmate, *v.* dar mate.

cheek, *n.* mejilla *f.*

cheer, **1.** *n.* alegría *f.;* aplauso *m.* **2.** *v.* alegrar; aplaudir.

cheerful, *a.* alegre.

cheerfully, *adv.* alegremente.

cheerfulness, *n.* alegría *f.*

cheerless, *a.* triste.

cheery, *a.* alegre.

cheese, *n.* queso *m.* **cottage c.**, requesón *m.*

chef, *n.* cocinero en jefe.

chemical, **1.** *a.* químico. **2.** *n.* reactivo *m.*

chemically, *adv.* químicamente.

chemist, *n.* químico *m.*

chemistry, *n.* química *f.*

chemotherapy, *n.* quimioterapia *f.*

chenille, *n.* felpilla *f.*

cherish, *v.* apreciar.

cherry, *n.* cereza *f.*

cherub, *n.* querubín *m.*

chess, *n.* ajedrez *m.*

chest, *n.* arca *f.;* (physiology) pecho *m.*

chestnut, *n.* castaña *f.*

chevron, *n.* sardineta *f.*

chew, *v.* mascar, masticar.

chewer, *n.* mascador *m.*

chic, *a.* elegante, paquete.

chicanery, *n.* trampería *f.*

chick, *n.* pollito.

chicken, *n.* pollo *m.,* gallina *f.*

chicken-hearted, *a.* cobarde.

chicken pox, *n.* viruelas locas *f.*

chicle, *n.* chicle *m.*

chicory, *n.* achicoria *f.*

chide, *v.* regañar, reprender.

chief, **1.** *a.* principal. **2.** *n.* jefe *m.*

chiefly, *adv.* principalmente, mayormente.

chieftain, *n.* caudillo *m.;* (Indian c.) cacique *m.*

chiffon, *n.* chifón *m.*

chilblain, *n.* sabañón *m.*

child, *n.* niño -ña; hijo -ja.

childbirth, *n.* parto *m.*

childhood, *n.* niñez *f.*

childish, *a.* pueril.

childishness, *n.* puerilidad *f.*

childless, *a.* sin hijos.

childlike, *a.* infantil.

Chilean, *a.* & *n.* chileno -na.

chili, *n.* chile ají *m.*

chill, **1.** *n.* frío; escalofrío *m.* **2.** *v.* enfriar.

chilliness, *n.* frialdad *f.*

chilly, *a.* frío; friolento.

chimes, *n.* juego de campanas.

chimney, *n.* chimenea *f.*

chimpanzee, *n.* chimpancé *m.*

chin, *n.* barba *f.*

china, *n.* loza *f.*

chinchilla, *n.* chinchilla *f.*

Chinese, *a.* & *n.* chino -na.

chink, *n.* grieta *f.*

chintz, *n.* zaraza *f.*

chip, 1. n. astilla f. **2.** v. astillar.

chiropodist, n. pedicuro m.

chiropractor, n. quiroprático m.

chirp, 1. n. chirrido m. **2.** v. chirriar, piar.

chisel, 1. n. cincel m. **2.** v. cincelar, talar.

chivalrous, a. caballeroso.

chivalry, n. caballería f.

chive, n. cebollino m.

chloride, n. cloruro m.

chlorine, n. cloro m.

chloroform, n. cloroformo m.

chlorophyll, n. clorófila f.

chock-full, a. repleto, colmado.

chocolate, n. chocolate m.

choice, 1. a. selecto, escogido. **2.** n. selección f.; escogimiento m.

choir, n. coro m.

choke, v. sofocar, ahogar.

cholera, n. cólera f.

choleric, a. colérico, irascible.

choose, v. elegir, escoger.

chop, 1. n. chuleta, costilla f. **2.** v. tajar; cortar.

chopper, n. tajador m.

choppy, a. agitado.

choral, a. coral.

chord, n. cuerda f.

chore, n. tarea f., quehacer m.

choreography, n. coreografía f.

chorister, n. corista m.

chorus, n. coro m.

christen, v. bautizar.

Christendom, n. cristiandad f.

Christian, a. & n. cristiano -na.

Christianity, n. cristianismo m.

Christmas, n. navidad f., pascua f. **Merry C.,** felices pascuas. **C. Eve,** nochebuena f.

chromatic, a. cromático.

chromium, n. cromo m.

chromosome, n. cromosoma m.

chronic, a. crónico.

chronicle, n. crónica f.

chronological, a. cronológico.

chronology, n. cronología f.

chrysalis, n. crisálida f.

chrysanthemum, n. crisantemo m.

chubby, a. regordete.

chuck, v. (cluck) cloquear; (throw) echar, tirar.

chuckle, v. reír entre dientes.

chum, n. amigo m.; compinche m.

chummy, a. íntimo.

chunk, n. trozo m.

chunky, a. fornido, trabado.

church, n. iglesia f.

churchman, n. eclesiástico m.

churchyard, n. cementerio m.

churn, 1. n. mantequera f. **2.** v. agitar, revolver.

chute, n. conducto m.; canal f.

cicada, n. cigarra, chicharra f.

cider, n. sidra f.

cigar, n. cigarro, puro m.

cigarette, n. cigarrillo, pitillo m. **c. case,** cigarrillera f. **c. lighter,** encendedor m.

cinchona, n. cinchona f.

cinder, n. ceniza f.

cinema, n. cine m.

cinnamon, n. canela f.

cipher, n. cifra f.

circle, n. círculo m.

circuit, n. circuito m.

circuitous, a. tortuoso.

circuitously, adv. tortuosamente.

circular, a. circular, redondo.

circularize, v. hacer circular.

circulate, v. circular.

circulation, n. circulación f.

circulator, n. diseminador m.

circulatory, a. circulatorio.

circumcise, v. circuncidar.

circumcision, n. circuncisión f.

circumference, n. circunferencia f.

circumlocution, n. circunlocución f.

circumscribe, v. circunscribir; limitar.

circumspect, a. discreto.

circumstance, n. circunstancia f.

circumstantial, a. circunstancial, indirecto.

circumstantially, adv. minuciosamente.

circumvent, v. evadir, evitar.

circumvention, n. trampa f.

circus, n. circo m.

cirrhosis, n. cirrosis f.

cistern, n. cisterna f.

citadel, n. ciudadela f.

citation, n. citación f.

cite, v. citar.

citizen, n. ciudadano -na.

citizenship, n. ciudadanía f.

citric, a. cítrico.

city, n. ciudad f.

civic, a. cívico.

civics, *n.* ciencia del gobierno civil.

civil, *a.* civil; cortés.

civilian, *a.* & *n.* civil *m.*

civility, *n.* cortesía *f.*

civilization, *n.* civilización *f.*

civilize, *v.* civilizar.

civil service, *n.* servicio civil oficial *m.*

civil war, *n.* guerra civil *f.*

clabber, 1. *n.* cuajo *m.* **2.** *v.* cuajarse.

clad, *a.* vestido.

claim, 1. *n.* demanda; pretensión *f.* **2.** *v.* demandar, reclamar.

claimant, *n.* :reclamante *m.*

clairvoyance, *n.* clarividencia *f.*

clairvoyant, *a.* clarividente.

clam, *n.* almeja *f.*

clamber, *v.* trepar.

clamor, 1. *n.* clamor *m.* **2.** *v.* clamar.

clamorous, *a.* clamoroso.

clamp, 1. *n.* prensa de sujeción *f.* **2.** *v.* asegurar, sujetar.

clan, *n.* tribu *f.*

clandestine, *a.* clandestino.

clandestinely, *adv.* clandestinamente.

clangor, *n.* estruendo *m.,* estrépito *m.*

clannish, *a.* unido; exclusivista.

clap, *v.* aplaudir.

clapboard, *n.* chilla *f.*

claque, *n.* claque *f.*

claret, *n.* clarete *m.*

clarification, *n.* clarificación *f.*

clarify, *v.* clarificar.

clarinet, *n.* clarinete *m.*

clarinetist, *n.* clarinero *m.*

clarity, *n.* claridad *f.*

clash, 1. *n.* choque *m.* **2.** *v.* chocar.

clasp, 1. *n.* broche *m.* **2.** *v.* abrochar.

class, *n.* clase *f.*

classic, classical, *a.* clásico.

classicism, *n.* clasicismo *m.*

classifiable, *a.* clasificable, calificable.

classification, *n.* clasificación *f.*

classify, *v.* clasificar.

classmate, *n.* compañero de clase.

classroom, *n.* sala de clase.

clatter, 1. *n.* alboroto *m.* **2.** *v.* alborotar.

clause, *n.* cláusula *f.*

claustrophobia, *n.* claustrofobia *f.*

claw, *n.* garra *f.*

clay, *n.* arcilla *f.;* barro *m.*

clean, 1. *a.* limpio. **2.** *v.* limpiar.

cleaner, *n.* limpiador -ra.

cleanliness, *n.* limpieza *f.*

cleanse, *v.* limpiar, purificar.

cleanser, *n.* limpiador *m.,* purificador *m.*

clear, *a.* claro.

clearance, *n.* espacio libre. **c. sale,** venta de liquidación.

clearing, *n.* despejo *m.;* desmonte *m.*

clearly, *adv.* claramente, evidentemente.

clearness, *n.* claridad *f.*

cleavage, *n.* resquebradura *f.*

cleaver, *n.* partidor *m.,* hacha *f.*

clef, *n.* clave, llave *f.*

clemency, *n.* clemencia *f.*

clench, *v.* agarrar.

clergy, *n.* clero *m.*

clergyman, *n.* clérigo *m.*

clerical, *a.* clerical. **c. work,** trabajo de dependientes.

clericalism, *n.* clericalismo *m.*

clerk, *n.* dependiente, escribiente *m.*

clerkship, *n.* escribanía *f.,* secretaría *f.*

clever, *a.* diestro, hábil.

cleverly, *adv.* diestramente, hábilmente.

cleverness, *n.* destreza *f.*

cliché, *n.* cliché *m.*

client, *n.* cliente *m.*

clientele, *n.* clientela *f.*

cliff, *n.* precipicio, risco *m.*

climate, *n.* clima *m.*

climatic, *a.* climático.

climax, *n.* colmo *m.,* culminación *f.*

climb, *v.* escalar; subir.

climber, *n.* trepador *m.,* escalador *m.;* (bot.) enredadera *f.*

clinch, *v.* afirmar.

cling, *v.* pegarse.

clinic, *n.* clínica *f.*

clinical, *a.* clínico.

clinically, *adv.* clinicalmente.

clip, 1. *n.* grapa *f.* **paper c.,** gancho *m.* **2.** *v.* prender; (shear) trasquilar.

clipper, *n.* recortador *m.;* (aero.) clíper *m.*

clipping, *n.* recorte *m.*

clique, *n.* camarilla *f.,* compadraje *m.*

cloak, *n.* capa *f.,* manto *m.*

clock, *n.* reloj *m.* **alarm c.,** despertador *m.*

clod, *n.* terrón *m.;* césped *m.*

clog, *v.* obstruir.

cloister, *n.* claustro *m.*

clone, *m.* ser viviente reproducido a base de las células de otro.

close, 1. *a.* cercano. **2.** *adv.* cerca. **c. to,** cerca de. **3.** *v.* cerrar; tapar.

closely, *adv.* (near) de cerca; (tight) estrechamente; (care) cuidadosamente.

closeness, *n.* contigüidad *f.,* apretamiento *m.;* (airless) falta de ventilación *f.*

closet, *n.* gabinete *m.* **clothes c.,** ropero *m.*

clot, 1. *n.* coagulación *f.* **2.** *v.* coagularse.

cloth, *n.* paño *m.;* tela *f.*

clothe, *v.* vestir.

clothes, clothing, *n.* ropa *f.*

clothing, *n.* vestidos *m.,* ropa *f.*

cloud, *n.* nube *f.*

cloudburst, *n.* chaparrón *m.*

cloudiness, *n.* nebulosidad *f.;* obscuridad *f.*

cloudless, *a.* despejado, sin nubes.

cloudy, *a.* nublado.

clove, *n.* clavo *m.*

clover, *n.* trébol *m.*

clown, *n.* bufón *m.*

clownish, *a.* grosero; bufonesco.

cloy, *v.* saciar.

club, 1. *n.* porra *f.;* (social) círculo, club *m.;* (cards) basto *m.* **2.** *v.* golpear con una porra.

clubfoot, *n.* pateta *m.,* pie zambo *m.*

clue, *n.* seña, pista *f.*

clump, *n.* grupo *m.,* masa *f.*

clumsiness, *n.* tosquedad *f.,* desmaña *f.*

clumsy, *a.* torpe, desmañado.

cluster, 1. *n.* grupo *m.;* (fruit) racimo *m.* **2.** *v.* agrupar.

clutch, 1. *n.* (auto.) embrague *m.* **2.** *v.* agarrar.

clutter, 1. *n.* confusión *f.* **2.** *v.* poner en desorden.

coach, 1. *n.* coche, vagón *m.;*

coche ordinario; (sports) entrenador *m.* **2.** *v.* entrenar.

coachman, *n.* cochero *m.*

coagulate, *v.* coagular.

coagulation, *n.* coagulación *f.*

coal, *n.* carbón *m.*

coalesce, *v.* unirse, soldarse.

coalition, *n.* coalición *f.*

coal oil, *n.* petróleo *m.*

coal tar, *n.* alquitrán *m.*

coarse, *a.* grosero, burdo; (material) tosco, grueso.

coarsen, *v.* vulgarizar.

coarseness, *n.* grosería; tosquedad *f.*

coast, 1. *n.* costa *f.,* litoral *m.* **2.** *v.* deslizarse.

coastal, *a.* costanero.

coast guard, *n.* costanero *m.*

coat, 1. *n.* saco *m.,* chaqueta *f.;* (paint) capa *f.* **2.** *v.* cubrir.

coat of arms, *n.* escudo *m.*

coax, *v.* instar.

cobalt, *n.* cobalto *m.*

cobbler, *n.* zapatero *m.*

cobblestone, *n.* guijarro *m.*

cobra, *n.* cobra *f.*

cobweb, *n.* telaraña *f.*

cocaine, *n.* cocaína *f.*

cock, *n.* (rooster) gallo *m.;* (water, etc.) llave *f.;* (gun) martillo *m.*

cockfight, *n.* riña de gallos *f.*

cockpit, *n.* gallera *f.;* reñidero de gallos *m.*

cockroach, *n.* cucaracha *f.*

cocktail, *n.* coctel *m.*

cocky, *a.* confiado, atrevido.

cocoa, *n.* cacao *m.*

coconut, *n.* coco *m.*

cocoon, *n.* capullo *m.*

cod, *n.* bacalao *m.*

code, *n.* código *m.;* clave *f.*

codeine, *n.* codeína *f.*

codfish, *n.* bacalao *m.*

codify, *v.* compilar.

coeducation, *n.* coeducación *f.*

coequal, *a.* mutuamente igual.

coerce, *v.* forzar.

coercion, *n.* coerción *f.*

coercive, *a.* coercitivo.

coexist, *v.* coexistir.

coffee, *n.* café *m.* **c. plantation,** cafetal *m.* **c. shop,** café *m.*

coffer, *n.* cofre *m.*

coffin, *n.* ataúd *m.*

cog, *n.* diente de rueda *m.*

cogent, a. convincente.

cogitate, v. pensar, reflexionar.

cognizance, n. conocimiento m., comprensión f.

cognizant, a. conocedor, informado.

cogwheel, n. rueda dentada f.

cohere, v. pegarse.

coherent, a. coherente.

cohesion, n. cohesión f.

cohesive, a. cohesivo.

cohort, n. cohorte f.

coiffure, n. peinado, tocado m.

coil, 1. n. rollo m.; (naut.) adujada f. **2.** v. enrollar.

coin, n. moneda f.

coinage, n. sistema monetario f.

coincide, v. coincidir.

coincidence, n. coincidencia; casualidad f.

coincident, a. coincidente.

coincidental, a. coincidental.

coincidentally, adv. coincidentalmente, al mismo tiempo.

colander, n. colador m.

cold, n. & n. frío m.; (med.) resfriado m. **to be c.,** tener frío; (weather) hacer frío.

coldly, adv. friamente.

coldness, n. frialdad f.

collaborate, v. colaborar.

collaboration, n. colaboración f.

collaborator, n. colaborador m.

collapse, 1. n. desplome m.; (med.) colapso m. **2.** v. desplomarse.

collar, n. cuello m.

collarbone, n. clavícula f.

collate, v. comparar.

collateral, 1. a. colateral. **2.** n. garantía f.

collation, n. comparación f.; (food) colación f., merienda f.

colleague, n. colega m. & f.

collect, v. cobrar; recoger; coleccionar.

collection, n. colección f.

collective, a. colectivo.

collectively, adv. colectivamente, en masa.

collector, n. colector -ra; coleccionista m. & f.

college, n. colegio m.; universidad f.

collegiate, a. colegiado m.

collide, v. chocar.

collision, n. choque m.

colloquial, a. familiar.

colloquially, adv. familiarmente.

colloquy, n. conversación f., coloquio m.

collusion, n. colusión f., connivencia f.

Colombian, a. & n. colombiano -na.

colon, n. colon m.; (punct.) dos puntos.

colonel, n. coronel m.

colonial, a. colonial.

colonist, n. colono m.

colonization, n. colonización f.

colonize, v. colonizar.

colony, n. colonia f.

color, 1. n. color; colorido m. **2.** v. colorar; colorir.

coloration, n. colorido m.

colored, a. de color.

colorful, a. vívido.

colorless, a. descolorido, sin color.

colossal, a. colosal.

colt, n. porto m.

column, n. columna f.

coma, n. coma m.

comb, 1. n. peine m. **2.** v. peinar.

combat, 1. n. combate m. **2.** v combatir.

combatant, n. combatiente m.

combative, a. combativo.

combination, n. combinación f.

combine, v. combinar.

combustible, a. & n. combustible m.

combustion, n. combustión f.

come, v. venir. **c. back,** volver. **c. in,** entrar. **c. out,** salir. **c. up,** subir. **c. upon,** encontrarse con.

comedian, n. cómico -ca.

comedienne, n. cómica f., actriz f.

comedy, n. comedia f.

comet, n. cometa m.

comfort, 1. n. confort m.; solaz m. **2.** v. confortar; solazar.

comfortable, a. cómodo.

comfortably, adv. cómodamente.

comforter, n. colcha f.

comfortingly, adv. confortantemente.

comfortless, a. sin consuelo; sin comodidades.

comic, comical, a. cómico.

coming, 1. n. venida f., llegada f. **2.** a. próximo, que viene, entrante.

comma, *n.* coma *f.*

command, **1.** *n.* mando *m.* **2.** *v.* mandar.

commandeer, *v.* reclutar forzosamente, expropiar.

commander, *n.* comandante *m.*

commander in chief, *n.* generalísimo, jefe supremo.

commandment, *n.* mandato; mandamiento *m.*

commemorate, *v.* conmemorar.

commemoration, *n.* conmemoración *f.*

commemorative, *a.* conmemorativo.

commence, *v.* comenzar, principiar.

commencement, *n.* comienzo *m.;* graduación *f.*

commend, *v.* encomendar.

commendable, *a.* recomendable.

commendably, *adv.* loablemente.

commendation, *n.* recomendación *f.*

commensurate, *a.* proporcionado.

comment, **1.** *n.* comento *m.* **2.** *v.* comentar.

commentary, *n.* comentario *m.*

commentator, *n.* comentador -ra.

commerce, *n.* comercio *m.*

commercial, *a.* comercial.

commercialism, *n.* comercialismo *m.*

commercialize, *v.* mercantilizar, explotar.

commercially, *a. & adv.* comercial.

commiserate, *v.* compadecerse.

commissary, *n.* comisario *m.*

commission, **1.** *n.* comisión *f.* **2.** *v.* comisionar.

commissioner, *n.* comisionista *m. & f.*

commit, *v.* cometer.

commitment, *n.* compromiso *m.*

committee, *n.* comité *m.*

commodious, *a.* cómodo.

commodity, *n.* mercadería *f.*

common, *a.* común; ordinario.

commonly, *adv.* comúnmente, vulgarmente.

commonplace, *a.* trivial, banal.

commonwealth, *n.* estado *m.;* nación *f.*

commotion, *n.* tumulto *m.*

communal, *a.* comunal, público.

commune, **1.** *n.* distrito municipal *m.;* comuna *f.* **2.** *v.* conversar.

communicable, *a.* comunicativo.

communicate, *v.* comunicar.

communication, *n.* comunicación *f.*

communicative, *a.* comunicativo.

communion, *n.* comunión *f.* **take c.**, comulgar.

communiqué, *n.* comunicación *f.*

communism, *n.* comunismo *m.*

communist, *n.* comunista *m. & f.*

communistic, *a.* comunístico.

community, *n.* comunidad *f.*

commutation, *n.* conmutación *f.*

commuter, *n.* empleado que viaja diariamente desde su domicilio hasta la ciudad donde trabaja.

compact, **1.** *a.* compacto. **2.** *n.* pacto *m.;* (lady's) polvera *f.*

companion, *n.* compañero -ra.

companionable, *a.* sociable.

companionship, *n.* compañerismo *m.*

company, *n.* compañía *f.*

comparable, *a.* comparable.

comparative, *a.* comparativo.

comparatively, *a.* relativamente.

compare, *v.* comparar.

comparison, *n.* comparación *f.*

compartment, *n.* compartimiento *m.*

compass, *n.* compás *m.;* (naut.) brújula *f.*

compassion, *n.* compasión *f.*

compassionate, *a.* compasivo.

compassionately, *adv.* compasivamente.

compatible, *a.* compatible.

compatriot, *n.* compatriota *m. & f.*

compel, *v.* obligar.

compensate, *v.* compensar.

compensation, *n.* compensación *f.*

compensatory, *a.* compensatorio.

compete, *v.* competir.

competence, *n.* competencia *f.*

competent, *a.* competente, capaz.

competently, *adv.* competentemente.

competition, *n.* concurrencia *f.;* concurso *m.*

competitive, *a.* competidor.

competitor, *n.* competidor -ra.

compile, *v.* compilar.

complacency, *n.* complacencia *f.*
complacent, *a.* complaciente.
complacently, *adv.* complaciente-
mente.
complain, *v.* quejarse.
complaint, *n.* queja *f.*
complement, *n.* complemento *m.*
complete, 1. *a.* completo **2.** *v.*
completar.
completely, *adv.* completamente,
enteramente.
completeness, *n.* integridad *f.*
completion, *n.* terminación *f.*
complex, *a.* complejo.
complexion, *n.* tez *f.*
complexity, *n.* complejidad *f.*
compliance, *n.* consentimiento *m.*
in c. with, de acuerdo con.
compliant, *a.* dócil; complaciente.
complicate, *v.* complicar.
complicated, *a.* complicado.
complication, *n.* complicación *f.*
complicity, *n.* complicidad *f.*
compliment, 1. *n.* flor *f.* **2.** *v.* felicitar; echar flores.
complimentary, *a.* galante, obse-
quioso, regaloso.
comply, *v.* cumplir.
component, *n.* & *a.* componente
m.
comport, *v.* portarse.
compose, *v.* componer.
composed, *a.* tranquilo; (made
up) compuesto.
composer, *n.* compositor -ra.
composite, *a.* compuesto.
composition, *n.* composición *f.*
composure, *n.* serenidad *f.*;
calma *f.*
compote, *n.* compota *f.*
compound, *a.* & *n.* compuesto *m.*
comprehend, *v.* comprender.
comprehensible, *a.* comprensible.
comprehension, *n.* comprensión
f.
comprehensive, *a.* comprensivo.
compress, 1. *n.* cabezal *m.* **2.** *v.*
comprimir.
compressed, *a.* comprimido.
compression, *n.* compresión *f.*
compressor, *n.* compresor *m.*
comprise, *v.* comprender; abarcar.
compromise, 1. *n.* compromiso
m. **2.** *v.* comprometer.

compromiser, *n.* compromisario
m.
compulsion, *n.* compulsión *f.*
compulsive, *a.* compulsivo.
compulsory, *a.* obligatorio.
compunction, *n.* compunción *f.*;
escrúpulo *m.*
computation, *n.* computación *f.*
compute, *v.* computar, calcular.
computer, *n.* computadora *f.*, ordenador *m.*
computerize, *v.* procesar en computadora.
comrade, *n.* camarada *m.* & *f.*;
compañero -ra.
comradeship, *n.* camaradería *f.*
concave, *a.* cóncavo.
conceal, *v.* ocultar, esconder.
concealment, *n.* ocultación *f.*
concede, *v.* conceder.
conceit, *n.* amor propio; engreimiento *m.*
conceited, *a.* engreído.
conceivable, *a.* concebible.
conceive, *v.* concebir.
concentrate, *v.* concentrar.
concentration, *n.* concentración
f.
concept, *n.* concepto *m.*
conception, *n.* concepción *f.*;
concepto *m.*
concern, 1. *n.* interés *m.*; inquietud *f.*; (com.) negocio *m.* **2.** *v.*
concernir.
concerning, *prep.* respecto a.
concert, *n.* concierto *m.*
concerted, *a.* convenido.
concession, *n.* concesión *f.*
conciliate, *v.* conciliar.
conciliation, *n.* conciliación *f.*
conciliator, *n.* conciliador *m.*
conciliatory, *a.* conciliatorio.
concise, *a.* conciso.
concisely, *adv.* concisamente.
conciseness, *n.* concisión *f.*
conclave, *n.* cónclave *m.*
conclude, *v.* concluir.
conclusion, *n.* conclusión *f.*
conclusive, *a.* conclusivo, decisivo.
conclusively, *adv.* concluyentemente.
concoct, *v.* confeccionar.
concomitant, *n.* & *a.* concomitante.
concord, *n.* concordia *f.*
concordat, *n.* concordato *m.*

concourse, n. concurso m.; confluencia f.

concrete, a. concreto.

concretely, adv. concretamente.

concubine, n. concubina, amiga f.

concur, v. concurrir.

concurrence, n. concurrencia f.; casualidad f.

concurrent, a. concurrente.

concussion, n. concusión f.; (c. of the brain) conmoción cerebral f.

condemn, v. condenar.

condemnable, a. culpable, condenable.

condemnation, n. condenación f.

condensation, n. condensación f.

condense, v. condensar.

condenser, n. condensador m.

condescend, v. condescender.

condescension, n. condescendencia f.

condiment, n. condimento m.

condition, 1. n. condición f.; estado m. **2.** v. acondicionar.

conditional, a. condicional.

conditionally, adv. condicionalmente.

condole, v. condolerse.

condolence, n. pésame m.

condominium, n. apartamento en propiedad m.

condone, v. condonar.

conducive, a. conducente.

conduct, 1. n. conducta f. **2.** v. conducir.

conductivity, n. conductividad f.

conductor, n. conductor m.

conduit, n. caño m., canal f.; conducto m.

cone, n. cono m. **ice-cream c.,** barquillo de helado.

confection, n. confitura f.

confectioner, n. confitero m.

confectionery, n. dulcería f.

confederacy, n. federación f.

confederate, a. & n. confederado m.

confederation, n. confederación f.

confer, v. conferenciar; conferir.

conference, n. conferencia f.; congreso m.

confess, v. confesar.

confession, n. confesión f.

confessional, 1. n. confesionario m. **2.** a. confesional.

confessor, n. confesor m.

confetti, n. confetti m.

confidant, confidante, n. confidente m. & f.

confide, v. confiar.

confidence, n. confianza f.

confident, a. confiado; cierto.

confidential, a. confidencial.

confidentially, adv. confidencialmente, en secreto.

confidently, adv. confiadamente.

confine, 1. n. confín m. **2.** v. confinar; encerrar.

confirm, v. confirmar.

confirmation, n. confirmación f.

confiscate, v. confiscar.

confiscation, n. confiscación f.

conflagration, n. incendio m.

conflict, 1. n. conflicto m. **2.** v. oponerse; estar en conflicto.

conform, v. conformar.

conformation, n. conformación f.

conformer, n. conformista m. & f.

conformist, n. conformista m. & f.

conformity, n. conformidad f.

confound, v. confundir.

confront, v. confrontar.

confuse, v. confundir.

confusion, n. confusión f.

congeal, v. congelar, helar.

congealment, n. congelación f.

congenial, a. congenial.

congenital, a. congénito.

congenitally, adv. congenitalmente.

congestion, n. congestión f.

conglomerate, 1. v. conglomerar. **2.** a. conglomerado.

conglomeration, n. conglomeración f.

congratulate, v. felicitar.

congratulation, n. felicitación f.

congratulatory, a. congratulatorio.

congregate, v. congregar.

congregation, n. congregación f.

congress, n. congreso m.

conic, 1. n. cónica f. **2.** a. cónico.

conjecture, 1. n. conjetura f. **2.** v. conjeturar.

conjugal, a. conyugal, matrimonial.

conjugate, v. conjugar.

conjugation, n. conjugación f.

conjunction, n. conjunción f.

conjunctive, 1. n. (gram.) conjunción f. **2.** a. conjuntivo.

conjunctivitis, n. conjuntivitis f.

conjure, v. conjurar.

connect, v. juntar; relacionar.

connection, n. conexión f.

connivance, n. consentimiento m.

connive, v. disimular.

connoisseur, n. perito -ta.

connotation, n. connotación f.

connote, v. connotar.

connubial, a. conyugal.

conquer, v. conquistar.

conquerible, a. conquistable, vencible.

conqueror, n. conquistador m.

conquest, n. conquista f.

conscience, n. conciencia f.

conscientious, a. concienzudo.

conscientiously, adv. escrupulosamente.

conscious, a. consciente.

consciously, adv. con conocimiento.

consciousness, n. consciencia f.

conscript, 1. n. conscripto m., recluta m. **2.** v. reclutar, alistar.

conscription, n. conscripción f., alistamiento m.

consecrate, v. consagrar.

consecration, n. consagración f.

consecutive, a. consecutivo, seguido.

consecutively, adv. consecutivamente, de seguida.

consensus, n. consenso m., acuerdo general m.

consent, 1. n. consentimiento m. **2.** v. consentir.

consequence, n. consecuencia f.

consequent, a. consiguiente.

consequential, a. importante.

consequently, adv. por lo tanto, por consiguiente.

conservation, n. conservación f.

conservatism, n. conservatismo m.

conservative, a. conservador, conservativo.

conservatory, n. (plants) invernáculo m.; (school) conservatorio m.

conserve, v. conservar.

consider, v. considerar.

considerable, a. considerable.

considerably, adv. considerablemente.

considerate, a. considerado.

considerately, adv. consideradamente.

consideration, n. consideración f.

considering, prep. visto que, en vista de.

consign, v. consignar.

consignment, n. consignación f., envío m.

consist, v. consistir.

consistency, n. consistencia f.

consistent, a. consistente.

consolation, n. consolación f.

console, v. consolar.

consolidate, v. consolidar.

consommé, n. caldo m.

consonant, n. consonante f.

consort, 1. n. conyuge m. & f.; socio. **2.** v. asociarse.

conspicuous, a. conspicuo.

conspicuously, adv. visiblemente, llamativamente.

conspicuousness, n. visibilidad f.; evidencia f.; fama f.

conspiracy, n. conspiración f.; complot m.

conspirator, n. conspirador -ra.

conspire, v. conspirar.

conspirer, n. conspirante m. & f.

constancy, n. constancia f., lealdad f.

constant, a. constante.

constantly, adv. constantemente, de continuo.

constellation, n. constelación f.

consternation, n. consternación f.

constipation, n. constipación f.

constituency, n. distrito electoral m.

constituent, 1. a. constituyente. **2.** n. elector m.

constitute, v. constituir.

constitution, n. constitución f.

constitutional, a. constitucional.

constrain, v. constreñir.

constraint, n. constreñimiento m., compulsión f.

constrict, v. apretar, estrechar.

construct, v. construir.

construction, n. construcción f.

constructive, a. constructivo.

constructively, adv. constructivamente; por deducción.

constructor, n. constructor m.

construe, v. interpretar.

consul, n. cónsul m.

consular, a. consular.

consulate, n. consulado m.
consult, v. consultar.
consultant, n. consultante m. & f.
consultation, n. consulta f.
consume, v. consumir.
consumer, n. consumidor -ra.
consummation, n. consumación f.
consumption, n. consumo m.
consumptive, 1. n. tísico m. **2.** a. consuntivo.
contact, 1. n. contacto m. **2.** v. ponerse en contacto con.
contagion, n. contagio m.
contagious, a. contagioso.
contain, v. contener.
container, n. envase m.
contaminate, v. contaminar.
contemplate, v. contemplar.
contemplation, n. contemplación f.
contemplative, a. contemplativo.
contemporary, n. & a. contemporáneo -nea.
contempt, n. desprecio m.
contemptible, v. vil, despreciable.
contemptuous, a. desdeñoso.
contemptuously, adv. desdeñosamente.
contend, v. contender; competir.
contender, n. competidor m.
content, 1. a. contento. **2.** n. contenido m. **3.** v. contentar.
contented, a. contento.
contention, n. contención f.
contentment, n. contentamiento m.
contest, 1. n. concurso m. **2.** v. disputar.
contestable, a. contestable.
context, n. contexto m.
contiguous, a. contiguo.
continence, n. continencia f., castidad f.
continent, n. continente m.
continental, a. continental.
contingency, n. eventualidad f., casualidad f.
contingent, a. contingente.
continual, a. continuo.
continuation, n. continuación f.
continue, v. continuar.
continuity, n. continuidad f.
continuous, a. continuo.
continuously, adv. continualmente.
contour, n. contorno m.
contraband, n. contrabando m.

contraception, n. contracepción f.
contraceptive, n. & a. anticeptivo m.
contract, 1. n. contrato m. **2.** v. contraer.
contraction, n. contracción f.
contractor, n. contratista m.
contradict, v. contradecir.
contradiction, n. contradicción f.
contradictory, a. contradictorio.
contralto, n. contralto m.
contrary, a. & n. contrario m.
contrast, 1. n. contraste m. **2.** v. contrastar.
contribute, v. contribuir.
contribution, n. contribución f.
contributive, contributory, a. contribuyente.
contributor, n. contribuidor m.
contrite, a. contrito.
contrition, n. contrición f.
contrivance, n. aparato m.; estratagema f.
contrive, v. inventar, tramar; darse maña.
control, 1. n. control m. **2.** v. controlar.
controllable, a. controlable, dominable.
controller, n. interventor m., contralor m.
controversial, a. contencioso.
controversy, n. controversia f.
contusion, n. contusión f.
convalesce, v. convalecer.
convalescence, n. convalecencia f.
convalescent, n. convaleciente m. & f.
convene, v. juntarse; convocar.
convenience, n. comodidad f.
convenient, a. cómodo. **to be c.,** convenir.
conveniently, adv. cómodamente.
convent, n. convento m.
convention, n. convención f.
conventional, a. convencional.
conventionally, adv. convencionalmente.
converge, v. convergir.
convergence, n. convergencia f.
convergent, a. convergente.
conversant, a. versado; entendido (de).
conversation, n. conversación, plática f.

conversational, *a.* de conversación.

conversationalist, *n.* conversador *m.*

converse, *v.* conversar.

conversely, *adv.* a la inversa.

convert, 1. *n.* convertido *m.* **2.** *v.* convertir.

converter, *n.* convertidor *m.*

convertible, *a.* convertible.

convex, *a.* convexo.

convey, *v.* transportar; comunicar.

conveyance, *n.* transporte; vehículo *m.*

conveyor, *n.* conductor *m.;* (mech.) transportador *m.*

convict, 1. *n.* reo *m.* **2.** *v.* probar de culpa.

conviction, *n.* convicción *f.*

convince, *v.* convencer.

convincing, *a.* convincente.

convivial, *a.* cónvival.

convocation, *n.* convocación; asamblea *f.*

convoke, *v.* convocar, citar.

convoy, *n.* convoy *m.;* escolta *f.*

convulse, *v.* convulsionar; agitar violentamente.

convulsion, *n.* convulsión *f.*

convulsive, *a.* convulsivo.

cook, 1. *n.* cocinero -ra. **2.** *v.* cocinar, cocer.

cookbook, *n.* libro de cocina *m.*

cooky, *n.* galleta dulce *f.*

cool, 1. *a.* fresco. **2.** *v.* refrescar.

cooler, *n.* enfriadera *f.*

coolness, *n.* frescura *f.*

coop, 1. *n.* jaula *f.* **chicken c.,** gallinero *m.* **2.** *v.* enjaular.

cooperate, *v.* cooperar.

cooperation, *n.* cooperación *f.*

cooperative, *a.* cooperativo.

cooperatively, *adv.* cooperativamente.

coordinate, *v.* coordinar.

coordination, *n.* coordinación *f.*

coordinator, *n.* coordinador *m.*

cope, *v.* contender. **c. with,** superar, hacer frente a.

copier, *n.* copiadora *f.*

copious, *a.* copioso, abundante.

copiously, *adv.* copiosamente.

copiousness, *n.* copia *f.,* abundancia *f.*

copper, *n.* cobre *m.*

copy, 1. *n.* copia *f.;* ejemplar *m.* **2.** *v.* copiar.

copyist, *n.* copista *m.* & *f.*

copyright, *n.* derechos de propiedad literaria *m.pl.*

coquetry, *n.* coquetería *f.*

coquette, *n.* coqueta *f.*

coral, *n.* coral *m.*

cord, *n.* cuerda *f.*

cordial, *a.* cordial.

cordiality, *n.* cordialidad *f.*

cordially, *adv.* cordialmente.

cordovan, *n.* cordobán *m.*

corduroy, *n.* pana *f.*

core, *n.* corazón; centro *m.*

cork, *n.* corcho *m.*

corkscrew, *n.* tirabuzón *m.*

corn, *n.* maíz *m.*

cornea, *n.* córnea *f.*

corner, *n.* rincón *m.;* (of street) esquina *f.*

cornet, *n.* corneta *f.*

cornetist, *n.* cornetín *m.*

cornice, *n.* cornisa *f.*

cornstarch, *n.* maicena *f.*

corollary, *n.* corolario *m.*

coronary, *a.* coronario.

coronation, *n.* coronación *f.*

corporal, 1. *a.* corpóreo. **2.** *n.* cabo *m.*

corporate, *a.* corporativo.

corporation, *n.* corporación *f.*

corps, *n.* cuerpo *m.*

corpse, *n.* cadáver *m.*

corpulent, *a.* corpulento.

corpuscle, *n.* corpúsculo *m.*

corral, 1. *n.* corral *m.* **2.** *v.* acorralar.

correct, 1. *a.* correcto. **2.** *v.* corregir.

correction, *n.* corrección; enmienda *f.*

corrective, *n.* & *a.* correctivo.

correctly, *adv.* correctamente.

correctness, *n.* exactitud *f.*

correlate, *v.* correlacionar.

correlation, *n.* correlación *f.*

correspond, *v.* corresponder.

correspondence, *n.* correspondencia *f.*

correspondent, *a.* correspondiente.

corresponding, *a.* correspondiente.

corridor, *n.* corredor, pasillo *m.*

corroborate, *v.* corroborar.

corroboration, n. corroboración f.

corroborative, a. corroborante.

corrode, v. corroer.

corrosion, n. corrosión f.

corrugate, v. arrugar; ondular.

corrupt, 1. a. corrompido. 2. v. corromper.

corruptible, a. corruptible.

corruption, n. corrupción f.

corruptive, a. corruptivo.

corset, n. corsé m., (girdle) faja f.

cortege, n. comitiva f., séquito m.

corvette, n. corbeta f.

cosmetic, a. & n. cosmético.

cosmic, a. cósmico.

cosmopolitan, a. & n. cosmopolita m. & f.

cosmos, n. cosmos m.

cost, 1. n. coste m.; costa f. 2. v. costar.

Costa Rican, a. & n. costarricense m. & f.

costly, a. costoso, caro.

costume, n. traje; disfraz m.

cot, n. catre m.

coterie, n. camarilla f.

cotillion, n. cotillón m.

cottage, n. casita f.

cottage cheese, n. requesón m.

cotton, n. algodón m.

cottonseed, n. semilla del algodón f.

couch, n. sofá m.

cougar, n. cuguar m.

cough, 1. n. tos f. 2. v. toser.

council, n. consejo, concilio m.

counsel, 1. n. consejo; (law) abogado m. 2. v. aconsejar. **to keep one's c.**, no decir nada.

counselor, n. consejero; (law) abogado m.

count, 1. n. cuenta f.; (title) conde m. 2. v. contar.

countenance, 1. n. aspecto m.; cara f. 2. v. aprobar.

counter, 1. adv. **c. to**, contra, en contra de. 2. v. mostrador m.

counteract, v. contrariar.

counteraction, n. oposición f.

counterbalance, 1. n. contrapeso m. 2. v. contrapesar.

counterfeit, 1. a. falsificado. 2. v. falsear.

countermand, v. contramandar.

counteroffensive, n. contraofensiva f.

counterpart, n. contraparte f.

countess, n. condesa f.

countless, a. innumerable.

country, n. campo m.; (pol.) país m.; (homeland) patria f.

countryman, n. paisano m. **fellow c.**, compatriota m.

countryside, n. campo, paisaje m.

county, n. condado m.

coupé, n. cupé m.

couple, 1. n. par m. 2. v. unir.

coupon, n. cupón, talón m.

courage, n. valor m.

courageous, a. valiente.

course, n. curso m. **of c.**, por supuesto, desde luego.

court, 1. n. corte f.; cortejo m.; (of law) tribunal m. 2. v. cortejar.

courteous, a. cortés.

courtesy, n. cortesía f.

courthouse, n. palacio de justicia m., tribunal m.

courtier, n. cortesano m.

courtly, n. cortés, galante.

courtroom, n. sala de justicia f.

courtship, n. corte f.

courtyard, n. patio m.

cousin, n. primo -ma.

covenant, n. contrato, convenio m.

cover, 1. n. cubierta, tapa f. 2. v. cubrir, tapar.

covet, v. ambicionar, suspirar por.

covetous, a. codicioso.

cow, n. vaca f.

coward, n. cobarde m. & f.

cowardice, n. cobardía f.

cowardly, a. cobarde.

cowboy, n. vaquero, gaucho m.

cower, v. agacharse.

cowhide, n. cuero m.

coy, a. recatado, modesto.

coyote, n. coyote m.

cozy, a. cómodo y agradable.

crab, n. cangrejo m.

crab apple, n. manzana silvestre f.

crack, 1. n. hendedura f.; (noise) crujido m. 2. v. hender; crujir.

cracker, n. galleta f.

cradle, n. cuna f.

craft, n. arte m.

craftsman, n. artesano m.

craftsmanship, n. mano de obra f.

crafty, a. ladino.

crag, n. despeñadero m.

cram, v. rellenar, hartar.

cramp, n. calambre m.

cranberry, n. arándano m.

crane, 1. n. (bird) grulla f.; (mech.) grúa f.

cranium, n. cráneo m.

crank, n. (mech.) manivela f.

cranky, a. chiflado, caprichoso.

crash, 1. n. choque; estallido m. **2.** v. estallar.

crate, n. canasto m.

crater, n. cráter m.

crave, v. desear; anhelar.

craven, a. cobarde.

craving, n. sed m., anhelo m.

crawl, v. andar a gatas, arrastrarse.

crayon, n. creyón; lápiz m.

crazy, a. loco.

creak, v. crujir.

creaky, a. crujidero.

cream, n. crema f.

creamery, n. lechería f.

crease, 1. n. pliegue m. **2.** v. plegar.

create, v. crear.

creation, n. creación f.

creative, a. creativo, creador.

creator, n. criador -ra.

creature, n. criatura f.

credence, n. creencia f.

credentials, n. credenciales f.pl.

credibility, n. credibilidad f.

credible, a. creíble.

credit, 1. n. crédito m. **on c.,** al fiado. **2.** v. (com.) abonar.

creditable, a. fidedigno.

credit card, n. tarjeta de crédito f.

creditor, n. acreedor -ra.

credo, n. credo m.

credulity, n. credulidad f.

credulous, a. crédulo.

creed, n. credo m.

creek, n. riachuelo m.

creep, v. gatear.

cremate, v. cremar.

crematory, n. crematorio m.

creosote, n. creosota f.

crepe, n. crespón m.

crescent, a. & n. creciente f.

crest, n. cresta; cima f.; (heraldry) timbre m.

cretonne, n. cretona f.

crevice, n. grieta f.

crew, n. tripulación f.

crib, n. pesebre m.; camita de niño.

cricket, n. grillo m.

crime, n. crimen m.

criminal, a. & n. criminal.

criminologist, n. criminólogo m.

criminology, n. criminología f.

crimson, a. & n. carmesí m.

cringe, v. encogerse, temblar.

cripple, 1. n. lisiado -da. **2.** v. estropear, lisiar.

crisis, n. crisis f.

crisp, a. crespo, fresco.

crispness, n. encrespadura f.

crisscross, a. entrelazado.

criterion, n. criterio m.

critic, n. crítico m.

critical, a. crítico.

criticism, n. crítica; censura f.

criticize, v. criticar; censurar.

critique, n. crítica f.

croak, 1. n. graznido m. **2.** v. graznar.

crochet, 1. n. crochet m. **2.** v. hacer crochet.

crock, n. cazuela f.; olla de barro f.

crockery, n. loza f.

crocodile, n. cocodrilo m.

crony, n. compinche m.

crooked, a. encorvado; deshonesto.

croon, v. canturrear.

crop, n. cosecha f.

croquet, n. juego de croquet m.

croquette, n. croqueta f.

cross, 1. a. enojado, mal humorado. **2.** n. cruz f. **3.** v. cruzar, atravesar.

crossbreed, 1. n. mestizo m. **2.** v. cruzar.

cross-examine, v. interrogar.

cross-eyed, a. bisco.

cross-fertilization, n. alogamia f.

crossing, crossroads, n. cruce m.

cross section, n. corte transversal m.

crotch, n. bifurcación f.; (anat.) bragadura f.

crouch, v. agacharse.

croup, n. (med.) crup m.

croupier, n. crupié m.

crow, n. cuervo m.

crowd, 1. n. muchedumbre f. tropel m. **2.** v. apretar.

crowded, a. lleno de gente.

crown, 1. n. corona f. **2.** v. coronar.

crown prince, n. príncipe heredero m.

crucial, a. crucial.

crucible, n. crisol m.

crucifix, n. crucifijo m.

crucifixion, n. crucifixión f.

crucify, v. crucificar.

crude, a. crudo; (oil) bruto.

crudeness, n. crudeza.

cruel, a. cruel.

cruelty, n. crueldad f.

cruet, n. vinagrera f.

cruise, 1. n. viaje por mar. **2.** v. navegar.

cruiser, n. crucero m.

crumb, n. miga; migaja f.

crumble, v. desmigajar; desmoronar.

crumple, v. arrugar; encogerse.

crusade, n. cruzada f.

crusader, n. cruzado m.

crush, v. aplastar.

crust, n. costra f.

crustacean, n. crustáceo m.

crutch, n. muleta f.

cry, 1. n. grito m. **2.** v. gritar; (weep) llorar.

cryosurgery, n. criocirugía f.

crypt, n. gruta f., cripta f.

cryptic, a. secreto.

cryptography, n. criptografía f.

crystal, n. cristal m.

crystalline, a. cristalino, transparente.

crystallize, v. cristalizar.

cub, n. cachorro m.

Cuban, n. & a. cubano -na.

cube, n. cubo m.

cubic, a. cúbico.

cubicle, n. cubículo m.

cubic measure, n. medida de capacidad f.

cubism, n. cubismo m.

cuckoo, n. cuco m.

cucumber, n. pepino m.

cuddle, v. abrazar.

cudgel, n. palo m.

cue, n. apunte m.; (billiards) taco m.

cuff, n. puño de camisa. **c. links,** gemelos.

cuisine, n. arte culinario f.

culinary, a. culinario.

culminate, v. culminar.

culmination, n. culminación f.

culpable, a. culpable.

culprit, n. criminal; delincuente m.

cult, n. culto m.

cultivate, v. cultivar.

cultivated, a. cultivado.

cultivation, n. cultivo m.; cultivación f.

cultivator, n. cultivador m.

cultural, a. cultural.

culture, n. cultura f.

cultured, a. culto.

cumbersome, a. pesado, incómodo.

cumulative, a. acumulativo.

cunning, 1. a. astuto. **2.** n. astucia f.

cup, n. taza, jícara f.

cupboard, n. armario, aparador m.

cupidity, n. avaricia f.

curable, a. curable.

curator, n. guardián m.

curb, 1. n. freno m. **2.** v. refrenar.

curd, n. cuajada f.

curdle, v. cuajarse, coagularse.

cure, 1. n. remedio m. **2.** v. curar, sanar.

curfew, n. toque de queda m.

curio, n. objeto curioso m.

curiosity, n. curiosidad f.

curious, a. curioso.

curl, 1. n. rizo m. **2.** v. rizar.

curly, a. rizado.

currant, n. grosella f.

currency, n. circulación f.; dinero m.

current, a. & n. corriente f.

currently, adv. corrientemente.

curriculum, n. plan de estudio m.

curse, 1. n. maldición f. **2.** v. maldecir.

cursory, a. sumario.

curt, a. brusco.

curtail, v. reducir; restringir.

curtain, n. cortina f.; (theat.) telón m.

curtsy, 1. n. reverencia f. **2.** v. hacer una reverencia.

curvature, n. curvatura f.

curve, 1. n. curva f. **2.** v. encorvar.

cushion, n. cojín m.; almohada f.

cuspidor, n. escupidera f.

custard, n. flan m.; natillas f.

custodian, n. custodio m.

custody, n. custodia f.

custom, n. costumbre f.

customary, *a.* acostumbrado, usual.

customer, *n.* cliente *m. & f.*

customhouse, customs, *n.* aduana *f.*

cut, 1. *n.* corte *m.;* cortada *f.;* tajada *f.;* (printing) grabado *m.* **2.** *v.* cortar; tajar.

cute, *a.* mono, lindo.

cut glass, *n.* cristal tallado *m.*

cuticle, *n.* cutícula *f.*

cutlery, *n.* cuchillería *f.*

cutlet, *n.* coteleta, chuleta *f.*

cutter, *n.* cortador -ra; (naut.) cúter *m.*

cutthroat, *n.* asesino *m.*

cyclamate, *n.* ciclamato *m.*

cycle, *n.* ciclo *m.*

cyclist, *n.* ciclista *m. & f.*

cyclone, *n.* ciclón, huracán *m.*

cyclotron, *n.* ciclotrón *m.*

cylinder, *n.* cilindro *m.*

cylindrical, *a.* cilíndrico.

cymbal, *n.* címbalo *m.*

cynic, *n.* cínico *m.*

cynical, *a.* cínico.

cynicism, *n.* cinismo *m.*

cypress, *n.* ciprés *m.* **c. nut,** piñuela *f.*

cyst, *n.* quiste *m.*

D

dad, *n.* papá *m.,* papito *m.*

daffodil, *n.* narciso *m.*

dagger, *n.* puñal *m.*

dahlia, *n.* dalia *f.*

daily, *a.* diario, cotidiano.

daintiness, *n.* delicadeza *f.*

dainty, *a.* delicado.

dairy, *n.* lechería, quesería *f.*

dais, *n.* tablado *m.*

daisy, *n.* margarita *f.*

dale, *n.* valle *m.*

dally, *v.* holgar; perder el tiempo.

dam, *n.* presa *f.;* dique *m.*

damage, 1. *n.* daño *m.* **2.** *v.* dañar.

damask, *n.* damasco *m.*

damn, *v.* condenar.

damnation, *n.* condenación *f.*

damp, *a.* húmedo.

dampen, *v.* humedecer.

dampness, *n.* humedad *f.*

damsel, *n.* doncella *f.*

dance, 1. *n.* baile *m.;* danza *f.* **2.** *v.* bailar.

dancer, *n.* bailador -ra; (professional) bailarín -na.

dancing, *n.* baile *m.*

dandelion, *n.* amargón *m.*

dandruff, *n.* caspa *f.*

dandy, *n.* petimetre *m.*

danger, *n.* peligro *m.*

dangerous, *a.* peligroso.

dangle, *v.* colgar.

Danish, *a. & n.* danés -sa; dinamarqués -sa.

dapper, *a.* gallardo.

dare, *v.* atreverse, osar.

daredevil, *n.* atrevido *m.,* -da *f.*

daring, 1. *a.* atrevido. **2.** *n.* osadía *f.*

dark, 1. *a.* obscuro; moreno. **2.** *n.* obscuridad *f.*

darken, *v.* obscurecer.

darkness, *n.* obscuridad *f.*

darkroom, *n.* cámara obscura *f.*

darling, *a. & n.* querido, amado.

darn, *v.* zurcir.

darning needle, *n.* aguja de zurcir *m.*

dart, *n.* dardo *m.*

dash, *n.* arranque *m.;* (punct.) guión *m.*

data, *n.* datos *m.*

data processing, proceso de datos *m.*

date, *n.* fecha *f.;* (engagement) cita *f.;* (fruit) dátil *m.*

daughter, *n.* hija *f.*

daughter-in-law, *n.* nuera *f.*

daunt, *v.* intimidar.

dauntless, *a.* intrépido.

davenport, *n.* sofá *m.*

dawn, 1. *n.* alba, madrugada *f.* **2.** *v.* amanecer.

day, *n.* día *m.* **good d.,** buenos días.

daybreak, *n.* alba, madrugada *f.*

daydream, *n.* fantasía *f.*

daylight, *n.* luz del día *f.*

daze, *v.* aturdir.

dazzle, *v.* deslumbrar.

deacon, *n.* diácono *m.*

dead, *a.* muerto.

deaden, *v.* amortecer.

deadline, *n.* límite absoluto *m.*

deadlock, *n.* paro *m.*

deadly, *a.* mortal.

deaf, *a.* sordo.

deafen, *v.* ensordecer.

deaf-mute, *n.* sordomudo *m.*

deafness, *n.* sordera *f.*

deal, 1. n. trato m.; negociación f. **a great d., a good d.,** mucho. **2.** v. tratar; negociar.

dealer, n. comerciante m., (at cards) tallador -ra.

dean, n. decano m.

dear, a. querido; caro.

dearth, n. escasez f.

death, n. muerte f.

deathless, a. inmortal.

debacle, n. desastre m.

debase, v. degradar.

debatable, a. discutible.

debate, 1. n. debate m. **2.** v. disputar, deliberar.

debauch, v. corromper.

debilitate, v. debilitar.

debit, n. débito m.

debonair, a. cortés; alegre, vivo.

debris, n. escombros m.pl.

debt, n. deuda f.

debtor, n. deudor -ra.

debunk, v. traer a la realidad.

debut, n. debut, estreno m.

debutante, n. debutante f.

decade, n. década f.

decadence, n. decadencia f.

decadent, a. decadente.

decaffeinated, a. descafeinado.

decalcomania, n. calcomanía f.

decanter, n. garrafa f.

decapitate, v. descabezar.

decay, 1. n. descaecimiento m.; (dental) caries f. **2.** v. decaer; (dental) cariarse.

deceased, a. muerto, difunto.

deceit, n. engaño m.

deceitful, a. engañoso.

deceive, v. engañar.

December, n. diciembre m.

decency, n. decencia f.; decoro m.

decent, a. decente.

decentralize, v. descentralizar.

deception, n. decepción f.

deceptive, a. deceptivo.

decibel, n. decibelio m.

decide, v. decidir.

decimal, a. decimal.

decipher, v. descifrar.

decision, n. decisión f.

decisive, a. decisivo.

deck, n. cubierta f.

declamation, n. declamación f.

declaration, n. declaración f.

declarative, a. declarativo.

declare, v. declarar.

declension, n. declinación f.

decline, 1. n. decadencia f. **2.** v. decaer; negarse; (gram.) declinar.

decompose, v. descomponer.

decongestant, n. descongestionante m.

decorate, v. decorar, adornar.

decoration, n. decoración f.

decorative, a. decorativo.

decorator, n. decorador m.

decorous, a. correcto.

decorum, n. decoro m.

decrease, v. disminuir.

decree, n. decreto m.

decrepit, a. decrépito.

decry, v. descreditar.

dedicate, v. dedicar; consagrar.

dedication, n. dedicación f.; dedicatoria f.

deduce, deduct, v. deducir.

deduction, n. rebaja f.

deductive, a. deductivo.

deed, n. acción f.; hazaña f.

deem, v. estimar.

deep, a. hondo, profundo.

deepen, v. profundizar, ahondar.

deep freeze, n. congelación f.

deeply, adv. profundamente.

deer, n. venado, ciervo m.

defamation, n. calmunia f.

defame, v. difamar.

default, 1. n. defecto m. **2.** v. faltar.

defeat, 1. n. derrota f. **2.** v. derrotar.

defect, n. defecto m.

defective, a. defectivo.

defend, v. defender.

defendant, n. acusado -da.

defender, n. defensor -ra.

defense, n. defensa f.

defensive, a. defensivo.

defer, v. aplazar; deferir.

deference, n. deferencia f.

defiance, n. desafío m.

defiant, a. desafiador.

deficiency, n. defecto m.

deficient, a. deficiente.

deficit, n. déficit, descubierto m.

defile, 1. n. desfiladero m. **2.** v. profanar.

define, v. definir.

definite, a. exacto; definitivo.

definitely, adv. definidamente.

definition, n. definición f.

definitive, *a.* definitivo.
deflation, *n.* desinflación *f.*
deflect, *v.* desviar.
deform, *v.* deformar.
deformity, *n.* deformidad *f.*
defraud, *v.* defraudar.
defray, *v.* costear.
deft, *a.* diestro.
defy, *v.* desafiar.
degenerate, 1. *a.* degenerado. **2.** *v.* degenerar.
degeneration, *n.* degeneración *f.*
degradation, *n.* degradación *f.*
degrade, *v.* degradar.
degree, *n.* grado *m.*
deign, *v.* condescender.
deity, *n.* deidad *f.*
dejected, *a.* abatido.
dejection, *n.* tristeza *f.*
delay, 1. *n.* retardo *m.,* demora *f.* **2.** *v.* tardar, demorar.
delegate, 1. *n.* delegado -da. **2.** *v.* delegar.
delegation, *n.* delegación *f.*
delete, *v.* suprimir.
deliberate, 1. *a.* premeditado. **2.** *v.* deliberar.
deliberately, *adv.* deliberadamente.
deliberation, *n.* deliberación *f.*
deliberative, *a.* deliberativo.
delicacy, *n.* delicadeza *f.*
delicate, *a.* delicado.
delicious, *a.* delicioso.
delight, *n.* deleite *m.*
delightful, *a.* deleitoso.
delinquency, *n.* delincuencia *f.*
delinquent, *a. & n.* delincuente.
delirious, *a.* delirante.
deliver, *v.* entregar.
deliverance, *n.* liberación; salvación *f.*
delivery, *n.* entrega *f.;* (med.) parto *m.*
delude, *v.* engañar.
deluge, *n.* inundación *f.*
delusion, *n.* decepción *f.;* engaño *m.*
delve, *v.* cavar, sondear.
demagogue, *n.* demagogo *m.*
demand, 1. *n.* demanda *f.* **2.** *v.* demandar; exigir.
demarcation, *n.* demarcación *f.*
demeanor, *n.* conducta *f.*
demented, *a.* demente, loco.
demilitarize, *v.* desmilitarizar.
demobilize, *v.* desmovilizar.

democracy, *n.* democracia *f.*
democrat, *n.* demócrata *m. & f.*
democratic, *a.* democrático.
demolish, *v.* demoler.
demon, *n.* demonio *m.*
demonstrate, *v.* demostrar.
demonstration, *n.* demostración *f.*
demonstrative, *a.* demostrativo.
demoralize, *v.* desmoralizar.
demure, *a.* modesto, serio.
den, *n.* caverna *f.;* retrete *m.*
denature, *v.* alterar.
denial, *n.* negación *f.*
denim, *n.* tela para jeans, azul de Vergara.
Denmark, *n.* Dinamarca *f.*
denomination, *n.* denominación; secta *f.*
denote, *v.* denotar.
denounce, *v.* denunciar.
dense, *a.* denso, espeso; estúpido.
density, *n.* densidad *f.*
dent, 1. *n.* abolladura *f.* **2.** *v.* abollar.
dental, *a.* dental.
dentist, *n.* dentista *m.*
dentistry, *n.* odontología *f.*
denture, *n.* dentadura *f.*
denunciation, *n.* denunciación *f.*
deny, *v.* negar, rehusar.
deodorant, *n.* desodorante *m.*
depart, *v.* partir; irse, marcharse.
department, *n.* departamento *m.*
departmental, *a.* departamental.
departure, *n.* salida; desviación *f.*
depend, *v.* depender.
dependability, *n.* confiabilidad *f.*
dependable, *a.* confiable.
dependence, *n.* dependencia *f.*
dependent, *a. & n.* dependiente *m.*
depict, *v.* pintar; representar.
deplete, *v.* agotar.
deplorable, *a.* deplorable.
deplore, *v.* deplorar.
deport, *v.* deportar.
deportation, *n.* deportación *f.*
deportment, *n.* conducta *f.*
depose, *v.* deponer.
deposit, 1. *n.* depósito *m.* **2.** *v.* depositar.
depositor, *n.* depositante *m. & f.*
depot, *n.* depósito *m.;* (railway) estación *f.*
depravity, *n.* depravación *f.*

deprecate, v. deprecar.

depreciate, v. depreciar.

depreciation, n. depreciación f.

depredation, n. depredación f.

depress, v. deprimir; desanimar.

depression, n. depresión f.

deprive, v. privar.

depth, n. profundidad, hondura f.

depth charge, n. carga de profundidad f.

deputy, n. diputado m.

deride, v. burlar.

derision, n. burla f.

derivation, n. derivación f.

derivative, a. derivativo.

derive, v. derivar.

derogatory, a. derogatorio.

derrick, n. grúa f.

descend, v. descender, bajar.

descendant, n. descendiente m. & f.

descent, n. descenso m.; origen m.

describe, v. describir.

description, n. descripción f.

descriptive, a. descriptivo.

desecrate, v. profanar.

desert, 1. n. desierto m. 2. v. abandonar.

deserter, n. desertor m.

desertion, n. deserción f.

deserve, v. merecer.

design, 1. n. diseño m. 2. v. diseñar.

designate, v. señalar, apuntar.

designation, n. designación f.

designer, n. diseñador -ra; (technical) proyectista m. & f.

desirability, n. conveniencia f.

desirable, a. deseable.

desire, 1. n. deseo m. 2. v. desear.

desirous, a. deseoso.

desist, v. desistir.

desk, n. escritorio m.

desolate, 1. a. desolado. 2. v. desolar.

desolation, n. desolación, ruina f.

despair, 1. n. desesperación f. 2. v. desesperar.

despatch, dispatch, 1. n. despacho m.; prontitud f. 2. v. despachar.

desperado, n. bandido m.

desperate, a. desesperado.

desperation, n. desesperación f.

despicable, a. vil.

despise, v. despreciar.

despite, prep. a pesar de.

despondent, a. abatido; desanimado.

despot, n. déspota m.

despotic, a. despótico.

dessert, n. postre m.

destination, n. destinación f.

destine, v. destinar.

destiny, n. destino m.

destitute, a. destituido.

destitution, n. destitución f.

destroy, v. destrozar, destruir.

destroyer, n. destruidor m.; (naval) destróyer m.

destruction, n. destrucción f.

destructive, a. destructivo.

desultory, a. inconexo; casual.

detach, v. separar, desprender.

detachment, n. (mil.) destacamento m.

detail, 1. n. detalle m. 2. v. detallar.

detain, v. detener.

detect, v. descubrir.

detection, n. detección f.

detective, n. detective m.

detente, n. détente f.

detention, n. detención; cautividad f.

deter, v. disuadir.

detergent, n. & a. detergente m.

deteriorate, v. deteriorar.

deterioration, n. deterioración f.

determination, n. determinación f.

determine, v. determinar.

deterrence, n. disuasión f.

detest, v. detestar.

detonate, v. detonar.

detour, n. desvío m.

detract, v. disminuir.

detriment, n. detrimento m., daño m.

detrimental, a. dañoso.

devaluate, v. depreciar.

devastate, v. devastar.

develop, v. desarrollar; (phot.) revelar.

developing nation, nación en desarrollo.

development, n. desarrollo m.

deviate, v. desviar.

deviation, n. desviación f.

device, n. aparato; artificio m.

devil, n. diablo, demonio m.

devious, a. desviado.

devise, v. inventar.
devoid, a. desprovisto.
devote, v. dedicar, consagrar.
devoted, a. devoto.
devotee, n. aficionado m.
devotion, n. devoción f.
devour, v. devorar.
devout, a. devoto.
dew, n. rocío, sereno m.
dexterity, n. destreza f.
dexterous, a. diestro.
diabetes, n. diabetes f.
diabolic, a. diabólico.
diadem, n. diadema f.
diagnose, v. diagnosticar.
diagnosis, n. diagnóstico m.
diagonal, a. diagonal f.
diagram, n. diagrama f.
dial, n. cuadrante m., carátula f.
dialect, n. dialecto m.
dialogue, n. diálogo m.
diameter, n. diámetro m.
diamond, n. diamante, brillante m.
diaper, n. pañal m.
diarrhea, n. diarrea f.
diary, n. diario m.
diathermy, n. diatermia f.
dice, n. dados m.pl.
dictate, 1. n. dictamen m. **2.** v. dictar.
dictation, n. dictado m.
dictator, n. dictador m.
dictatorship, n. dictadura f.
diction, n. dicción f.
dictionary, n. diccionario m.
die, 1. n. matriz f.; (game) dado m. **2.** v. morir.
diet, n. dieta f.
dietary, a. dietético.
dietitian, n. dietista m. & f.
differ, v. diferir.
difference, n. diferencia f. **to make no d.,** no importar.
different, a. diferente, distinto.
differential, n. diferencial f.
differentiate, v. diferenciar.
difficult, a. difícil.
difficulty, n. dificultad f.
diffident, a. tímido.
diffuse, v. difundir.
diffusion, n. difusión f.
dig, v. cavar.
digest, 1. n. extracto m. **2.** v. digerir.
digestible, a. digerible.
digestion, n. digestión f.

digestive, a. digestivo.
digital, a. digital.
digitalis, n. digital f.
dignified, a. digno.
dignify, v. dignificar.
dignitary, n. dignitario m.
dignity, n. dignidad f.
digress, v. divagar.
digression, n. digresión f.
dike, n. dique m.
dilapidated, a. dilapidado.
dilapidation, n. dilapidación f.
dilate, v. dilatar.
dilatory, a. dilatorio.
dilemma, n. dilema m.
dilettante, n. diletante m. & f.
diligence, n. diligencia f.
diligent, a. diligente, aplicado.
dilute, v. diluir.
dim, 1. a. oscuro. **2.** v. oscurecer.
dimension, n. dimensión f.
diminish, v. disminuir.
diminution, n. disminución f.
diminutive, a. diminutivo.
dimness, n. oscuridad f.
dimple, n. hoyuelo m.
din, n. alboroto m.
dine, v. comer, cenar.
diner, n. coche comedor m.
dingy, a. deslucido, deslustrado.
dining room, n. comedor m.
dinner, n. comida, cena f.
dinosaur, n. dinosauro m.
diocese, n. diócesis f.
dip, v. sumergir, hundir.
diphtheria, n. difteria f.
diploma, n. diploma m.
diplomacy, n. diplomacia f.
diplomat, n. diplomático m.
diplomatic, a. diplomático.
dipper, n. cucharón m.
dire, a. horrendo.
direct, 1. a. directo. **2.** v. dirigir.
direction, n. dirección f.
directive, n. directivo m.
directly, adv. directamente.
director, n. director -ra.
directory, n. directorio m., guía f.
dirigible, n. dirigible m.
dirt, n. basura f.; (earth) tierra f.
dirty, a. sucio.
disability, n. inhabilidad f.
disable, v. incapacitar.
disabuse, v. desengañar.
disadvantage, n. desventaja f.
disagree, v. desconvenir; disentir.
disagreeable, a. desagradable.

disagreement, n. desacuerdo m.
disappear, v. desaparecer.
disappearance, n. desaparición f.
disappoint, v. disgustar, desilusionar.
disappointment, n. disgusto m., desilusión f.
disapproval, n. desaprobación f.
disapprove, v. desaprobar.
disarm, v. desarmar.
disarmament, n. desarme m.
disarrange, v. desordenar; desarreglar.
disaster, n. desastre m.
disastrous, a. desastroso.
disavow, v. repudiar.
disavowal, n. repudiación f.
disband, v. dispersarse.
disbelieve, v. descreer.
disburse, v. desembolsar, pagar.
discard, v. descartar.
discern, v. discernir.
discerning, a. discernidor, perspicaz.
discernment, n. discernimiento m.
discharge, v. descargar; despedir.
disciple, n. discípulo m.
disciplinary, a. disciplinario.
discipline, n. disciplina f.
disclaim, v. repudiar.
disclaimer, n. negador m.
disclose, v. revelar.
disclosure, n. descubrimiento m.
disco, n. discoteca f.
discolor, v. descolorar.
discomfort, n. incomodidad f.
disconcert, v. desconcertar.
disconnect, v. desunir; desconectar.
disconnected, a. desunido.
disconsolate, a. desconsolado.
discontent, n. descontento m.
discontented, a. descontento.
discontinue, v. descontinuar.
discord, n. discordia f.
discordant, a. disonante.
discotheque, n. discoteca f.
discount, n. descuento m.
discourage, v. desalentar, desanimar.
discouragement, n. desaliento, desánimo m.
discourse, n. discurso m.
discourteous, a. descortés.
discourtesy, n. descortesía f.
discover, v. descubrir.

discoverer, n. descubridor -ra.
discovery, n. descubrimiento m.
discreet, a. discreto.
discrepancy, n. discrepancia f.
discretion, n. discreción f.
discriminate, v. distinguir; diferenciar parcialmente.
discrimination, n. discernimiento m.; discriminación f.
discuss, v. discutir.
discussion, n. discusión f.
disdain, 1. n. desdén m. **2.** v. desdeñar.
disdainful, a. desdeñoso.
disease, n. enfermedad f., mal m.
disembark, v. desembarcar.
disentangle, v. desenredar.
disfigure, v. desfigurar.
disgrace, 1. n. vergüenza; deshonra f. **2.** v. deshonrar.
disgraceful, a. vergonzoso.
disguise, 1. n. disfraz m. **2.** v. disfrazar.
disgust, 1. n. fastidio m. **2.** v. fastidiar.
dish, n. plato m.
dishearten, v. desanimar; descorazonar.
dishonest, a. deshonesto.
dishonesty, n. deshonestidad f.
dishonor, 1. n. deshonra f. **2.** v. deshonrar.
dishonorable, a. deshonroso.
disillusion, 1. n. desengaño m. **2.** v. desengañar.
disinfect, v. desinfectar.
disinfectant, n. desinfectante m.
disinherit, v. desheredar.
disintegrate, v. desintegrar.
disinterested, a. desinteresado.
disk, n. disco m.
dislike, 1. n. antipatía f. **2.** v. no gustar de.
dislocate, v. dislocar.
dislodge, v. desalojar.
disloyal, a. desleal; infiel.
disloyalty, n. deslealtad f.
dismal, a. lúgubre.
dismantle, v. desmantelar.
dismay, 1. n. consternación f. **2.** v. consternar.
dismiss, v. despedir.
dismissal, n. despedida f.
dismount, v. apearse.
disobedience, n. desobediencia f.
disobedient, a. desobediente.
disobey, v. desobedecer.

disorder, n. desorden m.

disorderly, a. desarreglado, desordenado.

disown, v. repudiar.

dispassionate, a. desapasionado; templado.

dispatch, 1. n. despacho m. **2.** v. despachar.

dispel, v. despersar.

dispensary, n. dispensario m.

dispensation, n. dispensación f.

dispense, v. dispensar.

dispersal, n. dispersión f.

disperse, v. dispersar.

displace, v. dislocar.

display, 1. n. despliegue m., exhibición f. **2.** desplegar, exhibir.

displease, v. disgustar; ofender.

displeasure, n. disgusto, sinsabor m.

disposable, a. disponible.

disposal, n. disposición f.

dispose, v. disponer.

disposition, n. disposición f.; indole f., genio m.

dispossess, v. desposeer.

disproportionate, a. desproporcionado.

disprove, v. confutar.

dispute, 1. n. disputa f. **2.** v. disputar.

disqualify, v. inhabilitar.

disregard, 1. n. desatención f. **2.** v. desatender.

disrepair, n. descompostura f.

disreputable, a. desacreditado.

disrespect, n. falta de respeto.

disrespectful, a. irrespetuoso.

disrobe, v. desvestir.

disrupt, v. romper; desbaratar.

dissatisfaction, n. descontento m.

dissatisfy, v. descontentar.

dissect, v. disecar.

dissemble, v. disimular.

disseminate, v. diseminar.

dissension, n. disensión f.

dissent, 1. n. disensión f. **2.** v. disentir.

dissertation, n. disertación f.

dissimilar, a. desemejante.

dissipate, v. disipar.

dissipation, n. disipación f.; libertinaje m.

dissolute, a. disoluto.

dissolution, n. disolución f.

dissolve, v. disolver; derretirse.

dissonant, a. disonante.

dissuade, v. disuadir.

distance, n. distancia f. **at a d., in the d.,** a lo lejos.

distant, a. distante, lejano.

distaste, n. disgusto, sinsabor m.

distasteful, a. desagradable.

distill, v. destilar.

distillation, n. destilación f.

distillery, n. destilería f.

distinct, a. distinto.

distinctive, a. distintivo; característico.

distinctly, adv. distintamente.

distinction, n. distinción f.

distinguish, v. distinguir.

distinguished, a. distinguido.

distort, v. falsear; torcer.

distract, v. distraer.

distraction, n. distracción f.

distraught, a. aturrullado; demente.

distress, 1. n. dolor m. **2.** v. afligir.

distribute, v. distribuir.

distribution, n. distribución f.; reparto m.

distributor, n. distribuidor -ra.

district, n. distrito m.

distrust, 1. n. desconfianza f. **2.** v. desconfiar.

distrustful, a. desconfiado; sospechoso.

disturb, v. incomodar; inquietar.

disturbance, n. disturbio m.

ditch, n. zanja f.; foso m.

divan, n. diván m.

dive, 1. n. clavado m.; (coll.) leonera f. **2.** v. echar un clavado; bucear.

diver, n. buzo m.

diverge, v. divergir.

divergence, n. divergencia f.

divergent, a. divergente.

diverse, a. diverso.

diversion, n. diversión f.; pasatiempo m.

diversity, n. diversidad f.

divert, v. desviar; divertir.

divest, v. desnudar, despojar.

divide, v. dividir.

dividend, n. dividendo m.

divine, a. divino.

divinity, n. divinidad f.

division, n. división f.

divorce, 1. n. divorcio m. **2.** v. divorciar.

divorcee, n. divorciada f.

divulge, v. divulgar, revelar.

dizziness, n. vértigo, mareo m.

dizzy, a. mareado.

do, v. hacer.

docile, a. dócil.

dock, 1. n. muelle m. **dry d.,** astillero m. **2.** v. entrar en muelle.

doctor, n. médico m.; doctor -ra.

doctrine, n. doctrina f.

document, n. documento m.

documentary, a. documental.

documentation, n. documentación f.

dodge, 1. n. evasión f. **2.** v. evadir.

doe, n. gama f.

dog, n. perro m.

dogma, n. dogma m.

dogmatic, a. dogmático.

dogmatism, n. dogmatismo m.

doily, n. servilletita f.

doleful, a. triste.

doll, n. muñeca f.

dollar, n. dólar m.

dolorous, a. lastimoso.

dolphin, n. delfín m.

domain, n. dominio m.

dome, n. domo m.

domestic, a. doméstico.

domesticate, v. domesticar.

domicile, n. domicilio m.

dominance, n. dominación f.

dominant, a. dominante.

dominate, v. dominar.

domination, n. dominación f.

domineer, v. dominar.

domineering, a. tiránico, mandón.

dominion, n. dominio; territorio m.

domino, n. dominó m.

donate, v. donar; contribuir.

donation, n. donación f.

donkey, n. asno, burro m.

doom, 1. n. perdición, ruina f. **2.** v. perder, ruinar.

door, n. puerta f.

doorman, n. portero m.

doorway, n. entrada f.

dope, n. narcótico m.

dormant, a. durmiente.

dormitory, n. dormitorio m.

dosage, n. dosificación f.

dose, n. dosis f.

dot, n. punto m.

double, 1. a. doble. **2.** v. duplicar.

double-breasted, a. cruzado.

double-cross, v. traicionar.

doubly, adv. doblemente.

doubt, 1. n. duda f. **2.** v. dudar.

doubtful, a. dudoso, incierto.

doubtless, 1. a. indudable. **2.** adv. sin duda.

dough, n. pasta, masa f.

doughnut, n. buñuelo m.

dove, n. paloma f.

dowager, n. viuda f.

down, 1. adv. abajo. **2.** prep. **d. the street,** etc. calle abajo, etc.

downcast, a. cabizbajo.

downfall, n. ruina, perdición f.

downhearted, a. descorazonado.

downpour, n. chaparrón m.

downright, a. absoluto, completo.

downstairs, 1. adv. abajo. **2.** n. primer piso.

downtown, adv. al centro, en el centro.

downward, 1. a. descendente. **2.** adv. hacia abajo.

dowry, n. dote m.

doze, v. dormitar.

dozen, n. docena f.

draft, 1. n. dibujo m.; (com.) giro m.; (mil.) conscripción f. **2.** v. dibujar; (mil.) reclutar.

draftee, n. conscripto m.

drag, v. arrastrar.

dragon, n. dragón m.

drain, 1. n. desaguadero m. **2.** v. desaguar.

drainage, n. drenaje m.

drama, n. drama m.

dramatic, a. dramático.

dramatics, n. dramática f.

dramatist, n. dramaturgo m.

dramatize, v. dramatizar.

drape, n. cortina f.

drapery, n. colgaduras f.pl.; ropaje m.

drastic, a. drástico.

draw, v. dibujar; atraer. **d. up,** formular.

drawback, n. desventaja f.

drawer, n. cajón m.

drawing, n. dibujo m.; rifa f.

dread, 1. n. terror m. **2.** v. temer.

dreadful, a. terrible.

dreadfully, adv. horrendamente.

dream, 1. n. sueño, ensueño m. **2.** v. soñar.

dreamer, n. soñador -ra; visionario -ia.

dreamy, *a.* soñador, contemplativo.

dreary, *a.* monótono y pesado.

dredge, 1. *n.* rastra *f.* 2. *v.* rastrear.

dregs, *n.* sedimento *m.*

drench, *v.* mojar.

dress, 1. *n.* vestido; traje *m.* 2. *v.* vestir.

dresser, *n.* (furniture) tocador *m.*

dressing, *n.* (med.) curación *f.;* (cookery) relleno *m.*

dressing gown, *n.* batá *f.*

dressmaker, *n.* modista *m. & f.*

drift, 1. *n.* tendencia *f.;* (naut.) deriva *f.* 2. *v.* (naut.) derivar; (snow) amontonarse.

drill, 1. *n.* ejercicio *m.;* (mech.) taladro *m.* 2. *v.* (mech.) taladrar.

drink, 1. *n.* bebida *f.* 2. *v.* beber, tomar.

drinkable, *a.* potable, bebible.

drip, *v.* gotear.

drive, 1. *n.* paseo *m.* 2. *v.* impeler; (auto.) guiar, conducir.

driver, *n.* chofer *m.* **d.'s license,** permiso de conducir.

driveway, *n.* entrada para coches.

drizzle, 1. *n.* llovizna *f.* 2. *v.* lloviznar.

dromedary, *n.* dromedario *m.*

droop, *v.* inclinarse.

drop, 1. *n.* gota *f.* 2. *v.* soltar; dejar, caer.

dropout, *n.* joven que abandona sus estudios.

dropper, *n.* cuentagotas *f.*

dropsy, *n.* hidropesía *f.*

drought, *n.* seca, sequía *f.*

drove, *n.* manada *f.*

drown, *v.* ahogar.

drowse, *v.* adormecer.

drowsiness, *n.* somnolencia *f.*

drowsy, *a.* soñoliento.

drudge, *n.* ganapán *m.*

drudgery, *n.* trabajo penoso.

drug, 1. *n.* droga *f.* 2. *v.* narcotizar.

druggist, *n.* farmacéutico, boticario *m.*

drugstore, *n.* farmacia, botica, droguería *f.*

drum, *n.* tambor *m.*

drummer, *n.* tambor *m.*

drumstick, *n.* palillo *m.;* (leg) pierna *f.*

drunk, *a. & n.* borracho.

drunkard, *n.* borrachón *m.*

drunken, *a.* borracho; ebrio.

drunkenness, *n.* embriaguez *f.*

dry, 1. *a.* seco, árido. 2. *v.* secar.

dry cell, *n.* pila seca *f.*

dry-cleaner, *n.* tintorero *m.*

dryness, *n.* sequedad *f.*

dual, *a.* doble.

dubious, *a.* dudoso.

duchess, *n.* duquesa *f.*

duck, 1. *n.* pato *m.* 2. *v.* zabullir; (avoid) esquivar.

duct, *n.* canal *m.*

due, 1. *a.* debido; (com.) vencido. **2. dues,** *n.* cuota *f.*

duel, *n.* duelo *m.*

duelist, *n.* duelista *m.*

duet, *n.* dúo *m.*

duke, *n.* duque *m.*

dull, *a.* apagado, desteñido; sin punta; (fig.) pesado, soso.

dullness, *n.* estupidez; pesadez *f.;* deslustre *m.*

duly, *adv.* debidamente.

dumb, *a.* mudo; (coll.) estúpido.

dumbwaiter, *n.* montaplatos *m.*

dumfound, *v.* confundir.

dummy, *n.* figurón *m.*

dump, 1. *n.* depósito *m.* 2. *v.* descargar.

dune, *n.* duna *f.*

dungeon, *n.* calabozo *m.*

dunk, *v.* mojar.

dupe, *v.* engañar.

duplicate, 1. *a. & n.* duplicado *m.* 2. *v.* duplicar.

duplication, *n.* duplicación *f.*

duplicity, *n.* duplicidad *f.*

durability, *n.* durabilidad *f.*

durable, *a.* durable, duradero.

duration, *n.* duración *f.*

duress, *n.* compulsión *m.;* encierro *m.*

during, *prep.* durante.

dusk, *n.* crepúsculo *m.*

dusky, *a.* oscuro; moreno.

dust, 1. *n.* polvo *m.* 2. *v.* polvorear; despolvorear.

dusty, *a.* empolvado.

Dutch, *a.* holandés -sa.

dutiful, *a.* respetuoso.

dutifully, *adv.* respetuosamente, obedientemente.

duty, *n.* deber *m.;* (com.) derechos *m.pl.*

duty-free, *a.* libre de derechos.

dwarf, 1. n. enano -na. **2.** v. achicar.

dwell, v. habitar, residir. **d. on,** espaciarse en.

dwelling, n. morada, casa f.

dwindle, v. disminuirse.

dye, 1. n. tintura f. **2.** v. teñir.

dyer, n. tintorero -ra.

dynamic, a. dinámico.

dynamite, n. dinamita f.

dynamo, n. dínamo m.

dynasty, n. dinastía f.

dysentery, n. disentería f.

dyslexia, n. dislexia f.

dyspepsia, n. dispepsia f.

E

each, 1. a. cada. **2.** pron. cada uno -na. **e. other,** el uno al otro.

eager, a. ansioso.

eagerly, adv. ansiosamente.

eagerness, n. ansia f.

eagle, n. águila f.

ear, n. oído m.; (outer) oreja f., (of corn) mazorca f.

earache, n. dolor de oído m.

earl, n. conde m.

early, a. & adv. temprano.

earn, v. ganar.

earnest, a. serio.

earnestly, adv. seriamente.

earnings, n. ganancias f.pl.; (com.) ingresos m.pl.

earphone, n. auricular m.

earring, n. pendiente, arete m.

earth, n. tierra f.

earthquake, n. terremoto m.

ease, 1. n. reposo m.; facilidad f. **2.** v. aliviar.

easel, n. caballete m.

easily, adv. fácilmente.

east, n. oriente, este m.

Easter, n. Pascua Florida.

eastern, a. oriental.

eastward, adv. hacia el este.

easy, a. fácil.

eat, v. comer.

eaves, n. socarrén m.

ebb, 1. n. menguante f. **2.** v. menguar.

ebony, n. ébano m.

eccentric, a. excéntrico.

eccentricity, n. excentricidad f.

ecclesiastic, a. & n. eclesiástico. m.

ecclesiastical, a. eclasiástico.

echelon, n. escalón m.

echo, n. eco m.

eclipse, 1. n. eclipse m. **2.** v. eclipsar.

ecological, a. ecológico.

ecology, n. ecología f.

economic, a. económico.

economical, a. económico.

economics, n. economía política.

economist, n. economista m.

economize, v. economizar.

economy, n. economía f.

ecstasy, n. éxtasis m.

Ecuadorian, a. & n. ecuatoriano -na.

ecumenical, a. ecuménico.

eczema, n. eczema f.

eddy, 1. n. remolino m. **2.** v. remolinar.

edge, 1. n. filo; borde m. **2.** v. e. one's way, abrirse paso.

edible, a. comestible.

edict, n. edicto m.

edifice, n. edificio m.

edify, v. edificar.

edition, n. edición f.

editor, n. redactor m.

editorial, n. editorial m. **e. staff,** redacción f.

educate, v. educar.

education, n. instrucción; enseñanza f.

educational, a. educativo.

educator, n. educador, pedagogo m.

eel, n. anguila f.

efface, v. tachar.

effect, 1. n. efecto m. **in e.,** en vigor. **2.** v. efectuar, realizar.

effective, a. eficaz; efectivo; en vigor.

effectively, adv. eficazmente.

effectiveness, n. efectividad f.

effectual, a. eficaz.

effeminate, a. afeminado.

efficacy, n. eficacia f.

efficiency, n. eficiencia f.

efficient, a. eficaz.

efficiently, adv. eficazmente.

effigy, n. efigie m.

effort, n. esfuerzo m.

effrontery, n. impudencia f.

effusive, a. expansivo.

egg, n. huevo m. **fried e.,** huevo frito. **soft-boiled e.,** h. pasado por agua. **scrambled eggs,** huevos revueltos.

eggplant, *n.* berenjena *f.*

egoism, egotism, *n.* egoísmo *m.*

egoist, egotist, *n.* egoísta *m. & f.*

egotism, *n.* egotismo *m.*

egotist, *n.* egotista *m.*

Egypt, *n.* Egipto *m.*

Egyptian, *a. & n.* egipcio -ia.

eight, *a. & pron.* ocho.

eighteen, *a. & pron.* dieciocho.

eighth, *a.* octavo.

eightieth, *n.* octogésimo *m.*

eighty, *a. & pron.* ochenta.

either, 1. *a. & pron.* cualquiera de los dos. **2.** *adv.* tampoco. **3.** *conj.*

either . . . or, o . . . . o.

ejaculate, *v.* exclamar.

eject, *v.* expeler.

ejection, *n.* expulsión *f.*

elaborate, 1. *a.* elaborado. **2.** *v.* elaborar; ampliar.

elapse, *v.* transcurrir; pasar.

elastic, *a. & n.* elástico *m.*

elasticity, *n.* elasticidad *f.*

elate, *v.* exaltar.

elation, *n.* exaltación *f.*

elbow, *n.* codo *m.*

elder, 1. *a.* mayor. **2.** *n.* anciano *m.*

elderly, *a.* de edad.

eldest, *a.* mayor.

elect, *v.* elegir.

election, *n.* elección *f.*

elective, *a.* electivo.

electorate, *n.* electorado *m.*

electric, electrical, *a.* eléctrico.

electrician, *n.* electricista *m.*

electricity, *n.* electricidad *f.*

electrocardiogram, *n.* electrocardiograma *m.*

electrocute, *v.* electrocutar.

electrode, *n.* electrodo *m.*

electrolysis, *n.* electrólisis *f.*

electron, *n.* electrón *m.*

electronics, *n.* electrónica *f.*

elegance, *n.* elegancia *f.*

elegant, *a.* elegante.

elegy, *n.* elegía *f.*

element, *n.* elemento *m.*

elemental, *a.* elemental.

elementary, *a.* elemental.

elephant, *n.* elefante *m.*

elevate, *v.* elevar.

elevation, *n.* elevación *f.*

elevator, *n.* ascensor *m.*

eleven, *a. & pron.* once.

eleventh, *a.* undécimo.

elf, *n.* duende *m.*

elicit, *v.* sacar; despertar.

eligibility, *n.* elegibilidad *f.*

eligible, *a.* elegible.

eliminate, *v.* eliminar.

elimination, *n.* eliminación *f.*

elixir, *n.* elixir *m.*

elk, *n.* alce *m.*, anta *f.*

elm, *n.* olmo *m.*

elocution, *n.* elocución *f.*

elongate, *v.* alargar.

elope, *v.* fugarse.

eloquence, *n.* elocuencia *f.*

eloquent, *a.* elocuente.

eloquently, *adv.* elocuentemente.

else, *adv.* más. **someone e.,** otra persona. **something e.,** otra cosa. **or e.,** de otro modo.

elsewhere, *adv.* en otra parte.

elucidate, *v.* elucidar.

elude, *v.* eludir.

elusive, *a.* evasivo.

emaciated, *a.* enflaquecido.

emanate, *v.* emanar.

emancipate, *v.* emancipar.

emancipation, *n.* emancipación *f.*

emancipator, *n.* libertador *m.*

embalm, *v.* embalsamar.

embankment, *n.* malecón, dique *m.*

embargo, *n.* embargo *m.*

embark, *v.* embarcar.

embarrass, *v.* avergonzar; turbar.

embarrassing, *a.* penoso, vergonzoso.

embarrassment, *n.* turbación; vergüenza *f.*

embassy, *n.* embajada *f.*

embellish, *v.* hermosear, embellecer.

embellishment, *n.* embellecimiento *m.*

embezzle, *v.* apropiarse dinero ilícitamente.

emblem, *n.* emblema *m.*

embody, *v.* incorporar.

embrace, 1. *n.* abrazo *m.* **2.** *v.* abrazar.

embroider, *v.* bordar.

embroidery, *n.* bordado *m.*

embryo, *n.* embrión *m.*

embryonic, *a.* embrionario.

emerald, *n.* esmeralda *f.*

emerge, *v.* salir.

emergency, *n.* emergencia *f.*

emergent, *a.* emergente.

emery, *n.* esmeril *m.*

emetic, *n.* emético *m.*

emigrant, *a.* & *n.* emigrante *m.* & *f.*

emigrate, *v.* emigrar.

emigration, *n.* emigración *f.*

eminence, *n.* altura; eminencia *f.*

eminent, *a.* eminente.

emissary, *n.* emisario *m.*

emission, *n.* emisión *f.*

emit, *v.* emitir.

emolument, *n.* emolumento *m.*

emotion, *n.* emoción *f.*

emotional, *a.* sensible.

emperor, *n.* emperador *m.*

emphasis, *n.* énfasis *m.* or *f.*

emphasize, *v.* acentuar, recalcar.

emphatic, *a.* enfático.

empire, *n.* imperio *m.*

empirical, *a.* empírico.

employ, *v.* emplear.

employee, *n.* empleado -da.

employer, *n.* patrón -ona.

employment, *n.* empleo *m.*

empower, *v.* autorizar.

emptiness, *n.* vaciedad; futilidad *f.*

empty, 1. *a.* vacío. 2. *v.* vaciar.

emulate, *v.* emular.

emulsion, *n.* emulsión *f.*

enable, *v.* capacitar; permitir.

enact, *v.* promulgar, decretar.

enactment, *n.* ley *f.*, estatuto *m.*

enamel, 1. *n.* esmalte *m.* 2. *v.* esmaltar.

enamored, *a.* enamorado.

enchant, *v.* encantar.

enchantment, *n.* encanto *m.*

encircle, *v.* circundar.

enclose, *v.* encerrar. **enclosed,** (in letter) adjunto.

enclosure, *n.* recinto *m.*; (in letter) incluso *m.*

encompass, *v.* circundar.

encounter, 1. *n.* encuentro *m.* 2. *v.* encontrar.

encourage, *v.* animar.

encouragement, *n.* estímulo *m.*

encroach, *v.* usurpar; meterse.

encyclical, *n.* encíclica *f.*

encyclopedia, *n.* enciclopedia *f.*

end, 1. *n.* fin, término, cabo; extremo; (aim) propósito *m.* 2. *v.* acabar; terminar.

endanger, *v.* poner en peligro.

endear, *v.* hacer querer.

endeavor, 1. *n.* esfuerzo *m.* 2. *v.* esforzarse.

ending, *n.* conclusión *f.*

endless, *a.* sin fin.

endorse, *v.* endosar; apoyar.

endorsement, *n.* endoso *m.*

endow, *v.* dotar, fundar.

endowment, *n.* dotación *f.*, fundación *f.*

endurance, *n.* resistencia *f.*

endure, *v.* soportar, resistir, aguantar.

enema, *n.* enema; lavativa *f.*

enemy, *n.* enemigo -ga.

energetic, *a.* enérgico.

energy, *n.* energía *f.*

enervate, *v.* enervar.

enervation, *n.* enervación *f.*

enfold, *v.* envolver.

enforce, *v.* ejecutar.

enforcement, *n.* ejecución *f.*

engage, *v.* emplear; ocupar.

engaged, (to marry) comprometido.

engagement, *n.* combate; compromiso; contrato *m.*; cita *f.*

engine, *n.* máquina *f.* (railroad) locomotora *f.*

engineer, *n.* ingeniero; maquinista *m.*

engineering, *n.* ingeniería *f.*

England, *n.* Inglaterra *f.*

English, *a.* & *n.* inglés *m.*

Englishman, *n.* inglés *m.*

Englishwoman, *n.* inglesa *f.*

engrave, *v.* grabar.

engraver, *n.* grabador *m.*

engraving, *n.* grabado *m.*

engross, *v.* absorber.

enhance, *v.* aumentar en valor; realzar.

enigma, *n.* enigma *m.*

enigmatic, *a.* enigmático.

enjoy, *v.* gozar de; disfrutar de. **e. oneself,** divertirse.

enjoyable, *a.* agradable.

enjoyment, *n.* goce *m.*

enlarge, *v.* agrandar; ampliar.

enlargement, *n.* ensanchamiento *m.*, ampliación *f.*

enlarger, *n.* amplificador *m.*

enlighten, *v.* informar.

enlightenment, *n.* esclarecimiento *m.*; cultura *f.*

enlist, *v.* reclutar; alistarse.

enlistment, *n.* alistamiento *m.*

enliven, *v.* avivar.

enmesh, v. entrampar.

enmity, n. enemistad f.

enormity, v. enormidad f.

enormous, a. enorme.

enough, n. & adv. bastante. **to be e.,** bastar.

enrage, v. enfurecer.

enrich, v. enriquecer.

enroll, v. registrar; matricularse.

enrollment, n. matriculación f.

ensign, n. bandera f.; (naval) sub-teniente m.

enslave, v. esclavizar.

ensue, v. seguir, resultar.

entail, v. envolver.

entangle, v. enredar.

enter, v. entrar.

enterprise, n. empresa f.

enterprising, a. emprendedor.

entertain, v. entretener; divertir.

entertainment, n. entretenimiento m.; diversión f.

enthrall, v. esclavizar.

enthusiasm, n. entusiasmo m.

enthusiast, n. entusiasta m. & f.

enthusiastic, a. entusiasmado.

entice, v. inducir.

entire, a. entero.

entirely, adv. enteramente.

entirety, n. totalidad f.

entitle, v. autorizar; (book) titular.

entity, n. entidad f.

entrails, n. entrañas f.pl.

entrance, n. entrada f.

entrant, n. competidor m.

entreat, v. rogar, suplicar.

entreaty, n. ruego m., súplica f.

entrench, v. atrincherar.

entrust, v. confiar.

entry, n. entrada f.; (com.) partida f.

enumerate, v. enumerar.

enumeration, n. enumeración f.

enunciate, v. enunciar.

enunciation, n. enunciación f.

envelop, v. envolver.

envelope, n. sobre m., cubierta f.

enviable, a. envidiable.

envious, a. envidioso.

environment, n. ambiente m.

environmentalist, n. activista ecológico, ecologista m.

environmental protection, protección del ambiente.

environs, n. alrededores m.

envoy, n. enviado m.

envy, 1. n. envidia f. **2.** v. envidiar.

eon, n. eón m.

ephemeral, a. efímero.

epic, 1. a. épico. **2.** n. epopeya f.

epicure, n. epicúreo m.

epidemic, 1. a. epidémico. **2.** n. epidemia f.

epidermis, n. epidermis f.

epigram, n. epigrama f.

epilepsy, n. epilepsia f.

epilogue, n. epílogo m.

episode, n. episodio m.

epistle, n. epístola f.

epitaph, n. epitafio m.

epithet, n. epíteto m.

epitome, n. epítome m.

epoch, n. época, era f.

equal, 1. a. & n. igual m. **2.** v. igualar; equivaler.

equality, n. igualdad f.

equalize, v. igualar.

equanimity, n. ecuanimidad f.

equate, v. igualar.

equation, n. ecuación f.

equator, n. ecuador m.

equatorial, n. & a. ecuatorial f.

equestrian, 1. n. jinete m. **2.** a. ecuestre.

equilibrium, n. equilibrio m.

equinox, n. equinoccio m.

equip, v. equipar.

equipment, n. equipo m.

equitable, a. equitativo.

equity, n. equidad, justicia f.

equivalent, a. & n. equivalente m.

equivocal, a. equívoco, ambiguo.

era, n. era, época, edad f.

eradicate, v. extirpar.

erase, v. borrar.

eraser, n. borrador m.

erasure, n. borradura f.

erect, 1. a. derecho, erguido. **2.** v. erigir.

erection, erectness, n. erección f.

ermine, n. armiño m.

erode, v. corroer.

erosion, n. erosión f.

erotic, a. erótico.

err, v. equivocarse.

errand, n. encargo, recado m.

errant, a. errante.

erratic, a. errático.

erroneous, a. erróneo.

error, n. error m.

erudite, a. erudito.

erudition, n. erudición f.

eruption, *n.* erupción, irrupción *f.*

escalate, *v.* realizar una escalada.

escalator, *n.* escalera mecánica *f.*

escapade, *n.* escapada *f.*; correría *f.*

escape, 1. *n.* fuga, huída *f.* **fire e.,** escalera de salvamento. **2.** *v.* escapar; fugarse.

eschew, *v.* evadir.

escort, 1. *n.* escolta *f.* **2.** *v.* escoltar.

escrow, *n.* plica *f.*

escutcheon, *n.* escudo de armas *m.*

esophagus, *n.* esófago *m.*

esoteric, *a.* esotérico.

especially, *adv.* especialmente.

espionage, *n.* espionaje *m.*

essay, *n.* ensayo *m.*

essayist, *n.* ensayista *f.*

essence, *n.* esencia *f.*; perfume *m.*

essential, *a.* esencial.

essentially, *adv.* esencialmente.

establish, *v.* establecer.

establishment, *n.* establecimiento *m.*

estate, *n.* estado *m.*; hacienda *f.*; bienes *m.pl.*

esteem, 1. *n.* estima *f.* **2.** *v.* estimar.

estimable, *a.* estimable.

estimate, 1. *n.* cálculo; presupuesto *m.* **2.** *v.* estimar.

estimation, *n.* estimación *f.*; cálculo *m.*

estrange, *v.* extrañar; enajenar.

estuary, *n.* estuario *m.*

etching, *n.* grabado al agua fuerte.

eternal, *a.* eterno.

eternity, *n.* eternidad *f.*

ether, *n.* éter *m.*

ethereal, *a.* etéreo.

ethical, *a.* ético.

ethics, *n.* ética *f.*

ethnic, *a.* étnico.

etiquette, *n.* etiqueta *f.*

etymology, *n.* etimología *f.*

eucalyptus, *n.* eucalipto *m.*

eugenic, *a.* eugenésico.

eugenics, *n.* eugenesia *f.*

eulogize, *v.* elogiar.

eulogy, *n.* elogio *m.*

eunuch, *n.* eunuco *m.*

euphonious, *a.* eufónico.

Europe, *n.* Europa *f.*

European, *a.* & *n.* europeo -pea.

euthanasia, *n.* eutanasia *f.*

evacuate, *v.* evacuar.

evade, *v.* evadir.

evaluate, *v.* avaluar.

evaluation, *n.* valoración *f.*

evangelist, *n.* evangelista *m.*

evaporate, *v.* evaporarse.

evaporation, *n.* evaporación *f.*

evasion, *n.* evasión *f.*

evasive, *a.* evasivo.

eve, *n.* víspera *f.*

even, 1. *a.* llano; igual. **2.** *adv.* aun; hasta. **not e.,** ni siquiera.

evening, *n.* noche, tarde *f.* **good e.,** buenas noches.

evenness, *n.* uniformidad *f.*

event, *n.* acontecimiento, suceso *m.*

eventful, *a.* memorable.

eventual, *a.* eventual.

ever, *adv.* alguna vez; (after *not*) nunca. **e. since,** desde que.

everlasting, *a.* eterno.

every, *a.* cada, todos los.

everybody, *pron.* todo el mundo; cada uno.

everyday, *a.* ordinario, de cada día.

everyone, *pron.* cada uno; cada cual; todos.

everything, *pron.* todo *m.*

everywhere, *adv.* por todas partes, en todas partes.

evict, *v.* expulsar.

eviction, *n.* evicción *f.*

evidence, *n.* evidencia *f.*

evident, *a.* evidente.

evidently, *adv.* evidentemente.

evil, 1. *a.* malo; maligno. **2.** *n.* mal *m.*

evince, *v.* revelar.

evoke, *v.* evocar.

evolution, *n.* evolución *f.*

evolve, *v.* desenvolver; desarrollar.

ewe, *n.* oveja *f.*

exact, 1. *a.* exacto. **2.** *v.* exigir.

exacting, *a.* exigente.

exactly, *adv.* exactamente.

exaggerate, *v.* exagerar.

exaggeration, *n.* exageración *f.*

exalt, *v.* exaltar.

exaltation, *n.* exaltación *f.*

examination, *n.* examen *m.*; (legal) interrogatorio *m.*

examine, *v.* examinar.

example, *n.* ejemplo *m.*

exasperate, *v.* exasperar.

exasperation, n. exasperación f.

excavate, v. excavar, cavar.

exceed, v. exceder.

exceedingly, adv. sumamente, extremadamente.

excel, v. sobresalir.

excellence, n. excelencia f.

Excellency, n. (title) Excelencia f.

excellent, a. excelente.

except, 1. prep. salvo, excepto. **2.** v. exceptuar.

exception, n. excepción f.

exceptional, a. excepcional.

excerpt, n. extracto.

excess, n. exceso m.

excessive, a. excesivo.

exchange, 1. n. cambio; canje m. **stock e.,** bolsa f. **telephone e.,** central telefónica. **2.** v. cambiar, canjear.

exchangeable, a. cambiable.

excise, 1. n. sisa f. **2.** v. extirpar.

excite, v. agitar; provocar; emocionar.

excitement, n. agitación, conmoción f.

exciting, a. emocionante.

exclaim, v. exclamar.

exclamation, n. exclamación f.

exclamation point or mark, n. punto de admiración m.

exclude, v. excluir.

exclusion, n. exclusión f.

exclusive, a. exclusivo.

excommunicate, v. excomulgar, descomulgar.

excommunication, n. excomunión f.

excrement, n. excremento m.

excruciating, a. penosísimo.

exculpate, v. justificar.

excursion, n. excursión f.; jira f.

excuse, 1. n. excusa f. **2.** v. excusar, perdonar; dispensar; disculpar.

execrable, a. execrable.

execute, v. ejecutar.

execution, n. ejecución f.

executioner, n. verdugo m.

executive, a. & n. ejecutivo m.

executor, n. testamentario m.

exemplary, a. ejemplar.

exemplify, v. ejemplificar.

exempt, 1. a. exento. **2.** v. exentar.

exercise, 1. n. ejercicio m. **2.** v. ejercitar.

exert, v. esforzar.

exertion, n. esfuerzo m.

exhale, v. exhalar.

exhaust, 1. n. (auto.) escape m. **2.** v. agotar.

exhaustion, n. agotamiento m.

exhaustive, a. agotador.

exhibit, 1. n. exhibición, exposición f. **2.** v. exhibir.

exhibition, n. exhibición f.

exhilarate, v. alegrar; estimular.

exhort, v. exhortar.

exhortation, n. exhortación f.

exhume, v. exhumar.

exigency, n. exigencia f., urgencia f.

exile, 1. n. destierro m., (person) desterrado m. **2.** v. desterrar.

exist, v. existir.

existence, n. existencia f.

existent, a. existente.

exit, n. salida f.

exodus, n. éxodo m.

exonerate, v. exonerar.

exorbitant, a. exorbitante.

exorcise, v. exorcizar.

exotic, a. exótico.

expand, v. dilatar; ensanchar.

expanse, n. espacio m.; extensión f.

expansion, n. expansión f.

expansive, a. expansivo.

expatiate, v. espaciarse.

expatriate, 1. n. & a. expatriado m. **2.** v. expatriar.

expect, v. esperar; contar con.

expectancy, n. esperanza f.

expectation, n. esperanza f.

expectorate, v. expectorar.

expediency, n. conveniencia f.

expedient, 1. a. oportuno. **2.** n. expediente m.

expedite, v. acelerar, despachar.

expedition, n. expedición f.

expel, v. expeler, expulsar.

expend, v. desembolsar, expender.

expenditure, n. desembolso; gasto m.

expense, n. gasto m.; costa f.

expensive, a. caro, costoso.

expensively, adv. costosamente.

experience, 1. n. experiencia f. **2.** v. experimentar.

experienced, *a.* experimentado, perito.

experiment, 1. *n.* experimento *m.* **2.** *v.* experimentar.

experimental, *a.* experimental.

expert, *a. & n.* experto *m.*

expiate, *v.* expiar.

expiration, *n.* expiración *f.*

expire, *v.* expirar; (com.) vencerse.

explain, *v.* explicar.

explanation, *n.* explicación *f.*

explanatory, *a.* explicativo.

expletive, 1. *n.* interjección *f.* **2.** *a.* expletivo.

explicit, *a.* explícito, claro.

explode, *v.* estallar, volar; refutar.

exploit, 1. *n.* hazaña *f.* **2.** *v.* explotar.

exploitation, *n.* explotación *f.*

exploration, *n.* exploración *f.*

exploratory, *a.* exploratorio.

explore, *v.* explorar.

explorer, *n.* explorador *m.*

explosion, *n.* explosión *f.*

explosive, *a.* explosivo.

export, 1. *n.* exportación *f.* **2.** *v.* exportar.

exportation, *n.* exportación *f.*

expose, *v.* exponer; descubrir.

exposition, *n.* exposición *f.*

expository, *a.* expositivo.

expostulate, *v.* altercar.

exposure, *n.* exposición *f.*

expound, *v.* exponer, explicar.

express, 1. *a. & n.* expreso *m.* **e. company,** compañía de porteo. **2.** *v.* expresar.

expression, *n.* expresión *f.*

expressive, *a.* expresivo.

expressly, *adv.* expresamente.

expressman, *n.* empresario de expresos *m.*

expropriate, *v.* expropriar.

expulsion, *n.* expulsión *f.*

expunge, *v.* borrar, expurgar.

expurgate, *v.* expurgar.

exquisite, *a.* exquisito.

extant, *a.* existente.

extemporaneous, *a.* improvisado.

extend, *v.* extender.

extension, *n.* extensión *f.*

extensive, *a.* extenso.

extensively, *adv.* por extenso.

extent, *n.* extensión *f.*; grado *m.*

to a certain e., hasta cierto punto.

extenuate, *v.* extenuar.

exterior, *a. & n.* exterior *m.*

exterminate, *v.* exterminar.

extermination, *n.* exterminio *m.*

external, *a.* externo, exterior.

extinct, *a.* extinto.

extinction, *n.* extinción *f.*

extinguish, *v.* extinguir, apagar.

extol, *v.* alabar.

extort, *v.* exigir dinero sin derecho.

extortion, *n.* extorsión *f.*

extra, 1. *a.* extraordinario; adicional. **2.** *n.* (newspaper) extra *m.*

extract, 1. *n.* extracto *m.* **2.** *v.* extraer.

extraction, *n.* extracción *f.*

extraneous, *a.* extraño; ajeno.

extraordinary, *a.* extraordinario.

extravagance, *n.* extravagancia *f.*

extravagant, *a.* extravagante.

extreme, *a. & n.* extremo *m.*

extremity, *n.* extremidad *f.*

extricate, *v.* desenredar.

exuberant, *a.* exuberante.

exude, *v.* exudar.

exult, *v.* regocijarse.

exultant, *a.* triunfante.

eye, 1. *n.* ojo *m.* **2.** *v.* ojear.

eyeball, *n.* globo del ojo.

eyebrow, *n.* ceja *f.*

eyeglasses, *n.* lentes *m.*

eyelash, *n.* pestaña *f.*

eyelid, *n.* párpado *m.*

eyesight, *n.* vista *f.*

F

fable, *n.* fábula; ficción *f.*

fabric, *n.* tejido *m.*, tela *f.*

fabricate, *v.* fabricar.

fabulous, *a.* fabuloso.

façade, *n.* fachada *f.*

face, 1. *n.* cara *f.* **to make faces,** hacer muecas. 2. encararse con. **f. the street,** dar a la calle.

facet, *n.* faceta *f.*

facetious, *a.* chistoso.

facial, 1. *n.* masaje facial *m.* **2.** *a.* facial.

facile, *a.* fácil.

facilitate, *v.* facilitar.

facility, *n.* facilidad *f.*

facsimile, n. facsímile m.

fact, n. hecho m. **in f.,** en realidad.

faction, n. facción f.

factor, n. factor m.

factory, n. fábrica f.

factual, a. verdadero.

faculty, n. facultad f.

fad, n. boga; novedad f.

fade, v. desteñirse; (flowers) marchitarse.

fail, 1. n. without f., sin falta. 2. v. fallar; fracasar. **not to f. to,** no dejar de.

failure, n. fracaso m.

faint, 1. a. débil; vago; pálido. 2. n. desmayo m. 3. v. desmayarse.

faintly, adv. débilmente; indistintamente.

fair, 1. a. razonable, justo; (hair) rubio; (weather) bueno. 2. n. feria f.

fairly, adv. imparcialmente; regularmente; claramente; bellamente.

fairness, n. justicia f.

fairy, n. hada f., duende m.

faith, n. fe; confianza f.

faithful, a. fiel.

fake, 1. a. falso; postizo. 2. n. imitación; estafa f. 3. v. imitar; fingir.

faker, n. imitador m.; farsante m.

falcon, n. halcón m.

fall, 1. n. caída; catarata f.; (season) otoño m.; (in price) baja f. 2. v. caer; bajar. **f. asleep,** dormirse; **f. in love,** enamorarse.

fallacious, a. falaz.

fallacy, n. falacia f.

fallible, a. falible.

fallout, n. precipitación resultante de una explosión nuclear.

fallow, a. sin cultivar.

false, a. falso; postizo.

falsehood, n. falsedad; mentira f.

falseness, n. falsedad, perfidia f.

falsetto, n. falsete m.

falsification, n. falsificación f.

falsify, v. falsificar.

falter, v. vacilar; (in speech) tartamudear.

fame, n. fama f.

familiar, a. familiar; conocido. **to be f. with,** estar familiarizado con.

familiarity, n. familiaridad f.

familiarize, v. familiarizar.

family, n. familia; especie naje m.

famine, n. hambre; carestía f.

famished, a. muerto de hambre.

famous, a. famoso, célebre.

fan, n. abanico; ventilador m. (sports) aficionado -da.

fanatic, a. & n. fanático -ca.

fanatical, a. fanático.

fanaticism, n. fanatismo m.

fanciful, a. caprichoso; fantástico.

fancy, 1. a. fino, elegante. **f. foods,** novedades f.pl. 2. n. fantasía f.; capricho m. 3. v. imaginar.

fanfare, n. fanfarria f.

fang, n. colmillo m.

fantastic, a. fantástico.

fantasy, n. fantasía f.

far, 1. a. lejano, distante. 2. adv. lejos. **how f.,** a qué distancia. **as f. as,** hasta. **so f., thus f.,** hasta aquí.

farce, n. farsa f.

fare, n. pasaje m.

farewell, 1. n. despedida f. **to say f.** despedirse. 2. interj. ¡adiós!

farfetched, a. forzado.

farm, 1. n. granja; hacienda f. 2. v. cultivar, labrar la tierra.

farmer, n. labrador, agricultor m.

farmhouse, n. hacienda, alquería f.

farming, n. agricultura f.; cultivo m.

fascinate, v. fascinar, embelesar.

fascination, n. fascinación f.

fascism, n. fascismo m.

fashion, 1. n. moda; costumbre; guisa f. 2. v. formar.

fashionable, a. de moda, en boga.

fast, 1. a. rápido, veloz; (watch) adelantado; (color) firme. 2. adv. ligero, de prisa. 3. n. ayuno m. 4. v. ayunar.

fasten, v. afirmar, atar; fijar.

fastener, n. asegurador m.

fastidious, a. melindroso.

fat, 1. a. gordo. 2. n. grasa, manteca f.

fatal, a. fatal.

fatality, n. fatalidad f.

fatally, adv. fatalmente.

fate, n. destino m.; suerte f.

fateful, a. fatal; ominoso.

father, n. padre m.

fatherhood, n. paternidad f.

father-in-law, n. suegro m.

fatherland, n. patria f.

fatherly, 1. a. paternal. **2.** adv. paternalmente.

fathom, 1. n. braza f. **2.** v. sondar; (fig.) penetrar en.

fatigue, 1. n. fatiga f., cansancio m. **2.** v. fatigar, cansar.

fatten, v. engordar, cebar.

faucet, n. grifo m., llave f.

fault, n. culpa f.; defecto m. **at f.,** culpable.

faultless, a. sin tacha, perfecto.

faultlessly, adv. perfectamente.

faulty, a. defectuoso, imperfecto.

favor, 1. n. favor m. **2.** v. favorecer.

favorable, a. favorable.

favorite, a. & n. favorito -ta.

favoritism, n. favoritismo m.

fawn, 1. n. cervato m. **2.** v. halagar, adular.

faze, v. desconcertar.

fear, 1. n. miedo, temor m. **2.** v. temer.

fearful, a. temeroso, medroso.

fearless, a. intrépido; sin temor.

fearlessness, n. intrepidez f.

feasible, a. factible.

feast, n. banquete m.; fiesta f.

feat, n. hazaña f.; hecho m.

feather, n. pluma f.

feature, 1. n. facción f.; rasgo m.; (movies) película principal. **2.** v. presentar como atracción especial.

February, n. febrero m.

federal, a. federal.

federation, n. confederación, federación f.

fee, n. honorarios m.pl.

feeble, a. débil.

feebleminded, a. imbécil.

feebleness, n. debilidad f.

feed, 1. n. pasto m. **2.** v. alimentar; dar de comer. **fed up with,** harto de.

feedback, n. feedback m., retroalimentación f.

feel, 1. n. sensación f. **2.** v. sentir; palpar. **f. like,** tener ganas de.

feeling, n. sensación; sensibilidad f.

feign, v. fingir.

felicitate, v. felicitar.

felicitous, a. feliz.

felicity, n. felicidad f., dicha f.

feline, a. felino.

fellow, n. compañero; socio m.; (coll.) tipo m.

fellowship, n. compañía, (for study) beca f.

felon, n. reo m., felón m.

felony, n. felonía f.

felt, n. fieltro m.

female, a. & n. hembra f.

feminine, a. femenino.

fence, 1. n. cerca f. **2.** v. cercar.

fender, n. guardabarros m.

ferment, 1. n. fermento m.; (fig.) agitación f. **2.** v. fermentar.

fermentation, n. fermentación f.

fern, n. helecho m.

ferocious, a. feroz; fiero.

ferociously, adv. ferozmente.

ferocity, n. ferocidad, fiereza f.

ferry, n. transbordador m., barca de transporte.

fertile, a. fecundo; (land) fértil.

fertility, n. fertilidad f.

fertilization, n. fertilización f.

fertilize, v. fertilizar, abonar.

fertilizer, n. abono m.

fervency, n. ardor m.

fervent, a. ferviente.

fervently, adv. fervorosamente.

fervid, a. férvido.

fervor, n. fervor m.

fester, v. ulcerarse.

festival, n. fiesta f.

festive, a. festivo.

festivity, n. festividad f.

festoon, 1. n. festón m. **2.** v. festonear.

fetch, v. ir por; traer.

fete, n. fiesta f. **2.** v. festejar.

fetid, a. fétido.

fetish, n. fetiche m.

fetter, 1. n. grillete m. **2.** v. engrillar.

fetus, n. feto m.

feud, n. riña f.; feudo m.

feudal, a. feudal.

feudalism, n. feudalismo m.

fever, n. fiebre f.

feverish, a. febril.

feverishly, adv. febrilmente.

few, a. pocos. **a. f.,** algunos, unos cuantos.

fiancé, fiancée, n. novio -via.

fiasco, n. fiasco m.

fiat, n. fiat m., orden f.

fib, 1. *n.* mentira *f.* **2.** *v.* mentir.

fiber, *n.* fibra *f.*

fibrous, *a.* fibroso.

fickle, *a.* caprichoso.

fickleness, *n.* inconstancia *f.*

fiction, *n.* ficción *f.;* (literature) novelas *f.pl.*

fictitious, *a.* ficticio.

fidelity, *n.* fidelidad *f.*

fidget, *v.* inquietar.

field, *n.* campo *m.*

fiend, *n.* demonio *m.*

fiendish, *a.* diabólico, malvado.

fierce, *a.* fiero, feroz.

fiery, *a.* ardiente.

fiesta, *n.* fiesta *f.*

fife, *n.* pífano *m.*

fifteen, *a.* & *pron.* quince.

fifteenth, *n.* & *a.* décimoquinto.

fifth, *a.* quinto.

fifty, *a.* & *pron.* cincuenta.

fig, *n.* higo *m.* **f. tree,** higuera *f.*

fight, 1. *n.* lucha, pelea *f.* **2.** *v.* luchar, pelear.

fighter, *n.* peleador -ra, luchador -ra.

figment, *n.* invención *f.*

figurative, *a.* metafórico.

figuratively, *adv.* figuradamente.

figure, 1. *n.* figura; cifra *f.* **2.** *v.* figurar; calcular.

filament, *n.* filamento m.

file, 1. *n.* archivo *m.;* (instrument) lima *f.;* (row) fila *f.* **2.** *v.* archivar; limar.

filial, *a.* filial.

filigree, *n.* filigrana *f.*

fill, *v.* llenar.

fillet, *n.* filete *m.*

filling, *n.* relleno *m.;* (dental) empastadura *f.* **f. station,** bomba *f.*

film, 1. *n.* película *f.,* film *m.* 2. *v.* filmar.

filter, 1. *n.* filtro *m.* **2.** *v.* filtrar.

filth, *n.* suciedad, mugre *f.*

filthy, *a.* sucio.

fin, *n.* aleta *f.*

final, 1. *a.* final, último. **2.** *n.* examen final. **finals,** (sports) final *f.*

finalist, *n.* finalista *f.*

finally, *adv.* finalmente.

finances, *n.* recursos, fondos *m.pl.*

financial, *a.* financiero.

financier, *n.* financiero m.

find, 1. *n.* hallazgo *m.* **2.** *v.* hallar;

encontrar. **f. out,** averiguar, enterarse, saber.

fine, 1. *a.* fino; bueno. **2.** *adv.* muy bien. **3.** *n.* multa *f.* **4.** *v.* multar.

finery, *n.* gala *f.,* adorno *m.*

finesse, 1. *n.* artificio *m.* **2.** *v.* valerse de artificio.

finger, *n.* dedo *m.*

finger bowl, *n.* enjuagatorio *m.*

fingernail, *n.* uña *f.*

fingerprint, 1. *n.* impresión digital *f.* **2.** *v.* tomar las impresiones digitales.

finicky, *a.* melindroso.

finish, 1. *n.* conclusión *f.* **2.** *v.* acabar, terminar.

finished, *a.* acabado.

finite, *a.* finito.

fir, *n.* abeto *m.*

fire, 1. *n.* fuego; incendio *m.* **2.** *v.* disparar, tirar; (coll.) despedir.

fire alarm, *n.* alarma de incendio *f.*

firearm, *n.* arma de fuego.

firecracker, *n.* triquitraque *m.,* buscapiés *m.,* petardo *m.*

fire engine, *n.* bomba de incendios *f.*

fire escape, *n.* escalera de incendios *f.*

fire extinguisher, *n.* matafuego *m.*

firefly, *n.* luciérnaga *f.*

fireman, *n.* bombero *m.;* (railway) fogonero *m.*

fireplace, *n.* hogar, fogón *m.*

fireproof, *a.* incombustible.

fireside, *n.* hogar *m.* fogón *m.*

fireworks, *n.* fuegos artificiales.

firm, 1. *a.* firme. **2.** *n.* casa de comercio.

firmness, *n.* firmeza *f.*

first, *a.* & *adv.* primero. **at f.,** al principio.

first aid, *n.* primeros auxilios *m.*

first-class, *a.* de primera clase.

fiscal, *a.* fiscal.

fish, 1. *n.* (food) pescado *m.;* (alive) pez *m.* **2.** *v.* pescar.

fisherman, *n.* pescador *m.*

fishhook, *n.* anzuelo *m.*

fishing, *n.* pesca *f.* **to go f.,** ir de pesca.

fishmonger, *n.* pescadero *m.*

fission, *n.* fisura *f.*

fissure, *n.* grieta *f.*, quebradura *f.*

fist, *n.* puño *m.*

fit, 1. *a.* capaz; justo. 2. *n.* corte, talle *m.;* (med.) convulsión *f.* 3. *v.* caber; quedar bien, sentar bien.

fitful, *a.* espasmódico; caprichoso.

fitness, *n.* aptitud; conveniencia *f.*

fitting, 1. *a.* conveniente. **to be f.,** convenir. 2. *n.* ajuste *m.*

five, *a.* & *pron.* cinco.

fix, 1. *n.* apuro *m.* 2. *v.* fijar; arreglar; componer, reparar.

fixation, *n.* fijación *f.;* fijeza *f.*

fixed, *a.* fijo.

fixture, *n.* instalación; guarnición *f.*

flabby, *a.* flojo.

flaccid, *a.* flojo; flácido.

flag, *n.* bandera *f.*

flagellant, *n.* & *a.* flagelante *m.*

flagon, *n.* frasco *m.*

flagrant, *a.* flagrante.

flagrantly, *adv.* notoriamente.

flair, *n.* afición *f.*

flake, 1. *n.* lámina *f.;* copo de nieve. 2. *v.* romperse en láminas.

flamboyant, *a.* flamante, llamativo.

flame, 1. *n.* llama *f.* 2. *v.* llamear.

flaming, *a.* llameante, flamante.

flamingo, *n.* flamenco *m.*

flank, 1. *n.* ijada *f.;* (mil.) flanco *m.* 2. *v.* flanquear.

flannel, *n.* franela *f.*

flap, 1. *n.* cartera *f.* 2. *v.* aletear; sacudirse.

flare, 1. *n.* llamarada *f.* 2. *v.* brillar; (fig.) enojarse.

flash, 1. *n.* resplandor *m.;* (lightning) rayo, relámpago *m.;* (fig.) instante *m.* 2. *v.* brillar.

flashcube, *n.* cubo de flash *m.*

flashlight, *n.* linterna eléctrica.

flashy, *a.* resplandeciente; ostentoso.

flask, *n.* frasco *m.*

flat, 1. *a.* llano; (tire) desinflado. 2. *n.* llanura *f.;* apartamento *m.*

flatness, *n.* llanura *f.*

flatten, *v.* aplastar, allanar; abatir.

flatter, *v.* adular, lisonjear.

flatterer, *n.* lisonjero -ra. zalamero -ra.

flattery, *n.* adulación, lisonja *f.*

flaunt, *v.* ostentar.

flavor, 1. *n.* sabor *m.* 2. *v.* sazonar.

flavoring, *n.* condimento *m.*

flaw, *n.* defecto *m.*

flax, *n.* lino *m.*

flay, *v.* despellejar; excoriar.

flea, *n.* pulga *f.*

fleck, 1. *n.* mancha *f.* 2. *v.* varetear.

flee, *v.* huir.

fleece, 1. *n.* vellón *m.* 2. *v.* esquilar.

fleet, 1. *a.* veloz. 2. *n.* flota *f.*

fleeting, *a.* fugaz, pasajero.

flesh, *n.* carne *f.*

fleshy, *a.* gordo; carnoso.

flex, 1. *n.* doblez *m.* 2. *v.* doblar.

flexibility, *n.* flexibilidad *f.*

flexible, *a.* flexible.

flier, *n.* aviador -ra.

flight, *n.* vuelo *m.;* fuga *f.*

flight attendant, *n.* azafata *f.;* ayudante de vuelo *m.*

flimsy, *a.* débil.

flinch, *v.* acobardarse.

fling, *v.* lanzar.

flint, *n.* pedernal *m.*

flip, *v.* lanzar.

flippant, *a.* impertinente.

flippantly, *adv.* impertinentemente.

flirt, 1. *n.* coqueta *f.* 2. *v.* coquetear, flirtear.

flirtation, *n.* coqueteo *m.*

float, *v.* flotar.

flock, 1. *n.* rebaño *m.* 2. *v.* congregarse.

flog, *v.* azotar.

flood, 1. *n.* inundación *f.* 2. *v.* inundar.

floor, 1. *n.* suelo, piso *m.* 2. *v.* derribar.

floral, *a.* floral.

florid, *a.* florido.

florist, *n.* florista *m.* & *f.*

flounce, 1. *n.* (sewing) volante *m.* 2. *v.* pernear.

flounder, *n.* rodaballo *m.*

flour, *n.* harina *f.*

flourish, 1. *n.* floreo *m.* 2. *v.* florecer; prosperar; blandir.

flow, 1. *n.* flujo *m.* 2. *v.* fluir.

flower, 1. *n.* flor *f.* 2. *v.* florecer.

flowerpot, *n.* maceta de flores *f.*

flowery, *a.* florido.

fluctuate, v. fluctuar.

fluctuation, n. fluctuación f.

flue, n. humero m.

fluency, n. fluidez f.

fluent, a. fluente.

fluffy, a. velloso.

fluid, a. & n. flúido m.

fluidity, n. fluidez f.

fluoroscope, n. fluoroscopio m.

flurry, n. agitación f.

flush, 1. a. bien provisto. **2.** n. sonrojo m. **3.** v. limpiar con un chorro de agua; sonrojarse.

flute, n. flauta f.

flutter, 1. n. agitación f. **2.** v. agitarse.

flux, n. flujo m.

fly, 1. n. mosca f. **2.** v. volar.

foam, 1. n. espuma f. **2.** v. espumar.

focal, a. focal.

focus, 1. n. enfoque m. **2.** v. enfocar.

fodder, n. forraje m.

foe, n. adversario -ria, enemigo -ga.

fog, n. niebla f.

foggy, a. brumoso.

foil, v. frustrar.

foist, v. emponer.

fold, 1. n. pliegue m. **2.** v. doblar, plegar.

folder, n. circular m.; (for filing) carpeta f.

foliage, n. follaje m.

folio, n. infolio; folio m.

folklore, n. folklore m.

folks, n. gente, familia f.

follicle, n. folículo m.

follow, v. seguir.

follower, n. partidario -ria.

folly, n. locura f.

foment, v. fomentar.

fond, a. cariñoso, tierno. **be f. of,** ser aficionado a.

fondle, v. acariciar.

fondly, adv. tiernamente.

fondness, n. afición f.; cariño m.

food, n. alimento m.; comida f.

foodstuffs, n.pl. comestibles, víveres m.pl.

fool, 1. n. tonto -ta; bobo -ba; bufón -ona. **2.** v. engañar.

foolhardy, a. temerario.

foolish, a. bobo, tonto, majadero.

foolproof, a. seguro.

foot, n. pie m.

footage, n. longitud en pies.

football, n. fúbol, balompié m.

foothold, n. posición establecida.

footing, n. base f.; fundamento m.

footlights, n.pl. luces del proscenio.

footnote, n. nota al pie de una página.

footprint, n. huella f.

footstep, n. paso m.

footstool, n. escañuelo m., banqueta f.

fop, n. petimetre m.

for, 1. prep. para; por. **as f.,** en cuanto a. **what f.,** ¿para qué? **2.** conj. porque, pues.

forage, 1. n. forraje m. **2.** v. forrajear.

foray, n. correría f.

forbear, v. cesar; abstenerse.

forbearance, n. paciencia f.

forbid, v. prohibir.

forbidding, a. repugnante.

force, 1. n. fuerza f. **2.** v. forzar.

forceful, a. fuerte; enérgico.

forcible, a. fuerte; enérgico.

ford, n. vado m. **2.** v. vadear.

fore, 1. a. delantero. **2.** n. delantera f.

fore and aft, de popa a proa.

forearm, n. antebrazo m.

forebears, n.pl. antepasados m.pl.

forebode, v. presagiar.

foreboding, n. presentimiento m.

forecast, 1. n. pronóstico m.; profecía f. **2.** v. pronosticar.

forecastle, n. (naut.) castillo de proa.

forefather, n. antepasado m.

forefinger, n. índice m.

forego, v. renunciar.

foregone, a. predeterminado.

foreground, n. primer plano.

forehead, n. frente f.

foreign, a. extranjero.

foreign aid, ayuda exterior.

foreigner, n. extranjero -ra; forastero -ra.

foreleg, n. pierna delantera.

foreman, n. capataz m.

foremost, 1. a. primero. **2.** adv. er primer lugar.

forenoon, n. mañana f.

forensic, a. forense.

forerunner, n. precursor -ra.

foresee, v. prever.

foreshadow, v. prefigurar, anunciar.

foresight, n. previsión f.

forest, n. bosque m.; selva f.

forestall, v. anticipar; prevenir.

forester, n. silvicultor; guardamonte m.

forestry, n. silvicultura f.

foretell, v. predecir.

forever, adv. por siempre, para siempre.

forevermore, adv. siempre.

forewarn, v. advertir, avisar.

foreword, n. prefacio m.

forfeit, 1. n. prenda, multa f. **2.** v. perder.

forfeiture, n. decomiso m., multa f.

forgather, v. reunirse.

forge, 1. n. fragua f. **2.** forjar; falsear.

forger, n. forjador; falsificador m.

forgery, n. falsificación f.

forget, v. olvidar.

forgetful, a. olvidadizo.

forgive, v. perdonar.

forgiveness, n. perdón m.

fork, 1. n. tenedor m.; bifurcación f. **2.** v. bifurcarse.

forlorn, a. triste.

form, 1. n. forma f.; (document) formulario m. **2.** v. formar.

formal, a. formal; ceremonioso. **f. dance,** baile de etiqueta. **f. dress,** traje de etiqueta.

formality, n. formalidad f.

formally, adv. formalmente.

format, n. formato m.

formation, n. formación f.

formative, a. formativo.

former, a. anterior; antiguo. **the f.,** aquél.

formerly, adv. antiguamente.

formidable, a. formidable.

formless, a. sin forma.

formula, n. fórmula f.

formulate, v. formular.

formulation, n. formulación f.; expresión f.

forsake, v. abandonar.

fort, n. fortaleza f.; fuerte m.

forte, a. & adv. (mus.) forte, fuerte.

forth, adv. adelante. **back and f.,** de aquí allá. **and so f.,** etcétera.

forthcoming, a. futuro, próximo.

forthright, a. franco.

forthwith, adv. inmediatamente.

fortification, n. fortificación f.

fortify, v. fortificar.

fortissimo, a. & adv. (mus.) fortisimo.

fortitude, n. fortaleza; fortitud f.

fortnight, n. quincena f.

fortress, n. fuerte m., fortaleza f.

fortuitous, a. fortuito.

fortunate, a. afortunado.

fortune, n. fortuna f.; suerte f.

fortune-teller, n. sortílego, adivino m.

forty, a. & pron. cuarenta.

forum, n. foro m.

forward, 1. a. delantero; atrevido. **2.** adv. adelante. **3.** v. trasmitir, reexpedir.

foster, 1. a. **f. child,** hijo adoptivo. **2.** v. fomentar, criar.

foul, a. sucio; impuro.

found, v. fundar.

foundation, n. fundación f.; (of building) cimientos m.pl.

founder, 1. n. fundador -ra. **2.** v. irse a pique.

foundry, n. fundición f.

fountain, n. fuente f.

four, a. & pron. cuatro.

fourteen, a. & pron. catorce.

fourth, a. & n. cuarto m.

fowl, n. ave f.

fox, n. zorro -rra.

fox trot, n. foxtrot m.

foxy, a. astuto.

foyer, n. salón de entrada.

fracas, n. riña f.

fraction, n. fracción f.

fracture, 1. n. fractura, rotura f. **2.** v. fracturar, romper.

fragile, a. frágil.

fragment, n. fragmento, trozo m.

fragmentary, a. fragmentario.

fragrance, n. fragancia f.

fragrant, a. fragante.

frail, a. débil, frágil.

frailty, n. debilidad, fragilidad f.

frame, 1. n. marco; armazón f.; cuadro, cuerpo m. **2.** v. fabricar; formar; encuadrar.

frame-up, n. (coll.) conspiración f.

framework, n. armazón m.

France, n. Francia f.

franchise, n. franquicia f.

frank, 1. a. franco. **2.** n. carta franca. **3.** v. franquear.

frankfurter, n. salchicha f.

frankly, adv. francamente.

frankness, n. franqueza f.

frantic, a. frenético.

fraternal, a. fraternal.

fraternity, n. fraternidad f.

fraternization, n. fraternización f.

fraternize, v. confraternizar.

fratricide, n. fratricida m. & f.

fraud, n. fraude m.

fraudulent, a. fraudulento.

fraudulently, adv. fraudulenta-mente.

fraught, a. cargado.

freak, n. rareza f.

freckle, n. peca f.

free, 1. a. libre; gratis. **2.** v. liber-tar, librar.

freedom, n. libertad f.

freeze, v. helar, congelar.

freezer, n. heladora f.

freight, 1. n. carga f.; flete m. **2.** v. cargar; fletar.

freighter, n. (naut.) fletador m.

French, a. & n. francés m.

Frenchman, n. francés m.

frenzied, a. frenético.

frenzy, n. frenesí m.

frequency, n. frecuencia f.

frequency modulation, modula-ción de frequencia.

frequent, a. frecuente.

frequently, adv. frecuentemente.

fresco, n. pintura al fresco.

fresh, a. fresco. **f. water,** agua dulce.

freshen, v. refrescar.

freshness, n. frescura f.

fret, v. quejarse, irritarse.

fretful, a. irritable.

fretfully, adv. de mala gana.

fretfulness, n. mal humor.

friar, n. fraile m.

fricassee, n. fricasé m.

friction, n. fricción f.

Friday, n. viernes m. **Good F.,** Viernes Santo.

fried, a. frito.

friend, n. amigo -ga.

friendless, a. sin amigos.

friendliness, a. amistad f.

friendly, a. amistoso.

friendship, n. amistad f.

fright, n. susto m.

frighten, v. asustar, espantar.

frightful, a. espantoso.

frigid, a. frígido, frío.

frill, n. (sewing) lechuga f.

fringe, n. fleco; borde m.

frisky, a. retozón.

fritter, n. fritura f.

frivolity, n. frivolidad f.

frivolous, a. frívolo.

frivolousness, n. frivolidad f.

frock, n. vestido de mujer. **f. coat,** levita f.

frog, n. rana f.

frolic, 1. n. retozo m. **2.** v. retozar.

from, prep. de; desde.

front, n. frente; (of building) fa-chada f. **in f. of,** delante de.

frontal, a. frental.

frontier, n. frontera f.

frost, n. helada, escarcha f.

frosty, a. helado.

froth, n. espuma f.

frown, 1. n. ceño m. **2.** v. fruncir el entrecejo.

frowzy, a. desaliñado.

frozen, a. helado; congelado.

fructify, v. fructificar.

frugal, a. frugal.

frugality, n. frugalidad f.

fruit, n. fruta f.; (benefits) frutos m.pl. **f. tree,** árbol frutal.

fruitful, a. productivo.

fruition, n. fruición f.

fruitless, a. inútil, vano.

frustrate, v. frustrar.

frustration, n. frustración f.

fry, v. freír.

fuel, n. combustible m.

fugitive, a. & n. fugitivo -va.

fugue, n. (mus.) fuga f.

fulcrum, n. fulcro m.

fulfill, v. cumplir.

fulfillment, n. cumplimiento m.; realización f.

full, a. lleno; completo; pleno.

fullness, n. plenitud f.

fulminate, v. volar; fulminar.

fulmination, n. fulminación, de-tonación f.

fumble, v. chapucear.

fume, 1. n. humo m. **2.** v. humear.

fumigate, v. fumigar.

fumigator, n. fumigador m.

fun, n. diversión f. **to make f. of,** burlarse de. **to have f.,** divertirse.

function, 1. n. función f. **2.** v. fun-cionar.

functional, a. funcional.

fund, n. fondo m.
fundamental, a. fundamental.
funeral, n. funeral m.
fungus, n. hongo m.
funnel, n. embudo m.; (of ship) chimenea f.
funny, a. divertido, gracioso. **to be f.,** tener gracia.
fur, n. piel f.
furious, a. furioso.
furlough, n. permiso m.
furnace, n. horno m.
furnish, v. surtir, proveer; (a house) amueblar.
furniture, n. muebles m.pl.
furrow, 1. n. surco m. 2. v. surcar.
further, 1. a. & adv. más. 2. v. adelantar, fomentar.
furthermore, adv. además.
fury, n. furor m.; furia f.
fuse, 1. n. fusible m. 2. v. fundir.
fuss, 1. n. alboroto f. 2. v. preocuparse por pequeñeces.
fussy, a. melindroso.
futile, a. fútil.
future, 1. a. futuro. 2. n. porvenir m.
futurology, n. futurología f.

G

gag, n. chiste m.
gaiety, n. alegría f.
gain, 1. n. ganancia f. 2. v. ganar.
gait, n. paso m.
gale, n. ventarrón m.
gall, n. hiel f.; (fig.) amargura f.; descaro m.
gallant, 1. a. galante. 2. n. galán m.
gallery, n. galería f.; (theat.) paraíso m.
gallon, n. galón m.
gallop, 1. n. galope m. 2. v. galopar.
gallows, n. horca f.
gamble, 1. n. riesgo m. 2. v. jugar; aventurar.
game, n. juego m.; (match) partida f.; (hunting) caza f.
gang, n. cuadrilla f.; pandilla f.
gangster, n. rufián m.
gap, n. raja f.
gape, v. boquear.
garage, n. garaje m.
garbage, n. basura f.

garden, n. jardín m.; (vegetable) huerta f.
gardener, n. jardinero -ra.
gargle, 1. n. gárgara f. 2. v. gargarizar.
garland, n. guirnalda f.
garlic, n. ajo m.
garment, n. prenda de vestir.
garrison, n. guarnición f.
garter, n. liga f.; ataderas f.pl.
gas, n. gas m.
gasohol, n. gasohol m.
gasoline, n. gasolina f.
gasp, 1. n. boqueada f. 2. v. boquear.
gate, n. puerta; entrada f.
gather, v. recoger; inferir; reunir.
gaudy, a. brillante; llamativo.
gauge, 1. n. manómetro, indicador m. 2. v. medir; estimar.
gaunt, a. flaco.
gauze, n. gasa f.
gay, 1. a. alegre; homosexual. 2. n. homosexual.
gaze, 1. n. mirada f. 2. v. mirar con fijeza.
gear, n. engranaje m. **in g.,** en juego.
gem, n. joya f.
gender, n. género m.
general, a. & n. general m.
generality, n. generalidad f.
generalize, v. generalizar.
generation, n. generación f.
generator, n. generador m.
generosity, n. generosidad f.
generous, a. generoso.
genial, a. genial.
genius, n. genio m.
gentle, a. suave; manso; benigno.
gentleman, n. señor, caballero m.
gentleness, n. suavidad f.
genuine, a. genuino.
genuineness, n. pureza f.
geographical, a. geográfico.
geography, n. geografía f.
geometric, a. geométrico.
geranium, n. geranio m.
germ, n. germen; microbio m.
German, a. & n. alemán -mana.
Germany, n. Alemania f.
gesticulate, v. gesticular.
gesture, 1. n. gesto m. 2. v. gesticular, hacer gestos.
get, v. obtener; conseguir; (become) ponerse. **go and g.,** ir a

buscar; **g. away,** irse; escaparse; **g. together,** reunirse; **g. on,** subir; **g. off,** bajar; **g. up,** levantarse; **g. there,** llegar.

ghastly, a. pálido; espantoso.

ghost, n. espectro, fantasma m.

giant, n. gigante m.

gift, n. regalo, don; talento m.

gild, v. dorar.

gin, n. ginebra f.

ginger, n. jengibre m.

gingerbread, n. pan de jengibre.

gingham, n. guinga f.

gird, v. ceñir.

girdle, n. faja f.

girl, n. muchacha, niña, chica f.

give, v. dar; regalar. **g. back,** devolver. **g. up,** rendirse; renunciar.

giver, n. dador -ra; donador -ra.

glacier, n. ventisquero m.

glad, a. alegre, contento. **to be g.,** alegrarse.

gladly, adj. con mucho gusto.

gladness, n. alegría f.; placer m.

glamor, n. encanto m.; elegancia f.

glamorous, a. encantador, elegante.

glance, 1. n. vistazo m., ojeada f. **2.** v. ojear.

gland, n. glándula f.

glare, 1. n. reflejo; brillo m. **2.** v. deslumbrar; echar miradas indignadas.

glass, n. vidrio; vaso m.; **(eyeglasses),** lentes anteojos m.pl.

gleam, 1. n. fulgor m. **2.** v. fulgurar.

glee, n. alegría f.; júbilo m.

glide, v. deslizarse.

glimpse, 1. n. vistazo m. **2.** v. ojear.

glisten, 1. n. brillo m. **2.** v. brillar.

glitter, 1. n. resplandor m. **2.** v. brillar.

globe, n. globo; orbe m.

gloom, n. oscuridad; tristeza f.

gloomy, a. oscuro; sombrío, triste.

glorify, v. glorificar.

glorious, a. glorioso.

glory, n. gloria, fama f.

glossary, n. glosario m.

glove, n. guante m.

glow, 1. n. fulgor m. **2.** v. relucir; arder.

glue, 1. n. cola f. **2.** v. encolar, pegar.

glum, a. de mal humor.

glutton, n. glotón -ona.

gnaw, v. roer.

go, v. ir, irse. **g. away,** irse, marcharse. **g. back,** volver, regresar. **g. down,** bajar. **g. in,** entrar. **g. on,** seguir. **g. out,** salir. **g. up,** subir.

goal, n. meta f.; objeto m.

goat, n. cabra f.

goblet, n. copa f.

God, n. Dios m.

gold, n. oro m.

golden, a. áureo.

good, 1. a. bueno. **2.** n. bien m.pl.; **(com.)** géneros m.pl.

good-bye, 1. n. adiós m. **2.** interj. ¡adiós!; ¡hasta la vista!; ¡hasta luego! **to say g. to,** despedirse de.

goodness, n. bondad f.

goose, n. ganso m.

gooseberry, n. uva crespa f.

gooseneck, 1. n. cuello de cisne m. **2.** a. curvo.

goose step, n. paso de ganso m.

gore, 1. n. sangre f. **2.** v. acornear.

gorge, 1. n. gorja f. **2.** v. engullir.

gorgeous, a. magnífico; precioso.

gorilla, n. gorila f.

gory, a. sangriento.

gosling, n. gansarón m.

gospel, n. evangelio m.

gossamer, 1. n. telaraña f. **2.** a. delgado.

gossip, 1. n. chisme m. **2.** v. chismear.

Gothic, a. gótico.

gouge, 1. n. gubia f. **2.** v. escoplear.

gourd, n. calabaza f.

gourmand, n. glotón m.

gourmet, a. gastrónomo -ma.

govern, v. gobernar.

governess, n. aya, institutriz f.

government, n. gobierno m.

governmental, a. gubernamental.

governor, n. gobernador m.

governorship, n. gobernatura f.

gown, n. vestido m. **dressing g.,** bata f.

grab, v. agarrar, arrebatar.

grace, n. gracia; gentileza; merced f.

graceful, *a.* agraciado.

graceless, *a.* réprobo.

gracious, *a.* gentil, cortés.

grackle, *n.* grajo *m.*

grade, 1. *n.* grado; nivel *m.;* pendiente; nota; calidad *f.* 2. *v.* graduar.

grade crossing, *n.* paso a nivel *m.*

gradual, *a.* gradual.

gradually, *adv.* gradualmente.

graduate, 1. *n.* graduado -da, diplomado -da. 2. *v.* graduar; diplomarse.

graft, 1. *n.* injerto *m.;* soborno público. 2. *v.* injertar.

graham, *a.* centeno; acemita.

grail, *n.* grial *m.*

grain, *n.* grano; cereal *m.*

grain alcohol, *n.* alcohol de madera *m.*

gram, *n.* gramo *m.*

grammar, *n.* gramática *f.*

grammarian, *n.* gramático *m.*

grammar school, *n.* escuela elemental *f.*

grammatical, *a.* gramatical.

gramophone, *n.* gramófono *m.*

granary, *n.* granero *m.*

grand, *a.* grande, ilustre; estupendo.

grandchild, *n.* nieto -ta.

granddaughter, *n.* nieta *f.*

grandee, *n.* noble *m.*

grandeur, *n.* grandeza *f.*

grandfather, *n.* abuelo *m.*

grandiloquent, *a.* grandílocuo.

grandiose, *a.* grandioso.

grand jury, *n.* gran jurado *m.*

grandly, *adv.* grandiosamente.

grandmother, *n.* abuela *f.*

grand opera, *n.* ópera grande *f.*

grandparents, *n.* abuelos *m.pl.*

grandson, *n.* nieto *m.*

grandstand, *n.* andanada *f.,* tribuna *f.*

grange, *n.* granja *f.*

granger, *n.* labriego *m.*

granite, *n.* granito *m.*

granny, *n.* abuelita *f.*

grant, 1. *n.* concesión; subvención *f.* 2. *v.* otorgar; conceder; conferir. take for granted, tomar por cierto.

granular, *a.* granular.

granulate, *v.* granular.

granulation, *n.* granulación *f.*

granule, *n.* gránulo *m.*

grape, *n.* uva *f.*

grapefruit, *n.* toronja *f.*

grapeshot, *n.* metralla *f.*

grapevine, *n.* vid; parra *f.*

graph, *n.* gráfia *f.*

graphic, *a.* gráfico.

graphite, *n.* grafito *m.*

graphology, *n.* grafología *f.*

grapple, *v.* agarrar.

grasp, 1. *n.* puño; poder; conocimiento *m.* 2. *v.* empuñar agarrar; comprender.

grasping, *a.* codicioso.

grass, *n.* hierba *f.;* (marijuana) marijuana *f.*

grasshopper, *n.* saltamontes *m.*

grassy, *a.* herboso.

grate, *n.* reja *f.*

grateful, *a.* agradecido.

gratify, *v.* satisfacer.

grating, 1. *n.* enrejado *m.* 2. *a.* discordante.

gratis, *adv. & a.* gratis.

gratitude, *n.* agradecimiento *m.*

gratuitous, *adv.* gratismente.

gratuity, *n.* propina *f.*

grave, 1. *a.* grave. 2. *n.* sepultura; tumba *f.*

gravel, *n.* cascajo *m.*

gravely, *adv.* gravemente.

gravestone, *n.* lápida sepulcral *f.*

graveyard, *n.* cementerio *m.*

gravitate, *v.* gravitar.

gravitation, *n.* gravitación *f.*

gravity, *n.* gravedad; seriedad *f.*

gravure, *n.* grabado *m.*

gravy, *n.* salsa *f.*

gray, *a.* gris; (hair) cano.

grayish, *a.* pardusco.

gray matter, *n.* substancia gris *f.*

graze, *v.* rozar; (cattle) pastar.

grazing, *a.* pastando.

grease, 1. *n.* grasa *f.* 2. *v.* engrasar.

greasy, *a.* grasiento.

great, *a.* grande, ilustre; estupendo.

Great Dane, *n.* mastín danés *m.*

greatness, *n.* grandeza *f.*

Greece, *n.* Grecia *f.*

greed, greediness, *n.* codicia, voracidad *f.*

greedy, *a.* voraz.

Greek, *a. & n.* griego -ga.

green, *a. & n.* verde *m.* greens, *n.* verduras *f.pl.*

greenery, *n.* verdor *m.*

greenhouse, n. invernáculo m.

greet, v. saludar.

greeting, n. saludo m.

gregarious, a. gregario.

grenade, n. granada; bomba f.

greyhound, n. galgo m.

grid, n. parrilla f.

griddle, n. tortera f.

griddlecake, n. tortita de harina f.

gridiron, n. parrilla f., campo de fútbol m.

grief, n. dolor m.; pena f.

grievance, n. pesar; agravio m.

grieve, v. afligir.

grievous, a. penoso.

grill, 1. n. parrilla f. 2. v. asar a la parrilla.

grillroom, n. restaurante de servicio rápido m.

grim, a. ceñudo.

grimace, 1. n. mueca f. 2. v. hacer muecas.

grime, n. mugre f.

grimy, a. sucio; mugroso.

grin, 1. n. sonrisa f. 2. v. sonreír.

grind, v. moler; afilar.

grindstone, n. esmeriladora f.

gringo, n. gringo; yanqui m.

grip, 1. n. maleta f. 2. v. agarrar.

gripe, 1. v. agarrar. 2. n. asimiento m., opresión f.

grippe, n. gripe f.

grisly, a. espantoso.

grist, n. molienda f.

gristle, n. cartílago m.

grit, n. arena f., entereza f.

grizzled, a. tordillo.

groan, 1. n. gemido m. 2. v. gemir.

grocer, n. abacero m.

grocery, n. tienda de comestibles, bodega f.

grog, n. brebaje m.

groggy, a. medio borracho; vacilante.

groin, n. ingle f.

groom, n. (of horses) establero; (at wedding) novio m.

groove, 1. n. estria f. 2. v. acanalar.

grope, v. tentar; andar a tientas.

gross, 1. a. grueso; grosero. 2. n. gruesa f.

grossly, adv. groseramente.

grossness, n. grosería f.

grotesque, a. grotesco.

grotto, n. gruta f.

grouch, n. gruñón; descontento m.

ground, n. tierra f.; terreno; suelo; campo; fundamento m.

groundhog, n. marmota f.

groundless, a. infundado.

groundwork, n. base f., fundamento m.

group, 1. n. grupo m. 2. v. agrupar.

groupie, n. muchacha que acompaña a un grupo de música moderna.

grouse, n. chachalaca f.

grove, n. arboleda f.

grovel, v. rebajarse; envilecerse.

grow, v. crecer; cultivar.

growl, 1. n. gruñido m. 2. v. gruñir.

grown, a. crecido; desarrollado.

grownup, n. adulto m.

growth, n. crecimiento m.; vegetación f.; (med.) tumor m.

grub, n. gorgojo m., larva f.

grubby, a. guasarapiento.

grudge, n. rencor m. **bear a g.,** guardar rencor.

gruel, 1. n. atole m. 2. v. estropear.

gruesome, a. horripilante.

gruff, a. ceñudo.

grumble, v. quejarse.

grumpy, a. gruñón; quejoso.

grunt, v. gruñir.

guarantee, 1. n. garantía f. 2. v. garantizar.

guarantor, n. fiador m.

guaranty, n. garantía f.

guard, 1. n. guardia m. or f. 2. v. vigilar.

guarded, a. cauteloso.

guardhouse, n. prisión militar f.

guardian, n. guardián m.

guardianship, n. tutela f.

guardsman, n. centinela m.

guava, n. guayaba f.

gubernatorial, a. gubernativo.

guerrilla, n. guerrillero m.

guess, 1. n. conjetura f. 2. v. adivinar; (coll.) creer.

guesswork, n. conjetura f.

guest, n. huésped m. & f.

guffaw, n. risotada f.

guidance, n. dirección f.

guide, 1. n. guía m. & f. 2. v. guiar.

guidebook, *n.* guía *f.*
guidepost, *n.* poste indicador *m.*
guild, *n.* gremio *m.*
guile, *n.* engaño *m.*
guillotine, 1. *n.* guillotina *f.* **2.** *v.* guillotinar.
guilt, *n.* culpa *f.*
guiltily, *adv.* culpablemente.
guiltless, *a.* inocente.
guilty, *a.* culpable.
guinea fowl, *n.* gallina de Guinea *f.*
guinea pig, *n.* cobayo *m.*
guise, *n.* modo *m.*
guitar, *n.* guitarra *f.*
gulch, *n.* quebrada *f.*
gulf, *n.* golfo *m.*
gull, *n.* gaviota *f.*
gullet, *n.* esófago *m.*; zanja *f.*
gullible, *a.* crédulo.
gully, *n.* barranca *f.*
gulp, 1. *n.* trago *m.* **2.** *v.* tragar.
gum, 1. *n.* goma *f.*; (anat.) encía *f.* chewing g., chicle *m.* **2.** *v.* engomar.
gumbo, *n.* quimbombó *m.*
gummy, *a.* gomoso.
gun, *n.* fusil; cañón *m.*
gunboat, *n.* cañonero *m.*
gunman, *n.* bandido *m.*
gunner, *n.* artillero *m.*
gunpowder, *n.* pólvora *f.*
gunshot, *n.* escopetazo *m.*
gunwale, *n.* borda *f.*
gurgle, 1. *n.* gorgoteo *m.* **2.** *v.* gorgotear.
guru, *n.* gurú *m.*
gush, 1. *n.* chorro *m.* **2.** *v.* brotar, chorrear.
gusher, *n.* pozo de chorro de petróleo *m.*
gust, *n.* soplo *m.*; ráfaga *f.*
gustatory, *a.* del sentido del gusto.
gusto, *n.* gusto; placer *m.*
gusty, *a.* borrascoso.
gut, *n.* intestino *m.*, tripa *f.*
gutter, *n.* canal; zanja *f.*
guttural, *a.* gutural.
guy, *n.* tipo *m.*
guzzle, *v.* engullir; tragar.
gym, *n.* gimnasio *m.*
gymnasium, *n.* gimnasio *m.*
gymnast, *n.* gimnasta *m.*
gymnastic, *a.* gimnástico.
gymnastics, *n.* gimnasia *f.*
gynecology, *n.* ginecología *f.*

gypsum, *n.* yeso *m.*
Gypsy, *a.* & *n.* gitano -na.
gyrate, *v.* girar.
gyroscope, *n.* giroscopio *m.*

H

habeas corpus, *n.* habeas corpus *m.*
haberdasher, *n.* camisero *m.*
haberdashery, *n.* camisería *f.*
habiliment, *n.* vestuario *m.*
habit, *n.* costumbre *f.*, hábito *m.* be in the h. of, estar acostumbrado a; soler.
habitable, *a.* habitable.
habitat, *n.* habitación *f.*, ambiente *m.*
habitation, *n.* habitación *f.*
habitual, *a.* habitual.
habituate, *v.* habituar.
habitué, *n.* parroquiano *m.*
hack, 1. *n.* coche de alquiler. **2.** *v.* tajar.
hackneyed, *a.* trillado.
hacksaw, *n.* sierra para cortar metal *f.*
haddock, *n.* merluza *f.*
haft, *n.* mango *m.*
hag, *n.* bruja *f.*
haggard, *a.* trasnochado.
haggle, *v.* regatear.
hail, 1. *n.* granizo; (greeting) saludo *m.* **2.** *v.* granizar; saludar.
Hail Mary, *n.* Ave María *f.*
hailstone, *n.* piedra de granizo *f.*
hailstorm, *n.* granizada *f.*
hair, *n.* pelo; cabello *m.*
haircut, *n.* corte de pelo.
hairdo, *n.* peinado *m.*
hairdresser, *n.* peluquero *m.*
hairpin, *n.* horquilla *f.*; gancho *m.*
hair's-breadth, *n.* ancho de un pelo *m.*
hairspray, *n.* aerosol para cabello.
hairy, *a.* peludo.
halcyon, 1. *n.* alcedón *m.* **2.** *a.* tranquilo.
hale, *a.* sano.
half, 1. *a.* medio. **2.** *n.* mitad *f.*
half-and-half, *a.* mitad y mitad.
half-baked, *a.* medio crudo.
half-breed, *n.* mestizo *m.*

half brother, n. medio hermano m.

half-hearted, a. sin entusiasmo.

half-mast, a. & n. media asta m.

halfpenny, n. media penique m.

halfway, adv. a medio camino.

half-wit, n. bobo m.

halibut, n. hipogloso m.

hall, n. corredor m.; (for assembling) sala f. **city h.,** ayuntamiento m.

hallmark, n. marca del contraste f.

hallow, v. consagrar.

Halloween, n. víspera de Todos los Santos f.

hallucination, n. alucinación f.

hallway, n. pasadizo m.

halo, n. halo m.; corona f.

halt, 1. a cojo. **2.** n. parada f. **3.** v. parar. **4.** interj. ¡alto!

halter, n. cabestro m.

halve, v. dividir en dos partes.

halyard, n. driza f.

ham, n. jamón m.

hamburger, n. albóndiga f.

hamlet, n. aldea f.

hammer, 1. n. martillo m. **2.** v. martillar.

hammock, n. hamaca f.

hamper, n. canasta f., cesto m.

hamstring, 1. n. tendón de la corva m. **2.** v. desjarretar.

hand, 1. mano f. **on the other h.,** en cambio. **2.** v. pasar. **h. over,** entregar.

handbag, n. cartera f.

handball, n. pelota f.

handbook, n. manual m.

handcuff, n. esposas f.

handful, n. puñado m.

handicap, n. desventaja f.

handicraft, n. artífice m.

handiwork, n. artefacto m.

handkerchief, n. pañuelo m.

handle, 1. n. mango m. **2.** v. manejar.

handmade, n. hecho a mano m.

handmaid, n. criada de mano f.

hand organ, n. organillo m.

handsome, a. guapo; hermoso.

hand-to-hand, adv. de mano a mano.

handwriting, n. escritura f.

handy, a. diestro; útil; a la mano.

hang, v. colgar; ahorcar.

hangar, n. hangar m.

hangdog, a. & n. camastrón m.

hanger, n. colgador, gancho m.

hanger-on, n. dependiente; mogollón m.

hang glider, n. aparato para vuelo libre.

hanging, 1. n. ahorcadura f. **2.** a. colgante.

hangman, n. verdugo m.

hangnail, n. padrastro m.

hang out, v. enarbolar.

hangup, n. tara (psicológica) f.

hank, n. madeja f.

hanker, n. ansiar; apetecer.

haphazard. a. casual.

happen, v. acontecer, suceder, pasar.

happening, n. acontecimiento m.

happiness, n. felicidad; dicha f.

happy, a. feliz; contento; dichoso.

happy-go-lucky, a. & n. descuidado m.

harakiri, n. harakiri (suicidio japonés) m.

harangue, 1. n. arenga f. **2.** v. arengar.

harass, v. acosar; atormentar.

harbinger, n. presagio m.

harbor, 1. n. puerto; albergue m. **2.** v. abrigar.

hard, 1. a. duro; difícil. **2.** adv. mucho.

hard coal, antracita m.

harden, v. endurecer.

hard-headed, a. terco.

hard-hearted, a. empedernido.

hardiness, n. vigor m.

hardly, adv. apenas.

hardness, n. dureza; dificultad f.

hardship, n. penalidad f.; trabajo m.

hardware, n. ferretería f.

hardwood, n. madera dura f.

hardy, a. fuerte, robusto.

hare, n. liebre f.

harebrained, a. tolondro.

harelip, n. labio leporino m. **2** a. labihendido.

harem, n. harén m.

hark, v. escuchar: atender.

Harlequin, n. arlequín m.

harlot, n. ramera f.

harm, 1. n. mal, daño; perjuicio m. **2.** v. dañar.

harmful, a. dañoso.

harmless, a. inocente.

harmonic, *n.* armónico *m.*

harmonica, *n.* armónica *f.*

harmonious, *a.* armonioso.

harmonize, *v.* armonizar.

harmony, *n.* armonía *f.*

harness, *n.* arnés *m.*

harp, *n.* arpa *f.*

harpoon, *n.* arpón *m.*

harridan, *n.* vieja regañona *f.*

harrow, 1. *n.* rastro *m.;* grada *f.* **2.** *v.* gradar.

harry, *v.* acosar.

harsh, *a.* áspero.

harshness, *n.* aspereza *f.*

harvest, 1. *n.* cosecha *f.* **2.** *v.* cosechar.

hash, *n.* picadillo *m.*

hashish, *n.* haxis *m.*

hasn't, *v.* no tiene (neg. + tener).

hassle, *n.* lío *m.,* molestia *f.;* controversia *f.*

hassock, *n.* cojín *m.*

haste, *n.* prisa *f.*

hasten, *v.* apresurarse, darse prisa.

hasty, *a.* apresurado.

hat, *n.* sombrero *m.*

hatch, 1. *n.* (naut.) cuartel *m.* **2.** *v.* incubar; (fig.) tramar.

hatchery, *n.* criadero *m.*

hatchet, *n.* hacha pequeña.

hate, 1. *n.* odio *m.* **2.** *v.* odiar, detestar.

hateful, *a.* detestable.

hatred, *n.* odio *m.*

haughtiness, *n.* arrogancia *f.*

haughty, *a.* altivo.

haul, 1. *n.* (fishery) redada *f.* **2.** *v.* tirar, halar.

haunch, *n.* anca *f.*

haunt, 1. *n.* lugar frecuentado. **2.** *v.* frecuentar, andar por.

have, *v.* tener; haber.

haven, *n.* puerto; asilo *m.*

haven't, *v.* no tiene (neg. + tener).

havoc, *n.* ruina *f.*

hawk, *n.* halcón *m.*

hawker, *n.* buhonero *m.*

hawser, *n.* cable *m.*

hawthorn, *n.* espino *m.*

hay, *n.* heno *m.*

hay fever, *n.* catarro anual de la nariz *m.;* alergia nasal.

hayfield, *n.* henar *m.*

hayloft, *n.* henil *m.*

haystack, *n.* hacina de heno *f.*

hazard, 1. *n.* azar *m.* **2.** *v.* aventurar.

hazardous, *a.* peligroso.

haze, *n.* niebla *f.*

hazel, *n.* avellano *m.*

hazy, *a.* brumoso.

he, *pron.* él *m.*

head, 1. *n.* cabeza *f.;* jefe *m.* **2.** *v.* dirigir; encabezar.

headache, *n.* dolor de cabeza.

headband, *n.* venda para cabeza *f.*

headfirst, *adv.* de cabeza.

headgear, *n.* tocado *m.*

headlight, *n.* linterna delantera *f.,* farol de tope *m.*

headline, *n.* encabezado *m.*

headlong, *a.* precipitoso.

head-on, *adv.* de frente.

headquarters, *n.* jefatura *f.;* (mil.) cuartel general.

headstone, *n.* lápida mortuoria *f.*

headstrong, *a.* terco.

headwaters, *n.* cabeceras *f.*

headway, *n.* avance *m.,* progreso *m.*

headwork, *n.* trabajo mental *m.*

heady, *a.* impetuoso.

heal, *v.* curar, sanar.

health, *n.* salud *f.*

healthful, *a.* saludable.

healthy, *a.* sano; salubre.

heap, *n.* montón *m.*

hear, *v.* oír. **h. from,** tener noticias de. **h. about, h. of,** oír hablar de.

hearing, *n.* oído *m.*

hearsay, *n.* rumor *m.*

hearse, *n.* ataúd *m.*

heart, *n.* corazón *m.;* ánimo *m.* **by h.,** de memoria.

heartache, *n.* angustia *f.*

heartbreak, *n.* angustia *f.;* pesar *m.*

heartbroken, *a.* acongojado.

heartburn, *n.* acedía *f.*

heartfelt, *a.* sentido.

hearth, *n.* hogar *m.,* chimenea *f.*

heartless, *a.* empedernido.

heartsick, *a.* desconsolado.

heart-stricken, *a.* afligido.

heart-to-heart, *adv.* franco; sincero.

hearty, *a.* cordial; vigoroso.

heat, 1. *n.* calor; ardor *m.;* calefacción *f.* **2.** *v.* calentar.

heated, *a.* acalorado.

heater, n. calentador m.
heath, n. matorral m.
heathen. a. & n. pagano -na.
heather, n. brezo m.
heatstroke, n. insolación f.
heat wave, n. onda de calor f.
heave, v. tirar.
heaven, n. cielo m.
heavenly, a. divino.
heavy, a. pesado; oneroso.
Hebrew, a. & n. hebreo -ea.
hectic, a. turbulento.
hedge, n. seto m.
hedgehog, n. erizo m.
hedonism, n. hedonismo m.
heed, 1. n. cuidado m. 2. v. atender.
heedless, a. desatento; incauto.
heel, n. talón m.; (of shoe) tacón m.
heifer, n. novilla f.
height, n. altura f.
heighten, v. elevar; exaltar.
heinous, a. nefando.
heir, heiress, n. heredero -ra.
helicopter, n. helicóptero m.
heliotrope, n. heliotropo m.
helium, n. helio m.
hell, n. infierno m.
Hellenism, n. helenismo m.
hellish, a. infernal.
hello, interj. ¡hola!; (on telephone) aló; bueno.
helm, n. timón m.
helmet, n. yelmo, casco m.
helmsman, n. limonero m.
help, 1. n. ayuda f. **help!** ¡socorro! 2. v. ayudar. **h. oneself,** servirse. **can't help (but),** no poder menos de.
helper, n. ayudante m.
helpful, a. útil; servicial.
helpfulness, n. utilidad f.
helpless, a. imposibilitado.
hem, 1. n. ribete m. 2. v. ribetear.
hemisphere, n. hemisferio m.
hemlock, n. abeto m.
hemoglobin, n. hemoglobina f.
hemophilia, n. hemofilia f.
hemorrhage, n. hemorragia f.
hemorrhoid, n. hemorriodes f.pl.
hemp, n. cáñamo m.
hemstitch, 1. n. vainica f. 2. v. hacer una vainica.
hen, n. gallina f.
hence, adv. por lo tanto.

henceforth, adv. de aquí en adelante.
henchman, n. paniaguado m.
henna, n. alheña f.
her, 1. a. su. 2. pron. ella; la; le
herald, n. heraldo m.
heraldic, a. heráldico.
heraldry, n. heráldica f.
herb, n. yerba, hierba f.
herbaceous, a. herbáceo.
herbarium, n. herbario m.
herd, 1. n. hato, rebaño m. 2. v. reunir en hatos.
here, adv. aquí; acá.
hereafter, adv. en lo futuro.
hereby, adv. por éstas, por la presente.
hereditary, a. hereditario.
heredity, n. herencia f.
herein, adv. aquí dentro; incluso
heresy, n. herejía f.
heretic, 1. a. herético. 2. n. hereje m. & f.
heretical, a. herético.
heretofore, adv. hasta ahora.
herewith, adv. con esto, adjunto
heritage, n. herencia f.
hermetic, a. hermético.
hermit, n. ermitaño m.
hernia, n. hernia f.
hero, n. héroe m.
heroic, a. heroico.
heroically, adv. heroicamente.
heroin, n. heroína f.
heroine, n. heroína f.
heroism, n. heroísmo m.
heron, n. garza f.
herring, n. arenque m.
hers, pron. suyo, de ella.
herself, pron. sí, sí misma, se. **she h.,** ella misma. **with h.,** consigo
hertz, n. hertzio m.
hesitancy, n. hesitación f.
hesitant, a. indeciso.
hesitate, v. vacilar.
hesitation, n. duda; vacilación f
heterogeneous, a. heterogéneo.
heterosexual, a. heterosexual.
hexagon, n. hexágono m.
hibernate, v. invernar.
hibernation, n. invernada f.
hibiscus, n. hibisco m.
hiccup, 1. n. hipo m. 2. v. tener hipo.
hickory, n. nogal americano m.
hidden, a. oculto; escondido.

hide, 1. n. cuero m.; piel f. **2.** v. esconder; ocultar.

hideous, a. horrible.

hide-out, n. escondite m.

hierarchy, n. jerarquía f.

high, a. alto, elevado; (in price) caro.

highbrow, n. erudito m.

high fidelity, de alta fidelidad.

highly, adv. altamente; sumamente.

high school, n. escuela secundaria f.

highway, n. carretera f.; camino real m.

hijacker, n. secuestrador, pirata de aviones m.

hike, n. caminata f.

hilarious, a. alegre, bullicioso.

hilariousness, hilarity, n. hilaridad f.

hill, n. colina f.; cerro m.; **down h.,** cuesta abajo. **up h.,** cuesta arriba.

hilt, n. puño m. **up to the h.,** a fondo.

him, pron. él; lo; le.

himself, pron. si, sí mismo; se. **he h.,** él mismo. **with h.,** consigo.

hinder, v. impedir.

hindmost, a. último.

hindquarter, n. cuarto trasero m.

hindrance, n. obstáculo m.

hinge, 1. n. gozne m. **2.** v. engoznar. **h. on,** depender de.

hint, 1. n. insinuación f.; indicio m. **2.** v. insinuar.

hip, n. cadera f.

hippopotamus, n. hipopótamo m.

hire, v. alquilar.

his, 1. a. su. **2.** pron. suyo, de él.

Hispanic, a. hispano.

hiss, v. silbar; sisear.

historian, n. historiador m.

historic, historical, a. histórico.

histrionic, a. histriónico.

history, n. historia f.

hit, 1. n. golpe m.; (coll.) éxito m. **2.** v. golpear, dar.

hitch, v. amarrar; enganchar.

hither, adv. acá, hacia acá.

hitherto, adv. hasta ahora.

hive, n. colmena f.

hives, n. urticaria f.

hoard, 1. n. acumulación f. **2.** v. acaparar; atesorar.

hoarse, a. ronco.

hoax, 1. n. engaño m. **2.** v. engañar.

hobby, n. afición f., pasatiempo m.

hobgoblin, n. trasgo m.

hobnob, v. tener intimidad.

hobo, n. vagabundo m.

hockey, n. hockey m. **ice-h.,** hockey sobre hielo.

hod, n. esparavel m.

hodgepodge, n. baturillo m.; mezcolanza f.

hoe, 1. n. azada f. **2.** v. cultivar con azada.

hog, n. cerdo, puerco m.

hoist, 1. n. grúa f., elevador m. **2.** v. elevar, enarbolar.

hold, 1. n. presa f.; agarro m.; (naut.) bodega f. **to get h. of,** conseguir, apoderarse de. **2.** v. tener; detener; sujetar; celebrar.

holder, n. tenedor m. **cigarette h.,** boquilla f.

holdup, n. salteamiento m.

hole, n. agujero; hoyo; hueco m.

holiday, n. día de fiesta.

holiness, n. santidad f.

Holland, n. Holanda f.

hollow, 1. a. hueco. **2.** n. cavidad f. **3.** v. ahuecar; excavar.

holly, n. acebo m.

hollyhock, n. malva real f.

holocaust, n. holocausto m.

hologram, n. holograma m.

holography, n. holografía f.

holster, n. pistolera f.

holy, a. santo.

holy day. n. disanto m.

Holy See, n. Santa Sede f.

Holy Spirit, n. Espíritu Santo m.

Holy Week, n. Semana Santa f.

homage, n. homenaje m.

home, n. casa, morada f; hogar m. **at h.,** en casa. **to go h.,** ir a casa.

homeland, n. patria f.

homely, a. feo; casero.

home rule, n. autonomía f.

homesick, a. nostálgico.

homespun, a. casero; tocho.

homeward, adv. hacia casa.

homicide, n. homicida m. & f.

homily, n. homilía f.

homogeneous, a. homogéneo.

homogenize, v. homogenizar.

homosexual, n. & a. homosexual m.

Honduras, n. Honduras f.

hone, 1. n. piedra de afilar f. **2.** v. afilar.

honest, a. honrado, honesto; sincero.

honestly, adv. honradamente; de veras.

honesty, n. honradez, honestidad f.

honey, n. miel f.

honeybee, n. abeja obrera f.

honeymoon, n. luna de miel.

honeysuckle, n. madreselva f.

honor, 1. n. honra f.; honor m. **2.** v. honrar.

honorable, a. honorable; ilustre.

honorary, a. honorario.

hood, n. capota f.; capucha f.; (auto.) cubierta del motor.

hoodlum, n. pillo m., rufián m.

hoof, n. pezuña f.

hook, 1. n. gancho m. **2.** v. enganchar.

hoop, n. cerco m.

hop, 1. n. salto m. **2.** v. saltar.

hope, 1. n. esperanza f. **2.** v. esperar.

hopeful, a. lleno de esperanzas.

hopeless, a. desesperado; sin remedio.

horde, n. horda f.

horehound, n. marrubio m.

horizon, n. horizonte m.

horizontal, a. horizontal.

hormone, n. hormón m.

horn, n. cuerno m.; (music) trompa f.; (auto.) bocina f.

hornet, n. avispón m.

horny, a. córneo; calloso.

horoscope, n. horóscopo m.

horrendous, a. horrendo.

horrible, a. horrible.

horrid, a. horrible.

horrify, v. horrorizar.

horror, n. horror m.

horse, n. caballo m. **to ride a h.,** cabalgar.

horseback, n. **on h.,** a caballo. **to ride h.,** montar a caballo.

horsefly, n. tábano m.

horsehair, n. pelo de caballo m.; tela de crin f.

horseman, n. jinete m.

horsemanship, n. manejo m., equitación f.

horsepower, n. caballo de fuerza m.

horseradish, n. rábano picante m.

horseshoe, n. herradura f.

hortatory, a. exhortatorio.

horticulture, n. horticultura f.

hose, n. medias f.pl; (garden) manguera f.

hosiery, n. calcetería f.

hospitable, a. hospitalario.

hospital, n. hospital m.

hospitality, n. hospitalidad f.

hospitalization, n. hospitalización f.

hospitalize, v. hispitalizar.

host, n. anfitrión m., dueño de la casa; (rel.) hostia f.

hostage, n. rehén m.

hostel, n. hostería f.

hostelry, n. fonda f., parador m.

hostess, n. anfitriona f., dueña de la casa.

hostile, a. hostil.

hostility, n. hostilidad f.

hot, a. caliente; (sauce) picante. **to be h.,** tener calor; (weather) hacer calor.

hotbed, n. estercolero m. (fig.) foco m.

hotel, n. hotel m.

hot-headed, a. turbulente, alborotadizo.

hothouse, n. invernáculo m.

hound, 1. n. sabueso m. **2.** v. perseguir; seguir la pista.

hour, n. hora f.

hourglass, n. reloj de arena m.

hourly, 1. a. por horas. **2.** adv. a cada hora.

house, 1. casa f.; (theat.) público m. **2.** v. alojar, albergar.

housefly, n. mosca ordinaria f.

household, n. familia; casa f.

housekeeper, n. ama de llaves.

housemaid, n. criada f., sirvienta f.

housewife, n. ama de casa.

housework, n. tareas domésticas f.

hovel, n. choza f.

hover, v. revolotear.

hovercraft, n. hovercraft m.

how, adv. cómo. **h. much,** cuánto. **h. many,** cuántos. **h. far,** a qué distancia.

however, adv. como quiera; sin embargo.

howl, 1. n. aullido m. **2.** v. aullar

hub, n. centro m.; eje m. **h. of a wheel**, cubo de la rueda m.

hubbub, n. alborota f., bulla f.

hue, n. matiz; color m.

hug, 1. n. abrazo m. 2. v. abrazar.

huge, a. enorme.

hulk, n. casco de buque m.

hull, 1. n. cáscara f.; (naval) casco m. 2. v. decascarar.

hum, 1. n. zumbido m. 2. v. tararear; zumbar.

human, a. & n. humano -na.

humane, a. humano, humanitario.

humanism, n. humanidad f.; benevolencia f.

humanitarian, a. humanitario.

humanity, n. humanidad f.

humanly, a. humanamente.

humble, a. humilde.

humbug, n. farsa f., embaucador m.

humdrum, a. monótono.

humid, a. húmedo.

humidity, n. humedad f.

humiliate, v. humillar.

humiliation, n. mortificación f.; bochorno m.

humility, n. humildad f.

humor, 1. n. humor; capricho m. 2. v. complacer.

humorist, n. humorista m.

humorous, a. divertido.

hump, n. joroba f.

humpback, n. jorobado m.

humus, n. humus m.

hunch, n. giba f.; (idea) corazonada f.

hunchback, n. jorobado m.

hundred, 1. a. & pron. cien, ciento. **200**, doscientos. **300**, trescientos. **400**, cuatrocientos. **500**, quinientos. **600**, seiscientos. **700**, setecientos. **800**, ochocientos. **900**, novecientos. 2. n. centenar m.

hundredth, n. & a. centésimo m.

Hungarian, a. & n. húngaro -ra.

Hungary, Hungría f.

hunger, n. hambre f.

hungry, a. hambriento. **to be h.**, tener hambre.

hunt, 1. n. caza f. 2. v. cazar. **h. up**, buscar.

hunter, n. cazador m.

hunting, n. caza f. **to go h.**, ir de caza.

hurdle, n. zarzo m., valla f.; dificultad f.

hurl, v. arrojar.

hurricane, n. huracán m.

hurry, 1. n. prisa f. **to be in a h.**, tener prisa. 2. v. apresurar; darse prisa.

hurt, 1. n. daño, perjuicio m. 2. v. dañar; lastimar; doler; ofender.

hurtful, a. perjudicial, dañino.

hurtle, v. lanzar.

husband, n. marido, esposo m.

husk, 1. n. cáscara f. 2. v. descascarar.

husky, a. fornido.

hustle, v. empujar.

hut, n. choza f.

hyacinth, n. jacinto m.

hybrid, a. híbrido.

hydrangea, n. hortensia f.

hydraulic, a. hidráulico.

hydroelectric, a. hidroeléctrico.

hydrogen, n. hidrógeno m.

hydrophobia, n. hidrofobia. f.

hydroplane, n. hidroavión m.

hydrotherapy, n. hidroterapia f.

hyena, n. hiena f.

hygiene, n. higiene f.

hygienic, a. higiénico.

hymn, n. himno m.

hymnal, n. himnario m.

hypercritical, a. hipercrítico.

hyphen, n. guión m.

hyphenate, v. separar con guión.

hypnosis, n. hipnosis f.

hypnotic, a. hipnótico.

hypnotism, n. hipnotismo m.

hypnotize, v. hipnotizar.

hypochondria, n. hipocondría f.

hypochondriac, n. & a. hipocondríaco m.

hypocrisy, n. hipocresía f.

hypocrite, n. hipócrita m. & f.

hypocritical, a. hipócrita.

hypodermic, a. hipodérmico.

hypotenuse, n. hipotenusa f.

hypothesis, n. hipótesis f.

hypothetical, a. hipotético.

hysterectomy, n. histerectomía f.

hysteria, **hysterics**, n. histeria f.

hysterical, a. histérico.

I

I, pron. yo.

iambic, a. yámbico.

ice, n. hielo m.

iceberg, n. iceberg m.

icebox, n. refrigerador m.

ice cream, n. helado, mantecado m.; **i-c. cone**, barquillo de helado.

ice skate, n. patín de cuchilla m.

icon, n. icón m.

icy, a. helado; indiferente.

idea. n. idea f.

ideal, a. ideal.

idealism, n. idealismo m.

idealist, n. idealista m. & f.

idealistic, a. idealista.

idealize, v. idealizar.

ideally, adv. idealmente.

identical, a. idéntico.

identifiable, a. identificable.

identification, n. identificación f. **i. papers**, cédula de identidad f.

identify, v. identificar.

identity, n. identidad f.

ideology, n. ideología f.

idiocy, n. idiotez f.

idiom, n. modismo m.; idioma m.

idiot, n. idiota m. & f.

idiotic, a. idiota, tonto.

idle, a. desocupado; perezoso.

idleness, n. ociosidad, pereza f.

idol, n. ídolo m.

idolatry, n. idolatría f.

idolize, v. idolatrar.

idyl, n. idilio m.

idyllic, a. idílico.

if, conj. si. **even if**, aunque.

ignite, v. encender.

ignition, n. ignición f.

ignoble, a. innoble, indigno.

ignominious, a. ignominioso.

ignoramus, n. ignorante m.

ignorance, n. ignorancia f.

ignorant, a. ignorante. **to be i. of**, ignorar.

ignore, v. desconocer, pasar por alto.

ill, a. enfermo, malo.

illegal, a. ilegal.

illegible, a. ilegible.

illegibly, adv. ilegiblemente.

illegitimacy, n. ilegitimidad f.

illegitimate, a. ilegítimo; desautorizado.

illicit, a. ilícito.

illiteracy, n. analfabetismo m.

illiterate, a. & n. analfabeto -ta.

illness, n. enfermedad, maldad f.

illogical, a. ilógico.

illuminate, v. iluminar.

illumination, n. iluminación f.

illusion, n. ilusión f.; ensueño m.

illusive, a. ilusivo.

illustrate, v. ilustrar; ejemplificar.

illustration, n. ilustración f.; ejemplo; grabado m.

illustrative, a. ilustrativo.

illustrious, a. ilustre.

ill will, n. malevolencia f.

image, n. imagen, estatua f.

imagery, n. imaginación f.

imaginable, a. imaginable.

imaginary, a. imaginario.

imagination, n. imaginación f.

imaginative, a. imaginativo.

imagine, v. imaginarse, figurarse

imbecile, n. & a. imbécil m.

imitate, v. imitar.

imitation, n. imitación f.

imitative, a. imitativo.

immaculate, a. inmaculado.

immanent, a. inmanente.

immaterial, a. inmaterial; sin importancia.

immature, a. inmaturo.

immediate, a. inmediato.

immediately, adv. inmediatamente.

immense, a. inmenso.

immerse, v. sumergir.

immigrant, n. & a. inmigrante m

immigrate, v. inmigrar.

imminent, a. inminente.

immobile, a. inmóvil.

immoderate, a. inmoderado.

immodest, a. inmodesto; atrevido.

immoral, a. inmoral.

immorality, n. inmoralidad f.

immorally, adv. licenciosamente

immortal, a. inmortal.

immortality, n. inmortalidad f.

immortalize, v. inmortalizar.

immune, a. inmune.

immunity, n. inmunidad f.

immunize, v. inmunizar.

impact, n. impacto m.

impair, v. empeorar, perjudicar.

impale, v. empalar.

impart, v. impartir, comunicar.

impartial, a. imparcial.

impatience, n. impaciencia f.

impatient, a. impaciente.

impede, v. impedir, estorbar.

impediment, n. impedimento m.

impel, v. impeler.

impenetrable, a. impenetrable.

impenitent, n. & a. impenitente m.

imperative, a. imperativo.

imperceptible, a. imperceptible.

imperfect, a. imperfecto.

imperfection, n. imperfección f.

imperial, a. imperial.

imperialism, n. imperialismo m.

imperious, a. imperioso.

impersonal, a. impersonal.

impersonate, v. personificar; imitar.

impersonation, n. personificación f.; imitación f.

impertinence, n. impertinencia f.

impervious, a. impermeable.

impetuous, a. impetuoso.

impetus, n. impetú m., impulso m.

impinge, v. tropezar; infringir.

implacable, a. implacable.

implant, v. implantar; inculcar.

implement, n. herramienta f.

implicate, v. implicar; embrollar.

implication, n. inferencia f.; complicidad f.

implicit, a. implícito.

implied, a. implícito.

implore, v. implorar.

imply, v. significar; dar a entender.

impolite, a. descortés.

import, 1. n. importación f. **2.** v. importar.

importance, n. importancia f.

important, a. importante.

importation, n. importación f.

importune, v. importunar.

impose, v. imponer.

imposition, n. imposición f.

impossibility, n. imposibilidad f.

impossible, a. imposible.

impotence, n. impotencia f.

impotent, a. impotente.

impregnable, a. impregnable.

impregnate, v. impregnar; fecundizar.

impresario, n. empresario m.

impress, v. impresionar.

impression, n. impresión f.

impressive, a. imponente.

imprison, v. encarcelar.

imprisonment, n. prisión, encarcelación f.

improbable, a. improbable.

impromptu, a. extemporáneo.

improper, a. impropio.

improve, v. mejorar; progresar.

improvement, n. mejoramiento; progreso m.

improvise, v. improvisar.

imprudent, a. descarada.

impugn, v. impugnar.

impulse, n. impulso m.

impulsive, a. impulsivo.

impunity, n. impunidad f.

impure, a. impuro.

impurity, n. impureza f.; deshonestidad f.

impute, v. imputar.

in, 1. prep. en; dentro de. **2.** adv. adentro.

inadvertent, a. inadvertido.

inalienable, a. inalienable.

inane, a. mentecato.

inaugural, a. inaugural.

inaugurate, v. inaugurar.

inauguration, n. inauguración f.

Inca, n. inca m.

incandescent, a. incandescente.

incantation, n. encantación f., conjuro m.

incapacitate, v. incapacitar.

incarcerate, v. encarcelar.

incarnate, a. encarnado; personificado.

incarnation, n. encarnación f.

incendiary, a. incendario.

incense, 1. n. incienso m. **2.** v. indignar.

incentive, n. incentivo m.

inception, n. cimienzo m.

incessant, a. incesante.

incest, n. incesto m.

inch, n. pulgada f.

incidence, n. incidencia f.

incident, n. incidente m.

incidental, a. incidental.

incidentally, adv. incidentalmente; entre paréntesis.

incinerator, n. incinerador m.

incipient, a. incipiente.

incision, n. incisión f.; cortadura f.

incisive, a. incisivo; mordaz.

incisor, n. incisivo m.

incite, v. incitar, instigar.

inclination, n. inclinación f.; declive m.

incline, 1. n. pendiente m. **2.** v. inclinar.

inclose, *v.* incluir.

include, *v.* incluir.

including, *prep.* incluso.

inclusive, *a.* inclusivo.

incognito, *n. & adv.* incógnito *m.*

income, *n.* renta *f.*; ingresos *m.pl.*

incomparable, *a.* incomparable.

inconvenience, 1. *n.* incomodidad *f.* **2.** *v.* incomodar.

inconvenient, *a.* incómodo.

incorporate, *v.* incoporar; dar cuerpo.

incorrigible, *a.* incorregible.

increase, *v.* crecer; aumentar.

incredible, *a.* increíble.

incredulity, *n.* incredulidad *f.*

incredulous, *a.* incrédulo.

increment, *n.* incremento *m.,* aumento *m.*

incriminate, *v.* incriminar.

incrimination, *n.* incriminación *f.*

incrust, *v.* incrustar.

incubator, *n.* incubadora *f.*

inculcate, *v.* inculcar.

incumbency, *n.* incumbencia *f.*

incumbent, *a.* obligatorio; colocado sobre.

incur, *v.* incurrir.

incurable, *a.* incurable.

indebted, *a.* obligado; adeudado.

indeed, *adv.* verdaderamente, de veras. **no i.,** de ninguna manera.

indefatigable, *a.* incansable.

indefinite, *a.* indefinido.

indefinitely, *adv.* indefinidamente.

indelible, *a.* indeleble.

indemnify, *v.* indemnizar.

indemnity, *n.* indemnificación *f.*

indent, 1. *n.* diente *f.,* mella *f.* **2.** *v.* indentar, mellar.

indentation, *n.* indentación *f.*

independence, *n.* independencia *f.*

independent, *a.* independiente.

in-depth, *adj.* en profundidad.

index, *n.* índice *m.;* (of book) tabla *f.*

India, *n.* India *f.*

Indian, *a. & n.* indio -dia.

indicate, *v.* indicar.

indication, *n.* indicación *f.*

indicative, *a. & n.* indicativo *m.*

indict, *v.* encausar.

indictment, *n.* (law) sumaria *m.;* denuncia *f.*

indifference, *n.* indiferencia *f.*

indifferent, *a.* indiferente.

indigenous, *a.* indígena.

indigent, *a.* indigente, pobre.

indigestion, *n.* indigestión *f.*

indignant, *a.* indignado.

indignation, *n.* indignación *f.*

indignity, *n.* indignidad *f.*

indirect, *a.* indirecto.

indiscreet, *a.* indiscreto.

indiscretion, *n.* indiscreción *f.*

indiscriminate, *a.* promiscuo.

indispensable, *a.* indispensable.

indisposed, *a.* indispuesto.

individual, *a. & n.* individuo *m.*

individuality, *n.* individualidad *f.*

individually, *adv.* individualmente.

indivisible, *a.* indivisible.

indoctrinate, *v.* doctrinar, enseñar.

indolent, *a.* indolente.

indoor, *a.* interior. **indoors,** *adv.* en casa; bajo techo.

indorse, *v.* endosar.

induce, *v.* inducir, persuadir.

induct, *v.* instalar, iniciar.

induction, *n.* introducción *f.;* instalación *f.*

inductive, *a.* inductivo; introductor.

indulge, *v.* favorecer. **i. in,** entregarse a.

indulgence, *n.* indulgencia *f.*

indulgent, *a.* indulgente.

industrial, *a.* industrial.

industrialist, *n.* industrial *m.*

industrious, *a.* industrioso, trabajador.

industry, *n.* industria *f.*

ineligible, *a.* inelegible.

inept, *a.* inepto.

inert, *a.* inerte.

inertia, *n.* inercia *f.*

inevitable, *a.* inevitable.

inexplicable, *a.* inexplicable.

infallible, *a.* infalible.

infamous, *a.* infame.

infamy, *n.* infamia *f.*

infancy, *n.* infancia *f.*

infant, *n.* nene *m.;* criatura *f.*

infantile, *a.* infantil.

infantry, *n.* infantería *f.*

infatuated, *a.* infatuado.

infect, *v.* infectar.

infection, *n.* infección *f.*

infectious, *a.* infeccioso.

infer, *v.* inferir.

inference, *n.* inferencia *f.*

inferior, *a.* inferior.

infernal, *a.* infernal.

inferno, *n.* infierno *m.*

infest, *v.* infestar.

infidel, 1. *n.* infiel *m.;* pagano *m.* **2.** *a.* infiel.

infidelity, *n.* infidelidad *f.*

infiltrate, *v.* infiltrar.

infinite, *a.* infinito.

infinitesimal, *a.* infinitesimal.

infinitive, *n.* & *a.* infinitivo *m.*

infinity, *n.* infinidad *f.*

infirm, *a.* enfermizo.

infirmary, *n.* hospital *m.,* enfermería *f.*

infirmity, *n.* enfermedad *f.*

inflame, *v.* inflamar.

inflammable, *a.* inflamable.

inflammation, *n.* inflamación *f.*

inflammatory, *a.* inflamante; (med.) inflamatorio.

inflate, *v.* inflar.

inflation, *n.* inflación *f.*

inflection, *n.* inflexión *f.;* (of the voice) modulación de la voz *f.*

inflict, *v.* infligir.

infliction, *n.* imposición *f.*

influence, 1. *n.* influencia *f.* **2.** *v.* influir en.

influential, *a.* influyente.

influenza, *n.* gripe *f.*

inform, *v.* informar. **i. oneself,** enterarse.

informal, *a.* informal.

information, *n.* informaciones *f.pl.*

infringe, *v.* infringir.

infuriate, *v.* enfurecer.

ingenious, *a.* ingenioso.

ingenuity, *n.* ingeniosidad; destreza *f.*

ingredient, *n.* ingrediente *m.*

inhabit, *v.* habitar.

inhabitant, *n.* habitante *m.* & *f.*

inhale, *v.* inhalar.

inherent, *a.* inherente.

inherit, *v.* heredar.

inheritance, *n.* herencia *f.*

inhibit, *v.* inhibir.

inhibition, *n.* inhibición *f.*

inhuman, *a.* inhumano.

inimical, *a.* hostil.

inimitable, *a.* inimitable.

iniquity, *n.* iniquidad *f.*

initial, *a.* & *n.* inicial *f.*

initiate, *v.* iniciar.

initiation, *n.* iniciación *f.*

initiative, *n.* iniciativa *f.*

inject, *v.* inyectar.

injection, *n.* inyección *f.*

injunction, *n.* mandato *m.;* (law) embargo *m.*

injure, *v.* herir; lastimar; ofender.

injurious, *a.* perjudicial.

injury, *n.* herida; afrenta *f.* perjuicio *m.*

injustice, *n.* injusticia *f.*

ink, *n.* tinta *f.*

inland, 1. *a.* interior. **2.** *adv.* tierra adentro.

inlet, *n.* entrada *f.;* ensenada *f.;* estuario *m.*

inmate, *n.* residente *m.;* (of a prison) preso *m.*

inn, *n.* posada *f.;* mesón *m.*

inner, *a.* interior. **i. tube,** cámara de aire.

innocence, *n.* inocencia *f.*

innocent, *a.* inocente.

innocuous, *a.* innocuo.

innovation, *n.* innovación *f.*

innuendo, *n.* insinuación *f.*

innumerable, *a.* innumerable.

inoculate, *v.* inocular.

inoculation, *n.* inoculación *f.*

input, *n.* aducto *m.*

inquest, *n.* indagación *f.*

inquire, *v.* preguntar; inquirir.

inquiry, *n.* pregunta; investigación *f.*

inquisition, *n.* escudriñamiento *m.;* (church) Inquisición *f.*

insane, *a.* loco. **to go i.,** perder la razón; volverse loco.

insanity, *n.* locura *f.;* demencia *f.*

inscribe, *v.* inscribir.

inscription, *n.* inscripción; dedicatoria *f.*

insect, *n.* insecto *m.*

insecticide, *n.* & *a.* insecticida *f.*

inseparable, *a.* inseparable.

insert, *v.* insertar, meter.

insertion, *n.* cosa insertada *f.*

inside, 1. *a.* & *n.* interior *m.* **2.** *adv.* adentro, por dentro. **i. out,** al revés. **3.** *prep.* dentro de.

insidious, *a.* insidioso.

insight, *n.* perspicacia *f.;* comprensión *f.*

insignia, *n.* insignias *f.pl.*

insignificance, *n.* insignificancia *f.*

insignificant, *a.* insignificante.

insinuate, *v.* insinuar.

insinuation, *n.* insinuación *f.*

insipid, *a.* insípido.

insist, *v.* insistir.

insistence, *n.* insistencia *f.*

insistent, *a.* insistente.

insolence, *n.* insolencia *f.*

insolent, *a.* insolente.

insomnia, *n.* insomnio *m.*

inspect, *v.* inspeccionar, examinar.

inspection, *n.* inspección *f.*

inspector, *n.* inspector *m.*

inspiration, *n.* inspiración *f.*

inspire, *v.* inspirar.

install, *v.* instalar.

installation, *n.* instalación *f.*

installment, *n.* plazo *m.*

instance, *n.* ocasión *f.* **for i.,** por ejemplo.

instant, *a.* & *n.* instante *m.*

instantaneous, *a.* instantáneo.

instantly, *adv.* al instante.

instead, *adv.* en lugar de eso. **i. of,** en vez de, en lugar de.

instigate, *v.* instigar.

instill, *v.* instilar.

instinct, *n.* instinto *m.*

instinctive, *a.* instintivo.

institute, 1. *n.* instituto *m.* 2. *v.* instituir.

institution, *n.* institución *f.*

instruct, *v.* instruir.

instruction, *n.* instrucción *f.*

instructive, *a.* instructivo.

instructor, *n.* instructor *m.*

instrument, *n.* instrumento *m.*

instrumental, *a.* instrumental.

insufficient, *a.* insuficiente.

insular, *a.* insular; estrecho de miras.

insulate, *v.* aislar.

insulation, *n.* aislamiento *m.*

insulator, *n.* aislador *m.*

insulin, *n.* insulina *f.*

insult, 1. *n.* insulto *m.* 2. *v.* insultar.

insuperable, *a.* insuperable.

insurance, *n.* seguro *m.*

insure, *v.* asegurar.

insurgent, *a.* & *n.* insurgente *m.*

insurrection, *n.* insurrección *f.*

intact, *a.* intacto.

intangible, *a.* intangible, impalpable.

integral, *a.* íntegro.

integrate, *v.* integrar.

integrity, *n.* integridad *f.*

intellect, *n.* intelecto *m.*

intellectual, *a.* & *n.* intelectual *m. & f.*

intelligence, *n.* inteligencia *f.*

intelligent, *a.* inteligente.

intelligible, *a.* inteligible.

intend, *v.* pensar; intentar; destinar.

intense, *a.* intenso.

intensify, *v.* intensificar.

intensity, *n.* intensidad *f.*

intensive, *a.* intensivo.

intent, *n.* intento *m.*

intention, *n.* intención *f.*

intentional, *a.* intencional.

intercede, *v.* interceder.

intercept, *v.* interceptar; detener.

intercourse, *n.* tráfico *m.;* comunicación *f.;* coito *m.*

interest, 1. *n.* interés *m.* 2. *v.* interesar.

interesting, *a.* interesante.

interface, *n.* aparato o zona de contacto.

interfere, *v.* meterse; intervenir. **i. with,** estorbar.

interference, *n.* intervención *f.;* obstáculo *m.*

interior, *a.* interior.

interject, *v.* interponer; intervenir.

interjection, *n.* interjección *f.;* interposición *f.*

interlude, *n.* intervalo *m.;* (theat.) intermedio *m.;* (music) interludio *m.*

intermediary, *n.* intermediario *m.*

intermediate, *a.* intermedio.

interment, *n.* entierro.

intermission, *n.* intermisión *f.;* (theat.) entreacto *m.*

intermittent, *a.* intermitente.

intern, 1. *n.* interno *m.* 2. *v.* internar.

internal, *a.* interno.

international, *a.* internacional.

internationalism, *n.* internacionalismo *m.*

interne, *n.* practicante de hospital *m.*

interpose, *v.* interponer.

interpret, *v.* interpretar.

interpretation, *n.* interpretación *f.*

interpreter, n. intérprete m. & f.

interrogate, v. interrogar.

interrogation, n. interrogación; pregunta f.

interrogative, a. interrogativo.

interrupt, v. interrumpir.

interruption, n. interrupción f.

intersect, v. cortar.

intersection, n. intersección f.; (street) bocacalle f.

intersperse, v. entremezclar.

interval, n. intervalo m.

intervene, v. intervenir.

intervention, n. intervención f.

interview, 1. n. entrevista f. **2.** v. entrevistar.

intestine, n. intestino m.

intimacy, n. intimidad; familiaridad f.

intimate, 1. a. íntimo, familiar. **2.** n. amigo íntimo. **3.** v. insinuar.

intimidate, v. intimidar.

intimidation, n. intimidación f.

into, prep. en, dentro de.

intonation, n. entonación f.

intone, v. entonar.

intoxicate, v. embriagar.

intoxication, n. embriaguez f.

intravenous, a. intravenoso.

intrepid, a. intrépido.

intricacy, n. intrincación f.; enredo m.

intricate, a. intrincado; complejo.

intrigue, 1. n. intriga f. **2.** v. intrigar.

intrinsic, a. intrínseco.

introduce, v. introducir; (a person) presentar.

introduction, n. presentación; introducción f.

introductory, a. introductivo.

introvert, n. & a. introverso m.

intrude, v. entremeterse.

intruder, n. intruso -sa.

intuition, n. intuición f.

intuitive, a. intuitivo.

inundate, v. inundar.

invade, v. invadir.

invader, n. invasor m.

invalid, a. & n. inválido -da.

invariable, a. invariable.

invasion, n. invasión f.

invective, 1. n. invectiva f. **2.** a. ultrajante.

inveigle, v. seducir.

invent, v. inventar.

invention, n. invención f.

inventive, a. inventivo.

inventor, n. inventor m.

inventory, n. inventario m.

invertebrate, n. & a. invertebrado m.

invest, v. investir; (com.) invertir.

investigate, v. investigar.

investigation, n. investigación f.

investment, n. inversión f.

inveterate, a. inveterado.

invidious, a. difamatorio.

invigorate, v. vigorizar, fortificar.

invincible, a. invencible.

invisible, a. invisible.

invitation, n. invitación f.

invite, v. invitar, convidar.

invocation, n. invocación f.

invoice, n. factura f.

invoke, v. invocar.

involuntary, a. involuntario.

involve, v. envolver; implicar.

involved, a. complicado.

invulnerable, a. invulnerable.

inward, adv. hacia adentro.

inwardly, adv. interiormente.

iodine, n. iodo m.

irate, a. encolerizado.

Ireland, n. Irlanda f.

iris, n. (anat.) iris m.; (botany) flor de lis f.

Irish, a. irlandés.

irk, v. fastidiar.

iron, 1. n. hierro m.; (appliance) plancha f. **2.** v. planchar.

ironical, a. irónico.

irony, n. ironía f.

irrational, a. irracional; ilógico.

irregular, a. irregular.

irregularity, n. irregularidad f.

irrelevant, a. ajeno.

irresistible, a. irresistible.

irresponsible, a. irresponsable.

irreverent, a. irreverente.

irrevocable, a. irrevocable.

irrigate, v. regar; (med.) irrigar.

irrigation, n. riego m.

irritability, n. irritabilidad f.

irritable, a. irritable.

irritant, n. & a. irritante f.

irritate, v. irritar.

irritation, n. irritación f.

island, n. isla f.

isolate, v. aislar.

isolation, n. aislamiento m.

isosceles, a. isósceles.

issuance, n. emisión f.; publicación f.

issue, 1. n. emisión; edición; progenie f.; número m.; punto en disputa. **2.** v. emitir; publicar.

isthmus, n. istmo m.

it, pron. ello; él, ella; lo, la.

Italian, a. & n. italiano -na.

Italy, n. Italia f.

itch, 1. n. picazón f. v. picar.

item, n. artículo; detalle m.; inserción f.; (com.) renglón m.

itemize, v. detallar.

itinerant, 1. n. viandante m. **2.** a. ambulante.

itinerary, n. itinerario m.

its, a. su.

itself, pron. sí; se.

ivory, n. marfil m.

ivy, n. hiedra f.

J

jab, 1. n. pinchazo m. **2.** v. pinchar.

jack, n. (for lifting) gato m.; (cards) sota f.

jackal, n. chacal m.

jackass, n. asno m.

jacket, n. chaqueta f.; saco m.

jack-of-all-trades, n. estuche m.

jade, n. (horse) rocín m.; (woman) picarona f.; (mineral) jade m.

jaded, a. rendido.

jagged, a. mellado.

jaguar, n. jaguar m.

jail, n. cárcel f.

jailer, n. carcelero m.

jam, 1. n. conserva f.; apretura f. **2.** v. apiñar, apretar; trabar.

janitor, n. portero m.

January, n. enero m.

Japan, n. Japón m.

Japanese, a. & n. japonés -esa.

jar, 1. n. jarro m. **2.** v. chocar; agitar.

jargon, n. jerga f.

jasmine, n. jazmín m.

jaundice, n. ictericia f.

jaunt, n. paseata f.

javelin, n. jabalina f.

jaw, n. quijada f.

jay, n. grajo m.

jazz, n. jazz m.

jealous, a. celoso. **to be j.,** tener celos.

jealousy, n. celos m.pl.

jeans, n. jeans m.pl.

jeer, 1. n. burla f., mofa f. **2.** v. burlar, mofar.

jelly, n. jalea f.

jellyfish, n. aguamar m.

jeopardize, v. arriesgar.

jeopardy, n. riesgo m.

jerk, 1. n. sacudida f. **2.** v. sacudir.

jerky, a. espasmódico.

Jerusalem, n. Jerusalén m.

jest, 1. n. broma f. **2.** v. bromear.

jester, n. bufón m.; burlón m.

Jesuit, 1. n. jesuita m. **2.** a. jesuítico.

Jesus Christ, n. Jesucristo m.

jet, n. chorro m.; (gas) mechero m.

jet lag, n. fatiga que sufre un viajero en avión, por causa del cambio de horas.

jetsam, n. echazón f.

jettison, v. echar mercancias al mar.

jetty, n. muelle m.

Jew, n. judío -día.

jewel, n. joya f.

jeweler, n. joyero m.

jewelry, n. joyería f. **j. store,** joyería f.

Jewish, a. judío.

jib, n. (naut.) foque m.

jiffy, n. instante m.

jig, n. jiga f. **j-saw,** sierra de vaivén f.

jilt, v. dar calabazas.

jingle, 1. n. retintín m.; rima pueril f. **2.** v. retiñir.

jinx, 1. n. aojo m. **2.** v. aojar.

jittery, a. nervioso.

job, n. empleo m.

jobber, n. destajista m., remendero m.

jockey, n. jockey m.

jocular, a. jocoso.

jog, 1. n. empujoncito m. **2.** v. empujar; estimular. **to j. along,** ir a un trote corto.

join, v. juntar; unir.

joiner, n. ebanista m.

joint, n. juntura f.

jointly, adv. conjuntamente.

joke, 1. n. broma, chanza f.; chiste m. **2.** v. bromear.

joker, *n.* bromista *m. & f.*

jolly, *a.* alegre, jovial.

jolt, 1. *n.* sacudido *m.* **2.** *v.* sacudir.

jonquil, *n.* junquillo *m.*

jostle, *v.* rempujar.

journal, *n.* diario *m.;* revista *f.*

journalism, *n.* periodismo *m.*

journalist, *n.* periodista *m. & f.*

journey, 1. *n.* viaje *m.;* jornada *f.* **2.** *v.* viajar.

journeyman, *n.* jornalero *m.,* oficial *m.*

jovial, *a.* jovial.

jowl, *n.* carrillo *m.*

joy, *n.* alegría *f.*

joyful, joyous, *a.* alegre, gozoso.

jubilant, *a.* jubiloso.

jubilee, *n.* jubileo *m.*

Judaism, *n.* judaísmo *m.*

judge, 1. *n.* juez *m.* **2.** *v.* juzgar.

judgment, *n.* juicio *m.*

judicial, *a.* judicial.

judiciary, *a.* judiciario *m.*

judicious, *a.* juicioso.

jug, *n.* jarro *m.*

juggle, *v.* escamotear.

juice, *n.* jugo, zumo *m.*

juicy, *a.* jugoso.

July, *n.* julio *m.*

jumble, 1. *n.* revoltillo *m.* **2.** *v.* arrebujar, revolver.

jump, 1. *n.* salto *m.* **2.** *v.* saltar, brincar.

junction, *n.* confluencia *f.;* (railway) empalme *m.*

juncture, *n.* junta *f.*

June, *n.* junio *m.*

jungle, *n.* selva *f.*

junior, *a.* menor; más joven. **Jr.** *n.* hijo.

juniper, *n.* enebro *m.*

junk, *n.* basura *f.*

junket, 1. *n.* leche cuajado *f.* **2.** *v.* festejar.

jurisdiction, *n.* jurisdicción *f.*

jurisprudence, *n.* jurisprudencia *f.*

jurist, *n.* jurista *m.*

juror, *n.* jurado *m.*

jury, *n.* jurado *m.*

just, 1. *a.* justo; exacto. **2.** *adv.* exactamente; (only) sólo. **j. now,** ahora mismo. **to have j.,** acabar de.

justice, *n.* justicia *f.;* (person) juez *m.*

justifiable, *a.* justificable.

justification, *n.* justificación *f.*

justify, *v.* justificar.

jut, *v.* sobresalir.

jute, *n.* yute *m.*

juvenile, *a.* juvenil.

K

kaleidoscope, *n.* calidoscopio *m.*

kangaroo, *n.* canguro *m.*

karakul, *n.* caracul *m.*

karat, *n.* quilate *m.*

karate, *n.* karate *m.*

keel, 1. *n.* quilla *f.* **2.** *v.* **to k. over,** volcarse.

keen, *a.* agudo; penetrante.

keep, *v.* mantener, retener; guardar; preservar. **k. on,** seguir, continuar.

keeper, *n.* guardián *m.*

keepsake, *n.* recuerdo *m.*

keg, *n.* barrilito *m.*

kennel, *n.* perrera *f.*

kerchief, *n.* pañuelo *m.*

kernel, *n.* pepita *f.;* grano *m.*

kerosene, *n.* kerosén *m.*

ketchup, *n.* salsa de tomate *f.*

kettle, *n.* caldera, olla *f.*

kettledrum, *n.* tímpano *m.*

key, *n.* llave *f.;* (music) clave *f.;* (piano) tecla *f.*

keyhole, *n.* bocallave *f.*

khaki, *a.* caqui.

kick, 1. *n.* patada *f.* **2.** *v.* patear; (coll.) quejarse.

kid, 1. *n.* cabrito *m.;* (coll.) niño -ña, chico -ca. **2.** *v.* (coll.) bromear.

kidnap, *v.* secuestrar.

kidnaper, *n.* secuestrador *m.*

kidney, *n.* riñón *m.*

kidney bean, *n.* frijol *m.*

kill, *v.* matar.

killer, *n.* matador *m.*

kiln, *n.* horno *m.*

kilogram, *n.* kilogramo *m.*

kilohertz, *n.* kilohertzio *m.*

kilometer, *n.* kilómetro *m.*

kilowatt, *n.* kilovatio *m.*

kin, *n.* parentesco *m.;* parientes *m.pl.*

kind, 1. *a.* bondadoso, amable. **2.** *n.* género *m.;* clase *f.* **k. of,** algo, un poco.

kindergarten, n. kindergarten m.
kindle, v. encender.
kindling, n. encendimiento m. **k. wood,** leña menuda f.
kindly, a. bondadoso.
kindness, n. bondad f.
kindred, n. parentesco m.
kinetic, a. cinético.
king, n. rey m.
kingdom, n. reino m.
kink, n. retorcimiento m.
kiosk, n. kiosco m.
kiss, 1. n. beso m. **2.** v. besar.
kitchen, n. cocina f.
kite, n. cometa f.
kitten, n. gatito -ta.
kleptomania, n. cleptomanía f.
kleptomaniac, n. cleptómano m.
knack, n. don m., destreza f.
knapsack, n. alforja f.
knead, v. amasar.
knee, n. rodilla f.
kneecap, n. rodillera f.
kneel, v. arrodillarse.
knickers, n. calzón corto m., pantalones m.
knife, n. cuchillo m.
knight, n. caballero m.; (chess) caballo m.
knit, v. tejer.
knob, n. tirador m.
knock, 1. n. golpe m.; llamada f. **2.** v. golpear; tocar, llamar.
knot, 1. n. nudo; lazo m. **2.** v. anudar.
knotty, a. nudoso.
know, v. saber; (a person) conocer.
knowledge, n. conocimiento, saber m.
knuckle, n. nudillo m. **k. bone,** jarrete m. **to k. under,** ceder a.
Korea, n. Corea f.

L

label, 1. n. rótulo m. **2.** v. rotular; designar.
labor, 1. n. trabajo m.; la clase obrera. **2.** v. trabajar.
laboratory, n. laboratorio m.
laborer, n. trabajador, obrero m.
laborious, a. laborioso, difícil.
labor union, n. gremio obrero m.
labyrinth, n. laberinto m.

lace, 1. n. encaje m.; (of shoe) lazo m. **2.** v. amarrar.
lacerate, v. lacerar, lastimar.
laceration, n. laceración f., desgarro m.
lack, 1. n. falta f. **2.** faltar, carecer.
lackadaisical, a. indiferente; soñador.
laconic, a. lacónico.
lacquer, 1. n. laca f., barniz m. **2.** v. laquear, barnizar.
lactic, a. láctico.
lactose, n. lactosa f.
ladder, n. escalera f.
ladle, 1. n. cucharón m. **2.** v. servir con cucharón.
lady, n. señora, dama f.
ladybug, n. mariquita f.
lag, 1. n. retraso m. **2.** v. quedarse atrás.
lagoon, n. laguna f.
laid-back, a. de buen talante.
laity, n. laicidad f.
lake, n. lago m.
lamb, n. cordero m.
lame, 1. a. cojo; estropeado. **2.** v. estropear.
lament, 1. n. lamento m. **2.** v. lamentar.
lamentable, a. lamentable.
lamentation, n. lamento m.; lamentación f.
laminate, a. laminado.
lamp, n. lámpara f.
lampoon, 1. n. pasquín m. **2.** v. pasquinar.
lance, 1. n. lanza f. **2.** v. (med.) abrir.
land, 1. n. país m.; tierra f. **native l.,** patria f. **2.** v. desembarcar; (plane) aterrizar.
landholder, n. hacendado m.
landing, n. (of stairs) descanso m.; (ship) desembarcadero m.; (airplane) aterrizaje m.
landlady, landlord, n. propietario -ria.
landmark, n. mojón m., señal f.; rasgo sobresaliente m.
landscape, n. paisaje m.
landslide, n. derrumbe m.
lane, n. senda f.
language, n. lengua f., idioma m.; lenguaje m.
languid, a. lánguido.
languish, v. languidecer.

languor, n. languidez f.

lanolin, n. lanolina f.

lantern, n. linterna f.; farol m.

lap, 1. n. regazo m.; falda f. **2.** v. lamer.

lapel, n. solapa f.

lapse, 1. n. lapso m. **2.** v. pasar; decaer; caer en error.

larceny, n. ratería f.

lard, n. manteca f.

large, a. grande.

largely, v. ampliamente; mayormente; muy.

largo, n. & a. (mus.) largo m.

lariat, n. lazo m.

lark, n. (bird) alondra f.

larva, n. larva f.

laryngitis, n. laringitis f.

larynx, n. laringe f.

lascivious, a. lascivo.

laser, n. láser m.

lash, 1. n. azote, latigazo m. **2.** v. azotar.

lass, n. doncella f.

lassitude, n. lasitud f.

lasso, 1. n. lazo m. **2.** v. enlazar.

last, 1. a. pasado; (final) último. **at l.,** por fin. **2.** v. durar.

lasting, a. duradero.

latch, n. aldaba f.

late, 1. a. tardío; (deceased) difunto. **to be l.,** llegar tarde. **2.** adv. tarde.

lately, adv. recientemente.

latent, a. latente.

lateral, a. lateral.

lather, 1. n. espuma de jabón. **2.** v. enjabonar.

Latin, n. latín m.

Latin America, n. Hispanoamérica, América Latina f.

Latin American, a. & n. hispanoamericano -na.

latitude, n. latitud f.

latrine, n. letrina f.

latter, a. posterior. **the l.,** éste.

lattice, n. celosía f.

laud, v. loar.

laudable, a. laudable.

laudanum, n. láudano m.

laudatory, a. laudatorio.

laugh, 1. n. risa, risotada f. **2.** v. reír. **l. at,** reírse de.

laughable, a. risible.

laughter, n. risa f.

launch, 1. n. (naut.) lancha f. **2.** v. lanzar.

launder, v. lavar y planchar la ropa.

laundry, n. lavandería f.

laundryman, n. lavandero m.

laureate, n. & a. laureado m.

laurel, n. laureado.

lava, n. lava f.

lavatory, n. lavatorio m.

lavender, n. lavándula f.

lavish, 1. a. pródigo. **2.** v. prodigar.

law, n. ley f.; derecho m.

lawful, a. legal.

lawless, a. sin ley.

lawn, n. césped; prado m.

lawsuit, n. pleito m.

lawyer, n. abogado m.

lax, a. flojo, laxo.

laxative, n. purgante m.

laxity, n. laxidad f.; flojedad f.

lay, 1. a. secular. **2.** v. poner.

layer, n. capa f.

layman, n. lego, seglar m.

lazy, a. perezoso.

lead, 1. n. plomo m.; (theat.) papel principal. **to take the l.,** tomar la delantera. **2.** v. conducir; dirigir.

leaden, a. plomizo; pesado; abatido.

leader, n. líder; jefe; director m.

leadership, n. dirección f.

leaf, n. hoja f.

leaflet, n. (bot.) hojilla f.; folleto m.

league, n. liga; (measure) legua f.

leak, 1. n. escape; goteo m. **2.** v. gotear; (naut.) hacer agua.

leakage, n. goteo m., escape m.; pérdida f.

leaky, a. llovedizo; resquebrajado.

lean, 1. a. flaco, magro. **2.** v. apoyarse, arrimarse.

leap, 1. n. salto m. **2.** v. saltar.

leap year, n. año bisiesto m.

learn, v. aprender; saber.

learned, a. erudito.

learning, n. erudición f., instrucción f.

lease, 1. n. arriendo m. **2.** v. arrendar.

leash, 1. n. correa f. **2.** v. atraillar.

least, a. menor; mínimo. **the l.,** lo menos. **at l.,** por lo menos.

leather, n. cuero m.

leathery, a. coriáceo.

leave, 1. *n.* licencia *f.* **to take l.,** despedirse. **2.** *v.* dejar; (depart) salir, irse. **l. out,** omitir.
leaven, 1. *n.* levadura *f.* **2.** *v.* fermentar, imbuir.
lecherous, *a.* lujurioso.
lecture, *n.* conferencia *f.*
lecturer, *n.* conferencista *m.;* catedrático *m.*
ledge, *n.* borde *m.;* capa *f.*
ledger, *n.* libro mayor *m.*
lee, *n.* sotavento *m.*
leech, *n.* sanguijuela *f.*
leek, *n.* porro *m.*
leer, *v.* mirar de soslayo.
leeward, *n.* sotavento.
left, *a.* izquierdo. **the l.,** la izquierda. **to be left,** quedarse.
leftist, *n.* izquierdista *m. & f.*
leg, *n.* pierna *f.*
legacy, *n.* legado *m.,* herencia *f.*
legal, *a.* legal.
legalize, *v.* legalizar.
legation, *n.* legación, embajada *f.*
legend, *n.* leyenda *f.*
legendary, *a.* legendario.
legible, *a.* legible.
legion, *n.* legión *f.*
legislate, *v.* legislar.
legislation, *n.* legislación *f.*
legislator, *n.* legislador *m.*
legislature, *n.* legislatura *f.*
legitimate, *a.* legítimo.
legume, *n.* legumbre *f.*
leisure, *n.* desocupación *f.;* horas libres.
leisurely, 1. *a.* deliberado. **2.** *adv.* despacio.
lemon, *n.* limón *f.*
lemonade, *n.* limonada *f.*
lend, *v.* prestar.
length, *n.* largo *m.;* duración *f.*
lengthen, *v.* alargar.
lengthwise, *adv.* a lo largo.
lengthy, *a.* largo.
lenient, *a.* indulgente.
lens, *n.* lente *m. or f.*
Lent, *n.* cuaresma *f.*
Lenten, *a.* cuaresmal.
lentil, *n.* lenteja *f.*
leopard, *n.* leopardo *m.*
leper, *n.* leproso *m.*
leprosy, *n.* lepra *f.*
lesbian, *n.* lesbiana *f.*
lesion, *n.* lesión *f.*
less, *a. & adv.* menos.
lessen, *v.* disminuir.

lesser, *a.* menor; más pequeño.
lesson, *n.* lección *f.*
lest, *conj.* para que no.
let, *v.* dejar; permitir; arrendar.
lethal, *a.* letal.
lethargic, *a.* letárgico.
lethargy, *n.* letargo *m.*
letter, *n.* carta; (of alphabet) letra *f.*
letterhead, *n.* membrete *m.*
lettuce, *n.* lechuga *f.*
leukemia, *n.* leucemia *f.*
levee, *n.* recepción *f.*
level, 1. *a.* llano, nivelado. **2.** *n.* nivel *m.;* llanura *f.* **3.** *v.* allanar; nivelar.
lever, *n.* palanca *f.*
levity, *n.* levedad *f.*
levy, 1. *n.* leva *f.* **2.** *v.* imponer.
lewd, *a.* lascivo.
lexicon, *n.* léxico *m.*
liability, *n.* riesgo *m.;* obligación *f.*
liable, *a.* sujeto; responsable.
liaison, *n.* vinculación *f.,* enlace *m.;* concubinaje *m.*
liar, *n.* embustero -ra.
libel, 1. *n.* libelo *m.* **2.** *v.* difamar.
libelous, *a.* difamatorio.
liberal, *a.* liberal; generoso.
liberalism, *n.* liberalismo *m.*
liberality, *n.* liberalidad *f.*
liberate, *v.* libertar.
liberty, *n.* libertad *f.*
libidinous, *a.* libidinoso.
librarian, *n.* bibliotecario *m.*
library, *n.* biblioteca *f.*
libretto, *n.* libreto *m.*
license, *n.* licencia *f.;* permiso *m.*
licentious, *a.* licencioso.
lick, *v.* lamer.
licorice, *n.* regaliz *m.*
lid, *n.* tapa *f.*
lie, 1. *n.* mentira *f.* **2.** *v.* mentir. **l. down,** acostarse, echarse.
lieutenant, *n.* teniente *m.*
life, *n.* vida *f.*
lifeboat, *n.* bote salvavidas *m.*
life buoy, *n.* buya *f.*
life insurance, *n.* seguro de vida *m.*
lifeless, *a.* sin vida.
life preserver, *n.* salvavidas *m.*
life style, *n.* modo de vida *m.*
lift, *v.* levantar, alzar, elevar.
ligament, *n.* ligamento *m.*
ligature, *n.* ligadura *f.*

light, 1. *a.* ligero; liviano; (in color) claro. 2. *n.* luz; candela *f.* 3. *v.* encender; iluminar.

lighten, *v.* aligerar; aclarar; iluminar.

lighter, *n.* encendedor *m.*

lighthouse, *n.* faro *m.*

lightness, *n.* ligereza; agilidad *f.*

lightning, *n.* relámpago *m.*

like, 1. *a.* semejante. 2. *prep.* como. 3. *v.* **I like . . .** me gusta, me gustan . . . **I should like,** quisiera.

likeable, *a.* simpático, agradable.

likelihood, *n.* probabilidad *f.*

likely, *a.* probable; verosímil.

liken, *v.* comparar; asemejar.

likeness, *n.* semejanza *f.*

likewise, *adv.* igualmente.

lilac, *n.* lila *f.*

lilt, 1. *n.* cadencia alegre *f.* 2. *v.* cantar alegremente.

lily, *n.* lirio *m.*

lily of the valley, *n.* muguete *m.*

limb, *n.* rama *f.*

limber, *a.* flexible. **to l. up,** ponerse flexible.

limbo, *n.* limbo *m.*

lime, *n.* cal *f.;* (fruit) limoncito *m.,* lima *f.*

limestone, *n.* piedra caliza *f.*

limewater, *n.* agua de cal *f.*

limit, 1. *n.* límite *m.* 2. *v.* limitar.

limitation, *n.* limitación *f.*

limitless, *a.* ilimitado.

limousine, *n.* limousine *f.*

limp, 1. *n.* cojera *f.* 2. *a.* flojo. 3. *v.* cojear.

limpid, *a.* límpido.

line, 1. *n.* línea; fila; raya *f.;* (of print) renglón *m.* 2. *v.* forrar; rayar.

lineage, *n.* linaje *m.*

lineal, *a.* lineal.

linear, *a.* lineal, longitudinal.

linen, *n.* lienzo, lino *m.;* ropa blanca.

liner, *n.* vapor *m.*

linger, *v.* demorarse.

lingerie, *n.* ropa blanca *f.*

linguist, *n.* lingüista *m. & f.*

linguistic, *a.* lingüístico.

liniment, *n.* linimento *m.*

lining, *n.* forro *m.*

link, 1. *n.* eslabón; vínculo *m.* 2. *v.* vincular.

linoleum, *n.* linóleo *m.*

linseed, *n.* linaza *f.;* simiente de lino *f.*

lint, *n.* hilacha *f.*

lion, *n.* león *m.*

lip, *n.* labio *m.*

lipstick, *n.* lápiz de labios.

liqueur, *n.* cordial *m.*

liquid, *a. & n.* líquido *m.*

liquidate, *v.* liquidar.

liquidation, *n.* liquidación *f.*

liquor, *n.* licor *m.*

lisp, 1. *n.* ceceo *m.* 2. *v.* cecear.

list, 1. *n.* lista *f.* 2. *v.* registrar.

listen (to), *v.* escuchar.

listless, *a.* indiferente.

litany, *n.* letanía *f.*

liter, *n.* litro *m.*

literal, *a.* literal.

literary, *a.* literario.

literate, *a.* literato.

literature, *n.* literatura *f.*

litigant, *n. & a.* litigante *m.*

litigation, *n.* litigio, pleito *m.*

litter, 1. *n.* litera *f.;* cama de paja. 2. *v.* poner en desorden.

little, *a.* pequeño; (quantity) poco.

liturgical, *a.* litúrgico.

liturgy, *n.* liturgia *f.*

live, 1. *a.* vivo. 2. *v.* vivir.

livelihood, *n.* subsistencia *f.*

lively, *a.* vivo; rápido; animado.

liver, *n.* hígado *m.*

livery, *n.* librea *f.*

livestock, *n.* ganadería *f.*

livid, *a.* lívido.

living, 1. *a.* vivo. 2. *n.* sustento *m.* **to earn (make) a living,** ganarse la vida.

lizard, *n.* lagarto *m.,* lagartija *f.*

llama, *n.* llama *f.*

load, 1. *n.* carga *f.* 2. *v.* cargar.

loaf, 1. *n.* pan *m.* 2. *v.* holgazanear.

loam, *n.* marga *f.*

loan, 1. *n.* préstamo *m.* 2. *v.* prestar.

loathe, *v.* aborrecer, detestar.

lobby, *n.* vestíbulo *m.*

lobe, *n.* lóbulo *m.*

lobster, *n.* langosta *f.*

local, *a.* local.

locale, *n.* localidad *f.*

locality, *n.* localidad *f.,* lugar *m.*

localize, *v.* localizar.

locate, *v.* situar; hallar.

location, *n.* sitio *m.;* posición *f.*

lock, 1. n. cerradura f.; (pl.) cabellos m.pl. **2.** v. cerrar con llave.

locker, n. cajón m.; ropero m.

locket, n. guardapelo m., medallón m.

lockjaw, n. trismo m.

locksmith, n. cerrajero m.

locomotive, n. locomotora f.

locust, n. cigarra f., saltamontes m.

locution, n. locución f.

lode, n. filón m., vena f.

lodge, 1. n. logia; (inn) posada f. **2.** v. fijar; alojar, morar.

lodger, n. inquilino m.

lodging, n. posada f.

loft, n. piso m., sobrado m.

lofty, a. alto; altivo.

log, n. tronco de árbol; (naut.) barquilla f.

loge, n. palco m.

logic, n. lógica f.

logical, a. lógico.

loin, n. lomo m.

loiter, v. haraganear.

lone, a. solitario.

loneliness, n. soledad f.; tristeza f.

lonely, lonesome, a. solo y triste.

lonesome, a. solitario; triste.

long, 1. a. largo. **a l. time,** mucho tiempo. **2.** adv. mucho tiempo. **how l.,** cuánto tiempo. **no longer,** ya no. **3.** v. l. for, anhelar.

longevity, n. longevidad f.

longing, n. anhelo m.

longitude, n. longitud m.

look, 1. n. mirada f.; aspecto m. **2.** v. parecer; mirar. l. at, mirar. l. for, buscar. l. like, parecerse a. l. out!, ¡cuidado! l. up, buscar; ir a ver, venir a ver.

looking glass, n. espejo m.

loom, 1. n. telar m. **2.** v. asomar.

loop, n. vuelta f.

loophole, n. abertura f., mirador m.

loose, a. suelto; flojo.

loosen, v. soltar; aflojar.

loot, 1. n. botín m., saqueo m. **2.** v. saquear.

lopsided, a. desequilibrado.

loquacious, a. locuaz.

lord, n. señor m.; (Brit. title) lord m.

lordship, n. señorío m.

lose, v. perder.

loss, n. pérdida f.

lost, a. perdido.

lot, n. suerte f. **building l.,** solar m. **a lot (of), lots of,** mucho.

lotion, n. loción f.

lottery, n. lotería f.

loud, 1. a. fuerte; ruidoso. **2.** adv. alto.

loudspeaker, n. altavoz m.

lounge, n. sofá m.; salón de fumar m.

louse, n. piojo m.

love, 1. n. amor m. **in l.,** enamorado. **to fall in l.,** enamorarse. **2.** v. querer; amar; adorar.

lovely, a. hermoso.

lover, n. amante m.

low, a. bajo; vil.

lower, v. bajar; (in price) rebajar.

lowly, a. humilde.

loyal, a. leal, fiel.

loyalist, n. lealista m. & f.

loyalty, n. lealtad f.

lozenge, n. pastilla f.

lubricant, n. lubricante m.

lubricate, v. engrasar, lubricar.

lucid, a. claro, lúcido.

luck, n. suerte; fortuna f.

lucky, a. afortunado. **to be l.,** tener suerte.

lucrative, a. lucrativo.

ludicrous, a. ridículo.

luggage, n. equipaje m.

lukewarm, a. tibio.

lull, 1. n. momento de calma. **2.** v. calmar.

lullaby, n. arrullo m.

lumbago, n. lumbago m.

lumber, n. madera f.

luminous, a. luminoso.

lump, n. protuberancia f.; (of sugar) terrón m.

lunacy, n. locura f.

lunar, a. lunar.

lunatic, a. & n. loco -ca.

lunch, luncheon, 1. n. merienda f., almuerzo m. **2.** v. merendar, almorzar.

lung, n. pulmón m.

lunge, 1. n. estocada f. **2.** v. dar un estocada.

lure, v. atraer.

lurid, a. rojizo; fantástico.

lurk, v. esconderse; espiar.

luscious, a. sabroso, delicioso.

lust, n. sensualidad; codicia f.

luster, n. lustre m.

lustful, a. sensual, lascivo.
lusty, a. vigoroso.
lute, n. laúd m.
Lutheran, n. & a. luterano m.
luxuriant, a. exuberante, frondoso.
luxurious, a. lujoso.
luxury, n. lujo m.
lying, a. mentiroso.
lymph, n. linfa f.
lynch, v. linchar.
lyre, n. lira f.
lyric, a. lírico.
lyricism, n. lirismo m.

M

macabre, a. macabre.
macaroni, n. macarrones m.
machine, n. máquina f.
machine gun, n. ametralladora f.
machinery, n. maquinaria f.
machinist, n. maquinista, mecánico m.
macho, n. machista.
mackerel, n. escombro m.
mad, a. loco; furioso.
madam, n. señora f.
mafia, n. mafia f.
magazine, n. revista f.
magic, 1. a. mágico. 2. n. magia f.
magician, n. mágico m.
magistrate, n. magistrado m.
magnanimous, a. magnánimo.
magnate, n. magnate m.
magnesium, n. magnesio m.
magnet, n. imán m.
magnetic, a. magnético.
magnificence, n. magnificencia f.
magnificent, a. magnífico.
magnify, v. magnificar.
magnitude, n. magnitud f.
mahogany, n. caoba f.
maid, n. criada f. **old m.,** soltera f.
maiden, a. soltero.
mail, 1. n. correo m. **air m.,** correo aéreo. **by return m.,** a vuelta de correo. 2. v. echar al correo.
mailbox, n. buzón m.
mailman, n. cartero m.
maim, v. multilar.
main, a. principal.
mainframe, n. componente central de una computadora.
mainland, n. continente m.

maintain, v. mantener; sostener.
maintenance, n. mantenimiento; sustento m.; conservación f.
maize, n. maiz m.
majestic, a. majestuoso.
majesty, n. majestad f.
major, 1. a. mayor. 2. n. (mil.) comandante m.; (study) especialidad f.
majority, n. mayoría f.
make, 1. n. marca f. 2. v. hacer; fabricar; (earn) ganar.
maker, n. fabricante m.
makeshift, a. provisional.
make-up, n. cosméticos m.pl.
malady, n. mal m., enfermedad f.
malaria, n. paludismo m.
male, a. & n. macho m.
malevolent, a. malévolo.
malice, n. malicia f.
malicious, a. malicioso.
malign, 1. v. difamar. 2. a. maligno.
malignant, a. maligno.
malnutrition, n. desnutrición f.
malt, n. malta m. & f.
mammal, n. mamífero m.
man, n. hombre; varón m.
manage, v. manejar; dirigir; administrar; arreglárselas. **m. to,** lograr.
management, n. dirección, administración f.
manager, n. director m.
mandate, n. mandato m.
mandatory, a. obligatorio.
mandolin, n. mandolina f.
mane, n. crines f.
maneuver, 1. n. maniobra f. 2. v. maniobrar.
manganese, n. manganeso m.
manger, n. pesebre m.
mangle, 1. n. planchadora mecánica. 2. v. mutilar.
manhood, n. virilidad f.
mania, n. manía f.
maniac, a. & n. maníático m.
manicure, n. manicuro m.
manifest, 1. a. & n. manifiesto m. 2. v. manifestar.
manifesto, n. manifesto m.
manifold, 1. a. muchos. 2. n. (auto.) tubo múltiple.
manipulate, v. manipular.
mankind, n. humanidad f.
manly, a. varonil.

manner, *n.* manera *f.,* modo *m.*
manners, modales *m.pl.*
mannerism, *n.* manerismo *m.*
mansion, *n.* mansión *f.*
mantel, *n.* manto de chimenea.
mantle, *n.* manto *m.*
manual, *a. & n.* manual *m.*
manufacture, *v.* fabricar.
manufacturer, *n.* fabricante *m.*
manufacturing, *n.* fabricación *f.*
manure, *n.* abono, estiércol *m.*
manuscript, *n.* manuscrito *m.*
many, *a.* muchos. **how m., so m.,** tantos. **too m.,** demasiados, cuántos. **as m. as,** tantos como.
map, *n.* mapa *m.*
maple, *n.* arce *m.*
mar, *v.* estropear; desfigurar.
marble, *n.* mármol *m.*
march, 1. marcha *f.* **2.** *v.* marchar.
mare, *n.* yegua *f.*
margarine, *n.* margarina *f.*
margin, *n.* margen *m. or f.*
marijuana, *n.* marijuana *f.*
marine, 1. *a.* marino. **2.** *n.* soldado de marina.
mariner, *n.* marinero *m.*
marionette, *n.* marioneta *f.*
marital, *a.* marital.
maritime, *a.* marítimo.
mark, 1. *n.* marca *f.* **2.** *v.* marcar.
market, *n.* mercado *m.* **meat m.,** carnicería *f.* **stock m.,** bolsa *f.*
marmalade, *n.* mermelada *f.*
maroon, *a. & n.* color rojo oscuro.
marquis, *n.* marqués *m.*
marriage, *n.* matrimonio *m.*
married, *a.* casado. **to get m.,** casarse.
marrow, *n.* medula *f.;* substancia *f.*
marry, *v.* casarse con; casar.
marsh, *n.* pantano *m.*
marshal, *n.* mariscal *m.*
marshmallow, *n.* malvarisco *m.;* bombón de altea *m.*
martial, *a.* marcial. **m. law,** gobierno militar.
martyr, *n.* mártir *m. & f.*
martyrdom, *n.* martirio *m.*
marvel, 1. *n.* maravilla *f.* **2.** *v.* maravillarse.
marvelous, *a.* maravilloso.
mascot, *n.* mascota *f.*
masculine, *a.* masculino.

mash, *v.* majar. **mashed potatoes,** puré de papas *m.*
mask, *n.* máscara *f.*
mason, *n.* albañil *m.*
masquerade, *n.* mascarada *f.*
mass, *n.* masa *f.;* (rel.) misa *f.* **to say m.,** cantar misa. **m. production,** producción en serie.
massacre, 1. *n.* carnicería, matanza *f.* **2.** *v.* matar attrozmente, destrozar.
massage, 1. *n.* masaje *m.;* soba *f.* **2.** *v.* sobar.
masseur, *n.* masajista *m. & f.*
massive, *a.* macizo, sólido.
mast, *n.* palo, árbol *m.*
master, 1. *n.* amo; maestro *m.* **2.** *v.* domar, dominar.
masterpiece, *n.* obra maestra.
mastery, *n.* maestría *f.*
mat, 1. *n.* estera; palleta *f.* **2.** *v.* enredar.
match, 1. *n.* igual *m.;* fósforo *m.;* (sport) partida, contienda *f.;* (marriage) noviazgo; casamiento. **2.** *v.* ser igual a; igualar.
mate, 1. *n.* consorte *m. & f.;* compañero -ra. **2.** *v.* igualar; casar.
material, *a. & n.* material *m.* **raw materials,** materias primas.
materialism, *n.* materialismo *m.*
materialize, *v.* materializar.
maternal, *a.* materno.
maternity, *n.* maternidad *f.*
mathematical, *a.* matemático.
mathematics, *n.* matemáticas *f.pl.*
matinee, *n.* matiné *m.*
matrimony, *n.* matrimonio *m.*
matron, *n.* matrona; directora *f.*
matter, 1. *n.* materia *f.;* asunto *m.* **what's the m.?,** ¿qué pasa? **2.** *v.* importar.
mattress, *n.* colchón *m.*
mature, 1. *a.* maduro. **2.** *v.* madurar.
maturity, *n.* madurez *f.*
maudlin, *a.* sentimental en exceso; peneque.
maul, *v.* maltratar a golpes.
maxim, *n.* máxima *f.*
maximum, *a. & n.* máximo.
may, *v.* poder.
May, *n.* mayo *m.*
maybe, *adv.* quizá, quizás, tal vez.
mayonnaise, *n.* mayonesa *f.*
mayor, *n.* alcalde *m.*

maze, n. laberinto m.

me, pron. mí; me. **with me,** conmigo.

meadow, n. prado m.; vega f.

meager, a. magro; pobre.

meal, n. comida; (flour) harina f.

mean, 1. a. bajo; malo. **2.** n. medio (see also **means**). **3.** v. significar; querer decir.

meaning, n. sentido, significado m.

means, n.pl. medios, recursos m. **by all m.,** sin falta. **by no m.,** de ningún modo. **by m. of,** por medio de.

meanwhile, adv. mientras tanto.

measles, n. sarampión m.

measure, 1. n. medida f.; (music) compás m. **2.** v. medir.

measurement, n. medida, dimensión f.

meat, n. carne f.

mechanic, n. mecánico m.

mechanical, a. mecánico.

mechanism, n. mecanismo m.

mechanize, v. mecanizar.

medal, n. medalla f.

meddle, v. meterse, entremeterse.

mediate, v. mediar.

medical, a. médico.

medicine, n. medicina f.

medieval, a. medioeval.

mediocre, a. mediocre.

mediocrity, n. mediocridad f.

meditate, v. meditar.

meditation, n. meditación f.

Mediterranean, n. Mediterráneo m.

medium, 1. a. mediano, medio. **2.** n. medio m.

medley, n. mezcla f., ensalada f.

meek, a. manso; humilde.

meekness, n. modestia; humildad f.

meet, 1. a. propio. **2.** n. concurso m. **3.** v. encontrar; reunirse; conocer.

meeting, n. reunión f.; mitin m.

megahertz, n. megahertzio m.

megaphone, n. megáfono m.

melancholy, 1. a. melancólico. **2.** n. melancolía f.

mellow, a. suave; blando; maduro.

melodious, a. melodioso.

melodrama, n. melodrama m.

melody, n. melodía f.

melon, n. melón m.

melt, v. derretir.

meltdown, n. fundición resultante de un accidente en un reactor nuclear.

member, n. socio -ia; miembro m.

membership, n. membrecía f.

membrane, n. membrana f.

memento, n. recuerdo m.

memoir, n. memoria f.

memorable, a. memorable.

memorandum, n. memorándum, volante m.

memorial, 1. a. conmemorativo. **2.** n. memorial m.

memorize, v. aprender de memoria.

memory, n. memoria f.; recuerdo m.

menace, 1. n. amenaza f. **2.** v. amenazar.

mend, v. reparar, remendar.

menial, 1. a. servil. **2.** n. sirviente m.

menopause, n. menopausia f.

menstruation, n. menstruación f.

menswear, n. ropa de caballeros f.

mental, a. mental.

mentality, n. mentalidad f.

menthol, n. mentol m.

mention, 1. n. mención f. **2.** v. mencionar.

menu, n. menú m., lista f.

mercantile, a. mercantil.

mercenary, a. & n. mercenario -ria.

merchandise, n. mercancía f.

merchant, 1. n. mercante. **2.** n. comerciante m.

merciful, a. misericordioso, compasivo.

merciless, a. cruel, inhumano.

mercury, n. mercurio m.

mercy, n. misericordia; merced f.

mere, a. mero, puro.

merely, adv. solamente; simplemente.

merge, v. unir, combinar.

merger, n. consolidación, fusión.

meringue, n. merengue m.

merit, 1. n. mérito m. **2.** v. merecer.

meritorious, a. meritorio.

mermaid, n. sirena f.

merriment, n. regocijo m.

merry, *a.* alegre, festivo.

merry-go-round, *n.* caballitos *m.*

mesh, *n.* malla *f.*

mess, 1. *n.* lío *m.;* confusión *f.;* (mil.) salón comedor, rancho *m.* **2.** *v.* **m. up,** ensuciar; enredar.

message, *n.* mensaje, recado *f.*

messenger, *n.* mensajero -ra.

messy, *a.* confuso, desarreglado.

metabolism, *n.* metabolismo *m.*

metal, *n.* metal *m.*

metallic, *a.* metálico.

metaphysics, *n.* metafísica *f.*

meteor, *n.* metéoro *m.*

meteorology, *n.* meteorología *f.*

meter, *n.* medidor; (measure) metro *m.*

method, *n.* método *m.*

meticulous, *a.* meticuloso.

metric, *a.* métrico.

metropolis, *n.* metrópoli *f.*

metropolitan, *a.* metropolitano.

Mexican, *a. & n.* mexicano -na.

Mexico, *n.* México *m.*

mezzanine, *n.* entresuelo *m.*

microbe, *n.* microbio *m.*

microfiche, *n.* microficha *f.*

microfilm, *n.* microfilm *m.*

microform, *n.* microforma *f.*

microphone, *n.* micrófono *m.*

microscope, *n.* microscopio *m.*

microscopic, *a.* microscópico.

mid, *a.* medio.

middle, *a. & n.* medio *m.* **in the m. of,** en medio de, a mediados de.

middle-aged, *a.* de edad madura.

Middle East, *n.* Medio Oriente *m.*

midget, *n.* enano -na.

midnight, *n.* medianoche *f.*

midwife, *n.* partera *f.*

might, *n.* poder *m.,* fuerza *f.*

mighty, *a.* poderoso.

migraine, *n.* migraña *f.;* jaqueca *f.*

migrate, *v.* emigrar.

migration, *n.* emigración *f.*

migratory, *a.* migratorio.

mild, *a.* moderado, suave; templado.

mildew, *n.* añublo *m.,* moho *m.*

mile, *n.* milla *f.*

militant, *a.* militante.

militarism, *n.* militarismo *m.*

military, *a.* militar.

militia, *n.* milicia *f.*

milk, 1. *n.* leche *f.* **2.** *v.* ordeñar.

milkman, *n.* lechero *m.*

milky, *a.* lácteo; lechoso.

mill, 1. *n.* molino *m.;* fábrica *f.* **2.** *v.* moler.

miller, *n.* molinero *m.*

millimeter, *n.* milímetro *m.*

milliner, *n.* modista *m. & f.*

millinery, *n.* sombrerería *f.*

million, *n.* millón *m.*

millionaire, *n.* millonario -ria.

mimic, 1. *n.* mimo *m.* **2.** *v.* imitar.

mind, 1. *n.* mente; opinión *f.* **2.** *v.* obedecer. **never m.,** no se ocupe.

mindful, *a.* atento.

mine, 1. *pron.* mío *f.* **2.** *n.* mina *f.* **3.** *v.* minar.

miner, *n.* minero *m.*

mineral, *a. & n.* mineral *m.*

mine sweeper, *n.* dragaminas *f.*

mingle, *v.* mezclar.

miniature, *n.* miniatura *f.*

miniaturize, *v.* miniaturizar.

minimize, *v.* menospreciar.

minimum, *a. & n.* mínimo *m.*

mining, *n.* minería *f.*

minister, 1. *n.* ministro; (rel.) pastor *m.* **2.** *v.* ministrar.

ministry, *n.* ministerio *m.*

mink, *n.* visón *m.;* (fur) piel de visón *m.*

minor, 1. *a.* menor. **2.** *n.* menor de edad.

minority, *n.* minoría *f.*

minstrel, *n.* juglar *m.*

mint, 1. *n.* menta *f.;* casa de moneda. **2.** *v.* acuñar.

minus, *prep.* menos.

minute, 1. *a.* minucioso. **2.** *n.* minuto, momento *m.*

miracle, *n.* milagro *m.*

miraculous, *a.* milagroso.

mirage, *n.* miraje *m.*

mire, *n.* lodo *m.*

mirror, *n.* espejo *m.*

mirth, *n.* alegría; risa *f.*

misbehave, *v.* portarse mal.

miscellaneous, *a.* misceláneo.

mischief, *n.* travesura, diablura *f.*

mischievous, *a.* travieso, dañino.

miser, *n.* avaro -ra.

miserable, *a.* miserable; infeliz.

miserly, *a.* avariento, tacaño.

misfortune, *n.* desgracia *f.,* infortunio, revés *m.*

misgiving, *n.* recelo *m.,* desconfianza *f.*

mishap, n. desgracia f., contratiempo m.

mislead, v. extraviar, despistar; pervertir.

misplaced, a. extraviado.

mispronounce, v. pronunciar mal.

miss, **1.** n. señorita f. **2.** v. perder; echar de menos, extrañar. **be missing**, faltar.

missile, n. proyectil m.

mission, n. misión; comisión f.

missionary, n. misionero -ra.

mist, n. niebla, bruma f.

mistake, **1.** n. equivocación f.; error m. **to make a m.**, equivocarse.

mistaken, a. equivocado.

mister, n. señor m.

mistletoe, n. muérdago m.

mistreat, v. maltratar.

mistress, n. ama; señora; concubina f.

mistrust, v. desconfiar; sospechar.

misty, a. nebuloso, brumoso.

misunderstand, v. entender mal.

misuse, v. maltratar; abusar.

mite, n. pizca f., blanca f.

mitten, n. mitón, confortante m.

mix, v. mezclar. **m. up**, confundir.

mixture, n. mezcla, mixtura f.

mix-up, n. confusión f.

moan, **1.** n. quejido, gemido m. **2.** v. gemir.

mob, n. muchedumbre f.; gentío m.

mobilization, n. movilización f.

mobilize, v. movilizar.

mock, v. burlar.

mockery, n. burla f.

mod, a. a la última; en boga.

mode, n. modo m.

model, **1.** n. modelo m. **2.** v. modelar.

moderate, **1.** a. moderado. **2.** v. moderar.

moderation, n. moderación; sobriedad f.

modern, a. moderno.

modernize, v. modernizar.

modest, a. modesto.

modesty, n. modestia f.

modify, v. modificar.

modulate, v. modular.

moist, a. húmedo.

moisten, v. humedecer.

moisture, n. humedad f.

molar, n. molar m.

molasses, n. molaza f.

mold, **1.** n. molde; moho m. **2.** v. moldar, formar; enmohecerse.

moldy, a. mohoso.

mole, n. lunar m.; (animal) topo m.

molecule, n. molécula f.

molest, v. molestar.

mollify, v. molificar.

moment, n. momento m.

momentary, a. momentáneo.

momentous, a. importante.

monarch, n. monarca m.

monarchy, n. monarquía f.

monastery, n. monasterio m.

Monday, n. lunes m.

monetary, a. monetario.

money, n. dinero m. **m. order**, giro postal.

mongrel, **1.** n. mestizo m. **2.** a. mestizo, cruzado.

monitor, n. amonestador m.

monk, n. monje m.

monkey, n. mono -na.

monocle, n. monóculo m.

monologue, n. monólogo m.

monopolize, v. monopolizar.

monopoly, n. monopolio m.

monosyllable, n. monosílabo m.

monotone, n. monotonía f.

monotonous, a. monótono.

monotony, n. monotonía f.

monsoon, n. monzón m.

monster, n. monstruo m.

monstrosity, n. monstruosidad f.

monstrous, a. monstruoso.

month, n. mes m.

monthly, a. mensual.

monument, n. momumento m.

monumental, a. monumental.

mood, n. humor m.; (gram.) modo m.

moody, a. caprichoso, taciturno.

moon, n. luna f.

moonlight, n. luz de la luna.

moor, **1.** n. páramo m. **2.** v. anclar.

mop, **1.** n. estropajo m. **2.** v. fregar.

moped (vehicle), n. velomotor m.

moral, **1.** a. moral. **2.** n. moraleja f. **morals**, moralidad f.

morale, n. espíritu m.

moralist, n. moralista m.

morality, n. moralidad f.

morbid, a. mórbido.

more, *a. & adv.* más. **m. and m.,** cada vez más.

moreover, *adv.* además.

morgue, *n.* necrocomio *m.*

morning, *n.* mañana *f.* **good m.,** buenos días.

morose, *a.* malhumorado.

morphine, *n.* morfina *f.*

morsel, *n.* bocado *m.*

mortal, *a. & n.* mortal *m.*

mortality, *n.* mortalidad *f.*

mortar, *n.* mortero *m.*

mortgage, 1. *n.* hipoteca *f.* **2.** *v.* hipotecar.

mortify, *v.* mortificar.

mosaic, *n. & a.* mosaico *m.*

mosquito, *n.* mosquito *m.*

moss, *n.* musgo *m.*

most, 1. *a.* más. **2.** *adv.* más; sumamente. **3.** *pron.* **m. of,** la mayor parte de.

mostly, *adv.* principalmente; en su mayor parte.

moth, *n.* polilla *f.*

mother, *n.* madre *f.*

mother-in-law, *n.* suegra *f.*

motif, *n.* tema *m.*

motion, 1. *n.* moción *f.;* movimiento *m.* **2.** *v.* hacer señas.

motionless, *a.* inmóvil.

motion picture, *n.* película *f.*

motivate, *v.* motivar.

motive, *n.* motivo *m.*

motor, *n.* motor *m.*

motorboat, *n.* bote de gasolina.

motorcycle, *n.* motocicleta *f.*

motorist, *n.* motorista *m. & f.*

motto, *n.* lema *m.*

mound, *n.* terrón; montón *m.*

mount, 1. *n.* monte *m.;* (horse) montura *f.* **2.** *v.* montar; subir.

mountain, *n.* montaña *f.*

mountaineer, *n.* montañés *m.*

mountainous, *a.* montañoso.

mourn, *v.* lamentar, llorar; llevar luto.

mournful, *a.* triste.

mourning, *n.* luto; lamento *m.*

mouse, *n.* ratón, ratoncito *m.*

mouth, *n.* boca *f.;* (of river) desembocadura *f.*

movable, *a.* movible, movedizo.

move, 1. *n.* movimiento *m.;* mudanza. **2.** *v.* mover; mudarse; conmover, mudarse. **m. away,**

movement, *n.* movimiento *m.*

movie, *n.* película *f.* **m. theater, movies,** cine *m.*

moving, *a.* conmovedor; persuasivo.

mow, *v.* guadañar, segar.

Mr., *title.* Señor (Sr.).

Mrs., *title.* Señora (Sra.).

much, *a. & adv.* mucho. **how m.,** cuánto; no *f.,* tanto. **too m.,** demasiado. **as m. as,** tanto como.

mucilage, *n.* mucilago *m.*

mucous, *a.* mucoso.

mucous membrane, *n.* mucosa *f.*

mud, *n.* fango, lodo *m.*

muddy, 1. *a.* lodoso; turbio. **2.** *v.* ensuciar; enturbiar.

muff, *n.* manguito *m.*

muffin, *n.* panecillo *m.*

mug, *n.* cubilete *m.*

mulatto, *n.* mulato *m.*

mule, *n.* mula *f.*

mullah, *n.* mullah *m.*

multinational, *a.* multinacional.

multiple, *a.* múltiple.

multiplication, *n.* multiplicación *f.*

multiplicity, *n.* multiplicidad *f.*

multiply, *v.* multiplicar.

multitude, *n.* multitud *f.*

mummy, *n.* momia *f.*

mumps, *n.* poperas *f.pl.*

municipal, *a.* municipal.

munificent, *a.* munífico.

munition, *n.* municiones *f.*

mural, *a. & n.* mural *m.*

murder, 1. *n.* asesinato; homicidio *m.* **2.** *v.* asesinar.

murderer, *n.* asesino -na.

murmur, 1. *n.* murmullo *m.* **2.** *v.* murmurar.

muscle, *n.* músculo *m.*

muscular, *a.* muscular.

muse, 1. *n.* musa *f.* **2.** *v.* meditar.

museum, *n.* museo *m.*

mushroom, *n.* seta *f.,* hongo *m.*

music, *n.* música *f.*

musical, *a.* musical; melodioso.

musician, *n.* músico *m.*

muslin, *n.* muselina *f.,* percal *m.*

must, *v.* deber; tener que.

mustache, *n.* bigotes *m.pl.*

mustard, *n.* mostaza *f.*

muster, 1. *n.* (mil.) revista *f.* **2.** *v.* agregar.

mute, *a. & n.* mudo *m.*

mutilate, *v.* mutilar.

mutiny, 1. *n.* motín *m.* **2.** amotinarse.

mutter, *v.* refunfuñar, gruñir.

mutton, *n.* carnero *m.*

mutual, *a.* mutuo.

muzzle, 1. *n.* hocico *m.;* bozal *m.* **2.** *v.* embozar.

my, *a.* mi.

myriad, *n.* miríada *f.*

myrtle, *n.* mirto *m.*

myself, *pron.* mi, mí mismo; me. **I m.,** yo mismo.

mysterious, *a.* misterioso.

mystery, *n.* misterio *m.*

mystic, *a.* místico.

mystify, *v.* confundir.

myth, *n.* mito *m.*

mythical, *a.* mítico.

mythology, *n.* mitología *f.*

N

nag, 1. *n.* jaca *f.* **2.** *v.* regañar; sermonear.

nail, 1. *n.* clavo *m.;* (finger) uña *f.* **n. polish,** esmalte para las uñas. **2.** *v.* clavar.

naïve, *a.* ingenuo.

naked, *a.* desnudo.

name, 1. *n.* nombre *m.;* reputación *f.* **2.** *v.* nombrar, mencionar.

namely, *adv.* a saber; es decir.

namesake, *n.* tocayo *m.*

nap, *n.* siesta *f.* **to take a n.,** echar una siesta.

naphtha, *n.* nafta *f.*

napkin, *n.* servilleta *f.*

narcissus, *n.* narciso *m.*

narcotic, *a. & n.* narcótico *m.*

narrate, *v.* narrar.

narrative, 1. *a.* narrativo. **2.** *n.* cuento, relato *m.*

narrow, *a.* estrecho, angosto. **n.-minded,** intolerante.

nasal, *a.* nasal.

nasty, *a.* desagradable.

nation, *n.* nación *f.*

national, *a.* nacional.

nationalism, *n.* nacionalismo *m.*

nationality, *n.* nacionalidad *f.*

nationalization, *n.* nacionalización *f.*

nationalize, *v.* nacionalizar.

native, 1. *a.* nativo. **2.** *n.* natural; indígena *m. & f.*

nativity, *n.* natividad *f.*

natural, *a.* natural.

naturalist, *n.* naturalista *m.*

naturalize, *v.* naturalizar.

naturalness, *n.* naturalidad *f.*

nature, *n.* naturaleza *f.;* índole *f.;* humor *m.*

naughty, *a.* travieso, desobediente.

nausea, *n.* náusea *f.*

nauseous, *a.* nauseoso.

nautical, *a.* náutico.

naval, *a.* naval.

nave, *n.* nave *f.*

navel, *n.* ombligo *m.*

navigable, *a.* navegable.

navigate, *v.* navegar.

navigation, *n.* navegación *f.*

navigator, *n.* navegante *m.*

navy, *n.* marina *f.*

near, 1. *a.* cercano, próximo. **2.** *adv.* cerca. **3.** *prep.* cerca de.

nearby, 1. *a.* cercano. **2.** *adv.* cerca.

nearly, *adv.* casi.

nearsighted, *a.* corto de vista.

neat, *a.* aseado; ordenado.

neatness, *n.* aseo *m.*

nebulous, *a.* nebuloso.

necessary, *a.* necesario.

necessity, *n.* necesidad *f.*

neck, *n.* cuello *m.*

necklace, *n.* collar *m.*

necktie, *n.* corbata *f.*

nectar, *n.* néctar *m.*

need, 1. *n.* necesidad; (poverty) pobreza *f.* **2.** *v.* necesitar.

needle, *n.* aguja *f.*

needless, *a.* innecesario, inútil.

needy, *a.* indigente, necesitado, pobre.

nefarious, *a.* nefario.

negative, 1. *a.* negativo. **2.** *n.* negativa *f.*

neglect, 1. *n.* negligencia *f.;* descuido *m.* **2.** *v.* descuidar.

negligee, *n.* negligée *m.,* bata de casa *f.*

negligent, *a.* negligente, descuidado.

negligible, *a.* insignificante.

negotiate, *v.* negociar.

negotiation, *n.* negociación *f.*

Negro, *n.* negro -ra.

neighbor, *n.* vecino -na.

neighborhood, *n.* vecindad *f.*

neither, 1. *a. & pron.* ninguno de

los dos. **2.** *adv.* tampoco. **3.** *conj.* neither . . . nor, ni . . . ni.

neon, *n.* neón *m.* **n. light,** tubo neón *m.*

nephew, *n.* sobrino *m.*

nerve, *n.* nervio *m.; (coll.)* audacia *f.*

nervous, *a.* nervioso.

nest, *n.* nido *m.*

net, 1. *a.* neto. **2.** *n.* red *f.* **hair n.,** albanega *f.* **3.** redar; *(com.)* ganar.

netting, *n.* red *m.;* obra de malla *f.*

network, *n.* (radio) red radiodifusora.

neuralgia, *n.* neuralgia *f.*

neurology, *n.* neurología *f.*

neurotic, *a.* neurótico.

neutral, *a.* neutral.

neutrality, *n.* neutralidad *f.*

neutron, *n.* neutrón *m.*

neutron bomb, bomba de neutrones *f.*

never, *adv.* nunca, jamás; **n. mind,** no importa.

nevertheless, *adv.* no obstante, sin embargo.

new, *a.* nuevo.

news, *n.* noticias *f.pl.*

newsboy, *n.* vendedor de periódicos.

newspaper, *n.* periódico *m.*

New Testament, *n.* Nuevo Testamento *m.*

new year, *n.* año nuevo *m.*

next, 1. *a.* próximo; siguiente; contiguo. **2.** *adv.* luego, después. **n. door,** al lado de. **n. to,** al lado de.

nibble, *v.* picar.

nice, *a.* simpático, agradable; amable; hermoso; exacto.

nick, *n.* muesca *f.,* picadura *f.* **in the n. of time,** apunto.

nickel, *n.* níquel *m.*

nickname, 1. *n.* apodo, mote *m.* **2.** *v.* apodar.

nicotine, *n.* nicotina *f.*

niece, *n.* sobrina *f.*

niggardly, *a.* mezquino.

night, *n.* noche *f.* **good n.,** buenas noches. **last n.,** anoche. **n. club,** cabaret *m.*

nightclub, *n.* cabaret *m.*

nightgown, *n.* camisa de dormir.

nightingale, *n.* ruiseñor *m.*

nightly, *adv.* todas las noches.

nightmare, *n.* pesadilla *f.*

nimble, *a.* ágil.

nine, *a.* & *pron.* nueve.

nineteen, *a.* & *pron.* diecinueve.

ninety, *a.* & *pron.* noventa.

ninth, *a.* noveno.

nipple, *n.* teta *f.;* pezón *m.*

nitrogen, *n.* nitrógeno *m.*

no, 1. *a.* ninguno. **no one,** nadie. **2.** *adv.* no.

nobility, *n.* nobleza *f.*

noble, *a.* & *n.* noble *m.*

nobleman, *n.* noble *m.*

nobody, *pron.* nadie.

nocturnal, *a.* nocturno.

nocturne, *n.* nocturno *m.*

nod, 1. *n.* seña con la cabeza. **2.** *v.* inclinar la cabeza; (doze) dormitar.

no-frills, *a.* sin extras.

noise, *n.* ruido *m.*

noiseless, *a.* silencioso.

noisy, *a.* ruidoso.

nominal, *a.* nominal.

nominate, *v.* nombrar.

nomination, *n.* nombramiento *m.,* nominación *f.*

nominee, *n.* nombrado *m.*

nonaligned (in political sense) *a.* no alineado.

nonchalant, *a.* indiferente.

noncombatant, *n.* no combatiente *m.*

noncommittal, *a.* evasivo; reservado.

nondescript, *a.* difícil de describir.

none, *pron.* ninguno.

nonentity, *n.* nulidad *f.*

nonpartisan, *a.* sin afiliación.

non-proliferation, *n.* no proliferación *m.*

nonsense, *n.* tontería *f.*

noodle, *n.* fideo *m.*

noon, *n.* mediodía *m.*

noose, *n.* lazo corredizo *m.;* dogal *m.*

nor, *conj.* ni.

normal, *a.* normal.

north, *n.* norte *m.*

North America, *n.* Norte América *f.*

North American, *a.* & *n.* norte americano -na.

northeast, *n.* nordeste *m.*

northern, *a.* septentrional.

North Pole, *n.* polo norte *m.*

northwest, n. noroeste m.

Norway, n. Noruega f.

Norwegian, a. & n. noruego -ga.

nose, n. nariz f.

nostalgia, n. nostalgia f.

nostril, n. ventana de la nariz; (pl.) narices.

not, adv. no. **n. at all,** de ninguna manera. **n. even,** ni siquiera.

notable, a. notable.

notary, n. notario m.

notation, a. notación f.

notch, n. muesca f.; corte m.

note, 1. n. nota f.; apunte m. **2.** v. notar.

notebook, n. libreta f., cuaderno m.

noted, a. célebre.

notepaper, n. papel de notas m.

noteworthy, a. notable.

nothing, pron. nada.

notice, 1. n. aviso m.; noticia f. **2.** v. observar, fijarse en.

noticeable, a. notable.

notification, n. notificación f.

notify, v. notificar.

notion, n. noción; idea f.; (pl.) novedades f.pl.

notoriety, n. notoriedad f.

notorious, a. notorio.

noun, n. nombre, sustantivo m.

nourish, v. nutrir, alimentar.

nourishment, n. nutrimento, alimento m.

novel, 1. a. nuevo, original. **2.** n. novela f.

novelist, n. novelista m. & f.

novelty, n. novedad f.

November, n. noviembre m.

novena, n. novena f.

novice, n. novicio -cia, novato -ta.

Novocaine, n. novocaína f.

now, adv. ahora. **n. and then,** de vez en cuando. **by n.,** ya. **from n. on,** de ahora en adelante. **just n.,** ahorita. **right n.,** ahora mismo.

nowhere, adv. en ninguna parte.

nozzle, n. boquilla f.

nuance, n. matiz m.

nuclear, a. nuclear.

nuclear warhead, cabeza nuclear f.

nuclear waste, desechos nucleares m.pl.

nucleus, n. núcleo m.

nude, a. desnudo.

nuisance, n. molestia f.

nuke, n. armamento o reactor nuclear.

nullify, v. anular.

number, 1. n. número m.; cifra f. **license n.,** matrícula f. **2.** v. numerar, contar.

numerical, a. numérico.

numerous, a. numeroso.

nun, n. monja f.

nuptial, a. nupcial.

nurse, 1. n. enfermera f.; (child's) ama, niñera f. **2.** v. criar, alimentar, amamantar; cuidar.

nursery, n. cuarto destinado a los niños; (agr.) plantel, criadero m.

nurture, v. nutrir.

nut, n. nuez f.; (mech.) tuerca f.

nutrition, n. nutrición f.

nutritious, a. nutritivo.

nylon, n. nilón m.

nymph, n. ninfa f.

O

oak, n. roble m.

oar, n. remo m.

oasis, n. oasis m.

oat, n. avena f.

oatmeal, n. harina de avena f.

oath, n. juramento m.

obedience, n. obediencia f.

obedient, a. obediente.

obese, a. obeso, gordo.

obey, v. obedecer.

obituary, n. obituario m.

object, 1. n. objeto m.; (gram.) complemento m. **2.** v. oponerse; objectar.

objection, n. objeción f.

objectionable, a. censurable.

objective, a. & n. objetivo m.

obligation, n. obligación f.

obligatory, a. obligatorio.

oblige, v. obligar; complacer.

oblique, a. oblicuo.

obliterate, v. borrar; destruir.

oblivion, n. olvido m.

oblong, a. oblongo.

obnoxious, a. ofensivo, odioso.

obscene, a. obsceno, indecente.

obscure, 1. a. obscuro. **2.** v. obscurecer.

observance, n. observancia; ceremonia f.

observation, n. observación f.

observatory, n. observatorio m.

observe, v. observar; celebrar.

observer, n. observador -ra.

obsession, n. obsesión f.

obsolete, a. anticuado.

obstacle, n. obstáculo m.

obstetrician, a. obstétrico m.

obstinate, a. obstinado, terco.

obstruct, v. obstruir, impedir.

obstruction, n. obstrucción f.

obtain, v. obtener, conseguir.

obtuse, a. obtuso.

obviate, v. obviar.

obvious, a. evidente, obvio.

occasion, 1. n. ocasión f. 2. v. ocasionar.

occasional, a. ocasional.

occult, a. oculto.

occupant, n. ocupante m.; inquilino -na.

occupation, n. ocupación f.; empleo m.

occupy, v. ocupar; emplear.

occur, v. ocurrir.

occurrence, n. ocurrencia f.

ocean, n. océano m.

o'clock: it's one o., es la una. **it's two o.,** son las dos, etc. **at . . . o.,** a las . . .

octagon, n. octágono m.

octave, n. octava f.

October, n. octubre m.

octopus, n. pulpo m.

oculist, n. oculista m.

odd, a. impar; suelto; raro.

odious, a. odioso.

odor, n. olor m.; fragancia f.

of, prep. de.

off, adv. (see under verb: **stop off, take off,** etc.)

offend, v. ofender.

offender, n. ofensor -ra; delincuente m.

offense, n. ofensa f.; crimen m.

offensive, 1. a. ofensivo. 2. n. ofensiva f.

offer, 1. n. oferta f. 2. v. ofrecer.

offering, n. oferta f.

office, n. oficina f.; despacho m.; oficio, cargo m.

officer, n. oficial m. **police o.,** agente de policía.

official, 1. a. oficial. 2. n. oficial, funcionario m.

officiate, v. oficiar.

officious, a. oficioso.

offspring, n. hijos m.pl.; progenie f.

often, adv. muchas veces, a menudo. **how o., con** qué frecuencia.

oil, 1. n. aceite; óleo m.; petróleo m. 2. v. aceitar; engrasar.

oily, a. aceitoso.

ointment, n. ungüento m.

okay, adv. bien; de acuerdo.

old, a. viejo; antiguo. **o. man, o. woman,** viejo -ja.

old-fashioned, a. fuera de moda.

Old Testament, n. Antiguo Testamento m.

olive, n. aceituna, oliva f.

ombudsman, n. ombudsman m.

omelet, n. tortilla de huevos.

omen, n. agüero m.

ominous, a. ominoso, siniestro.

omission, n. omisión f.; olvido m.

omit, v. omitir.

omnibus, n. ómnibus m.

omnipotent, a. omnipotente.

on, prep. en, sobre, encima de. 2. adv. adelante.

once, adv. una vez. **at o.,** en seguida. **o. in a while,** de vez en cuando.

one, a. & pron. uno.

oneself, pron. sí mismo; se. **with o.,** consigo.

onion, n. cebolla f.

only, 1. a. único, solo. 2. adv. sólo, solamente.

onward, adv. adelante.

opal, n. ópalo m.

opaque, a. opaco.

open, 1. a. abierto; franco. **o. air,** aire libre. 2. v. abrir.

opening, n. abertura f.

opera, n. ópera f. **o. glasses,** anteojos de ópera; gemelos m.pl.

operate, v. operar.

operation, n. operación f. **to have an o.,** operarse, ser operado.

operative, a. eficaz, operativo.

operator, n. operario -ria. **elevator o.,** ascensorista m. & f. **telephone o.,** telefonista m. & f.

operetta, n. opereta f.

ophthalmic, a. oftálmico.

opinion, n. opinión f.

opponent, n. antagonista m. & f.

opportunism, n. oportunismo m.

opportunity, n. ocasión, oportunidad f.

oppose, v. oponer.

opposite, 1. a. opuesto, contrario. **2.** prep. al frente de. **3.** n. contrario m.

opposition, n. oposición f.

oppress, v. oprimir.

oppression, n. opresión f.

oppressive, a. opresivo.

optic, a. óptico.

optician, n. óptico m.

optics, n. óptica f.

optimism, n. optimismo.

optimistic, a. optimista.

option, n. opción, elección f.

optional, a. discrecional, facultativo.

optometry, n. optometría f.

opulent, a. opulento.

or, conj. o, (before o-, ho-) u.

oracle, n. oráculo m.

oral, a. oral, vocal.

orange, n. naranja f.

oration, n. discurso m.; oración f.

orator, n. orador m.

oratory, n. elocuencia f.; (church) oratorio m.

orbit, n. órbita f.

orchard, n. huerto m.

orchestra, n. orquesta f. **o. seat,** butaca f.

orchid, n. orquídea f.

ordain, v. ordenar.

ordeal, n. prueba f.

order, 1. n. orden, m. or f.; clase f.; (com.) pedido m. **in o. that,** para que. **2.** v. ordenar; mandar; pedir.

orderly, a. ordenado.

ordinance, n. ordenanza f.

ordinary, a. ordinario.

ordination, n. ordenación f.

ore, n. mineral m.

organ, n. órgano m.

organdy, n. organdí m.

organic, a. orgánico.

organism, n. organismo m.

organist, n. organista m. & f.

organization, n. organización f.

organize, v. organizar.

orgy, n. orgía f.

orient, 1. n. oriente m. **2.** v. orientar.

Oriental, a. oriental.

orientation, n. orientación f.

origin, n. origen m.

original, a. & n. original m.

originality, n. originalidad f.

ornament, 1. n. ornamento m. **2.** v. ornamentar.

ornamental, a. ornamental, decorativo.

ornate, a. ornado.

ornithology, n. ornitología f.

orphan, a. & n. huérfano -na.

orphanage, n. orfanato m.

orthodox, a. ortodoxo.

ostentation, n. ostentación f.

ostentatious, a. ostentoso.

ostrich, n. avestruz m.

other, a. & pron. otro. **every o. day,** un día sí otro no.

otherwise, adv. de otra manera.

ought, v. deber.

ounce, n. onza f.

our, ours, a. & pron. nuestro.

ourselves, pron. nosotros mismos; nos.

oust, v. desalojar.

ouster, n. desahucio m.

out, 1. adv. fuera, afuera. **out of,** fuera de. **2.** prep. por.

outbreak, n. erupción f.

outcast, n. paria m. & f.

outcome, n. resultado m.

outdoors, adv. fuera de casa; al aire libre.

outer, a. exterior, externo.

outfit, 1. n. equipo m.; traje m. **2.** v. equipar.

outgrowth, n. resultado m.

outing, n. paseo m.

outlaw, 1. n. bandido m. **2.** v. proscribir.

outlet, n. salida f.

outline, 1. n. contorno; esbozo m.; silueta f. **2.** v. esbozar.

outlive, v. sobrevivir.

out-of-date, a. pasado.

outpost, n. puesto avanzado.

output, n. capacidad f.; educto m.

outrage, 1. n. ultraje m.; atrocidad f. **2.** v. ultrajar.

outrageous, a. atroz.

outrun, v. exceder.

outside, 1. a. & n. exterior m. **2.** adv. afuera, por fuera. **3.** prep. fuera de.

outskirt, n. borde m.

outward, adv. hacia afuera.

outwardly, adv. exteriormente.

oval, 1. a. oval, ovalado. **2.** n. óvalo m.

ovary, n. ovario m.

ovation, n. ovación f.
oven, n. horno m.
over, 1. prep. sobre, encima de; por. **2.** adv. **o. here,** aquí. **o. there,** allí, por allí. **to be o.,** estar terminado.
overcoat, n. abrigo, sobretodo m.
overcome, v. superar, vencer.
overdue, a. restrasado.
overflow, 1. n. inundación f. **2.** v. inundar.
overhaul, v. repasar.
overhead, adv. arriba, en lo alto.
overkill, n. efecto mayor que el pretendido.
overlook, v. pasar por alto.
overnight, adv. **to stay or stop o.,** pasar la noche.
overpower, v. vencer.
overrule, v. predominar.
overrun, v. invadir.
oversee, v. superentender.
oversight, n. equivocación f.
overt, a. abierto.
overtake, v. alcanzar.
overthrow, 1. n. trastorno m. **2.** v. trastornar.
overture, n. obertura f.
overturn, v. trastornar.
overview, n. visión de conjunto f.
overweight, a. demasiado pesado.
overwhelm, v. abrumar.
overwork, v. trabajar demasiado.
owe, v. deber. **owing to,** debido a.
owl, n. lechuza f.
own, 1. a. propio. **2.** v. poseer.
owner, n. dueño -ña.
ox, n. buey m.
oxygen, n. oxígeno m.
oxygen tent, n. tienda de oxígeno f.
oyster, n. ostra f.

P

pace, 1. n. paso m. **2.** v. pasearse. **p. off,** medir a pasos.
pacific, a. pacífico.
pacifier, n. pacificador m.; (baby p.) chupete m.
pacifism, n. pacifismo m.
pacifist, n. pacifista m. & f.
pacify, v. pacificar.
pack, 1. n. fardo; paquete m.; (animals) muta f. **p. of cards,** ba-

raja f. **2.** v. empaquetar; (baggage) empacar.
package, n. paquete, bulto m.
pact, n. pacto m.
pad, 1. n. colchoncillo m. **p. of paper,** bloc de papel. **2.** v. rellenar.
paddle, 1. n. canalete m. **2.** v. remar.
padlock, n. candado m.
pagan, a. & n. pagano -na.
page, n. página f.; (boy) paje m.
pageant, n. espectáculo m.; procesión f.
pail, n. cubo m.
pain, 1. n. dolor m. **to take pains,** esmerarse.
painful, a. doloroso; penoso.
paint, 1. n. pintura f. **2.** v. pintar.
painter, n. pintor -ra.
painting, n. pintura f.; cuadro m.
pair, 1. n. par m.; pareja f. **2.** v. parear. **p. off,** emparejarse.
pajamas, n. pijama m.
palace, n. palacio m.
palatable, a. sabroso, agradable.
palate, n. paladar m.
palatial, a. palaciego, suntuoso.
pale, a. pálido. **to turn pale,** palidecer.
paleness, n. palidez f.
palette, n. paleta f.
pallbearer, n. andero m.
pallid, a. pálido.
palm, n. palma f. **p. tree,** palmera f.
palpitate, v. palpitar.
paltry, a. miserable.
pamper, v. mimar.
pamphlet, n. folleto m.
pan, n. cacerola f.
panacea, n. panacea f.
Pan-American, a. panamericano
pane, n. hoja f.; cuadro m.
panel, n. tablero m.
pang, n. dolor; remordimiento m.
panic, n. pánico m.
panorama, n. panorama m.
pant, v. jadear.
panther, n. pantera f.
pantomine, n. pantomima f.; mímica f.
pantry, n. despensa f.
pants, n. pantalones, m.pl.
panty hose, n. pantyhose m. (me dias hasta la cintura).
papal, a. papal.

paper, n. papel; periódico; artículo m.

paperback, n. libro en rústica m.

paper hanger, n. empapelador m.

par, n. paridad f.; (com.) par f.

parable, n. parábola f.

parachute, n. paracaídas m.

parade, 1. n. desfile m., procesión f. **2.** v. desfilar.

paradise, n. paraíso m.

paradox, n. paradoja f.

paraffin, n. parafina f.

paragraph, n. párrafo m.

parakeet, n. perico m.

parallel, 1. a. paralelo. **2.** v. correr parejas con.

paralysis, n. parálisis f.

paralyze, v. paralizar.

paramedic, n. paramédico m.

parameter, n. parámetro m.

paramount, a. supremo.

paraphrase, 1. n. paráfrasis f. **2.** v. parafrasear.

parasite, n. parásito m.

parcel, n. paquete m. **p. of land,** lote de terreno.

parchment, n. pergamino m.

pardon, 1. n. perdón m. **2.** v. perdonar.

pare, v. pelar.

parentage, n. origen m.; extracción f.

parenthesis, n. paréntesis f.

parents, n. padres m.pl.

parish, n. parroquia f.

Parisian, a. & n. parisiense m. f.

park, 1. n. parque m. **2.** v. estacionar.

parking lot, n. estacionamiento m.

parkway, n. bulevar m.

parley, n. conferencia f.; (mil.) parlamento m.

parliament, n. parlamento m.

parlor, n. sala f.; salón m.

parochial, a. parroquial.

parody, 1. n. parodia f. **2.** v. parodiar.

parole, 1. n. palabra f.; (mil.) santo y seña. **2.** v. poner en libertad bajo palabra.

paroxysm, n. paroxismo m.

parrot, n. loro, papagayo m.

parsimony, n. parsimonia f.

parsley, n. perejil m.

parson, n. párroco m.

part, 1. n. parte f.; (theat.) papel

m. **2.** v. separarse; partirse. **p. with,** desprenderse de.

partake, v. tomar parte.

partial, a. parcial.

participant, n. participante m. & f.

participate, v. participar.

participation, n. participación f.

participle, n. participio m.

particle, n. partícula f.

particular, a. & n. particular m.

parting, n. despedida f.

partisan, a. & n. partidario -ria.

partition, n. tabique m.

partly, adv. en parte.

partner, n. socio -cia; compañero -ra.

partridge, n. perdiz f.

party, n. tertulia, fiesta f.; grupo m.; (political) partido m.

pass, 1. n. pase; (mountain) paso m. **2.** v. pasar. **p. away,** fallecer.

passable, a. transitable; regular.

passage, n. pasaje; (corridor) pasillo m.

passé, a. anticuado.

passenger, n. pasajero -ra.

passerby, n. transeúnte m. & f.

passion, n. pasión f.

passionate, a. apasionado.

passive, a. pasivo.

passport, n. pasaporte m.

past, 1. a. & n. pasado m. **2.** prep. más allá de; después de.

paste, 1. n. pasta f. **2.** v. empastar; pegar.

pasteurize, v. pasteurizar.

pastime, n. pasatiempo m.; diversión f.

pastor, n. pastor m.

pastry, n. pastelería f.

pasture, 1. n. pasto m.; pradera f. **2.** v. pastar.

pat, 1. n. golpecillo m. **to stand p.,** mantenerse firme. **2.** v. dar golpecillos.

patch, 1. n. remiendo m. **2.** v. remendar.

patent, 1. a. & n. patente f. **2.** v. patentar.

patent leather, n. charol m.

paternal, a. paterno, paternal.

paternity, n. paternidad f.

path, n. senda f.

pathetic, a. patético.

pathology, n. patología f.

pathos, *n.* rasgo conmovedor *m.*

patience, *n.* paciencia *f.*

patient, 1. *a.* paciente. **2.** *n.* enfermo, paciente *m.*

patio, *n.* patio *m.*

patriarch, *n.* patriarca *m.*

patriot, *n.* patriota *m.*

patriotic, *a.* patriótico.

patriotism, *n.* patriotismo *m.*

patrol, 1. *n.* patrulla *f.* **2.** *v.* patrullar.

patrolman, *n.* vigilante *m.;* patrullador *m.*

patron, *n.* patrón *m.*

patronize, *v.* condescender; patrocinar; ser cliente de.

pattern, *n.* modelo *m.*

pauper, *n.* indigent *m. & f.*

pause, *n.* *n.* pausa *f.* **2.** *v.* pausar.

pave, *v.* pavimentar. **p. the way,** preparar el camino.

pavement, *n.* pavimento *m.*

pavilion, *n.* pabellón *m.*

paw, 1. *n.* pata *f.* **2.** *v.* patear.

pawn, 1. *n.* prenda *f.;* (chess) peón de ajedrez *m.* **2.** *v.* empeñar.

pay, 1. *n.* pago; sueldo, salario *m.;* **2.** *v.* pagar. **p. back,** pagar; vengarse de.

payment, *n.* pago *m.;* recompensa *f.*

pea, *n.* guisante *m.*

peace, *n.* paz *f.*

peaceable, *a.* pacífico.

peaceful, *a.* tranquilo.

peach, *n.* durazno, melocotón *m.*

peacock, *n.* pavo real *m.*

peak, *n.* pico, cumbre; máximo *m.*

peal, *n.* repique; estruendo *m.* **p. of laughter,** risotada *f.*

peanut, *n.* maní, cacahuete *m.*

pear, *n.* pera *f.*

pearl, *n.* perla *f.*

peasant, *n.* campesino -na.

pebble, *n.* guija *f.*

peck, 1. *n.* picotazo *m.* **2.** *v.* picotear.

peculiar, *a.* peculiar.

pecuniary, *a.* pecuniario.

pedagogue, *n.* pedagogo *m.*

pedagogy, *n.* pedagogia *f.*

pedal, *n.* pedal *m.*

pedant, *n.* pedante *m.*

peddler, *n.* buhonero *m.*

pedestal, *n.* pedestal *m.*

pedestrian, *n.* peatón -na.

pediatrician, *n.* pediatra *m. & f.*

pedigree, *n.* genealogía *f.*

peek, 1. *n.* atisbo *m.* **2.** *v.* atisbar.

peel, 1. *n.* corteza *f.;* (fruit) pellejo *m.* **2.** *v.* descortezar; pelar.

peep, *n.* ojeada *f.*

peer, 1. *n.* par *m.* **2.** *v.* mirar fijamente.

peg, *n.* clavija; estaquilla *f.;* gancho *m.*

pelt, 1. *n.* pellejo *m.* **2.** *v.* apedrear; (rain) caer con fuerza.

pelvis, *n.* pelvis *f.*

pen, *n.* pluma *f.;* corral *m.* **fountain p.,** pluma fuente.

penalty, *n.* pena; multa *f.;* castigo *m.*

penance, *n.* penitencia *f.* **to do p.,** penar.

penchant, *n.* propensión *f.*

pencil, *n.* lápiz *m.*

pending, *a.* pendiente. **to be p.,** pender.

penetrate, *v.* penetrar.

penetration, *n.* penetración *f.*

penicillin, *n.* penicilina *f.*

peninsula, *n.* península *f.*

penitent, *n. & a.* penitente *m.*

penknife, *n.* cortaplumas *f.*

penniless, *a.* indigente.

penny, *n.* penique *m.*

pension, *n.* pensión *f.*

pensive, *a.* pensativo.

penury, *n.* penuria *f.*

people, 1. *n.* gente *f.;* (of a nation) pueblo *m.* **2.** *v.* poblar.

pepper, *n.* pimienta *f.;* (plant) pimiento *m.*

per, *prep.* por.

perambulator, *n.* cochecillo de niño *m.*

perceive, *v.* percibir.

percent, *adv.* por ciento.

percentage, *n.* porcentaje *m.*

perceptible, *a.* perceptible.

perception, *n.* percepción *f.*

perch, *n.* percha *f.;* (fish) perca *f*

perdition, *n.* perdición *f.*

peremptory, *a.* perentorio; terminante.

perennial, *a.* perenne.

perfect, 1. *a.* perfecto. **2.** *v.* perfeccionar.

perfection, *n.* perfección *f.*

perforation, *n.* perforación *f.*

perform, v. hacer; ejecutar; (theat.) representar.

performance, n. ejecución f.; (theat.) representación f.

perfume, 1. n. perfume m.; fragancia f. 2. v. perfumar.

perfunctory, a. perfunctorio, superficial.

perhaps, adv. quizá, quizás, tal vez.

peril, n. peligro m.

perilous, a. peligroso.

perimeter, n. perímetro m.

period, n. período m.; (punct.) punto m.

periodic, a. periódico.

periodical, n. revista f.

periphery, n. periferia f.

perish, v. perecer.

perishable, a. perecedero.

perjury, n. perjurio m.

permanent, a. permanente. p. wave, ondulado permanente.

permeate, v. penetrar.

permissible, a. permisible.

permission, n. permiso m.

permit, 1. n. permiso m. 2. v. permitir.

pernicious, a. pernicioso.

perpendicular, n. & a. perpendicular m.

perpetrate, v. perpetrar.

perpetual, a. perpetuo.

perplex, v. confundir.

perplexity, n. perplejidad f.

persecute, v. perseguir.

persecution, n. persecución f.

perseverance, n. perseverancia f.

persevere, v. perseverar.

persist, v. persistir.

persistent, a. persistente.

person, n. persona f.

personage, n. personaje m.

personal, a. personal.

personality, n. personalidad f.

personnel, n. personal m.

perspective, n. perspectiva f.

perspiration, n. sudor m.

perspire, v. sudar.

persuade, v. persuadir.

persuasive, a. persuasivo.

pertain, v. pertenecer.

pertinent, a. pertinente.

perturb, v. perturbar.

peruse, v. leer con cuidado.

pervade, v. penetrar; llenar.

perverse, a. perverso.

perversion, n. perversión f.

pessimism, n. pesimismo m.

pestilence, n. pestilencia f.

pet, 1. n. favorito -ta. 2. v. mimar.

petal, n. pétalo m.

petition, 1. n. petición, súplica f. 2. v. pedir, suplicar.

petrify, v. petrificar.

petroleum, n. petróleo m.

petticoat, n. enagua f.

petty, a. mezquino, insignificante.

petulant, a. quisquilloso.

pew, n. banco de iglesia m.

pewter, n. peltre m.

phantom, n. espectro, fantasma m.

pharmacist, n. farmacéutico, boticario m.

pharmacy, n. farmacia, botica f.

phase, n. fase f.

pheasant, n. faisán m.

phenomenal, a. fenomenal.

phenomenon, n. fenómeno f.

philanthropy, n. filantropía f.

philately, n. filatelia f.

philosopher, n. filósofo m.

philosophical, a. filosófico.

philosophy, n. filosofía f.

phlegm, n. flema f.; frialdad de ánimo f.

phobia, n. fobia f.

phonetic, a. fonético.

phonograph, n. fonógrafo m.

phosphorus, n. fósforo m.

photocopier, n. fotocopiadora f.

photocopy, 1. n. fotocopia f. 2. v. fotocopiar.

photoelectric, a. fotoeléctrico.

photogenic, a. fotogénico.

photograph, 1. n. fotografía f. 2. v. fotografiar; retratar.

photography, n. fotografía f.

Photostat, n. fotocopia f.

phrase, 1. n. frase f. 2. v. expresar.

physical, a. físico.

physician, n. médico m.

physics, n. física f.

physiology, n. fisiología f.

physiotherapy, n. fisioterapia f.

physique, n. físico m.

pianist, n. pianista m. & f.

piano, n. piano m.

picayune, a. insignificante.

piccolo, n. flutín m.

pick, 1. *n.* pico *m.* 2. *v.* escoger. **p. up,** recoger.

picket, *n.* piquete *m.*

pickle, 1. *n.* salmuera *f.;* encurtido *m.* 2. *v.* escabechar.

pickpocket, *n.* cortabolsas *m. & f.*

picnic, *n.* picnic *m.*

picture, 1. *n.* cuadro; retrato *m.;* fotografía *f.;* (movie) película *f.* 2. *v.* imaginarse.

picturesque, *a.* pintoresco.

pie, *n.* pastel *m.*

piece, *n.* pedazo *m.;* pieza *f.*

pier, *n.* muelle *m.*

pierce, *v.* perforar; pinchar; traspasar.

piety, *n.* piedad *f.*

pig, *n.* puerco, cerdo, lechón *m.*

pigeon, *n.* paloma *f.*

pigeonhole, *n.* casilla *f.*

pigment, *n.* pigmento *m.*

pile, 1. *n.* pila *f.;* montón *m.pl.;* (med.) hemorroides *f.pl.* 2. *v.* amontonar.

pilfer, *v.* ratear.

pilgrim, *n.* peregrino -na, romero -ra.

pilgrimage, *n.* romería *f.*

pill, *n.* píldora *f.*

pillage, 1. *n.* pillaje *m.* 2. *v.* pillar.

pillar, *n.* columna *f.*

pillow, *n.* almohada *f.*

pillowcase, *n.* funda de almohada *f.*

pilot, 1. *n.* piloto *m.* 2. *v.* pilotear.

pimple, *n.* grano *m.*

pin, 1. *n.* alfiler; broche *m.;* (mech.) clavija *f.* 2. *v.* prender. **p. up,** fijar.

pinch, 1. *n.* pellizco *m.* 2. *v.* pellizcar.

pine, 1. *n.* pino *m.* 2. *v.* **p. away,** languidecer. **p. for,** anhelar.

pineapple, *n.* piña *f.,* ananá *m.*

pink, *a.* rosado.

pinnacle, *n.* pináculo *m.;* cumbre *f.*

pint, *n.* pinta *f.*

pioneer, *n.* pionero -ra.

pious, *a.* piadoso.

pipe, *n.* pipa *f.;* tubo; (of organ) cañón *m.*

piper, *n.* flautista *m. & f.*

piquant, *a.* picante.

pirate, *n.* pirata *m.*

pistol, *n.* pistola *f.*

piston, *n.* pistón *m.*

pit, *n.* hoyo *m.;* (fruit) hueso *m.*

pitch, 1. *n.* brea *f.;* grado de inclinación; (music) tono *m.;* 2. *v.* lanzar; (ship) cabecear.

pitchblende, *n.* pechblenda *f.*

pitcher, *n.* cántaro *m.;* (baseball) lanzador *m.*

pitchfork, *n.* horca *f.;* tridente *m.*

pitfall, *n.* trampa *f.,* hoya cubierta *f.*

pitiful, *a.* lastimoso.

pitiless, *a.* cruel.

pity, 1. *n.* compasión, piedad *f.* **to be a p.,** ser lástima. 2. *v.* compadecer.

pivot, 1. *n.* espiga *f.,* pivote *m.;* punto de partida *m.* 2. *v.* girar sobre un pivote.

pizza, *n.* pizza *f.*

placard, 1. *n.* cartel *m.* 2. *v.* fijar carteles.

placate, *v.* aplacar.

place, 1. *n.* lugar, sitio, puesto *m.* 2. *v.* colocar, poner.

placid, *a.* plácido.

plagiarism, *n.* plagio *m.*

plague, 1. *n.* plaga, peste *f.* 2. *v.* atormentar.

plain, 1. *a.* sencillo; puro; evidente. 2. *n.* llano *m.*

plaintiff, *n.* demandador -ra.

plan, 1. *n.* plan, propósito *m.* 2. *v.* planear; pensar. **p. on,** contar con.

plane, 1. *n.* plano; (tool) cepillo *m.* 2. *v.* allanar; acepillar.

planet, *n.* planeta *m.*

planetarium, *n.* planetario *m.*

plank, *n.* tablón *m.*

plant, 1. *n.* mata, planta *f.* 2. *v.* sembrar, plantar.

plantation, *n.* plantación *f.* **coffee p.,** cafetal *m.*

planter, *n.* plantador; hacendado *m.*

plasma, *n.* plasma *m.*

plaster, *n.* yeso; emplasto *m.* 2. *v.* enyesar; emplastar.

plastic, *a.* plástico.

plate, 1. *n.* plato *m.;* plancha de metal. 2. *v.* planchear.

plateau, *n.* meseta *f.*

platform, *n.* plataforma *f.*

platinum, *n.* platino *m.*

platitude, *n.* perogrullada *f.*

platter, *n.* fuente *f.;* platel *m.*

plaudit, *n.* aplauso *m.*

plausible, *a.* plausible.

play, **1.** *n.* juego *m.*; (theat.) pieza *f.* **2.** *v.* jugar; (music) tocar; (theat.) representar. **p. a part**, hacer un papel.

player, *n.* jugador -ra; (music) músico *m.*; (theat.) actor *m.*, actriz *f.*

playful, *a.* juguetón.

playground, *n.* campo de deportes; patio de recreo.

playmate, *n.* compañero -ra de juego.

playwright, *n.* dramaturgo *m.*

plea, *n.* ruego *m.*; súplica *f.*; (legal) declaración *f.*

plead, *v.* suplicar; declararse. **p. a case**, defender un pleito.

pleasant, *a.* agradable.

please, **1.** *v.* gustar, agradar. **Pleased to meet you**, Mucho gusto en conocer a Vd. **2.** *adv.* por favor. **Please . . .** Haga el favor de . . ., Tenga la bondad de . . ., Sírvase . . .

pleasure *n.* gusto, placer *m.*

pleat, **1.** *n.* pliegue *m.* **2.** *v.* plegar.

plebiscite, *n.* plebiscito *f.*

pledge, **1.** *n.* empeño *m.* **2.** *v.* empeñar.

plentiful, *a.* abundante.

plenty, *n.* abundancia *f.* **p. of**, bastante. **p. more**, mucho más.

pleurisy, *n.* pleuritis *f.*

pliable, **pliant**, *a.* flexible.

pliers, *n.pl.* alicates *m.pl.*

plight, *n.* apuro, aprieto *m.*

plot, **1.** *n.* conspiración; (of a story) trama; (of land) parcela *f.* **2.** *v.* conspirar; tramar.

plow, **1.** *n.* arado *m.* **2.** *v.* arar.

pluck, **1.** *n.* valor *m.* **2.** *v.* arrancar; desplumar.

plug, **1.** *n.* tapón; (elec.) enchufe *m.* **spark p.**, bujía *f.* **2.** *v.* tapar.

plum, *n.* ciruela *f.*

plumage, *n.* plumaje *m.*

plumber, *n.* plomero *m.*

plume, *n.* pluma *f.*

plump, *a.* regordete.

plunder, **1.** *n.* botín *m.*; despojos *m.pl.* **2.** *v.* saquear.

plunge, *v.* zambullir; precipitar.

plural, *a.* & *n.* plural *m.*

plus, *prep.* más.

plutocrat, *n.* plutócrata *m.* & *f.*

pneumatic, *a.* neumático.

pneumonia *n.* pulmonía *f.*

poach, *v.* (eggs) escalfar; invadir; cazar en vedado.

pocket, **1.** *n.* bolsillo *m.* **2.** *v.* embolsar.

pocketbook, *n.* cartera *f.*

podiatry, *n.* podiatría *f.*

poem, *n.* poema *m.*

poet, *n.* poeta *m.*

poetic, *a.* poético.

poetry, *n.* poesía *f.*

poignant, *a.* conmovedor.

point, **1.** *n.* punta *f.*; punto *m.* **2.** *v.* apuntar. **p. out**, señalar.

pointed, *a.* puntiagudo; directo.

pointless, *a.* inútil.

poise, **1.** *n.* equilibrio *m.*; serenidad *f.* **2.** *v.* equilibrar; estar suspendido.

poison, **1.** *n.* veneno *m.* **2.** *v.* envenenar.

poisonous, *a.* venenoso.

poke, **1.** *n.* empuje *m.*, hurgonada *f.* **2.** *v.* picar; haronear.

Poland, *n.* Polonia *f.*

polar, *a.* polar.

pole, *n.* palo; (geog.) polo *m.*

police, *n.* policía *f.*

policeman, *n.* policía *m.*

policy, *n.* política *f.* **insurance p.**, póliza de seguro.

Polish, *a.* & *n.* polaco *m.*

polish, **1.** *n.* lustre *m.* **2.** *v.* pulir, lustrar.

polite, *a.* cortés.

politic, **political**, *a.* político.

politician, *n.* político *m.*

politics, *n.* política *f.*

poll, *n.* encuesta *f.*; (pl.) urnas *f.pl.*

pollen, *n.* polen *m.*

pollute, *v.* contaminar.

polo, *n.* polo *m.*

polygamy, *n.* poligamia *f.*

polygon, *n.* polígono *f.*

pomp, *n.* pompa *f.*

pompous, *a.* pomposo.

poncho, *n.* poncho *m.*

pond, *n.* charca *f.*

ponder, *v.* ponderar, meditar.

ponderous, *a.* ponderoso, pesado.

pontiff, *n.* pontífice *m.*

pontoon, *n.* pontón *m.*

pony, *n.* caballito *m.*

pool, *n.* charco *m.* **swimming p.**, piscina *f.*

poor, *a.* pobre; (not good) malo.
pop, *n.* chasquido *m.*
popcorn, *n.* maíz tostado *m.*
pope, *n.* papa *m.*
popular, *a.* popular.
popularity, *n.* popularidad *f.*
population, *n.* población *f.*
porcelain, *n.* porcelana *f.*
porch, *n.* pórtico *m.;* galería *f.*
pore, *n.* poro *m.*
pork, *n.* carne de puerco.
pornography, *n.* pornografía *f.*
porous, *a.* poroso, esponjoso.
port, *n.* puerto; (naut.) babor *m.*
p. wine, oporto *m.*
portable, *a.* portátil.
portal, *n.* portal *m.*
portend, *v.* pronosticar.
portent, *n.* presagio *m.*, portento *m.*
porter, *n.* portero *m.*
portfolio, *n.* cartera *f.*
porthole, *n.* porta *f.*
portion, *n.* porción *f.*
portly, *a.* corpulento.
portrait, *n.* retrato *m.*
portray, *v.* pintar.
Portugal, *n.* Portugal *m.*
Portuguese, *a.* & *n.* portugués -sa.
pose, **1.** *n.* postura; actitud *f.* **2.** *v.* posar. **p. as,** pretender ser.
position, *n.* posición *f.*
positive, *a.* positivo.
possess, *v.* poseer.
possession, *n.* posesión *f.*
possessive, *a.* posesorio.
possibility, *n.* posibilidad *f.*
possible, *a.* posible.
post, **1.** *n.* poste; puesto *m.* **2.** *v.* fijar; situar; echar al correo. **postage,** *n.* porte de correo. **p. stamp,** sello *m.*
postal, *a.* postal.
post card, tarjeta postal.
poster, *n.* cartel, letrero *m.*
posterior, *a.* posterior.
posterity, *n.* posteridad *f.*
postgraduate, *a.* postgraduado.
postmark, *n.* matasellos *m.*
post office, casa de correos.
postpone, *v.* posponer, aplazar.
postscript, *n.* posdata *f.*
posture, *n.* postura *f.*
pot, *n.* olla, marmita; (marijuana) marijuana, hierba *f.*
flower p., tiesto *m.*

potassium, *n.* potasio *m.*
potato, *n.* patata, papa *f.* **sweet p.,** batata *f.*
potent, *a.* potente, poderoso.
potential, *a.* & *n.* potencial *f.*
potion, *n.* poción *f.,* pócima *f.*
pottery, *n.* alfarería *f.*
pouch, *n.* saco *m.;* bolsa *f.*
poultry, *n.* aves de corral.
pound, **1.** *n.* libra *f.* **2.** *v.* golpear
pour, *v.* echar; verter; llover a cántaros.
poverty, *n.* pobreza *f.*
powder, 1. *n.* polvo *m.;* (gun) pólvora *f.* **2.** *v.* empolvar; pulverizar.
power, *n.* poder *m.;* potencia *f.*
powerful, *a.* poderoso, fuerte.
powerless, *a.* impotente.
practical, *a.* prático.
practically, *adv.* casi; práticamente.
practice, 1. *n.* prática; costumbre; clientela *f.* **2.** *v.* practicar; ejercer.
practiced, *a.* experto.
practitioner, *n.* practicante *m.*
pragmatic, *a.* pragmática.
prairie, *n.* llanura; (So. Amer.) pampa *f.*
praise, 1. *n.* alabanza *f.* **2.** *v.* alabar.
prank, *n.* travesura *f.*
pray, *v.* rezar; (beg) rogar.
prayer, *n.* oración; súplica *f.,* ruego *m.*
preach, *v.* predicar; sermonear.
preacher, *n.* predicador *m.*
preamble, *n.* preámbulo *m.*
precarious, *a.* precario.
precaution, *n.* precaución *f.*
precede, *v.* preceder, anteceder.
precedent, *a.* & *n.* precedente *m*
precept, *n.* precepto *m.*
precinct, *n.* recinto *m.*
precious, *a.* precioso.
precipice, *n.* precipicio *m.*
precipitate, *v.* precipitar.
precise, *a.* preciso, exacto.
precision, *n.* precisión *f.*
preclude, *v.* evitar.
precocious, *a.* precoz.
predatory, *a.* de rapiña, rapaz.
predecessor, *n.* predecesor, antecesor *m.*
predicament, *n.* dificultad *f.,* apuro *m.*

predict, v. pronosticar, predecir.

predilection, n. predilección f.

predispose, v. predisponer.

predominant, a. predominante.

prefabricate, v. fabricar de antemano.

preface, n. prefacio m.

prefer, v. preferir.

preferable, a. preferible.

preference, n. preferencia f.

prefix, 1. n. prefijo m. **2.** v. prefijar.

pregnant, a. preñada.

prehistoric, a. prehistórico.

prejudice, n. prejuicio m.

prejudiced, a. prejuiciado.

preliminary, a. preliminar.

prelude, n. preludio m.

premature, a. prematuro.

premeditate, v. premeditar.

premier, n. premer ministro.

première, n. estreno m.

premise, n. premisa f.

premium, n. premio m.

premonition, n. presentimiento m.

prenatal, a. prenatal.

preparation, n. preparativo m.; preparación f.

preparatory, a. preparatorio. **p. to,** antes de.

prepare, v. preparar.

preponderant, a. preponderante.

preposition, n. preposición f.

preposterous, a. prepóstero, absurdo.

prerequisite, n. requisito previo.

prerogative, n. prerrogativa f.

prescribe, v. prescribir; (med.) recetar.

prescription, n. prescripción; (med.) receta f.

presence, n. presencia f.; porte m.

present, 1. a. presente. **to be present,** a, asistir a. **2.** n. presente; (gift) regalo m. **at p.,** ahora. **for the p.,** por ahora. **3.** v. presentar.

presentable, a. presentable.

presentation, n. presentación; introducción f.; (theat.) representación f.

presently, adv. luego; dentro de poco.

preservative, a. & n. preservativo m.

preserve, 1. n. conserva f.; (hunt-ing) vedado m. **2.** v. preservar.

preside, v. presidir.

presidency, n. presidencia f.

president, n. presidente -ta.

press, 1. n. prensa f. **2.** v. apretar; urgir; (clothes) planchar.

pressing, a. urgente.

pressure, n. presión f.

pressure cooker, n. cocina de presión f.

prestige, n. prestigio m.

presume, v. presumir; suponer.

presumptuous, a. presumtuoso.

presuppose, v. presuponer.

pretend, v. fingir. **p. to the throne,** aspirar al trono.

pretense, n. pretensión f.; fingimiento m.

pretension, n. pretensión f.

pretentious, a. presumido.

pretext, n. pretexto m.

pretty, 1. a. bonito, lindo. **2.** adv. bastante.

prevail, v. prevalecer.

prevailing, prevalent, a. predominante.

prevent, v. impedir; evitar.

prevention, n. prevención f.

preventive, a. preventivo.

preview, n. vista previa f.

previous, a. anterior, previo.

prey, n. presa f.

price, n. precio m.

priceless, a. sin precio.

prick, 1. n. punzada f. **2.** v. punzar.

pride, n. orgullo m.

priest, n. sacerdote, cura m.

prim, a. severamente modesto.

primary, a. primario, principal.

prime, 1. a. primero. **2.** n. flor f. **3.** v. alistar.

prime minister, n. primer ministro m.

primitive, a. primitivo.

prince, n. príncipe m.

princess, n. princesa f.

principal, 1. a. principal. **2.** n. principal; director m.

principle, n. principio m.

print, 1. n. letra f.; (art) grabado m. **2.** v. imprimir; estampar.

printing, n. imprenta f.

printing press, n. prensa f.

printout, n. impreso producido por una computadora.

priority, *n.* prioridad, precedencia *f.*

prism, *n.* prisma *m.*

prison, *n.* prisión, cárcel *f.*

prisoner, *n.* prisionero, preso *m.*

privacy, *n.* soledad *f.*

private, 1. *a.* particular. 2. *n.* soldado raso. **in p.,** en particular.

privation, *n.* privación *f.*

privet, *n.* ligustro *m.*

privilege, *n.* privilegio *m.*

privy, *n.* letrina *f.*

prize, 1. *n.* premio *m.* 2. *v.* apreciar, estimar.

probability, *n.* probabilidad *f.*

probable, *a.* probable.

probate, *a.* testamentario.

probation, *n.* prueba *f.;* probación *f.;* libertad condicional *f.*

probe, 1. *n.* indagación *f.* 2. *v.* indagar; tentar.

probity, *n.* probidad *f.*

problem, *n.* problema *m.*

procedure, *n.* procedimiento *m.*

proceed, *v.* proceder; proseguir.

process, *n.* proceso *m.*

procession, *n.* procesión *f.*

proclaim, *v.* proclamar, anunciar.

proclamation, *n.* proclamación *f.;* decreto *m.*

procrastinate, *v.* dilatar.

procure, *v.* obtener, procurar.

prodigal, *n.* & *a.* pródigo *m.*

prodigy, *n.* prodigio *m.*

produce, *v.* producir.

product, *n.* producto *m.*

production, *n.* producción *f.*

productive, *a.* productivo.

profane, 1. *a.* profano. 2. *v.* profanar.

profanity, *n.* profanidad *f.*

profess, *v.* profesar; declarar.

profession, *n.* profesión *f.*

professional, *a.* & *n.* profesional *m.*

professor, *n.* profesor -ra; catedrático *m.*

proficient, *a.* experto, proficiente.

profile, *n.* perfil *m.*

profit, 1. *n.* provecho *m.;* ventaja *f.;* (com.) ganancia *f.* 2. *v.* aprovechar; beneficiar.

profitable, *a.* provechoso, ventajoso, lucrativo.

profiteer, 1. *n.* explotador *m.* 2. *v.* explotar.

profound, *a.* profundo, hondo.

profuse, *a.* pródigo, profuso.

prognosis, *n.* pronóstico *m.*

program, *n.* programa *m.*

progress, 1. *n.* progresos *m.pl.* **in p.,** en marcha. 2. *v.* progresar; marchar.

progressive, *a.* progresivo; progresista.

prohibit, *v.* prohibir.

prohibition, *n.* prohibición *f.*

prohibitive, *a.* prohibitivo.

project, 1. *n.* proyecto *m.* 2. *v.* proyectar.

projectile, *n.* proyectil *m.*

projection, *n.* proyección *f.*

projector, *n.* proyector *m.*

proliferation, *n.* proliferación *f.*

prolific, *a.* prolífico.

prologue, *n.* prólogo *m.*

prolong, *v.* prolongar.

prominent, *a.* prominente; eminente.

promiscuous, *a.* promiscuo.

promise, 1. *n.* promesa *f.* 2. *v.* prometer.

promote, *v.* fomentar; estimular; adelantar.

promotion, *n.* promoción *f.;* adelanto *m.*

prompt, 1. *a.* pronto; puntual. 2. *v.* impulsar; (theat.) apuntar.

promulgate, *v.* promulgar.

pronoun, *n.* pronombre *m.*

pronounce, *v.* pronunciar.

pronunciation, *n.* pronunciación *f.*

proof, *n.* prueba *f.*

proofread, *v.* corregir pruebas.

prop, 1. *n.* apoyo *m.* 2. *v.* sostener.

propaganda, *n.* propaganda *f.*

propagate, *v.* propagar.

propel, *v.* propulsar.

propeller, *n.* hélice *f.*

propensity, *n.* tendencia *f.*

proper, *a.* propio; correcto.

property, *n.* propiedad *f.*

prophecy, *n.* profecía *f.*

prophesy, *v.* predecir, profetizar.

prophet, *n.* profeta *m.*

prophetic, *a.* profético.

propitious, *a.* propicio.

proponent, *n.* & *a.* proponente *f.*

proportion, *n.* proporción *f.*

proportionate, *a.* proporcionado

proposal, n. propuesta; oferta f.; (marriage) declaración f.

propose, v. proponer; pensar; declararse.

proposition, n. proposición f.

proprietor, n. propietario, dueño m.

propriety, n. corrección f., decoro m.

prosaic, a. prosaico.

proscribe, v. proscribir.

prose, n. prosa f.

prosecute, v. acusar, procesar.

prospect, n. perspectiva; esperanza f.

prospective, a. anticipado, presunto.

prosper, v. prosperar.

prosperity, n. prosperidad f.

prosperous, a. próspero.

prostitute, 1. n. prostituta f. 2. v. prostituir. 3. a. prostituido.

prostrate, 1. a. postrado. 2. v. postrar.

protect, v. proteger; amparar.

protection, n. protección f.; amparo m.

protective, a. protector.

protector, n. protector m.

protégé, n. protegido -da.

protein, n. proteína f.

protest, 1. n. protesta f. 2. v. protestar.

Protestant, a. & n. protestante m.

protocol, n. protocolo m.

proton, n. protón m.

protract, v. alargar, demorar.

protrude, v. salir fuera.

protuberance, n. protuberancia f.

proud, a. orgulloso.

prove, v. comprobar.

proverb, n. proverbio, refrán m.

provide, v. proporcionar; proveer.

provided, conj. con tal que.

providence, n. providencia f.

province, n. provincia f.

provincial, 1. a. provincial. 2. n. provinciano -na.

provision, 1. n. provisión f.; (pl.) comestibles m.pl. 2. v. abastecer.

provocation, n. provocación f.

provoke, v. provocar.

prowess, n. proeza f.

prowl, v. rondar.

proximity, n. proximidad f.

proxy, n. delegado m. **by p.**, mediante apoderado.

prudence, n. prudencia f.

prudent, a. prudente, cauteloso.

prune, n. ciruela pasa.

pry, v. atisbar; curiosear; (mech.) alzaprimar.

psalm, n. salmo m.

pseudonym, n. seudónimo m.

psychedelic, a. psiquedélico.

psychiatrist, n. psiquiatra m.

psychiatry, n. psiquiatría f.

psychoanalysis, n. psicoanálisis m. or f.

psychological, a. psicológico.

psychology, n. psicología f.

psychosis, n. psicosis.

ptomaine, n. tomaína f.

public, a. & n. público m.

publication, n. publicación; revista f.

publicity, n. publicidad f.

publish, v. publicar.

publisher, n. editor m.

pudding, n. pudín m.

puddle, n. charco, lodazal m.

Puerto Rico, n. Puerto Rico m.

Puerto Rican, a. & n. puertorriqueño -ña.

puff, 1. n. soplo m.; (of smoke) bocanada f. **powder p.**, polvera f. 2. v. jadear; echar bocanadas. **p. up**, hinchar; (fig.) engreír.

pugnacious, a. pugnaz.

pull, 1. n. tirón m.; (coll.) influencia f. 2. v. tirar; halar.

pulley, n. polla f.; motón m.

pulmonary, a. pulmonar.

pulp, n. pulpa; (of fruit) carne f.

pulpit, n. púlpito m.

pulsar, n. pulsar m.

pulsate, v. pulsar.

pulse, n. pulso m.

pump, 1. n. bomba f. 2. v. bombear. **p. up**, inflar.

pumpkin, n. calabaza f.

pun, n. juego de palabras.

punch, 1. n. puñetazo; (mech.) punzón; (beverage) ponche m. 2. v. dar puñetazos; punzar.

punctual, a. puntual.

punctuate, v. puntuar.

puncture, 1. n. pinchazo m., perforación f. 2. v. pinchar, perforar.

pungent, a. picante, pungente.

punish, v. castigar.

punishment, *n.* castigo *m.*

punitive, *a.* punitivo.

puny, *a.* encanijado.

pupil, *n.* alumno -na; (anat.) pupila *f.*

puppet, *n.* muñeco *m.*

puppy, *n.* perrito *m.*

purchase, 1. *n.* compra *f.* **2.** *v.* comprar.

pure, *a.* puro.

purée, *n.* puré *m.*

purge, *v.* purgar.

purify, *v.* purificar.

puritanical, *a.* puritano.

purity, *n.* pureza *f.*

purple, 1. *a.* purpúreo. **2.** *n.* púrpura *f.*

purport, 1. *n.* significación *f.* **2.** *v.* significar.

purpose, *n.* propósito *m.* **on p.,** de propósito.

purse, *n.* bolsa *f.*

pursue, *v.* perseguir.

pursuit, *n.* caza; busca; ocupación *f.* **p. plane,** caza *m.*

push, 1. *n.* empuje; impulso *m.* **2.** *v.* empujar.

put, *v.* poner, colocar. **p. away,** guardar. **p. in,** meter. **p. off,** dejar. **p. on,** ponerse. **p. out,** apagar. **p. up with,** aguantar.

putrid, *a.* podrido.

puzzle, 1. *n.* enigma; rompecabezas *m.* **2.** *v.* dejar perplejo. **p. out,** descifrar.

pyramid, *n.* pirámide *f.*

pyromania, *n.* piromanía *f.*

Q

quadrangle, *n.* cuandrángulo *m.*

quadraphonic, *a.* cuadráfonico.

quadruped, *a. & n.* cuadrúpedo *m.*

quail, 1. *n.* codorniz *f.* **2.** *v.* descorazonarse.

quaint, *a.* arcaico y curioso.

quake, 1. *n.* temblor *m.* **2.** *v.* temblar.

qualification, *n.* requisito *m.;* (pl.) preparaciones.

qualified, *a.* calificado, competente; preparado.

qualify, *v.* calificar, modificar; llenar los requisitos.

quality, *n.* calidad *f.*

quandary, *n.* incertidumbre *f.*

quantity, *n.* cantidad *f.*

quarantine, *n.* cuarentena *f.*

quarrel, 1. *n.* riña, disputa *f.* **2.** reñir, disputar.

quarry, *n.* cantera; (hunting) presa *f.*

quarter, *n.* cuarto *m.;* (pl.) vivienda *f.*

quarterly, 1. *a.* trimestral. **2.** *adv.* por cuartos.

quartet, *n.* cuarteto *m.*

quartz, *n.* cuarzo *m.*

quasar, *n.* quasar *m.*

quaver, *v.* temblar.

queen, *n.* reina *f.;* (chess) dama *f.*

queer, *a.* extraño, raro.

quell, *v.* reprimir.

quench, *v.* apagar.

query, 1. *n.* pregunta *f.* **2.** *v.* preguntar.

quest, *n.* busca *f.*

question, 1. *n.* pregunta; cuestión *f.* **q. mark,** signo de interrogación. **2.** *v.* preguntar; interrogar; dudar.

questionable, *a.* dudoso.

questionnaire, *n.* cuestionario *m.*

quick, *a.* rápido.

quicken, *v.* acelerar.

quicksand, *n.* arena movediza.

quiet, *n.* quieto, tranquilo; callado. **to be q., keep q.,** callarse. **2.** *n.* calma; quietud *f.* **3.** *v.* tranquilizar. **q. down,** callarse; calmarse.

quilt, *n.* colcha *f.*

quinine, *n.* quinina *f.*

quintet, *n.* (mus.) quinteto *m.*

quip, 1. *n.* pulla *f.* **2.** *v.* echar pullas.

quit, *v.* dejar; renunciar a. **q. doing** (etc.) dejar de hacer (etc.).

quite, *adv.* bastante; completamente. **not q.,** no precisamente; no completamente.

quiver, 1. *n.* aljabe *f.;* temblor *m.* **2.** *v.* temblar.

quixotic, *a.* quijotesco.

quorum, *n.* quórum *m.*

quota, *n.* cuota *f.*

quotation, *n.* citación; (com.) cotización *f.* **q. marks,** comillas *f.pl.*

quote, *v.* citar; (com.) cotizar.

R

rabbi, *n.* rabí, rabino *m.*

rabbit, *n.* conejo *m.*

rabble, *n.* canalla *f.*

rabid, *a.* rabioso.

rabies, *n.* hidrofobia *f.*

race, 1. *n.* raza; carrera *f.* 2. *v.* echar una carrera; correr de prisa.

rack, 1. *n.* (cooking) pesebre *m.;* (clothing) colgador *m.* 2. *v.* atormentar.

racket, *n.* (noise) ruido *m.;* (tennis) raqueta *f.;* (graft) fraude organizado.

radar, *n.* radar *m.*

radiance, *n.* brillo *m.*

radiant, *a.* radiante.

radiate, *v.* irradiar.

radiation, *n.* irradiación *f.*

radiator, *n.* colorífero *m.;* (auto.) radiador *m.*

radical, *a. & n.* radical *m.*

radio, *n.* radio *m. or f.* **r. station,** estación radiodifusora.

radioactive, *a.* radioactivo.

radish, *n.* rábano *m.*

radium, *n.* radio *m.*

radius, *n.* radio *m.*

raffle, 1. *n.* rifa, lotería *f.* 2. *v.* rifar.

raft, *n.* balsa *f.*

rafter, *n.* viga *f.*

rag, *n.* trapo *m.*

ragamuffin, *n.* galopín *m.*

rage, 1. *n.* rabia *f.* 2. *v.* rabiar.

ragged, *a.* andrajoso; desigual.

raid, *n.* (mil.) correría *f.*

rail, *n.* baranda *f.;* carril *m.;* **by r.,** por ferrocarril.

railroad, *n.* ferrocarril *m.*

rain, 1. *n.* lluvia *f.* 2. *v.* llover.

rainbow, *n.* arco iris *m.*

raincoat, *n.* impermeable *m.*

rainfall, *n.* precipitación *f.*

rainy, *a.* lluvioso.

raise, 1. *n.* aumento *m.* 2. *v.* levantar, alzar; criar.

raisin, *n.* pasa *f.*

rake, 1. *n.* rastro *m.* 2. *v.* rastrillar.

rally, 1. *n.* reunión *f.* 2. *v.* reunirse.

ram, *n.* carnero *m.*

ramble, *v.* vagar.

ramp, *n.* rampa *f.*

rampart, *n.* terraplén *m.*

ranch, *n.* rancho *m.*

rancid, *a.* rancio.

rancor, *n.* rencor *m.*

random, *a.* fortuito. **at r.,** a la ventura.

range, 1. *n.* extensión *f.;* alcance *m.;* estufa; sierra *f.;* terreno de pasto. 2. *v.* recorrer; extenderse.

rank, 1. *a.* espeso; rancio. 2. *n.* fila *f.;* grado *m.* 3. *v.* clasificar.

ransack, *v.* saquear.

ransom, 1. *n.* rescate *m.* 2. *v.* rescatar.

rap, 1. *n.* golpecito *m.* 2. *v.* golpear.

rapid, *a.* rápido.

rapport, *n.* armonía *f.*

rapture, *n.* éxtasis *m.*

rare, *a.* raro; (of food) a medio cocer.

rascal, *n.* pícaro, bribón *m.*

rash, 1. *a.* temerario. 2. *n.* erupción *f.*

raspberry, *n.* frambuesa *f.*

rat, *n.* rata *f.*

rate, 1. *n.* velocidad; tasa *f.;* precio *m.;* (of exchange; of interest) tipo *m.* **at any r.,** de todos modos. 2. *v.* valuar.

rather, *adv.* bastante; más bien, mejor dicho.

ratify, *v.* ratificar.

ratio, *n.* razón; proporción *f.*

ration, 1. *n.* ración *f.* 2. *v.* racionar.

rational, *a.* racional.

rattle, 1. *n.* ruido *m.;* matraca *f.* **r. snake,** culebra de cascabel. 2. *v.* matraquear; rechinar.

raucous, *a.* ronco.

ravage, *v.* pillar; destruir; asolar.

rave, *v.* delirar; entusiasmarse.

ravel, *v.* deshilar.

raven, *n.* cuervo *m.*

ravenous, *a.* voraz.

raw, *a.* crudo; verde.

ray, *n.* rayo *m.*

rayon, *n.* rayón *m.*

razor, *n.* navaja de afeitar. **r. blade,** hoja de afeitar.

reach, 1. *n.* alcance *m.* 2. *v.* alcanzar.

react, *v.* reaccionar.

reaction, *n.* reacción *f.*

reactionary, 1. *a.* reaccionario. **2.** *n.* (pol.) retrógrado *m.*

read, *v.* leer.

reader, *n.* lector *m.*; libro de lectura.

readily, *adv.* fácilmente.

reading, *n.* lectura *f.*

ready, *a.* listo, preparado; dispuesto.

real, *a.* verdadero; real.

realist, *n.* realista *m.* & *f.*

reality, *n.* realidad *f.*

realization, *n.* comprensión; realización *f.*

realize, *v.* darse cuenta de; realizar.

really, *adv.* de veras; en realidad.

realm, *n.* reino; dominio *m.*

reap, *v.* segar, cosechar.

rear, 1. *a.* posterior. **2.** *n.* parte posterior. **3.** *v.* criar; levantar.

reason, 1. *n.* razón; causa *f.*; motivo *m.* **2.** *v.* razonar.

reasonable, *a.* razonable.

reassure, *v.* calmar, tranquilizar.

rebate, *n.* rebaja *f.*

rebel, 1. *n.* rebelde *m.* & *f.* **2.** *v.* rebelarse.

rebellion, *n.* rebelión *f.*

rebellious, *a.* rebelde.

rebirth, *n.* renacimiento *m.*

rebound, *v.* repercutir; resaltar.

rebuff, 1. *n.* repulsa *f.* **2.** *v.* rechazar.

rebuke, 1. *n.* reprensión *f.* **2.** *v.* reprender.

rebuttal, *n.* refutación *f.*

recalcitrant, *a.* recalcitrante.

recall, *v.* recordar; acordarse de; hacer volver.

recapitulate, *v.* recapitular.

recede, *v.* retroceder.

receipt, *n.* recibo *m.*; (com., pl.) ingresos *m.pl.*

receive, *v.* recibir.

receiver, *n.* receptor *m.*

recent, *a.* reciente.

recently, *adv.* recién.

receptacle, *n.* receptáculo *m.*

reception, *n.* acogida; recepción *f.*

receptionist, *n.* recepcionista *m.* & *f.*

receptive, *a.* receptivo.

recess, *n.* nicho; retiro; recreo *m.*

recipe, *n.* receta *f.*

recipient, *n.* receptor, recipiente *m.*

reciprocate, *v.* corresponder; reciprocar.

recite, *v.* recitar.

reckless, *a.* descuidado; imprudente.

reckon, *v.* contar; calcular.

reclaim, *v.* reformar; (leg.) reclamar.

recline, *v.* reclinar; recostar.

recognition, *n.* reconocimiento *m.*

recognize, *v.* reconocer.

recoil, 1. *n.* culatada *f.* **2.** *v.* recular.

recollect, *v.* recordar, acordarse de.

recommend, *v.* recomendar.

recommendation, *n.* recomendación *f.*

recompense, 1. *n.* recompensa *f.* **2.** *v.* recompensar.

reconcile, *v.* reconciliar.

recondition, *v.* reacondicionar.

reconsider, *v.* considerar de nuevo.

reconstruct, *v.* reconstruir.

record, 1. *n.* registro; (sports) record *m.* **phonograph r.,** disco *m.* **2.** *v.* registrar.

record player, *n.* tocadiscos *m.*

recount, *v.* relatar; contar.

recover, *v.* recobrar; restablecerse.

recovery, *n.* recobro *m.*; recuperación *f.*

recruit, 1. *n.* recluta *m.* **2.** *v.* reclutar.

rectangle, *n.* rectángulo *m.*

rectify, *v.* rectificar.

recuperate, *v.* recuperar.

recur, *v.* recurrir.

recycle, *v.* reciclar.

red, *a.* rojo; colorado.

redeem, *v.* redimir, rescatar.

redemption, *n.* redención *f.*

reduce, *v.* reducir.

reduction, *n.* reducción *f.*

reed, *n.* caña *f.*, (S.A.) bejuco *m.*

reef, *n.* arrecife, escollo *m.*

reel, 1. *n.* aspa *f.*, carrete *m.* **2.** *v.* aspar.

refer, *v.* referir.

referee, *n.* árbitro *m.*

reference, *n.* referencia *f.*

refill, 1. *n.* relleno *m.* **2.** *v.* rellenar.

refine, *n.* refinar.

refinement, *n.* refinamiento *m.;* cultura *f.*

reflect, *v.* reflejar; reflexionar.

reflection, *n.* reflejo *m.;* reflexión *f.*

reflex, *a.* reflejo.

reform, 1. *n.* reforma *f.* **2.** *v.* reformar.

reformation, *n.* reformación *f.*

refractory, *a.* refractorio.

refrain, 1. *n.* estribillo *m.* **2.** *v.* abstenerse.

refresh, *v.* refrescar.

refreshment, *n.* refresco *m.*

refrigerator, *n.* refrigerador *m.*

refuge, *n.* refugio *m.*

refugee, *n.* refugiado -da.

refund, 1. *n.* reembolso *m.* **2.** *v.* reembolsar.

refusal, *n.* negativa *f.*

refuse, 1. *n.* basura *f.* **2.** *v.* negarse, rehusar.

refute, *v.* refutar.

regain, *v.* recobrar.

regal, *a.* real.

regard, 1. *n.* aprecio; respeto *m.* **with r. to,** con respecto a. **2.** *v.* considerar; estimar.

regarding, *prep.* en cuanto a, acerca de.

regardless (of), a pesar de.

regent, *n.* regente *m.*

regime, *n.* régimen *m.*

regiment, 1. *n.* regimiento *m.* **2.** *v.* regimentar.

region, *n.* región *f.*

register, 1. *n.* registro *m.* **cash r.,** caja registradora. **2.** *v.* registrar; matricularse; (a letter) certificar.

registration, *n.* registro *m.;* matrícula *f.*

regret, 1. *n.* pena *f.* **2.** *v.* sentir, lamentar.

regular, *a.* regular; ordinario.

regularity, *n.* regularidad *f.*

regulate, *v.* regular.

regulation, *n.* regulación *f.*

regulator, *n.* regulador *m.*

rehabilitate, *v.* rehabilitar.

rehearse, *v.* repasar; (theat.) ensayar.

reign, 1. *n.* reino, reinado *m.* **2.** *v.* reinar.

reimburse, *v.* reembolsar.

rein, 1. *n.* rienda *f.* **2.** *v.* refrenar.

reincarnation, *n.* reencarnación *f.*

reindeer, *n.* reno *m.*

reinforce, *v.* reforzar.

reinforcement, *n.* refuerzo *m.;* armadura *f.*

reiterate, *v.* reiterar.

reject, *v.* rechazar.

rejoice, *v.* regocijarse.

rejoin, *v.* reunirse con; replicar.

rejuvenate, *v.* rejuvenecer.

relapse, 1. *n.* recaída *f.* **2.** *v.* recaer.

relate, *v.* relatar, contar; relacionar. **r. to,** llevarse bien con.

relation, *n.* relación *f.;* pariente *m.* & *f.*

relative, 1. *a.* relativo. **2.** *n.* pariente *m.* & *f.*

relativity, *n.* relatividad *f.*

relax, *v.* descansar; relajar.

relay, 1. *n.* relevo *m.* **2.** *v.* retransmitir.

release, 1. *n.* liberación *f.* **2.** *v.* soltar.

relent, *v.* ceder.

relevant, *a.* pertinente.

reliability, *n.* veracidad *f.*

reliable, *a.* responsable; digno de confianza.

relic, *n.* reliquia *f.*

relief, *n.* alivio; (sculpture) relieve *m.*

relieve, *v.* aliviar.

religion, *n.* religión *f.*

religious, *a.* religioso.

relinquish, *v.* abandonar.

relish, 1. *n.* sabor; condimento *m.* **2.** *v.* saborear.

reluctant, *a.* renuente.

rely, *v.* **r. on,** confiar en; contar con; depender de.

remain, 1. *n.* (pl.) restos *m.pl.* **2.** *v.* quedar, permanecer.

remainder, *n.* resto *m.*

remark, 1. *n.* observación *f.* **2.** *v.* observar.

remarkable, *a.* notable.

remedial, *a.* reparador.

remedy, 1. *n.* remedio *m.* **2.** *v.* remediar.

remember, *v.* acordarse de, recordar.

remembrance, *n.* recuerdo *m.*

remind, *v.* **r. of,** recordar.

reminisce, *v.* pensar en o hablar de cosas pasadas.

remiss, *a.* remiso; flojo.

remit, *v.* remitir.

remorse, *n.* remordimiento *m.*

remote, *a.* remoto.

removal, *n.* alejamiento *m.;* eliminación *f.*

remove, *v.* quitar; remover.

renaissance, *n.* renacimiento *m.*

rend, *v.* hacer pedazos; separar.

render, *v.* dar; rendir; (theat.) interpretar.

rendezvous, *n.* cita *f.*

rendition, *n.* interpretación, rendición *f.*

renege, *v.* renunciar.

renew, *v.* renovar.

renewal, *n.* renovación; (com.) prórroga *f.*

renounce, *v.* renunciar a.

renovate, *v.* renovar.

renown, *n.* renombre *m.,* fama *f.*

rent, **1.** *n.* alquiler *m.* **2.** *v.* arrendar, alquilar.

repair, **1.** *n.* reparo *m.* **2.** *v.* reparar.

repatriate, *v.* repatriar.

repay, *v.* pagar; devolver.

repeat, *v.* repetir.

repel, *v.* repeler, repulsar.

repent, *v.* arrepentirse.

repentance, *n.* arrepentimiento *m.*

repercussion, *n.* repercusión *f.*

repertoire, *n.* repertorio *m.*

repetition, *n.* repetición *f.*

replace, *v.* reemplazar.

replenish, *v.* rellenar; surtir de nuevo.

reply, **1.** *n.* respuesta *f.* **2.** *v.* replicar; contestar.

report, **1.** *n.* informe *m.* **2.** *v.* informar, contar; denunciar; presentarse.

reporter, *n.* repórter, reportero *m.*

repose, **1.** *n.* reposo *m.* **2.** *v.* reposar; reclinar.

reprehensible, *a.* reprensible.

represent, *v.* representar.

representation, *n.* representación *f.*

representative, **1.** *a.* representativo. **2.** *n.* representante *m.*

repress, *v.* reprimir.

reprimand, **1.** *n.* regaño *m.* **2.** *v.* regañar.

reprisal, *n.* represalia *f.*

reproach, **1.** *n.* reproche *m.* **2.** *v.* reprochar.

reproduce, *v.* reproducir.

reproduction, *n.* reproducción *f.*

reproof, *n.* censura *f.*

reprove, *v.* censurar, regañar.

reptile, *n.* reptil *m.*

republic, *n.* república *f.*

republican, *a.* & *n.* republicano -na.

repudiate, *v.* repudiar.

repulsive, *a.* repulsivo, repugnante.

reputation, *n.* reputación; fama *f.*

repute, **1.** *n.* reputación *f.* **2.** *v.* reputar.

request, **1.** *n.* súplica *f.,* ruego *m.* **2.** *v.* pedir; rogar, suplicar.

require, *v.* requerir; exigir.

requirement, *n.* requisito *m.*

requisite, **1.** *a.* necesario. **2.** *n.* requisito *m.*

requisition, *n.* requisición *f.*

rescind, *v.* rescindir, anular.

rescue, **1.** *n.* rescate *m.* **2.** *v.* rescatar.

research, *n.* investigación *f.*

resemble, *v.* parecerse a, asemejarse a.

resent, *v.* resentirse de.

reservation, *n.* reservación *f.*

reserve, **1.** *n.* reserva *f.* **2.** *v.* reservar.

reservoir, *n.* depósito; tanque *m.*

reside, *v.* residir, morar.

residence, *n.* residencia, morada *f.*

resident, *n.* residente *m.* & *f.*

residue, *n.* residuo *m.*

resign, *v.* dimitir; resignar.

resignation, *n.* dimisión, resignación *f.*

resist, *v.* resistir.

resistance, *n.* resistencia *f.*

resolute, *a.* resuelto.

resolution, *n.* resolución *f.*

resolve, *v.* resolver.

resonant, *a.* resonante.

resort, **1.** *n.* recurso; expediente *m.* **summer r.,** lugar de veraneo. **2.** *v.* acudir, recurrir.

resound, *v.* resonar.

resource, *n.* recurso *m.*

respect, **1.** *n.* respeto *m.* **with r.**

to, con respecto a. 2. v. respetar.
respectable, a. respetable.
respectful, a. respetuoso.
respective, a. respectivo.
respiration, n. respiración f.
respite, n. pausa, tregua f.
respond, v. responder.
response, n. respuesta f.
responsibility, n. responsabilidad f.
responsible, a. responsable.
responsive, a. respondiente, sensible.
rest, 1. n. descanso; reposo m.; (music) pausa f. **the r.,** el resto, lo demás; los demás. **2.** v. descansar; rocostar.
restaurant, n. restaurante m.
restful, a. tranquilo.
restitution, n. restitución f.
restless, a. inquieto.
restoration, n. restauración f.
restore, v. restaurar.
restrain, v. refrenar.
restraint, n. limitación, restricción f.
restrict, v. restringir, limitar.
result, 1. n. resultado m. **2.** v. resultar.
resume, v. reasumir; empezar de nuevo.
resurgent, a. resurgente.
resurrect, v. resucitar.
retail, n. **at r.,** al por menor.
retain, v. retener.
retaliate, v. vengarse.
retard, v. retardar.
retention, n. retención f.
reticent, a. reticente.
retire, v. retirar.
retort, 1. n. réplica f.; (chem.) retorta f. **2.** v. replicar.
retreat, 1. n. retiro m.; (mil.) retirada, retreta f. **2.** v. retirarse.
retribution, n. retribución f.
retrieve, v. recobrar.
return, 1. n. vuelta f., regreso m.; torno m. **by r. mail,** a vuelta de correo. **2.** v. volver, regresar; devolver.
reunion, n. reunión f.
reveal, v. revelar.
revelation, n. revelación f.
revenge, n. venganza f. **to get r.,** vengarse.
revenue, n. renta f.
revere, v. reverenciar, venerar.

reverence, 1. n. reverencia f. **2.** v. reverenciar.
reverend, 1. a. reverendo. **2.** n. pastor m.
reverent, a. reverente.
reverse, 1. a. inverso. **2.** n. revés, inverso m. **3.** v. invertir; revocar.
revert, v. revertir.
review, 1. n. repaso m.; revista f. **2.** v. repasar; revistar.
revise, v. revisar.
revision, n. revisión f.
revival, n. reavivamiento m.
revive, v. avivar; revivir.
revoke, v. revocar.
revolt, 1. n. rebelión f. **2.** v. rebelarse.
revolution, n. revolución f.
revolutionary, a. & n. revolucionario -ria.
revolve, v. girar; dar vueltas.
revolver, n. revólver m.
reward, 1. n. pago m.; recompensa f. **2.** v. recompensar.
rhetoric, n. retórica f.
rheumatism, n. reumatismo m.
rhinoceros, n. rinoceronte m.
rhyme, 1. n. rima f. **2.** v. rimar.
rhythm, n. ritmo m.
rhythmical, a. rítmico.
rib, n. costilla f.
ribbon, n. cinta f.
rice, n. arroz m.
rich, a. rico.
rid, v. librar. **get r. of,** deshacerse de, quitarse.
riddle, n. enigma; rompecabezas m.
ride, 1. n. paseo (a caballo o en coche) m. **2.** v. cabalgar; ir en coche.
ridge, n. cerro m.; arruga f.; (of a roof) caballete m.
ridicule, 1. n. ridículo m. **2.** v. ridiculizar.
ridiculous, a. ridículo.
rifle, n. fusil m. **2.** v. robar.
rig, 1. n. aparejo m. **2.** v. aparejar.
right, 1. a. derecho; correcto. **to be r.,** tener razón. **2.** adv. bien, correctamente. **r. here,** etc., aquí mismo, etc. **all r.,** está bien, muy bien. **3.** n. derecho m.; justicia f. **to the r.,** a la derecha. **4.** v. corregir; enderezar.
righteous, a. justo.
rigid, a. rígido.

rigor, *n.* rigor *m.*

rigorous, *a.* riguroso.

rim, *n.* margen *m. or f.*; borde *m.*

ring, 1. *n.* anillo *m.*; sortija *f.*; círculo; campaneo *m.* **2.** *v.* cercar; sonar; tocar.

rinse, *v.* enjuagar, lavar.

riot, *n.* motín *f.*; alboroto *m.*

rip, 1. *n.* rasgadura *f.* **2.** *v.* rasgar; descoser.

ripe, *a.* maduro.

ripen, *v.* madurar.

ripoff, *n.* robo, atraco *m.*

ripple, 1. *n.* onda *f. or f.* **2.** *v.* ondear.

rise, 1. *n.* subida *f.* **2.** *v.* ascender; levantarse; (moon) salir.

risk, 1. *n.* riesgo *m.* **2.** *v.* arriesgar.

rite, *n.* rito *m.*

ritual, *a. & n.* ritual *m.*

rival, *n.* rival *m. & f.*

rivalry, *n.* rivalidad *f.*

river, *n.* río *m.*

rivet, 1. *n.* remache, roblón *m.* **2.** *v.* remachar, roblar.

road, *n.* camino *m.*; carretera *f.*

roam, *v.* vagar.

roar, 1. *n.* rugido, bramido *m.* **2.** *v.* rugir, bramar.

roast, 1. *n.* asado *m.* **2.** *v.* asar.

rob, *v.* robar.

robber, *n.* ladrón -na.

robbery, *n.* robo *m.*

robe, *n.* manto *m.*

robin, *n.* petirrojo *m.*

robust, *a.* robusto.

rock, 1. *n.* roca *f.*; (music) rock *m.*, musica (de) rock *f.* **2.** *v.* mecer; oscilar.

rocker, *n.* mecedora *f.*

rocket, *n.* cohete *m.*

rocky, *a.* pedregoso.

rod, *n.* varilla *f.*

rodent, *n.* roedor *m.*

rogue, *n.* bribón, pícaro *m.*

roguish, *a.* pícaro.

role, *n.* papel *m.*

roll, 1. *n.* rollo *m.*; lista *f.*; panecillo *m.* **to call the r.,** pasar lista. **2.** *v.* rodar. **r. up,** enrollar.

roller, *n.* rodillo, cilindro *m.*

Roman, *a. & n.* romano -na.

romance, 1. *a.* románico. **2.** *n.* romance *m.*; amorío *m.*

romantic, *a.* romántico.

romp, *v.* retozar; jugar.

roof, 1. *n.* techo *m.* **2.** *v.* techar.

room, 1. *n.* cuarto *m.*, habitación *f.*; lugar *m.* **2.** *v.* alojarse.

roommate, *n.* compañero -ra de cuarto.

rooster, *n.* gallo *m.*

root, *n.* raíz *f.* **to take r.,** arraigar.

rope, *n.* cuerda, soga *f.*

rose, *n.* rosa *f.*

rosy, *a.* róseo, rosado.

rot, 1. *n.* putrefacción *f.* **2.** *v.* pudrirse.

rotary, *a.* giratorio; rotativo.

rotate, *v.* girar; alternar.

rotation, *n.* rotación *f.*

rotten, *a.* podrido.

rouge, *n.* colorete *m.*

rough, *a.* áspero; rudo; grosero; aproximado.

round, 1. *a.* redondo. **r. trip,** viaje de ida y vuelta. **2.** *n.* ronda *f.*; (boxing) asalto *m.*

rouse, *v.* despertar.

rout, 1. *n.* derrota *f.* **2.** *v.* derrotar.

route, 1. *n.* ruta, vía *f.*

routine, 1. *a.* rutinario. **2.** *n.* rutina *f.*

rove, *v.* vagar.

rover, *n.* vagabundo -da.

row, 1. *n.* fila; pelea *f.* **2.** *v.* (naut.) remar.

rowboat, *n.* bote de remos.

rowdy, *a.* alborotoso.

royal, *a.* real.

royalty, *n.* realeza *f.*; (pl.) regalías *f.pl.*

rub, *v.* frotar. **r. against,** rozar. **r. out,** borrar.

rubber, *n.* goma *f.*; caucho *m.*; (pl.) chanclos *m.pl.*, zapatos de goma.

rubbish, *n.* basura *f.*; (nonsense) tonterías *f.pl.*

ruby, *n.* rubí *m.*

rudder, *n.* timón *m.*

ruddy, *a.* colorado.

rude, *a.* rudo; grosero; descortés.

rudiment, *n.* rudimento *m.*

rue, *v.* deplorar; lamentar.

ruffian, *n.* rufián, bandolero *m.*

ruffle, 1. *n.* volante fruncido *f.* **2.** *v.* fruncir; irritar.

rug, *n.* alfombra *f.*

rugged, *a.* áspero; robusto.

ruin, 1. *n.* ruina *f.* **2.** *v.* arruinar.

ruinous, *a.* ruinoso.

rule, 1. *n.* regla *f.* **as a r.,** por regla general. 2. v. gobernar; mandar; rayar.

ruler, n. gobernante; soberano m.; regla f.

rum, n. ron m.

rumble, v. retumbar.

rumor, n. rumor m.

run, v. correr; hacer correr. **r. away,** escaparse. **r. into,** chocar con.

runner, n. corredor -ra; mensajero -ra.

rupture, 1. n. rotura; hernia f. 2. v. reventar.

rural, a. rural, campestre.

rush, 1. n. prisa f.; (bot.) junco m. 2. v. ir de prisa.

Russia, n. Rusia f.

Russian, 1. a. & n. ruso -sa.

rust, 1. n. herrumbre m. 2. v. aherrumbrarse.

rustic, a. rústico.

rustle, 1. n. susurro m. 2. v. susurrar.

rusty, a. mohoso.

rut, n. surco m.

ruthless, a. cruel, inhumano.

rye, n. centeno m.

S

saber, n. sable m.

sable, n. cebellina f.

sabotage, n. sabotaje m.

sachet, n. perfumador m.

sack, 1. n. saco m. 2. v. (mil.) saquear.

sacred, a. sagrado, santo.

sacrifice, 1. n. sacrificio m. 2. v. sacrificar.

sacrilege, n. sacrilegio m.

sad, a. triste.

saddle, 1. n. silla de montar. 2. v. ensillar.

safe, 1. a. seguro; salvo. 2. n. caja de caudales.

safeguard, 1. n. salvaguardia f. 2. v. proteger, poner a salvo.

safety, n. seguridad, protección f.

safety pin, n. imperdible m.

sage, 1. a. sabio, sagaz. 2. n. sabio m.; (bot.) salvia f.

sail, 1. n. vela f.; paseo por mar. 2. v. navegar; embarcarse.

sailboat, n. barco de vela.

sailor, n. marinero m.

saint, n. santo -ta.

sake, n. **for the s. of,** por; por el bien de.

salad, n. ensalada f. **s. bowl,** ensaladera f.

salary, n. sueldo, salario m.

sale, n. venta f.

salesman, n. vendedor m.; viajante de comercio.

sales tax, impuesto sobre la venta.

saliva, n. saliva f.

salmon, n. salmón m.

salt, 1. a. salado. 2. n. sal f. 3. v. salar.

salute, 1. n. saludo m. 2. v. saludar.

salvage, v. salvar; recobrar.

salvation, n. salvación f.

salve, n. emplasto, ungüento m.

same, a. & pron. mismo. **it's all the s.,** lo mismo da.

sample, 1. n. muestra f. 2. v. probar.

sanatorium, n. sanatorio m.

sanctify, v. santificar.

sanction, 1. n. sanción f. 2. v. sancionar.

sanctity, n. santidad f.

sanctuary, n. santuario, asilo m.

sand, n. arena f.

sandal, n. sandalia f.

sandwich, n. sandwich m.

sandy, a. arenoso; (color) rufo.

sane, a. cuerdo; sano.

sanitary, a. higiénico, sanitario. **s. napkin,** toalla sanitaria.

sanitation, n. saneamiento m.

sanity, n. cordura f.

sap, 1. n. savia f.; (coll.) estúpido, bobo m. 2. v. agotar.

sapphire, n. zafiro m.

sarcasm, n. sarcasmo m.

sardine, n. sardina f.

sash, n. cinta f.

satellite, n. satélite m.

satin, n. raso m.

satire, n. sátira f.

satisfaction, n. satisfacción; recompensa f.

satisfactory, a. satisfactorio.

satisfy, v. satisfacer. **be satisfied that . . .,** estar convencido de que.

saturate, v. saturar.

Saturday, n. sábado m.

sauce, n. salsa; compota f.

saucer, *n.* platillo *m.*

saucy, *a.* descarado, insolente.

sausage, *n.* salchicha *f.*

savage, *a. & n.* salvaje *m.*

save, 1. *v.* salvar; guardar; ahorrar, economizar **2.** *prep.* salvo, excepto.

savings, *n.* ahorros *m.pl.*

savior, *n.* salvador *m.*

savor, 1. *n.* sabor *m.* **2.** *v.* saborear.

savory, *a.* sabroso.

saw, 1. *n.* sierra *f.* **2.** *v.* aserrar.

say, *v.* decir; recitar.

saying, *n.* dicho, refrán *m.*

scaffold, *n.* andamio; (gallows) patíbulo *m.*

scald, *v.* escaldar.

scale, 1. *n.* escala; (of fish) escama *f.*; (pl.) balanza *f.* **2.** *v.* escalar; escamar.

scalp, 1. *n.* pericráneo *m.* **2.** *v.* escalpar.

scan, *v.* hojear, repasar; (poetry) escandir.

scandal, *n.* escándalo *m.*

scant, *a.* escaso.

scar, *n.* cicatriz *f.*

scarce, *a.* escaso; raro.

scarcely, *adv. & conj.* apenas.

scare, 1. *n.* susto *m.* **2.** *v.* asustar. **s. away,** espantar.

scarf, *n.* pañuleta, bufanda *f.*

scarlet, *a.* escarlata *f.*

scatter, *v.* esparcir; dispersar.

scavenger, *n.* basurero *m.*

scenario, *n.* escenario *m.*

scene, *n.* vista *f.*, paisaje *m.*; (theat.) escena *f.* **behind the scenes,** bajo cuerda.

scenery, *n.* paisaje *m.*; (theat.) decorado *m.*

scent, 1. *n.* olor, perfume; (sense) olfato *m.* **2.** *v.* perfumar; (fig.) sospechar.

schedule, 1. *n.* programa, horario *m.* **2.** *v.* fijar la hora para.

scheme, 1. *n.* proyecto; esquema *m.* **2.** *v.* intrigar.

scholar, *n.* erudito; becado -da.

scholarship, *n.* beca; erudición *f.*

school, 1. *n.* escuela *f.*; colegio *m.*; (of fish) banco *m.* **2.** *v.* enseñar.

sciatica, *n.* ciática *f.*

science, *n.* ciencia *f.*

science fiction, *n.* ciencia ficción.

scientific, *a.* científico.

scientist, *n.* científico -ca.

scissors, *n.* tijeras *f.pl.*

scoff, *v.* mofarse, burlarse.

scold, *v.* regañar.

scoop, 1. *n.* cucharón *m.*; cucharada *f.* **2.** *v.* **s. out,** recoger, sacar.

scope, *n.* alcance; campo *m.*

scorch, 1. *n.* tantos *m.pl.*; (music) partitura *f.* **2.** *v.* marcar, hacer tantos.

scorn, 1. *n.* desprecio *m.* **2.** *v.* despreciar.

scornful, *a.* desdeñoso.

Scotch, *a.* escocés.

Scotland, *n.* Escocia *f.*

scour, *v.* fregar, estregar.

scourge, *n.* azote *m.*; plaga *f.*

scout, 1. *n.* explorador *m.* **2.** *v.* explorar, reconocer.

scramble, 1. *n.* ribatiña *f.* **2.** *v.* bregar. **scrambled eggs,** huevos revueltos.

scrap, 1. *n.* migaja *f.*; pedacito *m.*; (coll.) riña *f.* **s. metal,** hierro viejo. **s. paper,** papel borrador. **2.** *v.* desechar; (coll.) reñir.

scrape, 1. *n.* lío, apuro *m.* **2.** *v.* rascar; (feet) restregar.

scratch, 1. *n.* rasguño *m.* **2.** *v.* rasguñar; rayar.

scream, 1. *n.* grito, chillido *m.* **2.** *v.* gritar, chillar.

screen, *n.* biombo *m.*; (for window) tela metálica; (movie) pantalla *f.*

screw, 1. *n.* tornillo *m.* **2.** *v.* atornillar.

screwdriver, *n.* destornillador *m.*

scribble, *v.* hacer garabatos.

scroll, *n.* rúbrica *f.*; rollo de papel.

scrub, *v.* gregar, estregar.

scruple, *n.* escrúpulo *m.*

scrupulous, *a.* escrupuloso.

sculptor, *n.* escultor *m.*

sculpture, 1. *n.* escultura *f.* **2.** *v.* esculpir.

scythe, *n.* guadaña *f.*

sea, *n.* mar *m.* or *f.*

seabed, *n.* lecho marino *m.*

seafood, *n.* mariscos *m.pl.*

seal, 1. *n.* sello *m.*; (animal) foca *f.* **2.** *v.* sellar.

seam, *n.* costura *f.*

seaport, *n.* puerto de mar.

search, 1. n. registro m. **in s. of,** en busca de. **2.** v. registrar. **s. for,** buscar.

seasick, a. mareado. **to get s.,** marearse.

season, 1. n. estación; sazón; temporada f. **2.** v. sazonar.

seasoning, n. condimento m.

seat, 1. n. asiento m.; residencia, sede f.; (theat.) localidad f. **s. belt,** cinturón de seguridad. **2.** v. sentar. **be seated,** sentarse.

second, 1. a. & n. segundo m. **2.** v. apoyar, segundar.

secondary, a. secundario.

secret, a. & n. secreto m.

secretary, n. secretario -ria; (govt.) ministro m.; (furniture) papelera f.

sect, n. secta f.; partido m.

section, n. sección, parte f.

sectional, a. regional, local.

secular, a. secular.

secure, 1. a. seguro. **2.** v. asegurar; obtener; (fin.) garantizer.

security, n. seguridad; garantía f.

sedative, a. & n. sedativo m.

seduce, v. seducir.

see, v. ver; comprender. **s. off,** despedirse de. **s. to,** encargarse de.

seed, 1. n. semilla f. **2.** v. sembrar.

seek, v. buscar. **s. to,** tratar de.

seem, v. parecer.

seep, v. colarse.

segment, n. segmento m.

segregate, v. segregar.

seize, v. agarrar; apoderarse de.

seldom, adv. rara vez.

select, 1. a. escogido, selecto. **2.** v. elegir, seleccionar.

selection, n. selección f.

selective, a. escogedor.

selfish, a. egoísta.

selfishness, n. egoísmo m.

sell, v. vender.

semester, n. semestre m.

semicircle, n. semicírculo m.

senate, n. senado m.

senator, n. senador -ra.

send, v. mandar, enviar; (a wire) poner. **s. away,** despedir. **s. back,** devolver. **s. for,** mandar buscar. **s. off,** expedir. **s. word,** mandar recado.

senile, a. senil.

senior, 1. a. mayor; más viejo. **Sr.,** padre.

senior citizen, persona de edad.

sensation, n. sensación f.

sensational, a. sensacional.

sense, 1. n. sentido; juicio m. **2.** v. percibir; sospechar.

sensible, a. sensato, razonable.

sensitive, a. sensible; sensitivo.

sensual, a. sensual.

sentence, 1. n. frase; (gram.) oración; (leg.) sentencia f. **2.** v. condenar.

sentiment, n. sentimiento m.

sentimental, a. sentimental.

separate, 1. a. separado; suelto. **2.** v. separar, dividir.

separation, n. separación f.

September, n. septiembre m.

sequence, n. serie f. **in s.,** seguidos.

serenade, 1. n. serenata f. **2.** v. dar serenata a.

serene, a. sereno; tranquilo.

sergeant, n. sargento m.

serial, a. en serie, de serie.

series, n. serie f.

serious, a. serio; grave.

sermon, n. sermón m.

serpent, n. serpiente f.

servant, n. criado -da; servidor -ra.

serve, v. servir.

service, 1. n. servicio m. **at the s. of,** a las órdenes de. **to be of s.,** servir; ser útil. **2.** v. (auto.) reparar.

session, n. sesión f.

set, 1. a. fijo. **2.** n. colección f.; (of a game) juego; (mech.) aparato; (theat.) decorado m. **3.** v. poner, colocar; fijar; (sun) ponerse. **s. forth,** exponer. **s. off,** **s. out,** salir. **s. up,** instalar; establecer.

settle, v. solucionar; arreglar; establecerse.

settlement, n. caserío; arreglo; acuerdo m.

settler, n. poblador -ra.

seven, a. & pron. siete.

seventeen, a. & pron. diecisiete.

seventh, a. séptimo.

seventy, a. & pron. setenta.

sever, v. desunir; romper.

several, a. & pron. varios.

severe, a. severo; grave.

severity, *n.* severidad *f.*

sew, *v.* coser.

sewer, *n.* cloaca *f.*

sex, *n.* sexo *m.*

sexism, *n.* sexismo *m.*

sexist, *a.* & *n.* sexista.

sexton, *n.* sacristán *m.*

sexual, *a.* sexual.

shabby, *a.* haraposo, desalineado.

shade, **1.** *n.* sombra *f.;* tinte *m.;* (window) transparente *m.* **2.** *v.* sombrear.

shadow, *n.* sombra *f.*

shady, *a.* sombroso; sospechoso.

shaft, *n.* columna; (mech.) asta *f.*

shake, *v.* sacudir; agitar; temblar. **s. hands with,** dar la mano a.

shallow, *a.* poco hondo; superficial.

shame, **1.** *n.* vergüenza *f.* **to be a s.,** ser una lástima. **2.** *v.* avergonzar.

shameful, *a.* vergonzoso.

shampoo, *n.* champú *m.*

shape, **1.** *n.* forma *f.;* estado *m.* **2.** *v.* formar.

share, **1.** *n.* parte; (stock) acción *f.* **2** *v.* compartir.

shark, *n.* tiburón *m.*

sharp, *a.* agudo; (blade) afilado.

sharpen, *v.* aguzar; afilar.

shatter, *v.* estrellar; hacer pedazos.

shave, **1.** *n.* afeitada *f.* **2.** *v.* afeitarse.

shawl, *n.* rebozo, chal *m.*

she, *pron.* ella *f.*

sheaf, *n.* gavilla *f.*

shear, *v.* cizallar.

shears, *n.* cizallas *f.pl.*

sheath, *n.* vaina *f.*

shed, **1.** *n.* cobertizo *m.* **2.** *v.* arrojar, quitarse.

sheep, *n.* oveja *f.*

sheet, *n.* sábana; (of paper) hoja *f.*

shelf, *n.* estante, *m.,* repisa *f.*

shell, **1.** *n.* cáscara; (sea) concha *f.;* (mil.) proyectil *m.* **2.** *v.* desgranar; bombardear.

shellac, *n.* laca *f.*

shelter, **1.** *n.* albergue; refugio *m.* **2.** *v.* albergar; amparar.

shepherd, *n.* pastor *m.*

sherry, *n.* jerez *m.*

shield, **1.** *n.* escudo *m.* **2.** *v.* amparar.

shift, **1.** *n.* cambio; (work) turno *m.* **2.** *v.* cambiar, mudar. **s. for oneself,** arreglárselas.

shine, **1.** *n.* brillo, lustre *m.* **2.** *v.* brillar; (shoes) lustrar.

shiny, *a.* brillante, lustroso.

ship, **1.** *n.* barco *m.,* nave *f.* **2.** *v.* embarcar; (com.) enviar.

shipment, *n.* envío, embarque *m.*

shirk, *v.* faltar a.

shirt, *n.* camisa *f.*

shiver, **1.** *n.* temblor *m.* **2.** *v.* temblar.

shock, **1.** *n.* choque *m.* **2.** *v.* chocar.

shoe, *n.* zapato *m.*

shoelace, *n.* lazo *m.;* cordón de zapato.

shoemaker, *n.* zapatero *m.*

shoot, *v.* tirar; (gun) disparar. **s. away, s. off,** salir disparado.

shop, *n.* tienda *f.*

shopping, *n.* **to go s.,** hacer compras, ir de compras.

shore, *n.* orilla; playa *f.*

short, *a.* corto; breve; (in stature) pequeño, bajo. **a s. time,** poco tiempo. **in s.,** en suma.

shortage, *n.* escasez; falta *f.*

shorten, *v.* acortar, abreviar.

shortly, *adv.* en breve, dentro de poco.

shorts, *n.* calzoncillos *m.pl.*

shot, *n.* tiro, disparo *m.*

shoulder, **1.** *n.* hombro *m.* **2.** *v.* asumir; cargar con.

shout, **1.** *n.* grito *m.* **2.** *v.* gritar.

shove, **1.** *n.* empujón *m.* **2.** *v.* empujar.

shovel, **1.** *n.* pala *f.* **2.** *v.* traspalar.

show, **1.** *n.* ostentación *f.;* (theat.) función *f.;* espectáculo *m.* **2.** *v.* enseñar, mostrar; verse. **s. up,** destacarse; (coll.) asomar.

shower, *n.* chubasco *m.;* (bath) ducha *f.*

shrapnel, *n.* metralla *f.*

shrewd, *a.* astuto.

shriek, **1.** *n.* chillido *m.* **2.** *v.* chillar.

shrill, *a.* chillón, agudo.

shrimp, *n.* camarón *m.*

shrine, *n.* santuario *m.*

shrink, *v.* encogerse, contraerse, **s. from,** huir de.

shroud, 1. *n.* mortaja *f.* **2.** *v.* (fig.) ocultar.

shrub, *n.* arbusto *m.*

shudder, 1. *n.* estremecimiento *m.* **2.** *v.* estremecerse.

shun, *v.* evitar, huir de.

shut, *v.* cerrar. **s. in,** encerrar. **s. up,** (coll.) callarse.

shutter, *n.* persiana *f.*

shy, *a.* tímido, vergonzoso.

sick, *a.* enfermo. **s. of,** aburrido de, cansado de.

sickness, *n.* enfermedad *f.*

side, 1. *n.* lado *m.*; partido *m.*; parte *f.*; (anat.) costado *m.* **2.** *v.* **s. with,** ponerse del lado de.

sidewalk, *n.* acera, vereda *f.*

siege, *n.* asedio *m.*

sieve, *n.* cedazo *m.*

sift, *v.* cerner.

sigh, 1. *n.* suspiro *m.* **2.** *v.* suspirar.

sight, 1. *n.* vista *f.*; punto de interés. **to lose s. of,** perder de vista. **2.** *v.* divisar.

sign, 1. *n.* letrero; señal, seña *f.* **2.** *v.* firmar. **s. up,** inscribirse.

signal, 1. *n.* señal *f.* **2.** *v.* hacer señales.

signature, *n.* firma *f.*

significance, *n.* significación *f.*

significant, *a.* significativo.

signify, *v.* significar.

silence, 1. *n.* silencio *m.* **2.** *v.* hacer callar.

silent, *a.* silencioso; callado.

silk, *n.* seda *f.*

silken, silky, *a.* sedoso.

sill, *n.* umbral de puerta *m.*, solera *f.*

silly, *a.* necio, tonto.

silo, *n.* silo *m.*

silver, *n.* plata *f.*

silverware, *n.* artículos de plata.

similar, *a.* semejante, parecido.

similarity, *n.* semejanza *f.*

simple, *a.* sencillo, simple.

simplicity, *n.* sencillez *f.*

simplify, *v.* simplificar.

simulate, *v.* simular.

simultaneous, *a.* simultáneo.

sin, 1. *n.* pecado *m.* **2.** *v.* pecar.

since, 1. *adv.* desde entonces. **2.** *prep.* desde. **3.** *conj.* desde que; puesto que.

sincere, *a.* sincero.

sincerely, *adv.* sinceramente.

sincerity, *n.* sinceridad *f.*

sinew, *n.* tendón *m.*

sinful, *a.* pecador.

sing, *v.* cantar.

singe, *v.* chamuscar.

singer, *n.* cantante *m. & f.*

single, *a.* solo; (room) sencillo; (unmarried) soltero.

singular, *a. & n.* singular *m.*

sinister, *a.* siniestro.

sink, 1. *n.* fregadero *f.* **2.** *v.* hundir; (fig.) abatir.

sinner, *n.* pecador -ra.

sinuous, *a.* sinuoso.

sinus, *n.* seno; hueco *m.*

sip, 1. *n.* sorbo *m.* **2.** *v.* sorber.

siphon, *n.* sifón *m.*

sir, *title.* señor.

siren, *n.* sirena *f.*

sirloin, *n.* solomillo *m.*

sister, *n.* hermana *f.*

sister-in-law, *n.* cuñada *f.*

sit, *v.* sentarse; posar. **be sitting,** estar sentado. **s. down,** sentarse. **s. up,** incorporarse; quedar levantado.

site, *n.* sitio, local *m.*

sitting, *n.* sesión *f.*

situate, *v.* situar.

situation, *n.* situación *f.*

six, *a. & pron.* seis.

sixteen, *a. & pron.* dieciseis.

sixth, *a.* sexto.

sixty, *a. & pron.* sesenta.

size, *n.* tamaño *f.*; (of shoe, etc.) número *m.*

sizing, *n.* aderezo *m.*

skate, 1. *n.* patín *f.* **2.** *v.* patinar.

skateboard, *n.* monopatín *m.*

skein, *n.* madeja *f.*

skeleton, *n.* esqueleto *m.*

skeptic, *n.* escéptico -ca.

skeptical, *a.* escéptico.

sketch, 1. *n.* esbozo *m.* **2.** *v.* esbozar.

ski, 1. *n.* esquí *m.* **2.** *v.* esquiar.

skid, 1. *v.* resbalar. **2.** *n.* varadera *f.*

skill, *n.* destreza, habilidad *f.*

skillful, *a.* diestro, hábil.

skim, *v.* rasar; (milk) desnatar. **s. over, s. through,** hojear.

skin, 1. *n.* piel *m.*; (of fruit) corteza *f.* **2.** *v.* desollar.

skip, 1. *n.* brinco *m.* **2.** *v.* brincar. **s. over,** pasar por alto.

skirmish, n. escaramuza f.

skirt, n. falda f.

skull, n. cráneo m.

skunk, n. zorrillo m.

sky, n. cielo m.

skylight, n. tragaluz m.

skyscraper, n. rascacielos m.

slab, n. tabla f.

slack, a. flojo; descuidado.

slacken, v. relajar.

slacks, n. pantalones flojos.

slam, 1. n. portazo m. **2.** v. cerrar de golpe.

slander, 1. n. calumnia f. **2.** v. calumniar.

slang, n. jerga f.

slant, 1. n. sesgo m. **2.** v. sesgar.

slap, 1. n. bofetada, palmada f. **2.** v. dar una bofetada.

slash, 1. n. cuchillada f. **2.** v. acuchillar.

slat, 1. n. tablilla f. **2.** v. lanzar.

slate, 1. n. pizarra f.; lista de candidatos. **2.** n. destinar.

slaughter, 1. n. matanza f. **2.** v. matar.

slave, n. esclavo -va.

slavery, n. esclavitud f.

Slavic, a. eslavo.

slay, v. matar, asesinar.

sled, n. trineo m.

sleek, a. liso.

sleep, 1. n. sueño m. **to get much s.,** dormir mucho. **2.** v. dormir.

sleeping car, n. coche cama.

sleeping pill, n. pastilla para dormir.

sleepy, a. soñoliento. **to be s.,** tener sueño.

sleet, 1. n. cellisca f. **2.** v. cellisquear.

sleeve, n. manga f.

slender, a. delgado.

slice, 1. n. rebanada f.; (of meat) tajada f. **2.** v. rebanar; tajar.

slide, v. resbalar, deslizarse.

slide rule, n. regla de cálculo f.

slight, 1. n. desaire m. **2.** a. pequeño; leve. **3.** v. desairar.

slim, a. delgado.

slime, n. lama f.

sling, 1. n. honda f.; (med.) cabestrillo m. **2.** v. tirar.

slink, v. escabullirse.

slip, 1. n. imprudencia; (garment) combinación f.; (of paper) trozo m.; ficha f. **2.** v.

resbalar; deslizar. **s. up,** equivocarse.

slipper, n. chinela f.

slippery, a. resbaloso.

slit, 1. n. abertura f. **2.** v. cortar.

slogan, n. lema m.

slope, 1. n. declive m. **2.** v. inclinarse.

sloppy, a. desaliñado, chapucero.

slot, n. ranura f.

slot machine, n. máquina de servicio automático f.

slouch, 1. n. patán m. **2.** v. estar gacho.

slovenly, a. desaliñado.

slow, 1. a. lento; (watch) atrasado. **2.** v. **s. down, s. up,** retardar; ir más despacio.

slowly, adv. despacio.

slowness, n. lentitud f.

sluggish, a. perezoso, inactivo.

slum, n. barrio bajo m.

slumber, v. dormitar.

slur, 1. n. estigma m. **2.** v. menospreciar.

slush, n. fango m.

sly, a. taimado. **on the s.** a hurtadillas.

smack, 1. n. manotada f. **2.** v. manotear.

small, a. pequeño.

smallpox, n. viruela f.

smart, 1. a. listo; elegante. **2.** v. escocer.

smash, v. aplastar; hacer pedazos.

smear, 1. n. mancha; difamación f. **2.** v. manchar; difamar.

smell, 1. n. olor; (sense) olfato m. **2.** v. oler.

smelt, 1. n. eperlano m. **2.** v. fundir.

smile, 1. n. sonrisa f. **2.** v. sonreír.

smite, v. afligir; apenar.

smock, n. camisa de mujer f.

smoke, 1. n. humo m. **2.** v. fumar; (food) ahumar.

smokestack, n. chimenea f.

smolder, v. arder sin llama.

smooth, 1. a. liso; suave; tranquilo. **2.** v. alisar.

smother, v. sofocar.

smug, a. presumido.

smuggle, v. pasar de contrabando.

snack, n. bocadillo m.

snag, n. nudo m., obstáculo m.

snail, n. caracol m.
snake, n. culebra, serpiente f.
snap, 1. n. trueno m. **2.** v. tronar, romper.
snapshot, n. instantánea f.
snare, n. trampa f.
snarl, 1. n. gruñido m. **2.** v. gruñir; (hair) enredar.
snatch, v. arrebatar.
sneak, v. ir, entrar, salir (etc.) a hurtadillas.
sneaker, n. sujeto ruín m.
sneakers, n.pl. tenis m.pl.
sneer, 1. n. mofa f. **2.** v. mofarse.
sneeze, 1. n. estornudo m. **2.** v. estornudar.
snicker, n. risita m.
snob, n. esnob m.
snore, 1. n. ronquido m. **2.** v. roncar.
snow, 1. n. nieve f. **2.** v. nevar.
snowdrift, n. ventisquero m.
snub, v. desairar.
snug, a. abrigado y cómodo.
so, 1. adv. así; (also) también. **so as to,** para. **so that,** para que. **so . . . as,** tan . . . como. **so . . . that,** tan . . . que. **2.** conj. así es que.
soak, v. empapar.
soap, 1. n. jabón m. **2.** v. enjabonar.
soar, v. remontarse.
sob, 1. n. sollozo m **2.** v. sollozar.
sober, a. sobrio; pensativo.
sociable, a. sociable.
social, 1. a. social. **2.** n. tertulia f.
socialism, n. socialismo m.
socialist, a. & n. socialista m.
society, n. sociedad; compañía f.
sociology, n. sociología f.
sock, 1. n. calcetín; puñetazo m. **2.** v. dar un puñetazo a.
socket, n. cuenca f.; (elec.) enchufe m.
sod, n. césped m.
soda, n. soda; (chem.) sosa f.
sodium, n. sodio m.
sofa, n. sofá m.
soft, a. blando; fino; suave.
soft drink, n. bebida no alcohólica m.
soften, v. ablandar; suavizar.
soil, 1. n. suelo m. **2.** v. ensuciar.
sojourn, n. morada f., estancia f.
solace, 1. n. solaz m **2.** v. solazar.
solar, a. solar.
solar system, n. sistema solar m.

solder, 1. v. soldar. **2.** n. soldadura f.
soldier, n. soldado m.
sole, 1. n. suela m.; (of foot) planta f.; (fish) lenguado m. **2.** a. único.
solemn, a. solemne.
solemnity, n. solemnidad f.
solicit, v. solicitar.
solicitous, a. solícito.
solid, a. & n. sólido m.
solidify, v. solidificar.
solidity, n. solidez f.
solitary, a. solitario.
solitude, n. soledad f.
solo, n. solo m.
soloist, n. solista m.
soluble, a. soluble.
solution, n. solución f.
solve, v. solucionar; resolver.
solvent, a. solvente.
somber, a. sombrío.
some, a. & pron. algo (de), un poco (de); alguno; (pl.) algunos, unos.
somebody, someone, pron. alguien.
somehow, adv. de algún modo.
someone, n. alguien o alguno.
somersault, n. salto mortal m.
something, pron. algo, alguna cosa.
sometime, adv. alguna vez.
sometimes, adv. a veces, algunas veces.
somewhat, adv. algo, un poco.
somewhere, adv. en (or a) alguna parte.
son, n. hijo m.
song, n. canción f.
son-in-law, n. yerno m.
soon, adv. pronto. **as s. as possible,** cuanto antes. **sooner or later,** tarde o temprano. **no sooner . . . than,** apenas . . . cuando.
soot, n. hollín m.
soothe, v. calmar.
soothingly, adv. tiernamente.
sophisticated, a. sofisticado.
sophomore, n. estudiante de segundo año m.
soprano, n. soprano m. & f.
sorcery, n. encantamiento m.
sordid, a. sórdido.
sore, 1. n. llaga f. **2.** a. lastimado; (coll.) enojado. **to be s.,** doler.

sorority, *n.* hermandad de mujeres *f.*

sorrow, *n.* pesar, dolor *m.*; aflicción *f.*

sorrowful, *a.* doloroso; afligido.

sorry, *a.* to be s., sentir, lamentar. **to be s. for**, compadecer.

sort, **1**. *n.* tipo *m.*; clase, especie *f.* **s. of**, algo, un poco. **2**. *v.* clasificar.

soul, *n.* alma *f.*

sound, **1**. *a.* sano; razonable; firme. **2**. *n.* sonido *m.* **3**. *v.* sonar; parecer.

soup, *n.* sopa *f.*

sour, *a.* agrio; ácido; rancio.

source, *n.* fuente; causa *f.*

south, *n.* sur *m.*

South America, *n.* Sud América, América del Sur.

South American, *a.* & *n.* sudamericano -na.

southeast, *n.* sudeste *m.*

southern, *a.* meridional.

South Pole, *n.* polo sur *m.*

southwest, *n.* sudoeste *m.*

souvenir, *n.* recuerdo *m.*

sovereign, *n.* soberano *m.*

sovereignty, *n.* soberanía *f.*

Soviet Russia, *n.* Rusia Soviética *f.*

sow, **1**. *n.* puerca *f.* **2**. *v.* sembrar.

space, **1**. *n.* espacio *m.* **2**. *v.* espaciar.

space shuttle, *n.* vehículo que comunica a dos naves espaciales.

spacious, *a.* espacioso.

spade, **1**. *n.* laya; (cards) espada *f.* **2**. *v.* layar.

spaghetti, *n.* fideo *m.*

Spain, *n.* España *f.*

span, **1**. *n.* tramo *m.* **2**. *v.* extenderse sobre.

Spaniard, *n.* español -la.

Spanish, *a.* & *n.* español *m.*

spank, *v.* pegar.

spanking, *n.* tunda, zumba *f.*

spar, *v.* altercar.

spare, **1**. *a.* de respuesto. **2**. *v.* perdonar; ahorrar; prestar. **have . . . to s.**, tener . . . de sobra.

spark, *n.* chispa *f.*

sparkle, **1**. *n.* destello *m.* **2**. *v.* chispear. **sparkling wine**, vino espumoso.

spark plug, *n.* bujía *f.*

sparrow, *n.* gorrión *m.*

sparse, *a.* esparcido.

spasm, *n.* espasmo *m.*

spasmodic, *a.* espasmódico.

spatter, *v.* salpicar; manchar.

speak, *v.* hablar.

speaker, *n.* conferencista *m.* & *f.*

spear, *n.* lanza *f.*

special, *a.* especial. **s. delivery**, entrega inmediata, entrega urgente.

specialist, *n.* especialista *m.* & *f.*

specialty, *n.* especialidad *f.*

species, *n.* especie *f.*

specific, *a.* específico.

specify, *v.* especificar.

specimen, *n.* espécimen *m.*; muestra *f.*

spectacle, *n.* espectáculo *m.*; (pl.) lentes, anteojos *m.pl.*

spectacular, *a.* espectacular, aparatoso.

spectator, *n.* espectador -ra.

spectrum, *n.* espectro *m.*

speculate, *v.* especular.

speculation, *n.* especulación *f.*

speech, *n.* habla *f.*; lenguaje; discurso *m.* **part of s.**, parte de la oración.

speechless, *a.* mudo.

speed, **1**. *n.* velocidad; rapidez *f.* **2**. *v.* **s. up**, acelerar, apresurar.

speedometer, *n.* velocímetro *m.*

speedy, *a.* veloz, rápido.

spell, **1**. *n.* hechizo; rato; (med.) ataque *m.* **2**. *v.* deletrear; relevar.

spelling, *n.* ortografía *f.*

spend, *v.* gastar; (time) pasar.

spendthrift, *n.* pródigo; manirroto *m.*

sphere, *n.* esfera *f.*

spice, **1**. *n.* especia *f.* **2**. *v.* especiar.

spider, *n.* araña *f.*

spike, *n.* alcayata *f.*

spill, *v.* derramar.

spillway, *n.* vertedero *m.*

spin, *v.* hilar; girar.

spinach, *n.* espinaca *f.*

spine, *n.* espinazo *m.*

spinet, *n.* espineta *m.*

spinster, *n.* solterona *f.*

spiral, *a.* & *n.* espiral *m.*

spire, *n.* caracol *m.*, espira *f.*

spirit, *n.* espíritu; ánimo *m.*

spiritual, *a.* espiritual.

spiritualism, *n.* espiritismo *m.*

spit, v. escupir.

spite, n. despecho m. **in s. of**, a pesar de.

splash, 1. n. salpicadura f. **2.** v. salpicar.

splendid, a. espléndido.

splendor, n. esplendor m.

splice, 1. v. empalmar. **2.** n. empalme m.

splint, n. tablilla f.

splinter, 1. n. astilla f. **2.** v. astillar.

split, 1. n. división f. **2.** v. dividir, romper en dos.

splurge, 1. v. fachendear. **2.** n. fachenda f.

spoil, 1. n. (pl.) botín m. **2.** v. echar a perder; (a child) mimar.

spoke, n. rayo (de rueda) m.

spokesman, n. interlocutor m.

sponge, n. esponja f.

sponsor, 1. n. patrocinador m. **2.** v. patrocinar; costear.

spontaneity, n. espontaneidad f.

spontaneous, a. espontáneo.

spool, n. carrete m.

spoon, n. cuchara f.

spoonful, n. cucharada f.

sporadic, a. esporádico.

sport, n. deporte m.

sportsman, 1. a. deportivo. **2.** n. deportista m.

spot, 1. n. mancha f.; lugar, punto m. **2.** v. distinguir.

spouse, n. esposo (o esposa) m. or f.

spout, 1. n. chorro; (of teapot) pico m. **2.** v. correr a chorro.

sprain, 1. n. torcedura f. **2.** v. torcerse.

sprawl, v. tenderse.

spray, 1. n. rociada f. **2.** v. rociar.

spread, 1. n. propagación; extensión; (for bed) colcha f. **2.** v. propagar; extender.

spree, n. parranda f.

sprig, n. ramita f.

sprightly, a. garboso.

spring, 1. n. resorte, muelle m.; (season) primavera f.; (of water) manantial m.

springboard, n. trampolín m.

sprinkle, v. rociar; (rain) lloviznar.

sprint, n. carrera f.

sprout, n. retoño m.

spry, a. ágil.

spun, a. hilado.

spur, 1. n. espuela f. **on the s. of the moment**, sin pensarlo. **2.** v. espolear.

spurious, a. espurio.

spurn, v. rechazar, despreciar.

spurt, 1. n. chorro m.; esfuerzo supremo. **2.** v. salir en chorro.

spy, 1. n. espía m. & f. **2.** v. espiar.

squabble, 1. n. riña f. **2.** v. reñir.

squad, n. escuadra f.

squadron, n. escuadrón m.

squalid, a. escuálido.

squall, n. borrasca f.

squalor, n. escualidez f.

squander, v. malgastar.

square, 1. a. cuadrado. **2.** n. cuadrado m.; plaza f.

square dance, n. contradanza f.

squat, v. agacharse.

squeak, 1. n. chirrido m. **2.** v. chirriar.

squeamish, a. escrupuloso.

squeeze, 1. n. apretón m. **2.** v. apretar; (fruit) exprimir.

squirrel, n. ardilla f.

squirt, 1. n. chisguete m. **2.** v. jeringar.

stab, 1. n. puñalada f. **2.** v. apuñalar.

stability, n. estabilidad f.

stabilize, v. estabilizar.

stable, 1. a. estable, equilibrado. **2.** n. caballeriza f.

stack, 1. n. pila f. **2.** v. apilar.

stadium, n. estadio m.

staff, n. personal m. **editorial s.**, cuerpo de redacción. **general s.**, estado mayor.

stag, n. ciervo m.

stage, 1. n. etapa; (theat.) escena f. **2.** v. representar.

stagflation, n. estagnación e inflación a la vez.

stagger, v. tambalear.

stagnant, a. estancado.

stagnate, v. estancarse.

stain, 1. n. mancha f. **2.** v. manchar.

staircase, stairs, n. escalera f.

stake, n. estaca; (bet) apuesta f. **at s.**, en juego; en peligro.

stale, a. rancio.

stalemate, n. estancación f., tablas.

stalk, n. caña f.; (of flower) tallo m.

stall, 1. *n.* tenderete; (for horse) pesebre *m.* **2.** *v.* demorar; (motor) atascar.

stallion, *n.* garañón *m.*

stalwart, *a.* fornido.

stamina, *n.* vigor *m.*

stammer, *v.* tartamudear.

stamp, 1. *n.* sello *m.,* estampilla *f.* **2.** *v.* sellar.

stampede, *n.* estampida *f.*

stand, 1. *n.* puesto *m.;* posición; (speaker's) tribuna; (furniture) mesita *f.* **2.** *v.* estar; estar de pie; aguantar. **s. up,** pararse, levantarse.

standard, 1. *a.* normal, corriente. **2.** *n.* norma *f.* **s. of living,** nivel de vida.

standardize, *v.* uniformar.

standing, *a.* fijo; establecido.

standpoint, *n.* punto de vista *m.*

staple, *n.* materia prima *f.*

star, *n.* estrella *f.*

starboard, *n.* estribor *m.*

starch, 1. *n.* almidón *m.;* (in diet) fécula *f.* **2.** *v.* almidonar.

stare, *v.* mirar fijamente.

stark, 1. *a.* severo. **2.** *adv.* completamente.

start, 1. *n.* susto; principio *m.* **2.** *v.* comenzar, empezar; salir; poner en marcha; causar.

startle, *v.* asustar.

starvation, *n.* hambre *f.*

starve, *v.* morir de hambre.

state, 1. *n.* estado *m.* **2.** *v.* declarar, decir.

statement, *n.* declaración *f.*

stateroom, *n.* camarote *m.*

statesman, *n.* estadista *m.*

static, 1. *a.* estático. **2.** *n.* estática *f.*

station, *n.* estación *f.*

stationary, *a.* estacionario, fijo.

stationery, *n.* papel de escribir.

statistics, *n.* estadística *f.*

statue, *n.* estatua *f.*

stature, *n.* estatura *f.*

status, *n.* estado legal *m.*

statute, *n.* ley *f.*

staunch, *a.* fiel; constante.

stay, 1. *n.* estancia; vista *f.* **2.** *v.* quedar, permanecer; parar, alojarse. **s. away,** ausentarse. **s. up,** velar.

steadfast, *a.* inmutable.

steady, 1. *a.* firme; permanente; regular. **2.** *v.* sostener.

steak, *n.* biftec, bistec *m.*

steal, 1. *n.* plagio *m.* **2.** *v.* robar. **s. away,** escabullirse.

stealth, *n.* cautela *f.*

steam, *n.* vapor *m.*

steamboat, steamer, steamship, *n.* vapor *m.*

steel, 1. *n.* acero *m.* **2.** *v.* **s. one-self,** fortalecerse.

steep, *a.* escarpado, empinado.

steeple, *n.* campanario *m.*

steer, 1. *n.* buey *m.* **2.** *v.* guiar, manejar.

stellar, *a.* astral.

stem, 1. *n.* tallo *m.* **2.** *v.* parar. **s. from,** emanar de.

stencil, 1. *n.* estarcidor. **2.** *v.* estarcir.

stenographer, *n.* estenógrafo -fa.

stenography, *n.* taquigrafía *f.*

step, 1. *n.* paso *m.;* medida *f.;* (stairs) escalón *m.* **2.** *v.* pisar. **s. back,** retirarse.

stepladder, *n.* escalera de mano *f.*

stereophonic, *a.* estereofónico.

stereotype, 1. *n.* estereotipo *m.* **2.** *v.* estereotipar.

sterile, *a.* estéril.

sterilize, *v.* esterilizar.

sterling, *a.* esterlina, genuino.

stern, 1. *n.* popa *f.* **2.** *a.* duro, severo.

stethoscope, *n.* estetoscopio *m.*

stevedore, *n.* estibador *m.*

stew, 1. *n.* guisado *m.* **2.** *v.* estofar.

steward, *n.* camarero.

stewardess, *n.* azafata *f.,* aeromoza *f.*

stick, 1. *n.* palo, bastón *m.* **2.** *v.* pegar; (put) poner, meter.

sticky, *a.* pegajoso.

stiff, *a.* tieso; duro.

stiffness, *n.* tiesura *f.*

stifle, *v.* sofocar; (fig.) suprimir.

stigma, *n.* estigma *f.*

still, 1. *a.* quieto; silencioso. **to keep s.,** callarse. **2.** *adv.* todavía, aún; no obstante. **3.** *n.* alambique *m.*

stillborn, *n.* & *a.* nacido muerto *m.*

still life, *n.* naturaleza muerta *f.*

stillness, *n.* silencio *m.*

stilted, *a.* altisonante.

stimulant, *a.* & *n.* estimulante *m.*

stimulate, *v.* estimular.

stimulus, *n.* estímulo *m.*

sting, 1. *n.* picadura *f.* **2.** *v.* picar.

stingy, *a.* tacaño.

stipulate, *v.* estipular.

stir, 1. *n.* conmoción *f.* **2.** *v.* mover. **s. up,** conmover; suscitar.

stitch, 1. *n.* puntada *f.* **2.** *v.* coser.

stock, *n.* surtido *m.;* raza *f.;* (finance) acciones. *f.pl.* **in s.,** en existencia. **to take s. in,** tener fe en.

stock exchange, *n.* bolsa *f.*

stockholder, *n.* corredor de bolsa *m.*

stocking, *n.* media *f.*

stockyard, *n.* corral de ganado *m.*

stodgy, *a.* pesado.

stoical, *a.* estoico.

stole, *n.* estola *f.*

stolid, *a.* impasible.

stomach, *n.* estómago *m.*

stone, *n.* piedra *f.*

stool, *n.* banquillo *m.*

stoop, *v.* encorvarse; (fig.) rebajarse.

stop, 1. *n.* parada *f.* **to put a s. to,** poner fin a. **2.** *v.* parar; suspender; detener; impedir. **s. doing** (etc.), dejar de hacer (etc.).

stopgap, *n.* subterfugio *m.*

storage, *n.* almacenaje *m.*

store, 1. *n.* tienda; provisión *f.* **department s.,** almacén *m.* **2.** *v.* guardar; almacenar.

storm, *n.* tempestad, tormenta *f.*

stormy, *a.* tempestuoso.

story, *n.* cuento; relato *m.;* historia *f.* **short s.,** cuento.

stout, *a.* corpulento.

stove, *n.* hornilla; estufa *f.*

straight, 1. *a.* recto; derecho. **2.** *adv.* directamente.

straighten *v.* enderezar. **s. out,** poner en orden.

straightforward, *a.* recto, sincero.

strain, 1. *n.* tensión *f.* **2.** *v.* colar.

strainer, *n.* colador *m.*

strait, *n.* estrecho *m.*

strand, 1. *n.* hilo *m.* **2.** *v.* **be stranded,** encallarse.

strange, *a.* extraño; raro.

stranger, *n.* extranjero -ra. forastero -ra; desconocido -da.

strangle, *v.* estrangular.

strap, *n.* correa *f.*

stratagem, *n.* estratagema *f.*

strategic, *a.* estratégico.

strategy, *n.* estrategia *f.*

stratosphere, *n.* estratosfera *f.*

straw, *n.* paja *f.*

strawberry, *n.* fresa *f.*

stray, 1. *a.* vagabundo. **2.** *v.* extraviarse.

streak, 1. *n.* racha; raya *f.;* lado *m.* **2.** *v.* rayar.

stream, *n.* corriente *f.*

street, *n.* calle *f.*

streetcar, *n.* tranvía *m.*

strength, *n.* fuerza *m.*

strengthen, *v.* reforzar.

strenuous, *a.* estrenuo.

streptococcus, *n.* estreptococo *m.*

stress, 1. *n.* tensión *f.;* énfasis *m.* **2.** *v.* recalcar; acentuar.

stretch, 1. *n.* trecho *m.* **at one s.,** de un tirón. **2.** *v.* tender; extender; estirarse.

stretcher, *n.* camilla *f.*

strew, *v.* esparcir.

stricken, *a.* agobiado.

strict, *a.* estricto; severo.

stride, 1. *n.* tranco *m.;* (fig., pl.) progresos. **2.** *v.* andar a trancos.

strife, *n.* contienda *f.*

strike, 1. *n.* huelga *f.* **2.** *v.* pegar; chocar con; (clock) dar.

string, *n.* cuerda *f.;* cordel *m.*

string bean, *n.* habichuela *f.*

stringent, *a.* estricto.

strip, 1. *n.* tira *f.* **2.** despojar; desnudarse.

stripe, *n.* raya *f.;* (mil.) galón *m.*

strive, *v.* esforzarse.

stroke, *n.* golpe *m.;* (swimming) brazada *f.;* (med.) ataque *m.* **s. of luck,** suerte *f.*

stroll, 1. *n.* paseo *m.* **2.** *v.* pasearse.

stroller, *n.* vagabundo *m.*

strong, *a.* fuerte.

stronghold, *n.* fortificación *f.*

structure, *n.* estructura *f.*

struggle, 1. *n.* lucha *f.* **2.** *v.* luchar.

strut, 1. *n.* pavonada *f.* **2.** *v.* pavonear.

stub, 1. *n.* cabo; (ticket) talón *m.* **2.** *v.* **s. one's toe on,** tropezar con.

stubborn, *a.* testarudo.

stucco, 1. *n.* estuco. **2.** *v.* estucar.

student, *n.* alumno -na, estudiante -ta.

studio, *n.* estudio *m.*

studious, *a.* aplicado; estudioso.

study, 1. *n.* estudio *m.* **2.** *v.* estudiar.

stuff, 1. *n.* cosas *f.pl.* **2.** *v.* llenar; rellenar.

stuffing, *n.* relleno *m.*

stumble, *v.* tropezar.

stump, *n.* tronco *m.*

stun, *v.* aturdir.

stunt, 1. *n.* suerte *f.* **2.** *v.* impedir crecimiento.

stupendous, *a.* estupendo.

stupid, *a.* estúpido.

stupidity, *n.* estupidez *f.*

stupor, *n.* estupor *m.*

sturdy, *a.* robusto.

stutter, 1. *v.* tartamudear. **2.** *n.* tartamudeo *m.*

sty, *n.* pocilga *f.*

style, *n.* estilo *m.;* moda *f.*

stylish, *a.* elegante; a la moda.

suave, *a.* afable, suave.

subconscious, *a.* subconsciente.

subdue, *v.* dominar.

subject, 1. *n.* sujeto *m.* **2.** *n.* tema *m.;* (of study) materia *f.;* (pol.) súbdito -ta; (gram.) sujeto *m.* **3.** *v.* someter.

subjugate, *v.* sojuzgar, subjugar.

subjunctive, *a.* & *n.* subjuntivo *m.*

sublimate, *v.* sublimar.

sublime, *a.* sublime.

submarine, *a.* & *n.* submarino *m.*

submerge, *v.* sumergir.

submission, *n.* sumisión *f.*

submit, *v.* someter.

subnormal, *a.* subnormal.

subordinate, 1. *a.* & *n.* subordinado *m.* **2.** *v.* subordinar.

subscribe, *v.* aprobar; abonarse.

subscription, *n.* abono *m.*

subsequent, *a.* subsiguiente.

subservient, *a.* servicial.

subside, *v.* apaciguarse.

subsidy, *n.* subvención *f.*

substance, *n.* substancia *f.*

substantial, *a.* substancial; considerable.

substitute, 1. *a.* substitutivo. **2.** *n.* substituto *m.* **3.** *v.* substituir.

substitution, *n.* substitución *f.*

subterfuge, *n.* subterfugio *m.*

subtle, *a.* sutil.

subtract, *v.* substraer.

suburb, *n.* suburbio *m.;* (pl.) afueras *f.pl.*

subversive, *a.* subversivo.

subway, *n.* metro *m.*

succeed, *v.* lograr, tener éxito; (in office) suceder a.

success, *n.* éxito *m.*

successful, *a.* próspero; afortunado.

succession, *n.* sucesión *f.*

successive, *a.* sucesivo.

successor, *n.* sucesor -ra; heredero -ra.

succor, 1. *n.* socorro *m.* **2.** *v.* socorrer.

succumb, *v.* sucumbir.

such, *a.* tal.

suck, *v.* chupar.

suction, *n.* succión *f.*

sudden, *a.* repentino, súbito. **all of a s.,** de repente.

suds, *n.* jabonaduras *f.pl.*

sue, *v.* demandar.

suffer, *v.* sufrir; padecer.

suffice, *v.* bastar.

sufficient, *a.* suficiente.

suffocate, *v.* sofocar.

sugar, *n.* azúcar *m.*

suggest, *v.* sugerir.

suggestion, *n.* sugerencia *f.*

suicide, *n.* suicidio *m.;* (person) suicida *m.* & *f.* **to commit s.,** suicidarse.

suit, 1. *n.* traje; (cards) palo; (law) pleito *m.* **2.** *v.* convenir a.

suitable, *a.* apropiado; que conviene.

suitcase, *n.* maleta *f.*

suite, *n.* serie *f.,* séquito *m.*

suitor, *n.* pretendiente *m.*

sullen, *a.* hosco.

sum, 1. *n.* suma *f.* **2.** *v.* **s. up,** resumir.

summarize, *v.* resumir.

summary, *n.* resumen *m.*

summer, *n.* verano *m.*

summon, *v.* llamar; (law) citar.

summons, *n.* citación *f.*

sumptuous, *a.* suntuoso.

sun, 1. *n.* sol *m.* **2.** *v.* tomar el sol.

sunburn, *n.* quemadura de sol.

sunburned, *a.* quemado por el sol.

Sunday, *n.* domingo *m.*

sunken, *a.* hundido.

sunny, *a.* asoleado. **s. day,** día de

sol. **to be s.,** (weather) hacer sol.

sunshine, n. luz del sol.

suntan, n. bronceado m. **s. lotion,** loción bronceadora.

superb, a. soberbio.

superficial, a. superficial.

superfluous, a. superfluo.

superhuman, a. sobrehumano.

superintendent, n. superintendente m.; (of building) conserje m.; (of school) director general.

superior, a. & n. superior m.

superiority, n. superioridad f.

superlative, a. superlativo.

supernatural, a. sobrenatural.

supersede, v. reemplazar.

superstar, n. superstar m.

superstition, n. superstición f.

superstitious, a. supersticioso.

supervise, v. supervisar.

supper, n. cena f.

supplement, 1. n. suplemento m. **2.** v. suplementar.

supply, 1. n. provisión f.; (com.) surtido m.; (econ.) existencia f. **2.** v. suplir; proporcionar.

support, 1. n. sustento; apoyo m. **2.** v. mantener; apoyar.

suppose, v. suponer. **be supposed to,** deber.

suppress, v. suprimir.

suppression, n. supresión f.

supreme, a. supremo.

sure, a. seguro, cierto. **for s.,** con seguridad. **to make s.,** asegurarse.

surety, n. garantía f.

surf, n. marejada f.

surface, n. superficie f.

surge, n. surgir.

surgeon, n. cirujano m.

surgery, n. cirujía f.

surmise, v. suponer.

surmount, v. vencer.

surname, n. apellido m.

surpass, v. superar.

surplus, a. & n. sobrante m.

surprise, 1. n. sorpresa f. **2.** v. sorprender. **I am surprised . . . ,** me extraña . . .

surrender, 1. n. rendición f. **2.** v. rendir.

surround, v. rodear, circundar.

surveillance, n. vigilancia f.

survey, 1. n. examen estudio m. **2.** v. examinar; (land) medir.

survival, n. supervivencia f.

survive, v. sobrevivir.

susceptible, a. susceptible.

suspect, v. sospechar.

suspend, v. suspender.

suspense, n. incertidumbre f. **in s.,** en suspenso.

suspension, n. suspensión f.

suspension bridge, n. puente colgante m.

suspicion, n. sospecha f.

suspicious, a. sospechoso.

sustain, v. sustentar; mantener.

swallow, 1. n. trago m.; (bird) golondrina f. **2.** v. tragar.

swamp, 1. n. pantano m. **2.** v. (fig.) abrumar.

swan, n. cisne m.

swap, 1. n. trueque m. **2.** v. cambalachear.

swarm, n. enjambre m.

sway, 1. n. predominio m. **2.** v. bambolearse; (fig.) influir en.

swear, v. jurar. **s. off,** renunciar a.

sweat, n. sudor m. **2.** v. sudar.

sweater, n. suéter m.

Swede, n. sueco -ca.

Sweden, n. Suecia f.

Swedish, a. sueco.

sweep, v. barrer.

sweet, 1. a. dulce; amable, simpático. **2.** n. (pl.) dulces m.pl.

sweetheart, n. amante m.

sweetness, n. dulzura f.

swell, 1. a. (coll.) estupendo, excelente. **2.** n. (mar.) oleada f. **3.** v. hincharse; aumentar.

swelter, v. sofocar.

swift, a. rápido, veloz.

swim, 1. n. nadada f. **2.** v. nadar.

swindle, 1. n. estafa f. **2.** v. estafar.

swine, n. puercos m.pl.

swing, 1. n. columpio m. **in full s.,** en plana actividad. **2.** v. mecer; balancear.

swirl, 1. n. remolino m. **2.** v. arremolinar.

Swiss, a. & n. suizo -za.

switch, 1. n. varilla f.; (elec.) llave f., conmutador m.; (railway) cambiavía m. **2.** v. cambiar; trocar.

switchboard, n. cuadro conmutador m.

Switzerland, n. Suiza f.

sword, n. espada f.

syllable, n. sílaba f.

symbol, n. símbolo m.

sympathetic, a. compasivo. to be s., tener simpatía.

sympathy, n. lástima; condolencia f.

symphony, n. sinfonía f.

symptom, n. síntoma m.

synchronize, v. sincronizar.

syndicate, n. sindicato m.

syndrome, n. síndroma m.

synonym, n. sinónimo m.

synthetic, a. sintético.

syringe, n. jeringa f.

syrup, n. almíbar; (med.) jarabe m.

system, n. sistema m.

systematic, a. sistemático.

T

tabernacle, n. tabernáculo m.

table, n. mesa; (list) tabla f.

tablespoon, n. cuchara f.

tablespoonful, n. cucharada f.

tablet, n. tableta; (med.) pastilla f.

tack, n. tachuela f.

tact, n. tacto m.

tag, n. etiqueta f., rótulo m.

tail, n. cola f., rabo m.

tailor, n. sastre m.

take, v. tomar; llevar. t. away, quitar. t. off, quitarse. t. out, sacar. t. long, tardar mucho.

tale, n. cuento m.

talent, n. talento m.

talk, 1. n. plática, habla f.; discurso m. 2. v. hablar.

talkative, a. locuaz.

tall, a. alto.

tame, 1. a. manso, domesticado. 2. v. domesticar.

tamper, v. t. with, entremeterse en.

tampon, n. tampón m.

tan, 1. a. color de arena. 2. v. curtir; tostar.

tangible, a. tangible.

tangle, 1. n. enredo m. 2. v. enredar.

tank, n. tanque m.

tap, 1. n. golpe ligero. 2. v. golpear ligeramente; decantar.

tape, n. cinta f.

tape recorder, n. magnetófono m.

tapestry, n. tapiz m.; tapicería f.

tar, 1. n. brea f. 2. v. embrear.

target, n. blanco m.

tarnish, 1. n. deslustre m. 2. v. deslustrar.

task, n. tarea f.

taste, 1. n. gusto; sabor m. 2. v. gustar; progar. t. of, saber a.

tasty, a. sabroso.

taut, a. tieso.

tavern, n. taberna f.

tax, 1. n. impuesto m. 2. v. imponer impuestos.

taxi, n. taxi, taximetro m. t. driver, taxista m. or f.

tea, n. té m.

teach, v. enseñar.

teacher, n. maestro -tra, profesor -ra.

team, n. equipo m.; pareja f.

tear, 1. n. rasgón m.; lágrima f. 2. v. rasgar, lacerar; separar.

tease, v. atormentar; embromar.

teaspoon, n. cucharita f.

technical, a. técnico.

technique, n. técnica f.

tedious, a. tedioso.

telegram, n. telegrama m.

telegraph, 1. n. telégrafo m. 2. v. telegrafiar.

telephone, 1. n. teléfono m. t. book, directorio telefónico. 2. v. telefonear; llamar por teléfono.

telescope, 1. n. telescopio m. 2. v. enchufar.

television, n. televisión f.

tell, v. decir; contar; distinguir.

temper, 1. n. temperamento, genio m. 2. v. templar.

temperament, n. temperamento.

temperamental, a. sensible, emocional.

temperance, n. moderación; sobriedad f.

temperate, a. templado.

temperature, n. temperatura f.

tempest, n. tempestad f.

tempestuous, a. tempestuoso.

temple, n. templo m.

temporary, a. temporal, temporario.

tempt, v. tentar.

temptation, n. tentación f.

ten, a. & pron. diez.

tenant, n. inquilino -na.

tend, v. tender. t. to, atender.

tendency, n. tendencia f.

tender, 1. a. tierno. 2. v. ofrecer.

tenderness, n. ternura f.

tennis, n. tenis m.

tenor, *n.* tenor *m.*

tense, 1. *a.* tenso. **2.** *n.* tiempo *m.*

tent, *n.* tienda, carpa *f.*

tenth, *a.* décimo.

term, 1. *n.* término; plazo *m.* **2.** *v.* llamar.

terminal, *n.* terminal *f.*

terrace, *n.* terraza *f.*

terrible, *a.* terrible, espantoso.

territory, *n.* territorio *m.*

terror, *n.* terror, espanto *m.*

test, 1. *n.* prueba *f.*; examen *m.* **2.** *v.* probar, examinar.

testament, *n.* testamento *m.*

testify, *v.* atestiguar, testificar.

testimony, *n.* testimonio *m.*

text, *n.* texto; tema *m.*

textile, 1. *a.* textil. **2.** *n.* tejido *m.*

texture, *n.* textura *f.*; tejido *m.*

than, *conj.* que; de.

thank, *v.* agradecer, dar gracias; **thanks, th. you,** gracias.

thankful, *a.* agradecido; grato.

that, 1. *a.* ese, aquel. **2.** *dem. pron.* ése, aquél; eso, aquello. **3.** *rel. pron. & conj.* que.

the, *art.* el, la, los, las; lo.

theater, *n.* teatro *m.*

theft, *n.* robo *m.*

their, *a.* su.

theirs, *pron.* suyo, de ellos.

them, *pron.* ellos, ellas; los, las; les.

theme, *n.* tema; (mus.) motivo *m.*

themselves, *pron.* sí, sí mismos -as. **they th.,** ellos mismos, ellas mismas. **with th.,** consigo.

then, *adv.* entonces, después; pues.

thence, *adv.* de allí.

theology, *n.* teología *f.*

theory, *n.* teoría *f.*

there, *adv.* allí, allá, ahí. **there is, there are,** hay.

therefore, *adv.* por lo tanto, por consiguiente.

thermometer, *n.* termómetro *m.*

they, *pron.* ellos, ellas.

thick, *a.* espeso, grueso, denso; torpe.

thicken, *v.* espesar, condensar.

thief, *n.* ladrón -na.

thigh, *n.* muslo *m.*

thimble, *n.* dedal *m.*

thin, **1.** *a.* delgado; raro; claro; escaso. **2.** *v.* enrarecer; adelgazar.

thing, *n.* cosa *f.*

think, *v.* pensar; creer.

thinker, *n.* pensador -ra.

third, *a.* tercero.

Third World, *n.* Tercer Mundo *m.*

thirst, *n.* sed *f.*

thirsty, *a.* sediento. **to be th.,** tener sed.

thirteen, *a. & pron.* trece.

thirty, *a. & pron.* treinta.

this, 1. *a.* este. **2.** *pron.* éste; esto.

thorough, *a.* completo; cuidadoso.

though, 1. *adv.* sin embargo. **2.** *conj.* aunque. **as th.,** como si.

thought, *n.* pensamiento *m.*

thoughtful, *a.* pensativo; considerado.

thousand, *a. & pron.* mil.

thread, *n.* hilo *m.*; (of screw) rosca *f.*

threat, *n.* amenaza *f.*

threaten, *v.* amenazar.

three, *a. & pron.* tres.

thrift, *n.* economía, frugalidad *f.*

thrill, 1. *n.* emoción *f.* **2.** *v.* emocionar.

thrive, *v.* prosperar.

throat, *n.* garganta *f.*

throne, *n.* trono *m.*

through, 1. *prep.* por; a través de; por medio de. **2.** *a.* continuo. **th. train,** tren directo. **to be th.,** haber terminado.

throughout, 1. *prep.* por todo, durante todo. **2.** *adv.* en todas partes; completamente.

throw, 1. *n.* tiro *m.* **2.** *v.* tirar, lanzar. **th. away,** arrojar. **th. out,** echar.

thrust, 1. *n.* lanzada *f.* **2.** *v.* empujar.

thumb, *n.* pulgar *m.*

thunder, 1. *n.* trueno *m.* **2.** *v.* tronar.

Thursday, *n.* jueves *m.*

thus, *adv.* así, de este modo.

thwart, *v.* frustrar.

ticket, 1. *n.* billete, boleto *m.* **t. window,** taquilla *f.* **round trip t.,** billete de ida y vuelta.

tickle, 1. *n.* cosquilla *f.* **2.** *v.* hacer cosquillas a.

ticklish, *a.* cosquilloso.

tide, *n.* marea *f.*

tidy, 1. *a.* limpio, ordenado. **2.** *v.* poner en orden.

tie, 1. *n.* corbata *f.;* lazo; (game) empate *m.* **2.** *v.* atar; anudar.

tier, *n.* hilera *f.*

tiger, *n.* tigre *m.*

tight, *a.* apretado; tacaño.

tighten, *v.* estrechar, apretar.

tile, *n.* teja *f.,* azulejo *m.*

till, 1. *prep.* hasta. **2.** *conj.* hasta que. **3.** *n.* cajón *m.* **4.** *v.* cultivar, labrar.

tilt, 1. *n.* inclinación; justa *f.* **2.** *v.* inclinar; justar.

timber, *n.* madera *f.;* (beam) madero *m.*

time, *n.* tiempo *m.;* vez *f.;* (of day) hora *f.*

timetable, *n.* horario, itinerario *m.*

timid, *a.* tímido.

timidity, *n.* timidez *f.*

tin, *n.* estaño *m.;* hojalata *f.* **t. can,** lata *f.*

tint, 1. *n.* tinte *m.* **2.** *v.* teñir.

tiny, *a.* chiquito, pequeñito.

tip, 1. *n.* punta; propina *f.* **2.** *v.* inclinar; dar propina a.

tire, 1. *n.* llanta, goma *f.,* neumático *m.* **2.** *v.* cansar.

tired, *a.* cansado.

tissue, *n.* tejido *m.* **t. paper,** papel de seda.

title, 1. *n.* título *m.* **2.** *v.* titular.

to, *prep.* a; para.

toast, 1. *n.* tostada *f.;* (drink) brindis *m.* **2.** *v.* tostar; brindar.

tobacco, *n.* tabaco *m.* **t. shop,** tabaquería *f.*

today, *adv.* hoy.

toe, *n.* dedo del pie.

together, 1. *a.* juntos. **2.** *adv.* juntamente.

toil, 1. *n.* trabajo *m.* **2.** *v.* afanarse.

toilet, *n.* tocado; excusado, retrete *m.* **t. paper,** papel higiénico.

token, *n.* señal *f.*

tolerance, *n.* tolerancia *f.*

tolerate, *v.* tolerar.

tomato, *n.* tomate *m.*

tomb, *n.* tumba *f.*

tomorrow, *adv.* mañana. **day after t.,** pasado mañana.

ton, *n.* tonelada *f.*

tone, *n.* tono *m.*

tongue, *n.* lengua *f.*

tonic, *n.* tónico *m.*

tonight, *adv.* esta noche.

tonsil, *n.* amígdala *f.*

too, *adv.* también; demasiado. **t. much,** demasiado. **t. many,** demasiados.

tool, *n.* herramienta *f.*

tooth, *n.* diente *m.;* (back) muela *f.*

toothache, *n.* dolor de muela.

toothbrush, *n.* cepillo de dientes.

toothpaste, *n.* pasta dentífrica.

top, 1. *n.* parte de arriba. **2.** *v.* cubrir; sobrepasar.

topic, *n.* tópico *m.*

topical, *a.* tópico.

torch, *n.* antorcha *f.*

torment, 1. *n.* tormento *m.* **2.** *v.* atormentar.

torrent, *n.* torrente *m.*

torture, 1. *n.* tortura *f.* **2.** *v.* torturar.

toss, *v.* tirar; agitar.

total, 1. *a.* total, entero. **2.** *n.* total *m.*

totalitarian, *a.* totalitario.

touch, 1. *n.* tacto *m.* **in t.,** en comunicación. **2.** *v.* tocar; conmover.

tough, *a.* tosco; tieso; fuerte.

tour, 1. *n.* viaje *m.* **2.** *v.* viajar.

tourist, 1. *n.* turista *m.* & *f.* **2.** *a.* turístico.

tournament, *n.* torneo *m.*

tow, 1. *n.* remolque *m.* **2.** *v.* remolcar.

toward, *prep.* hacia.

towel, *n.* toalla *f.*

tower, *n.* torre *f.*

town, *n.* pueblo *m.*

toy, 1. *n.* juguete *m.* **2.** *v.* jugar.

trace, 1. *n.* vestigio; rastro *m.* **2.** *v.* trazar; rastrear; investigar.

track, 1. *n.* huella, pista *f.* **race t.,** hipódromo *m.* **2.** *v.* rastrear.

tract, *n.* trecho, tracto *m.*

tractor, *n.* tractor *m.*

trade, 1. *n.* comercio, negocio; oficio; canje *m.* **2.** *v.* comerciar, negociar; cambiar.

trader, *n.* comerciante *m.*

tradition, *n.* tradición *f.*

traditional, *a.* tradicional.

traffic, 1. *n.* tráfico *m.* **2.** *v.* traficar.

tragedy, *n.* tragedia *f.*

tragic, *a.* trágico.

trail, 1. *n.* sendero; rastro *m.* **2.** *v.* rastrear; arrastrar.

train, 1. *n.* tren *m.* **2.** *v.* enseñar; disciplinar; (sport) entrenarse.

traitor, *n.* traidor *m.*

tramp, 1. *n.* caminata *f.;* vagabundo *m.* **2.** *v.* patear.

tranquil, *a.* tranquilo.

tranquilizer, *n.* tranquilizante *m.*

tranquillity, *n.* tranquilidad *f.*

transaction, *n.* transacción *f.*

transfer, 1. traslado *m.;* boleto de transbordo. **2.** *v.* trasladar, transferir.

transform, *v.* transformar.

transfusion, *n.* transfusión *f.*

transition, *n.* transición *f.*

translate, *v.* traducir.

translation, *n.* traducción *f.*

transmit, *v.* transmitir.

transparent, *a.* transparente.

transport, 1. *n.* transporte *m.* **2.** *v.* transportar.

transportation, *n.* transporte *m.*

transsexual, *a.* transexual.

transvestite, *n.* travestí *m.*

trap, 1. *n.* trampa *f.* **2.** *v.* atrapar.

trash, *n.* desecho *m.;* basura *f.*

travel, 1. *n.* tráfico *m.;* (pl.) viajes *m.pl.* **2.** *v.* viajar.

traveler, *n.* viajero -ra.

traveler's check, *n.* cheque de viaje *m.*

tray, *n.* bandeja *f.*

tread, 1. *n.* pisada *f.;* (of a tire) cubierta *f.* **2.** *v.* pisar.

treason, *n.* traición *f.*

treasure, *n.* tesoro *m.*

treasurer, *n.* tesorero -ra.

treasury, *n.* tesorería *f.*

treat, *v.* tratar; convidar.

treatment, *n.* trato, tratamiento *m.*

treaty, *n.* tratado, pacto *m.*

tree, *n.* árbol *m.*

tremble, *v.* temblar.

tremendous, *a.* tremendo.

trench, *n.* foso *m.;* (mil.) trinchera *f.*

trend, 1. *n.* tendencia *f.* **2.** *v.* tender.

trespass, *v.* traspasar; violar.

triage, *n.* clasificación de los heridos después del combate.

trial, *n.* prueba *f.;* (leg.) proceso, juicio *m.*

triangle, *n.* triángulo *m.*

tribulation, *n.* tribulación *f.*

tributary, *a. & n.* tributario *m.*

tribute, *n.* tributo *m.*

trick, 1. *n.* engaño *m.;* maña *f.;* (cards) baza *f.* **2.** *v.* engañar.

trifle, 1. *n.* pequeñez *f.* **2.** *v.* juguetear.

trigger, *n.* gatillo *m.*

trim, 1. *a.* ajustado, acicalado. **2.** *n.* adorno *m.* **3.** *v.* adornar; ajustar; cortar un poco.

trinket, *n.* bagatela, chuchería *f.*

trip, 1. *n.* viaje *m.* **2.** *v.* tropezar.

triple, 1. *a.* triple **2.** *v.* triplicar.

trite, *a.* banal.

triumph, 1. *n.* triunfo *m.* **2.** *v.* triunfar.

triumphant, *a.* triunfante.

trivial, *a.* trivial.

trolley, *n.* tranvía *m.*

troop, *n.* tropa *f.*

trophy, *n.* trofeo *m.*

tropical, *a.* trópico.

tropics, *n.* trópico *m.*

trot, 1. *n.* trote *m.* **2.** *v.* trotar.

trouble, 1. *n.* apuro *m.;* congoja; aflicción *f.* **2.** *v.* molestar; afligir.

troublesome, *a.* penoso, molesto.

trough, *n.* artesa *f.*

trousers, *n.* pantalones, calzones *m.pl.*

trout, *n.* trucha *f.*

truce, *n.* tregua *f.*

truck, *n.* camión *m.*

true, *a.* verdadero; cierto, verdad.

trumpet, *n.* trompeta, trompa *f.*

trunk, *n.* baúl *m.;* (of a tree) tronco *m.*

trust, 1. *n.* confianza *f.* **2.** *v.* confiar.

trustworthy, *a.* digno de confianza.

truth, *n.* verdad *f.*

truthful, *a.* veraz.

try, 1. *n.* prueba *f.;* ensayo *m.* **2.** *v.* tratar; probar; ensayar; (leg.) juzgar. **t. on,** probarse.

T-shirt, *n.* camiseta *f.*

tub, *n.* tina *f.*

tube, *n.* tubo *m.*

tuberculosis, *n.* tuberculosis, tisis *f.*

tuck, 1. *n.* recogido *m.* **2.** *v.* recoger.

Tuesday, *n.* martes *m.*

tug, 1. *n.* tirada *f.;* (boat) remolcador *m.* **2.** *v.* tirar.

tuition, *n.* matrícula, colegiatura *f.*

tumble, 1. caída *f.* **2.** *v.* caer, tumbar; voltear.

tumult, *n.* tumulto, alboroto *m.*

tune, 1. *n.* tono *m.;* melodía, canción *f.* **2.** *v.* templar.

tunnel, *n.* túnel *m.*

turf, *n.* césped *m.*

Turkey, *n.* Turquía *f.*

Turkish, *a.* turco.

turmoil, *n.* disturbio *m.*

turn, 1. *n.* vuelta *f.;* giro; turno *m.* **2.** *v.* volver, tornear, girar; transformar. **t. around,** volverse. **t. on,** encender; abrir. **t. off, t. out,** apagar.

turnip, *n.* nabo *m.*

turret, *n.* torrecilla *f.*

turtle, *n.* tortuga *f.*

tutor, 1. *n.* tutor *m.* **2.** *v.* enseñar.

twelve, *a.* & *pron.* doce.

twenty, *a.* & *pron.* veinte.

twice, *adv.* dos veces.

twig, *n.* varita, ramita *f.;* vástago *m.*

twilight, *n.* crepúsculo *m.*

twin, *n.* gemelo -la.

twine, 1. *n.* guita *f.* **2.** *v.* torcer.

twinkle, *v.* centellear.

twist, *v.* torcer.

two, *a.* & *pron.* dos.

type, 1. *n.* tipo *m.* **2.** *v.* escribir a máquina.

typewriter, *n.* máquina de escribir.

typhoid fever, fiebre tifoidea.

typical, *a.* típico.

typist, *n.* mecanógrafo -fa.

tyranny, *n.* tiranía *f.*

tyrant, *n.* tirano *m.*

U

udder, *n.* ubre *f.*

ugly, *a.* feo.

ulcer, *n.* úlcera *f.*

ulterior, *a.* ulterior.

ultimate, *a.* último.

umbrella, *n.* paraguas *m.* **sun u.,** quitasol *m.*

umpire, *n.* árbitro *m.*

unable, *a.* incapaz. **to be u.,** no poder.

unanimous, *a.* unánime.

uncertain, *a.* incierto, inseguro.

uncle, *n.* tío *m.*

unconscious, *a.* inconsciente; desmayado.

uncover, *v.* descubrir.

under, 1. *adv.* debajo, abajo. **2.** *prep.* bajo, debajo de.

underestimate, *v.* menospreciar, subestimar.

undergo, *v.* sufrir.

underground, *a.* subterráneo.

underline, *v.* subrayar.

underneath, 1. *adv.* por debajo. **2.** *prep.* debajo de.

undershirt, *n.* camiseta *f.*

understand, *v.* entender, comprender.

undertake, *v.* emprender.

underwear, *n.* ropa interior.

undo, *v.* deshacer; desatar.

undress, *v.* desnudar, desvestir.

uneasy, *a.* inquieto.

uneven, *a.* desigual.

unexpected, *a.* inesperado.

unfair, *a.* injusto.

unfit, *a.* incapaz; inadecuado.

unfold, *v.* desplegar; revelar.

unforgettable, *a.* inolvidable.

unfortunate, *a.* desafortunado, desgraciado.

unhappy, *a.* infeliz.

uniform, *a.* & *n.* uniforme *m.*

unify, *v.* unificar.

union, *n.* unión *f.* **labor u.,** sindicato de obreros.

unique, *a.* único.

unisex, *a.* unisex.

unit, *n.* unidad *f.*

unite, *v.* unir.

unity, *n.* unidad *f.*

universal, *a.* universal.

universe, *n.* universo *m.*

university, *n.* universidad *f.*

unleaded, *a.* sin plomo.

unless, *conj.* a menos que, si no es que.

unlike, *a.* disímil.

unload, *v.* descargar.

unlock, *v.* abrir.

untie, *v.* desatar, soltar.

until, 1. *prep.* hasta. **2.** *conj.* hasta que.

unusual, *a.* raro, inusitado.

up, 1. *adv.* arriba. **2.** *prep.* **u. the street,** *etc.* calle arriba, etc.

uphold, *v.* apoyar, defender.

upholster, v. entapizar.

upon, prep. sobre, encima de.

upper, a. superior.

upright, a. derecho, recto.

uproar, n. alboroto, tumulto m.

upset, 1. n. trastorno m. **2.** v. trastornar.

uptight, a. (psicológicamente) tenso, tieso.

upward, adv. hacia arriba.

urge, 1. n. deseo m. **2.** v. instar.

urgency, n. urgencia f.

urgent, a. urgente. **to be u.,** urgir.

us, pron. nosotros -as; nos.

use, 1. n. uso m. **2.** v. usar, emplear. **u. up,** gastar, agotar. **be used to,** ser acostumbrado a.

useful, a. útil.

useless, a. inútil.

usher, 1. n. acomodador m. **2.** v. introducir.

usual, a. usual.

utensil, n. utensilio m.

utmost, a. sumo, extremo.

utter, 1. a. completo. **2.** v. proferir; dar.

utterance, n. expresión f.

V

vacancy, n. vacante f.

vacant, a. desocupado, libre.

vacation, n. vacaciones f.pl.

vaccinate, v. vacunar.

vacuum, n. vacuo, vacío m. **v. cleaner,** aspirador m.

vagrant, n. vagabundo.

vague, a. vago.

vain, a. vano; vanidoso. **in v.,** en vano.

valiant, a. valiente.

valid, a. válido.

valley, n. valle m.

valor, n. valor m., valentía f.

valuable, a. precioso. **to be v.,** valer mucho.

value, 1. n. valor, importe m. **2.** v. valorar; estimar.

vandal, n. vándalo m.

vanish, v. desaparecer.

vanity, n. vanidad f. **v. case,** polvera f.

vanquish, v. vencer.

vapor, n. vapor m.

variation, n. variación f.

variety, n. variedad f.

various, a. varios, diversos.

varnish, 1. n. barniz m. **2.** v. barnizar.

vary, v. variar; cambiar.

vase, n. vaso, jarrón m.

vasectomy, n. vasectomía f.

vassal, n. vasallo m.

vast, a. vasto.

vat, n. tina f., tanque m.

vault, n. bóveda f.

vegetable, 1. a. & n. vegetal m.; (pl.) legumbres, verderas f.pl.

vehement, a. vehemente.

vehicle, n. vehículo m.

veil, 1. n. velo m. **2.** v. velar.

vein, n. vena f.

velocity, n. velocidad f.

velvet, n. terciopelo m.

vengeance, n. venganza f.

vent, n. apertura f.

ventilate, v. ventilar.

venture, n. ventura f.

verb, n. verbo m.

verbose, a. verboso.

verdict, n. veredicto, fallo m.

verge, n. borde m.

verify, v. verificar.

versatile, a. versátil.

verse, n. verso m.

version, n. versión f.

vertical, a. vertical.

very, 1. a. mismo. **2.** adv. muy.

vessel, n. vasija f.; barco m.

vest, n. chaleco m.

veteran, a. & n. veterano -na.

veto, n. veto m.

vex, v. molestar.

via, prep. por la vía de; por.

viaduct, n. viaducto m.

vibrate, v. vibrar.

vibration, n. vibración f.

vice, n. vicio m.

vicinity, n. vecindad f.

vicious, a. vicioso.

victim, n. víctima f.

victor, n. vencedor m.

victorious, a. victorioso.

victory, n. victoria f.

videodisc, n. videodisco m.

videotape, n. video m., magnetoscopio m.

view, 1. n. vista f. **2.** v. ver.

vigil, n. vigilia, vela f.

vigilant, a. vigilante.

vigor, n. vigor m.

vile, a. vil, bajo.

village, n. aldea f.

villain, *n.* malvado *m.*

vindicate, *v.* vindicar.

vine, *n.* parra, vid *f.*

vinegar, *n.* vinagre *f.*

vintage, *n.* vendimia *f.*

violate, *v.* violar.

violation, *n.* violación *f.*

violence, *n.* violencia *f.*

violent, *a.* violento.

violin, *n.* violín *m.*

virgin, *n.* virgen *f.*

virile, *a.* viril.

virtual, *a.* virtual.

virtue, *n.* virtud *f.*

virtuous, *a.* virtuoso.

virus, *n.* virus *m.*

visa, *n.* visa *f.*

visible, *a.* visible.

vision, *n.* visión *f.*

visit, **1.** *n.* visita *f.* **2.** *v.* visitar.

visitor, *n.* visitante *m. & f.*

visual, *a.* visual.

vital, *a.* vital.

vitality, *n.* vitalidad *f.*

vitamin, *n.* vitamina *f.*

vivacious, *a.* vivaz.

vivid, *a.* vivo; gráfico.

vocabulary, *n.* vocabulario *m.*

vocal, *a.* vocal.

vogue, *n.* boga; moda *f.*

voice, **1.** *n.* voz *f.* **2.** *v.* expresar.

void, 1. *a.* vacío. **2.** *n.* vacío *m.* **3.** *v.* invalidar.

volume, *n.* volumen, tomo *m.*

voluntary, *a.* voluntario.

volunteer, 1. *n.* voluntario *m.* **2.** *v.* ofrecerse.

vomit, *v.* vomitar.

vote, **1.** *n.* voto *m.* **2.** *v.* votar.

voter, *n.* votante *m. & f.*

vouch, *v.* **v. for,** garantizar.

vow, **1.** *n.* voto *m.* **2.** *v.* jurar.

vowel, *n.* vocal *f.*

voyage, *n.* viaje *m.*

vulgar, *a.* vulgar; común.

vulnerable, *a.* vulnerable.

W

wade, *v.* vadear.

wag, *v.* menear.

wage, 1. *n.* (pl.) sueldo, salario *m.* **2.** *v.* **w. war,** hacer guerra.

wagon, *n.* carreta *f.*

wail, 1. *n.* lamento, gemido *m.* **2.** *v.* lamentar, gemir.

waist, *n.* cintura *f.*

wait, 1. *n.* espera *f.* **2.** *v.* esperar. **w. for,** esperar. **w. on,** atender.

waiter, waitress, *n.* camarero -ra.

waiting room, *n.* sala de espera.

wake, v. w. up, despertar.

walk, 1. *n.* paseo *m.;* vuelta; caminata *f.;* modo de andar. **2.** *v.* andar; caminar; ir a pie.

wall, *n.* pared; muralla *f.*

wallcovering, *n.* tapizado de pared *m.*

wallet, *n.* cartera *f.*

wallpaper, *n.* empapelado *m.*

walnut, *n.* nuez *f.*

waltz, *n.* vals *m.*

wander, *v.* vagar.

want, 1. *n.* necesidad *f.* **2.** *v.* querer.

war, *n.* guerra *f.*

ward, 1. *n.* (pol.) barrio *m.;* (hospital) cuadra *f.* **2.** *v.* **w. off,** parar.

wares, *n.* mercancías *f.pl.*

warlike, *a.* belicoso.

warm, 1. *a.* caliente; (fig.) caluroso. **to be w.,** tener calor; (weather) hacer calor. **2.** *v.* calentar.

warmth, *n.* calor *m.*

warn, *v.* advertir.

warp, *v.* alabear.

warrant, *v.* justificar.

warrior, *n.* guerrero *m.*

warship, *n.* navío de guerra.

wash, *v.* lavar.

wasp, *n.* avispa *f.*

waste, 1. *n.* gasto *m.;* desechos *m.pl.* **2.** *v.* gastar, perder.

watch, 1. *n.* reloj *m.;* (mil.) guardia *f.* **2.** *v.* observar, mirar. **w. for,** esperar. **w. out for,** tener cuidado con. **w. over,** guardar; velar por.

watchful, *a.* desvelado.

watchmaker, *n.* relojero *m.*

watchman, *n.* sereno *m.*

water, 1. *n.* agua *f.* **w. color,** acuarela *f.* **2.** *v.* aguar.

waterbed, *n.* cama de agua *f.*

waterfall, *n.* catarata *f.*

waterproof, *a.* impermeable.

wave, 1. *n.* onda; ola *f.* **2.** *v.* ondear; agitar; hacer señas.

waver, *v.* vacilar.

wax, 1. *n.* cera *f.* **2.** *v.* encerar.

way, *n.* camino; modo *m.*, manera *f.* **in a w.,** hasta cierto punto. **a long w.,** muy lejos. **by the w.,** a propósito. **this w.,** por aquí. **that w.,** por allí. **which w.,** por dónde.

we, *pron.* nosotros -as.

weak, *a.* débil.

weaken, *v.* debilitar.

weakness, *n.* debilidad *f.*

wealth, *n.* riqueza *f.*

wealthy, *a.* rico.

weapon, *n.* arma *f.*

wear, 1. *n.* uso, desgaste *m.;* (clothes) ropa *f.* **2.** *v.* usar, llevar. **w. out,** gastar; cansar.

weary, *a.* cansado, rendido.

weather, *n.* tiempo *m.*

weave, *v.* tejer.

weaver, *n.* tejedor -ra.

web, *n.* tela *f.*

wedding, *n.* boda *f.*

wedge, *n.* cuña *f.*

Wednesday, *n.* miércoles *m.*

weed, *n.* maleza *f.*

week, *n.* semana *f.* **w. end,** fin de semana.

weekday, *n.* día de trabajo.

weekly, *a.* semanal.

weep, *v.* llorar.

weigh, *v.* pesar.

weight, *n.* peso *m.*

weird, *a.* misterioso, extraño.

welcome, 1. *a.* bienvenido. **you're w.,** de nada, no hay de qué. **2.** *n.* acogida, bienvenida *f.* **3.** *v.* acoger, recibir bien.

welfare, *n.* bienestar *m.*

well, 1. *a.* sano, bueno. **2.** *adv.* bien; pues. **3.** *n.* pozo *m.*

well-done, *a.* (food) bien cocido.

well-known, *a.* bien conocido.

west, *n.* oeste, occidente *m.*

western, *a.* occidental.

westward, *adv.* hacia el oeste.

wet, 1. *a.* mojado. **to get w.,** mojarse. **2.** *v.* mojar.

whale, *n.* ballena *f.*

what, 1. *a.* qué; cuál. **2.** *interrog. pron.* qué. **3.** *rel. pron.* lo que.

whatever, 1. *a.* cualquier. **2.** *pron.* lo que; todo lo que.

wheat, *n.* trigo *m.*

wheel, *n.* rueda *f.* **steering w.,** volante *m.*

when, 1. *adv.* cuándo. **2.** *conj.* cuando.

whenever, *conj.* siempre que, cuando quiera que.

where, 1. *adv.* dónde, adónde. **2.** *conj.* donde.

wherever, *conj.* dondequiera que, adondequiera que.

whether, *conj.* si.

which, 1. *a.* qué. **2.** *interrog. pron.* cuál. **3.** *rel. pron.* que; el cual; lo cual.

whichever, *a. & pron.* cualquiera que.

while, 1. *conj.* mientras; mientras que. **2.** *n.* rato *m.* **to be worth w.,** valer la pena.

whip, 1. *n.* látigo *m.* **2.** *v.* azotar.

whirl, *v.* girar.

whirlpool, *n.* vórtice *m.*

whirlwind, *n.* torbellino *m.*

whisk broom, *n.* escobilla *f.*

whisker, *n.* bigote *m.*

whiskey, *n.* whisky *m.*

whisper, 1. *n.* cuchicheo *m.* **2.** *v.* cuchichear.

whistle, 1. *n.* pito; silbido *m.* **2.** *v.* silbar.

white, 1. *a.* blanco. **2.** *n.* (of egg) clara *f.*

who, whom, 1. *interrog. pron.* quién. **2.** *rel. pron.* que; quien.

whoever, whomever, *pron.* quienquiera que.

whole, 1. *a.* entero. **the wh.,** todo el. **2.** *n.* totalidad *f.* **on the wh.,** por lo general.

wholesale, *n.* **at wh.,** al por mayor.

wholesome, *a.* sano, saludable.

wholly, *adv.* enteramente.

whose, 1. *interrog. adj.* de quién. **2.** *rel. adj.* cuyo.

why, *adv.* por qué; para qué.

wicked, *a.* malo, malvado.

wickedness, *n.* maldad *f.*

wide, 1. *a.* ancho; extenso. **2.** *adv.* **w. open,** abierto de par en par.

widen, *v.* ensanchar; extender.

widespread, *a.* extenso.

widow, *n.* viuda *f.*

widower, *n.* viudo *m.*

width, *n.* anchura *f.*

wield, *v.* manejar, empuñar.

wife, *n.* esposa, señora, mujer *f.*

wig, *n.* peluca *f.*

wild, *a.* salvaje; bárbaro.

wilderness, *n.* desierto *m.*

wildlife, *n.* fauna silvestre *f.*

will, 1. *n.* voluntad *f.;* testamento

m. **2.** *v.* querer; determinar; (leg.) legar.

willful, *a.* voluntarioso; premeditado.

willing, *a.* to be w., estar dispuesto.

willingly, *adv.* de buena gana.

wilt, *v.* marchitar.

win, *v.* ganar.

wind, *n.* viento *m.* **2.** *v.* torcer; dar cuerda a.

window, *n.* ventana; (of car) ventanilla *f.*

windshield, *n.* parabrisas *m.*

windy, *a.* ventoso. to be w., (weather) hacer viento.

wine, *n.* vino *m.*

wing, *n.* ala *f.*; (theat.) bastidor.

wink, **1.** *n.* guiño *m.* **2.** *v.* guiñar.

winner, *n.* ganador -ra.

winter, *n.* invierno *m.*

wipe, *v.* limpiar; (dry) secar. w. out, destruir.

wire, **1.** *n.* alambre; hilo; telegrama *m.* **2.** *v.* telegrafiar.

wireless, *n.* telégrafo sin hilos.

wisdom, *n.* juicio *m.*; sabiduría *f.*

wise, *a.* sensato, juicioso; sabio.

wish, **1.** *n.* deseo; voto *m.* **2.** *v.* desear; querer.

wit, *n.* ingenio *m.*, sal *f.*

witch, *n.* bruja *f.*

with, *prep.* con.

withdraw, *v.* retirar.

wither, *v.* marchitar.

withhold, *v.* retener, suspender.

within, **1.** *adv.* dentro, por dentro. **2.** *prep.* dentro de; en.

without, **1.** *adv.* fuera, por fuera. **2.** *prep.* sin.

witness, **1.** *n.* testigo; testimonio *m.* **2.** *v.* presenciar; atestar.

witty, *a.* ingenioso, gracioso.

wizard, *n.* hechicero *m.*

woe, *n.* dolor *m.*; pena *f.*

wolf, *n.* lobo *m.*

woman, *n.* mujer *f.*

womb, *n.* entrañas *f.pl.*, matriz *f.*

wonder, **1.** *n.* maravilla; admiración *f.* for a w., por milagro. no w., no es extraño. **2.** *v.* preguntarse; maravillarse.

wonderful, *a.* maravilloso; estupendo.

woo, *v.* cortejar.

wood, *n.* madera; (for fire) leña *f.*

wooden, *a.* de madera.

wool, *n.* lana *f.*

word, **1.** *n.* palabra *f.* the words (of a song), la letra. **2.** *v.* expresar.

work, **1.** *n.* trabajo *m.*; (of art) obra *f.* **2.** *v.* trabajar; obrar; funcionar.

worker, *n.* trabajador -ra; obrero -ra.

workman, *n.* obrero *m.*

world, *n.* mundo *m.* w. war, guerra mundial.

worldly, *a.* mundano.

worldwide, *a.* mundial.

worm, *n.* gusano *m.*

worn, *a.* usado. w. out, gastado, cansado, rendido.

worry, **1.** *n.* preocupación *f.* **2.** *v.* preocupar.

worse, *a.* peor. to get w., empeorar.

worship, **1.** *n.* adoración *f.* **2.** *v.* adorar.

worst, *a.* peor.

worth, **1.** *a.* to be w., valer. **2.** *n.* valor *m.*

worthless, *a.* sin valor.

worthy, *a.* digno.

wound, **1.** *n.* herida *f.* **2.** *v.* herir.

wrap, **1.** *n.* (pl.) abrigos *m.pl.* **2.** *v.* envolver.

wrapping, *n.* cubierta *f.*

wrath, *n.* ira, cólera *f.*

wreath, *n.* guirnalda; corona *f.*

wreck, **1.** *n.* ruina *f.*; accidente *m.* **2.** *v.* destrozar, arruinar.

wrench, *n.* llave *f.* monkey w., llave inglesa.

wrestle, *v.* luchar.

wretched, *a.* miserable.

wring, *v.* retorcer.

wrinkle, **1.** *n.* arruga *f.* **2.** *v.* arrugar.

wrist, *n.* muñeca *f.* w. watch, reloj de pulsera.

write, *v.* escribir. w. down, apuntar.

writer, *n.* escritor -ra.

writhe, *v.* contorcerse.

wrong, **1.** *a.* equivocado; incorrecto. to be w., equivocarse; no tener razón. **2.** *adv.* mal, incorrectamente. **3.** *n.* agravio *m.* right and w., el bien y el mal. **4.** *v.* agraviar, ofender.

X, Y, Z

x-ray, *n.* rayo X *m.*
xylophone, *n.* xilófono *m.*
yacht, *n.* yate *m.*
yard, *n.* patio, corral *m.;* (measure) yarda *f.*
yarn, *n.* hilo.
yawn, 1. *n.* bostezo *m.* **2.** *v.* bostezar.
year, *n.* año *m.*
yearly, *a.* anual.
yearn, *v.* anhelar.
yell, 1. *n.* grito *m.* **2.** *v.* gritar.
yellow, *a.* amarillo.
yesterday, *adv.* ayer.
yet, *adv.* todavía, aún.
yield, *v.* producir; ceder.
yogurt, *n.* yogur *m.*
yoke, *n.* yugo *m.*
yolk, *n.* yema *f.*
you, *pron.* usted, (pl.) ustedes; lo, la, los, las; le, les; (familiar) tú, (pl.) vosotros -as; ti; te, (pl.) os. **with y.,** contigo.
young, *a.* joven.
your, *a.* su; (familiar) tu; (pl.) vuestro.
yours, *pron.* suyo; (familiar) tuyo; (pl.) vuestro.
yourself, -selves, *pron.* sí; se; (familiar) ti; te. **with y.,** consigo. **you y.,** usted mismo, ustedes mismos; tú mismo, vosotros mismos.
youth, *n.* juventud *f.;* (person) joven *m.*
youthful, *a.* juvenil.
zap, *v.* desintegrar, aniquilar.
zeal, *n.* celo, fervor *m.*
zealous, *a.* celoso, fervoroso.
zero, *n.* cero *m.*
zest, *n.* gusto *m.*
zip code, *n.* número de distrito postal.
zipper, *m.* cremallera *f.*
zone, *n.* zona *f.*
zoo, *n.* jardín zoológico.

Useful Phrases/Locuciones Útiles

Good day, Good morning.   Buenos días.
Good afternoon.   Buenas tardes.
Good night, Good evening.   Buenas noches.
Hello.   ¡Hola!
Welcome!   ¡Bienvenido!
See you later.   Hasta luego.
Goodbye.   ¡Adiós!
How are you?   ¿Cómo está usted?
I am fine, thank you.   Estoy bien, gracias.
I am pleased to meet you.   Mucho gusto en conocerle.
May I introduce...   Quisiera presentar...
Thank you very much.   Muchas gracias.
You're welcome.   De nada *or* No hay de qué.
Please.   Por favor.
Excuse me.   Con permiso.
Good luck.   ¡Buena suerte!
To your health.   ¡Salud!

Please help me.   Ayúdeme, por favor.
I don't know.   No sé.
I don't understand.   No entiendo.
Do you understand?   ¿Entiende usted?
I don't speak Spanish.   No hablo español.
Do you speak English?   ¿Habla usted inglés?
How do you say...in Spanish?   ¿Cómo se dice...en español?
What do you call this?   ¿Cómo se llama esto?
Speak slowly, please.   Hable despacio, por favor.
Please repeat.   Repita, por favor.
I don't like it.   No me gusta.
I am lost.   Ando perdido; Me he extraviado.

What is your name?   ¿Cómo se llama usted?
My name is...   Me llamo...
I am an American.   Soy norteamericano.
Where are you from?   ¿De dónde es usted?
I'm from ...   Soy de ...

How is the weather?   ¿Qué tiempo hace?
It's cold (hot) today.   Hace frío (calor) hoy.
What time is it?   ¿Qué hora es?

How much is it?   ¿Cuánto es?
It is too much.   Es demasiado.
What do you wish?   ¿Qué desea usted?
I want to buy...   Quiero comprar...
May I see something better?   ¿Podría ver algo mejor?
May I see something cheaper?   ¿Podría ver algo menos caro?
It is not exactly what I want.   No es exactamente lo que quiero.

I am hungry.   Tengo hambre.
I am thirsty.   Tengo sed.
Where is there a restaurant?   ¿Dónde hay un restaurante?
I have a reservation.   Tengo una reservación.
I would like...   Quisiera...; Me gustaría...
Please give me...   Por favor, déme usted...

272

Please bring me...   Por favor, tráigame usted...
May I see the menu?   ¿Podría ver el menú?
The bill, please.   La cuenta, por favor.
Is service included in the bill?   ¿El servicio está incluido en la cuenta?
Where is there a hotel?   ¿Dónde hay un hotel?
Where is the post office?   ¿Dónde está el correo?
Is there any mail for me?   ¿Hay correo para mí?
Where can I mail this letter?   ¿Dónde puedo echar esta carta al correo?

Take me to...   Lléveme a...
I believe I am ill.   Creo que estoy enfermo.
Please call a doctor.   Por favor, llame al médico.
Please call the police.   Por favor, llame a la policía.
I want to send a telegram.   Quiero poner un telegrama.
As soon as possible.   Cuanto antes.

Round trip.   Ida y vuelta.
Please help me with my luggage.   Por favor, ayúdeme con mi equipaje.
Where can I get a taxi?   ¿Dónde puedo coger un taxi?
What is the fare to...   ¿Cuánto es el pasaje hasta...?
Please take me to this address.   Por favor, lléveme a esta dirección.
Where can I change my money?   ¿Dónde puedo cambiar mi dinero?
Where is the nearest bank?   ¿Dónde está el banco más cercano?
Can you accept my check?   ¿Puede aceptar usted mi cheque?
Do you accept traveler's checks?   ¿Aceptan cheques de viaje?
What is the postage?   ¿Cuánto es el franqueo?
Where is the nearest drugstore?   ¿Dónde está la farmacia más cercana?
Where is the men's (women's) room?   ¿Dónde está el servicio de caballeros (de señoras)?
Please let me off at...   Por favor, déjeme bajar en...

Right away.   ¡Pronto!
Help.   ¡Socorro!
Who is it?   ¿Quién es?
Just a minute!   ¡Un momento no más!
Come in.   ¡Pase usted!
Pardon me.   Dispense usted.
Stop.   ¡Pare!
Look out.   ¡Cuidado!
Hurry.   ¡De prisa! *or* ¡Dése prisa!
Go on.   ¡Siga!
To (on, at) the right.   A la derecha.
To (on, at) the left.   A la izquierda.
Straight ahead.   Adelante.

Signs/Señales

Caution Precaución	**No smoking** Prohibido fumar
Danger Peligro	**No admittance** Entrada prohibida
Exit Salida	**One way** Dirección única
Entrance Entrada	**No entry** Dirección prohibida
Stop Alto	**Women** Señoras, Mujeres, Damas
Closed Cerrado	**Men** Señores, Hombres, Caballeros
Open Abierto	**Ladies' Room** El cuarto de damas
Slow Despacio	**Men's Room** El servicio

273

Food Terms/Alimentos

apple	manzana
artichoke	alcachofa
asparagus	espárrago
bacon	tocino
baked	al horno
banana	banana
bean	habichuela
beer	cerveza
beet	remolacha
biscuit	bizcocho
boiled	hervido
bread	pan
broiled	a la parrilla
butter	manteca
cake	torta
carrot	zanahoria
cauliflower	coliflor
celery	apio
cheese	queso
chicken	pollo
chocolate	chocolate
coffee	café
cognac	coñac
cookie	galleta dulce
crab	cangrejo
cream	crema
cucumber	pepino
dessert	postre
duck	pato
egg	huevo
fillet	filete
fish	pescado
fowl	ave
fried	frito
fruit	fruta
goose	ganso
grape	uva
grapefruit	toronja
ham	jamón
hamburger	hamburguesa
ice cream	helado
jelly	jalea
juice	jugo
lamb	cordero